Victorian Village

John Coker Egerton, Rector of Burwash 1867–88

Victorian Village

The Diaries of the Reverend
John Coker Egerton, Curate and
Rector of Burwash, East Sussex
1857–1888

Edited
by

Roger Wells

ALAN SUTTON

First published in the United Kingdom in 1992 by
Alan Sutton Publishing Limited
Phoenix Mill · Far Thrupp · Stroud · Gloucestershire

First published in the United States of America in 1992 by
Alan Sutton Publishing Inc · Wolfeboro Falls · NH 03896–0848

British Library Cataloguing in Publication Data

A catalogue record for this book is available from the British Library

ISBN 0 7509 0274 4 (hbk)
ISBN 0 7509 0287 6 (pbk)

Library of Congress Cataloging in Publication Data applied for

Typeset in 10/11 Bembo.
Typesetting and origination by
Alan Sutton Publishing Limited.
Printed in Great Britain by
The Bath Press, Avon.

Contents

Acknowledgements

In the mid-1970s, Judith Brent, presently the deputy county archivist for East Sussex, introduced me to Burwash, a particularly interesting village with above average historical documentation, including the originals of the diaries edited here. My thanks go to Mrs Brent for this introduction, and to her colleagues, particularly Christopher Whittick, for their unfailing assistance and advice during prolonged periods of study in their archive. I should also like to thank the staffs of the Public Record Office, the newspaper division of the British Library at Colindale, and especially the Brighton Reference Library, for supplying materials in their collections from which derive many of the details reproduced here to complement the diary.

As always, Mick Reed shared his unrivalled knowledge of eighteenth and nineteenth-century Sussex with me, thereby improving the quality of the commentary. Professor John Rule of the University of Southampton made any number of helpful observations. Dr Bruce Coleman of the University of Exeter provided some technical information about Anglican Church history. Thanks are also due to Alan Gillett and Jim Smith for their help in locating the photographs reproduced here. The complete manuscript was read by the Revd John Lowerson and Dr Keith Snell, respectively of the Universities of Sussex and Leicester, and I am grateful for their suggestions. The content and tone of the introduction was greatly enhanced by advice from my historically sensitive colleague, the book illustrator, John Vernon Lord. Responsibility for inadequacies and mistakes remains with the editor.

Roger Wells
Brighton, July 1992

Introduction

Reputation

In 1874, the ageing Burwash-born bricklayer George Harmer informed the Rector, John Coker Egerton, that over thirty years previously working men gossiping near Portsmouth, spoke 'of Burwash Wheel as the roughest public house they were ever in'. The parish to which Egerton first came as curate in 1857, had an unenviable reputation. This derived from at least the mid-eighteenth century when the village hosted associates of the infamous Hawkhurst gang of smugglers, who terrorized much of Sussex during their heyday. Continuing commitment to smuggling was vividly revealed by an 1826 *cause célèbre*, when innkeeper Benjamin Russell was poisoned; his wife, Hannah, and her lover, Daniel Leaney were both convicted of murder, and sentenced to death. Leaney was executed, but a public outcry over disputed medical evidence saved Hannah from the hangman's rope. Reprieved, she subsequently married the shoemaker Thomas Chandler, and was still the most notorious woman during Egerton's years in the parish. The incident no doubt consolidated the infamy of the Wheel, as this was Russell's establishment, which did several lines in smuggled and illicitly-distilled spirits.

Smuggling, however, was not the village's sole, or even primary notorious forte. During the prolonged agricultural depression following the end of the French Wars in 1815, extreme poverty underpinned the escalating intensity of social conflict in Burwash. The 'labouring Class', it was said, had 'become very dissatisfied . . . disrespectful and insolent to their superiors, riotous and turbulent . . . ready for extreme acts of depredation', including 'anonymous letters dropt . . . threatening the lives of individuals', and that most fearsome of weapons in the hands of nineteenth-century countryside protesters, incendiarism. Working-class villagers mobilized during the famed Captain Swing quasi-insurrection of 1830. Burwash was the third parish in Sussex to rise, forcing farmers to raise wages, social-security administrators to increase their payments, and the clergyman to reduce his tithe exactions. Having secured these victories at home, the leaders – fortified by advanced radical democratic political ideology – then clandestinely orchestrated parallel risings in adjacent parishes.

This militancy complemented the very high levels of crime in High Wealden communities. At Burwash, as elsewhere, criminal activities ranged from everyday poaching, to theft of all denominations; burglary and highway robbery, generated the most fear, but opportunistic criminals struck whenever circumstances suggested impunity. In addition to these violent characteristics, organized crime also stimulated much alarm, notably when the evidence suggested – as it correctly and recurrently did in the 1830s and '40s – that gangs were at work. On Egerton's arrival Burwash remained notorious 'for being the birth place or sheltering place of rick-burners, sheep stealers and thieves'. Farmers kept loaded firearms at their bedsides; commercial travellers, and others, went armed along Wealden highways. But Burwash especially, remained prone to 'Robbery, violence, and lawlessness of all kinds', the bulk of the inhabitants denominated as 'wild, ignorant, and lawless'.

Property and Power

Burwash was, at over 7,000 acres, a large parish. There were three principal settlements. The first, and biggest, comprised the nucleated village of Burwash itself. Secondly, that on Burwash Common, was adjacent to Burwash Weald. Alternatively known as the Wheel, after which the notorious inn was named, the name was a perversion of Weald, and derived from pronunciation difficulties. Another, much smaller hamlet lay at Witherenden Hill. Numerous farmhouses, some with cottages, lay dispersed throughout the higher ground in the parish. Anciently, Burwash was a market town; by Egerton's time only the fairs survived with their mixture of pleasure and business. But the village, and the settlement on the Common, lay on one of the major routes between the South-east, and the South, and on to the South-west. A constant stream of foot and horse-drawn traffic passed along this highway, crossed by minor north-south routes at both the village and the Common. Burwash itself, and to a lesser extent the Common, were also centres of the rural service industries, with large numbers of tradesmen, blacksmiths, saddlers and harness-makers, wheelwrights, carpenters, joiners, builders, brickmakers, tailors, thatchers, shoemakers, grocers, drapers, general shopkeepers, publicans, butchers, bakers, and even a coachbuilder. Agriculture and the service industries were both central to the parochial economy, symbolized by the fair number of tradesmen who farmed to degrees as well, and were classic dual-occupationists.

After his translation from being Curate to the Rectorship of Burwash, Egerton described himself as the village 'boss'. This self-perception – no doubt shared by his predecessors, the Revds Gould and Mackenzie – hinged on the absence of any squire. Two of the largest landowners in the parish, the aristocratic Ashburnhams, and the gentry Fullers, respectively with 867 and 683 acres, were absentees, together with other more modest owners, who rented their two to three hundred acres to tenant farmers. The Havilands, who directly farmed 430 of their 550 acres, could conceivably have aspired to squirearchial status, but the family went bankrupt in 1849. The successive generations of the families of Baldock and Philcox, who handed their stable legal partnership from fathers to sons, also bought their way into land; they effectively disqualified themselves, by remaining men of business, retaining the Clerkship to the local Bench, and acting as the Rector's steward, which included collecting the contentious tithe.

Landownership remained fluid; occasional sales meant that socially-aspirant newcomers, after prestige and shooting rights, bought their way into land, with fortunes secured in London and other urban-based businesses. Some, including the Pooley's and the Tilley's, converted modest farmhouses into substantial mansions, but like their successors from similar circles, among them the Newton's and the Breach's, did not stay long enough to achieve further upward special mobility. Only the Londoner, Andrew Gibbs, who 'built & occupied' Dudwell House, was eventually elevated to the Bench. And, it is clear from the tone of Egerton's diary entries, that while he was positive towards Gibbs, the relative newcomer had nothing of the social status automatically accruing to George Courthope, chair of the Petty Sessions who, with his long-established family seat at Whileigh, was the unambiguous squire of the neighbouring village of Ticehurst.

Power in the nineteenth century bore a very close relationship to property, as translated into relative rate payments. Because land was more heavily weighted in terms of rateable value than the business premises of tradesmen, the more substantial tenant and owner-occupying farmers tended to dominate parochial politics. Such criteria also reinforced the Rector's importance which, if based on his social position, was strengthened by his status as a principal ratepayer, on both his eighty acres of glebe land, and on his additional contribution deriving from the payments levied on the tithe. This oligarchic characteristic was given statutory expression by the so-called Select Vestry Act of 1819, which was speedily adopted; it gave one to six votes to ratepayers, dependent on their contributions, and ensured that the wealthier inhabitants elected men of their own ilk on to the select vestry. This was particularly important before 1835, as it gave control over the most expensive component of parochial administration – namely social-security – to the bigger farmers, who were also the greatest employers of labour. Under these rules, the tradesmen's influence in parochial affairs was reduced, and remained incommensurate with their numerical and economic importance. In some senses, the farmers were able to translate this dominance into securing pecuniary advantages, through manipulating poor-relief procedures under the parochial autonomy permitted by the Old Poor Law, which remained unaltered until 1835.

This local autonomy was a prime victim of the radical Poor Law Amendment Act. Under its regional implementation in 1835, Burwash was joined to eight other adjacent parishes, which thereafter comprised the Poor Law Union of Ticehurst. Henceforth, social security – which retained its role as the largest item of expenditure funded through the rates – was administered through a Board of Guardians. The Boards were subjected to the close control of a new body, the Poor Law Commissioners, from their base in Somerset House in London, which effectively terminated autonomous parochial control. Every magistrate had an *ex officio* place on the Board, the other members of which were elected on identical grounds to those promulgated in 1819. The electoral system preserved the realities of pre-1835 political power throughout the entire Victorian period, with men drawn from the ranks of the grander farmers invariably elected annually to represent Burwash.

Economy

Like most Wealden economies, that of Burwash was dominated by agriculture. Only a handful of farmers had over 190 acres at the time of the tithe survey in 1842, among them Edward Simes, who rented that 'one-eyed place', the two-hundred acre Poundsford Farm from the Earl of Ashburnham. The earl also directly farmed 277 acres of his own, while another absentee owner, Edward Hussey, kept ninety acres of his own; bailiffs effectively ran both these farms. Richard Barrow represented those who owned and rented land; Barrow farmed 183 acres, of which he owned 125. But 'the largest number' of farms were 'under 100 acres each', including the sixty-three acre Witherest Farm, owned and cultivated by George Fagg Gilbert, and the ninety-three acre Old Toft Farm, rented by Thomas Gillham. Many more farms, were between forty and fifty acres, even more were very modest – between fifteen and forty acres – 'peasant' farms, run almost exclusively by family labour. Crowhurst Bridge Farm was typical; its eighteen acres were farmed by fifty-two-year-old John Pennels in 1861, aided by his two grown up sons, John (26) and William (19), who no doubt found jobs for three other children aged between ten and twelve. Among the dual-occupationists in 1851 was the current proprietor of the Wheel, James Russell, officially described as 'farmer & alehousekeeper' in recognition of his thirty-five acres. But while the generalities described here obtained, the details reveal a fluid land-market, and constantly changing tenancies. By 1861 for example the eighty-year-old Gilbert was semi-retired, 'retaining in use six acres'; he had sold the rest of Witherest to a new absentee owner, Charles Ansell, who employed yet another member of the extensive Russell family, James, as bailiff. Gillham rented another farm across the Ticehurst border, and thus farmed over three times the acreage that his Burwash holding suggested in isolation, and he was also a considerable brickmaker through his non-Burwash interests.

The tradesmen likewise varied considerably. Some were at only half a remove from the labouring class. Joseph Blackford, the proprietor of the Woodman at the time of the 1861 census, described himself as a 'Beershop keeper and Agricultural Labourer', while Thomas Hicks' self-description was that of a 'fruiterer and ag. lab.'. Several businesses passed down from father to son across several generations – including the Pilbeams' blacksmithery, and that branch of the Noakes family who were clock and watchmakers – without experiencing any growth in scale. Conversely, some were wealthy. John Vigor, of the stable butchering family, specialized in cattle-dealing. John Buss Noakes was a 'general shopkeeper', but his business required four employees. Another relatively stable family firm – Thompson's the builders – employed an oscillating number of men, developed side lines, including ironmongering. Another family of tradesmen, the Woods, were initially carpenters, but grew into builders, and one member established a large and prosperous building firm in London, retaining his Burwash connections with annual works outings to the village.

The agrarian economy, and with it this sizeable trading sector, was relatively prosperous during the long years of the French Wars 1793–1815. High cereal prices dictated increased acreages, especially for wheat, while buoyant demand for meat and wool guaranteed plenty of business in the long-established practices of providing winter-time pasturage for Marshland sheep. With Waterloo, and the end of the war, the economy spiralled into a prolonged depression from 1815 through to the 1830s. Prices for farm produce collapsed. Farmers reduced their wheat acreages, and that which remained was farmed less intensively. Sheep interests were hit by the rot in some years. Many farmers diversified especially into meat and dairy cattle, most developed interests in that fast growing district specialism, namely chicken-fattening and, above all, farmers increased their hop-acreages. Hops were a notoriously fickle crop; they required heavy investment – above all in labour – but planters could never be sure that a combination of wildly oscillating yields, mercurial prices, and the vagaries of the excise exactions, would even return them their capital outlay. On the other hand, this capricious crop approximated to bingo, and in some years huge profits materialized, though vexatious to the last, neighbouring farmers could experience diametrically opposite results. But, in the main, adequate years outnumbered the disasterous, and hops commonly under-pinned farmers' fragile liquidity.

This prolonged depression also affected the craft and business sector of the parochial economy, as farmers cut down on all expenditure to ward off bankruptcy, not invariably successfully. Vicious economic circles were felt. If farmers reduced outlays on, for example, new harnesses, not only were the sadler's skills in shorter demand, but demand for leather fell; similarly, the important woodland sector of the economy was partially undermined by reduced consumption of wood, by builders, carpenters with fencing contracts, and others, though enhanced hop-acreages – not just locally but throughout the south-east – inflated demand for hop-poles, which also needed regular replacement. While we examine poverty below in greater detail, an under-employed and under-paid agrarian workforce, cut every possible iota of expenditure, thus compromising the turnovers of butchers, shoemakers, and possibly even publicans.

The economy remained essentially fragile throughout the nineteenth century. It was another, be it shorter depression between 1847 and 1851 which finished off the Havilands. The over-supply of labour was but marginally checked by migration and emigration between the end of the

1810s and the early 1840s. Employment remaind vicarious, with wintertime lay-offs owing to snow and prolonged wet a recurrent feature. Securing permanent employ remained a pipe-dream for many, while the earnings of most working-class women and children were restricted to the tying and picking of hops, in the spring and in September respectively. While the railways, in the form of the Tunbridge Wells to Hastings line opened in 1851, passing through Etchingham to the east, and the line to Uckfield constructed in 1858, and routed through adjacent Heathfield and Mayfield to the west, improved communications and brought key metropolitan markets into closer orbit, they did not greatly enhance demand for local labour, once they had been built. But some jobs were secured, the 1851 census recording early successes, among them the youthful railway labourers Stephen Hazelden and George Chandler. Nevertheless, towards the very end of Egerton's incumbency, the speedy shrinkage of wheat and especially hop-acreages, generated such employment problems that a solution could be anticipated only in renewed emigration to the colonies.

Poverty and Social Security

Four factors, namely combating the impact of wartime inflation on working families, the much broader questions over the effective relief of low wages, high under- and unemployment during the lengthy post-war depression, the huge and rapid increase in population notably between 1811 and 1821, and the continued fragile economic equilibrium after the 1830s, combined to ensure that Burwash had a major and continuous poverty problem; only its *severity* fluctuated.

Farmworkers with familes were the principal victims of wartime inflation of all living expenses, including the costs of rents and especially food. Parochial authorities in Burwash, in common with their counterparts in many similarly placed Southern villages, resorted to regular payments in-aid-of wages largely based on the number of children; these were *de facto* child allowances, and were usually paid from the second or third child under ten or twelve in the family. Additional aid came in the form of 'casual' payments to help meet the costs of replacement clothing and shoes, fuel, and rent subsidies. This regular outdoor relief, as it was known, was boosted massively with the combined effects of demobilization and demographic growth after 1815. The population of Burwash rose from 1,524 in 1801, to 1,603 in 1811, and then to 1,937 in 1821; outward migration and emigration kept subsequent growth to the 1,966 registered in the 1831 census, though it rose to 2,143 in 1861. Work shortages comprised the principal new post-war factor, symbolized by the adoption of the expression 'surplus labourers'.

This dismal situation was worsened by other developments; farmers not only employed a shrinking number of permanent hands commensurate with less intensive, and a partial switch to pastoral agriculture, but increasingly hired workers on a weekly, daily or even hourly basis. In conformity with statutory obligations, the vestry resisted recourse to simple unemployment pay, and sought to oblige claimants to work for their relief. Various experiments were tried, abandoned, and retried. Among them was the infamous 'Roundsmen' system, whereby workers were disturbed round the parish's farmers, on a ratio of workers to acreages, with the parish subsidizing the wages paid by the employer. At the worst moments this system was extended to journeymen craftsmen. Other major expedients included putting men to work on the roads; as the parish had additional responsibilities to maintain its highways, there was a logic here, though the numbers allocated to the 'waywardens' administratively responsible, frequently exceeded the workforce required, and 'loitering' assumed a new significance. The parish also hired quarries for other out-of-work labourers to dig the stone for road repairs. Finally, the parish obtained the ninety-six-acre Bough Farm on the edge of the Common, and from *circa* 1816 till the mid-1830s a large number of unemployed were allocated here; the calibre of the experience might be gauged from the fact that ploughs were not used. 'Spade husbandry' certainly created a huge increment to man hours, but once again the less than enthusiastic perform-ance of those working here did not make this much of a test of the claim that improved crop yields effectively financed this ultra-labour-intensive system.

The massive extension of direct employment by the parish was in addition to the continuation of child allowances to the parents of large families, and the considerable range of casual assistance payments. Further pressure on housing stocks meant that many workers' rent commitments had to be guaranteed by the parish before landlords would let, and this stimulus to increasing public housing stock by purchases was consolidated by enhanced use of the conglomerate of buildings known as the workhouse. In effect this was a poorhouse, simply a residential block, though it did facilitate some experiments in social control, including one initiative of insisting that the high proportion of youthful and unmarried men employed by the parish all live there, so that a stricter eye could be kept upon them. Indeed the vestry tried to exploit all facets of the extension of its authority to enforcing subordination. Moreover, the vestry continually sought to minimize expenditure; as the parish recurrently hovered on the verge of bankruptcy, there was a logic here, but it was totally lost on the claimants who bore the brunt of seemingly increasingly harsh and parsimonious cuts in their relief. Cost-cutting, and policing through benefit administration, turned the social-security system into a theatre of fierce conflict, much of it on straight-forward class lines. And, these experiences helped guarantee that the generations who bore the brunt of it had no unreal perception of the good-old-days, when representatives as elderly people in Egerton's time reminisced to his reverence over their younger days.

If social relationships were strained under the Old Poor Law, they were immeasurably aggravated by its notorious utilitarian successor, the Poor Law Amendment Act, or the Poor Man's Robbery Bill in popular parlance.

In addition to the abolition of parochial autonomy, outlined above, the Act's principal target was the payment of outdoor relief in any form, other than medical aid, to able-bodied male workers and their families. For Burwash, this dictated that a large category of existing claimants was subsequently entitled to public assistance, only in the workhouse. These institutions, which came to underpin and symbolize the Victorian social-security system, were designed to repel rather than invite claimants to become inmates; in them, husbands were separated from wives, and both from their children, and the adults subjected to a disciplinarian regime, with repetitive and mundane forms of work. Children, at least those under twelve, might expect elementary schooling, from poorly-qualified staff, but this was no compensation. From mid-1835 miserably-paid labouring folk in Burwash either got by on what they and their families could earn, now denied income supplementation for low wages, help towards fuel, clothes and rent, or face incarceration in the new Union workhouse, speedily erected across the parish boundary in Ticehurst, the centre of the new Poor Law Union.

Other categories of claimants were more ambiguously placed, and the resolution of their cases depended on the attitude of both the elected Guardians for the parish, and the entire Board. The least scope for negotiation concerned unmarried mothers, fiercely and chauvinistically discriminated against, if they failed to secure and remain in receipt of maintenance payments. Widows with children could qualify for weekly financial assistance, on condition that they, and all eligible children, obtained whatever work was available. Infirm and elderly married folk were best placed to secure a regular, if tiny, pension, to subsist upon in their own homes, but their security was never guaranteed, especially after the death of one partner. Finally, almost as if to add insult to injury, the close relatives of claimants, were liable to legally enforceable contributions towards the cost of aid. Offspring might find themselves in the Petty Sessions dock, and emerge with an order forcing them to make weekly payments for their widowed mother for example, irrespective of whether aid was provided in the home, or the workhouse.

In the event, the sheer scale of poverty, plus the fact that maintaining especially whole families in the workhouse was much costlier than relieving them at home, defeated the maintenance of the strictest principles of the Robbery Bill's architects. For example, the most inclement weeks of the winters, saw so many workers temporarily laid off that they could never be accommodated in the workhouse, and the sole alternative was the short-term payment of out-relief. Medical Officers clandestinely effected *de facto* outdoor relief by ordering food on the rates, notably small weekly supplies of mutton. Eventually, the passage of time, and bureaucratic inertia, diluted utilitarian enthusiasms, revealed for example in the weekly flour allowances made to the labouring fathers of large families.

Nevertheless, the Act's significance cannot be exaggerated. First, the workhouse literally loomed, an omnipresent representation of the disciplinary and threatening posture of the Victorian state. Nobody, even those of modest means, could rest assured that they were safely outside the workhouse's catchment category. Secondly, the Act did promote – as its authors envisaged – greater reliance on self-help, notably through enhanced recourse to Friendly Societies, a phenomenon strongly reflected in Burwash. Thirdly, under the Act, all householders were rated; this turned many workers into supplicants asking to be excused from meeting their liabilities, while the wealthier ratepayers benefitted handsomely from the considerable reductions in social-security costs secured under the new system.

Finally, the Robbery Bill was the first major piece of social legislation passed after the 1832 Reform Bill, with its modest alterations to parliamentary constituencies, and the even more modest extensions to the franchise, notably to the urban middle class, and in the county seats, which embraced Burwash, the extension of the vote to tenant farmers with a rental of £50 or more. This excluded a not inconsequential number of the smaller farmers in Burwash, together with all agricultural labourers, journeymen craftsmen, and a proportion of their employers. The blatant class bias of the Act served to reinforce existing perceptions of the need for futher political reform on democratic principles, with the implementation of at least manhood suffrage to ensure that the state's enactments served mass, not sectional interests.

Popular Politics and Protest

Tracing the dissemination of populist politics in the rural districts is difficult, but there is no doubt that Paineite democratic principles were entertained by some Burwash folk in the 1790s. After the war, the terrible impact of the depression unleashed repetitive petitions from the south-east to parliament demanding government intervention to offset the worst effects. Although they were principally orchestrated by the bigger farmers, the effects of their repeated rejections were not lost on a broader sector of society; as the perceptive squire George Courthope put it, they 'invariably produced the worst of consequences amongst the labouring population', namely the strengthening of radical political principles. As we saw, these were articulated by Swing activists from Burwash in the autumn of 1830.

The prolonged Reform Bill crisis which coincided with Swing's harsh repression, and lasted until June 1832 served to raise the political temperature, and by the time of the passage of the Act formal political organization had commenced among Burwash's lowlier residents. A branch of the National Union of the Working Classes functioned, and involved some of the smaller farmers in addition to labourers. Although neither Burwash, nor the Ticehurst Union, were caught up in the fierce protests against the implementation of the Robbery Bill in 1835, village radicals were organized adequately to respond quickly and effectively to a regional anti-Poor Law movement, launched in 1837. In 1838, a number of Burwash workers addressed a public meeting, outlining their experiences of 'half-filled bellies and burning hearts', before drafting a fierce parliamentary petition asserting that 'their rights extend to something *more* than POTATOES AND RAGS'. The address concluded with an uncompromisingly political analysis of high taxes on articles of everyday consumption, which generated the huge revenues 'lavished upon thousands of idle and profligate hangers on of the State'.

In the light of this history, it is not surprising that one of the Chartist movement's national speakers addressed a meeting in Burwash, or that the village hosted a Chartist organization in the late 1830s and early 1840s. Moreover, there were other clear expressions of class-consciousness, including a refusal of members of a new Friendly Society to accept any aid, or indeed influence over the society's rules, which 'did not originate from some of their own Class'. This comprised a sharp rebuke to those 'principal Gentry of the place' who wanted the society to husband its resources, and not pay out all remaining funds in dividends at the end of each financial year. Gentry influence, notably from Egerton's predecessor the Revd Gould, was effectively excluded, until 1842 when bankruptcy after an unprecedented run on the club funds, was evaded only through emergency subscriptions from the wealthy. The membership's unabated determination to ensure that dividends financed a feast accompanied by heavy drinking every anniversary day, nevertheless survived, and engaged Egerton's energies. Equally, the politicization which peaked in the Chartist years ensured that a considerable number of Burwash working-class folk continued to entertain and on occasion to give expression to radical political views throughout the rest of the nineteenth century. What commenced in obscurity, matured into a lasting theme in everyday village life.

Parish Policing

Traditional historiography has it that the annually elected parochial constables were ineffective, if not invariably corrupt. The situation in Burwash, with high levels of crime, including the organized variety, throughout the period prior to the 1840 creation of a professional police for East Sussex, should have rendered its amateur policeman even more impotent. In fact, the true situation was more complicated. For not only did the vestry commit hard-pressed funds to the periodic employment of extra officials, dubbed beadles, to combat vagrancy, disorder and crime in the 1820s, and further finances to the erection of a sturdy two cell lock-up to hold prisoners prior to court appearances, but energetic and recurrent actions by some of the wealthier villagers during that decade, led to the convictions of a surprisingly large number of criminals. Even the Swing episode seems to have produced no more than a temporary hiatus, and in the 1830s the parish again devoted finance under the 1833 Lighting and Watching Act, for the periodic payment of policeman when crime rose to intolerable levels. But there were grumbles, inevitably over the costs and, less predictably, over power relationships, as on this issue at least, the large number of small ratepayers were able to outvote the big payers from the ranks of the larger farmers. The experiment lapsed, and in 1838, when gangs again terrorized the place, the sole solution seemed to lay in hiring a professional from the relatively new Metropolitan Police.

The fierce county-wide debate over the expensive option of implementing the 1839 Rural Police Act found expression at Burwash. The Curate, the Revd Mann led an alliance comprising the grander farmers and some of the most affluent tradesmen, in lobbying hard for adoption of the Act, but once the matter was debated in an open general vestry meeting, the idea inevitably came under fire from the smaller ratepayers. The precise proposals were open to ridicule, notably the fact that a village with Burwash's population would warrant but one constable, which experience proved would be wholly inadequate. The projected costs were simply stated to be beyond the pockets of many ratepayers. In the event, a professional force was virtually imposed on the county against the wishes of an overwhelming majority of ratepayers, by the Quarter Sessions comprising the magistracy, who of course were unelected and therefore unanswerable to any constituency. Burwash was, realistically enough in view of its reputation, selected as one location for one of the few new police stations, to be staffed by a sergeant and a constable from the start of the new force.

The division between Burwash ratepayers was recurrently replayed. The new police's supporters provided the men for appointment as Local Constables, in effect a recasting of the ancient constables, except there were initially six, and placed under the close control of the professionals. The majority of ratepayers continued to filibuster about the costs, claimed erroneously that the force had no ameliorative effect on crime levels, and remained hostile. Village villains naturally hated the new men in blue, and the numbers of times frame-ups were alleged, suggest that the police may not have been invariably scrupulous. But these hostilities were shared by most working people, either on principle, or by being among those caught poaching. Indeed, the police crossed swords with all manner of people, among them farmers for working injured horses, carters for illegally riding on their vehicles, retailers for false weights and measures, and representatives from most – but certainly not every – social rank for drunkenness. If professional policemen were well established by Egerton's time, they were far from being universally accepted.

Religion and Education

The professionalization of the police was one factor in the imposition of more order on an unruly community; in the 1860s – within Egerton's first decade in the place – claims that both religious and educational provision were instrumental to the same end were being made, notably by Anglicans. The long-serving National Schoolmaster Cox penned reports on religious, educational and social events for the county press from the 1850s, and these served as propaganda exercises designed to lift the parish's reputation. In the 1860s Egerton seems to have largely taken over from Cox – who succumbed to alcoholism – increasing the flow of 'laudatory accounts of persons and events'. From the middle of the nineteenth century, Burwash attracted a smattering of new and wealthy residents, some of whom joined the local establishment, none more vigorously so than the three Trower spinsters, whose brother was the Anglican Bishop of Gibraltar. A typical account penned for publication by Egerton of a 'treat' for more than two hundred National schoolchildren, laid on by the Trower sisters, rhetorically asked

> what more clearly carries with its own reward, is more free from stain or thought of evil, is more morally wholesome, and is more directly suggestive of purity and innocence, than a good school feast, well done?

The parochial Anglican establishment was certainly expansive. The Revd Gould, initially Curate to an absentee Rector, and in sole charge of Burwash from 1824 to 1840, was credited with some of this after becoming Rector in 1840. A National School was built in Burwash village in 1843, and the ancient parish church, St Bartholomews, was rebuilt in 1856. But it was the Common, two miles west along the main road to which the greatest notoriety attached. In 1844 Gould converted part of the old workhouse, into what was technically a licensed room for worship, but which functioned as a chapel of ease. It was replaced by a new church, St Philips, erected in 1867, Gould's last public act being the laying of the foundation stone. By this time the Trowers were also determinedly on the scene, for example opening the Sunday school on the Common in 1865, a Church day school in 1866, which transferred to new premises in 1868. In 1877 St Philip's Church became the centre of a new parish, named after it, which effectively severed the Common from Burwash village, though the new parish – even with the inclusion of outlying districts of Heathfield and Mayfield – had under a thousand residents.

The High Weald hosted a strong non-conformist community, including many Calvinist sects, a tradition fully expressed in Burwash, with the Providence Chapel, housed in a new chapel constructed in 1829. Here, William Buss, a self-taught agricultural labourer, was the long-serving 'Minister of the Gospel'. The Burwash Independent Chapel, prided itself as the oldest 'Independent or Congregational' chapel in Sussex; the minister was financed from the tiny eighteen-acre Crowhurst Bridge Farm, bequeathed by Elizabeth Cruttenden in 1726, but by the nineteenth century, was dominated by the shopkeeping sector of the Noakes kin. Like so many of its ilk, it succumbed to successive secessions, and after mid-century, many villagers still went over the Wadhurst border to the Particular

Baptists' Shover's Green Chapel, as had their forbears after their allegedly amicable split from the Congregationalists in 1816. Finally, the Wesleyans had a modest Chapel, accommodating ninety-five worshippers, erected on the Common, relatively recently in 1843; the principal patrons were the Simes', the long-standing tenants of Poundsford Farm.

If the Anglicans had a long-running Sunday school, parallel commitment and provision by their Dissenting counterparts appears to have oscillated. There was none at the Congregational Church in 1851, the date of the only national religious census. Nor had non-Anglicans combined to produce a rival day-school, though this did not represent aquiescence in absolute Anglican educational hegemony. The main alternatives were to be found in the Dame Schools, notoriously difficult to track down in the evidence. The scale of such provision at any one time in Burwash eludes precision, but a fair proportion of those from the ranks of the middling tradesmen and the farmers probably received an education in such establishments. There also appears to have been some tradition of self-help in educational matters among working-class folk, of which the Revd Buss was a product, and a night school is known to have functioned at times on the Common around the turn of the century, under the auspices of William Budd, 'a poor man more learned than his fellows'.

John Coker Egerton

John came from a clerical line of the Egertons, one of the three most powerful families in Cheshire. His father, also John, was the incumbent at Bunbury in the county, from which he retired at the early age of fifty-two, in 1849, and went to live on an old but minor family property at Hextable, near Dartford, in Kent. The son, born in 1829, spent some of his boyhood at Bunbury, and took holidays there throughout his life. After graduation from Oxford in 1850, John became Curate at Nuncton in Wiltshire, but in typical nepotistic fashion, was soon invited to become Curate by his Uncle John Gould, who had bought the advowson in 1835 and became Rector of Burwash five years later. The diary, printed here, commences with the offer, and Egerton's arrival at Burwash in 1857.

With the exception of 1860–3, when he experimented with the curacy of a small inner-London parish, Egerton remained at Burwash – becoming Rector in 1867 – until his premature death early in 1888. The diary covers the entire period from 1857, with the exceptions of 1860 to 1867, and the last year of his life. As might be expected, the *de facto* professionalization of the Anglican Church in the middle decades of the nineteenth century, ensured Egerton was a very different type of clergyman from his later eighteenth and early nineteenth-century predecessors whose diaries have been published. The best-known of these, Parson Woodforde, whose long-term incumbency of a country parish just outside Norwich, joined the eighteenth and nineteenth centuries, was a typical high liver, whose diary is

more concerned with lavish meals and extended holidays, than the cure of
lowly village souls. Two more diarists, both incumbents of Somerset
parishes in the early years of the nineteenth century, were also poles apart.
The Revd Holland of Over Stowey had a stroke of genuine humour,
captured in the title of the published version – *Paupers and Pig-Killers* –
categories which figure prominently in his fascinating detail of village life,
as viewed from the parsonage. In some contrast was that of the widowed
Rector Skinner, whose intensifying paranoia – over his relationship with his
children, and his parishioners – constitutes an entertaining, if ultimately
tragic theme, severed when his Reverence, convinced that the Methodists
were about to rule the world, abruptly departed from it by shooting
himself.

Egerton was only too aware of religious and social divisions in the
village; if, on occasions, his experiences dampened his enthusiasm and
extended to self-doubt, he never capitulated absolutely with even that not
inconsiderable sector of the plebeian population dubbed 'roughs', who
remained essentially untamed. Egerton, who was a teetotaller for most of
his adult life, did however give up haranguing drunken people he encountered on his rounds, whether he knew them or not. His temper
remained ecumenical in spirit, and a hint of pride may be detected in his
references to his personal relationships with some Dissenters. Conversely,
relations with certain affluent newcomers, were strained. Egerton never
really got on with Andrew Gibbs, eventually elevated to the County Bench,
but whose religious affiliations hovered between very low church and
noncomformity. Even worse, was the brash London solicitor, Thomas
Bolton, sometime Liberal MP, who bought an estate which straddled the
Heathfield boundary, and with whom Egerton clashed publicly, especially
over the viciously divisive issue of the so-called extraordinary tithe in the
1880s. Egerton clearly thought that Bolton's profile was too inelegant for
him to be considered a proper gentleman.

The diaries are copious, and were partially kept as a deliberate record of
his ministrations for future reference. He recorded, for example, many of
his charitable donations of small sums of money to hard-up, but esteemable
parishioners. But there are relatively few references – other than repetitive
new year reviews of his self-perceived shortcomings – to personal matters.
There is precious little record of his courtship of Helen Breach, the daughter
of another wealthy, and relatively temporary, newcomer, whom Egerton
married when he was well over forty, and she equally well under thirty.
Thereafter, his wife's fragile health, the birth and incidents in the lives of his
five children, are matters of record, though rarely consistently so. The most
regular, and the most valuable for the historian, are his descriptions of many
aspects of everyday life. Egerton was perceptive and sympathetic; these
acute observations are spiced with many anecdotally oriented matters,
which especially older people told him. For Egerton had what should be
seen as a sociologist's eye for material. This was put to good use, through a
series of newpaper articles, later consolidated into a book, published in 1884

as *Sussex Folk and Sussex Ways*. A remarkable work for its time, though possibly reflective of some of the preconceptions of contemporary folk-lorists, *Sussex Folk* interested among others Thomas Hardy, and a copy – bound in vellum – was presented by Egerton to Queen Victoria.

Editor's Notes: Complementary Details, Text and Abbreviations

Egerton's diaries comprise a number of hard and soft-backed, large and unruled, exercise books. Internal evidence proves that he mainly wrote up the day's experiences before retiring to bed, though some entries appear to have been penned one or two days later. Very occasionally a day's report also includes detail omitted from a previous day's account. Historical and anecdotal information, and other chit-chat, deriving from his encounters with parishioners, are usually dated, but recorded, either at the start and end of volumes, or occupy a block in others. In still further volumes, only one side of the page is used, the other reserved for such details. By and large, undated entries of this calibre have not been printed below, but the more interesting ones which are dated, have been included here under the diary entry coinciding with the date of Egerton recording the detail. This method goes some way towards enhancing the impression of the diary as a receptacle for its keeper's experiences, thereby conveying a better flavour of the man's life and his daily encounters, however much on occasion, the topic matter represents a real miscellany.

The original records much repetitive detail; indeed hundreds of entries for whole days are purely repetitive. Many of Egerton's days – or rather his record of them – started with a morning visit to the National School in his effective charge throughout his incumbency, when he regularly but not invariably taught. He rarely recorded details, except over difficulties. Equally repetitive, and in the main identically uninformative, are his virtual listings of simply the names of parishioners, especially the sick, the elderly, and the widowed, on whom he called during his conscientious daily rounds. The same repetitive quality attaches to his very numerous, though inconsistently detailed, evenings spent in the drawing rooms of the more affluent, usually engaged in some musical activity. Music was Egerton's greatest love in life (in his later years, shared with his wife), both at these somewhat esoteric levels, and with his continuous – if oft frustrating – campaign to train his church choir to an unusual level of achievement. The former category of activity has largely been edited out; the second, and almost always less rich, though interesting brief notes on his recurrent problems with cussid men and insubordinate boys, has been included here, giving details central to Egerton's ministrations. He usually recorded texts used for his Sunday sermons, and regularly commented on the size of congregations from week to week; a selection of these is retained.

Before and after his marriage Egerton regularly journied to regional towns, including Tunbridge Wells, Hastings, and Brighton, commonly for personal reasons, including the pursuit of musical interests, and on professional business. He also went to London fairly regularly, normally on family and personal matters, in which musical activities were intermixed. He returned, at least once a year, to his previous parish near Salisbury, and equally often Bunbury in Cheshire where his father had been incumbent during his childhood and youth. After his marriage, he joined his wife – and later family – for part of their extended holidays spent usually in a southern coastal resort. He without fail returned to Oxford for the annual boat race. The details of these visits have been edited out in order to permit concentration on Burwash.

Although Egerton at one point records that parochial affairs dominated his life, and that he had little interest in a broader world, the diary in fact indicates that he kept abreast of developments, particularly the oft-traumatic divisions in his own Church, and also in the educational sphere, in both of which he had obvious professional interests. He also seems to have consistently followed home and foreign political affairs, though their lack of direct intrusion in parochial life, except on occasion like the first election in which any farmworkers exercised the franchise (1885), meant that he rarely recorded any detail. He did get involved in some major issues, including the debate over the legitimate roles of the state and the denominations in education, and also the heated, if only regionally relevant, furore over the issue of so-called extraordinary tithes, from which derived some of his income. On these he engaged publicly, through letters to the press, and on the public stage on occasion. His position dictated participation in public affairs, notably unofficial lobbying over social-security issues. This broader involvement is one reason why the diary zooms from one topic to another, and is partly responsible for the, at times, considerable commentary required to contextualize Egerton's own record. This editorial material is supplied in the footnotes.

The footnotes also contain much additional matter on parochial matters which come from other sources, including the regional press, and the records of social and criminal, and to a lesser extent religious administrations. This material is designed with a view to providing three principal functions. First, it often provides key supplementary details necessary to fully understand the diary entries. Secondly, it is also deployed as a form of control, a means of evaluating and balancing Egerton's perceptions, with others. Thirdly, purely factual information is provided, notably respecting biographical minutae of the villagers encountered and commented upon by Egerton, in order to complement it. This material is divided between very short editorial interventions in the text, giving, for example, a character's age and/or occupation, and the footnotes, where lengthier detail of similar nature is entered.

It is estimated that about nine per cent of the original text is reproduced below. Because many entries are repetitive, there are often time lapses between those printed here, though there are very few gaps – even of a day's duration – in the diaries themselves. For identical reasons, few daily entries appear in the entirety, the repetitive parts throughout, the beginning, during, and at the end, have been removed, though the convention of three or four full stops, indicating respectively the editing out of part, or whole sentence(s), is adopted.

Some effort has been made to preserve the flavour of the original, especially by using Egerton's own abbreviations, of which the most regularly used often take more than one form, or had two or three meanings. The most used appear below; others, like further editorial interventions in the text are explained and contained within square parenthesis; hence gr[and]. Finally, abbreviations used occasionally, but whose meaning is immediately obvious from their context, including 'cr.' and 'inns' (cricket and innings) are reproduced as in the original.

Cash sums in old pence, or shillings and pence, are recorded as paid to the needy in parenthesis, though the diarist usually recorded the sum without the brackets above the individual name. Here, for example, (2/6) denotes a payment of half a crown to whomsoever named. Egerton – perhaps somewhat archaically – usually made use of 'ye', technically perhaps as an abbreviation for 'the', and this is retained.

Abbreviations used in the Text

aft. . . . after, or afternoon, normally explained by the context.
agst. . . . against.
C. . . . called.
C. & R. . . . called and read.
C. & P. . . . called and prayed.
cd. . . . could.
Ch. . . . Church.
Cong: Congr, Congrg: . . . Congregation.
d. . . . daughter, or dined, or dinner: distinction between the latter two is
    virtually impossible.
Etchm. . . . Etchingham.
evg. . . . evening.
Husb. . . . husband.
morg. . . . morning.
N. . . . Nellie (Helen) Egerton's wife.
P. . . . Prayed.
pl. . . . pleasant.
Pr. . . . preached.
Ps. . . . psalm.
Rect. . . . Rectory.
s. . . . son.
Sch. . . . school.

shd. . . . should.
t. . . . talk, or talked.
w. . . . Either with, went, or walked. The context usually indicates which,
  though not invariably between went and walked.
wd. . . . would.
wh. . . . which.

Abbreviations used in Footnotes

Census, 1851. C.J. Barnes (ed.), *East Sussex Census: 1851 Index; Burwash,
  Ticehurst, Etchingham,* vol. 11 (Hastings, 1989).
ESCRO. East Sussex County Record Office.
PLB. Poor Law Board.
PRO. Public Record Office. HO. Home Office.
                        MH. Ministry of Health.
Sussex Folk. J. C. Egerton, *Sussex Folk and Sussex Ways,* (1924 edition).

1857

20 Feb. By morg. post from Uncle Joseph the offer of Curacy of Burwash; shewed the letter to the Vicar [of Nunton] who was at once generous & freed me from a promise I had given him to stay till Xmas. Uncle off[ered] £130 viz. £120 & surplice fees. I accepted it & wrote to the Bishop [of Salisbury] to resign Nunton. . . .

[He arrived in Burwash on 2 July.]

3 July. Looked at lodgings at a Mr. Taylors Vet[erinary] Surg[eon]. 12s. per week.

4 July. After R. w. Uncle to be introduced to some of the cottagers. . . . Pleased on the whole. Uncle in old carriage; horse fell in the carr. & hurt himself. . . .

Sun. 5 July. . . . in morg. at Burwash. . . . Day wet & showery, & a popular dissenting preacher close by: so congr: small. . . . An old yeoman farmer a Mr. Newington 83 walked part way with me to ye Rect. . . .

8 July [his 28th birthday]. . . . I am getting rapidly stout & I suppose a corporation is a sign of age.[1] . . . I went to boys & girls school & took a class in each. Boys 1st class not above the average I suppose. The Brit[ish] Sch. at Nunton wd. I fancy beat it hollow. Girls 2d cl. fairish; labouring hard at [three] R's with indifferent success. . . .

9 July. I w. uncle to call on several people to ask them to assist at School feast. At 2 oClock 280 children marched up and sang a rather doleful grace, then dispatched much beef & plum pudding. Games, sack running, scrambling for sugar plums, cricket, etc. etc. Previous to leaving they were drawn up under the trees sang God save the Queen . . . then listened to a speech in my behalf from [National Schoolmaster] Mr. Cox w. much fluency of speech wished me success in my work. I much obliged & the children departed about 8.30 or 45.

10 July. . . . Uncle & I parochialised. . . .

Sun. 12 July. School. . . . Wheel aft. congr: small.[2] Cherry orchard a counter attraction. . . .

14 July. To the school. Took 2d class; reading fair, writing not good, either in 1st or 2d class. Mr. & Mrs. Tilley called yesterday. . . . I called & R. w. Mrs. Isted & Mrs. Dann . . . of the Tott. C. on Mrs Wood of ye shop & Mrs Wood ye [Parish] Clerk's wife. R. w. an old couple named Hawkins beyond ye pay [toll] gate; liked them & R. w. Mrs Mepham . . . a cripple. Called on [surgeon] Mr. Combs[3] got a dose, as the heat has upset me rather. Mr. Tilley asked me to lunch. . . .

15 July. . . . Mr. Towers [Egerton's predecessor as Curate] called on me, & gave me the names of some of the old people. My shower bath came down from town. . . .

16 July. Lunched with Mr. Tilley. . . . Mr. & Mrs Towers came down. Mr. T. a good specimen of an English man of business. Shrewd, clear-headed, energetic, progressive, & yet with sympathies far above those of a merely materialist creed. . . .

17 July. To ye school, boys & girls. Singing in Church at 2 o'Clock. Funeral of one James Russell at 3. In the evg. took a letter for a man named John Pennells to his house near Crowhurst bridge. It contained the news of the death of his br[other]. . . .

18 July. Called on Mr. Combs. He came & helped me to set up my shower bath. Saw Mrs C[ombs]; Mr. Gibbs, Mrs Philcox, Mr. J. Philcox[4] & Mr. Foote called upon me. Uncle Philip called in evg. & I walked back part of the way to Brightling.

Sun. 19 July. Mr Izard [incumbent at Flimwell] pr: for me in morg. . . . Gave the domestics a short reading lesson. Began my shower bath.

20 July. Called & R. w. Mr. W. Newington at ye Green. R. w. James Waterhouse an old cripple. C. on a Mrs Balinger Farley a woman who has had 11 children & looks as young as a woman of 30. C. on Mrs Hetherington a cripple, bedridden; back to dinner. Then ye book club at ye Rose & Crown. Henry & Miss Young, Tilleys, Gibbs, Rush, Kirby, Combs there.[5] After club ye Franchise[6]; spent ye evg. archery; Gibbs, Mr. & two Miss Chards, his sister's. Mr. & Mrs Prothero there; ye latter played some Beethoven. . . .

21 July. To the school. Boys & girls. In aft. to Brightling. School feast, 166 children. Cheese, Bread, cake, tea, sack racing; one boy named Winchester an excellent jumper of high jumps. Sundry games, then ringing, & cheering & . . . away. . . .

25 July. . . . Aft. I walked to Glaziers Forge or Ford at the [South-eastern] extremity of the parish. Called en route on a Mrs Hyland of Park Hill; at the. . . . Forge live A. Clark & his wife & d. & s. in law ? Leeves or some such name: man terribly deaf. . . . In winter these places must be really inaccessible. . . .

27 July. A cricket match w. Waldron Club. I played; bowled out first ball. Waldron beat us by 70 or 80 runs. Our bowling shocking. Dined w. them afterwards at Rose & Crown. Made a short speech & left at 9 o'Clock: very orderly assembly as long as I saw them.[7]

30 July. Gave my domestic Ellen Hartfield her last lesson in reading & writing as she leaves tomorrow. Don't know what she will do. Handsome, ignorant, but well disposed; not 16 yet yet looks 20. I spoke plainly to her but kindly; hope she may have strength to go on well.

Sat. 1 Aug. . . . To the Wheel. Called on old Mr. Newington & son. C. on Waterhouse; gave a shilling to get them to put off tomorrow's service till 6.30 i.e. to get them to proclaim the putting off. C. on the new shopkeeper on the Common. C. & sat sometime w. Master Pilbeam. C. on Mrs Fussell a shopkeeper, looked like a non com[formist].

Sun. 9 Aug. Pr: in M[orning]. I Cor[inthians] 13. Aft. at Wheal. Matt. 25. 29. Extempore, my first attempt; about 26 min[utes]. Old Mr. Newington sat under the desk did not know it was Extempore: is that a compliment or not? It certainly was a great fallacy about extempore being necessary more from the heart than written. . . .

11 Aug. To ye Common; called on Waterhouse but out reaping & house locked up. . . . C. on Relfe ye Wheelwright at ye Wheal & on his mother an old woman at the Common who wd. go thro' her family history wh. was a long one, only she suppressed all mention of murder in that family.[8] . . . C. on either today or yesterday on a woman of name of Meopham at top of Bateman's Cart, she full of troubles; a woman of the name of Eyles (?) in house. . . .

Sun. 16 Aug. Aft. [afternoon Service] round by the road wh. leads from the Weald to Brightling; met a man who chaparoned me shewed me the boundaries of the parish wh. are intricate. His name was Budd.[9]

Mon. 17 Aug. At 1 (ought to have been at 12) the funeral of late farmer [James] Noakes. Smell very offensive; ought to have been buried on Saturday. I away to another funeral, of a woman named [Ann] Relf a pauper [who died in the workhouse, aged twenty-two]. The style of the two very different. Really the pauper funeral hardly decent; but I suppose it wd. not do to offer any premium to pauperism in any way whatever.[10]

21 Aug. Up to ye Common. C. on Mrs Pilbeam who keeps a day school a great contrast to ye new system. Still ye Children read nicely & spelt very well. She does not break up in harvest. . . .[11]

26 Aug. Up to the Common. C. on Miss Shavell who takes a few pupils of the better class of farmers. . . . Master Shavell a fiddler & has a tidy fiddle.[12]

3 Sept. At a "village party" comprising Mr. & Mrs Combs, Mr. Mrs Miss Tilley, Miss Hayward, Mr. & Mrs Barton, Mr. Gibbs, Mr. & Mrs Prothero; J. Philcox. A pleasant evg. Some discussion about the origin of the fly in the hop. Where does it come from. Mr. Barton thought it was brought by the wind.[13] Mrs Prothero played some Beethoven beautifully.

4 Sept. . . . up to the Common. . . . Met [John] Blunden the post man; he walks 15 miles a day & gets 11s a week. . . .

5 Sept. [Returning from Etchingham] . . . came through. . . . Font-ridge. . . . Found two or 3 consistent Churchmen up there amongst the cottagers. Tho' it is a long way off & perfectly isolated. Had some conversation with a Master [William] Buss [agricultural labourer, aged forty-three]. What a satisfactory sight a really religious & humble minded poor person is; thanks be to God. There are many such men even in Burwash.

Sun. 13 Sept. [After preaching] . . . Coming home spoke to one of a number of loungers near the Wheal Church. He was exceedingly rude, profane & blasphemous; professed himself an absolute unbeliever & expressed his conviction that when he died shd. die like a dog. I reasoned w. him sometime fortunately without losing my temper. The bystanders I find considered that the man treated me very "unhandsomely" & therefore I trust the feeling was agst. him; as it is painful where such a man can carry an audience with him. He was unusually shallow in his sceptical or rather atheistical arguments, but very profane. His name was I believe Buss & he works as I was told in the gardens at Brightling.

Sun. 20 Sept. [Burwash Wheel Church] . . . no loungers agst. ch. . . .

3 Oct. . . . to the school where there was an annual exhibition of large carrots, turnips, parsneps, & cabbage grown in the cottage gardens. I am not much of a judge & found that in cabbages, Savoys, a soft head is a virtue. Down to Bateman's where was a dinner to about 50. Good beef & pudding given by Uncle, so good appetites brought by ye men. Prizes then given away, & the party separated. . . . I walked up with Mr. Chard a stock-jobber who has two farms in the parish; the Boughs & Swing-gate.

Sun. 4 Oct. [Burwash Wheel Church] . . . 48 comm[unicants]; not many; some body took the bottle of wine out of the vestry during service time. . . .

6 Oct. The fair wh. was yesterday cleared out altogether to day. The results in penny trumpets & whistles not very troublesome.

8 Oct. [Ticehurst Agricultural Association annual show, which he attended with uncle Gould] . . . A pouring wet day. The show suffered accordingly. Beasts few but good. Uncle got two prizes, one for stock, one for Roots; he affects farming very much. A better attendance at dinner than expected. . . . Mr. Dixon was chairman & was a very good one; he came out well with a bonhommie wh. I thought cd. never have proceeded from such a generally demure personage. Speeches poor on the whole. We away about 8.30. Such entertainments interesting I think chiefly to the farmers immediately concerned. Cows, carrots, beet root, turnips & sheep, mysterious productions to me, tho' Uncle feels aggrieved that I do not comprehend them more.

16 Oct. . . . October fine weather is called about here "blackberry summer". . . .

Sun. 1 Nov. . . . A Wedding at 9. The man burst out laughing in trying to repeat the words after me. . . .[14]

3 Nov. . . . In aft. attended a meeting at the Bear for the purpose of discussing the ways of meeting the want of employment among the poor. Nothing much done, & it certainly is wonderful how the people will help themselves if they can get relief in no other way. It does seem that the only plan is to offer able-bodied relief in a repulsive form. It may seem hard, but again it seems fairest to all, for it separates between the idle ones, & the willing ones. . . .[15]

4 Nov. . . . Had a long talk with a man of ye name of Luck. He entertained a strong feeling agst. threshing machines, & said the feeling was general. . . .[16]

11 Nov. . . . After d. a long tour thro' the S[outh] W[est] wilds of the parish. C. on Mrs Syns [Simes] of Pounce Ford [Poundsford] also on Pankhurst of the Green Woods a most outlandish place; left w. 7 Childr. at home w[ife, Caroline, buried 1 Nov. aged thirty-nine] died a short time ago.

Sun. 15 Nov. [After Wheel service]. . . A drunken man at ye Wheel shouted out to me that he always found beer much more profitable to him than preaching; he also began to . . . [urinate] & told me he was coming to church as soon as he had done.

18 Nov. . . . I called on a farmer named Gillhum (?) [Gillham]. We got talking, & he turned out to be a regular Baptist. I promised him a few facts on the subject when I had time. We had a long & amicable talk.

20 Nov. . . . called on Mr. [David] Hyland about a character for a boy named James Caller [aged twenty-three, currently a farm labourer] who wants to be a policeman.

4 Dec. . . . Went up to meet Mr. [John] Coppard re. a poor woman . . . Grant who is to be sent to a lunatic asylum; she appeared very rational at times but clearly is liable to temporary attacks: weak from having had children so fast. . . .[17]

5 Dec. . . . I went down to Mrs Bartons at "the Lodge" to see Mr. Waghorn, the Builder, to get him to sign Caller's testimonials for the Police. He gave him an excellent character. . . .

7 Dec. . . . I signed the certif. for the poor woman . . . Grant to go to a Lunatic Asylum.

8 Dec. . . . gave a Man Fuller by name a shilling he having no work for a long time. Tried a razor I bought yesterday from an itinerant "Mr. Hobson". I might as well bought a ploughshare.

12 Dec. . . . Called on a Mrs. Pope, & had a scene w. her occasioned by my speaking to her about her habitually infamous language.

21 Dec. Dole day. I helped at the distribution at the Bear from 12.15 to about 5.30 PM; gave away about 50 stone of beef at [costing] 4s 1d per stone. One con man said a neighbour couldn't come because he had "electric fits" . . .[18]

22 Dec. . . . spoke to a man Leaney, a pensioner of marines; gave him 6d sorry as I fear he is not the steadiest character possible. . . .

23 Dec. To ye school to witness a public examination of a boy, Bishop, for taking wot wasn't his; humoured the occasion slightly. Aft: helped to decorate the church. . . . I called at ye Rectory. A woman by name Boots called; her husb: deserted her & satisfied she belongs by marr[iage] now to Warbleton I believe but as she was an Eastwood of Burwash comes back to her old place.[19]

24 Dec. . . . called on a Master Pankhurst, about privately baptizing his child; it was not ill, so said I cd. not do it.[20] His wife being dead, he has now a young woman as housekeeper, having a young child about 2 months old and having no girl of his own to take care of if he was obliged to get some one. The cottage is small, the family large & the chances of sin are very great; indeed the chances that sin is committed become almost a certainty. Gave one of his sons, a sharp lad, a shilling for shewing me the way out of the woods. C. & R. w. Mrs Clark of Glazier's Forge. She told me she had got "jumping twitely pains in her face, but that they sometimes left her face & got into her inside & then she said he tickled". . . . Helped at the distribution of prizes & of tea . . . to about 260 school children; they seemed to enjoy themselves.

25 Dec. . . . A wedding in the morg. The witnesses were a man & woman living in open sin, but we cannot refuse them or if we cd. the couple to whom they were witnesses, wd. never have been married most probably.[21] . . . James Caller having been rejected by Police Surgeon applied for character to get a sit[uation] on London, Brighton and South Coast Railway Company sent it him.

26 Dec. James Philcox sent me 27 oysters. Weather remarkably mild. Old Mr. Newington 83 recollects one such Xmas day only one. I heard the birds singing to day quite gaily, thrushes & blackbirds. Rhubard is sprouting in Mr. Taylor's Garden, the thermometer 51 in shade. The rustics all about sparrow shooting,[22] tho' at Brightling there is I am told a "pigeon shoot" to day. A holy day in Burwash & ye shops shut.

29 Dec. . . . Young Parks the butcher said he gathered ripe blackberries on Sunday at Brightling, & a mushroom is reported. . . .

30 Dec. . . . I c. on Mrs Barrow & on Mrs Hepworth both complaining of farmers prospects; the latter had many reasons to prove that they must be ruined. I c. on Mrs Edwards of Coppards hill to speak about her gr[and] ch[ild] at church. "Ah Sir" she groaned out "they are rudy they are rudy. They must be up to somethings that rubbidge"; their special rubbidge was cracking nuts at the Weald Church. C. to expostulate w. Haffenden & Collins boy for the same cause; they denied it. . . . Mrs Trower told me it is reported that "I am so angry with the girls hair that I am going to write to government about it"!!

Notes

1.   A pun on incorporated boroughs, many of which were of medieval or Tudor origin. At this time Egerton weighed $14\frac{1}{2}$ stone.
2.   At the Anglicans' licensed room on the Weald; see introduction, p. 18.
3.   Born 1829; qualified 1850, since when he was successively assistant surgeon in the Kent Poor-Law Unions, of Eastry, Bridge and Dartford. In September 1856 he was appointed surgeon to the Burwash medical division of the Ticehurst Union on a salary of £36 10s. Like most surgeons with Poor Law contracts, he was also a private practitioner. PRO. MH.12/13146.
4.   Gibbs and the Philcox's appear in the introduction.
5.   A lending library financed by the affluent, some of whom are named in the text. Egerton made as much use of it as any subscriber, and many further essentially repetitive references have been omitted.
6.   One of the largest farms in the parish, currently occupied by the relative newcomer, W.J. Tilley.
7.   The diary contains many brief entries respecting cricket matches which Egerton commonly watched for half hours while he was doing his rounds. In *Sussex Folk*, p. 110, he asserted that 'Cricket is, of course, our favourite summer game, though it rarely flourishes in any parish where there is not some resident gentleman

who, being himself fond of it, gives it his personal encouragement'. The fact that these cricketers then dined at the Rose and Crown with the opposition suggests that these players were relatively affluent. On the other hand, Egerton's comment on the maintenance of civilized behaviour while he remained, suggests that the sons of even the village affluent could become rowdy with drink.

8.   For the murder, see introduction, and esp. 18 Nov. 1859, p. 56 and note 17.

9.   William, a sixty-four-year-old agricultural labourer domiciled on the Common.

10.   Another dimension to the less eligibility concept behind the New Poor Law, vividly illustrated by the contrast here, which clearly shook Egerton, who took immediate, if not entirely comfortable refuge in utilitarian ideology, to the effect that even a decent publicly-funded funeral, could be said to favour dependency. ESCRO. Par.284/1/5/2.

11.   A typical Dame School. The fact that she did not close during the harvest suggests that a significant portion of her clientele were drawn from the tradesmen and shopkeeping elements.

12.   An interesting family; the father, William, born in Kensington, was fifty-one, and combined his occupation as a glazier with farming ten acres. His wife was also a Londoner, but daughter Ann, aged seventeen had been born in Romford, Essex, and later described herself as a 'Governess'. 1861 Census.

13.   The appearance, and then the potential damage caused by the fly – and other pests including fungi – was a subject of intense speculation from the spring, which intensified in the immediate run up to the hop-harvest in September. Most South-eastern newspapers printed reports from April through to the end of the harvest, many of which were submitted by local correspondents.

14.   Thomas, son of labourer William Twort married Lucy, daughter of the reprieved murderess Hannah Chandler, and her second husband, the deceased Thomas. ESCRO. Par.284/1/3/2.

15.   Wintertime lay-offs of a significant proportion of the workforce were the norm; in order to minimize parochial contributions to the Poor Law Union, farmers often came to unofficial agreements to employ married men with children, rather than single-men. Such arrangements could be more formally thrashed out at vestry meetings, where additional decisions to mitigate the winter-time poverty problem included, especially, road maintenance programmes. Once again Egerton seems to reluctantly accept the less-eligibility principle, namely limiting relief to only those able-bodied males who would take their families into the workhouse.

16.   There is some evidence that the introduction and use of threshing machines, was fundamentally retarded by the Swing explosion in 1830, especially outside East Anglia; elsewhere their re-introduction is said to belong to the 1850s. E.J. Hobsbawm and G. Rudé, *Captain Swing*, (1973 edition), esp. pp. 317–23. Some contemporaries claimed that in fact labourers disliked the long winter-time hours spent in the laborious task with hand-flails. However, populist expressions of anti-machinery sentiment encountered by Egerton were more likely to have been long-standing by this date, and their articulation at this season in the context of parochial meetings to consider winter-time working-class conditions, is significant.

17.   Caroline Grant, aged 48, was sent to a private lunatic asylum in Clerkenwell, early in December, as Sussex was resisting the implementation of the 1856 legislation enforcing the erection of County Asylums for 'Pauper Lunatics'. PRO. MH.12/13146. S. Williams, 'Institutional Care for the Pauper Insane in Sussex 1830–1880', (Unpublished MA dissertation, CNAA, Brighton Polytechnic, 1990), ch. 3.

18.   The implication is that this applicant tried to use false pretences to obtain his neighbour's share.

19.   Marriage conferred a settlement, and Mrs Boots belonged to Warbleton in the Hailsham Poor Law Union, from which she may have received outdoor relief; alternatively, relatives domiciled in Burwash may have provided for her.

20.   See above, p. 29, 11 Nov. Most baptisms of working-class babies were performed on Sundays. However, high infant mortality, notably in the first few days, led many parents to have a sickly infant baptized immediately and at home. See below, p. 36, 15 and 17 Feb. 1858.

21.   The witnesses were labourer John Vidler and Harriet Hodge, to the marriage of widower and bricklayer Elkanah Russell and Isabella Twort. In 1861, Vidler then aged forty-one, married Harriet, thirty-eight, witnessed by Elkanah, and Sarah Snashall. ESCRO. Par.284/1/3/2.

22.   Sparrow-shooting, was the poor-man's equivalent to game-shooting; it was a traditional Boxing Day sport, and whether organized or not, the tradition preserved participants from being mistaken for poachers.

1858

1 Jan. Blunden the postmaster's daughter married at Ashburnham, where-upon the bells at Burwash rang much. They will ring for a gallon of beer I am told. Singing with the school children. The new mistress came. I went to the boys' school.

[From 4 to 16 Jan. in London and Bath, including Sun. 10th: 'I preached for Mr. Harding at Bexley. . . . A rich & fashionable congregation, very different from Burwash'.]

18 Jan. . . . parish meeting about the poor. The idea of lowering the old people's pay was hinted at bec. it is higher than in other unions. I spoke up agst. it. Went thro' the relief list & didn't find any body to dock; added on a case or two.[1]

19 Jan. . . . C. on old Hawkins; he told me that he recollected in the old war time bread being 3/9½ a gallon for one week.[2] He mentioned a case of 3 idiots in one family in Burwash. . . . One was noted for running to a ram & butted him. . . .

20 Jan. . . . Yesterday . . . I had a long parley on matters musical with Brook ye musical tutor of Burwash an intelligent man.[3] Funeral of an Isted child; yesterday Sally Weston heard she had got a Queen's scholarship, having been put in the 2d class at the Examination.

22 Jan. Carman got the news of his Queen's scholarship, tho' he is but a 2d class, & not high in that; the fact is, he reads a great deal, but he is apathetic, & sadly wants energy. I congratulated him at the school. In the girls school I happened to look at the 1st class slates; they contained a character of Charles the 2d; most were very good. From one however, I gathered that Charles was eminently hypocritical & insincere; that there was a great plague in his reign; that many people in London died of it & that it destroyed 89 churches & several houses. . . .

23 Jan. Wrote sermon, based on J.H. Newman's parochial Sermons; really his sermons are remarkable productions, pregnant to a degree; there is not a needless sentence in a volume & they are extremely suggestive. After din. to Fontridge. C. in Wenham Brill on Mrs Sands who lives where Ballard did w. Edmund King. A very long talk w. a "young chap" named Ballard. He spoke sensibly about work: wages etc, tho' strongly agst. the army he had a brother in the Artillery, who was discharged at the reduction after the

Crimean War. He alleged that the victuals weren't sufficient, & that the liberty wasn't sufficient.

Sun. 24 Jan. . . . C. & P. w. old [sixty-five, Samuel] Waterhouse after the serv[ice]: he quite ill. Just as I came out the Dissenting preacher went in. I happened to have left my gloves & had to go back for them. I heard brother noncom[formist] halloing out to the deaf old man "Have you got Jesus X in you – the hope of glory?". . . .

25 Jan. . . . school. I had to turn 3 boys out Edwd. Watson Harmer & Pope for bad conduct in my absence: Pope's 2d time. . . .

27 Jan. In the morg. to the Common. C. & saw poor old Waterhouse as he lay dead. . . . C. on widow Hetherington about her boy being late at Sunday school.

28 Jan. . . . Uncle took me in his carr[iage] to Ticehurst to funeral of old Mr. Wetherell; met nearly all the neighbouring clergy; a rather swell funeral. . . . C. on Mrs Hyland's night school. Heard . . . that Whelwall Master of Tr[inity] Coll[ege] . . . in marrying Miss Hashall last week not being au fait in the marr. service, himself put the ring on Miss Hashall's finger, & said "w. this ring I thee wed" & on being chaffed afterwards said – Ah well I suppose I must give Marshall a 99 year lease of her – . Anne left, a day before her time, but she had become so unbearable that she was bundled off. Burwash servants are primitive. Mrs Radcliffe wanted a housemaid, a bold looking girl of about 15 by appearance applied: Mrs R, "You are but young are you to take a housemaid's place". Girl "Oh I am much older than I look". Mrs R. "But have you ever had a situation before". Girl "Oh yes lots!". . . .[4]

30 Jan. Sermon writing. Rain all the day almost. Two funerals old Waterhouse & [seventy-four-year-old, road haulier, William] Eastwood. The news of the death of a son of Waterhouse who had emigrated to Ohio as a labourer, came to London, Sunday. . . .

4 Feb. . . . A man called Edward Dann applied to me to help him into the Metrop[olitan] Police. Mr. Hyland mentioned something agst. him so I wrote a note to him telling him to call tomorrow.

5 Feb. To ye schools. Afterwards to ye Common. C. Mrs Luck (6d) & on young Dann who went to the police in Staffordshire about 7 weeks since. He crippled w. Rheumatism, a nice young fellow & he was glad to see me. . . . Lecture in evg. by a Mr Mackintosh on Astronomy; good room; people attentive & seemed to understand. It was a good lecture, tho' it wd. seem impossible almost to make such a subject clear to an audience who know nothing about it previously. E. Dann saw me & denied ye charges, of course, but as Mr. and Mrs Hyland affirmed them most strongly I declined to assist his case.

6 Feb. . . . Pankhursts (1/-) boys of Greenwoods asked for 1/- to get "the baby some clothes to be Xteened in". . . . John Harmer (1/-), poor man, 5 childr. & hardly any work for last 3 months; fine man, but looks half starved. . . .[5]

[Brief stay in London.]

15 Feb. Sent a note to Pankhurst of Greenwoods whose child died unbaptized. I am sorry for it, but I cd. not help it. I went up ye day before Xmas day; then the child was not ill, & he did not come again till it was too late. . . . Evg. school; I pronounced this year's session closed, as I can no longer spare the time. I shook each boy by the hand, & got one or two hearty shakes wh. repaid me well for all the trouble & money I have been at; several thanked me. I have liked the work much & hope it may have done good.

16 Feb. . . . Wrote to . . . traffic manager S[outh] E[astern] R[ailway] about a porter's place for R[ichar]d Pilbeam. Wrote yesterday to Officer Commanding R[oyal] Marines at Chatham about a lad Alfred Cornwall 81st Co[mpany] his mother being anxious about him.

17 Feb. . . . C. & sat w. Joe Blackford at Saller's Brook, a very amusing oldish man. . . . Pankhurst unbaptized child buried without service. . . . Wrote to ask Uncle [Gould] whether a woman called Crawford cd. have a child buried here; the child an orphan Rebecca Croft, the woman living at Shoyswell [just across the Etchingham border].

18 Feb. . . . Got a letter from Lieut. Thomas Adj[utan]t of R. M. saying that Cornwall was serving in China. . . . C. on old Mr. Newington; he very ill. R. & P. w. him. . . . C. on new police Sergt. Peerless; saw his wife; a very respectable looking person. C (yesterday) on Mrs Caller; no tidings of James who I fear must be in mischief.

19 Feb. Letter from Uncle declining to bury the girl, as being an out parishioner. . . .

Sun. 21 Feb. . . . My Bible class began 32 boys; I only pray that this may continue.

25 Feb. . . . C. & R. w. Mrs Watson & her grandson; had a long conversation w. her gr[and] d. who is living with a man Hyland by name. The girl wants to be married but the man won't marry her, alleging that he does not want to be burdened with a large family or he is growing old, that is calmly looking forward to throwing them on the parish. It certainly seems almost a premium on illeg. children that a man can have as many as he likes & then when he pleases send them & their mother into the workhouse.[6] . . . C. on the new Constable-Company. . . . C. & R. w. Mrs Pope. They say she is improved in conduct. God grant that it may be on right principles. Her cottage is almost as windy as the high road. . . .

26 Feb. . . . A boy Pope asked to day for ticket for adm[ission] to sch; did not know the [Christian] name of either Father or Mother!!

3 Mar. . . . C. on Mrs Balcombe (1/-) about her going into the Union. I cd. do nothing. . . .

4 Mar. A Woman Booth came up to ask me to write to the War Office about getting her husband who ran away, & enlisted in the Artillery & is now at Corfue to allow her something. After I to Rectory to search Register of bapt[isms] for a Mrs Luck née Budd; also extracted no of illeg. baptisms for various years (see end of book). . . .

7 Mar. . . . A travelling woman called in aft. having heard from one of the men whom I relieved yesterday that there was a "kind gentleman" in Burwash. She had heard it on the Lewes road. I had unwillingly to refuse her assistance as she seemed a woman of better class, but it will not do. I shd. soon be nothing more that a relieving officer for tramps.

11 Mar. . . . C. at Mrs Watson: she indulged me w. a tirade agst. her old husband for taking opium, wh. is I fear a habit w. several in Burwash. Old Wood delerious & cd. not see me.

12 Mar. . . . C. on old Mrs Edwards, a great sufferer w. asthma & dropsy; said she used to relieve beggars & has given them bonnets & shoes wh. her children have after wards picked up in ye fields and brought home again. . . .

16 Mar. . . . c. on Mrs Pilbeam heard some of her scholars read; they acquitted themselves fairly. . . . C. on Mrs Hook; she told me that the farmers are thinking of lowering the wages of their labourers to 10s. . . . I hear so too in other quarters. C. on Mr. Barton a person who is purchasing a good many little lots of property in Burwash. He stays at Lucks. I found him to be a very stout elderly stockbroker, apparently rich, but disposed to be kind to his tenants in the way of improving their cottages. I leant James Copper £1 to be paid when he can do it, towards purchasing the dog & ferrets of Twort who is going to Australia.[7]

18 Mar. . . . C. on Mrs Pope (1/-) near Rye Green. The man Smith who had the farm last left owing poor Pope £3:0:0 for labour. The loss is very

heavy to a labouring man. Smith was a drunken fellow & I fear that Pope
has not a chance of getting his money. C. on Mrs Gogmunden [?] of Rye
Green lately come to ye farm. Rent under Mr. Sargeat who seems a hardish
sort of man. The husb: is a Dissenter. The wife was 6 y[ea]rs servant to Mr.
Courthope. The farm is 67 acres, the rent £60.

Sun. 21 Mar. . . . C. & R. w. Pennels; worse again. There is something sad
& painful in seeing an able bodied man lying at death's door: it is a very
diff[erent] sight from the death-bed of a child or an old person. Bible class
25.

22 Mar. . . . Dined at Rectory. Mr. Morland there. He afterwards gave a
lecture in Natn. School on China & the Tea Trade. A good audience. I liked
the lecture; many did not care much about it. . . .

[25-7 Mar. in London.]

Sun. 28 Mar. Bible class smaller & not the right class of boys, being young
boys & those who come to Sunday School & day school . . .

Good Friday, 2 Apl. School & Church. Fair congregation of middle
class. . . . Aft. to Weald . . . congreg. but poor. It is the custom among the
Burwash "young chaps" to play marbles in the road all Good Friday & there
was plenty of it to day tho' snow in the aft. dispersed a good many
assembleys.

Sun. 4 Apl. 67 at Holy Comm. tho' only 3 poor men. Aunt Harriet sent me
£5 to distribute in charity at Burwash. . . . Bible Class 18 or 19.

5 Apl. C. on J. Hilder (1/-), Ham lane. Day for giving up ye sheep wh. have
been kept in Burwash by the farmers during ye winter. Mr. Piper of
Hawkhurst has I think 1300, wh. pay about 7s a head.

6 Apl. . . . C. on Pope of Brooks Marl. He is ill of Ague & no wonder; his
wife is enough to give a dozen men the Ague, a dirty wretched looking
woman & the children a sad mixture of natural rosiness & artificial squalor.
I talked w. the man about Sunday observance. God only can make one's
words anything more than mere words, but the man said he wd. see about
it when he got well. . . .

7 Apl. . . . c. N. Pennells. Found that Uncle had been in the habit of giving
them rice *every* week. . . . Just looked in on H. Pennells (6d); a terrible boil
on his neck.

17 Apl. C. & R. w. a man named Stephen Elliott living w. a woman named
? Vergill. Talked very seriously to him for a considerable time. He is a man

who has evidently read a good deal of the Bible, tho' his knowledge has not hindered his sin. Had been ill before when Uncle was able to visit him, but without apparent results; however as he is now clearly ill I sent him up some brandy.

18 Apl. . . . Being a moonlight night I met many couples walking together & many girls who had better have been in doors.

23 Apr. C. on Cramp at ye Bough [Farm]; he has had a most wonderful escape from being killed in a thrashing machine: his wife showed me his clothes wh. had not a piece a foot square belonging to them. The man only bruised in the leg. . . .[8]

Sun. 25 Apl. . . . the road home [from the Weald] made one sorrowful; young men & women out together in a manner wh. however harmless it may be w. other classes, we know to be full of danger for them.

26 Apl. . . . Mr. Taylor told me the disheartening news that 6 or 7 girls, if not more, close at hand in the vill. were in the family way. It indeed is sad beyond expression. . . . Such a fact makes one almost a sceptic as to schools or anything else. . . . Still it is not right to doubt. . . . Bad as things are, they surely cd. be worse if the voice of warning & exhortation to turn to Xy [Christianity] were altogether dumb.

29 Apl. . . . I don't know how it is but we have a great number of ague cases this winter & spring; more I am told than have ever been known simultaneously before.

30 Apl. . . . walked round by Perrimans & Etchingham by Fontridge. Wild outlandish place. C. on an old woman Balcombe (1/-). Cottage hardly fit for a pig pound. Husb: drinks away all his money. Her son (1/-) a big strong fellow ill of ague. A German band (1/-), a tolerably good one in ye village. . . . I had them before my house.

1 May. Sundry May garlands & May poles; some pretty others the reverse. . . .

3 May. . . . C. & talked w. Elliott (1/-). Suffering from hunger. The woman & children must go into the Union [workhouse] clearly. . . . Coppard came up about ye case of Elliott & others. He is a capital man for overseer [of the poor] a shrewd head & a kind heart are not often found in closer conjunction than w. him.

7 May. Singing; the children terribly flat, so that I dismissed them somewhat before their time. I can't tell why it is, but every now & then they are radically or hopelessly flat. A funeral at 4.15; a Jenner Child.

Sun. 9 May. . . . In aft: at ye Wheel. . . . A good congregation; larger than usual owing to there being no service at ye [Wesleyan] Chapel. . . .

10 May. Refused a Mrs Tom Vidler a ticket of admission to the school for her child, as it was not 6 and didn't know all its letters. Really schools now-a-days save parents trouble enough, a mother need not think it hard that she shd. be called upon to teach her children their letters. After d. looked in at school. Then w. down to Testers at the Park Farm. 100 acres of hops grubbed this year in Burwash; tho' 20 perhaps have come into bearing, the decrease is only about 80 acres.[9]

12 May. Burwash fair; not much stirring. . . .

Sun. 16 May. . . . A nigger c. on me aft: serv[ice] & abruptly asked me to give him a new Bible for his old one. I could not doubt that he was a hypocrit so I bundled him off.

3 June. I had a funeral; the woman died of fever & the coffin was taken at once to the grave. The custom is here to do the rest of ye service in ye church after ye burial.[10]

Sun. 20 June. [At Wheel licensed room]. . . . Had to speak again to some godless geniuses who were loitering about. Only got laughed at, but I try nevertheless to speak as quietly & seriously as I can.

22 June. To ye school. I have a plan now wh. I think answers in improving ye boys reading. One boy reads a piece out of a book while the next stands up & looks over. He then takes it & reads while the next to him stands up & so on. I am using Monros True Stories about cottagers & I find the boys keep up their interest & I hope mend in their style of elocution.

Sun. 27 June. [Wheel]. . . . Spoke to some young men who were going away from church. They laughed & passed on. Spoke to a man Hawkins . . . son of old Richard Hawkins; he appears a Chapelite & apparently knew me tho' I did not know him.

28 June. . . . C. Mrs Baker wife of ye new tenant of Honeysetts Mill & Mr. Laws house; finds Burwash dull never having lived in ye country before.

1 July. . . . c. on Mrs Edwards to speak to her grandsons about idling away Sunday tho' sent to Church. Only one wd. let me get near him; the others bolted. . . . On Tues: she presented me w. an oak walking stick, as a memorial of her regard.

12 July. . . . gave my watch to [watchmaker, John] Noakes to put in a new spring; he lent me a silver watch.[11]

16 July. School. Took also girls 1st cl. in Bible. They want the supervision of a higher mind than that of a pupil teacher, who I find takes them chiefly.

17 July. . . . C. on Mrs Barrow. Had a long talk with Levi Luck on the subject of living together without being married. The woman's husband ran away 12 y[ea]rs ago to America & has not been heard of; still I do not suppose she cannot marry, & I fear they will not separate.[12]

30 July. Inspected Cottage gardens with Mr. Tilley & Uncle; only three claimants, Eastwood, Pennells, Waterhouse. . . .[13]

Table, at end of volume of births and illegitimate births for selected years.

Year:	Total Births.	Illegitimate.	Year.	Total Births.	Illegitimate.
1821	73	7	1845	63	4
1825	60	4	1850	56	3
1826	70	6	1855	62	3
1831	67	6	1856	49	7
1836	80	5	1857	61	8 (one of
1840	45	4			mothers aged 14

1 Aug. School thinner owing to harvest.

4 Aug. . . . A meeting about relief of ye poor. I did not go tho' I was invited.

7 Aug. In aft. some time looking over old letters & old papers an occupation I every now & then like very much. A good many from poor people of different sorts. Simple & warm hearted. Old school exercises etc. all bring back reminiscences of interest, if not all of pleasure. . . . James Copper pd. back a sovereign wh. I leant him in the early spring.

8 Aug. . . . Tea w. Mr. & Mrs Dunk of Perch Hill; pleasant & I believe good old people; he 74 & a most active old man. Formerly a volunteer & appointed also to drive off the cattle in the neighbourhood in case Buonoparte landed.[14] He recollects bread for a long time at 3s 4d a gallon [loaf].[15] I recollect it 10d. . . .[16] Old Hawkins recollects in 1816 or 17 Ice being on the wheat when he went to reap in ye morg. . . . Heard that James Caller died last week in London. Poor lad. I did not expect anything of the sort when I tried to get him in as policemen in the spring. I shd. not be surprised if his br[other] a corporal in the . . . [army] in India was dead, as they have not heard for some time. [Added later: 'he was'.]

Sun. 22 Aug. [Wheel]. . . . One set of men about 5 in number seems to take a delight in just meeting me as one is going into Ch: & again when one comes out.

30 Aug. . . . spoke to [farmers] John Dann & Frank Russell & to the Edwards . . . of Copper's Hill . . . about hopping, asking them to stop picking at 12 on Saturdays [following decision to this effect at Rural Deanery meeting on 26th] so as to let the people do their baking & washing etc. on Sat. not on Sunday. Some said they wd. others said they wd. consider.

31 Aug. W. Uncle & Mr. Tilley to inspect cottages & gardens for the prizes.

3 Sept. Sands funeral. Mr Combs had a post mortem exam. & found that the poor man had been a fearful sufferer. The poor will seldom allow such a thing as a post mortem but in this case I am thankful it was allowed as the man had been considered a shammer.[17] . . . Cous[in] Ellen told me that old Mrs Cruttenden of ye Tot objected once to a tract bec. it spoke ill of Judas Iscariot wh. it was wrong to do when a man was dead!

7 Sept. W. Uncle over Mr. Tilley's ground. Very wet at intervals, about 4 brace killed.

11 Sept. c. on old Mrs Hawkins. She very facetious indeed & asked me whether I thought yesterday that she had gone out hopping! Said her old man too comes home very "testy" & does not like to be asked how many bushels he has picked. . . .

13 Sept. Out shooting w. Uncle, or rather walking w. him while he shot. . . . Uncle killed 6 or 7 brace I think. . . .

14 Sept. . . . Funeral of old [sixty-three, Henry] Waterhouse, poor man. I wish I cd. read the service w. as much hope over more of my parishioners as I did over him.

16 Sept. . . . Funeral of Relf child w. died suddenly. 1st Coroner's inq[uest] in parish since I have been here.[18]

17 Sept. . . . Coming into ye vill. met a Mr. Franks just returned from Tasmania where he had been since 1820. Walked w. him some little time & was interested. Very little change in Burwash for the time certainly.

Sun. 19 Sept. At ye school, had to call in Mr. Cox to ye 1st cl. By a sharp & vigorous movement he soon produced discipline & handed me over the class quite subdued. I have not the power or rather do not think it seemly to proceed to extremities wh. is a power wh. every now & then must be used & in hoppicking time the boys get uncommonly free & easy. . . .[19]

Sun. 26 Sept. [Wheel]. . . . No chapel service & so a better congregation. After Ch. a stranger asked me for a tract, but I fear he was a humbug as I think he had been drinking. He said he came from Devonport in Wales; now there is no such place, I believe! [in Wales].

28 Sept. . . . at 10 a wedding, two hoppers, the man Jos. Pittfold, a widower, much affected at thoughts of last wife. I feared he wd. not be able to go thro' the ceremony, but his best man exhorted him "Come Joe – stand up man". Mary [Taylor's domestic servant] left foolish girl; from what she says she will not better herself. I fear it is a fancy. . . . Tonbridge Wells is her rendezvous & the person who has engaged her is "quite a gentleman", that is his name is on a brassplate. Whereupon I comments of course he can't be a gentleman or else he wd. not have his name on the door. A good instance of the common acceptation that a gentleman is one who does not work for his living. . . . Up to the Windmill field to look on while Mr. Gould, Tilley & [owner-occupying farmer George Fagg] Gilbert inspected allotments. . . .

29 Sept. . . . some nice conversation w. two Misses Hagley & Miss Eaton tho' really single ladies who are no longer young are apt to be rather dangerous members of society, inasmuch as they say sharpish things.

2 Oct. In morg. awards to Cottagers vegetables made in School Room. Afterwards dinner to 66 tenants at Batemans. Uncle, Mr. Tilley & myself spoke; men very attentive, tho' they had a good deal of advice given them.[20] One man spoke up well & said that if those thrashing machines were done away with all wd. be right. I argued with him; poor man, it is but an indifferent consolation to say that they cannot stop the use of machinery & that however hard it presses they must submit but this is the long and short of it.[21]

4 Oct. School, better numbers. Discovered that ye singing boys had entered into an agreement yesterday not to come singing in ye afternoon; ye young varlets. . . . James Smith wanted me to sign a certif. that I had known him 4 years, he having been in the parish 2, & I one & a 1/4: he too living with a woman & not being married. Considerable cheek I think.

5 Oct. School. Corn came in as the subject of a reading lesson so I tried a little Political Economy. Some of the answers sensible, perhaps quite as sensible as the questions. . . . Went by Lades past a little farm [Glyddish, seventeen acres] wh. one [Richard] Balcombe uses. The wife said that till a month ago neither Rector nor Curate for 9 years had been to the House; it certainly is much out of the way. . . . About 9 a young farmer named Bagshawe a Northamptonshire man who is going to take Mr. Gibbs farm came down. An intelligent young fellow apparently, tho' I question whether he knows what he is coming to.

9 Oct. . . . C. on Pankhurst of Pump Court & read a letter from her s. John
H.M. 9th Lancers. A good & sensible letter, giving a very clear account of
ye campaign [in India] tho' written I fancy by a comrade & not by himself.
Made out a list of Burwash men serving in different parts of H.M. Service;
15 men & a boy, 3 Cavalry, 4 R. M., 4 R. N.

Sun. 10 Oct. School. . . . Singing boys I fear conspiring again to be
troublesome. No responses & hardly any singing. It is very odd, but they
have no just cause of complaint that I am aware of. . . .

11 Oct. . . . c. on Henry Pennalls; neither he nor Eliot any work, I fear there
is every prospect of a terrible winter.[22] . . . Talked for sometime about
Emigration to a young man by name of Balcombe who wants to go to
Australia, but says his mother tells him that she wd. "as soon follow him to
the grave" as let him go. A very common saying;[23] what is to be done, is
mother to be obeyed.

16 Oct. C. on Mrs Head tried to combat the idea wh. a woman broached
that ye Poor Law "Officers" take much of the money wh. shd. go to the
poor. . . .[24]

19 Oct. Walked to Brightling. Wet, but large [Rural Deanery] meeting. . . .
Jackson tried to speak for a few minutes continuously on the way of treating
High Calvinism, but private talking as usual, soon began again; he divided
the matter I think well. 1st. How are we to defend our own people. 2dly
how are we to influence the Calvinists themselves. Nothing very definite
resulted, as is our misfortune. Conversation at dinner, above the average for
life, if not for intellect.

25 Oct. . . . W. over to Stonegate, nearly got taken up as a poacher having
lost my way, & got near a preserve, where the gamekeeper met me; he
shewed me ye way. . . . [While returning] I woke a man who was drunk &
asleep on ye parapet of Crowhurst bridge; one roll ye wrong way & he wd.
have been drowned. He gratefully called me a d[amned] blackguard Bobby.

1 Nov. . . . Night school opened with 28. One of the old ones dead, some
left the parish & others for various reasons away so, many new recruits.
Young ones chiefly.

2 Nov. . . . Some travelling auctioneers w. cheap goods c. at Hyland's
[while Egerton was visiting] & sold some things. They are staying at the
Bell & hold their auction every night. The goods are I am told very
rubbishy pretending to be bankrupt stock, but the men take a good deal of
money. . . .

8 Nov. . . . 30 boys at night school.

10 Nov. . . . C. on Mrs Waterhouse, she says her husband wants very much to learn to read & that he is now "man enough" to put 3 letters together. . . . Had a long talk on Political Economy with [labourer] George Luck. . . . Night school 40. I stated my intention of closing ye school [with prayers].

12 Nov. . . . Night school closed in prayer. I trust it is not an idle form but that it is an earnest acknowledgement of our need of God's help if the work is to be blessed.

15 Nov. . . . Had a conversat[io]n w. a Burwash man Sergt. Major Bond 11th Huss[ars]. Medal & 4 clasps for Crimea & French war medal in 19 yrs. in ye service; a fine man. Night school 39.

16 Nov. . . . drove to Waldron [Rural Deanery; eight present]. . . . A more profitable meeting than many. . . . A long discussion on ye best means of dealing w. ye High Calvinism prevalent in this neighbourhood. . . .

18 Nov. . . . C. on John Dann. He says he is sure that if a good master cd. be got there are 30 or 40 boys & men on the Common who wd. pay willingly 3d a week for night schooling.

25 Nov. . . . Night School [convened today] as tomorrow is club night.

26 Nov. . . . Presided at ye Club quarterly meeting in ye school room. A truly self-governing & independent association. A very good specimen it struck me of the turn wh. the English disposition naturally takes when left to itself. I was pleased with what I saw & heard. The rules are read over every quarter night & indicate a love of order: a full desire that every body shd. have justice that every question concerning the Club shd. have a full & frank discussion; that after discussion the minority should submit quietly to the decision of the majority.

29 Nov. . . . Wrote to a man Elis Eaton who c. on me on Friday night about emigration. I am sorry to say that the Commissioners from whom I heard yesterday only take out now [virtually free of charge] female domestic servants & married agricultural labourers with 2 children or less.[25]

2 Dec. . . . C. & R. w. Mrs Mepham. T. to her son & d. in law about emigrating. They wd. not go on the water for a house full of gold; they wd. rather starve at home first. . . .

Sun. 5 Dec. . . . I had to turn a boy Wm. Eyles, a big boy a generally speaking one of my best boys, out of my night school for bullying. I found out afterwards the little boy had been "aggravation" & "contradicting" but still I cannot allow bullying in school.

21 Dec. . . . I assisted at the Dole distribution, given out this year in ye school, wh. is a great improvement.[26] I subscrib[ed] £1:3:4 not that I altogether like this system of indiscriminate Charity, & yet it has perhaps this good that once a year human judgement of evil-doers is suspended, & all are treated equally, excepting of course those who are living in open sin such as living together without being married. We gave away about 91 stones of beef at 4s 3d a stone, 2d higher than last year.

22 Dec. . . . Called on Mrs Radcliffe about decorations. I saw [William] Shoosmith about holly.[27] N.B. This year I took care that no premiums shd. be offered for stolen holly by giving money to "any" boy who brought holly & I wrote notes to the proprietors of holly.[28] N. School, only about 33.

23 Dec. Boys kept bringing up holly. . . .

24 Dec. Helped to decorate the Church. Mrs Radcliffe & Miss Tilley the chief designers. . . . The police have got Tom Relf of the Rocks & R[ichar]d Chandler for stealing oats from Mr. [Joel] Newington of the Green.[29] Also James Payne for poaching;[30] so two of my eye sores are removed. . . . Boys singing Carols came about 7. The whole village vocal the melodies uniform; not much ingenuity or skill in the performance. Hemings Blunden & Co the proprietors of the traditions of "Xmas Singing" came about 10.45. They sang such pieces as Hail smiling morn, The Red Cross Knight . . . Foresters round the cheerful horn, Life's a Bumper, & a County Son. . . . One carol, "While Shepherd's watched", gave the performance a Xmas character, & that was all; they came again about 4 or 5 o'Clock on Xmas morg. I gave 1s.

26 Dec. [Wheel] . . . only about 40 there. People I suppose have their friends for a holyday & dont look upon going to church as an element of a holyday.

27 Dec. After d. to Mrs Bull of Brooks Marl to speak about her d's marriage. The d. was born before the mother was married. The mother's name was Bowles; but she being married soon after, the girl was always c. by the father's name Bull. The mother has the d's name put up in the banns as Bowles being told that this was right. Uncle alters it to Bull wh. is the legal name, being "that by wh. the girl is known"; the banns of course were asked at Hawkhurst in the name of Bowles. The young man is afraid of the chaff consequent on a change of Banns & wants to know what to do. . . . N[ight] S[chool] only 6 so I gave it up for this week. "A sparrow shoot" & a raffle for a pig together with "a ball" at ye Rose & Crown the Burwash Xmas amusements. . . .

31 Dec. I baptized privately a child of a woman named Ellis who lives with R[ichar]d Relf. I spoke to her most seriously, but as her only refuge on leaving the man wd. be to "the house" she prefers living in sin to leaving him.[31] Baptized Mrs Combs little child wh. is in a bad way. Buried Wm. Newington. The first funeral I ever had where the coffin wd. not go into the grave wh. in this case had to be lengthened.

Notes

1. Clearly, the vestry hoped to reveal claimants whose regular relief payments could be reduced, or even terminated, only to discover legitimate additional claimants.
2. Either 1799–1801 or 1810–12, and possibly both periods.
3. In *Sussex Folk*, Egerton mentions only the Fleming family in a musical context. See below, pp. 123, 127–8, 14 Feb., 29 June, 2 and 3 July 1872.
4. Domestic servants were normally hired by the year. This story appears, almost verbatum, in *Sussex Folk*, pp. 37–8.
5. At this time the Ticehurst Board of Guardians reported that workhouse accommodation for able-bodied males was full, and that Burwash was particularly hard hit by poverty, because, unlike other parishes in the Union, special arrangements to maximize employment on the roads had not been made. It was said that Burwash 'farmers are much embarrassed by the depression of the price of hops and out of humour at the recent addition [enhancement of the police rate owing to] . . . the Police Act' of 1856. There were 79 Burwash inhabitants in the House. The Union would have to 'fall back' on the labour test for Burwash claimants, an emergency procedure last adopted in 1847. Meanwhile some claimants had no alternative to begging. One, James Payne, a father of three children under eight, directly approached the PLB in mid-March to represent that both he and his wife were ill; he had requested to have an order for the workhouse for his family, but was refused: 'i do not like to see my children suffer before my eyes and Mr combs our Medical gentman gave me a paper to certify that my wife and i was not able to work and i give that to our relieving offercer' to no effect. The Guardians, responding to these allegations, confirmed that he was not given the option of the workhouse in mid-March, but had been offered work at 10/- per week. He refused to take employment under 12/-, and again rejected the workhouse towards the end of the month. Union Clerk, 5, 10 and 18 Feb., and 5 Apl., and Payne, 16 Mar. 1858, to the PLB., PRO. MH.12/13146.
6. The mothers of illegitimate children who, unable to secure maintenance payments, were commonly forced into the workhouse with their offspring.
7. Thomas and Nancy Twort, both aged 23, and childless, received £2 towards their emigration from the Union, in addition to other costs being met by the Government, as emigration from Burwash was 'much wanted'. Statement, and covering letter from Union Clerk to the PLB. 18 Feb. 1858, PRO. MH.12/13146.
8. Threshing machines were regularly responsible for injuries and fatalities to farmworkers operating them.
9. This shrinkage of the hop acreage, with its concomitant reduction in demand for labour, proved transitory; a chronic decline in acreages set in during the 1880s.
10. In fact, two women were buried, Matilda Jarrett, twenty-five, and Mary Watson, thirty-one, but the cause of death is not given. ESCRO. Par.284/1/5/2.

11.   Country watchmakers usually lent a replacement timepiece while repairing more affluent customers' watches.

12.   'Thatcher & Pig Killer' Levi's cohabitee is unknown; he described himself as a widower in 1871, when his unmarried adult offspring, Matilda (25) and labourer Levi (19) lived with him, together with daughter Martha, and four grandchildren, aged one to eight, whose precise parentage is unknown. Levi was also something of bruiser and a boozer, with minor convictions for assault and drunkenness. Census, 1871. *Brighton Gazette*, 22 May 1845, 14 June 1847 and 23 Oct. 1856. Summary returns, ESCRO. QR/905, E1003. See also below, p. 210, 16 July 1878.

13.   For the prizes distributed by the Ticehurst Agricultural Association, for the two best cottage gardens in each of the Ticehurst Union parishes.

14.   Presumably in the invasion scares of 1801 and 1803.

15.   See above, p. 34, 19 Jan. 1858, and note 2.

16.   Probably in 1847.

17.   Agricultural labourer Stephen Sands, sixty-eight, buried on the 4th. ESCRO. Par.284/1/5/2.

18.   Lucy Relf, aged seven months, was found dead in her cot, and her mother admitted at the inquest to 'having given the child small quantities of gin', a practice 'condemned' by surgeon Combs for 'children of this age'; he nevertheless attributed death to 'congestion of the brain', and the jury returned a natural death verdict. *Sussex Agricultural Express*, 18 Sept. 1858.

19.   Social order virtually collapsed during the hop-picking period owing to the huge influx of entire families of workers, notably from the towns; drunkenness, rows, fights, strikes, and an upsurge in petty thieving, invariably occurred, commonly producing a crop of cases at Petty and Quarter Sessions. Such working-class children who remained at school, rather than join their parents in their work, were no doubt particularly fractious. See also below, 24 Sept. 1886, p. 348 and note 9.

20.   Each speaker spoke 'at some length', though a patronizing press report reiterated that they were 'listened to with great attention', following a consider-able 'beef and pudding' dinner for between sixty and seventy exhibitors at the 'annual exhibition of vegetable produce by the tenants of' allotments. Twenty prizes were awarded, the most valuable being the 12/- first prize for the best allotment, which went to Benjamin Thompson; he also picked up two 5/- prizes, for mangold weazel, and the six best white swedes. *Sussex Agricultural Express*, 12 Oct. 1858.

21.   Another example of popular hostility to threshing machines, and, given the context, a brave intervention by whomsoever it was.

22.   However, Poor Law records suggest that there was no repetition of the previous year's winter-time unemployment.

23.   Which implies that a strong residual prejudice remained against emigration, despite the many labourers who had left the country, commonly with public assistance, since 1819.

24.   An argument which initially derived from the numbers of officials appointed in the mid-1830s under the new Poor Law Amendment Act. Subsequently, there was only a small increase in officials, but the articulation of this argument nearly a quarter of a century after the commencement of the reformed social-security system, reveals both the endurance of the popular argument, which was doubtlessly reinforced by the unpopularity of officials, notably the Relieving Officers in the front line.

25.   Eli, an agricultural labourer, aged forty-one and wife Ann, thirty-seven, had

Elizabeth (17), Eliza (13), Emily (11), Eli (8), Edwin (2) and newly-born Ephrain. Censuses, 1851 and 1861.

26. Previously distributed from one of the public houses.

27. A forty-seven-year-old gardener employed by the Rector. Census 1851. *Sussex Advertiser*, 10 Oct. 1865.

28. Although Egerton made no relevant diary entry for his first Christmas at Burwash, this statement suggests that in the previous year he had offered cash to children who supplied holly to him, thereby enraging farmers and others with holly trees; the theft of holly for Christmas decorative purposes was endemic. Much of that stolen found its way to urban markets. Hence Egerton's arrangement with gardener Shoosmith.

29. Relf and Chandler came up at the Petty Sessions on 31 Dec. charged with the theft of six bushels, value 12/-. Relf pleaded guilty, and received four months hard labour. Chandler elected for trial at the Quarter Sessions where the Grand Jury threw out the case. Egerton makes no mention of an earlier grain robbery case in December, when six men fled on being seen by a policeman 'who was out watching'; only two men, George Relf and Henry Hawkins were charged with the theft of eleven bushels of wheat, and this case collapsed as 'no evidence could be obtained of whose wheat it was'. *Brighton Gazette*, 2 Dec. 1858 and 6 Jan. 1859.

30. Payne was summoned with thirty-year-old John Isted; on 21 Dec. they were disturbed while poaching in Park Wood by one of Fuller Meyrick's gamekeepers; Payne levelled his gun at the keeper and 'exclaimed "Stand back, if you come one inch further I'll blow your brains out"' in what had all the makings of yet another exemplar of vicious confrontations between poachers and keepers. However, the gamekeeper 'stood still', and when his colleague arrived on the scene, Payne and Isted decamped. Payne was identified by the keepers, while PC Maynard 'compared' Isted's 'boots . . . with the footprints' at the scene and 'they exactly corresponded'. Both defendants received three months hard labour, and were also ordered on release to find sureties not to offend again within a year, or in default, a further six months' imprisonment. *Brighton Gazette*, 6 Jan. 1859. For John Isted, see below, esp. 5 Dec. 1867, 7 Apl. 1868, Mar. 1869 (for his family budget), and 17 Dec. 1869, pp. 72–3, 85–6.

31. Egerton recorded the baptism of William James Relf, son of Mary Ann Ellis, spinster, ESCRO. Par.284/1/2/3.

1859–60

25 Jan. . . . C. on Mrs Relf. I had a long talk with James Russell. He seemed to say that a Mr. Pennells a Gardener who had bought a farm in Heathfield holds very free & easy ideas on religious points. C. on Mrs Hooker. Met Mr. Tilley; he complains sadly of the want of deference wh. Burwash men & boys shew to their employers & says it is the school's fault. I fear not altogether; our discipline is good in school, but the home influence is so bad: what to do I dont know. I think some of our Radical publications do much in destroying the feeling wh. ought to subsist between the upper & lower classes. Independence & Impudence are not the same things, tho' they may think so. . . .

27 Jan. School. I wish I cd. get ye 1st cl. to be more reverent in ye Bible lesson. I don't mean to say that their behaviour is bad, but I fear they look upon ye Bible as a book to be studied for its facts, its history, & its geography rather than as a guide for mens souls, teaching how to be holy & happy both in this world & the world to come. . . . C. & R. w. Newington in ye Vill. Met Mr. Baker [master shoemaker]; he I fear will soon leave Burwash, he can't stand it much longer. Place dull & no trade to be done. N. S. instead of tomorrow wh. is club [quarterly] night.

Sun. 30 Jan. . . . On Friday [he picked up from weekend gossip] out of 9 cases before ye magistrate at Hurst Green 6 were from Burwash.[1] One man [William Isted] never in work fined £4.0.0. wh. he paid at once. Another £1.5.0 & so on all paid. I don't know how it is that they find the money. It is said there is a club for the purpose of helping one another in trouble.[2]

31 Jan. . . . N.S. A long discussion concerning a case in wh. one of my young men [George Blackford] was fined on Friday. . . . Some very plain speaking wh. I was glad of as their claim to plain speech gave me a right to the same claim. Clearly the policeman is unpopular, being stricter than our old ones . . .[3]

1 Feb. School; Boys & girls. After meeting of School Committee at "The Office", passed a resolution that henceforth the 3 first children of any family pay 1d each; over 3 gratis. School Inc[ome] from all sources I think £180.0.0. Exp[enses] about £150.0.0. Aft. meeting Mr J. Philcox went over the case of the Police Constable v. Blackford & judging by what I understood, the case was clear & the PC was sober. . . .

2 Feb. . . . C. on Mrs Brabon, her son has enlisted on 16th F[oo]t is at

Templemoe & ye depot. C. on Mr. Smith. I like him: he shewed me over his house.

5 Feb. After C[hurch] C. on Mrs Caller to get particulars of her son George a Corp[oral] in 3d Batt. Rifle Brig: she heard last by letter dated Lucknow April 7th 1858 & fears he is dead. I wrote to War Office. C. on Dann, Eastwood, Pankhurst & Budd (1/-) at ye Forge. Mary Pankhurst wants to go to Australia. Wrote to [Emigration] Commissioners. C. on Alfred Tussell above Willingford. He out of work a day or two wet so turns his hand to making chicken coops. It is a great pity more men of the labouring class are not handier than they are . . .

6 Feb. . . . Had to reject a child from baptism, it having no Godfather.

7 Feb. . . . C. on Bagshawe; he seems quite an intelligent & rather superior young fellow; he differs on sundry points of farming from the natives. . . . N. S. 24. The boys begin to get on I think in reading.

12 Feb. Two funerals Mrs Relf & Panktellow child. . . . C. on Mrs Pennalls; she has 15 children alive & well. Mrs Taylor had 12 Aunts & Uncles all married & living at one time; there are 11 alive now. W. to Brook's Marl; spoke to Haffenden & Pope about confirm[ation]: the latter unpersuadable. Farming on his land after rain is no joke, as I discovered in walking behind Noakes' wagon up to ye Brooks Marl stables. C. at ye Rect. I had an offer of a school at Monmouth in ye gift of ye Haberdasher's Comp[an]y thro' Mr. Carter & Aunt Nathaniel who seemed to say that my interest wd. probably get it for me. It is worth £250 a year & an unfinished house. I must decline it, as my lot is thrown in for parochial work. Wrote sermon.

14 Feb. . . . I c. on Francis Fuller (1/-) at Willingford to recommend Emigration. C. on old Master Russell (1/-). His wife said she used to be "girl maid" to Mr Baldock's mother; quere "girl maid". C. on Mrs Clark to speak about the refusal on Sunday week of her child when brought to be bapt[ised] as it had no god-father. The man disappointed her. . . . N.S. only 13 or 14.

16 Feb. . . . N.S. The boys now have spelling matches wh. are amusing.

17 Feb. To Rect. in morg. to search for key of parish chest: but cd. not find it, so married Fuller (gentleman Fuller) & Price without [formally registering]; they must register tomorrow. Uncle Joseph had locked it up yesterday when he went to Brighton. He had to break open a cupboard to get the register book for Pat[t]en's marriage.

18 Feb. . . . Fullers signed.[4] N.S. Closed it for this season. Shook hands w.

each boy as he went out. I am well satisfied w. the result. One must not expect too much, but at any rate I learn to know the boys & they learn to know me, & I hope that the good may appear in the rising generation. I have closed the school w. prayer every night & have never once had to find the slightest fault with behaviour. At a penny a week I have received £1-19-3 this year agst. £1-15-8 last year. 53 boys on the books this y[ea]r against 47 last year.

23 Feb. . . . Spoke to Dann & Horace Russell; the latter [aged twenty-three] said he wd. come [to confirmation preparation classes]. Spoke to Stephen Barden; he wd. not promise to come. C. on Edwards; saw ye d. Spoke to David ye [eighteen-year-old] Son; he said he wd. not come. He is afraid of criticisms of his mates, & this I dare say the case with others. C. on some new Comers ab[out] ye Green. Mittens by name. . . .

26 Feb. . . . C. & sat with old Hawkins. He says "he never was at a . . . grammatical school" & so he can't pretend to much education, but he was always of "an inquisitive temper" & so he has "picked up" "a good deal". He is a nice old man. . . .

1 Mar. . . . Spoke to a boy named Russell about confirmation & said that if he wd. come up to me I wd. try & explain to him the difference between "Church n Chapel". Confirm. Class.

7 Mar. . . . The first brick of ye new Schoolroom laid . . .[5]

12 Mar. . . . my new dog a retriever arrived.

16 Mar. C & R w. a man of the name of [Thomas] Eastwood on ye Common; a painful case; he living w. a woman & says he hopes he has no cause to trouble about another World. P[rayed] for him that he might be softened & his eyes opened.[6]

19 Mar. Comm[on]: C. & R. w. Eastwood. . . . a new beer shop is being built on ye Common. I fear the publicans beat the parsons too much without adding to their number. I do think "the Beershop Act" was a most mischievous one . . .[7]

Sun. 20 Mar. Pr. in morg. from Rem. 2, 23 (V). Larger cong: than usual. Pr. in aft. from 2 St Peter 2. . . . Ext[empore] Large congreg. Chairs & some in passage. What are mothers of little children to do; if they come to church their babies cry & yet one doesn't like to see women stay away altogether, as many do.

21 Mar. . . . A lad named Cain brought me a very interesting letter from an Aunt in Canada. She says things are not as they used to be & that the price of land is very much increased, but still that hard work will secure what it does not always do in England – independence.

24 Mar. In Evg. I gave my Lect[ure] on What is an Englishman. Well attended. Uncle there; he moved a very cold vote of thanks. I had rather by half had [John] Payne the shoemaker do it . . .[8]

25 Mar. . . . C. on Mrs Barrow & an old Newington who made me drink parsnup wine. It was good & tasted exceedingly like commonish sherry, only more pure. . . . Parish dinner;[9] only 15 & they not tip top representatives of Burwash. However all harmonious.

26 Mar. . . . 2 Sisters Relf signed their name in 3 diff[erent] ways Relf Relph Ralph. . . .

28 Mar. Filled up Emigr[ation] paper for [George] Blackford.[10] . . . C. & had a long & serious talk w. [James] Jarvis ye Innkeeper.[11]

31 Mar. . . . Eastwood died yesterday; was living in sin I fear up to the last; one can only hope that there may be extenuating circumstances in his case wh. God can see where we cannot. Mr. Cox's lect[ure] on Columbus. Interesting & pleasing. I moved a vote of thanks. . . . An intelligent Stone Mason at ye school [under construction]. I have talked to him about Trade unions & strikes & about Masons Politics. He holds that the Unions are justified in preventing non-Union men from working when there is a strike, for he says that seeing how the Unions keep up prices for the good of all it is very hard that a non-union man who has been benefiting by the Union without the expense of subscribing to them shd. con[tinue] to take work when the Unions are holding out. I don't quite agree with him that Unions do permanently keep up prices, but I cannot be positive as the subj[ect] is one on wh. I don't know much.

1 Apl. . . . c. on Tom Waterhouse's wife; badly off, but bears not a good character; still she is in distress & must be helped. . . .[12]

2 Apl. . . . Married G. Blackford (22) & Hannah Relf (17) going to Emig[rate]. Did not take fee.

4 Apl. . . . Began to see ye boys privately. I received some satisfaction; one boy John told me he had been able to leave off bad language since their preparation for Conf[irmation]. One or two half determined to come to the Lord's supper but I fear the force of public opinion will weigh on them sadly.

5 Apl. Buried Eastwood. Certainly the burial service requires a considerable latitude of interpretation on the score of charity in some cases, & this is one of them. My chief dislike to certain expressions in the service in such a case as the present is grounded on the fear that the bystanders misinterpret them. I believe half the people take one at any rate as if we read it "in sure & certain hope of (his) resurrection to Eastwood's life".[13]

7 Apl. . . . Saw more boys. A nice lot of lads on ye whole certainly; but they manifest great reluctance on the subj[ect] of "The Lords Supper". Why is it so universal? There is some undefined notion about sin being worse after it than it wd. have been if they had not communicated. I want a short answer to this & also to the formula "I go where I get most good".

Sat. 9 Apl. . . . A drunken row outside ye Bell; strangers, natives.

Sun. 10 Apl. Morg. Serv. at ye Weald; very wet. 17 Adults, 3 Hobbledehog girls & 5 children. . . . Aft. Confirmation 60 Candidates 30 boys, 30 girls. A very large congr:. . . . The Bishop's Charge I h[ou]r 10 m[inutes]; matter good, but voice not strong & manner dry. Children very well behaved. One cannot help being anxious about them. God grant that they may have grace to carry out their good relations & their promises for Xt's sake. The Village very quiet & orderly, thanks to the policeman. Dined at ye Rectory; nothing very striking. . . .

11 Apl. . . . C. on Mr. Smith, liked my interview much: he has been a domestic serv[an]t & for many years was steward to a Mr. Napper a man of great wealth in Ireland. . . . Smith got the 1st Medal given by the Royal Agricultural Soc. of Ireland, at least so understood him to say. . . . Had a talk with Russell the shop-keeper about Confirmation.

16 Apl. . . . c. & P. w. an old man [Thomas] Parsons at 90 who is ill of a stoppage; lodges at [John] Parsons ye beer shopkeeper [Blacksmith's Arms]; poor man, he must suffer cruel pain . . .[14]

18 Apl. . . . Had a talk on religious matters w. ye stone mason. He a churchman but says there is much dissent & much infidelity among masons, tho' they are a more sober respectable class than they used to be.

22 Apl. Good Friday. Pr: in morg. from S. Luke 24. Fair congreg: The village devoted to marbles. Eastwood died last night. Poor man, he has been called quickly to his account, tho' think he must have expected his end for several days. . . . To ye Weald in aft: . . . Better congr: than I expected. C. on John Dann. He said "Good Friday always seems to me such a droll sort of day; some at work. Some at Church". We now have a 3d policeman stationed on ye Common.

23 Apl. . . . In aft: over to Stonegate. Saw Mrs Dawson in ye . . . [illegible] it is hard work in some cases to believe a person innocent, & yet legal proof may be difficult. Had a long talk with Mr. Dawson's clerk.

25 Apl. . . . Totty Eastwood buried; his death seemed to create quite a sensation among his mates. . . .[15]

5 May. . . . W. up to Rect. to see ye Guardian [of the Poor, either Edward Simes or Thomas Gillham]. Aft. went to watch a game of cricket wh. the Rectory employees had got up. Uncle's Tithe audit poorly attended & worse payments.

Sun. 8 May. . . . The policeman has ordered the loungers on Sundays at ye Weald to move off. This is pleasanter to the eye but about the wisdom of it *animi frendo*; when they were at the Weald one knew the worst; now they may be doing worse; still they annoyed people who were coming to church.

10 May. . . . I c. & R. w. Mary Noakes at Payn the shoemakers. Had a long talk with him; he a Unitarian. His great point is that there surely can be no such thing as eternal punishment; his arguments are a priori, not talking about what the Bible says is but arguing what can be & what cannot be.

14 May. Committee meeting of school. Boys av[era]g[e] of y[ea]r. 92. Have attended 176 days & upw[ards] 59, tho' many don't pay enough to entitle us to capitation fees.

18 May. Club. I Pr. Phil. 1. 27. . . . dinner but not many farmers or gentlemen; speeches & then Uncle left. I staid on. I sung 2 songs The Sailors grace & "When the heart is young" having an opportunity of speaking agst. bad songs. I left about 8.30; things very quiet then.

20 May. G. Blackford & his wife left . . . for Australia. I gave them the Careless Xtian by Wodehouse & her father G. Elliott gave his d. the Pilgrims Progress wh. I let him have for 4d if he ever repays me. . . .

21 May. I was sent for by old Mrs Pankhurst to read to her a letter from her son in 9th Lancers; he coming home w. ye Regt. wh. left Engl[and] in May 1842. It returns 250 strong 150 having volunteered to stop in India. I up to ye Comm[on] C. on John Dann; he worsts sadly. . . . A drunken man Amos Wickins stopped me on the street. I said you are committing sin in the sight of God: he said "What if I be, who made me sin; how did sin come into the world". "Who made the devil?" Deep agitations for a drunken man.

[Egerton's departure for a regular visit to Wiltshire including his old parish, Nunton, follows; there is one observation, on 12 June that 'The great point I believe to be the fact that I personally knew all my parishioners, a thing impossible in a large parish', clearly indicating an element of frustration with Burwash. There are no further entries respecting Burwash until the beginning of November.]

4 Nov. . . . Stopped to speak w. Edwards, a beershop keeper on ye Common for allowing yesterday a pitched battle in his field.[16]

Sat. 5 Nov. . . . Looked into ye Church. Sundry effective alterations in pews. . . . Hermitage Day coming to be curate. . . . to Little Common. Saw ye house wh. was an old telegraph station; very small but cosy looking.

16 Nov. . . . On talking today w. Uncle & his [game] beaters about the chance of a French invasion, the men volunteered the statement that Burwash chaps haven't heart enough to go for soldiers. Indeed the Burwash people don't affect any claim to personal courage.

17 Nov. . . . C. on Ellis at the shop, on Russell at the shop & on Daw at the shop asking them to put up notices of [fund raising] sermons for ye school. Took tea w. Mr. Smith. I gave him papers of Pennybank & he asked me for a Missionary box.

18 Nov. . . . Called at several cottages; a Master Funnell, living by the Woodman. Then Wm. Skinner a forty shilling freehold proprietor. Then old Mrs Chandler, she who was convicted of murdering her husband.[17] Then Grinder Weston & then Mrs Bridges (1/-): the latter confined a few hours after I had left, tho' did not show any great signs of the approaching event then.

23 Nov. . . . N.S. A figure of a man w. a blacksmiths apron stuck up over sign of Rose & Crown. The figure called "Old Clem" to day being S[t]. Clements day, but meet tonight to have a dinner. I had to go to the girls school, & be very angry with two girls in ye 1st class for gross insubordination. Miss Ellison wd. not let them go out. . . . I had a long confer[ence] w. Miss Ellison on discipline: she greatly grieved that moral force will not do altogether.

26 Nov. . . . C. on old [ex-road worker, sixty-nine year old John] Clapson (1/-): no furniture; I cd. not sit down. He has nevertheless a great horror of "ye House". Tea w. Mr. Combs. Penny bank; 20 depositors in all.

28 Nov. . . . C. on Relf at public house; he keeps his child at home because "part of his field is in plough & part grass" is to keep the cow from the plough part. I found from old bearded [seventy-one, Jesse] Relf that stone cardings 3/4 a y[ar]d & stone digging (both hard stone) 1/3 a yd. . . .[18]

2 Dec. . . . A young man & of but indifferent character had been keeping company w. the girl for 4 y[ea]rs & under promises of marr[iage] having had the banns put up & having even fixed the day had seduced her. As local morality goes, it is a hard case as the girl might fully have calculated a marriage. N.S. – 25 only paid this week. I think I shall give Burwash a rest next yr. & take a turn up the Weald where N.S. will be new.

3 Dec. A wedding between a J. Ralph & Caroline Cheesman; both laughed much & behaved themselves very lightly. I had to rebuke the man, & he I suppose thinking himself "taught by the priest" repeated my rebuke word for word. . . .

7 Dec. . . . C. on Mrs Hetherington. Spoke seriously to F. Read who lives in the house. C. on Hanna Hartfield & on a woman named Weeks about being married. Spoke to a young Edwards about being separated from his wife; she apparently no great shakes & she wants him to go for a divorce, but he says she may if she likes, he won't. . . . C. on Mrs Potten & insisted on the duty of her son marrying Russell girl.[19]

9 Dec. . . . c. . . . on Pope; child in 1st class & on Mallins a Sandhurst man, carter to Whatman. His house has part of the outside wall out, protected only by an old sack. Whatman wd. not leave his stable in that state I think. . . .

12 Dec. . . . had a marriage. Jos. Harmer & Hannah Hartfield. . . .

14 Dec. . . . no class did well with ye singing. . . .

Sat. 21 Dec. . . . Penny Bank. Tom Shadwell ye Bulls eye manufacturer says my bank is a downright robbery. The shop attractions have told on my deposit tonight.[20]

21 Dec. . . . Dole day. Relieved more than 200 families at 1lb each adult about $\frac{1}{2}$ to each child. Beef 4/3 a stone, about 100 stone. . . .

22 Dec. Extra dole was given away as we did not distribute quite enough yesterday. I w. into Mrs Radcliffes to help in making the Ch. ornaments. Miss Finch & Sally Weston helped. In aft. in Taylors field had a long conversation w. him on Education. Jo Snashall said that he thought that a poor man who liked work & who had nothing on his mind that is "who wasn't afraid of being took up for nothing" [arrested for a criminal offence] had less anxiety & trouble than lots of little farmers & tradesmen. . . .[21]

29 Dec. . . . School treat & rewards at 2.30; being wet most of ye Children came. . . . Boys had about 1lb of cake a piece. Rewards. Shirts, Frocks, books. Girls bonnets, books, Frocks. . . . NS & Singing we get on capitally so far.

31 Dec. . . . had a long interview w. a young Mr. Hutchinson? a dissenting preacher whom I met in a railway carriage [while returning from Hastings] on Monday & who does duty occasionally at the Independent Chapel; he is going to be a student at Cheshunt Coll[ege]. We talked amicably for some time on points such as Church Discipline & baptism & we ended with prayer: he shewed me the questions proferred to candidates for admission to Cheshunt Coll. & the 15 articles of their creed, many of which are taken toteden from our XXXIX Art [Anglican 39 Articles] . . .

1860

2 Jan. . . . down on ye 7.18 train [to London]. J.Snashall drove me [to Etchingham station]; he says quaint things at times; he was telling me that he had had a character for 25 yrs honesty from the late Mr. D.Hyland & added carries you thro' life Sir like honesty. Good principles Sir, good principles; some then allus turns up as makes then pay.[22]

16 Jan. . . . Funeral of old Master Ryley or Riley or Reilly; an old Irish R[oman] C[atholic] long resident in Burwash.[23]

26 Jan. Sch: & at Rect: gave a lect[ure] to ye 1st class on ye steam engine, taking them down to a st[eam] threshing machine at work in Jarvis' yard. . . .

27 Jan. . . . Attended Club meeting to explain [pro-]Ch. Rate petition: got a good many signatures . . .[24]

Sun. 29 Jan. . . . Wh[eel] Aft. Luke 14. 18 . . . some of the idlers now put me off saying they are coming to church & then do not come. . . .

30 Jan. C. on Chard about the Ch. Rates. He said he shd. remain neutral & sign neither way. C. on John Hyland; got his signature. N.S. singing.

31 Jan. . . . I attended a farmers' meeting at Rose & Crown. Discussed Ch: Rates for 1½ hours. Got no signatures, only a promise of one. Rochester late Ch: W[arden] chief opponent; he all for the voluntary principle. Several Dissenters Gillham & others influenced ye meeting. . . .

2 Feb. Sch: I started out & C. on old Newington; he signed; on Relf ye Wheeler; he signed; on James Russell a long arg[ument] but he signed; on Dowler; he signed; on Frank Russell, an hour's talk but he wd. not sign. On St[ephen] Hyland; he signed; on Mr. Christian; he signed; on old Edwards, he said of course he ought to stick to ye Church, as we all knew it had lasted from ye foundation of ye world but then you see Sir, says he, I'm partners in the farm with my son & never buys up bullocks nor nothing without consulting him. So I think I'll consult him before I sign this petition. I sent

Snashall for Wigan & then d. at Rect. meeting Dr. Giles. Lecture fairly attended. In parts rather mild but many were I believe satisfied. It was Notes on Norway. . . .

4 Feb. Letter fron Col. Lecard; he cannot get Buss a porter's place. . . . Had a convers[ation] in barn w. Jack Buss & Buss pére, who is a superior man if he didn't drink. N.S. & Singing.

5 Feb. . . . Had a long talk with Mrs Lusted who was very irate indeed w. Mrs Dungate for Locking her out of her seat [pew] on a Sunday or two ago. Those people who go the least often make the most fuss. . . .[25]

6 Feb. Took the petition up to the Rect. as it must go tonight.

23 Feb. . . . C. on Waterhouse. Mr. Claris' carter found a woman there who is living w. a man unmarried; she said that she did not know what it was wrong, but that she shd. not marry him; he was too old:[26] what can one do where the moral is gone. . . . C. on Edwin Harmer; very hard up. Wife confined & nothing to give her: no work, 2/6.

26 Feb. . . . C. on Frank Russell; saw he could not live many hours. He was out & about in Burwash on Wed: & was out twice yesterday; an old smuggler, but he has amassed a good deal of Money; at 83, & had a child less than 2 y[ea]rs ago of his own begetting.[27]

28 Feb. . . . In Evg. attended a farmers' meeting at Rose & Crown; a large audience. Made an explanation of ye Ch. Rate difficulty of 4 y[ea]rs ago wh. I believe was the true explanation. Then on I fancy a preconcerted arrangement I was shewn an anti-Ch. rate petition & was asked to read it out. I did so; then Payne ye shoemaker tackled me, & ever went at it for about an hour & $\frac{1}{2}$ very ardently. Payne was a very fair opponent & kept his temper very well. It resolved itself into a question of the rightfulness or wrongfulness of compulsory payments for Religious purposes. The audience tho' agst. me very civil. Such discussions I am persuaded do good.[28]

1 Mar. . . . C. on Mr. Simes found his father in his 83d year digging in the garden, having in the morg. walked all round the farm; has lived 53 yrs in that "one eyed" place [Great] Poundsford. Says Burwash Common is much improved.[29] Spoke to him & to Mrs about employing an old man on who is living with a young unmarried woman. Spoke to the man himself.

2 Mar. . . . C. on Honeysett he told me that 6 farmers signed the [anti-compulsion] petition on Tues: [28 Feb.] & one man a shop-assistant signed it having signed ours too.

10 Mar. . . . J[ame]s Haffenden . . . said that living where he did [Little Pookhill] & coming home tired there was a good deal of "slavery" in attending night School . . .

13 Mar. . . . Looked in at ye Farmers' meeting, but nothing particular going on.

15 Mar. . . . People say that bad as Burwash may be it can boast what its neighbours often cannot viz honest lawyers, & I do believe that the firm Philcox, Baldock & Philcox is composed of 3 as honest men as can be commonly found.

16 Mar. Offer of Charlton P[arish] C[hurch]. . . . I declined it as I do not want to leave this parish & Charlton is so small that I shd. prove terribly idle. . . .

17 Mar. . . . C. on Rover [?] Maynard's wife; odd to think of her as the mother of a lad who will probably become a man of eminence in Tasmania; he was a pupil teacher here, Queen's Scholar at Knoller Hall under Temple & is now a Schoolmaster in Hobart Town. We have also several young fellows doing well where they are. We have the Sgt Major of 10th Husars & Sergt (Brown) in Military Train, a Sergt. Russell in 16th Lancers & a lad just enlisted Douglas Weston [aged eighteen] is on trial as Depot Schoolmaster. . . .

24 Mar. C. & R. w. an old woman [widow Sarah] Dunk by name at Mutton's. . . . C. on Piper next door house not fit for a horse to live in. The walls in places broken thro' to ye open air. . . .

26 Mar. . . . Dined at parish dinner [at end of parochial administrative year] only 14 there very amicable. Speaking of old times when ye parish hired ye Bough farm for men out of work to work upon. Fleming said that somebody killed a robin there, & it was agreed that the robin shd. have a grand funeral. The loss of time about wh. cost ye parish £20![30]

Notes

1. Richard Chandler, George Hilder, and William Blackford, were convicted of rabbiting on surgeon Combs' land. Chandler (who had been fined 10/-, with 9/6 costs, for stealing a ferret, at the same court one month previously) was fined 30/-, and 9/6 costs, and his co-defendants (both with minor criminal records) 5/- with 9/6 costs.
  A Christmas Day incident resulted in the very heavy fine of £3, with 26/- costs being imposed on twenty-two-year-old William Isted for assaulting constable

Maynard, while George Blackford, was fined 2/- with 5/- costs for drunkenness. Isted had been convicted of drunkenness in 1856; for him see below, pp. 76, 89, 8 Aug. 1868 and esp. 28 May 1869.

Thomas Watson, convicted of breaking Thomas Hilder's windows in what appears to have been a dispute between roughs, was ordered to pay 8d damages and 14/- costs. *Brighton Gazette*, 3 Feb. 1859. Summary returns, ESCRO. QR/E975, 996.

2. An intriguing possibility, though more likely limited to payment of poaching fines, than those imposed for assaulting the police in cases unrelated to game. For similar collections to pay fines imposed for petty theft, and for breaking the notorious Master and Servants Act, see below, pp. 137, 157, 22–3 Apl. 1873, and 1 Apl. 1875 respectively.

3. This was clearly Blackford's response, but when Egerton discussed the case with lawyer Philcox, who was also Clerk to the Hurst Green Petty Sessions (see next entry), the evidence was clearly against the twenty-one-year-old, whose claim that PC Maynard was himself drunk – commonly advanced by defendants in parallel cases – was also false.

4. Possibly a branch of the landowning Fuller family, but Alfred, a fruiterer like his father Thomas, was illiterate, as was his bride, Frances, a labourer's daughter. ESCRO. Par.284/1/3/2.

5. The new schoolroom was built to relieve 'the present crowded condition of the boys' school', and 'more discipline' was anticipated by the HMI once in use. *Sussex Agricultural Express*, 15 Mar. 1859.

6. Aged sixty-four and an agricultural labourer. Eastwood had a relatively minor criminal record, with one year's hard labour term imposed in Aug. 1821 for stealing 'divers articles of wearing apparel, a sack and 28lbs of currents' from a waggon. On his release he could not find employment, and was allocated to parish quarrying. He also had at least one poaching conviction. *Sussex Weekly Advertiser*, 20 and 27 Aug. 1821. Vestry minute, 21 Dec. 1822; summary conviction return, Feb. 1828, ESCRO. Par.284/12/1; QR/E. Mich. 1828.

7. The 1830 Beer Act liberalized the licensing laws, and facilitated a mushrooming of retail establishments, able to sell beer only. They were immediately attacked as forums for disaffected plebeians in the countryside, where Captain Swing risings were planned, an allegation which was not without foundation. In the longer-term they were continuously censured as seminaries of miscellaneous vices, and attacked – again with some justification – as resorts of criminals and receivers of stolen goods.

8. Aged sixty-eight, a political radical, and virtually inevitably, a Dissenter. See above, pp. 55, 59, 10 May 1859 and 28 Feb. 1860.

9. Ladyday; traditionally the day for vestry meeting to audit accounts and elect new officials, churchwardens, overseers, highway surveyors, and local constables. Usually dominated by the richer ratepayers, though the more numerous lesser contributors could turn out when contentious (which usually meant potentially expensive) issues were on the agenda. Followed by a dinner for those who could afford it.

10. George was engaged to seventeen-year-old Hannah Relf. They married on 2 Apl., and the paperwork for their emigration was finalized in May. Clerk, Ticehurst Union, to the PLB., 7 May 1859, PRO. MH.12/13147.

11. James Thomas Jarvis was in fact a long-established beershop proprietor; accused of illegal opening on a Sunday in 1849, he was acquitted at the Petty Sessions, but warned that he was not free from 'suspicion'. He appears to have taken

the hint, though Egerton's intervention suggests that Jarvis was merely adequately cautious to avoid being caught. *Brighton Gazette*, 6 Sept. and 4 Oct. 1849.

12.   Mrs Waterhouse's reputation may have been more of a reflection of her sixty-four-year-old husband's record. Although he had won an award in 1849 for the best cottage garden, he had been formally evicted from a parish house in 1828, and served short prison terms in 1829 (with a privately-inflicted flogging), 1856, and 1857, for petty thefts. Vestry minute, 26 July 1828, ESCRO. Par.284/12/1. *Sussex Advertiser*, 20 Apl. and 4 May 1829. *Maidstone Gazette*, 9 Oct. 1849. *Brighton Gazette*, 2 Apl. 1856 and 24 Dec. 1857.

13.   Thomas, from the road-haulage family, aged sixty-two; although he had served one term of a year's imprisonment for theft, and had been fined heavily for poaching, his formal criminal record was slight compared to his son Thomas's. *Sussex Weekly Advertiser*, 20 and 27 Aug. 1821. ESCRO. QE/E Easter 1828; Par.284/1/5/2.

14.   Thomas had been a workhouse inmate in 1851, but now lived with his son or nephew. It is difficult to categorically identify members of this family in many records. Some were among the more substantial tenant farmers in the later eighteenth and early nineteenth centuries, while others were – including the nonagenerian – farmworkers. Several of John's predecessors had had interests in the licensed trade, and he farmed in addition to being the proprietor of the Blacksmith's Arms, one of the parish's tougher establishments, and the scene of many incidents.

15.   George Eastwood, aged thirty-eight, was a colourful character, who had led something of a charmed life. Part of the road-haulage family, he remained carting after his marriage to the recently-widowed licensee of the Admiral Vernon, Mary Pilbeam, in 1846. A court case soon established that Mary was not obliged to transfer the licence to her new husband, and from whatever precise cause, relations between sectors of the Eastwood clan, and the blacksmithing branch of the Pilbeams, were poor thereafter. Events included an attempt to rig a theft case against George Eastwood, who was eventually fined severely for a murderous assault on the notorious elder William Pilbeam (for him, see below, 14 Feb. 1881, pp. 242–3 and note 4). George was charged and acquitted on three minor counts of theft, was in further trouble for rescuing his impounded horse, and was formally warned against driving offences by the police. *Brighton Gazette*, 1 Oct. 1846, 25 Feb. 1847, 4 May, 22 June and 19 Oct. 1848, 22 Mar. and 12 Apl. 1849. *Brighton Herald*, 9 Jan. 1847. Summary returns, Quarter Sessions indictments, and jail registers, ESCRO. QR/E921, 928, 935, 939, 993.

16.   Probably a well-organized, if illegal, boxing match.

17.   The most notorious woman in the parish since July 1826, when she was convicted at the Assizes, with her lover Daniel Leaney, of the murder by poisoning of her husband Benjamin Russell. Both Hannah and Leaney were sentenced to death, and Leaney was hanged, while Hannah was at first respited, owing to legal technicalities, and then pardoned when the medical evidence under which both had been convicted was compromised.

The Russell family were typically Wealden; there were several branches, which included the innkeeper and smallholder, a substantial tenant farmer, a miller, and several labourers. Benjamin's uncle, Frank, farmed together with general dealing, smuggling, and fencing stolen goods. (See 26 Feb. 1860, below, for Egerton's knowledge of Frank's antecedents). In 1825 Benjamin went to the United States, and during his absence, Hannah, then aged thirty-three, commenced the affair with the teenaged Leaney. Benjamin returned, and with Hannah ran the infamous Wheel pub on the Common at the time of Benjamin's death. Leaney's relationship with Hannah was no secret, and both men lived at the pub, Hannah frequently engaging in ferocious rows with her husband, while demonstrating her affections for Leaney to all and sundry.

The Russells had disapproved of the marriage, and after Benjamin's death orchestrated a vestry decision to finance the prosecution of Hannah and Leaney, which gave rise to claims of a witch hunt, enflamed further by the printing and sale of an alleged confession. The Leaney's hit back by spreading rumours that at the time of his death, Benjamin was retrieving stolen, not smuggled goods, effectively replacing a broadly-favoured, by a largely reprobated activity in the estimations of Burwash's middling ranks.

Hannah was freed in February 1827, returned to Burwash, and within four months was cohabitating with cordwainer Thomas Chandler, whom she subsequently married – though not before the vestry promptly cancelled his contract to supply shoes to paupers.

Currently widowed, Hannah lived with her thirty-nine-year-old unmarried daughter, Mary Russell, and her twenty-year-old son, Richard Chandler, a farmworker.

Sussex Advertiser, especially 1 Aug. 1825, 22 May, 31 July, 20 Nov. and 4 Dec. 1826, 26 Feb, 5 and 19 Mar. 1827. Baron Graham, trial judge's report, 20 Dec. 1826, and a mass of supporting documentation, PRO. HO.47/71. Burwash vestry minutes, 5 July 1826 and June 1827; H. Russell to vestry, nd. [1825], ESCRO. Par.284/12/1; 284/35/109. Census, 1861.

18. Jesse described himself as a 'stone-cutter' in the 1851 census.

19. Egerton's expostulation had a somewhat delayed effect. Only on 27 Dec. 1861 did twenty-eight-year-old, illiterate labourer, John Potten, a labourer like his father John, marry twenty-three-year-old Hannah Russell, daughter of another labourer, Samuel; she signed the register, ESCRO. Par.284/1/3/2.

20. A 'fruiterer' in Census 1851, and a 'master fruiterer' in Census 1861.

21. In *Sussex Folk*, p. 76 this emerges somewhat differently; it is attributed to 'one of my poor parishioners, whom I used to take with me when I drove anywhere at night', said '"Well sir, in my opinion, a working man who likes work, and who has got work to do, when he comes home at night ought to be one of the happiest men alive, if he ain't afeared of being took for nothin"'.

22. An eloquent testimony to the importance attached by at least the 'respectable' sector of the working population to their reputations for honesty, hard work, and acceptable style of living.

23. James, an agricultural labourer, aged almost eighty.

24. Subsequent entries reveal that Egerton obtained more signatures by the direct lobbying of individuals, as opposed to collectively; at the vestry on 31 Jan. he did not get even one, but Burwash ratepayers were a parsimonious lot, and even Anglicans, like churchwarden Rochester, were quite happy to shield themselves behind Dissenters, in refusing to lend support to Anglican efforts to prevent the end of statutory compulsion to pay church-rates.

25. Private pews at St Bartholomew's were abolished when the church was rebuilt in 1856. However, individual worshippers usually sat in the same pew, and perhaps had a proprietorial perception, which extended down the social scale to agricultural labourer's wives, including Mrs Lusted.

26. Although the identity of Claris's carter at this juncture is unknown, this is one

of the few definitive examples of how Egerton got to know the identities of cohabitees who did not, of course, attend his church.

27. For the Russell family, including their smuggling activities, see the introduction, and especially note 17, pp. 62–3.

28. Compulsory Anglican Church rates were a recurrent political issue before their eventual abolition in 1868. It flared again in 1860 with fierce campaigning by both sides, and even in Dissenting strongholds like Cranbrook, Anglicans were able to mobilize impressive support. *Sussex Agricultural Express*, 21 Feb. 1860.

29. This relatively rosy view of what was still the roughest part of the parish would be far more obvious to an octogenerian, than even the historically-minded Egerton.

30. The farm had been hired for precisely these purposes between 1815 and the early 1830s, as alluded to in the introduction. Such local make-work schemes achieved a notoriety, exaggerated by the 1832–4 Royal Commission on the Poor Laws, and was illegalized under the resultant 1834 Poor Law Amendment Act. The story of the robin's funeral may be apocryphal, but it sybolizes the costs of such policies, and their liability to abuse, in this case by workers in public employ contriving an elaborate wake for a dead song-bird. It was of course natural that such reminiscences should be a topic of conversations at this type of annual parochial event. The tale was rehearsed in *Sussex Folk*, p. 45.

1867–68

20 Mar. I was this day Inducted to & so finally & fully made Rector & Vicar of this benefice.

21 Mar. . . . Uncle [Nathaniel Wetherell] & self called on Mr. Gibbs to congratulate him on his new dignity as a County Magistrate. The recommendation of him by the parishioners & neighbours I sent to Mr. Courthope, I think, last May or June. Mr. C. advised my Uncle to write to the Lord Lieutenant who conceiving 9 months ago there was no hurry has in due time brought forth the [formal] Commission.[1]

22 Mar. . . . A long letter from Mr. Courthope about a man & his wife named John [and Fanny] Relf.[2]

23 Mar. C. & P. w. Mrs Carman. Overtaken by Walter Morris who was in a most piteous trouble because his poor old father had just put an end to his life by hanging himself. . . . C. & P. w. the poor Morris's at Valenciennes; fearfully distressed, but as the old man was notedly quiet & well conducted, & to his light a religious man, I cd. sincerely assure them that this particular act did not affect my opinion of his prospects for eternity; these I shd. judge of as I shd. in any other case by their life & known character.[3] C. on Master Leaney (1/-). Injured his ribs very much by a cart accident a fortnight ago; in bed ever since. . . .

25 Mar. . . . Saw John Relf; he will try to live with his wife again. . . . Officers elected to day . . . Parish meeting at 12. I chairman as Rector. Kept on till 3. . . . [Poor Law] Guardians Mr. E. Simes Poundsford & Mr. W. Newton Franchise. "Overseers" [of the Poor] Mr. G. Hinde & Mr. J. Barrow. About 14 persons present & all civil & kindly.

26 Mar. . . . Went up to see whether J. Relf's wife had come home, but cd. not find her. . . .

27 Mar. . . . Mr. Courthope came into ye vestry to speak to me.

29 Mar. . . . Aft. lunch I had my aristocratic singing class in my room at Taylors. Mrs Roger & Alice. Mrs W. Newton & Miss Cooke. Mrs W. Hinde & 2 Misses Hinde. Miss Fanny Burton. . . . Aft. d. the night school children taught by Miss S. Trower twice a week for 18 weeks this winter came to tea. They were Ch. Russell, John Luck, Th. Luck, Levi Luck, M.

Thompson, Jn. Thompson, Wm. Holmes & Edwards, this last a subscr[iber] to Savings bank & also invited instead of St[ephen] Pilbeam who
wd. not come. We had prayers, then tea, then a display of things wh. the
boys cd. buy below cost price, as knives, writing cases etc. One boy L.
Luck took a 5/- concertina, another J. Luck a 3/6 flute. Altogether a very
pleasant evg. Miss S. Trower has a marvellously happy way w. boys. The
coming of Miss Trower to Burwash Common has been a very great
blessing. . . .[4]

2 Apl. . . . C. on W. Isted; his wife says that John Relf will not go back to
his wife. . . .

3 Apl. . . . d. & pr. at Ticehurst. The congregation much thinned by the
presence in the village of a circus wh. drew large crowds. The proprietor
(Ginnatt) gives a prize for the best local conundrum, to be decided by the
applause of the audience. The prize tonight was won by Mr. Clapson,
Tailor, for the following "If you want a meal of victuals had you better go
to the Establishment or to the Vicarage?" Ans[wer] to the Establishment,
for there you're going to get Bacon (an employee there) but at the Vicarage
you'll only find Bones. . . .[5]

8 Apl. Mr. Baillie of Wardour Street, Stained glass Artist came down about
ye Windows in ye New Church. I had a long talk w. him. He very full of a
memorial window to Chaucer wh. he is putting up in Westminster Abbey,
in Poets Corner. He will do our 3 windows for £60.[6] . . . Had a long talk
also with Mr. Noakes ye Clocksmith on religious matters. He a Deist, &
says that it is no use talking for that he cannot feel religious. . . .

12 Apl. [While on three day visit to London]. . . . The last about the
B[isho]p of Oxford Old Lady – Have you heard that the Bp. of Oxford has
now got so high Church that he turns his back upon the people, & reads the
lessons from the Rectum!

15 Apl. Sch: I spoke to Tom Pilbeam & to young Wm. [Pilbeam]; the latter
took what I said in very good part & I pray for that he may be enabled to
return to his former better life – drink drink drink – it is a curse & no
mistake. . . .[7]

20 Apl. . . . C. on Miss Pilbeam. Had a long talk to a young Relf girl who
lodges there.

22 Apl. . . . Vestry meeting; only Mr J[ame]s Philcox, Mr. J. Coppard, Mr.
J. Barrow, Mr. C. Taylor, Martin Coppard & self present. Audited
accounts: passed them. I made Ch. Rate at 2d in the £ & Loan rate at 2d in £.
I appointed Mr. Cramp my Ch. W[arden]. I had asked Mr. Barrow to be
my CH.W. but he is Overseer already & tho' Mr. Philcox knew my desire

to app[oin]t him Ch: W. before he was appt. Overseer, he did not tell me that a difficulty might arise thro' Barrow holding the two offices inasmuch as for signing rates a majority of the Officers is of the 2 Ch. W. & 2 overseers is needed; consequently if only 3 men in office no rate cd. be signed unless all 3 were in residence at the same time & as thro' accident this now & then might happen not to be the case, trouble wd. arise. I was therefore persuaded to appt. Mr. Cramp Ch. W. *for this year*; next year I trust that Mr. Barrow will resign his overseership & become my Ch. W. I explained all this to Mr. Barrow, but I was much annoyed at not being able to keep my word to him: however I lay the blame on Mr. Philcox for not suggesting this difficulty when I had mentioned the matter to Mr. Barrow. I had mentioned it to him. I hope that Mr. Barrow understood the case; he said he did entirely. . . .

25 Apl. . . . C. & R. on the Elliss's. Read for them a long letter from their son Tom in Wisconsin State U.S. doing well. Had a talk in the rain w. old Mr. Daw on politics. He thinks that if it came to war Prussia will win "Because you see Sir Prussia is a liberal government, & there is no doubt that the Almighty favours those principles more than" tyranny he explained that he meant wh. is what he calls Napoleon's govt. C. on a new comer a Mrs Hewett husb: a small farmer. Norfolk people, come down in the world I shd. think. . . .

27 Apl. Married Jas. Oliver & Louisa Clapson; ought to have been married years ago. . . .

1 May. . . . Evg. concert, greater success still. Everybody apparently pleased. The class was encored in "Sleep gentle Lady". . . . We took about £22. Such a day as this must I think do good in a place, & I cannot but feel that it raises the esprit de corps of our people, & prevents them from feeling that Burwash is a name not in good odour w. the public.[8]

2 May. . . . The Londoners [performers, down for the concert] for a drive in Blackford's van to Silver Hill, & so back to Etchingham. They have been very kind in helping us; have I hope enjoyed themselves. . . .

4 May. . . . Stopped to look at Sidney Hurstfield's application of a steam threshing engine to a [wood] sawing machine. Ingeneous & very success-ful. . . . Sam. Hazalden, a labourer from the Common brought me back 2 Vols. of Macaulay's His[tory] wh. I lent him some time ago & wh. he says he read very quickly as they were so fascinating. High taste this for Burwash labourer, but he is a very intelligent man.

8 May. . . . C. . . . on Mrs Gibbs (1/-), who plainly told me that she was much better now that her epileptic d. was in the Union as she got more to eat. . . .

11 May. Went over the Glebe with Mr. J. Coppard looking at timber proposed [for] repair of ch. y[ar]d fence. He suggested that we shd. wait a year or two before we went into anything big. . . .

15 May. Litany & address at 8a.m. 16 persons present. Serv. at 11.45. Orderly Congrg. I pr. from 1 Cor. 8, 9 Ext. Afterwards to dine; aft. dinn. many of the members seceded to K. Weller [Bell Inn] who had got up a counter attraction. I away before 6.[9]

16 May. . . . I hear that there was a row last night between some Wheelers & Burwash lads. I am sorry, as I had hoped that things were getting quieter.

18 May. . . . Spoke to Lizzy Vigor a kitchenmaid from Burwash whom I recommended. She is doing very well. Spoke about her earrings & a ring on the finger wh. she wore at my concert. She wept & said Father had told her she ought to do as other girls did. The ornament question is a difficult one; a pretty girl cannot believe in the power of her unaided face, & a neat simple style of dress: however Lizzy is so far a good girl & took well what I had to say.

22 May. [After an early morning visit to Ashburnham, and a lift back to Brightling] . . . I walked to ye Wheel. W. ye club to Mr. Breach's. He not at home. Dearsley [of Bodle Street Green, Warbleton] preached to ye Club. Litany . . . Ps. & Sermon. Dearsley & I to Miss Trowers. Then to dinner – good dinner – Speeches & I away at 4.55.[10] . . . A regular snow storm today about 1.40 & snow again in ye aft.

27 May. . . . Poor Mr. Evenden very ill. He one of [Congregationalist pastor] Buss' followers, so I did not go up. . . . Mr. Taylor purchased for me 2 Cottages near the School in Bell Ally for £305. A poor thing for me, but almost necessary for the school. . . .

28 May. . . . Pd. Js. Philcox £75 in add[ition] to £30 depos[it] for ye cottages. . . . Saw Miss Trower about the school wh. is to be brick & not stone & plain for £380 . . . C. on Baldock ye publican to say that I understand that the Club was very quiet.

31 May. Sch: C. on one or two parents to urge them to make their children learn at home. . . . To [village] Benefit Club 13 new members elected, & only one left: now 188 or thereabouts.

[Following his customary visit to old parish in Wiltshire.]

23 June. . . . Public Opinion much excited on the subject of Mr. Combs having bought John Barrows house over his head.[11]

1 July. . . . C. on Mrs Barrow; found her br. in law Mr. Buss the Mayfield

Sol[icito]r there. He and I together urged concessions, or rather a concil-
iatory spirit. . . .

4 July. Sch: had to punish a boy for thieving. . . .

5 July. . . . Russell bought the mill & and wh. belonged to his father for
£1650.

12 July. . . . c. on old Mrs Hewland who had very nearly put an end to
herself by an extra dose of opium, whether accidental or not I don't know.
She not yet sensible. . . .

15 July. . . . Signed an application for Employment in East Sussex County
Police on behalf of Alfr[ed] Butler. . . .

20 July. Mr. Slater [architect] . . . much dissatisfied w. the progress of the
Ch: [being built on the Common] & very angry at Piper ye Clerk of ye
works. . . .[12]

24 July. Making prep[arations]. The school was nicely decorated. Dist[rict]
visitors rather helped. Day fine Dawson [incumbent at Stonegate Chapelry]
came early about 10 min. to ye time. About 160 or 165 took tea. We had
prep[ared] for 100 but managed fairly well. After tea I began w. a hymn
(Pour down Thy Spirit Lord). . . . Then a statement of my object in
suggesting the meeting. Brotherly Union of fellowship as Churchmen. To
encourage one another to more private prayer, more earnest worship in
God's house & more communion in the Lords Supper. Then a hymn (Oh
for a clear[?] walk with God). Dawson then spoke of what he has by God's
help been able to do at Stonegate in the way of a Ch[ristian] Brotherhood
during the last 7 years. I summed up. A hymn (Jesus shall reign where'er the
Sun), & the blessing. I think good was done & people said they felt so. Poor
Tatham [the incumbent at Dallington] cd. not come. Mrs was taken w. the
pains of a premature confinement at about 8 o'Clock & died at 10.30 PM.
Poor Tatham, he has lost a wife such as is given to few men, & his children
(8) a mother who was a mother indeed & in truth. May God be with him &
wish them, & give them comfort under their bitter trial.

29 July. . . . At 10.30 . . . to Dallington Funeral, the most touching service
I think that I ever took part in. Mr. Dunn read it beautifully. Poor Tatham
bore up excellently. He sent for me after the service. I was to have been
Godfather to the child. . . . Dear Mrs Tatham was indeed a woman whom
to know was to love.

30 July. . . . Attended a parish meeting in the vestry at 7.15 about revaluing
the woods in the parish [for rating purposes]. The present assessment seems
to average about 5/- per acre; the meeting agreed to raise it 15 per cent. The

memorial window [in St Philip's] to my Uncle put up yesterday. Opinions on the whole favourable.

1 Aug. Our school feast this year my Aunt [Gould's widow] gave it, & gave tea & not dinner. The children seemed to enjoy one as much as the other. 105 girls & 99 boys. Fine day, tho' very cold for the time of the year. I introduced rounders wh. seemed to take. Cricket, Swings & Scrambling the other amusement. Also throwing a ball from a distance of 5 or 6 yards thro' the ring. This I varied by making them throw apples. The apples wh. went thro' belonging to the throwers side: the misses belonging to the opponents. Nearly all our local parochial aristocracy present. . . .

Sun. 4 Aug. I to Dallington. Pr. from St Matt. 4. 19 (ON). Poor Tatham very low; had the most touching conversation w. him after Ch. There is something very touching in the deep sorrow of a really Xtrian man. It seems to differ almost in kind from the sorrow of a mind wh. has no specially Xtrian sympathies. A large congr: & much affected. I was much tried in preaching, but tho' I faltered, I am thankful that I did not break down.

9 Aug. . . . Mr. Edwards Mr. Slater's Clerk came down & inspected. Baldock the contractors there, he says things shall be ready.

28 Aug. I w. early to ye Church w. pick & shovel for nearly 4 hours. A great deal of cleaning going on, & things are beginning to look better. Mr. Pooley sent up two horses & carts & 4 men also fruit & flowers by his son. . . . w. Ellen to Whileigh. The Bishop & his son Mr. Wimble . . .

29 Aug. I took up at 9 am the two Misses Honeysetts. Got to Holyhurst about 9.30. Lovely day. B[isho]p however came in good time [for dedication service at St Philip's]. A larger congr. . . . The Bishop of Chichester growing feeble. I read prayers. Bp. of Ch. Comm[union] Serv[ice]. Mr. Sergison [bishop's chaplain] Ep. Bp. w. Gospel. Bp. Trower preached a truly admirable sermon from 1 Cor. 14. 8. The verbal Explanation does certainly give many ideas as "battle" "trumpet" "clear" "stirring" "ringing" etc. However it was an excellent discourse. Collection during Offertory . . . note £5.0.0. Gold £58.0.0. Silver £14.7.3. Copper 1s.0½ making a total of £77.8.3½ towards the debt of £150. At the lunch, I as Rector was in the chair. . . . I proposed The Queen, Prince & Princess of W[ales] Bp. of Gibralter [Trower], Arch[itect] & Builders (Mr. Slater) Church wardens & Officers of ye parish (Mr. Taylor). "Parish of Burwash may it flourish root & branch" (Mr. Jas Philcox). Mr. Ley proposed the Bp. The Bp. proposed the Misses Trower. Bp. Trower proposed mine. I received very many warm congratulations on the manner in wh. I acted the part of Chairman, but I felt unusually inspired. . . .

4 Sept. . . . An anonymous friend, thro' Mr. Courthope gives us a Communion Plate. . . . C. & R. w. old Mrs Thompson (1/-). I asked her whether Stephen was likely to come to church now. Well Sir says the old woman "I don't know, for since he left off working at the stone for the Church he's been so drunk". C. on Dame Luck. She gives up Sunday worship for sake of morg. serv. . . .

11 Sept. Notice of a workhouse funeral for Friday. How curious, just the day when I am away. C. on Mr. Barton [Rector of Etchingham] on my way to the station & got him to take it.

16 Sept. . . . C. on G. Honeysett & J. Noakes to explain that in not asking them to sing at the opening of the new Ch. on the 29th I did not mean any offence, but cd. not ask more than I did.

14 Oct. . . . C. & P. w. Mrs J. Isted who gave me a wonderful idea of the shifts to wh. poor people are put in managing. Flour now 1/6 a gall[on] before baking. . . .

29 Oct. . . . I gave a dinner party, Mr. Gibbs, Mr. Mrs Miss Prothero, Clarke, Capt. Rogers, Mr. & Miss Philcox, myself. My cook did her part admirably. Philcox sent me a splendid piece of cod. Mr. Gibbs lent plate. James [Philcox's] Aunt sent grapes & pears, so I did pretty well. A pleasant evg. & some delightful music from Mrs Prothero.

1 Nov. . . . C. & R. w. Mrs Lusted a poor creature newly come into the parish behind Edward's [premises]. . . . C. on Mrs Reed, better; she told me that her sister Mrs Lusted suffered as much from fixed grief at having been deserted by a young man who had had two children by her, as from anything. She added I really believe she downright loved him; they were asked, but he cut her adrift.

6 Nov. . . . Tithe dinner; about 79. Mr. Breach, Mr. W. Newton, the Ch: Wardens, Guardians & nearly all the farmers dined. Philcox prop. my health. Pleasant Aft. & a good spirit among the guests.

9 Nov. . . . A young man Hawes by name applied to me to help him into the County Police. Fr[ank] Russell Jnr. came in & had a long talk. A most intelligent young Man one who has read & thought a great deal. He is going to teach in Sun: Sch: for me. . . .

Sun. 10 Nov. . . . On my way home had a long t. with St[ephen] Fielder [aged twenty-four, and an agricultural labourer like his father] who under all his rough outside has something quite winning in him. The shrewedness & clear sense of some of our uneducated men is to me remarkable.

29 Nov. . . . Committee meeting of Club. The Committee took a liberal view of the case & voted full pay in a question of doubt. One member said, Ours is called a friendly society, let it be so . . .

30 Nov. . . . Saml. Hazelden called. He has a bad hand & is going on his club so cannot teach at N. Sch. next week.[13] We discussed Gibbon's chapter agst. Xtianity as Hazelden is reading the Decline & Fall. He does not think much of the arguments.

4 Dec. . . . C. & took tea with Mr. & Mrs Rochester, by long invitation of the latter. A typical farmer's family. Comfortable & independent, a lot of sons who work on the farm & help their father not a little. . . .

5 Dec. C. & had a t. w. Mrs J. Isted; she overjoyed to tell me of her good fortune last week. Mr. W. Newton her husband's employer had made him a present of £2 for hop drying wh. he did not expect. A truly pleasant half hour in her cottage. . . .

6 Dec. . . . Mr. Gibbs. C. about Robt. Ireland's lunatic wife: on the question whether RI ought to be helped at the parish's expense. . . .

11 Dec. . . . Saw poor J[ohn] Cruttenden starting for himself for the Union. If his father, a well to do farmer & owner of land, had come to life again, & had seen him, he wd. have been shocked & yet his bringing up of the poor fellow had much to do w. it.[14]

12 Dec. Sch. Penny Popular. Audience small: took only 18/4. Performances tidy. Miss P[ooley] encored in both her songs. . . .

13 Dec. Sch: Vestry Meeting at 11 about the paths thro' the Village. The question being who is bound to repair them? Occupiers or the parish. A large meeting 14 in number. Adjourned to Lady-Tide. . . .[15]

21 Dec. Dole Mr. Barrow. M. Coppard. Mr. Taylor Mr. Cramp & old Mr. J. Coppard got thro' it completely by 2.30: gave away 89 stones at 4/3 – last year 4/10.

1868

23 Jan. . . . C. & R. w. old Beards Relf. He said that for 40 years he had never gone to bed without giving thanks to his Maker, that is when he is sober "Of course he didn't do it when he was Drunk"! . . .

1 Feb. Terrible gale last night & this morg. Part of the Roof of ye new Church blew off. Ye roof of Taylor's barn in great danger.[16]

5 Feb. . . . I wonder why I am called old fellow. Mr. J. said Good bye old fellow. Mr. Cox calls me old fellow & W.W. Townsend last autumn writing to me addresses me dear old fellow. I hope it is complimentary, but I can't quite explain it.

13 Feb. Sch. Uncle Nathan & Dixon called in ye morg. about Sch: acc[ounts] We went thro' them & found a deficit of about £150. I wrote a lot of letters – some begging ones. . . .

21 Feb. . . . Vestry meeting for appointment of Constables. . . .[17]

5 Mar. . . . Penny Pop[ular concert] good performance & largish audience tho' chiefly penny folks; so not so much money tho' the right sort of people. Miss Pooley sang admirably: Spirit of Spring. . . .

16 Mar. . . . To day died in the Ticehurst Workhouse John Cruttenden the last survivor in this parish of a name by wh. has flourished within the parish for 220 years . . . [Added later: 'no there is one more, an old man, an idiot'.]

25 Mar. Sch. Vestry meeting adj[ourned] to Bear. The pavement of the village question brought together the ratepayers. By a majority of one the pavement was negatived. . . .[18]

30 Mar. Mr. J. Fuller opened his school; terms 10/6 a quarter. About 2 or 3 have left us. . . .

7 Apl. C. on Mrs J. Isted; her husb: in trouble foor fellow. I c. on him in ye hop garden & had a long talk. A little drink on an empty stomach does sad mischief.[19]

8 Apl. . . . Clarke c. in ye evg. about a poor Collins girl who evinces a fixed repugnance of going into the Union Infirm[ary].

9 Apl. . . . C. on . . . [illegible] Clarke; not in. His mother treated the whole question of her 2 Sons' illegitmate children in the most matter of fact way. The idea of "sin" does not seem to attach to the question. . . .

13 Apl. School Committee in my room at 11. Mr. Gibbs, Newton, Breach, Clarke, Taylor & self present. It was resolved that I shd. write to Mr. Cox to say that unless the school is in a much more satisfactory state at the next Inspection we must request him to resign. It wd. be hard upon him but what can we do?[20] We then went to ye Vestry meeting. Looked round the Ch: yard wh. is not satisfactory. The Vestry had in [Parish Clerk] Benjn. Wood & told him that he cd. be re-elected only on condition that he did his work as the Ch: Wardens wished him to do it.

Sun. 19 Apl. Catt dr[ove] me up to Labour in Vain[21] as it was very wet. H[oly] C[ommunion] in morg. . . .

20 Apl. . . . C. on Mrs A. Russell she consulted me about Emigr[ation].

24 Apl. I w. up to H[urst] Green by 11. John Isted's case [at Petty Sessions] wd. not come on till last, so went up to Iridge. Lunch, & back to ye George [inn where the Petty Sessions convened]. Gave witness in favour of J. Isted's Char[acter]; he was fined 1/- & costs 13/4. . . . J. Philcox br[ought] me home in his carr[iage]. Circus (Ginnetts) in ye town – everybody there.

5 May. Sch. Drove Clarke to Waldron to Cler[ical] Meeting. Signed a pet[ition] agst. disestablishment, tho' it was curious how little agreement there was in the principle on wh. we opposed. Discuss[ion] about ye Report on Ritualism. Truly the words "Protestant Religion" are words wh. stick in the nostrils of many of the brethren. However we had a very pleasant meeting. . . .[22]

8 May. . . . C. on Mr J. Isted & had a long talk; poor thing he has troubles, no mistake.

9 May. . . . C. on Mrs Lusted, poor woman, she misses the diet she had for 6 months in the [workhouse] infirmary. . . .

Sun. 10 May. . . . Congr: very thin of young men, or men of any sort. . . .

14 May. . . . Concert at 3; aud[ience] not so large as it has been. Perform-ance best I have ever had. Class sang excellently. Miss Nelly Breach [Egerton's future wife] & Lucy played very well & Fraulein Mehlhorn created a great sensation. Mr. Bridge sang admirably; altogether a very pleasant entertainment. Dinner at 6. Evg. Concert better still; audience more demonstrative. Takings. Morg. £12:1:6. Evg. £7:16:9. . . .

15 May. . . . I sat up till 2.30 writing acc[oun]t of Concert for Sussex Express. Posted it by mailman at 2.30[a.m.].[23]

[Lengthy stay in Wiltshire.]

14 June. Sch. Mr. Anset has made a great difference already; the children being much more quiet & in better discipline. . . .

16 June. I c. on poor Cox (yesterday). He of course much upset & looking upon himself as a persecuted man but it cannot be helped. I am heartily & deeply grieved that his case shd. be as it is, but he cannot stop as master. . . .

17 June. . . . At 3 PM Committee meetg. Mr. Gibbs, Mr. Clarke, Mr. Taylor & myself. We agreed to offer ye School to Mr. Anset & to make Mr. Cox a don[atio]n of £15:0:0: I wrote to the Comm's resolution to Mr. Cox a private note of my own. . . .

18 June. Sch. A cr[icket] match Flimwell v. Burwash. Fl. won by 7 wickets. I to ye ground & sent several truants to school.

22 June. . . . Pleaded with Wilsher on behalf of old Tom Pankhurst . . .[24]

2 July. Woke up at 3 AM by two drunken tramps. The man kicking ye woman. I had to go over to Higham to give evidence. Mr L[uxford JP] out so w. back to Iridge staid aft:. . . . To Higham at 6.30. Mr. L. returned at 7.15. Man & woman fined 2/6 each & exp[enses i.e. costs]: total 17/-. . . .

10 July. Sch. Discipline much impr[oved]. . . .

13 July. . . . C. on J. Sweatman. Inspected Cottage Garden; good: took a cup of tea & some biscuit as I was hungry & thirsty. Honest respectable couple. Had a talk w. Mr. St[ephen] Gillett over his hedge. . . . C. on old Master (1/-) Hyland. Had worked 71 years & brought up 16 children before he applied to ye parish for anything [public assistance]. . . .

18 July. . . . C. on old Beard's Relf & had a scene. His family accuse him of using horribly bad lang[uage] an imputation wh. makes him very angry. . . . C. on old Mrs Thompsett who told me she had a visit from "The Pope's Wife" a statement to wh. she stuck, till it turned out to be B[isho]p Trower's wife. . . . C. on S. Hazelden (1/-) who is labouring under a false accusation of working while on ye Club whose [club] pay is stopped in ye meantime. . . .

20 July. . . . Committee meeting at Sch: in a matter of Hazelden. He was not turned out of ye Club.[25]

30 July. . . . Made some extracts from [Parish] Registers for a Mr. Henty, beginning about 1701. Found in the [Parish] chest a piece of Old Communion plate bearing date 1568. To an evg. party at Mrs Combs. Mr. Mrs Wm. Newton; Miss Cooke, Mr. Mrs Bourne & Miss Jones Woodknowle. Js. Philcox, Capn. Roger & a fr[iend] of Mrs Bourne. Captn. Roger was asked merely to save the number 13 & to make it 14. A piece of superstition wh. I shd. really have thought impossible in these days.

2 Aug. . . . Mr. Kitchin ye Bailiff at Mr. Companes' says that owing to our harvest being nearly simultaneous w. that on ye hills men are very scarce indeed. . . .[26]

3 Aug. Sch: only 50 Boys[27]; the girls a few more. . . .

4 Aug. . . . Saml. Waterhouse has lost his cow; about £15; not insured. . . .
C. on Dame Luck. The poor old dog "Papper" shot last night. Dame Luck
says she misses him terribly. . . .

7 Aug. . . . C. on Mr. Breach about Subscr[iption] to a fund for carrying a
Conserv[ative] member for East Sussex. He off[ere]d £5. C. on Mr.
Newton for the same purp[oses] Mr. Gibbs there. Had a long talk. Mr.
Newton will vote for the Liberals unless they go in for the Liberation
Soc[iety]:[28] then he sticks to Ch; & State. Mr. Gibbs off. £5 in case the
Candidate comes out on the True Protestant platform. A True Protestant
being this . . . if the Judicial Committee decide that Ritualism is according
to the Ch: of Engl[and] law, will agitate for an alteration of the law. . . .

8 Aug. C. on Mrs J. Isted: her husb: & his br[other] William there; sat
talking some time. 2 men killed by ye sun on the next farm to that on wh.
Wm. Isted was Harvesting nr. Falmer. . . .[29]

16 Aug. . . . Spoke on my way back [from St. Philip's] to old George
Waddell & said, Master Waddell I have often been told you say that if you
had y[ou]r life to lead over again, you wd. lead just such a one again as you
have led, is that so. No Sir. . . . I never said no such thing as that but I have
often said that if I had plenty of money I'd keep a cry of dogs! . . .[30]

17 Aug. Started at Etchingham at 9.35 w. 31 of my Singing Class for the
Crystal Palace. Had a carriage to ourselves. . . . arrived about 12.30. Mr.
Anset met us there. One girl (the only London born girl we had) left her
dinner on the train. . . . We had hard work to get into the 5.36 train, half
the people being left behind, but we did manage it, & reached Lond[on]
Br[idge] Station, 6.10 saving S[outh] E[astern] R[ailway] train by about 4 or
5 minutes. Too narrow a shave to be pleasant as 31 Children & young
women on one's hand for the night in London wd. have been no joke. . . .
Got to Etchingham at 8.40. . . .

22 Aug. A great storm of wind & rain; did much damage in the hop gardens,
in some places blowing down nearly all the poles & levelling altogether so
that they say 4 Acres wh. Mr. Bennett of Mountfield (the watchmaker of
Cheapside) has been growing on the new system of strings. . . .[31]

26 Aug. . . . Had my first Rectoral dinner party. Young W. Prideaux,
A. Wace, J. Foley, G.J. Courthope, Frank Courthope, Fred: Courthope,
R. Rudyard, H.W. Hussey, Sidney Spurin, Gibbs & myself. Very
pleasant evg. . . . Mrs Styles was my cook. Aunt Harriet leant me
plate. . . . [Hired] Pratt a professional waiter from ye Station Inn, Etchingham. . . .

27 Aug. Gave away to various poor people the remains of last night. Calculated that ye entertainment cost me about 10/- a head wh. is too much. . . .

28 Aug. . . . Dawson & Pupil at Cricket for a wonder I took a bat & they did not put me out tho' of course they cd. have done if they had bowled swift, wh. they did not for my eyes' sake. . . .

3 Sept. . . . C. on old Kemp. Poor old man into ye Union where he will be I think more comfortable. . . .

5 Sept. C. on Philcox. Bateman's sold to Mr. Jesse Piper for a Mr. Whitehead of London for £5100.

Sun. 6 Sept. . . . Master Lulham accused me of treating his boy very unjustly, & after his saying that Miss Irwin has done more good in the parish than all the rest of us, I had to tell him she was the very one who wd. not have his son in her class any longer.

7 Sept. . . . Chapter meeting. Small attendance. It was agreed that the best way of acting under the new Ch. Rate law will be to pass a Rate as usual, & to collect what we can. . . .[32]

9 Sept. . . . The pavement in ye street being mended at Aunt Harriett's expense. It is too bad, but the householders won't do it, & the parish won't do it. Nobody will go to law about it & who is to do it?

10 Sept. . . . My Aunt I find has sublet the Glebe to Mr. Philcox & Mr. Whatman, without saying a word to me. I certainly never meant to sublet it. If she wanted it for her own use, she might have it as she has had it this year for £50, but if she did not want it for herself, I meant that it should revert to me. However, she will make such a fuss that I suppose I must leave it. Still, I look upon it as rather sharp practice. . . .

12 Sept. . . . M. Coppard came in ye aft. & went thro' the list of voters w. me. Conservative a sm[all] majority on new list in Burwash.

18 Sept. . . . read over a good deal of my diary of years gone by. Of course the greater part of it fearful rubbish, but interesting to me here and there.

19 Sept. W. Taylor to inspect Cottage gardens. H. Morris 1st Pr[ize]; John Pennell 2d, both very good. . . . Sweatman's gard. very good, but not so good as ye others. . . .

1 Oct. . . . At 6 PM to my Aunts hop-treat. Tippler Weston sang a song wh. shewed that the current view of a husband coming home occasionally drunk is not a severe one. His d. Mrs Hilder sang a really good song; her voice is excellent and her pronounc[iation] very pure. I sang "Ye Village Blacksmith" & "When the heart is young"; away about 8.30. The last cricket match of our Season but a very poor affair. Merely a home match & very few there.

5 Oct. Fair day: more carts than customers. Sch. very small. I hunted up some of the boys but without much success. . . .

8 Oct. . . . On my way back [from school and parishioners] terribly abused by a drunken drover on the principle "You are one of the idle lot who do no work, & we help to keep you". I into ye Windmill field to speak to ye men about ye Allotments. Repassed ye Drover sunk past further controversy in ye ditch.

14 Oct. . . . I saw several boys & had serious conv[ersations] w. them. Was very much pleased as I always am at such times. I believe that the more directly spiritual intercourse one has w. one's parishioners, the more invariable reward does one get. . . .

29 Oct. Mr. Cox's sale; things I believe went well. Poor man I am truly sorry for him, but drink has so far utterly ruined him. . . .

2 Nov. . . . C. on Mr. & Miss Jobbins of Gingerbreads. He a retired biscuit maker from London, said to be quite hard baked himself, but I own I did not find it out. Has built an odd house & in country matters is reported very crotchety & cranky. . . . N.S. 35 men & boys, very attentive & business like. . . .

9 Nov. I to speak to Willsher ye Relieving Officer pretty sharply about some irregularities in ye delivery of wine to ye poor. He had nothing to say & was submissive. . . .[33]

13 Nov. . . . Called to talk w. a young man Punch Dann a soldier of the 90th F[oo]t, a Burwash man in custody in the lock up for a drunken row.[34]

21 Nov. C. on Mrs Isted, long talk w. her & w. her husband. The shifts to wh. poor people are put to get a living are really wonderful. . . . C. on Philcox. A long talk about ye living & ye possibility of my ever occupying ye Rectory. He thinks I cd. I think not.

23 Nov. . . . C. on Miss Trower. Mrs Cartwright there looking very well & full of politics. She & the Miss Trower high Tories as all ladies ought to be, but still putting Matters such as Ch: & state on such high ground that I cd. not quite agree. Proving too much is a dangerous fallacy. . . .

24 Nov. Taylor drove me to Mayfield in morg. Great crush at ye polling wh. was in ye Sch: room. Blue colours (Liberal) in great force. One blue non-voter solemnized for my benefit "I'm for fat pigs & less fat parsons". Home by 2 o'Clock. . . .[35]

25 Nov. . . . C. & R. w. Mrs Saml. Eyles; poor woman, she has been confined 14 times without any child living. . . .

26 Nov. Mr. Ladd [of Wadhurst] told a good story when a friend of his heard in Court in Maidstone. Sergt. Somebody was bullying a witness by insisting on he saying how he got the black eye w. wh. he appeared in ye witness box. After much hesitation the witness said, Well, Sir, if you must know I got it in the same way as you got y[ou]r silk gown (the Sergt had just been made Sergt) by my impudence! . . .

Sun. 29 Nov. . . . A good congr: A poor woman Knight? by name toils up from Socknersh on my Sundays & is amply rewarded if she shakes hands & speaks with me. One ought to take more pains than one does to preach the Gospel to one such as she. . . .

1 Dec. . . . Two women to day Bommy Whitten's wife & Syratt's housekeeper, insulted poor Clarke in ye Ch: Yard after a wedding by bringing out of ye Bell 2 glasses of gin & water & offering them to him & wanting him to drink.

[Short visit to Wiltshire.]

14 Dec. Sch: the Discipline becoming excellent. . . . C. on Saml. Hezelden, his hand better. It is odd to find a labouring man entering into conversation about the decline & fall of the Roman Empire, but he is on the Xth vol[ume] of Gibbon. . . . To N.S. a terrible night & only 11 or 12 there. John Hyland lent me his great coat & I got home safely. . . .

15 Dec. J. Jenner c. on me he is not well poor lad; gave him a bottle of Port wine. . . .

17 Dec. . . . C. on Mrs J. Isted. She let me take down on paper her income & outgoings. It is a sharp struggle. She has been married 15 years next Xmas day has had 11 confinements & 13 ch. 6 are alive. . . .[36]

18 Dec. . . . A Cheap Jack borrowed ye School hall w. wh. to cry his wares. . . .

21 Dec. St. Thomas's day, being wet for ye poor dolers. Sat in Sch. from 10.35 to 3.20. Gave away about £20 worth of beef. Many men I fear out of work. . . .

26 Dec. . . . Ben Wood C. on me. He doing well as a young Carpenter. . . .[37]

Notes

1.   From 1854 Andrew Gibbs lived in Burwash after buying land. A Londoner by birth, a bachelor now aged fifty-six, he employed a valet, cook, housemaid and a scullery maid at Dudwell House. Census, 1871.

2.   An example of inter-personal communications between Courthope, chairman of the Petty Sessions, and Egerton, in this case the socio-legal problems over John Relf's separation from his wife.

3.   Seventy-one-year-old Joseph Morris strangled himself, and was found by his wife, after losing his job as collector at the Weald toll-gate when the Lewes–Hurst Green turnpike trust was liquidated in Nov. 1866. The inquest brought in a suicide verdict. *Sussex Advertiser*, 27 Mar. 1867. *Sussex Agricultural Express*, 30 Mar. 1867.

4.   See introduction, p. 18.

5.   The Newington family's private mental hospital in Ticehurst was known colloquially at the Establishment; successive generations of the Newingtons were also philanthropists.

6.   The three stained-glass windows in the new church, St Philip's, paid for by Ellen Gould in memory of her husband. Kelly's, *Directory of Sussex*, (1878). *Sussex Agricultural Express*, 6 Aug. 1867.

7.   Neither man had much of a record, at least not through convictions in the local court. Thomas was fined in 1865 for a Sunday night fracas with one of the Pankhursts; after being separated in the street by Sergeant Pocock, they went off to continue it in a meadow: 'Both . . . admitted the offence, saying it would not have happened if they had not been drinking'. William had been convicted, on police evidence, of drunkenness and riotous behaviour in 1863. *Sussex Advertiser*, 2 May 1865. Summary returns, ESCRO. QR/E1023.

8.   The annual concerts given by the 'Burwash Singing Class', 'assisted by some professional and amateur musicians', at 3 and again at 7 p.m. attracted substantial audiences, with over two hundred present for the evening performance. *Sussex Agricultural Express*, 7 May 1867.

9.   The thirty-second anniversary of the Burwash Friendly Society; the substantial dividend of 7/- was paid, and the society had but one resignation, and several candidates for election. *Sussex Agricultural Express*, 21 May 1867.

10.   This anniversary of the 'Burwash Common Provident Society' was the subject of a very long letter to the local press, nominally from 'Visitor', but whose sentiments could – and perhaps did – come from Egerton's pen. The booth near the Railway Inn was 'filled with clean healthy folks'. Egerton spoke at some length, acknowledged that club members were healthy as only nine of the seventy-two had drawn on the funds, and that there were 'no "skulkers", no members pretending to be ill'. He praised the chair, John Hyland as a 'worthy man' and 'good parishioner', and secretary Sam Hazleden, who taught at night school, 'and when I tell you that he is reading some of my *hard books* you have a guarantee' that this official continued to do everything possible for further self-improvement. Egerton also addressed the hoary question of honorary members' subscriptions, to the effect that all monies from this source should be put into a reserve fund, rather than towards annual dividends; donors would then increase their contributions, thereby ensuring that 'when your club reaches mature age the old members should have something to look back upon, and not be subject to the sudden breaking up of what they had paid to for years', and as a 'proof of your vitality, and an earnest of keeping faith with members when they become old'. *Sussex Agricultural Express*, 28 May 1867.

11.   Thereby pre-empting the sitting tenant's opportunity of buying the property.
12.   'Neither' William Baldock not his partner Brooker 'had any capital when they commenced business' as builders based in Hurst Green, 'with their first contract . . . for repairing the church on Burwash Common', worth £1500. They lost between £50 and £200 on the job, but their partnership survived until 1879, when Baldock was bankrupted. *Sussex Agricultural Express*, 24 Jan. 1887.
13.   It is not known whether Egerton paid his less-affluent helpers at the Night Schools. Hazelden could have, of course, continued teaching, but if he were paid for it, the Common friendly society might well have ruled – illiberally – that he had thereby forfeited his benefit right.
14.   Cruttenden, now aged 74, had occupied 118 acre Tott Farm in 1842, and was employing six men there in 1851. 1842, Tithe. 1851 Census.
15.   'The frosts of last winter lifted yards of the pavement . . . there are risings in places and holes in others, which are positively dangerous'. In fact the meeting continued unofficially, and unknown to Egerton, afterwards in the pub, several 'opulent farmers advocated . . . a special rate . . . paid for by the inhabitants of the village to repair the . . . pavement', a neat device to circumvent costs falling on the highway rate paid by all ratepayers, including many farmers, domiciled outside the village. *Sussex Advertiser*, 2 Nov. 1867. See below, 25 Mar. 1868, p. 73 and note 18.
16.   The gale, 'one of the most violent hurricanes' for years did widespread damage, and falling masonry made it dangerous to walk in village streets. *Sussex Agricultural Express*, 8 Feb. 1868.
17.   Parish or Local Constables continued to be appointed annually despite the creation of the professional East Sussex police under the 1839–40 legislation; they were technically under the direction of the professionals. R. Wells, 'Implementation and Non-implementation of the 1839–40 Police Acts in East and West Sussex', *Policing and Society*, (1991). Frederick Cramp, Richard and William Hobden, were each appointed to their first term of office, joining farmworker William Pilbeam, who had served since 1853; it was Pilbeam's last year. ESCRO. QAC/3/E8. Egerton rarely attended these meetings.
18.   Representing a victory for the farmers (probably joined by some villagers) against the Highway Rate being used to finance footway repairs; presumably the villagers had rejected a special rate on just them for repairs. See above, 13 Dec. 1867, and for the issue's resolution, below, 9 Sept. 1868.
19.   John Isted was arrested for being drunk and disorderly in the village on 4 Apl. ESCRO. QR/E1042. See below, p. 74, 24 Apl. 1868.
20.   In the event, the long-serving schoolmaster forty-eight-year-old Alfred Cox, was forced to resign, apparently on the grounds of alcoholism, but as this occurred during Egerton's Wiltshire sojourn, there are no details, except that Egerton called to offer commiserations on his return; see below, p. 74, 16 June 1868.
21.   A 'beershop opened as such by Edmund Hilder, under the title of "Labour in Vain" with the sign of a "blackamoor in a tub with a white man trying to scrub the black off". This elaborate work of art was painted by Master Thomas Upfield who lived near "Haffle" church. The sign was suggested to Master Hilder by a travelling cloth pack man who said he had seen the sign in the "Sheeres"'. Egerton received this information from the then eighty-one-year-old Hilder on 22 May 1876; by that date the beershop had become a fully-licensed inn, known as the Railway Tavern. Hilder's days as a proprietor were over by 1847, when he was a field labourer. ESCRO. Add.Mss.5637/7. *Brighton Gazette*, 1 Sept. 1842. 19 Feb. 1847, list of

able-bodied male recipients of temporary outdoor relief, PRO. MH.12/13143. 1851 Census. Very briefly mentioned in *Sussex Folk*, pp. 125–6.

22. Disestablishment of the Anglican Church was a long-term radical demand, which had some supporters in the Liberal Party, in stark contrast to the Tories. Egerton's references to the lack of unity over principles, and even aversion to the use of Protestant Religion were reflections of the ritualistic High-Churchmen present, some of whom were no doubt crypto-Catholics, not curbed until the 1874 passage of the Public Worship Act.

23. Again, professionals dominated proceedings, though the fifty-strong choir was 'entirely parochial', and Egerton used Mehlhorn's performance to suggest that such piano soloists were almost on a par with professionals. *Sussex Agricultural Express*, 19 May 1868.

24. Pankhurst was seventy-nine; presumably Egerton put the case to Relieving Officer Willsher against Pankhurst's incarceration in the workhouse.

25. A guilty verdict would have invariably seen his expulsion; agricultural labourers' club rights were normally the greatest investment they had, though the same was not necessarily true of master craftsmen.

26. Normally, harvesting on the Downs preceded the Weald by a fortnight, permitting Wealden workers to migrate temporarily to the Downs, before returning to harvest the crops in their home parishes. This year Downland farmers complained of labour shortages, sufficiently severe not 'to get their crops cut fast enough'. *Sussex Agricultural Express*, 14 and 25 July 1868.

27. Another reflection of labour shortages.

28. Since its 1853 foundation, the Liberation Society supported, either directly or indirectly through inter-personnel connections, so many non-conformist and radical causes, that the precise issue which would lead Newton to vote Tory is not clear, but Liberal insistence on disestablishment and disendowment of the Anglican Church of Ireland seems likely at this juncture.

29. The second case, which was reported involved the death of a sixty-four-year-old harvester; as death through sunstroke was diagnosed, an inquest was deemed unnecessary. *Sussex Agricultural Express*, 28 July 1868.

30. A slightly different version appears in *Sussex Folk*, p. 105, where Egerton also asserts that Waddell's addiction to hunting with beagles 'and other means, had wasted a fair income and had come to poverty'. In fact, Waddell was one of the modest tenant farmers (54 acres in 1835, 95 acres in 1842) reduced between 1842 and 1851 to farm labouring. He took out a game-licence after a poaching conviction at Battle in December 1833, but failed to renew it in 1840, when he was fined again. His ability to engage in sports collapsed with his status. 1842, Tithe. 1851, Census. *Sussex Advertiser*, 16 Mar. and 7 Sept. 1835, 12 Sept. 1836, 23 Sept. 1839 and 11 May 1840.

31. The storm, high winds and heavy rain, did '"a world of damage". Poles down, branches blown off, and a general deterioration of the crop is now the true statement', according to the regular reporter on Burwash hops: 'This is one of the glorious uncertainties of hop growing . . .'. *Sussex Agricultural Express*, 25 Aug. 1868.

32. The Compulsory Church Rate Abolition Act, 31 and 32 Victoria, c.109.

33. Wine was regularly prescribed as a tonic by the Union Medical Officers.

34. Nobody appears to have been prosecuted as a result of this altercation.

35. The 1867 Reform Act's extension of the franchise applied only to borough constituencies, and the working-class majority of rural inhabitants remained

without the vote until at least 1884–5. However, the unfranchised often joined in at the hustings, and polling days were usually accompanied by heavy drinking.

36. Christmas Day was favoured for weddings by some. The expenditure, element of the Isted budget (reproduced in much greater detail below, pp. 85–6) was published in *Sussex Folk*, pp. 81–2, together with the observation that a common saying among such people is that a week comprised 'A feast and a fast'.

37. Aged twenty-one, the son of Benjamin also a carpenter and long-serving parish clerk, he was to migrate to London where he became a successful and substantial builder. See below, p. 223 note 10.

1869

1 Jan. . . . I to ye Common. . . . C. on old Jesse Relf. He at ye age of 82 teaching himself to read very fairly on ye N[ew] Test[ament].[1] . . . C. on old Mrs Thompsett (1/-); ill in bed & locked up by herself poor soul. . . .

10 Jan. . . . Young G. Langridge C. to say good bye, he going to Mr. Warton's to service tomorrow.

11 Jan. . . . A Rebecca Pennells living w. a Soldier at Shoeburyness had been passing herself off as the wife of one Wm. Peacock who married Halls d. saying that Monteith the soldier w. whom she is living m[arried] her in the n[ame] of Peacock. C. on N.Pennells saw his wife. . . .

[After a visit to London.]

22 Jan. . . . letter from Mrs S.E.Gordon, Shoeburyness thanking me for enquiries about Rebecca Pennells . . .

29 Jan. . . . to Club meeting. Qu[estion] what to do about paying the death money for Amos Wickens, as his friends take no notice of him & let him it seems be buried by ye parish. No decision, as not a quorum of committee.

3 Feb. . . . penny Reading. Young Barton read Tennyson's Dora excellently. Hussey who reads admirably gave a touching story of Mrs Gaskell called "The Sexton's Hero" written years ago for a Capesthorned Fete in behalf of ye Macclesfield Infirmary I think, & then publ[ished] by Johnson, Rawson & Co. Corporation Strt. Manchester. He also read Boob at the Holly Tree Inn wh. was very good. Ch. I read Alonzo the brave & the fair Imogeme. The brass band played & I sang "A thousand a year" & " When the heart is young". . . .

8 Feb. C. on master Collins in Hams L[ane]; he sent for me to intercede w. ye Guardians about relief for his d. I saw Mr. Combs & Willsher, but I feel sure all the G[uardians] will do will be to offer to take her into the Infirmary. C. on poor old Mrs Hyland & R. w. her. She is I suppose dying. She is a good old soul & will be much missed.

9 Feb. Poor Mrs Hyland died this morg. about 6 o'Clock. Quietly & without pain. Her husb: died on Easter Monday 1859. To ye Sch: I c. on poor Miss H. & saw Mrs; she looked wonderfully peaceful & calm. . . .

11 Feb. . . . C. on Rebecca Pennells. . . . C. on Daws. Gave him 7/6 for Rebecca Pennells. . . .

Sun. 14 Feb. . . . C. on old Luck (1/-) He turned 80. Confined to bed & only grieving because he was a trouble to his niece. A Chapel man. . . .

16 Feb. . . . C. & had a long chat w. Mrs Alfred Russell. She said that her husb: got much good under [the Rev.] Whitlock: that one day he came home from hearing him threw his arms round her neck & kissed her & said I will be different to you Mary for time to come, & his wife says So he was. I C. on G. Isted's wife. She very ill. P. w. her. gave Parsons a 1/- for looking after her. . . .

18 Feb. . . . C. on Mrs Fieldwick; 10 children, only one I fear can read & write. . . . C. on Daw's got to him 5/- for Rebecca Pennalls. . . . Coming away met Relfe late of ye Wheel Inn. He was very angry with me because I had told him his w[ife] ought to behave herself better. . . .[2]

22 Feb. . . . I wrote to Mr. Yates of Ron Hill an apology or explanation for my having at the Butler's suggestion taken lunch at Ron Hill when I called, in ye absence of Mr. & Mrs Yates, a proceeding wh. seems to have riled them.

1 Mar. By Expr[ess] to Ch[aring] X. Then to 3 Whitehall Gardens. Saw Mr. Fuller; by his advice to see Mr. Chard at ye Stock Exch[ange]. Had a talk w. him & got him to come down £250 in his price for Paddock Farm. He now says he will take £6250. . . .

J. I[sted] Married 15 years. Wife confined 11 times, besides mishaps; has had 13 children, once 3 at a birth; 6 now living, eldest 14: none of them earn anything except the eldest who is a girl & does a little hop-tying & a little hop-picking tho' the biggest part of this last she lost having to attend her mother, who is permanent invalid.

Income:				Outgoings per week	
Husbands day wages	13	6d			
Wife allowed by friend	1	0	Rent	2s.	0.
	14	6	7 gall[on]s flour	7	0
Parish allowance of flour	2	0	2 lbs. Dutch cheese	1	3
	—		1 lb Butter	1	4
	16	6	½ lb soap		2
			Soda ½ Blue ½		1

£ – s – d

52 at 13/6	35	2	0	Day wage
	2	12	0	Charity
	5	4	0	Do
	10	0	0	Extra work
	52	18	0	

Salt & pepper		½
1 lb & ½ Candles		10½
2 oz tea		4
2lb sugar		7
Schooling		7
Cotton 1d Mustard		3
Milk per week 1/4 p[in]t daily		3½
Washing	1	0
Mangling		1
	15	10½

pr week.

Piece work & extra earnings:

£ s d

Hoppicking – daughter	1– 0–0
Acorns picked up	15 0
Hop Tying	1 0 0
5 days harvesting over & above day wages	1 5 0
Hop drying 4 weeks at 30/- less 2/6 extra food & 12/6 day wages.	2 16 0
Mowing over & above day wages	2 0 0
Profit on Two pigs	2 0 0
	9 16 0

Extra outgoings per annum:

Benefit Club	1	0 0
Daughters School Club		4 4
Wifes Clothing Club		8 8
Daughters boots		12 0
Husbands boots		12 0
Faggots	2	0 0
5 childrens boots at 6/-	1	10 0
Husbands clothes	1	0 0
Tools		7 0
	7	14 0

Leaving £3-14 a year for Coals, meat & clothing, beyond what the Clothing Clubs give.

March 1869–71 volume commences with Egerton's own income:

Income	£	s	d	Deductions	£	s	d
Tithe say	1100	0	0	Curate	135	0	0
Glebe	122	0	0	Vicar of Stonegate	20	0	0
				Local Tax on House			
	1122	0	0	Gardens	30	0	0
				Insurance	1	10	0
Less deductions	479	0	0	Income Tax AB	5	0	0
Left to spend	£752	0	0		191	10	0
				Poor Rate Highway R	208	10	0
				Sundry outgoings	50	0	0
				Rates etc	20	0	0
				Income Tax			
					278	10	0

8 Mar. Discussed some poor law cases w. some of the local authorities. . . .

13 Mar. I had a letter from F. Fuller Esq. . . . saying that yesterday Mr. Chard had written a note to say that he accepted Mrs Holland's offer of £6000 for the Blacktown or Paddock Farm. 175 acres timber included. For this I truly thank God, as I believe that Mrs Holland will be a great help to the west part of our parish, not only materially but spiritually. My first letter to Mrs Holland seems to have been written on the 30th of June since wh. time I have written 17 letters to her on the subject, 3 to Mr. Fuller, & 2 or 3 to Mr. Chard. She is the Honourable Mrs F. Holland, a d. of the late Lord Denham sister of Houble G. Denman & C[onservative] MP. . . . C. on poor Mr. Brown the miller, he in great pecuniary trouble. . . . C. on old Mrs Thompsett in difficulties (2/-) about rent. . . .

20 Mar. . . . C. on Mrs J. Isted. Sally really a remarkable girl, at 15, & able to attend to all house duties as well as most women.

22 Mar. . . . To ye Sch. I took class & inspected copybooks & slates. Polly Thompson needs more systematic help in teaching: the numbers are too great & the initial ignorance of the children too uniform to give her a fair chance [as a Pupil Teacher]. She works hard & conscientiously, tho' she lacks all enthusiasm. Still she is a good mistress. . . . C. on old Relf(6d). His is a marvellous constitution. He is at the age of 82 getting stronger from a paralytic stroke, tho' he is still in bed.

23 Mar. . . . Mr. Frank Trower still engaged on ye "Burwash" article for ye

Sussex Archaeological Collection.[3] . . . C. on Hannah Chandler, a wonderfully tough old woman & clings to life very tightly. . . .

25 Mar. . . . The Parish meeting. Adjourned from the Vestry to my room. Not many present. Messrs. Philcox, Simes, Wm. Newton, Taylor, Noakes, Cramp, Gilham. J. Coppard Snr. Martin C[oppard], Mr. Barrow. We went thro' the Doctor's list of persons receiving mutton . . . as the Board [of Guardians] complains of its length but we cd. not find in our heart to strike off more than one or two. . . . dinner at the Admiral. . . . We had a very friendly meeting . . .[4]

27 Mar. . . . I c. on Mrs J. Isted. Inquired of her about a pig wh. her husb: had just sold for £5 & wh. was causing talk as he is receiving parish relief. She owed £2-15-0 of the money for it's keep & out of the rest wh. he got boots 13/6, Trowsers 10/-, R[ound] Fr[ock] 8/6. She is a good little woman & very thankful for sympathy. John also much improved of late years & works hard for his family. . . .

Sun. 28 Mar. Easter day. Snow & cold. Much humbled to day. Small congr: no men in ye Choir. Only 38 Comm[unicants] & this a G[od's] D[ay]. O how much of this carelessness of the people may be owing to my own want of zeal & energy. God grant that I may do more for Him in this place. . . .

29 Mar. . . . In matter of Ch: Rates agreed to pass a 2d rate as usual & collect what we cd.

1 Apl. To ye Rect. [where large gathering]. . . . Old Johnston told ye story about ye High Ch: Clergyman being "in bad odour w. his congr: by turning his back upon the people, & reading the lesson from the rectum", & on my saying that I knew the story, he added that it wonderful how quickly some stories travel, to wh. I replied that this particular story no doubt travelled like "wind". . . .

2 Apl. . . . D. at Rect. 1st dinner party since Uncle's death. . . .

5 Apl. . . . C. on Lizzy Gibbs, her mother died last week. I did not even know that the poor woman was ill. . . .[5]

6 Apl. . . . C. & R. w. Master Lee (1/-); he a hawker, 5 children under 12 & another close at hand, his wife said "our's isn't a living, its only a being"[6] & I fear that she is right. Cottage not much larger than a couple of bandboxes. . . .

9 Apl. . . . Committee meeting of ye Club in ye aft. about Amos Wickens money. When he had no wife no friends to claim the death subscription. So a majority of the Committee voted that the money shd. be divided pro rata amongst his creditors. . . . I sent out 35 concert circulars.

Sun. 18 Apl. . . . Baptisms & aft. Baptism of two adults Janet Fairway Waters & Ester Mann Waters. Interesting service: the eldest is so like Miss Payne as to keep me all the time in mind of her. . . .

26 Apl. . . . Nicky Crowhurst just come out of the Union & very drunk wanted to talk to me about religion. I declined. . . .

30 Apl. . . . In evg. to Committee of Benefit Club at ye School. Fined two members for breach of rules. Wrote to Uncle Nathan opinions of ye men & Mr. Taylor, Barrow & others, about allotments. All seemed to agree that 1/8 of an acre better than 1/4.[7]

[Visit to Wiltshire.]

19 May. . . . I gave leave to ye Club to have ye dinn. in ye Schoolroom. I pr. to ye Club from 15 John 5.5. (Ext). I felt unusually interested in the service & the large number of men present made one pray much for power to reach their hearts. . . . Dinner, I presided, made speeches sang "A thousand a year" & "When the heart is young" & came away about 7.30. Mr. Barrow staid till 10.50 when the room was shut up & said that altogether from the Bell & elsewhere he saw only 5 men led home, wh. I consider a favourable account.[8]

20 May. . . . I c. on John Isted; he I am thankful to say survived yesterday's temptations unhurt & said that when he was treated to drink he "drank pretty light many times"; just the example of restraint wh. I little hoped to find, & I am proportionately thankful. . . .

26 May. A most lovely day for the Common Club. I pr; to them from 15 John 5. 5 (Ext) Congr: large & orderly & very attentive. One of the band accompanied the 100th Ps[alm] with his Saxhorn & the effect was very good. . . . Dinner at a tent. Mr. H. Edwards, Mr. Combs, Mr. Dearsley, & an itinerant dealer in pills the visitors at the High Table. After dinner one man had to be removed for bad language, otherwise the conduct of the members was very good & proper. Tom Fielder said it was his intention to go home & go to bed, as it was his way when he had his belly full of victuals (and he had & no mistake) to go home & "nourish" [digest] it. He however did not go. Dearsley & I away about 5.30. He drove me home. . . .

28 May. . . . I c. on Mrs Wm. Isted whose husband was convicted this morg. at H[urst] Green, & sent to prison for two months for being on Clarke's premises on Sun: for an unlawful purpose.[9] The poor woman . . . with a fearful black eye from her husband's violence; in great grief at his sentence. C. on J. Hyland; his wife in; gave a good acc[oun]t of ye Club as did Hazelden who was there. So that I hope that on the whole things were satisfactory. . . . I presided over the 1st meeting of the Burwash Club for the new [club] year. Mr. J. Fuller elected Clerk; 3/6 a week, permanent relief after a twelve month voted henceforth instead of 5/- at present. . . .[10]

Sun. 30 May. Sch: Publicly rebuked Walter Baker for swearing.

10 June. . . . I c. on Mrs J. Isted; gave her a bottle of essence of ginger as a small token of my thankfulness that John was enabled to escape ye temptations of ye Fair & Club day. . . . At 7.30 a Mr. Stevens & Mr. Kemp addressed a meeting in ye Sch: room. They are a sort of Evangelists as they are called – Hussatarian [?] Revivalists: they gave very earnest addresses. Mr. Kemp spoke well. Few people there & nearly all Dissenters . . .

17 June. . . . C. on Polly Thompson about ye Singing. Home & singing at ye School w. ye men. Spoke to them again about ye Choir. I don't know what they will do, but it is a great shame when they can sing as they do, that they do not care more for helping in God's House.

24 June. . . . I c. on old Beard's Relf (6d). Surprised at his Scriptural knowledge. He has taught himself to read since he has been paralysed & bed ridden & since he was 80. . . .

Sat. 3 July. . . . C. on Mrs Isted, saw John, he going up to ye Vill: said he shd. be back at 7. I wonder whether he was, poor fellow, he has been mowing all ye week from 4am till 8 or 9 PM & who can wonder at his wanting a little relaxation on Sat. evg. I only wish men cd. get it without ye temptations wh. surround it in England. . . .

Sun. 4 July. . . . A Swarm of bees during morg. service wh. Luck aft. Ch. hived, getting stung twice, but making no account of it. . . .

8 July. My 40th birthday. Thought much of time wasted, & little done, made resolutions & determined to try to serve God more but I am sadly weak & irresolute. . . .

10 July. Started w. Choir Children at 10. They in two Vans. I drove Miss Bower & Flora Manwairing, Annie Park, & Sally Harmer in my trap. Enjoyed our day at Bodiam exceedingly. Many of ye children had never been beyond Etchingham & none had been in a boat. Dinner at one. Rowing on ye moat from 2 till ½ past 4. Some singing. Tea at 5. Cricket & hide & seek. God save the Queen & then home. . . .

Sun. 11 July. . . . Between Services . . . Mrs Holland . . . begged me to expostulate w. her son Dick aged 11 on his idle dawdling habits. He limp & irresolute by nature. . . .

17 July. . . . S. Cruttendon c. & returned his last vol. of Gibbon: he has now read the whole work with great interest. I have lent him Butlers Analogy.

Sun. 18 July. I married Harry Relf at 8.45. This is his 4th wife; 3 have been Elizabeth he tells me, one Harriett. There is in the Ch: Yard a stone erected by one Newington to the Affectionate Memory of his 4 wives. . . .

19 July. . . . C. on old Mrs Thompsett. Her wretched daughter Ruth Hartfield Conf[ined] of an illeg. ch[ild] within 10 Months of her husb: death. . . . C. on old Mr. & Mrs Dunk. The old man not well. His wife a worthy old Chatter box said Dunk is rather deaf Sir, & he does not say much. Dunk was sharp enough to hear this & said, "Not much occasion for my saying much when you are by". . . .

2 Aug. . . . C. on Mrs Wm. Isted. . . .

9 Aug. . . . I had in old [aged seventy-nine] John Vigor to supper & to tell me something about Burwash of olden days; nothing very remarkable in our history.

18 Aug. . . . C. on Mrs J. Isted (2/6) she is fu[rther] trouble as poor John is once more in the hands of the police for being drunk . . .[11]

24 Aug. . . . to look at a cricket match in Swan meadow between Burwash Common & Burwash town. Mr. Frank Trower & his Son pl[ayed] for ye Common. I persuaded poor Wm. Pilbeam & J[ame]s Farley both drunk & noisy to go home, the latter lecturing me in a loud voice on the uselessness of trying to live without prayer to the Almighty for forgiveness; sad in the extreme. To croquet at Mr. Newtons . . .

25 Aug. . . . To John Isted; he happened to come in, poor fellow, he is much ashamed, & promises to try teetotalism. I got him to allow his wife to tell me of the first beginnings of any future outbreak. . . .

26 Aug. I w. up to Miss Trowers. I noticed the heat more than I think I ever remember before. I put a cabbage leaf in my hat, but whether it did much good I cannot say. . . .

29 Aug. . . . dear Aunty Ellen died about 10 o'Clock [after a short illness] . . .

9 Sept. . . . C. & t. w. old Farley. How was he to overcome his drinking habits. I don't know. He spoke most reasonably & thanked me for my good advice; always I fear a sign of a somewhat hopeless case. . . .

13 Sept. . . . Gave Mrs Mallion in the hop garden 2/6 to compensate in a small degree for her disappointment in not getting the family prize,[12] wh. goes to Mrs. Wenham who has 8 ch. under 16 years of age. Harris (1/-) who lives at Burwash w. Russell in the Square on the sick list sitting watching the hoppers. . . .

15 Sept. . . . C. on Mrs Isted, she in great trouble about the chance of John's losing his work owing to ye changes at ye Franchise [Farm]. I wr[ote] to Mr. Gillham & Whatman for him. . . .

16 Sept. The s[inging] class in my room. It died today a natural death. . . .

19 Sept. Terrible storm again last night. G[rea]t loss of hops in Burwash; very serious. . . .

22 Sept. A Mr. Ch[arles] Cooper Clarke of 22 Torrington Squr London c. on me to ask if I cd. tell him where to get photographs of Burwash. His mother was born in Burwash, her name was I think he said Collins, & her father married a 2d time, one Luck. I gave him 2 photos. . . .

24 Sept. A letter from Lizzie Cox to say that her poor father died on Wed. at the Castle Inn Sandgate [Kent]. Poor man. His sun has set under a dark cloud & yet it cannot be denied that for some years in our school it shone very brightly. I wrote a short notice of him & sent it to Ed[itor] Sussex Expr.[13] I w. thro' Mr. Jarvis' hop garden. Old Mrs Pilbeam actually able to do some hopping. . . .

14 Oct. To Ticehurst Ag[ricultural] Assoc. meeting: not very good, tho' the beasts good in quality. . . .

18 Oct. . . . C. on John Isted; no work. . . . to Stonegate . . . & I also for a few minutes spoke to Mr. Courthope about some poor law matters. . . .

27 Oct. . . . I c. & R. w. Mrs Pilbeam (2/6) poor woman she suffers sad trouble. Her d's husb: has now taken to rough & cruel ways. . . . Singing good but no men. This is very tiresome as we cd. do very well if they wd. come.

1 Nov. . . . Some men on digging on ye road. I wheeled a barrow load & paid my footing. They began to day. The work will I hope employ some hands thro' the winter. . . .

2 Nov. C. & T. w. old Beards Relf. He really reads & learns a great deal of the Bible, paralytic & 80 tho' he be. C. & R. w. old Mrs Thompsett she simply joyful because Stephen has been 3 times to Church & Chapel. C. on Mrs John Harmer. C. on old Mrs Morris, née Hawkins, sister to old R[ichar]d Hawkins. Talking & reading to 3 deaf ones in succession, very trying. . . . Old Relf told me about the "mobbing" in the times of scarcity & gave the names of the uprisers "quorum pars magna fuit" as he calmly said he was one of the 3 who began it. They were undoubtedly half starved.

4 Nov. Held a court martial on two boys for rudeness to the girls in Ch. Had the father of one boy as a witness of the trial. Dismissed one culprit from the choir & suspended the other for a month from his office as a teacher in the [Sunday] sch. . . . Aft. at 2.30 to tithe dinner. 50 in upper room 23 in lower. Mr. Simes & Mr. Bourne, my two supporters on one side, Mr. Philcox on ye other. As usual nobody answered too ye Army, Navy, Militia, Yeomanry & Volunteers. So Mr. Bourne suggested add "The Parish Constable" wh. I did, but Joseph Noakes wd. not rise.[14] We discussed the labour question, but without much result. People seemed to enjoy themselves & the personal feeling shewn towards Mr. Philcox, Mr. Simes, & myself was very pleasant. I certainly value their good opinion, & hope that I never do anything so as to justly forfeit it. . . . The round of beef was very tough & was supposed to be old cow beef, a fact expressed by Mr. Simes in the phrase "She's had a good many songs sung under her". . . .

5 Nov. . . . A great many bonfires: only 5 boys in N.S. . . .

6 Nov. . . . master C. Crabb [?] in trouble thro' his Protestant zeal last night wh. led him to seize some of Mr. Gillham's tar for torches.[15] . . . John Isted has I much hope got a steady place at Mr. Spencer's of Bowmans [Farm]. . . .

Sun. 7 Nov. . . . Sch: Mr. Rochester has taken away his 3 boys from the singing because I ejected one & Park has done the same w. his girl.

12 Nov. . . . Had a long t. w. Rochester about his boy: he of course cd. not see that I had taken ye right view of ye case. . . .

25 Nov. . . . w. Mrs Pomfray . . . took a long parochial walk with her. Pomfray out shooting. I cannot say when I have enjoyed an afternoon as I did this. Mrs Pomfray is a delightful woman. Surely sensible, clever, right-minded, & warm hearted. Her manner in the cottages was a perfect lesson. We c. on one old man who had been a [game]keeper, & who is now hard on 80 & who suffers much from a very severe skin disease. He was a fiddler. I espied & tried his fiddle. . . .

21 Dec. Dole day; sat from 10.10 to 2.30 gave away about £20-0-0 in beef. Not much trouble. One or two cases of immorality refused. . . .

27 Dec. . . . C. on Mrs Hearse wife of ye gardener at Southover formerly Schoolmistress at Inf[an]t Sch: at Beatheston nr. Bath, on leaving wh. ye ladies of ye parish gave her £20. She here finds fearfully dull; her husb. very steady. She asserts that he is always at home exc[ept] when he goes up for shop things on Sat. night; that he gives her 20s out of 21/- per week & never asks her for money! wd. that there were more such husbands. . . .

Notes

1.   Mentioned, but not by name, in *Sussex Folk*, p. 42.
2.   The licence was transferred back to the Russell family, in the person of James jnr. in Aug. 1868. Relf had taken over a beershop, and his wife's adultery with William Crossingham was soon notorious. See below, 26 Aug. 1870, p. 102 and note 21. *Sussex Agricultural Express*, 1 Sept. 1868.
3.   The article was published in vol. 21 of the Society's *Collections* later this year.
4.   The orders for most recipients of mutton were issued for the elderly and sick, by the Medical Officer. The attempted review of recipients was in response to increased costs following the Board of Guardians' 25 Feb. decision to capitulate to local butchers raising mutton from 7 to 8d per pound. ESCRO. G10/1a/11.
5.   There is an element of self-reproach here; it is the first, but not the only entry to the effect that he had not been informed of a parishioner's serious illness.
6.   In *Sussex Folk*, p. 49, this statement is ascribed to an eighty-six-year-old lady.
7.   An old debate, still current since its inception in the 1820s, over the optimum size of allotments for farmworkers. While many gentry advocated generous allotment provision, especially after the 1830 Swing uprising, the farmers, as the employers, argued that larger allotments would lead to farmworkers conserving their strength to till their land, at the employers' expense. Hence the preference, surprisingly endorsed by the labourers, for an eighth rather than a quarter of an acre.
8.   The annual celebrations of the benefit clubs were notoriously drunken affairs, commonly ending in breaches of the peace, among other infractions of social decorum. For which, see below, p. 159, 25 May 1875.
9.   William Isted was formally convicted of vagrancy, for being found on the 'enclosed' premises of the Revd Charles Granville Clarke, and was sentenced to two months hard labour. Summary returns, ESCRO. QR/E1046.
10.   A sure sign that the club's finances were weakening.
11.   Arrested on 2 Aug. for being drunk at Burwash, he was fined 5/- with 13/- costs on the 27th. Summary returns, ESCRO. QR/E1047.
12.   The family prize related to the joint earnings of families during the harvest, awarded by Agricultural Societies, and by some village worthies; other prizes were awarded for those who brought up the largest families without recourse to social-security payments.
13.   A very brief obituary notice neatly linked Cox's contribution as 'one of the most skilful teachers in this part of the country, possessing as he did in a high degree the power of imparting knowledge and of awakening the intelligence of his pupils', to a large part of the incumbency of the late Revd Gould as Rector. *Sussex Agricultural Express*, 28 Sept. 1869.
14.   Noakes was serving his sole year as a Local Constable; presumably, none of the others currently serving, John Hyland, John Beaney and Charles Yates, were present. ESCRO. QAC/3/E8.
15.   Guy Fawkes' Day often saw impromptu seizures of materials to facilitate traditional celebrations; however, in this case the matter seems to have been settled privately without recourse to the courts.

1870

17 Jan. . . . To ye Common. C. on Maskell & spent a most pleasant half hour chatting to him & his wife. Their attachment to each other is something unusual, at any rate in its manifestation, amongst the poor. They hit it off to a t. . . . The best writer of the lot [in Miss Trower's night school class] a young Brabon brought up at the Ticehurst Union Sch: wh. he left 4 years since. He writes capitally. On my way home called on Jesse Isted to sympathise w. him in the trouble caused him by the police most unwarrantably searching his house for stolen goods.

19 Jan. . . . Jesse Isted c. poor fellow this evg. Mr. J. Coppard Snr, not his immediate master who J.I. said cried over it, turned him away. J.I. lost his temper . . . & swore at him for wh. he was very sorry but says that Mr. C. was nagging at him for $\frac{1}{2}$ an hour first. J.I. went away saying he felt comforted & I was glad I was at home.[1]

21 Jan. . . . Poor Mrs Manwaring's funeral; her 6 little Children a piteous sight, & indeed there was much genuine grief amongst the mourners. . . . W. home with J[ohn] I. & another. I somewhat fear for J.I. for tho' he is stirring to amend, I fear that he has never yet seen his past life in its true colours, & therefore I fear that his amendment is not on a safe basis. However he is very diff[erent] from what he was.

24 Jan. Sch. . . . Committee meet[in]g raised Anset's Salary £5 for last year & £1-5-0 a quarter for next.

29 Jan. . . . Aft. c. on Mrs Moore at Platt's, a poor creature, whose husb: drinks, so that they fare badly. C. next door on Mrs G. Gilbert (1/-) a superior woman, clean, managing, & educated; her husb: only a day lab[ourer] w. Schroeter but far better than ye Moore's. Such is management. . . .

31 Jan. . . . N.S. 20. Really they seem most anxious to learn.

1 Feb. . . . N.S. about 30, including a lot of navvies now relaying the road [permanent way] nr. Ticeh[urst] Rd. Station, a most interesting set of men.

5 Feb. . . . C on Mrs Maskall her husband gone to his father's for a change. Mrs told me with the greatest naivity.[2] . . . She is a very superior woman in mind & some of her aphorisms on domestic management are worth remembering. "My mother was a woman that always stood to her word, &

whatever she promised me I always know'd I shd. get it, whether it was a bull's eye or a hiding".[3] I c. on Higgs Mr. Breach's gardener, found him a well read & most intelligent young man. He came up in ye evg. & borrowed Macaulay's Hist[ory of England] Vol. 5 he having read the rest, & ye 1st Vol. of Macaulay's Essays. . . .

7 Feb. . . . Sent books 15 Vols down to ye class room wh. is to be open tonight for ye navvies. . . . N.S. 19 in spite of the wet. On my way home passed Relfe's beer shop just in time to put a stop to an imminent fight.

10 Feb. A letter from Mr. Courthope about putting Burwash with Soc[iety] for prom[oting] Xtianity among ye Jews. I answered it, saying that as I can not do good unto all men I feel constrained to do it especially to them that are of the household, viz. neglected Xtians & then to those who have not heard of Xt; to the heathen, rather than to those who have rejected Him as the Jews. I hope that he will not be riled as I value his good opinion much. . . . C. on old Granny Watson (1/-), she will talk till she dies poor old body. . . .

12 Feb. . . . I was shewn a singularly precocious production of Mabel Trower cet 10. Mr. F. Trower little d. entitled I think a History of Burwash w. special reference to Hollyhurst & including practical advice on all bachelors to marry! . . .

Sun. 13 Feb. Most bitterly cold. Sponge, water jug, & bath water all frozen. I w. to ye Common, very sm[all] congr: only 3 adults I think beside Hollyhurst folks. Luck told me that he never did know pigs ears to be freezed afore but their pigs' ears had freezed in the night! . . .

14 Feb. St Valentine's day, & bitter enough to freeze every bit of sentiment out of a human being. . . . C. on Mr. J.B.Noakes; he has been away from home for sometime, & I had quite missed him; he says our Burwash poor are now very short of money.[4] C on old Jesse Relf; he said he was cold in bed, so I bought a blanket at B.Fuller's & lent it to him. He will not I think live long. C. on Mrs W. Maskall (1/-), a truly cheery body. I helped her in w. a truck load of wood wh. she had dragged all ye way from below Park Hill. She said that she had overheard her little children talking in bed, & saying what shd. they do if mother went, who wd. bake the bread for them, father couldn't but they were in no trouble about father's going, mother cd. bake for them . . .

21 Feb. Chapter meeting; large attendance. Education bill discussed. G.H. agst. it; others all in favour I think. . . .

28 Feb. . . . Saw Willsher; my representations to ye Board [of Guardians] have had effect. Widow Pilbeam gets 6d a week extra! making 1/6 & a gallon of flour. John Isted gets 4 gallons of flour [weekly] for a time. . . .

7 *Mar.* . . . C. on Mr. Fuller about a cottage for Wm. Maskall. . . .

Tues. 8 Mar. . . . C. & P. w. old Christian who is I fear dying. Taken with bronchitis last night at 80 & was at work yesterday & certainly on Sat. . . . C. on Lydia Luck & tasted some really remarkable good home-made wine made by Mrs Eastwood who lives there. Blackberry 20 years old – currant too. . . .

9 *Mar.* . . . C. & P. w. old Christian who was quite clear in his mind, but who died about 2½ hours after I saw him at 79. He was earning days wages till Sat. night. . . .

17 *Mar.* My letter appeared in Sussex Expr[ess] & was favourably noticed in leading art[icle]. . . .⁵

16 *Mar.* [Confined to bed with acutely inflamed foot] I cd. not go to Wadhurst. Almost ye first time in 15 years that I have been unable to keep an appointment for duty. . . .⁶

23 *Mar.* Sch: gave away ye prizes wh. cost me nearly £6. However the children seemed to value them & I hope they will be an encouragement to them. . . .

24 *Mar.* I to Mr. Philcox to plead for John Isted as his tenant a cott[age] being vacant at Elphick's. . . . Aft. Mr. Atherton c. & had a long talk about ye state of the poor on wh. he has theories.⁷ . . . Mr. P. refuses John Isted on grounds wh. he will not disclose, but wh. he says "if I knew all wd. surprize me", this I think unfair & I fancy that Mr. P. wd. think it unfair if I refused to keep him on as my tenant for the same reason. However I must urge J.I. to keep up his heart. It is hard to get rid of a bad name, but the man is trying, & by God's help he will win.

25 *Mar.* . . . JP. c. on me & explained. The matters wh. wd. surprize me are not matters wh. refer to J.I's character, wh. was my chief concern. Under the circumstances, JP. cd. not have asked otherwise than he did, tho' JI. all the same is most unfairly treated. Vestry meeting. Adj[ourned] to ye Bear. An important road case, involving the liability of the parish to keep in repair two miles of shocking road from ye Common to Watkin's down, brought forward by Mr. Smith a new comer at Gingerbreads: nothing determined. I dined w. the meeting; about 16 at dinner. I c. on Mrs J.I. she much upset by my failure. Met J.I. on his way home & had a long t. I will try to see him right and some how. He will I hope some day quite conquer by God's help his fondness for drink. . . .

1 Apl. . . . c. . . . on Mrs Cornfoot (1/-) poor thing she is a great sufferer & thinks she ought to have more from the parish. It is hard to be obliged to tell her that she already has more than her share, but so it is. . . .

4 Apl. . . . At Fuller's shop sat & looked over some of the current periodical literature ordered by young Burwash; a miserable commentary on our education certainly. Weekly pennyworths of tales made up of murders, & the like that is if one may judge by the horrible similarity of the woodcuts in all of them. . . .

5 Apl. Oddly enough after writing last night what I have just said about the juvenile literature I found this morg. a strong article in the Pall Mall Gazette on the very subject. . . .[8]

8 Apl. . . . C. on Mrs J. Isted (1/-). Staid longer than I meant to. . . . C. and had some t[ea] w. St[even] Manwairing, whom I like much.

11 Apl. Mr. J.B.Noakes c. to expl[ain] a case of reputed scandal on the part of a poor man whom he is befriending. The report I am persuaded is simply false. . . . C. on old John Vigor, gave Mrs Relf 10/- on his behalf for rent. . . . I c. in at Mr. Combs. He told me something about ye case of scandal wh. made me suspend my judgement.

12 Apl. Sch. I had in [blank: name deliberately omitted] who in a most categorical manner deposed to having witnessed the evil complained of, & to having spoken to the parties, that I must alter my judgement. I c. on [blank again] but she denied it all. The man I cd. not see.[9] . . . On my way home t. politics w. young J. Russell. He remarkably intelligent. . . .

13 Apl. C. on Mrs J.Isted. C. on Hobden about a cottage for J.I. not in, wrote a note. The Australian meat trade has begun in Burwash & Mr. Noakes says that some of the poor people are buying it. I took some circulars about an Education meeting to be copied at the School. . . .

15 Apl. Good Friday. . . . Serv: at 11. Fair congr: a good many Dissenters as they had no service. . . . Mr. Courthope sent me a copy of a petition wh. he is getting signed in Wadhurst & Ticehurst. I think he is stirred up about ye Ed[ucation] bill. He also very kindly says that they will be glad to see me any time as a friend.

18 Apl. I had the sing[ing] boys & girls at Ch: & gave them a present of 1/- or 9d each accord[ing] to attendance. 15 g. & 16 boys, it cost me £1-9-3. . . . Vestry meeting. Amicable. Mr. J.Barrow resigned. Mr. Taylor my Ch; W[arden]. Mr. Breach for ye parish. Agreed to raise money by Voluntary contribution [presumably without even setting a nominal rate]. . . .

21 Apl. A burglary reported at Martin Coppard's last night; £55 in money, the parish books, Poor Law assessment & collecting books I believe, & some food stolen. . . . Part of the food found in the garden. . . . I c. on Mrs J. Isted (1/-). Still in trouble about a house. . . .

[One page covering 27 to 30 Apl. has been torn out.[10]]

9 May. . . . Looked in at Jarvis brickfield, & watched Tom Pankhurst filling the kiln for burning; it holds about 27000. . . . C. on Mr. Combs. He suddenly sent for to see a woman who was said to be lying dead by the road side at Willenden Hill.

10 May. Old Park the butcher at 82 committed suicide this morg. about 6 o'Clock by hanging. He had been suffering great pain in his head for some time. I c. to say that I thought it better not to toll the church bell in such a case. I saw the body.[11] It is feared that the woman who was found dead last night had been killed & knocked about. She was not a woman of good character if I am rightly informed & had a husband living at Hightown. . . . Vestry meeting at 7 o'Clock. Large attendance. Deficit in highway accts. £54-15-9 wh. Mr. J. Coppard Snr. guaranteed £25, I £10 & John Fuller who is now appointed deputy Surveyor £19-15-9. Mr. J.C. Snr. & myself went to Martin [Coppard] & persuaded him to appear in the vestry. I made his submission for him as humbly as I cd: it was more kindly received than I expected. The parish now being guaranteed agst. loss no further steps probably will be taken . . . but I hope it will be a lifelong lesson to Martin.[12] Robertson thanked me for the correction of his speech wh. appeared in Saturday's Express with the addition "the mistake was ours".[13]

14 May. . . . Witnessed w. Thomas Potten Mrs Cartwright sign her will. Home, funeral of Nancy Gibbs ye woman who was killed by Harry Hazelgrove who is committed on ch[arges] of manslaughter. . . .[14]

18 May. . . . Club. I pr. to an most attentive congr: from Ps 71. 16 (Ext). Dinner; speeches . . . till 1/4 to 8. I then to c. on Mrs Isted. Escorted Sally up to ye booth to see her father sworn [probably into a club office]. Listened to a Cheap Jack who was amusing, but coarse in the extreme. The evening passed off I really think very quietly. Certainly up till 9 o'Clock. I saw very little untoward. Mr. Wood's band improved much.

23 May. . . . I did an hour & a half navvying at Ellen's house wheeling barrow for barrow w. the best. A man came along looks for a job. He professed to be a carpenter, but one man said he looked more "like a running footman to a French pickpocket". . . .

24 May. Sch. I c. & R. W. Mrs J. Pennells (1/6) recovering. I w. Miss Trower. Mrs Holland . . . there. To ye Sch: heard ch[oir] sing ye hymns composed for ye occ[asion]. Buried old Mrs Dunk at 82 at 12 O'Cl. Foundation stone laid at Oakdown by me at 4.15. I made an address. Mr Ballard a Wesleyan preacher proposed 3 cheers for me! he being pleased w. my speech.[15] Mr G. Holland there. I w. him afterwards & J. Hyland round ye farm. Mrs H. gave me a lift home.

[In West Country and Oxford from 7 to 18 June.[16]]

21 June. . . . Brought from Maskall's a piece of meat full of maggots wh. had been supplied on parish acc[ount]. yesterday by Park. Old Mrs Park said the people ought to pick them out a bit of cheek wh. riled me. Park said he had not served it as they had not a piece of loin in the shop. . . .

Sun. 26 June. . . . C. on J. Russell at ye beershop or rather ye public house now. His wife was a decent sort of person, died this morg. about 3a.m. having been ill since Fri: broke blood vessels.

30 June. . . . C. on Mrs Isted (5/-); have moved into their old cottage; have papered it themselves, landlord done nothing. . . .

1 July. Sch. The epidemic of scarlet fever, & scarlative thins the numbers greatly, many keeping away thro' fear, rather than because they are ill. I in aft. to Mr. Gibbs to speak about ye Ch: Steeple wh. Mr. Taylor says wants looking to. Mr. Gibbs showed me his improvements to his grounds. He gets some ornamental water & a better view. . . .

2 July. Mr. Gibbs examind. the steeple & reported it wanted certain repair – tho' still substantially sound he thinks.

5 July. . . . I c. on James Russell. suggested to him Prov[erbs] 31. 28 for his wife's tombstone. . . . W. part way h[ome] w. Elkanah Russell & young Thompson. Russell said that W. Cramp's house built by S. Hartfield was so damp that they frequently gathered fungi from the walls. . . . J.Sinden c. to ask me to be chairman at a cricket dinner next week – gladly [do] it. I am at home. Old Harry Relf stopped me to ask whether our member [of Parliament] was not a Puseyite, as he had voted agst. the use of the Bible in schools. I did my best to dispel the muddle & delusion & left R. persuaded that Mr. G[oschen] voted for religious instruction in schools, that he was a good Conservative, & no Puseyite.[17]

7 July. . . . C. on Mr. Stevenson at Fisher's & inspected two cottages wh. Mr. Clements his landlord is building. Party walls only $4\frac{1}{2}$ inches thick as usual, they really ought to be 9 in. . . . Sounds of all kinds easily penetrate $4\frac{1}{2}$ work & families are for ever liable to be annoyed by troublesome neighbours. . . .[18]

8 July. . . . Sch. terribly thinned by ye fever; boys 54 girls 46.

18 July. C. on Mrs Holland who wanted to ask my opinion as to what her son at Zurich shd. do about coming home. I said I wd. write to Victor Buckley in the Foreign Office [about Franco-German situation]. . . .

19 July. . . . Passing by Thompson's ye blacksmith's found a tea meeting on behalf of a little preaching room at Witherendon Hill. They seized me & put me in the chair. Funny, ye Rector chairman of a Dissenting tea party, & yet I enjoyed it heartily. Ye good people have no enmity agst. ye ch: & are only doing their best in their way to do good. I said a few Words, wishing them well in their crusade agst. ignorance & sin. A Mr. Carwell a retired soldier & employed by some society to counteract Popery at Mayfield wanted ye schoolroom for an anti-popery lecture. I declined, our People know nothing about Popery & why shd. they; why stir up bitterness without need. I gave him leave for a lect: on ye early British Church, but said if I was in the chair I shd. keep him to his text. Left ye good people with feelings of much sympathy. Their head man John Hall a chicken fatter says that he got his "first impressions" "under me" but left because I suppose we did not keep them up, we are I fear somewhat unsympathetic with newly awakened souls.

23 July. C. on Mrs Holland as I have heard from Victor Buckley, who thinks that any Englishman who wd. hold his tongue wd. be safe in France, Switzerland or Germany. . . .

25 July. . . . C. & had a long t. w. Mrs Pilbeam. There is obviously a secession from ye Wesleyan chapel all along of Miss S & J P. I am sorry, as I fear that it will . . . more than counterbalance the increased activity of ye new cause. . . .

30 July. C. & had a long t. w. Master Maskell & wife of Winnisford. . . . This family is a most serious charge to ye parish.

1 Aug. C. on Mrs J. Isted, found her on a little bed on the kitchen floor, she had fainting fits from exhaustion in watching & overseeing her children last week. . . .

2 Aug. C. & R. w. Mrs J. Isted, gave her 2/- from Aunt Susan. She in bed & very weak, Mr. Combs unfortunately at ye Assizes. . . .[19]

17 Aug. By 8.35 to Tonbridge . . . Spoke to Burw[ash] man (Blackford I think) who has a public h[ouse] in Tonbridge, where H. W. Piper I imagine was. . . .[20]

19 Aug. School feast. I go to ye sch. at 2.30. Called ye roll & took down boys to ye Rect: 121 entitled to come, only about 85 there; many at harvest w[ork]. Good Games. Football, French & Germans, Trap bat, cricket, Races, Catching half pence on the back of a chair, scrambling, sack racing, three legged races & the like. Plenty to eat & drink & away at dusk.

22 Aug. . . . I c. on Mrs J. Isted. Willsher ye Rel[ieving] Off[icer] has neglected her wine & tho' the omission is not perhaps a great one on his part, the loss to her is great as she is very weak.

26 Aug. Dr[ove] to H[urst] Green, it being Licensing day. I gave evidence agst. James Relf of ye beer shop (vide Feb: 7). His renewal adjourned for a month. He very angry with me, but it was my duty to speak. The house is a bad one. . . .[21]

Sun. 28 Aug. . . . Funeral aft. Ch. in aft: another child of sc[arlet] fever, making I think 11. . . .

7 Sept. . . . Aft. to inspect J. Hilder's garden w. Mr. Taylor. C. on J. Noakes to get his signature to one paper [for a competition] candidate. I was in a fix about signature. What is a sober man. He is notoriously a hard-working man, loses no time by drink, does not get into rows & yet spends lots of money at the public house, & is much dist[ressed] for rent. Is he technically a sober man? I signed with much hesitation. . . .

10 Sept. . . . Looked over some capital new cottages wh. Uncle has built near ye T[urn] Pike gate at Ticehurst. I wish all ye party walls were 9" thick; nothing less seems to keep out ye sound & a drunken man in one house, sorely annoys his neighbours in ye next. . . .

22 Sept. . . . To Ticehurst Committee of Ticeh. Agric[ultural] Soc. I asked ye Comm. what is a reasonable def[inition] of a sober man & they seemed to think, at least ye farmers, that a man is sober enough to justify me in signing for him, who does not lose his time, or get into trouble, tho' he may be tipsy most Saturday nights. Mr. Courthope in ye chair. . . .

27 Sept. H.Jarvis yest[erday] & to day [for individual grammar lesson] Really Engl: Grammar is a curious & somewhat empirical study. How a foreigner ever acquires it, I cannot imagine. . . .

30 Sept. Dr[ove] to H. Green. The license was renewed, tho' doing so Mr. Courthope called an unpleasant duty. Mr. Philbrick appeared in support of applicant. . . .

Sun 2 Oct. . . . in aft: pr: Eze[kiel] 13. 12 (ext). Much distressed to see the benches wh. used to be filled w. young men very empty. I really cannot tell the reason for the change, unless it be the novelty of ch: going [to the new

church for the inhabitants of the Common and the Weald] is wearing
out. . . .

4 Oct. . . . The horrid fair carts & shows staying another day I fear. . . .

Thurs. 6 Oct. To the Common. A crowded congregation [for harvest
festival], the largest I have seen since the opening day. Ch: capitally
decorated w. wheat, hops, apples, flowers. potatoes, etc. & Mr. Breach's
Brighton lamps added wonderfully to the light. . . . Collection to Dio-
c[esan] Assoc: £6-0-0. A good collection at the old Wheel Chapel used to be
about 10/- or 12/-. . . .

8 Oct. . . . On my way back [from Brightling] found a poor man who had
been lying in ye road all ye morg. Sent a cart from G. Brookers to take him
to ye Union [workhouse]. . . .

13 Oct. Dr. to Wadhurst. . . . Before dinner I had outside ye Inn a long
discussion w. a violent radical named Jesse Thompsett; who turned out to
be a regular & old accustomed orator. His abuse of the "bloody" aristocracy
was vehement, if not to the point as regards truth. At dinner I sat next to
Mr. Bacon the Ed. of ye Sussex Advertiser. I had much t. w. him & found
him most agreeable & full of anecdote. . . .

18 Oct. . . . Mr. Frank Trower c. & had a chat about Burwash local
antiquarian matters, & ye University Tests Bill. . . .[22]

20 Oct. C. on G. Maskell (1/-), has suffered great pain. Compound &
comminuted fracture of ye leg & a shoulder out, but is doing well. . . .

Sun. 23 Oct. . . . I was much disheartened by hearing the boys before I
came down [to Sunday School] singing out one of the anthems in mockery.
I hardly know what to do with them. I spoke very seriously, & boxed the
ears of the chief offenders. . . .

24 Oct. . . . N.S. 24. G.Relf asked for me to speak for him at H[urst] Green,
he being summoned for assaulting Wm. Crossingham the man whose
conduct w. G.R's mother is so sad.[23] C. & P. w. G.Maskell; poor fellow he
suffers much. . . .

25 Oct. . . . C. & t.w. G.Mallion (1/-) about taking a carter's place. Mrs J.
Brook came up to consult me about a neighbours quarrels. When flint &
steel come into contact, there are sparks but wh. is fairly answerable for
them I don't know. . . . A young man Newett c. on me about a place as
coachman to Miss Naghter at Millbrook but it wd. not suit him. . . .

26 Oct. Mr. Fuller at the shop tells me that no more French eggs can be had at Dover at any rate, or Normandy butter, & very little Hambro' bacon [owing to Franco-Prussian war]. . . .

1 Nov. . . . Tithe dinner. Ye Audit & dinner this year for the first time at ye school; good change, & people I think satisfied; about 65 dined, payments not quite so good. Guests friendly & kindly disposed. Most left rather early. A few staid later, & I sang "When the heart is young" & "A thousand a year". . . . J. Vigor sang "Burial of Sir J.Moore" very well for a man of 78. . . .

Sun. 6 Nov. [After afternoon service]. . . . Sch. Some of ye boys gave me much trouble again by annoying the girls in their way home. There is manifestly a bad spirit among the boys, & it seems from what I hear that I am in some degree answerable for it. Several times when they have been very careless, & have told me, as in one or two instances has been the case, a story, I have boxed the offenders' ears, & this has caused ill-feeling. I am sorry if I have given cause for annoyance, but the manifest combination wh. there has been amongst the boys not to do their best, has I feel led me into treatment wh. had better have been avoided. I must try & set things straight.

8 Nov. . . . Gave Mr. Anset the Government papers about the Educational accommodation afforded in Burwash to fill up. . . .

9 Nov. . . . Dr. to Wadhurst, d. w. J. Foley met his br[other] Edw. Mr. Rowley Hill the Rector of Frant & the great Evangelical light of the neighbourhood. Did not greatly affect [take to] him. . . .

10 Nov. . . . Went into Hannah Watson's Sch: Very nice, but the poor thing is losing her voice & will I fear have to give up. . . .

Sun. 13 Nov. . . . Singing; had to eject W. Langridge. It is a great nuisance, but there are still some sulky spirits in ye class who pull agst. one. . . .

14 Nov. . . . C. on Mr. Gibbs, lunched, & he then w. me to school, where he took accurate measurements for Govt. . . .

16 Nov. Sch: Found lamentable Scriptural ignorance, greater than I had expected. . . .

19 Nov. Poor old Isaac [Hyland, a seventy-one-year-old agricultural labourer who Egerton visited on 18th] d[ied] this morg. having been ill only 2 or 3 days. I c. . . . on old Granny Watson, she told me that morg. she had on getting up put her toe into the heel of her stocking, on wh. she knew somebody wd. die soon, & sure enough old Isaac was the one. . . .

22 Nov. About 20 min. past one o'Clock this morg. I was called by Willy Eyles to see Mrs Wood. I had not gone to bed & went down in about 5 min. Mr. Combs was with her, & said she cd. not live above a few minutes. The poor creature was unconscious, breathing heavily, & the mouth was filled with froth. Mr. Combs stood w. his finger upon her pulse & at $\frac{1}{2}$ past 1 he simply said "gone" & all was over. That ceasing of the pulse to beat cd. have made such a difference as the difference between time & eternity, was an awful thought, as I stood watching the still unchanged form of as good a woman as perhaps I ever knew. For 36 years she had been mistress in our schools, & a more faithful consistent God fearing teacher it wd. be hard to find. Her memory will long be green amongst us. I said a few words in prayer w. her nieces, Mrs Jenner who been sent for, & Tessa Baker. In the morg. I went into the girls school, & spoke to the children who were very much affected. . . .

25 Nov. . . . At one O'Clock I buried poor Mrs Wood. Many of the inhabitants of all classes & a large number of school ch. attended & many were very much affected. . . .

Sun. 27 Nov. I took ye morg. serv[ice] at Burw: [taken normally by his Curate] as I wanted to speak of poor Mrs Wood. Pr. from Matt. 22. 24 (Ext.) Many of the congr: in mourning & many much affected. It is encouraging to find how little rank & position has to do with the respect in wh. a person is held, more people felt genuine sorrow round poor Mrs Wood's grave than feel it round the grave of many a peer of the realm. . . .[24]

29 Nov. . . . old Parsons stopped me to thank me as he said for having hindered him selling his brick to Miss Gould. I don't know quite what he means. C. on Maskells; he mending. . . . C. & had long t. w. Mr. Smith of Seaview Cott[age]. Civil but very non-conforming. . . .

2 Dec. Sch. . . . Saw Mr. Anset about arranging Mrs Bull to supply temporarily poor Mrs Wood pl[ace]. C. & R. w. Miss Tr[ower]. N.S. 35 & home w. a lot of boys of ye NS who were coming up all ye way to Burwash to get a tamborine for a Xmas band. Coming past Bateman's lane, one says "How that oak holds its leaves", to wh. another answered, "I think it rather a backward sort, like me".

10 Dec. I c. on Mr. Gibbs to argue a question about a pauper lunatic, ye d. of a man who cd. well keep her if sane, but who cannot pay for her at a pr[ivate] asylum. Mr. Gibbs holds that the woman is not a pauper lunatic. . . . I wrote to Mr. Goschen [MP] on the point. . . .

12 Dec. . . . The wretched woman Mrs Relf & Wm. Crossingham up in the lock up for threatening Mrs Wm C[rossingham]'s life. . . .[25]

14 Dec. . . . C & P. w. old Granny Watson who is worse, & said that she cd. hardly speak tho' for twenty one minutes by the clock she kept talking without intermission till I stopped her. . . . C. on Mrs Blunden, she rather weakening so did not stop long. . . .

16 Dec. Was terribly grieved to find that the Missionary box had been opened & the money 9d taken out. It is very sad, but every now & again it happens. The last time was 8 or 9 years ago. . . .

17 Dec. . . . I down to the sch: to see the decoration workers, very busy. . . . I wish I cd. be more use. She [Miss Tyler] "Well you wd. be more useful if you were a bunch of holly". I – If I were "yew" I think I shd. be more useful still. She. I am very sorry that I can't return the compliment. Whereupon being shut up, I disappeared. C. on Mrs Isted (2/6) . . .

19 Dec. Signed at Mr. Combs a certificate for the removal of Jane Brown on being a person of unsound mind to the County Lunatic Asylum at Hayward's Heath, the poor thing was discharged from Bethlehem Hosp-[ital] incurable.[26] C. on G.Maskell; he actually able to go for a change into Kent. . . .

20 Dec. Sch: I called on Mr. Gibbs & wheeled sundry barrow loads of clay for him in his pond works. . . .

21 Dec. Dole day. I down at 10 but ye distribution did not begin till eleven; done by 3.30. This year after much arg[umen]t with Mr. Taylor I relaxed my opposition to the idea of giving dole to illegitimate children belonging to people now married or living respectably. I used to object greatly to this as tending in my mind to encourage lax notions about the sin of living together unmarried, but it was argued so strongly that the rule irritates by continually keeping in memory old sins, rather than amend, that I gave in . . .

23 Dec. . . . Sch: treat about 3[p.m.]; about 213 invited, about 200 present. I gave notice that I shd. hereafter give Xmas treat only to Sunday Scholars, eith[er] Ch. or Chapel, & that my minimum of attendance wd. be 40 Sundays. Ellen much discomposed by this rule, but I think I must try it for a year at any rate . . .

24 Dec. . . . C. on Mrs J.Braban of Willingford Lane. 8 ch. eldest not 11, how they all live is a mystery. . . .

29 Dec. C. on Mrs Isted (2/6). She very grateful for the kindness of friends this Xmas. . . .

Notes

1.   The clear implication is that Isted was sacked over suspicions of dishonesty, despite the failure to find incriminating goods at his house.
2.   Egerton's scepticism derives from the common popular usage of a 'change' to denote marital breakdown, temporary or otherwise; it also had connotations of extra-marital activity.
3.   Published verbatum in *Sussex Folk*, p. 69.
4.   Owing, no doubt to the farmers laying off more and more men as the freezing weather reduced outdoor work.
5.   The issue was the burgeoning argument over the religious details in the current Education Bill, eventually passed during the summer, and known after its parliamentary sponsor. W.E. Forster, vice-chair of the Privy Council Committee on Education. Forster's Act aimed to make public provision of elementary education, in places where existing parochial accommodation, under either, or both, Anglican National Schools, or Dissenting British Schools, was inadequate. Here, School Boards would raise the necessary rates, erect and manage schools. Egerton supported the government, thought that the issue ought not to be party-political, and argued that expressions of support must be orchestrated in the rural districts where people had as great an interest as their urban counterparts. Egerton was unconvinced that sectarianism was strengthened by existing education. 'As far as my experience goes, there is little time in school to do much more than teach those Bible facts and lessons which are the common property of all Christians. If children have much acquaintance with the distinctive tenets of different bodies of Christians, that knowledge is chiefly gained . . . in the Sunday school', with which the current Bill was unconcerned. The leader, principally on the Irish problem, gave a sentence praising Egerton's position, and thus helped to stimulate a controversy in the correspondence columns. *Sussex Agricultural Express*, 12 Mar. 1870. Other commentators anticipated serious developments at parochial levels, including an East Sussex farmer, who foresaw 'War in the vestry, bitter and continuous, will result from the powers of controlling the compulsory and religious provisions of the bill. The peace of villages will be disturbed, and friendly relations will be interrupted and perhaps destroyed'; further conflict would be spawned between farmers and tradesmen ratepayers. *Pall Mall Gazette*, 2 Apl. 1870.
6.   Neighbouring clergymen often deputized for each other, permitting short or longer breaks from duties.
7.   Henry Atherton, had retired from the Bengal Civil Service, and was currently a tenant farmer in Brightling. His sixteen page pamphlet, *An Acre of Land in His Native Parish the Right of Every British Subject . . .*, was published at Battle in mid-1869. He was among the first of a tiny minority of farmers to publicly support the foundation of the Kent Labourers Union in 1872, writing to this effect to the union's press, and adding his support for labourers' rights to work, to the vote, and attendance at the church of their own choosing, not their employers. *Kent Messenger and Maidstone Times*, 18 May 1872.
8.   A strong but relatively common denunciation entitled 'Thieves' literature', it referred to a criminal case against a gang of boys *c.* 1865, each of whom had adopted the nick-name of a renowned criminal, including Blueskin, Sixteen-string Jack, Jonathan Wild, Jack Sheppard and Dick Turpin, as empirical proof of the impact of 'spicy gallows literature' on working-class youths. Among those singled out from the 'filthy heap of penny numbers' – or dreadfuls – were *The Dance of Death and the*

108 *Victorian Village*

Hangman's Plot, The Boy King of the Smugglers, and *The Wild Boys of London,* all priced 1d, comprising eight pages with 'wood engravings showing the performance of some crime, or the indulgence of some vice'. *Pall Mall Gazette,* 5 Apl. 1870.

9.   The details of this scandal, clearly of a sexual character, cannot be traced in other sources.

10.   The missing entries no doubt includes reference to the well-attended meeting, organized and chaired by Egerton, to promote support for the Education Bill, as he had recently advocated in the press (see above, note 5). Egerton asserted that the Bill as it stood 'secures religious liberty in elementary education, far more truly' than the Dissenter orchestrated Education League's proposed amendments, which were represented as inflated 'interference with managers of schools on religious matters'. *Sussex Advertiser,* 4 May 1870.

11.   Park was found hanging in the kitchen by his son; many years before, Park had suffered a fractured skull, and had informed surgeon Combs a couple of years previously, that he would commit suicide in the event of any recurrence of devastating head-pains. *Sussex Advertiser,* 18 May 1870.

12.   John Coppard had been in trouble over his accounts in 1865, 1866, 1868 and again in 1869; then, son Martin, who assisted his father, and was clearly intended to succeed him, explained that during John's prolonged illness, a brother also helped with the paperwork. Having survived potentially damaging assertions of incompetence, which were compounded by the notorious difficulty in extracting cash from Burwash ratepayers, the family's 1870 crisis was much more serious. Burglars were unaccustomed to burdening themselves with parochial account books, a 'somewhat surprising' fact in the eyes of the press; even the food stolen and 'wantonly cast into a cesspool at the back of the premises', had a ring of suspicion, and there was a remarkable coincidence concerning the £55 'in gold and notes' stolen, and the deficiency in the highway account mentioned by Egerton. Full enquiry revealed that 'The Son alleged that he had been the subject of a burglarous attack on the night before the Audit, in which his Father's Books had been abstracted'. Martin confessed to his illegal subterfuge to the vestry which then rallied round the father, with key vestrymen, including Egerton, contributing money to cover the debts. John's contract was renewed, and the Board of Guardians explained that they had no intention of over-ruling 'the views of the parishioners' in such appointments, and John's rehabilitation was also supported by an un-named JP, probably Courthope. But Ticehurst parish, for which John was also collector, was not so magnanimous, and he was forced to resign that post thereby becoming 'a severe sufferer'. The Union auditor subsequently resorted to formally summoning Martin, and further deficiencies led to John being surcharged, which he paid, though he continued to claim that the whole business derived 'entirely from my Son . . . getting into confusion with his accounts'. The Poor Law Board insisted that John's old sureties, totalling only £300 were inadequate, and demanded new ones to the tune of £500, which were provided by a Brightling farmer, and William Coppard, a Solicitor's Clerk at Philcox's law firm. See also below, 25 Mar. 1871. Endorsement on accounts, Dec. 1865; letters to the Poor Law Board from J.Coppard, 9 Jan. 1866, 24 July 1868, and 18 July 1870, M.Coppard 3 Dec. 1869, Clerk, and Auditor, to Ticehurst Poor Law Union, 21 May, and 25 June 1870, PRO. MH.12/13147–9. Board of Guardian minutes, esp. 16 July 1868, 30 Dec. 1869, 13 and 27 Jan., 10 and 24 Mar., 7 and 21 Apl., and 19 May 1870, ESCRO. G10/1a/11–12. *Sussex Advertiser,* 26 Apl. 1870.

13.   This followed the *Express*'s report of the meeting chaired by Egerton on 28

Apl. The *Express* got guest speaker Isaiah Robertson's argument completely opposite to what he said. *Sussex Agricultur~l Express*, 7 and 10 May 1870.

14.   Harry Hazelgrove was a thirty-seven-year-old farmworker, currently employed in Ticehurst; he had lived with Nancy Gibbs for some years, and they had a daughter, Mary Gibbs. On the day of Nancy's death, Harry complained to a workmate that Nancy 'was on the "drink", that he had broken the earthenware, that he should set fire to the furniture, and that he would kill the woman . . . she was "free to any one"'. That evening, more or less immediately after work, Harry encountered Nancy 'sitting on the bank' near Ticehurst Road Station. John West, who witnessed events, later deposed in the Assize court, that Harry 'came along and said to her "I have heard all about you: get up and come home". She tried to get up but fell down again without anybody touching her, as she was so intoxicated'. Harry 'then got hold of both of her feet and dragged her to and fro in the middle of the road for about four yards. He then let her feet go, but after this he kicked her as though he wanted her to get up. . . . He did not give me the notion that he was ill using her. I have seen many such jobs as that so that I didn't take much notice (laughter). . . . After she got up he gave her a shove, and she fell backwards on the road. He then took her in his arms about the waist and pulled her into the hedge . . . she appeared to draw breath very slowly', but Harry 'said she was shamming'. Once he realized she was not, Harry tried to summon help, but Nancy died, and Harry went to the police. At his trial for manslaughter, the judge established that 'there were big rough stones in the road. . . . She went "smack" down in the road' before Harry touched her. Surgeon Combs, who performed a post mortem, testified that the 'brain was in a state of congestion, arising from drink, which alone caused death. Violence would accelerate it, but there were other indications of intemperance, in fact, almost all her body was diseased. There was quite sufficient, independent of the blows, to account for death at the time'; on this, the judge directed an acquittal. *Sussex Agricultural Express*, 6 Aug. 1870.

15.   The house, Oakdown was entirely new, but not ready for occupation by Mrs Holland until July 1871. J.C. Egerton, *Village Instruction; Twelve Sermons*, (Tunbridge Wells, 1892), pp. 118–9.

16.   In Egerton's absence tragic scenes occurred on the Common over the sudden death of thirty-eight-year-old William John Olive; a neighbour first on the scene saw the 'children begging and praying, and saying that their papa would die'. Olive, a literate man, who composed letters for others, including the relatively prosperous fly proprietor Robert Blackford, had a history of respiratory troubles, and was a notoriously 'very great drinker'. Surgeon Combs attributed death to heart disease, adding somewhat gratuitously – not to say hypocritically – at the inquest, that his patient of eight years standing 'could not eat much, but drank a good deal'. *Sussex Advertiser*, 18 June 1870.

17.   The term Puseyism, after Edward Pusey, was coined in 1838 as one of the alternative names for the crypto-Catholic Oxford Movement.

18.   Egerton made similar observations in *Sussex Folk*, p. 68. Many families, including those with six or more children, lived in cottages with only two bedrooms and a very modest living room. Such cramped conditions exposed children to the 'various tempers and passions of a father and mother', 'every sound of a crying child or groaning sick person', together with 'the ordinary worries and irritations of life, aggravated now and then by a little beer, and less money, on a Saturday night'. He realistically concluded that not only was 'surprise . . . if some poor cottages are not exactly schools of patience, resignation, good temper and refinement', ridiculous,

but that they were inappropriate venues for 'the not over-soothing effect of a lecture from a clergyman or district visitor'.

19.   Giving evidence in the manslaughter case against Hazelgrove. Although the aunt would have seen Combs as a private patient, the diary entry suggests that poor-law surgeons did not necessarily ensure cover when absent for short periods.

20.   There are no corroborative details. The most likely explanation for Egerton's enquiry while in Tunbridge on other business, was that Piper had either deserted his family, or was failing to make remittances home for their support whilst working away.

21.   The police usually gave details against wayward licensees at the annual Brewster Petty Sessions, though at this meeting the police had no complaints against any of the renewal applicants. Egerton's intervention went unreported in the press. The Bench would feel obliged to act positively on a report from a clergyman of Egerton's discriminating character, but the penalty imposed, the effective suspension of the licence for a month, was a regular penalty against slightly errant licensees, like Relf, who it appears had no recent conviction for offences. He was the victim, of an assault by Michael Sawyer, in the last case in which he was involved, on 28 Apl. 1868. Relf's wife's adulturous relationship with William Crossingham, was a major cause of friction. See below, pp. 103, 113, esp. 24 Oct. 1870 and 28 Apl. 1871. Summary returns, ESCRO. QR/E1042. *Sussex Agricultural Express*, 3 Sept. 1870.

22.   Proposed legislation, introduced annually – and which finally became law in 1871 – ending subscription to the Thirty-Nine Articles of the Anglican Church for admission to the Theology Faculties at the Universities of Oxford and Cambridge.

23.   The case came up at the Petty Sessions on the 28th; the derisory fine of 6d imposed on Relf, and the Bench's refusal to award costs to Crossingham, speak for themselves. Summary returns, ESCRO. QR/E1052.

24.   The press reported that Eliza Wood had been at the school for thirty-six years, 'for the greater part of the time as principal and latterly under new government regulations, as assistant mistress'. Her funeral was attended by many 'principal inhabitants . . . by many pupils of a former generation, and by a large number of the children . . . amongst whom she had been occupied as usual till within a few hours of her death' at sixty-two. *Sussex Agricultural Express*, 29 Nov. 1870.

25.   However, no prosecutions followed this incident.

26.   Presumably the case referred to on 10 Dec. Bethlehem Hospital – or Bedlam – in London was the most famous lunatic asylum. Once doctors pronounced Jane incurable, there was no point in continuing her relatively expensive treatment in London. Jane's transfer to Hayward's Heath suggests that Egerton's opinion that she qualified as a pauper lunatic prevailed over justice Gibbs' assertion that her family could afford her maintenance.

1871

[In London from 9 to 14 January.]

26 Jan. C on a number of families, leaving 2/6 being Miss Tilley's generosity [£5 for the poor given to Egerton on 22 Jan.]. . . . C. at ye Budds of Kings Hill. He has a housekeeper out of the Union, a young single woman w. a child; how is immorality to be avoided.[1] C. on old Mrs Sukey Thompson, so deaf that I had to write on a slate. . . .

28 Jan. C. on King in the wood. Walks 4 miles to work & back each day, poor fellow. . . .[2]

30 Jan. . . . A great many applicants for relief called on me today [as workers were laid off following heavy snow falls]. . . .

31 Jan. . . . C. and had a long discussion in evg. w. Mr. J. Noakes about ye relief of ye poor. It seems almost impossible to get at the right of all the cases.[3] . . . Married Edgar Bowner & Sophia Hall, ye bridegroom a labouring man who couldn't sign his name but he came in kid gloves nevertheless & drove up in a fly.

4 Feb. . . . Buried old [farmer George Fagg] Gilbert at 1 o'clock: his age given as 90. Fancy a man buried to day who was 12 years old when Louis XVI was beheaded! & 34 years old when the battle of Waterloo was fought.

6 Feb. . . . saw Mr. Breach on ye road & had a long t. w. him about some poaching troubles. . . .[4]

8 Feb. . . . At 5.30 my guests arr[ived] at ye sch. room about 95; "Parish Officers & members of ye congr.". Tea at 6. Then music. Mr. Gibbs electrifying machine, Stereoscopic puzzles. I spoke a few words; then ended w. Anthem, Hallelujah Chorus. . . . ye Singers were Mrs Hollands class. . . . altogether a very pl[easant] evg, finished about 10.[5]

13 Feb. . . . C. on Mrs Langridge (1/6), She full of trouble, & really when one hears her case as she puts it, it seems one for parish relief & yet the parish authorities steadily refuse. . . . A long t. w. Mr. Taylor about ye question of "relief". . . .

27 Feb. Several poor women whose husband's parish allowances was lowered on Mon: last called upon me, but I cd. not help them, it is hard for them & yet I do not feel sure that the lowering was unjust. . . . C. to see Mrs R.Relfe found that the poor thing died yesterday. Her d. Mrs Butcher there never rose, never looked, never spoke. . . .

4 Mar. . . . C. on Noakes about ye Chapel: built in 1713. . . .

17 Mar. . . . Spoke to Js. Russell about ye fees for Steeped [?] grave, head-stone & body-stone for his wife. He calmly said that he did not know there was anything to pay! . . .

20 Mar. Wrote a letter of explanation [re. 'the decision of ye Judicial Committee about ye Surplice to use it now in preaching as well as in all other ministrations' – 16 Mar.] to Mr. Gibbs, who is our chief Protestant, tho' not a communicant. . . .[6]

23 Mar. There is a common opinion amongst us that men of the present generation in Burwash are not as strong as the men of 50 years ago. Today . . . I was speaking to old Master Weeks carter to Mr. Simes of Poundsford, & was asking him about the truth of a feat of strength wh. I had heard attributed to him. He assured me that it was absolutely true that when he was a young man, nearly fifty years ago, a waggon load of wheat wh. he was taking to the mill (Relfe's mill), tilted over by accident into a pond, & that he then jumped in, & fetched out one by one the 15 sacks of wheat (a sack is 4 bushels at about 62lbs a bushel . . . I have been told & tho' I forgot to ask him, that he got them out so quickly that the corn did not need drying before it was ground). The old man added that at the time he thought nothing of what he had done. I have also been told within the last few days of a man of 40 or 50 years ago, known by the nick-name of "Rudy-boy" who is "reported" to have carried a pair of 6 inch wheels on his shoulders across a fallow field! & also to have lain on his back on the ground under a waggon with a thousand of bricks in it, & to have lifted it off the ground with his feet!![7]

24 Mar. . . . C. on Mr. J.B.Noakes about parish matters. Mr. Gibbs c. on me about ye surplice question. I cannot clear myself of the charge of ulterior motives & of forcing my own opinions upon ye cong: It is hard to feel that after 14 years in Burwash one is still living in such an atmosphere of suspicion but so it is. . . .

25 Mar. Parish meeting. Some difficulty in finding Officers. The farmers do not like the trouble & the tradesmen cannot spare the time. Mr. G. Simes & Mr. G. Hinde nom[inated] as [Poor Law] Guardians. Mr. James Lade, Mr. W. Kemp ye Overseers. Mr. J. Fuller Road Surveyor. Mr. J. Coppard called upon me for my £10 guarantee, tho' when I gave the guarantee he stated himself to be £193 worse off thro' Martin [Coppard] that he afterwards turned out to be. Not many at dinner, only 9. At the end when

Mr. Jos. Noakes, Mr. Boorman, & Mr. Taylor were there I opened the question of obedience to the Judgement: they personally very civil, but I did not enter into my views at all. . . .

Sun. 26 Mar. . . . I stated . . . that "my motives in giving notice about ye use of ye surplice in preaching having been greatly misunderstood, the notice is withdrawn". I hope this will make peace. . . . In aft. I repeated ye statement. only using "meaning" instead of "motives". . . . After Ch. a very enjoyable walk w. young Irwin . . . a particularly nice, right minded, & able young fellow, one on whom Oxford seems to be exercising no ill influence, as it does on many intellects. He felt that Burwash Philistinism was rather unreasonable. . . .

10 Apl. A Mr. Heath c. on me at b[reakfast] time & br[ought] a card from Mr. Jackson [incumbent] of Heathfield, said he was collecting information about ye Sussex peasantry. I answered a few questions & he departed.[8] . . . Ye voluntary rate £1:13:6 deficient. Expences for ye year £44:18:7¼. Mr. Taylor & Mr. Breach, I am sorry to say resigned. I nominated Mr. Cramp & ye parish Capt. Roger. I sent ye Police Sergt. to look at a team of Master Russells of Perryman's [Farm] Shamefully poor.[9] . . . Mr. Fuller gave me a copy of our Census return for 1871. Our pop. now is 2232, in 1861 2143, in 1851 2227.[10] Inhabited houses 443. Average occupants of a house 5 1/26. Old Russell came up about his horses, & argued the question perfectly calmly, a funny old being. . . .

12 Apl. . . . C. on Mrs Fieldwick [of Rampyndene]. She showed me ye date of ye House, or rather a date on some bricks in ye wall, 1731. . . .

14 Apl. Morning Prayer at 8.0. Five or 6 people there. I cannot help observing that daily prayer has a tendency to beget a somewhat hurried & perfunctory style of doing the service, or I ought to say perhaps what seems to be a perfunctory style. . . .

28 Apl. . . . Presided over Benefit Club, settled the question of the reserve Fund, nothing to be left back, except the Subscr[iption] of Honorary members. . . .[11] Wm. Crossingham has deserted his wife & run off w. Relf's wife at ye beer shop, thereby fully justifying all I have done about the house.

29 Apl. . . . C. on Mrs Reed (1/-), Short (1/-) going to leave, as Mr. Daw gives up spinning, so one of our manufacturers perishes.[12]

1 May. . . . An old parish chest wh. has been missing brought in from the Hotel where it had been laid up when the Ch: was restored in 1855. We examined the contents, not of any great interest. Parish poor relief books & accounts of about 170 years old.[13]

14 May. . . . C. on Lulham to complain of their boys in Ch: he out but
c[ame] later & gave me his mind, wh. is that I do not preach the Gospel in
the matter of Xt dying for all, a curious criticism of my teaching founded on
hearing me once a year at ye Club, & as it happens an utter mistake, that I
am grossly overpaid, that I do no work, that I buy people to come to Ch. a
statement wh. I refuted by my "Charity" book, that I never do near as
much good as Mr. Gould did, a statement wh. I cd. not deny, that all my
tithes & everybody else's property came from the labourer on the land, a bit
of Political Economy wh. I shd. have liked Professor Fawcett[14] to have
explained to him, that he wanted his boy to have education, as might get
into places where they wouldn't have much hard work, but having no hard
work being an accusation agst. me, & that he & his eldest boy went to
Chapel, he wished the others to come to Sunday Sch: that they might not
lose the chance of a frock or a shirt as a prize. Altogether it was a spicy
interview. However we shook hands, & parted I hope as good friends as a
radical, dissenting, poor man, & a parson can well be. . . .

17 May. . . . Newton Taylor c. I signed his paper as cand[idate] for
reliev[in]g off[icer]. . . .

18 May. . . . Dr. to Ticehurst Comm[ittee] of Agric. Assoc: in moribund
state, Messrs Courthope, Eden [Rector of Ticehurst] & Foley, Mr. Bennett
ye new Sol[icitor, recently made Clerk to the Ticehurst Union] &
others. . . .

20 May. . . . C. on Miss Bullock, took her the address for outside sheet of
ye new "Burwash Parish Magazine" wh. Miss Hughes & herself have been
getting up. It is a magazine ed[ited] by her br[other] Revd. Bullock of
Worcester. . . .[15]

24 May. . . . C. . . . on Maskell (1/-). Wm. Maskell's Child told me her
mother had gone to Tunbridge, & naively added "to see the races". . . .

25 May. . . . I d. w. ye Club: no speeches. Music by Artillery Volunteer
band, Hastings, pretty good & singing good, but ye band master Herr
Hessler wanted me to hear his little son sing. I stopped for this & cd. only
feel what sad things some of ye Comic songs are. This was "Wait till I'm a
man" how the girls cuddled & kissed him now & how he'd turn the tables
when he was a man etc. . . . Met Mr. Simes. Mary Ann Hyland & Willy
gone to "the House" today. She is ill & it cd. not be helped. . . .

[In Wiltshire from 26 May to 3 June.]

5 June. . . . Mr. Fowler curate of Christchurch, Hants, came all ye way
over to see the [vacant] curacy. He declined it on ye ground that he wanted
to go where people are thicker together. He seemed pleasant, tho' I feel that

he wd. not have liked Burwash wh. wd. have been too dull. He slept at ye Bell.

6 June. . . . Relf John, ill, I read w. him, & found him very intelligent, & apparently right minded. he told me a good deal about ye Oddfellows, wh. certainly is a good soc[iety].[16] . . . ye Burwash Parish Magazine or Home Words localized out, w. an address from myself.

9 June. . . . I to ye Comm[on]. . . . Saw Mrs Wm. Crossingham there, she poor thing going into ye [work] house at Hellingly. . . .[17]

11 June. . . . I c. . . . Mr. Js. Russell who promised to pay ye fee for gravestone. . . .

15 June. . . . Newton Taylor elected Guardian. I am very glad. . . .[18]

16 June. . . . Mr. Barrow c. on me & amongst other things told me that it is all over for [John] Isted now, at any rate for a time. I dare not protect him any more. May God grant that he does not become reckless. For a whole twelvemonth he had been sober, but being on the club & having nothing to do, here is the sad end. It really grieves me to feel that a man who, bad as he had been, was I believe stirring to do better, shd. have so fallen.

17 June. . . . C. on Mrs John Harmer; has started a sewing machine, ye first on ye common. . . .

22 June. . . . Attended Committee meeting of club re. John Isted, he was fined. . . .[19]

23 June. . . . C. & had a long t. w. John Isted (1/6) & wife. He apparently very humble; a sad business. . . .

28 June. Sch: Punished w. the cane two boys for telling lies about taking flowers from Uncle Joseph's grave. When even in spite of direct evidence, a boy stoutly sticks to it that the evidence is wrong it is hard to know what to do. To do nothing wd. very possibly be merely holding out a premium for lying, & yet it is a cruel damage to a boy to punish him if he is innocent. One boy confessed to his lie, the other did not, tho' the evidence to my mind was conclusive & so I punished. I did some mowing in Mr. Taylor's field. It is curious how little one forgets, tho' touching a scythe only once a year. . . .

29 June. . . . Looked in at ye school, gave half a holyday as it was ye Foresters' club day;[20] ye French band engaged from T[unbridge] Wells, a very good one. . . . A large number of farmers & tradesmen dined. Some good music. I away about 5. . . .

17 July. . . . Holley's curacy dates from today. . . . [Over next few weeks, many visits with his new curate to introduce Holley, mostly to that sector of the community that Egerton dubbed 'the aristocracy'.]

2 Aug. My School Feast. 184 Children & about 60 other people, ye farmers etc. . . . Tea & cake to ye betters in ye dining room. Bread & Jam, br. & butter, & cake to ye ch. I spoke a few words before breaking up, saying ye treat was to those children whose parents took care they shd. go to School somewhere either Ch. or Chapel on Sunday. . . .[21]

16 Aug. I lent my trap to Holley for cr[icket] match at Wadh[urst]. . . .

9 Sept. . . . C. on Mrs Pope, her husb: w. ye threshing machine, a beautiful new one used yesterday for first time. . . .

10 Sept. . . . A serious fire at Mr. White's of Hammerden. Caused by a stranger's child playing w. lucifer matches. . . .

30 Sept. . . . C. on Mr. Walter at ye Beer shop, quite respectable . . . C. on Mrs P. Sawyer, recom[mended] Tom her poaching son to get an under-keeper's [assistant gamekeeper] place. I wd. say he knew all about his business. . . .[22]

2 Oct. . . . C. on Mr. Smith ye new Innkeeper at ye Bell, used to be gardener & musical entrepreneur at Rose-hill.

7 Oct. C. on Mrs Hayward in ye wood. Poor shiftless creature, but the cott[age] in wh. she lives disgraceful to her landlord. . . .

9 Oct. Meeting about ye spire. Marvellous discrepancies in tenders. Jon: Sinden £122-0-0. Sam. Waterhouse £114. J.Brook, £83-0-0 accepted w. misgivings. . . .[23]

16 Oct. . . . In evg. w. Taylor & Holley to Mr. Whatman's harv[est] home. Excellent gathering. Messrs. Gilham, Whatman, Boorman & J. Noakes united [celebration] & about 200 sat down to supper. I was asked to take ye chair. Holley on my left. Speeches & Songs. G. Waterhouse gave a recitation of poetry very creditably. Bentham Fuller sang "Nil desperandum". I sang When the heart is young, & "a Thousand a year". Holley spoke well to his own health, I prop. ye health of ye hosts. Holley & I came away at 8.30 or 8.45. I enjoyed myself greatly, & everybody else seemed to do so too. Danced till I believe 3 or 4 o'Clock AM! & yet not a bad word heard or any excess seen of any sort; this is as it shd. be.

17 Oct. I set out at 7.45 to drive to Lewes. . . . Ye Grand jury to our surprise threw out ye bill agst. Hilder, Meopham & Pennells, the Meopham at any rate had confessed & Hilder had bolted. . . .[24] A Mr. Basley a barrister defending a prisoner disgusted me horribly by his bullying treatment of ye witnesses. However he got his man off. . . .

18 Oct. Wrote out acct. of harv. home for Suss[ex] Expr[ess]. Showed it to Miss Noakes for approval. They well pleased with Monday night, much of the success owing to them. . . .[25]

25 Oct. . . . C. on Mrs Wren ye new comer at Hyland's house. She [illegible] a Cong[regational] Ind[ependent] Sun. Sch. Teacher at Westham. Certainly the social element is a stronger bond amongst Noncon[formists] than among ourselves. She evidently wd. not have missed the Sunday gathering of teachers for something. . . .

26 Oct. . . . Met ye Ticehurst Miss[ionary] Min[ister] coming to Burwash Weald for ye Wesleyans Missy. meeting. Shook hands & wished him God speed. Surely there is room for both. . . .

30 Oct. Sch; the ignorance of some of the children on matters concerning the very first elements of Xtianity. . . . G.Meopham c. to get a character for his Son. I after much hesitation wrote thoroughly sober. I have known him drunk twice, but under circumstances wh. I think so extenuate the fact as to entitle one to write them off as utterly exceptional cases. . . .

Mon. 6 Nov. . . . Night cold, people seemed to be trying to warm it by lighting fires in ye open air. Things however quiet. The police are a considerable check upon over exuberant Protestantism, & it is well. It is terrible what a substitute for religion many people seem to make the cry of "No Popery". 20 at night school notwithstanding. . . .

7 Nov. . . . Simes says we have 20 "in the house". Poor creatures they go in there & are forgotten. . . .[26]

11 Nov. . . . Ed: Jenner (1/-) c. to seem me he has enlisted in ye 1 Batt. 24th F[oo]t in the Compy. same as young Wm. Pope. I then said good bye to Mr. D. Charlie, Sissy, & Miss. K. I am sorry to leave the house in wh. I have been so kindly & considerately treated for 12 years. Home. House very lonely, but "study" comfortable. . . .[27]

12 Nov. . . . My good housemaid Charlotte Gillett very neat & respectful, & a credit to the house. Ye Cook Mary Raynor seems likely to be a good servt. So far I am fortunate . . .

25 Nov. . . . They have begun the steeple repairs. . . .

2 Dec. . . . Coming home overtaken by Blunden from whom I learnt about

Mr. Smiths singing meeting at ye Bell on Mondays: all my old class there exc[ept] B. Fuller. They pay 2d a week I think to go to a dinner at ye end of ye season & visitors pay 3d. . . . It is disappointing to hear one's old labours . . . being reproduced at ye public house when I can't get ye singers to come near me. . . .

Sun. 3 Dec. . . . Holley's serm[on] to day much praised. I am told that he certainly does preach well & indeed altogether, I am very thankful that he is in Burwash.

4 Dec. . . . Small N.S. I took Rover w. me, he lay pretty quiet in ye school for his first time. . . .

5 Dec. . . . Took the funeral of old Big headed Jack Fuller who died in the Union. His coffin was the plainest I ever remember. Absolutely "parish", not an initial, nor a date, simply a box. . . . C. on Widow Dann (1/-). She told me that there is a great talk about how somebody sent me ½ a bushel of ground oats with a spoon in it a propos to my notice about the use of oatmeal & water as a drink in hot weather in the Burwash Magazine for August. Of course it is a myth, but it seems to please the people with whom it appears that I am ceasing to be popular, in as much as I do not give much away. I really think that the imputation is unfair, as my account book will shew. I wd. rather be popular than not of course, but it is more difficult to be popular as Rector than it was as Curate. Expectations increase with increased wealth, more rapidly than one's power of satisfying them. . . .

6 Dec. . . . Heard of a cruel piece of neglect in the matter of not cleansing a cottage in wh. a family of Russells had had fever, owing to wh. humanly speaking a s. & ye mother lost their lives. Representations were made so I am informed to Mr. G.B.Gregory, by the medical officer, Mr. Eden, & the Inspector of nuisances; no real notice was taken & the two people died. If the facts are truly stated, Mr. G. is very guilty. . . .[28]

21 Dec. . . . to ye sch: at 10.30 for dole, but business didn't begin till 11.30. I came away at 1.30. Much difficulty in deciding what to do about giving to the workmen of farmers who will not subscribe anything [towards funding the Christmas beef distribution]. I pd. 4/- for four recusants so technically escaping the difficulty. . . .

25 Dec. I married Wm. Eaton a Serg[ean]t Gren[adier] Guards to Henrietta Price. A largish & somewhat rough crowd at ye West Door, disappointed by ye bridal party coming out at ye South door. . . . I d. w. Mr. Philcox as usual. His dependants not quite so numerous owing to deaths etc. . . .

Notes

1.   While Egerton's disapproval was automatic, this arrangement was economical as it saved the costs of the woman and child's residence in the workhouse, while providing the essential home help which the widower Budd needed for his children, thereby facilitating his employment.

2.   Unusual distance to walk for farmworkers in Wealden villages, but quite common elsewhere, especially for labourers living in towns, and working in neighbouring villages.

3.   In fact, out-door relief was chaotic, owing to successful fraudulent claims, compounded further by Relieving Officer Willsher's conduct. He unilaterally supplied flour to some families 'because I knew they where quite, Destitute, and it was an Ergent Necessity because I would not break up there homes before our Board Met, all, Parties have large families. I Can only say that if I have done wrong I am truly sorry, but I did what I believed to be wrigh'. Willsher's financial accounts were anarchic, and indeed the official enquiry currently commencing and which terminated in his forced resignation, discovered that 'postponed payments' facilitated 'the use for his own purposes of the money'. In Burwash, unpaid debts included Benjamin Wood's fees as sexton for the burials of paupers Hannah Chandler (aged eighty) and Betty Pattenden (aged fifteen), on 28 Jan. and 1 Feb. 1871 respectively, and carpenter John Sinden's bill for their coffins. An unnamed butcher, and a publican, who supplied meat and wine ordered by the Medical Officers, were also owed consequential sums. Various letters to Chairman, and Clerk, of Union, including Wood, and grocer E. Honeysett, 21 Jan. and 18 Mar.; letters to the PLB from Willsher, Clerk, and Auditor (enclosing further letters from Willsher), 7 Mar., 11 Apl. and 17 June; annual workhouse report from Inspector Longley, 30 Nov. 1871, PRO. MH.12/13149–50. ESCRO. Par.284/1/5/2. See also 7 Nov. 1871 and note 26 below.

4.   There were no convictions for poaching at this period, and it is possible that Egerton counselled against prosecutions, given the peaking poverty problem.

5.   The guests included the parochial 'aristocracy', including Mrs Holland 'and her party', Gibbs and Breach, the non-resident landowner Fuller, together with surgeon Combs, the wealthier farmers, including Gillham and Barrow, the schoolteaching Ansets, and Egerton's close friend, the vet Charles Taylor, almost all members of the congregations of either St Bartholomew's or St Philip's. Tea was provided by Kathy Weller of the Bell Inn. *Sussex Advertiser*, 15 Feb. 1871.

6.   One of the attempts to clarify rubrics over vestments and ceremonies, deriving from recent reports of the ritual commission, which – as at Burwash – antagonized relations between clergymen and parts of their congregations.

7.   These anecdotes were entered – oddly – in the current burial register, ESCRO. Par.284/1/1/6.

8.   This was certainly Richard Heath, who travelled extensively in the English countryside between 1870 and 1874, and wrote many articles on rural conditions; in the Burwash context, he published 'Sussex Commons and Sussex Songs' in *Golden Hours*, (1871), but his principal observations related to Mayfield and Rotherfield. Heath, *The Victorian Peasant*, (new edition, Gloucester, 1989, edited by K.Dockray), pp. ix–xxvii, and 89–96.

9.   The police enforced laws against working unfit horses, and commonly called in a RSPCA inspector to confirm evidence against that tiny minority of offenders who were prosecuted.

10.   The census figures were used to publicly project 'the healthiness of Burwash', illustrated by the numbers of elderly people; sixty-six were aged between seventy and eighty, and a further fourteen were over eighty. The decrease of population between 1851 and 1861 was attributed to the inclusion of forty railway navvies in the former year, and the 'unusually large number of young native females of the labouring class who had migrated to the great towns, attracted . . . by the large wages, as servants . . . as well as by the greater excitement and showiness of town life'. *Sussex Advertiser*, 19 Apl. 1871.

11.   Another exemplar of this recurrent problem, resolved yet again by the distribution of members' subscriptions through dividends, while reserving donations from honorary members for the next year's fund.

12.   Nothing is known about Daw's spinning enterprise, though the implications of Egerton's observation suggest that local domestic demand for wool was, or had been flourishing, and that household production of clothing items was considerable.

13.   These appear to have been preserved, nonetheless, and are in the ESCRO.

14.   Professor of political economy at Cambridge 1863–84, and an MP 1865–84, whom Egerton knew personally.

15.   The publishers of the Anglican magazine, *Leisure Hour*, also invited parochial distributors to compose their own village news, then printed on one or two sheets for inclusion in the main magazine. Burwash 'Parish Notes' commenced in 1871, but is extant only from 1875. Egerton was the main contributor. See also below, pp. 115, 118, 6 June and 5 Dec. 1871.

16.   The first of the affiliated Benefit Societies to develop on a national scale, based on sound scientific actuarial calculations respecting working men, and financially stable in stark contrast to many of the parochial Friendly Societies, including Burwash's. Oddfellows' lodges in Sussex swelled from sixteen in 1845 to forty-nine in 1875. P.H.J.H. Gosden, *The Friendly Societies in England 1815–75*, (Manchester UP, 1961), esp. pp. 11, 26, 31.

17.   A sad commentary on broken marriages under the Victorian Poor Law. Mrs Crossingham went to Hellingly workhouse, on the grounds that her legal settlement was in Hailsham Union and not Ticehurst; Hailsham immediately challenged this decision, and the Ticehurst Union accepted that the wife and her two children were legally settled in Burwash. Board of Guardians, minute, 13 July 1871, ESCRO. G10/1a/12.

18.   He meant Relieving Officer to replace Willsher who had been forced to resign. There was a strong field of six, mostly the younger sons of farmers and countryside professionals, including vets, who commonly sought jobs as farm bailiffs, as was the thirty-six-year-old Taylor, currently living at Wadhurst. The £100 salary offered for the full-time post exceeded that earned by many bailiffs, and was secure. Considerable behind-the-scenes lobbying naturally accompanied appointments, reflected in the relatively large number (twenty-two) of Guardians attending the election on 15 June. Formal notice, and Union Clerk to the Local Government Board, 19 Feb. 1871, PRO. MH.12/13149–50. Board of Guardians, minutes, 1 and 15 June 1871, ESCRO. G10/1a/12.

19.   As there is no record of any court appearance, and in the context of entries 22 and 23 June, it would seem that Isted defrauded his Friendly Society by working while claiming; if so, he was lucky to escape with a mere fine.

20.   The Foresters comprised the Oddfellows' principal competitor, and were equally financially sound. Their south-eastern (Sussex, Kent, Berkshire, Hampshire, Surrey) membership grew from under nine to over thirty-four thousand,

between 1858 and 1867, and exceeded fifty thousand in 1875. There is some evidence that it was more successful than its rival, in the recruitment of farm labourers. Gosden, op.cit., esp. pp. 44, 81.

21. The *Sussex Advertiser*, 9 Aug. 1871 reported that the 'children marched in procession, with their flags, from the School to the Rectory', played a variety of games, 'cricket, swings, dipping into water for money', watched by '70 to 80 . . . spectators of the ladies and gentlemen of this and the adjoining parishes'. This was the first year in which children who attended nonconformist Sunday schools were elegible for the Rector's 'treat', and Egerton stressed that his own innovation represented 'no sectarianism'.

22. Aged twenty-six, he had not been convicted of poaching by the local Petty Sessions.

23. James Brooks, father and son, were partners as carpenters. Sinden worked on a grander scale, employing three men. Waterhouse grandiosely described himself as 'Ag. Lab. & Landowner'. 1871 Census.

24. William Hilder may have made off at the time, but was subsequently arrested and currently in prison; his co-defendants George Mepham and James Pennalls had been bailed. These three, plus at least four other young labourers, had worked late at the seventy-acre Little Tott Farm, for Kitty Weller, who at this time, was also the well-established licensee at the Bell. They were fed, and allowed to drink at the pub until at least 1a.m., and were 'a little fresh' when they left with three quarts of beer. Subsequently, Mepham, Hilder and Pennalls were involved in breaking into the cellar at Tott House, the farmhouse, and the theft of eight bottles of 'home made Gooseberry Wine'. They were somewhat the worse for wear early in the morning when it was time to go to work. Various witnesses described them as 'freshy', and Mepham – who 'could not walk straight' – was vomiting, and simultaneously trying to get someone else to do his 'milkman's' round. Mepham indeed confessed, later in the day, when Sergeant Hawkins, who had established from tracks that three men were involved, called and found Mepham still incapacitated and lying on his bed. The Grand Jury's attitude is probably explained by the fact that Kitty Weller had herself broken the licensing laws, and by so doing had encouraged these young men's excessive drinking. Depositions of Catherine Weller, and several other witnesses, including Mepham's cousin, Joseph, 2–5 Aug. 1871, ESCRO. QR/E1059. Census, 1871.

25. Egerton's account of harvest festival activities at St. Bartholomew's and St. Philip's on the 15th, was subordinated to the politics of the 'entertainment' provided by these bigger farmers in Whatman's oasthouse. 'Would that such gatherings were more common. The icy barriers which too often separate employers and employed, masters and men in England . . . would . . . thaw and fairly melt away in such an atmosphere'. Presumably the editor added the concluding – and revealing – sentence: 'We are glad to hear on the best authority that neither in word nor in deed did anything occur during the whole evening to prevent the complete enjoyment of the meeting'. In his speech, Egerton with his customary historical sensitivity, also reported that George Hinde, 'the last representative in Burwash of the Gouldsmith's family which has flourished in this parish for several hundred years', was quitting Holton Farm, and leaving Sussex; the decision may have been relatively sudden, as Hinde was a current Guardian. *Sussex Agricultural Express*, 21 Oct. 1871. Election notice, Mar. 1871, PRO. MH.12/13149.

26. Although the Board of Guardians employed an Anglican chaplain, and facilitated visits by Nonconformist ministers, Egerton's diary does not mention one

pastoral visit to any parishioner inmate. Ironically, the next visit of the Local
Government Board inspector to the workhouse revealed that 'nearly 90 per cent of
paupers relieved are in receipt of out-relief', and in the inspector's hearing, a
Guardian unequivocally announced that 'one . . . Relieving Officer had *nothing to do
three days in the week*'. The Board's chairman privately admitted 'that the Guardians
were "imposed upon right and left"', and the Local Government Board endorsed
their inspector's recommendation 'for a more efficient supervision of out relief',
with 'more careful investigation' of claimants by Relieving Officers. Early in the
new year the Central Board started to implement a policy of radically reducing
outdoor relief, but the first stage of implementation was already under way in
Ticehurst Union: 'Overseers of most of the parishes examine the permanent
Out-Relief cases half-yearly, and make suggestions for the necessary alterations.
The Guardians occasionally do so', but subsequently would also monitor bi-annual
parochial investigations. Longley report, 30 Nov. and Local Government Board's
reply, 13 Dec. 1871, PRO.MH.12/13150. Board of Guardians, minute, 25 Jan. 1872,
ESCRO. G10/1a/12.
27.   Just prior to moving to the Rectory, Egerton chaired a vestry meeting when a
number of individual ratings were changed, including a reduction from £115 to £90
'on account of the dilapidated condition of the Rectory'; vestry minute, 7 Oct. 1871,
ESCRO. Par.284/12/2.
28.   This calibre of incident was common, and inasmuch as the historian can
penetrate the minutes of the relevant official bodies, and largely tame press
coverage, they suggest that the relatively recently professionalized sanitary officers
proved almost as unequal to the task of improving rural environmental conditions,
as their urban counterparts. George Burrough Gregory Esq. lived in Ticehurst.

1872

5 Jan. Sch: I am sorely troubled again. Some body has taken the Miss[ionar]y box out of the girls school. It is very disheartening, but what can one do. I spoke very seriously about it. . . .

15 Jan. . . . C. Mr. J.B.Noakes to speak about Harriet Fenner who died last week almost of actual starvation because she wd. not go into "the House". Mr. Noakes out of his own pocket has allowed her 2/6 a week for nearly 5 y[ea]rs!! besides giving her things. I had constantly relieved her[1] & had seen her just after dole day, & had urged her to go up into the Infirmary in ye House, but she wd. not. . . .

25 Jan. . . . Wm. Pope has been here for a week . . . but stupidly outstayed his leave & was had back [presumably arrested by the military authorities]. Eus[tace] Jenner was also at home but without leave & he will be tried by court martial. Stupid lads. . . .

27 Jan. . . . C. & R. w. Mrs Rich who has for years been living as wife to her husband's nephew. . . .

10 Feb. Paid my servants their 1st quarter's wages. It is an expensive dignity being the master of a house, still I am well satisfied & that is something. . . .

12 Feb. . . . C. on Mrs J. Isted. How gladly wd. I put a £10 note into the Savings Bank for Sally if I cd. spare it, to compensate her for staying at home w. her mother instead of going to service & earning something for a future day. . . .[2]

14 Feb. . . . [postmaster and church organist] Fleming told me that last night & this morning he stamped 1250 [mostly Valentine Day] letters. . . .

19 Feb. . . . Took exerc[ise] by digging in ye kitchen garden. How I envy ye physical strength of men who go hop-digging day after day. In half an hour I began to sweat like a Bull. . . . Wrote an answer to a circular by "A Tradesman" for Officer of Nat[iona]l Chamb[er] of Trade, 10 Duke Street. His line is that we country clergy who deal with co-operative stores are answerable for the bitter & unchristian feelings generated by not getting things in our own village. No doubt it is neighbourly to do what we can by dealing in the place, but many times we can get things so much better & cheaper in town that nothing but tyranny wd. prevent us doing so.

20 Feb. . . . Mrs Oliver c. on me to consult me about effecting a reconciliation between her husb: & herself. She 50 he 30. . . .

23 Feb. . . . attended quarterly Club meeting. Funds very low, will not admit of a dinner I fear. G[ibbs] spoke pretty freely about the gentry helping & seemed to intimate that they did not do much in that way. I spoke in defence & showed that in Schools, Dole, Honorary Subscri[bers] to Club Coals etc., more was done than he thought, but as he was a little bit "on" his arg[ument]s were not clear. He told me that Wm. Eyles, "the radical" had just died after a very short illness at Brighton, the only boy I ever turned out of night school, poor fellow, his has been a troubled life. Young Banks gone to Lewes [Gaol] for 3 months for stealing. I am really glad, he was corruption itself in this place.[3] C. & t. over Club matters w. Mr. Combs.

24 Feb. . . . C. on Polly Thompson as she wanted my opinion about joining a teachers' Assoc[iation] at Brighton. I advised her to do so, if she cd. manage the getting there. . . .

26 Feb. Sch: C. on Mr. J.B.N[oakes]. He told me of a case where I was called "hard cheese" because I had not done more. I know the poor man is in need, but how can one help all. . . . A [magisterial] sitting at ye [police] Station on Wm. Hicks, who was sent for trial, whereupon he kicked & bellowed greatly. The young Turk tells me a story that when he was a gaol last time in the black hole [punishment cell] for some offence when the Governor came to him & said "Hicks I'll forgive you this time if you will tell me whether there is any prison rule that you have not broken". Master Willy pondered for a moment & replied, "Well Sir I've never been out of bed before the bell rang"! Possibly this is a regular story of prison life, of wh. Master Willy makes himself the hero.[4] I dr[ove] to station to fetch Mr. Kitson. . . . Master Willy off by same train to Lewes. . . . Evg. damp & sadly poor meeting. However Mr. K. spoke earnestly . . . gave details of the wants of London & pleaded hard for the A.C.S. – result £2-3-4. . . .

17 Mar. . . . to ye Comm. w. Master Harmer. He talked most rationally on ye Subj[ect] of his weakness for drink, introducing the subj: himself & asking my advice. I strongly recommended him to begin a habit of Ch. going. He came twice to St. Ph. today. . . . He told me that his father's dying injunction to him was, "Mind you always keep better company than you be y[ou]rself". . . .[5]

23 Mar. . . . Sharp snow storm. Wembrannells Menagerie coming into the village. . . . Went into the managerie. Lion very noble. Rhinosceros a really great beast, on the whole I was much pleased. Mr. Anset very kindly undertook to collect subscriptions so as to let 200 children in at 30/- a hundred. I gave £1, Holley 10/-, Breachs' 14/6 & so on. The show well patronised. . . .

28 Mar. Got our report from ye Privy Council. Not very good. Requires much improvement both in Boys & Girls Department for another year. Got nevertheless a lot of money £90-1-9. . . .[6]

4 Apl. . . . Ch. finance. . . . In some slight deficit but on the whole ye expenses are fairly met. Mr. Courthope sugg[ested] a separation betw[een] fabric & Ch: expen[diture] ye latter to be paid by the worshippers & ye former by ye occupiers & owners [of land] on a voluntary rate. Well, as long as you have owners like himself, but a dissenting occupier & an infidel owner wd. not much regard a rate. Lunch in ye boys sch. 2/6 a head. Satisfactorily managed by Mr. Smith of ye Bell. After 1 [p.m.] business resumed but very desultory [discussion of 1870 Education Act]. I as worthy chairman hardly strict enough. Strong feeling agst. compulsion either direct, or indirect, ye latter being understood as an encroachment preventing employers employing children under a certain age who had not passed say standard 3. . . .

6 Apl. . . . Had t. w. old Harry Relf about his "estate" & his new buildings thereon. Kemp has bought James Russell's property, so out goes John Hall at Michaelmas who thought he was safe poor man. . . .

8 Apl. . . . Holley c. to tell me that owing to the death of Archdeacon Downall the living of Okehampton . . . is vacant & that he is going to be presented to it, so he leaves me this day 3 months. For my sake & the parish's sake I am very sorry as he suits us well, for his sake of course I am glad, tho' I think that if he had had to wait a year or two more it wd. have been better for him, & so he thinks too. . . .

20 Apl. . . . John Hall c. on me . . . to consult me as to what he shd. do in the way of getting a new house when he was to move at Michaelmas. I don't know how to help him poor man. Harry Jarvis c. about 9.30 to show me his Veterinary diplomas the Exam: for wh. he passed yesterday. He has distinguished himself by an Essay on "the digestion of horses", wh. has gained him the Fellowship of the Vet[erinary] Med[ical] Assoc: I always said he was the sharpest boy I ever had under me at the Nat[iona]l Sch; & having worked really honestly & hard since he has been in London. . . .[7]

25 Apl. . . . C. on poor Thompson: he feels it fearfully. Still I believe him to be humble & resigned about his great loss. His poor wife [Noani] was only 36 & had had 14 ch: & nearly always had had bad times. She did not expect to get over it. Adherent placenta & Haemorrhage were the causes of death. Surely in such a case & with the almost certain knowledge that another ch: bearing wd. be death they ought to have lived apart but they did not & they are parted now indeed. As a slight relief from anxiety her mother has come to keep house. . . .

26 Apl. . . . I asked Mr. Buss about Enos Braban's wife who is no better. Simple exhaustion I fear. Mrs Buss has taken the ch[ildren]: really it is good to have rough women sometimes; they just come in handy to help other rough ones whom nobody else wd. care to help. I can't think who else wd. have taken the Braban ch: & yet it was essential they shd. be taken. . . . Attended the Quarter night of the Club. Poor men I am very sorry that they cannot have a feast, but so it is. I hope it will not break the club up. I offered £5 as a help next year. . . .

12 May. . . . Whitaker pr. at Burwash & I heard favourable opinions of him. . . . I think he will come [as replacement curate].

13 May. . . . Kept a funeral waiting; first time I ever did so. I completely forgot it. Let the poor people off w. half fees in consequence. . . .[8]

14 May. . . . C. & had a long t. w. Mrs Isted; her husb: [John] discharged unfairly as he thinks & is very depressed about it. I did not see him, but wrote a note for him counselling submission & a request to be taken on again. I do hope it will have effect but see doubt in his fellow-workmen & others counsel resistance. . . .

[From 15 to 25 May in Wiltshire; on 20th at Nunton he attended a Friendly Society dinner, and recorded: 'no farmers who possibly do not like to face ye Men just now for fears of awkward questions about wages turning up. However all was quiet . . . '.[9]]

27 May. A Wedding . . . John Clifton (alias Holmes) & Frances Collins. . . . let them off my fee, as they had made up their minds to live respectably. . . . C. on Mrs J. Isted. Isted has been most dangerously ill. He came in & I argued with him for nearly an hour urging him to ask Mr. Whatman to take him on again. I do hope he will. . . . Rover got me into trouble by barking at a half drunk stranger who used fearful language.

28 May. . . . waylaid by H.Relf who gave me his version of ye misunderstanding between Mr. Breach & himself. . . . Last night I had a long conversation with [village shopkeeper] Alfred Hepworth about Co-Operative Stores wh. he says sensibly affect business.

1 June. C. on . . . Mrs Gilbert . . . gave me a bit of chaff applied to Harry Relf sometime after his marriage to his 4th wife. "Ah Master Relf so you've shoed the horse 'all round' at last". . . .

3 June. . . . C. on Mrs Isted: her husb; at home w. bad hand, times are certainly not very gay w. them just now. . . .

Tues. 4 June. . . . went to ye club service. Didn't come into Ch: till

12.5. . . . More men went in & out than common but those who remained were very attentive. . . . I always preach earnestly on Club days, as the temptations of the day seem real & tangible. Dinner in booth near ye hotel, about 135 members. I in ye chair, Mr. Jarvis opposite me, a good dinner, the afternoon comfortable. Ye members really grateful for the efforts made to secure them a feast. . . .

8 June. . . . I c. on Mrs Collins, better, but w. a filthy drain right under the house, how is she to be well. The landlord is a regular screw, & it wd. be of little use to ask him to set it to rights, so what is the poor woman to do. . . .

Sun. 9 June. Committee of [Privy] Council allow an Uncertified Teacher as substitute for [the sick] Mrs Anset if for not more than two months. . . . Only 6 men in ye choir, this matter really distresses me, & I don't know what to do. . . . it is becoming serious. . . . Sunday is often a disheartening day for me, & to day was so. It is a day wh. brings to the front all one's own shortcomings, & compels one to own that much that is not satisfactory in others is due to want of prayer, want of spirituality, want of earnestness in oneself.

10 June. . . . C. on John Isted & had a long oration again about Mr. Whatman's work. . . .

13 June. . . . Mr. J.Coppard gave me a lift home [from the station] in his tax cart[10] saying "an ordinary ride is better than a good walk".

19 June. . . . Ye funeral [to 'take' which he had returned early from Tunbridge Wells] kept me waiting 30 mins., ye poor woman [seventy-seven-year-old Jemina Pankhurst, domiciled at Cranbrook] had died of dropsy, & ye coffin leaked, so they had to get wooden bearers . . .

28 June. . . . C. & P. w. poor Fleming. I fear his time is short. He has a bad rupture & has not been wearing a truss. . . .

29 June. Poor Fleming died last night about 20 mins past 9. His heart gave way under ye exertion of getting out of bed. Poor man. I really liked him, he was always cheery, obliging & civil. He had been organist for 25 years, & had missed duty I believe only 3 Sundays in the whole time. . . . C. on Mrs Pope (1/-) & P. w. her. She ill of diarrhea. Told her to send some of ye well water up & I wd. get it tested. . . .

2 July. Poor Fleming's funeral at 2 o'Clock. Whitaker attended as well as myself. So did Mr. Breach, Gibbs & Capt. Roger, & a good many more. The choir sang "brief life is here our portion" from the Ch: Porch to ye grave, & the effect was very touching. Poor old man, every body liked him, & all are sorry that he is gone. . . .

3 July. . . . I . . . wrote notice of poor Fleming for Sussex Expr. & Parish Notes . . .[11]

18 July. . . . Capt. Roger says ye farmers are not going to subscribe towards ye organ bec[ause] they think ye bells & clock ought to be seen to first. Ye bells voted dangerous by both Mr. Slater & W. Milne, & so I cannot take ye responsibility of letting them be rehung & rung. . . .

22 July. Saw Newton Taylor about some poor law cases & only further convinced myself how difficult the whole subject is. The question of benefit clubs is a specially hard one. It is well to encourage prudence, & yet the parish cannot but consider income be it derived from what source it may. A fair appreciation seems to me such as this. A.B. not in a club wd. receive say 6/- from ye parish; he receives 7/6 from ye club, so let the parish give 3/-. So ye parish pays 3/- & ye man is 4/6 better off by being in ye Club. . . .[12]

23 July. . . . to ye Bear to explain about ye Ch. bells; not many farmers there, but I tried to shew that in ye face of Mr. Slater & Willy Milnes opinions I was not justified in taking ye responsibility of having ye bells rehung. . . .

27 July. . . . C. on Mrs J.Isted, sat longer than I meant. She very weak indeed & in bed. . . .

30 July. . . . Mr. Gibbs & Mr. Atherton c. ye latter got on his hobby of ye land & ye agricultural poor. It is more easy to recognise the evils of an existing system, than to devise a new system wh. shall be on the whole better, & I fancied that I saw many practical difficulties in friend A's suggestions, however he is very earnest. . . .

5 Aug. Bank Holyday. Hastings Pier opening & I grieve to say wet. Sch. I read out names for treat. Cannot accept less than 30 Sundays per ann: as qualification. Chapel children on same terms as Church. . . . Wrote invitations to farmers for school treat. . . .

11 Aug. . . . I looked at the Notice board in Ch. & saw ye Govt. Education Schedule. We are accredited w. accommodation for 343 Boys & girls & infants at ye Nat[iona]l School, Burwash, & for 111 at St Philips, total 454, wh. gave us acc[reditation] for a population of 2724 or one sixth of the whole pop. I am very thankful that we have not to build Sch.[13]

12 Aug. . . . C. on Mrs J.Isted, youngest child in bed w. ye measles. . . .

19 Aug. . . . C. on Mr. J.Noakes, & tried to clear myself from a charge of getting a workman away from him in an unfair way. I perfectly unconscious that I had been doing anything of ye sort, & I shd. be very willing to refer ye matter to any unprejudiced persons,[14] but he out & out set, & boldly avowed the doctrine that if any body trod on his toes, he tried to tred on theirs in return. I argued w. him about this but it was no use, right or wrong; that was his way, Bible or no Bible. It struck me at any rate he might pride himself that if he did tread on a man's toes, he didn't do it behind his back! Buried poor old master Buss ye minister of Providence Chapel in his 80th y[ear]. A truly good old man. Mr. Gibbs followed him to ye grave. . . .[15]

24 Aug. . . . Last night somebody, I can only hope in a drunken trick & not out of spite broke open Ellen [Gould's] greenhouse, took & destroyed a lot of grapes, let out the pigs, & took gates off ye hinges . . .[16]

3 Sept. C. on Mrs J.I: staid over my usual time, but it is very dull for her all day while everybody is out hopping & she is quite helpless in bed. . . .

15 Sept. . . . Poor Mrs Isted sent for Mr. C[ombs] thinking her conf[ine-men]t was coming on, poor thing. I pray she may live.

30 Sept. . . . Old [agricultural labourer John] Hicks came up [from the Common] on his 90th birthday. I gave him my annual 2/6 & a glass of hot brandy & water & some bread & butter. . . .

4 Oct. Burwash fair. A merry go round, peep show, & some cake stalls constituted ye fair. . . .

5 Oct. I w. round by ye old Etchm. road for a constitutional, broke my stick in attempting to make Rover feel ashamed of himself for hunting. . . .

17 Oct. . . . I c. on Mr. Spencer [of Tester's Farm] to plead for Mrs Debley's boy Matthew who had been stealing apples. I pleaded in vain. . . .[17]

26 Oct. Wedding at 10.30 Labourer & Labourress Js. Harmer & Caroline Walter, pretty wedding. Ye bridegro[om] in yellow kid gloves. Harry Head & wife witnesses; on going out a girl presented each of ye party w. a really nice little bouquet. The first time I have ever seen this done. . . .

28 Oct. . . . C. on Mrs J.Isted. On Sat [26th] night while all the Keeleys next door were "up town" somebody broke into the house & stole £20-10-0, all the hard earnings of Rob[er]t Keeley a very steady young fellow who was just going to be married. It is a cruel blow to the poor man, & I only hope that the thief may be found out.[18] . . . I c. on Mrs W. Isted (1/6) has b[een] ill for a week, but parish will not allow anything because it is so soon after hopping. In this case hopping just cleared debts leaving nothing over.[19] . . . I c. on Daw & argued the question of his Son's absence

from school. He very civil & we ended w. a compromise. He is to send a
note the day after his Son's absence, instead of on ye same day. . . . Opened
N.S. 36, a large number to begin with.

6 Nov. . . . My tithe dinner at 2 o'Clock. About the usual number. This
dinner signalized I fancy by an innovation. There were no toasts & no
speeches of any sorts. . . . A good dinner at the Bell, & the big room by
pulling down a partition just held the number. Some of the principal
farmers there. . . .

13 Nov. . . . I called at Mr. Whatman's late house; found there a labourer's
wife Fellowes by name; she did not care to see me . . .

15 Nov. . . . C. on Mrs Pope; in the field, to say that as she systematically
keeps her children away from school, I must decline to help when she
comes to beg. . . .

16 Nov. . . . a parish meeting at ye vestry, & adjourned to the Bear, to go
thro' the relief list, none lowered, one or two raised. . . .

23 Nov. . . . C. on Mrs Braban, not in, but represented by a lot of dark
eyed dirt-besmired children, as ignorant as Hottentots. C. on Mrs Oliver, a
very different sort. In Service 5 years at last pl[ace] w. 2 maiden ladies in
Hastings. Refined, educated, & religious, tho' her h[usband] only a labourer
at Mr. Hoadley's. She was a Hilder of Ashburnham. . . . Nonconform[ist].
C. on Mrs G. Maskell (1/-), Rough, honest, hardworking, ignorant. . . .

Sun. 24 Nov. . . . A most encouraging congr: a remarkable proportion of
men. . . .

25 Nov. Very wet. . . . Poor Mrs J. Sinden died last night of typhus fever, a
victim I believe to cesspools, drains & bad smells. I had not heard a word of
her being even poorly till Friday [22nd] afternoon, & only last night did I
hear that she was dangerously ill. . . . C. on poor Sinden, he in great
distress. . . .

26 Nov. . . . N.S. 42! I really was greatly interested in renewing my
acquaintance with so many of our young folks. One – Ben Mepham – who
did not seem quite bright, left on the score that he learnt nothing. . . .

27 Nov. . . . C. on Mrs Eastwood (1/-), advised her to go into the
house. . . .

2 Dec. . . . C. on Mrs J. Isted, gave the baby a 1/- for a feeding bottle. . . .
C. at Daws. He gave me a specimen of a new substitute for linseed cake viz
ground nut cake from Africa. D. w. Miss Trower. They lectured me about

not taking more pains to draw out shy & somewhat affected young ladies, the Miss Irwins for instance. What they said was possibly true, but when there are people who will talk & be sociable without all the crust breaking preliminaries, one is tempted to leave crusts unbroken. N.S. 28. C. & R. P. w. Bates & wife on my way home. What additional happiness; sympathy in the highest matters must give to married life. I enjoyed my visit very much.

3 Dec. Rain, rain. Poor people must be suffering greatly through loss of time, & farmers thro' loss of seed time. We ought to be humbled. . . .

16 Dec. . . . C. on Wm. Maskell (1/-). Another child, it really seems hard that a man costing the parish about 12/- a week as totally disabled shd. be able to keep on begatting child after child. . . .[20]

17 Dec. . . . Mrs Isted (2/-) taken very ill again. Has never got over her conf[inemen]t. . . .[21]

21 Dec. . . . Dole day. I went at 10.15, escaped for a bit & c. on Mrs J.I. who is very ill. Then back & staid till ye end. Gave away about 92 Stones at 5/- per stone. Refused only a few cases wh. are felt did not stand in need. Mr. Whatman helped part of the time. Mr. J.Fuller, Mr. Cramp, Mr. J.Coppard & Mr. Spencer all the time. The system is not altogether satisfactory, but on the whole I think well to be maintained. . . .

Sun. 22 Dec. [At St Philip's in the afternoon]. . . . A larger congr: & a remarkable number of men. . . .

25 Dec. . . . Attendance not large either morg. or aft. Holy-day merged in holiday. . . .

27 Dec. C. on Mrs J.Isted. She down stairs again but very weak & ill. I c. on Master Harmer of Shoyswell to see how he had managed this Xmas about his pledge. Saw his wife, she said he had been quite abstemious. I pray that he may keep on so. . . .

30 Dec. . . . To ye Common. . . . C. on Mrs Wm. Kemp. A drain thro' Cramp's garden blew up thro' a stoppage having lifted 8 or 10 feet of earth. C. & expl[ained] about the "no dole" to Mr. Arthur Leaves. They can hardly understand that if they "have nothing else than what they work for they can even be so well off as not to be objects of charity". . . . C. on Mr. Hallaway at the [Railway] Inn. He says he has had a very quiet time & at the same time remunerative Xmas. His is about the only trade wh. speaks of money being otherwise than short. . . .

Notes

1.   Fenner's name does not appear regularly in the diary, which suggests that Egerton's full record was kept separately in his 'charity' book.

2.   Ideally, girls who went into domestic service in their early teens, aimed to save a substantial proportion of their annually paid wages, which subsequently comprised an important contribution to the costs of setting-up home on marriage.

3.   Charles Banks, described as a 'respectably dressed young man', with no apparent criminal record, was sentenced by the Petty Sessions to three months hard labour; he had repeatedly stolen cash from grocer and draper Honeysett, on one day – 10 Feb. – visiting the shop six times for trifling things. He was trapped by coins marked by the police, one of which he spent in the Rose and Crown. *Sussex Agricultural Express*, 27 Feb. 1872.

4.   Fourteen-year-old Hicks had received two months imprisonment in Aug. 1870 for the theft of seven pears from J.B. Noakes' garden. On this later occasion, he was remanded in custody, and tried at the Assize for the theft of a sheepskin from butchers Jarvis and Sons. He took the skin across the parish border to Brightling, and sold it to the probably corrupt fellmonger, Gosling. Here Hicks purchased a pair of gloves, which he not only ostentaciously displayed when he popped into the Swan Inn, half a mile away, in the direct route to Burwash, but having said that they were too small, he responded to the barmaid's suggestion that he returned them by saying 'he should not do that'. Moreover, the barmaid, as she told the court, 'noticed him particularly because he was smoking, and he seemed very small to do that (laughter).' Undefended, Hicks 'cried profusely during the trial, declared his innocence, and said that the witnesses had spoken falsely'. On being found guilty, the judge learned from the local police that Hicks 'had robbed his father several times', in addition to his offence and earlier imprisonment, and was 'a very bad boy'. Sentencing him to three months hard labour, the judge told the lad – who was 'howling frightfully' – that another court appearance would lead to a heavy penal sentence. *Sussex Agricultural Express*, 23 Mar. 1872. Summary returns, ESRO. QR/E1051.

5.   It is impossible to identify which Harmer was referred to; none of the family appear to have been in trouble with officialdom at this stage.

6.   The report threatened to reduce the grant in 1873 unless some improvement was registered across a number of topics; arithmetic was 'not well done' throughout the upper school, the boys 'Upper Reading Standard is not good', and the managers must specifically address 'the absolute failure' among the girls at the sixth standard in composition. Finally, the Inspector insisted that in future a larger proportion of those eligible for examination on attendance criteria, should be entered as candidates. Dated 26 Feb. 1872, ESCRO. ESC.41/1.

7.   Henry was the son of corn-merchant James Thomas. He received his diploma from a college in Dover. *Sussex Agricultural Express*, 27 Apl. 1872.

8.   A non-parishioner too, namely eighty-year-old John Dean, whose connection with Burwash is unknown. As burial fees were doubled for out-parishioners, Egerton's generosity was somewhat muted. ESCRO. Par.284/1/5/2.

9.   By this date agrarian trade unionism had taken off in several parts of the country, and the Warwickshire men, under the soon-to-be legendary Joseph Arch, had already engaged in strike action. Hampshire farmworkers struck in early April, and their action spread to parts of Dorset. In the south-east, April also saw the foundation of the Kent Labourers Union. *The Beehive*, 13 and 20 Apl. 1872. *Kent*

Messenger and Maidstone Telegraph, 13 and 20 Apl. 1872. Egerton's visit to Wiltshire exposed him to ramifications of the movement. Whether Isted's colleagues' more beligerent attitude was affected by unionization, which was everyday and hotly debated national news, is unknown, but the Kent Union did not penetrate Sussex until 1873. See below, p. 135, 22 Feb. 1873.

10.   So-called as Coppard used it for his rate collection rounds.

11.   *Sussex Agricultural Express*, 9 July 1872. The obituary notice said that Fleming had missed only three Sundays since his appointment as organist in 1837. A man of 'cheery manners . . . steady answers, and . . . homely wit. . . . Never himself speaking ill of his fellow men, he made few enemies'. Egerton also praised Fleming in *Sussex Folk*, pp. 42–3, where he added that Fleming had also been 'choirmaster and general music director' for many years; he also composed and was a deft hand at mending musical instruments, and had built the church organ. The latter had to be replaced on Fleming's death, as nobody else understood the workings of the thing. His business as a wigmaker and hairdresser was taken over by a son, who remained choirmaster. Fleming also ran the Post Office, which was taken over by his son-in-law. However, there are surprisingly few references to either father or son in Egerton's diary, and the clergyman invariably had his hair cut on visits to London.

12.   The usual rule that men paid sickness benefits by Friendly Societies received no aid under the Poor Law, was felt by some to discriminate against those who committed parts of hard-earned wages to self-insurance. Here, Egerton clumsily posits a compromise by which recipients of benefit society payments, supplemented from the Poor Law, would mean that income levels during illness were lower for men who did not make independent provision.

13.   Egerton was particularly relieved that under the 1870 Education Act the current National School's accommodation sufficed. This meant that publicly-funded village education would remain under Anglican auspices. The increase of existing accommodation would have to be voluntarily funded, and if this proved inadequate, a compulsory rate would have been obligatory, together with a School Board, which in a place like Burwash was unlikely to see an elected Anglican majority.

14.   Disputes over minor economic matters in rural areas were commonly settled through reference to neutral, but local persons.

15.   William Buss, born 1794, was an agricultural labourer, who joined the chapel in 1820, but resigned after heavy personal involvement in an acerbic – though recurrently experienced among Nonconformist congregations – secession in 1828. Buss became a Calvinist Minister in Mar. 1843, when he took the oath of loyalty to Queen Victoria to secure his preaching licence. 1851 Census. Chapel minutes 1815–95: oath of allegiance, 6 Mar. 1843, ESCRO. NC3/1/2: QR/E891.

16.   All three forms of action, especially the latter two, were common types of both the exaction of private vengeance against an individual, and social protest in rural society. Detecting those responsible was next to impossible, and victims regularly could not be sure into which category they fell.

17.   Matthew had stolen three pears and five apples, valued at 1½d, from John Spencer's orchard, on the 5th. He was fined 5/-, with 1½d damages, and 14/- costs on the 25th, or fourteen days imprisonment in the event of non-immediate payment. Summary returns, ESCRO. QR/E1060.

18.   There is no evidence that this crime was ever solved, and Keeley was not married at St Bartholomew's.

19.   Poor-law authorities usually ruled against payments, even sickness pay, for a

month or two after the harvest and hop-picking seasons, despite the fact that such earnings were commonly absorbed totally in clearing debts with tradesmen.

20.   Disabled men were eligible for outdoor relief, though some more purist Boards of Guardians than that for the Ticehurst Union might well have forced this family to enter the workhouse. Aged thirty-eight, William moved to Burwash from Heathfield in 1864, and this latest addition to his family meant that he had seven children all under the age of 10. 1871, Census.

21.   Mrs Isted had a history of difficult births, including one of the earliest in 1861 when surgeon Combs was paid an additional £2 to his contracted 'midwifery' fee. Board of Guardians, minute, 7 Feb. 1861, ESCRO. G10/1a/9.

1873

1 Jan. . . . A Lamberhurst band playing about. A big drum the chief attraction. The most excrutiating version of "God save the Queen" I ever heard. Pr: at Ch: but no boys came, they following the drum, so they must wait for their money.

[From 7 to 18 Jan. in London.]

22 Jan. . . . C. on old Master Hicks (1/-). . . . He told me a story of some farmer named W.Skinner of ye Bough Farm being outlawed & doing penance in a white sheet in Ch. about . . . 1803. I wonder what it really was, & yet his father he says persuaded ye man to do it. . . .

27 Jan. . . . N.S. 10. I had to strictly admonish certain boys about rudeness & halloaing after Church on Sundays.

3 Feb. Sergt. Hawkins c. to ask for a Subscr. to Police Provident Fund. I gave 10/6. . . .

5 Feb. . . . Snow making ye roads very uncomfortable.

Thurs. 6 Feb. . . . Mr. Frewen's[1] Stag Hounds came over, but people really disappointed. State of ye ground prevented the animal from being unearthed. . . . Effects of ye stag hunt noticeable in ye public houses. Outside ye Bell a man wanted to fight me, & hit me.

21 Feb. . . . buried J[ames] Leaney at 3.15. He buried a pauper[2], & his old apprentice J.Sinden, now our head carpenter followed him to the grave. . . . Wages for day labour raised to 2s 6d a day.[3]

Sat. 22 Feb. . . . A sort of preliminary meeting of The Labourers' union at ye Rose & Crown, but I cd. learn no particulars, except that no resolutions were passed.[4]

17 Mar. . . . C. on Widow Russell. Her s. James ye Publican making her a pauper, selling all her things & sending her into the house to become chargeable: a fond filial proceeding.[5] . . . On ye way home stopped to listen to ye hired orator of the Agricultural Labourers Union a Mr. Nash who was haranguing in ye Admiral yard. Shamefully one sided talk. The Harristocrats & the Farmers the tyrants, the labourers the slaves: the Farmers rolling in luxury, on their pianos, & plate & carpets, 100 & 150 guinea hunters, waggonnettes, dog carts etc, the poor man's children crying for bread. I made a few remarks but Mr. Nash's chief argument was "that's a lie you're a liar" & the like.[6]

19 Mar. . . . Mr. Taylor spoke to me about the bitter feeling of resentment wh. I have aroused by taking notice of two cases of a child being born shortly after marriage. He thinks that marriage condones everything, but what am I to do? One case was that of a member of my choir, another was that of a woman who required me to perform the thanksgiving service for. I did the service, but spoke quietly to her the next day. It does not seem to me that merely for people who to [*sic*] ignore all discipline, is a dereliction of duty on the part of the clergyman, & till I am otherwise advised I must risk the consequences. . . .

22 Mar. . . . A letter from Ed[ucation] Committee of P[rivy] C[ouncil] saying that they cd. not consider our grant till we had given a promise that we wd. have an infant department. . . .

Sun. 23 Mar. . . . Bible Class, 12. It seems that bec[ause] I had to eject young Langridge on Sund. night for troublesomeness & telling a lie, Walter Harmer & [another] Langridge his mates have left also. It does seem impossible to exercise any discipline at all. . . .

24 Mar. . . . Ye Battle Blackbirds viz. a party of 17 men from Battle. Music fair but not more. I away at end of 1st part. People greatly pleased by the cock-crowing, bird imitation etc. just as people who have no taste for high art enjoy caricatures.[7]

25 Mar. Parish meeting, adjourned from the Vestry to the Rose & Crown. Mr. Breach & Mr. Gillham nominated the Guardians. . . . I persuaded Mr. B. to accept the office of Guardian. . . .[8]

26 Mar. . . . C. on St[even] Brown. He informed me that he was now a believer, & that he wished he always had been. He seems to have been unable to accept miracles. We had a long talk & the man really appears to have opened his heart to God's Spirit. . . .

29 Mar. . . . C. on Mrs Coleman (1/-) to sympathise w. her. She has indeed much trouble. Her husband is I fear very unkind & now her son's ill deed completely upsets her. . . .[9]

1 Apl. . . . C. on Mrs Lee (1/-) & had a long t. w. her & her husb: about his not taking work when it was offered him; his version made it seem all right. C. on Mrs Cramp (1/-), poor creature quite ill, sd. I wd. speak to the R[elieving] O[fficer]. . . . C. on "Lyddy" Luck & had a t. She has not slept away from home a single night for 29 years! . . .

5 Apl. . . . Sch: Committee meeting in aft. I offered to build the Night Sch: if the parish wd. keep the school going, but it was doubted whether the parish wd. agree to this as a voluntary rate is an unsavoury thing in Burwash eyes. Philcox however undertook to put it before the parish . . .

14 Apl. I c. on Newton Taylor about some relief cases. . . .

15 Apl. Vestry meeting. Mr. Cramp & Mr. Bourne Ch: Wardens. Mr. Barrow & self the only persons present besides C.Coppard the [rate] Collector. Ch. Loan rate all collected except 6/3. In Ch. Expence Fund a deficiency of £1.19.6 1/4 wh. I paid; the expences about £35. . . .

16 Apl. Rural deaneal conference. . . . Ye Burials Bill allowing Dissenters to be buried in ye Ch. yards w. their own service [previously denied], created much discussion. Mr Orr, Luxford, Howlett . . . & self in favour of ye Toleration [an euphemism for even such a mild ecumenical innovation], but the majority agst. it. . . .

22 Apl. Dr. to Mark Cross to intercede for Thos. Pilbeam who however got a week's imprisonment for stealing two rails value 8d. He asserted that he merely meant to use them to keep the fowls out of his garden & I believed him. However he was convicted. I am truly sorry. I hope it will not make him reckless. . . .

23 Apl. . . . C. on Mrs Pilbeam. Some neighbours subscribed £2 for T.Pilbeam last week, & gave it to his wife on Wed [23rd] morg; this I think says a good deal for his character in spite of his conviction. . . . C. on Mrs J. Isted. She sorely troubled by having been accused of writing to a man & impugning the character of a woman to whom he was engaged. I am sure that the accusation is false. . . .

2 May. . . . 3 boys Edw: Mepham being one not thinking I was at home came birds nesting to a tree near the front door. I saw them opened the door & halloaed their abject terror was most ludicrous, they bolted, & I after them. I caught Mepham. . . .

[10 to 17 May in London and Oxford.]

21 May. . . . Club. Was sorry to see a good many men worse for liquor before dinner, but as they did not dine till nearly 2.30 & did a lot of marching & calling at public houses, the effect of a little drink on empty stomachs is not to be wondered at. However in Ch. the congr: was most orderly & attentive. . . . but one farmer[10] & hardly any tradesmen dined. . . . no speeches or healths tho' Booth very full, & people seemed enjoying themselves. I away soon after 5. C. on Mrs J.Isted, she in great trouble about having to move. Isted came in from ye Club quite sober. . . .

22 May. . . . D. w. ye Club at Russells at ye Wheel. Very quiet, about 56 members. No speeches again, & Mr. Jarvis as yesterday ye only farmer, & he only because he is also butcher & supplies the meat. I away about 4. . . . An interview w. John Sawyers who I fear has bad companionship being going down lately, however he penitent & I hope in a better frame of mind. . . .

[27 May to 7 June in Wiltshire; on 2 June 'w. to Nunton & had an amusing convers[ation] w. two travelling chair menders. Agri[cultural] Lab. Union, not by my starting by their's: sensible men. . . .'[11]]

9 June. Sch. C. on Mrs Isted, her change of house is indeed a trial, as the rooms are close & small. . . .

18 June. . . . Have allowed Sally Isted to sleep at ye Rectory, seeing how small & close their house is, & how hot the weather is. . . .

20 June. . . . C. on Mr. Gibbs. . . . Convers[ation] on Cottages. He as usual dead agst. ye poor, & holds firmly to the doctrine that things will right themselves, & that interference [through statutory means] is impossible. . . . C. on Edmonds (6d). He belongs to a club, one of the rules of wh. is that members receiving sick pay at ye end of ye year are not re-elected. He has been in it many years, & in a fortnight will be stranded. He spoke w. no apparent perception of the absurdity of such a club . . .[12]

23 June. . . . C. on Mr. Taylor & paid interest in ye "cottages purchase money".[13] Oddly enough Mrs Parsons . . . described her cottage wh. she holds under Mr. Gibbs in the very terms I had been describing in horrible ones to him, of course he doesn't know the state it is in, but the coincidence is singular.[14]

24 June. . . . I c. & R. w. old Master Edwards of Rye Green. 68 years ago he lived as a boy w. Mr. Pattenden at Bateman's. I asked whether he had ever heard of any tradition as to who built Bateman's. He said he had not, but Mr. Pattenden had told him that at that time men worked for a penny a day! that somebody wanted to bate [abate] them something even of that, so the house was known as Bateman's![15] . . . C. on Mrs Relf, née Harriat Whybourne, not long married & looked very happy. House so low that she says her husband generally goes out of doors to put his coat on! . . .

25 June. Harry Rochester this morg. ceased to be pupil teacher, his engagement broken by reason of his grossly disobedient & idle conduct, his failure at his exams, & his continual tyrannizing over the boys. The Comm[ittee] of [the Privy] Council requests us to terminate ye eng[agement]. . . .

27 June. . . . In aft. to Osbornes to see about some fruit. Found them clearing out a stack bottom. 2 little girls & 3 little boys aiding with sticks to help kill ye mice & rats. Cruel amusement; killed 59 rats in about 40 minutes. What depredations ye farmers submit to thro' rats?

28 June. . . . Going home a long chat w. S. Pope jr; he says that in Burwash a carter may come away from ye stables by 8 o'Cl. AM, & need not go again till 5PM & then it is only to feed ye horses. . . . He thinks labourers wd. not have got their rise in wages but for the Union Club as he called it. . . .

3 July. . . . C. on . . . Mrs D. Edwards who seemed like the woman "who had so many children she didn't know what to do". . . .

5 July. Married Ch. Wm. Seamer, a bricklayer & Joanna Barden; bridegroom had been drinking & ye brides father also, such work upsets me. Ye bride a nice respectable looking girl. . . .

7 July. A young man John Thomas Hicks came up about a testimonial to Character for keeping a beer house. . . .

8 July. . . . C. on Mrs Ellis, her little boy aged 4 amuses himself & others much by going thro' the Ch: Service in ludicrous imitation of me. . . . C. on Master Harmer ye carter (1/-). He down w. a broken leg, broken by Joe Barden last night in a drunken fit. Sad goings on. . . . Signed testimonial for Reuben Walter for public house. . . .

9 July. Sch: only 41. The rest had taken French leave for ye Forester's Club. Ye band came up & played a selection from Martha at ye Rect. I dined w. them at 2 o'Clock. . . . Some good music. A few speeches & me away. . . .

10 July. . . . Master Weekes so Mr. Barrow tells me rails at me pretty much in ye public house for writing to Mr. Langridge about [farmer] Mr. Weekes annoyance to Miss Roger. Stupid old man, he must be stopped.

11 July. Sch: Aft. d. to ye Common. Took a class in Sch. Ditton ye Police Constable came in to frighten some children who had been bullying others on their way home. A Miss Hicks was put upon her defence. Why did you hit her (i.e. Miss Bowner) Please Sir She said I stunk! Verdict Guilty but under circumstances of much provocation. . . . Opened negotiations w. a Mr. H. Law[rence] Hussey of Putney Heath for letting this house for a month [in the summer].

14 July. . . . In evg. Mr. Taylor came up & t. about many things. He said that notice had been taken of Sally Isted's sleeping at the Rectory. It shows how little even an act of kindness is to be misunderstood.

15 July. . . . C. on Mrs Straker (?) in Bell Alley. Has been here about a fortnight, & already has been begging at Ashlands.

16 July. . . . Long t. w. Brusher Langridge & wife about their relief being taken off – he earns 21/6 & his boy 6/-. I don't expect that at present the board will restore it. . . .

18 July. . . . C. & R. w. Old Mrs Thompsett (6d) & put 6d in her Wesleyan Missionary box, the object of wh. she did not in the least understand, but thought it merely a box wh. Miss Simes had very kindly given her.

23 July. . . . Funeral of Bishop's child aged 15 m[onths]. Clarke tells me that it is said that [Egerton's dog] Rover upset the child wh. brought on an inflammation & mortification!! I was c. in to see old Stephen Brown who in a fit of low spirits had tried poor man to hang himself. He was all but gone, but I staid about an hour & 3/4, & in that time had come round a good deal. C. & t. w. his son Wm. who is also ill.

24 July. . . . C. on Brown who has quite revived. . . .

25 July. Sch: I asked F. Russell what was the meaning of "Ghost" a propos to the word in ye Catechism. He answered, "Something what people imagine". . . .

26 July. Yesterday being over St. James day the hop question is settled according to the old say[ing] "Till St. James's day be come & gone, There may be hops or may be none". We now look for a good half crop. . . .

6 Aug. C. on Mrs J.Isted in her new house. 3 beds in one room, & Sally sleeping in ye [kitchen] downstairs. It is too close. Mrs Isted quite poorly. I sat unnecessarily long.

9 Aug. . . . The trial Honeysett v. Fuller for £1000 damages for loss incurred thro' his mismanagement as bailiff on at Croydon today. Verdict for defendant. An iniquitous action, never ought to have been brought at all . . .[16]

11 Aug. . . . Heard from Mr. Fuller about ye trial.

29 Aug. . . . Two Burwash Commoners got punished today at H[urst] Green. Master Edward Hayward getting 6 weeks for an assault, & D.Edwards a fine of £5: both richly deserved.[17] Old Master Weekes had up for using threatening language to Capt. Roger. Willy Hicks came out of Lewes gaol, what he will do but relapse poor lad I cannot say.

[In Wiltshire from 4 to 6 Sept., before 9 Sept. to 4 Oct. trip, by coaster, to Scotland, and back overland via Bunbury, Cheshire.]

9 Oct. Poor Mr. John Coppard Snr. who was at Ch. last night died suddenly this morg. about 8. He was entirely a self-made man, but had risen to a high position of credit & trust amongst his fellow men. . . . will be much missed.[18]

11 Oct. . . . I drove Mr. Philcox to Brightling; followed Mr. Coppard's funeral; large following. . . .

24 Oct. . . . N.S. only 17 as a Labourers Union meeting had been advertised at ye Wheel. I came by on my way back at about 8.20 & no deputation [of speakers] had come then, & some of the men seemed to "doubt whether he wd. do much good if he did come".[19]

4 Nov. Sch. D. with Mrs Irwin. She asks what can be done to close ye sweet shops on Sundays, we must try . . .

5 Nov. . . . coming thro' ye village in ye evg. I was hit by young Master Farley w. a squib in ye back of ye neck, but not hurt. . . . To H[urst] Green to dine w. Mrs Hussey. We waited till 8.15 to see ye Bonfire procession & an effigy of George Noakes & ye inscription "From ye pond to ye fire", cleverly done, as also ye masks of ye mummers. Hundreds of people present. . . .[20]

18 Nov. C. on Mrs Hook. Ye new cott[age] wh. is being built will be better, their present one is horrible. . . . N.S. 21. . . .

24 Nov. . . . I c. on Mrs J.Isted whose baby aged 14 months died this morg. . . .

27 Nov. . . . I buried Mrs Isted's child. . . .

29 Nov. . . . I c. on Mrs J.Isted, gave 2/6 towards funeral expense. . . .

8 Dec. . . . Poor Mr. John Fuller comes in only a common creditor on John Honeysett's estate, & has to accept 6d in the pound for his £270. It is a cruel shame. . . .

16 Dec. . . . N.S. so, small that I did not take the money & dismissed ye scholars at 8.30. . . .

Notes

1.   The Frewens were big landowners at Northiam, some eight miles to the east.
2.   Aged seventy-six. Unlike many long-established tradesmen, Leaney clearly had not, or provided inadequately, for his retirement, and spent his last years in the workhouse.
3.   No doubt an attempted pre-emptive thrust as agrarian trade unionist activities intensified both regionally and nationally.
4.   This comprised part of the Kent Labourers' Union push across the county border, but as yet its own newspaper, the *Kent Messenger and Maidstone Telegraph*, made no mention of its progress. At this juncture none of the near ninety branches were outside Kent, in the published listings, and other details, but a representative of the 'Sussex District of the Kent Union' was present at meetings of several agrarian Unions held under the auspices of the London Trades Council, in the capital, at the end of Mar. ibid., 1 Feb. and 1 and 29 Mar. 1873.
5.   James Russell, of the Wheel. Ironically, while such action was possible, children of workhouse inmates could be forced by the courts to make a contribution towards, or to cover the costs of residential provision for aged parents.
6.   Egerton's observations, and even his language – notably 'hired orator' – were almost identical to the bulk of the press, which was hostile. Nash's career began with the chairmanship of the Cranbrook Branch, and he came to the fore over the fierce debate within the union after Joseph Arch's much more famous National Agricultural Labourers' Union poached the Kent's Wealden members, and even took over several West Kent branches. Nash's appointment as a paid delegate, responsible for lecturing at meetings held with the intention of creating new branches, commenced earlier in the year. These inaugural proceedings were commonly vitriolic, and Anglican clergymen in a number of villages intervened against unionization. For example, at Bethersden at the end of Feb. the General Secretary Alfred Simmons spoke against a 'continuous volley of abuse and interruption', and the Revd Clemenson formally moved 'that the meeting was very sorry "a stranger" had come there to interfere with the good feeling that had always existed between master and men'. There is no report of the Burwash meeting in the Union's newspaper, but the relevant issue is missing from the British Library's file. *Kent Messenger and Maidstone Telegraph*, 25 Jan., 1 Feb. and 8 Mar. 1873. *Tonbridge Free Press*, 8 and 15 Feb. 1873. Reporting a big rally at Wadhurst, the *Sussex Agricultural Express*, 22 Mar. 1873, denounced the speaker's 'clap-trap', and – in common with other reports – stressed that instead of encouraging 'good feeling' between farmers and their workers, the union had precisely the opposite intention.
7.   The Battle Blackbirds were 'a new body of minstrels' who performed before 'a crowded audience of all classes' in the school; the first half comprised songs 'interspersed with various comic dialogues, knotty questions, and conundrums, in the true nigger style'. The second half, missed by Egerton, opened with a flute solo, and was followed by dances, a 'comic sketch', and finally the audience was invited to join in with comic songs, accompanied by a banjo. *Sussex Advertiser*, 2 Apl. 1873.
8.   Guardianships were on the whole unpopular offices, especially so in larger villages, with greater numbers of potential claimants. Although elective, very few contests took place after 1840.
9.   Fifteen-year-old Thomas, employed for the past five months as living-in servant, with special responsibilities for looking after dairy cattle, at Burnt House Farm by Thomas Bartholomew, had developed a reputation for beastiality. As his

workmate William Langridge said, he had 'heard some people talk about it', but 'had never seen him do it before' 10 Mar. when, for 'about three or four minutes' he watched Thomas in the cow lodge, standing on a milking stool 'leaning forward over the hind part of the Cow. The Flaps of his Trousers were down I saw his Person . . . he was attempting to put part of his person in the Cow'. Bartholomew had caught Thomas in similar circumstances with the same cow – 'a gentle one' – some weeks ago, and reprimanded him, but as 'I thought he would not do it again . . . let it drop', as 'I did not wish to hurt him', by which he meant wreck his reputation at a very early age. This time Bartholomew sacked, and then prosecuted Thomas, who was committed to the Quarter Sessions on 27 Mar., only to be acquitted on 8 Apl. Depositions by Langridge and Bartholomew, ESCRO. QR/E1061. *Sussex Advertiser*, 9 Apl. 1873.

10.   A reflection of the growth of agrarian trades unionism, as at the Wheel the following day, where the only farmer was the dual occupationist, Alfred Jarvis.

11.   There is every probability that these two characters tried to bait Egerton, as Anglican clergymen were among the most outspoken opponents of agrarian unionism throughout the country.

12.   An exemplar of that numerous category of village benefit clubs, of ephemeral duration and dubious worth for precisely that type of self-defeating rule described here.

13.   Presumably the interest on whatever financial arrangement underpinned the cottages purchased, referred to above.

14.   It was commonly claimed that the owners of larger estates were ignorant as to the condition of workers' cottages which they rented out, not least as neither owners, nor even their stewards, ever inspected them.

15.   Doubtlessly apocryphal, though commensurate with the cynical outlook of many Burwash working folk. Recounted in *Sussex Folk*, p. 59.

16.   A complicated case which became something of a *cause célèbre*, commencing with an action in the Tunbridge Wells County Court in May, by Fuller for non-payment of expenses, whereupon Honeysett brought a counter-case at Kent Assize, from whence the case was removed for trial to the Surrey Assizes. One judge repeatedly asked lawyers representing both sides to reach an out-of-court agreement, as parts of the case revealed somewhat bizarre goings on, including a private investigator, an ex-member of the Metropolitan Police, being despatched to report on technical agrarian matters.

In 1855 John Honeysett inherited fifty-five-acre Dudwell Farm from his father. Honeysett retained his London coal-merchanting business, and for some of the intervening eighteen years the farm was managed by brother Edwin. In 1870 John Fuller, something of a failure as he was sometime schoolmaster, subsequently a grocer and draper, then a 'house agent', and currently highway surveyor, took over the management. The court cases hinged on Fuller's management of three hop-gardens of some five and a half acres, and as hops were such a notoriously fickle crop there was ample room for argument and counter-argument, which involved farmers, tradesmen, permanent and temporary workers (including women hop-tyers), from Burwash and adjacent villages, in addition to the private detective. The case finally involved the jury, 'mostly London men . . . [who] knew nothing about hops', as the foreman said whilst deciding that Honeysett had failed to establish a legally-binding contract with Fuller. *Sussex Advertiser*, 13 and 27 Aug. 1873. The case at least contributed to Honeysett's bankruptcy; see below, p. 141, 8 Dec. 1873.

17.   There was more to this than Egerton appreciated. Etchingham was the scene of

some excitement over the execution of a distress warrant by a Tunbridge Wells County Court bailiff, William Dampier, on local farmer William Elphick; his wife, Frances, assaulted the officer, and was fined £1 2s. 6d. on pain of fourteen days' imprisonment at the same Petty Sessions. The reason behind Hayward's and Edwards' presence in Etchingham had something to do with the execution of the warrant. Later that day, an unidentified elderly 'man came down the road [provocatively] singing a song'; Edwards emerged from the Eagle Inn, 'knocked him down', and continued to beat him. Joseph Young, repairing a fence on the railway embankment, intervened, whereupon Edwards called him a '—— navvy'. At this point Hayward pitched in, whereupon Edwards and Young 'had a fair fight for five or six rounds', a somewhat novel appreciation as Young 'had marks of teeth on the eye brow'.

During this mêlée, signalman Blaver went to investigate, only to be attacked by Hayward. This fight was progressing when ringing bells announced the imminent arrival of the 5p.m. train, with the necessity to close the level crossing gates. Hayward held on to Blaver, and if it had not been for the 'office lad' Oyles' dash to close the gates the signalman 'don't know what the consequence might have been'. Blaver fought free, returned to his signal box, pursued by Hayward who 'challenged me to a fight'. This invitation declined, Edwards and Hayward left the scene. When PC Tobutt arrived, he went to the Wheel Inn on Burwash Common and arrested both men on their identification by the station master. Hayward received a six-week hard labour term for assaulting Blaver, and a £1 fine plus 13/6 costs, or a further three weeks for assaulting Young. Hayward served both terms. Edwards' fine and costs for assaulting Young totalled the very heavy sum of £5-13-6, to be paid immediately or one month's hard labour. *Sussex Agricultural Express*, 9 Sept. 1873. Summary returns, ESCRO. QR/E1063.

18.   The generous obituary published in the *Sussex Advertiser*, 15 Oct. 1873, described Coppard as a farmer, with forty years experience first as salaried assistant-overseer, and then as rate-collector. His involvement in poor-law matters 'reached back to a time anterior to the passing of the existing poor law [1834]; to times . . . of frequent and great agricultural depression, and when the collecting of rates and management of parish affairs were matters of much greater difficulty than is the case . . . now. Often he has been heard to contrast 'the stormy, angry meetings held . . . in former times . . . and . . . the comparative smoothness indeed friendliness of similar meetings in the present day. . . . Coppard's lengthened experience gave weight to his opinions on all parochial subjects. His suggestions were always of a sound, practical character, and never failed . . . to be properly appreciated'.

19.   The Kent Union's second annual demonstration at Maidstone on 14 May 1873, attracted 11,000 workers and their families, including some 500 from Sussex. In the late spring and early summer, new Sussex branches included that at Crowborough, which the National tried to poach. By the autumn, farmers' defence associations had formed, with over a hundred unionists sacked and evicted from their tied cottages. The Union responded by supporting these victims, and stepping-up its emigration scheme. Etchingham and Wadhurst were represented at a delegate meeting in late July, and new branches created in Sussex over the summer, included those at Hailsham, Willingdon and Pevensey. The meeting to formally create a branch at Burwash was scheduled for 20 Sept., during Egerton's absence on holiday. The British Library's file of the union's newspaper ends with the issue of 8 Nov. 1873, and the reduced sources are silent on the union's activities in East Sussex, until the

new year, again covered by the union's press. *Kent Messenger and Maidstone Telegraph*, 3 and 17 May, 14 June, 2 and 30 Aug. 1873 *Sussex Agricultural Express*, 6, 20 and 27 May, and 17 June 1874.

20.   George Noakes, a 'retired farmer' and widower with ten children, in his early fifties, had moved from Burwash to Etchingham on his marriage to a widow in 1870. Marital difficulties, including Noakes' allegations of his wife's adultery with any number of candidates including innkeeper Pratt, the Revd Barton, the Rector of Etchingham, and either or both of his two sons, led to public altercations during which blows were exchanged between the couple, though the 'great deal of partisan spirit' subsequently raised, was principally directed against Noakes. He was subjected to traditional 'rough music' at midnight on 2 August 1873 when an assembly of masked people 'with tin kettles, and trays, horns and draining pipes', surrounded his house, allegedly encouraged by his wife. Later, a party returned, led by Henry and Arthur Barton, who broke into the house, tied up, and dragged Noakes down the stairs, threw him over the garden fence 'like a faggot', before tossing him into a pond and keeping him there for half an hour. Enjoined to treat his wife like a Christian, Noakes replied 'I was not a Christian', and he got another ducking. Six men, mysteriously excluding the Barton brothers, were fined £5 each for assaulting Noakes, while Noakes himself was fined £3 for assaulting his wife; charges of 'profane speech and scandalous language' on 24 and 29 July against him, were dropped. Guy Fawkes celebrants commonly substituted the effigy of the local and topically infamous. *Sussex Advertiser*, 1 Oct. 1873 and 24 Mar. 1874. *Sussex Agricultural Express*, 21 Mar. 1874.

1874

Sun. 4 Jan. . . . Went down to ye school to speak to ye boys about throwing stones at ye Chimney pot & breaking ye tiles. . . .

23 Jan. . . . [Somebody he does not identify] told me that a good deal of beer raffling during ye prohibited hours [viz. during Church Services] on Sunday goes on at one of ye public houses in Burwash.

23 Jan. . . . C. on ye Pooles. Knocked on ye door just as ye mother was threatening her child that if he didn't drop a certain stick, she'd lay it across his head, see how he liked that!? . . .

28 Jan. . . . [At Pashley for dinner] Uncle told me of two cases of overcrowding in Ticehurst & Flimwell in one wh. ye father occupied ye same bed as his two nearly grown up daughters, in ye other ye mother occ[upied] ye same bed as her two nearly grown up sons. I could not have imagined it. . . .

3 Feb. . . . C. on Mrs Sands; her little child the other day put its hand into the hopper of a turnip cutter, & a little Eastwood child next door duly began to turn the handle, but Sands child beginning to cry out, the one at the handle fled, & no more mischief was done. . . .

10 Feb. . . . C. & P. w. Mrs Maskall of ye Forge, gave her 4/- as ye rats last night eat a sovereigns worth of little chickens wh. the person whom she deputed to cover them up, she herself being nearly confined, did not do properly. . . .3 cottages at ye Forge empty.[1] Bought a loaf yesterday of Sally Isted's bakery, it was excellent bread.[2] . . . Mr. J.B.Noakes disgusted at Gladstone's minority. Encouragement of Popery. Vexation of tradesmen by Adulteration act, & by difficulties thrown in their way about the Grocers Wine License.[3]

12 Feb. . . . C. & had serious t. w. Moor (1/-) carter at Quayham [Farm]. Hurt his foot & nearly broke his neck a short time since. He professed his perfect ability to give up drink at any moment he liked, & also his complete knowledge that getting drunk is wrong. He half promised to make a fresh start. C. on Mrs J.Barden & her 5 daughters next door. Met old Weeks on ye road, drunk, he tackled me, & followed me ever so far, abusing me freely. Troublesome old man.

17 Feb. . . . I c. on Mr. Gibbs to speak for G[eorge] Baker who is accused, I think on very slight evidence, of taking some money from ye till at ye Rose & Crown.[4]. . . C. & R. w. Mrs Pope (1/-). Terribly Hottentot family. Cats live up in ye garret wh. is never cleaned out, ye d. w. illeg. ch. a sad girl. . . .

18 Feb. Sch: C. on Mrs Langridge, about her boy being away from sch: She used very big language, about her being persecuted, & trusting to God for help, all bec[ause] her boy had been caned. I cannot quite swallow such talk. . . .

10 Mar. . . . Buried Mrs Collins who survived her removal from her cottage [to the workhouse] only about a fortnight. . . .

14 Mar. . . . Met Mr. Barton who is a great [illegible] talking about ye action brought agst. him by George Noakes. The man a great brute bringing the most unfounded charges agst. all sorts of people & using horribly obscene lang[uage]. Still when men go into his house, pull him out of bed, duck him in a horse pond, tho' he deserves it all morally, they legally get into a mess. . . .[5]

20 Mar. . . . I took a class in sch: It seems impossible to assume that the ch[ildren] know anything. C. on Mrs Fairway & husb. they in great hope that Mr. Philcox will let them succeed their mother in ye farm, but they have no capital & ye farm will need £1000. C. on Mrs G.Harmer, pleaded hard for Sunday [observance]. Ye old man there: he said he had heard in his early days as far off at Fareham nr. Gosport talking of Burwash Wheel as the roughest public house they were ever in. . . .[6]

21 Mar. . . . C. on Shearman, & took his son a Bible & prayer & hymn book: he is to pay me a shilling: they cost me two. A long talk w. his father in ye field, he is Chairman of our branch of ye Ag[ricultural] Lab. Union: he says there are 74 members in Burwash. He is an intelligent man, & thinking of going to Queensland after hopping. . . .[7]

23 Mar. . . . C. on Mrs Isted (6d), she dangerously well. . . .Ye Guardians are now beginning a plan of giving Tickets to ye children of permanent paupers [those on permanent outdoor relief] wh. they must get filled up to certify that they have been at school.[8] A troublesome tramp wd. not leave ye back door, so Charlotte summoned me; he soon made tracks.

25 Mar. . . . To parish meeting; adj[ourned] to ye Bear: very amicable & comfortable. I dined, Whatman, Bourne, Jarvis, W.Kemp, J.Fuller, C.Coppard, Barrow, C.Taylor, Cramp, Mr. Love & Mr. Smith ye Corn dealer dined.

27 Mar. . . . Overtook & w. some way w. Mrs (Widow) "Cur-nata". She rather compromised my dignity by calling out to a man at a Cottage, "I've got a fresh sweetheart tonight, you mustn't tell any body"! . . .

30 Mar. . . . I attended a meeting at ye Bear for going thro' the relief list. Long discussion on some of ye cases, chiefly on those of chronic invalids who are supposed to be able to do some work. It is very difficult to do justice in these cases. . . .

2 Apl. . . . c. on Mrs J.Isted & told her that all her relief was taken off. . . .

13 Apl. Sch. Somebody again has stolen money during ye holydays. I offered 10/- reward: it is very sad. . . .

7 May. . . . Labourers Union meeting at ye Wheel. . . .

18 May. C. on Mrs J.Isted. In trouble again, has had to take Annie from Mrs Rogers thro' ill health, & that has riled ye R's who are very cross. . . .[9]

19 May. . . . C. at Hicks beer shop to threaten to report him for serving Mr. Fairway's carter who was already drunk: this drew his business & horrible lang[uage] on to me. . . .

Wed. 20 May. . . . aft. Serv. Cong: larger than usual & most satisfactorily attentive. . . . I pr. from Gal. 6 2 & spoke about ye Unions. . . .[10]

[22 to 30 May in Wiltshire. . . . 'Poor Rover died of kidney disease on Tues: night [26th]. I miss him sadly'.]

1 June. . . . Hyland & Hazelden came up to consult about ye Benefit Clubs, some members of wh. irregularly passed a resolution last Friday [29th] to shift ye meetings to ye Public House, & to stage [share] out ye Rescue fund! We called on Daw, & had a long t. He holds the money, & as the Club is not enrolled dealing in ye money & restraining dealing in it, is not easy. . . .[11]

2 June. . . . I dr. to Haviland's, gave Mrs Hazleden a lift from Pont's to ye Crown where ye Club was going on. Labourers' Union discussed at ye meeting. . . .[12]

4 June. . . . To the great joy of the village, the Buss family starting to Canada. . . .[13]

8 June. . . . Had a long t. in ye road . . . w. Ben Thompson, about matters concerning myself & my parishioners. I believe that the only people in ye parish who are not friends w. me are people to whom I have been obliged to speak about wrongdoing.

9 June. . . . Took ye funeral of poor [William] Ellis. First death of a member of the Hearts of Oak Club since its establishment 4 or 5 years ago, so the other members attended ye funeral in sashes. . . .

10 June. Ye Bishop came about 10. I took him round ye [Rectory] gardens wh. he admired. I carried ye crozier before him from ye Rectory to ye Church! & I was rather awkward with it. Serv. at 11. We presented 28 boys & 35 girls, & one boy (Gilbert) surrupticiously presented himself; Etchm. 22, Stonegate 15. Service delightfully orderly & reverent. Ye Bishop's address from St John 14 3. Very simple, very practical, very earnest & impressive. Hands laid on two at a time, & then they went away. I enjoyed the service much. After ye Confirmation ended ye Bishop congratulated ye new piece on the north side of Ch: yard. he, clergy, & choir w. round ye new part reading ye 49th Ps. Ye Bishop then offered prayer & signed ye deed in ye Church. . . . I carried back ye Crozier w. his lordship in procession to ye Rect. & thought I might have had to use it agst. an ill-intentioned bullock. . . .

12 June. . . . To ye School to preside over ye Club meeting. A few wanted to share out the revenue fund & some more to hold ye meetings up to Hallaways [the Railway Inn], ye latter prop[osition] rejected by 9 to 5, a number not voting, & ye former prop: dropped at last. Some very incisive & pointed talk. . . .

23 June. . . . C. & R. w. Lulham. He going to T[unbridge] Wells Police Force instead of Metropolitan. . . .

25 June. Sch. Aft. d[inner] c. on Mrs Pater (1/-) housekeeper to Master Budd. Widow w. 2 Ch[ildren]. Battle [Poor Law] Union very strict: won't allow anything for ye ch: out of ye house.[14]

6 July. C. on Mrs Isted. Gone with Farley for a drive to Ticehurst! All this freedom I believe owing to ye taking off of ye relief. She is now not afraid of being seen about. . . .

18 July. Sent for before br[eakfast] to see ye police Sergt: Hawkins . . . & his wife, both very ill. . . . C. again on Sergt. H; poor man dying.

19 July. Poor Sergt. H died last night at 10. Leaves 10 ch.[15]

23 July. . . . [at Frittenden, just across the Kent border] A few speeches & a great deal of chaff about Burwash as an unknown place supposed to be peopled by higglers & fair cart people. I don't think Frittenden got much change out of me. . . .

19 Aug. To ye schools: advised by boys & girls to shut up [close school]

owing to short attendance. . . . Mr Lewns c. w. Mr. Barns about a concert
on behalf of widow of Sergt. Hawkins . . .

21 Aug. . . . C. & R. w. [Irish, eighty-one-year-old] Mrs Riley (1/-). She
the most hopelessly ignorant person I have had to visit. R. Catholic, no
Pater-noster, no Ava-Marie, no anything. Says she cannot read because she
always had to mind her mother's turkeys! I asked her whether she had
thought about another world, she said No. I read another verse or two &
tried to explain, but the attempt seemed hopeless. Mrs Whatman there. C.
on Mrs Pennells (1/-). She very grumbling about ye parish pay being taken
off. . . . Watched a cricket match in Hicks field. C. on Mrs J[ame]s Braban
(1/-). The eldest of ye 2 ds. not in, having gone to try to get a place at Mrs
Kingston! I spoke to ye younger & persuaded her to try to get a place & not
to stay at home eating & drinking at her parents expense. Ye mother told
me a number of statements wh. she asserted were facts about the relief given
to families near. One does not like to encourage talk of one cottager against
another, but how is one to get a truth, if one never lets people speak. . . .

22 Aug. To Mrs Riley. Ye priest had just been from Mayfield, but ye old
lady professed not to like him or understand him, & no wonder as they say
he prayed in Latin to her. . . .

24 Aug. A man of ye name of Shearman of ye most appropriate [nick] name
"Ladder back" being very tall & upright, c. on me to get signature to
emigration papers. Ye Union helps him.[16]

26 Aug. . . . Concert good. Mr. J.Carleton really amusing not vulgar as a
Comic Singer. Mr. Slaughter (tenor) a nice voice, but lacking education
[training]. Mr. Duke pl[ayed] ye Eng[lish] Concertina simply but very
pleasantly. . . . A Mons[ieur] Pilbane a little Frenchman at ye Piano &
played "les Hirondelles par Streich" an old piece of Luigs. . . . Took
£8-11-6 for Hawkins widow. . . . I read out a letter of thanks from Mrs
Hawkins. . . .[17]

28 Aug. . . . Shearman came in & took leave.

[31 Aug to 25 Sept. in Scotland.]

28 Sept. . . . Met Whitaker in ye Street. I fear I have annoyed him by not
making some explicit arrangements when I went away, & so it seems
obliging him to take instructions from Mr. C[ourthope], but I honestly
thought that he wd. have settled such little matters w. Towers & Banks
without my intervention.[18]

30 Sept. [Harvest festival service]. . . . Wm. Weekes in liquor & trying to
sit along side Mrs F.Newton was prevented by Mr. Whatman & then began

to holloa: he was led out fortunately during ye singing: he assaults Mr. W. Mrs Sawyers fainted & there was a great tup; but it being while the sing[ing] was drowning it, it was not so noticeably distressing. . . .

29 Oct. . . . Old Mrs Thompson of Bell Alley died of wounds inflicted last Sunday [24th] by her idiotic grandson. . . .

30 Oct. . . . St Ph. Sch: took cl. Spoke about insubordination of a Master Harmer who being caned by Miss Press, & pleaded "that he shd. be all right if he'd got a teacher with any sense to teach him, why cd. n't she take his class": next day he threatened to do to the teachers what he had done to Miss Press, so he was ejected. . . . C. on Edwd: Harmer about his boy, not in. . . . Old Weekes has got a fortnight at Lewes [Gaol].[19] [Inquest] Verdict of died of wounds infl[icted] by her gr.s. he not being of sound mind, in case of old Mrs Th. . . .[20]

4 Nov. . . . I to Tithe dinn[er] Fair att[endance]. I said a few words expl[aining] that the average pr[ice] of Wheat, Barley & Oats during the last 7 yrs rules ye rise or fall of ye tithe, that this years rise I was sorry for . . . £20 gross.[21] . . . I spent £200 last year out of my own pocket to save ye ratepayers a school rate. . . . A good deal of chaff, but all very good humoured.

9 Nov. . . . C. on Mrs W.Isted (1/-). Prospect for ye winter bad enough to drive a woman almost to despair. . . . N.S. at St. Ph. 14 & very orderly & attentive. . . .

10 Nov. Sch . . . & looked over copy books. Some very amusing; one boy Albert Lusted, the most muddle headed narrator of events I think I ever met w. . . .

12 Nov. An uncivil Post Card from Wm. Kemp complaining of my "clouting" his son. I had on Tues. [10th] punished his S. for telling a lie, having publicly asked the class what it was for & they answered for telling a lie. Moreover I gave the boy two chances of proving that he told the truth. I to c. on Mr. Kemp, not at h[ome]. Saw Mrs & expl[ained] matters to her; they both Mr. & Mrs under a wrong impress[ion] as to fact. . . .

1 Dec. To St. Phil. to ye sch. Took ye juvenile class & Miss Sophia had ye 1st. Master Robert Kemp came back after having made apparently a reasonable submission. . . .

11 Dec. To St. Phil. Sch: Something must be done about ye children being late – 29 late yest[erday] morg. . . . C. on Tom Cramp. Cd. not get in. C. on ye Jones at ye rocks; poor people gone into ye house. . . .

17 Dec. . . . C. on Mrs Wm. Pope at ye Shrub to see about a reconciliation between her d. Harriet & her hus: Wm. Holmes: not much chance I fear. She in "ye House". He violent temper, she dirty, both immoral, I didn't know what to do. Their first night was in Novr. they slept in ye open air under a hedge.[22]

20 Dec. To St. Ph: roads very bad & slippery. I was a little late at starting owing to having to shave after breakfast! for the sake of hot water. I was delayed by writing my banns in the book at ye Ch; by Mr. Taylor stopping me to speak about a family up at Witherendon, he c. them Collins; they are Crofts, then by Mary Jeffreys serv[an]t at Laurelhurst stopped me to descant upon dear Miss Nellie's virtues. I cd. not well return . . . & ye end was that I was 7 mins. late at Ch; A thing I have never done I believe before in 20 years duty. . . .

21 Dec. To ye dole for a time. . . .

23 Dec. Mr. Brand & I attended to business about settlements;[23] all smooth. . . .

26 Dec. . . . saw . . . Mr. & Mrs Gadd . . . in ye street, they have left ye public h[ouse], & he is to work at his trade; better indeed. . . . C. on Mrs J.Isted, had to tell her that John her son & I cd. hit it off no longer at ye singing. I am sorry, but he is very troublesome. . . . Mr. S[impson] told me ye parish are going to make me some present, it is very kind of them. . . . ye street seemed noisy but Lusted told me that there was not so much doing at ye "houses" on Thurs. night Xmas Eve as often on a common Sat. night. . . .

27 Dec. . . . I published my own banns. It was rather a curious sensation, but I don't fancy that I betrayed any sanction. . . .[24]

Notes

1.   An unusual phenomenon, as heavy working-class demand for cottages was reflected in shortages throughout the nineteenth century at Burwash, and at least up until the 1850s and '60s in even the most advantaged Wealden parishes.
2.   This is the first mention of Sally Isted's bakery business, and there is no evidence as to how it was funded. Perhaps she took over an existing business, but the bakery trade required little capital, and was a traditional transitional stage for working-class folk's ascent into the lowest ranks of the shopocracy. Mrs Isted seems to have become involved in the enterprise, and ran it after Sally's marriage in 1880 after which she moved away. Egerton carefully patronized all the village bakers, who took it in turns to supply the Rectory. See below, esp. pp. 234, 288, 296, at 12 Nov. 1880, 7 June 1883 and 5 Jan. 1884.
3.   For the grocers' predicament see below, p. 160, 9 and 16 July 1875.

4.   Again Egerton's intervention on behalf of the accused was unsuccessful. Baker was charged with the theft of two florins at the pub on 3 Feb. He had been remanded to appear at the Petty Sessions in early Mar. The evidence against him was weak. When the landlady 'heard our money drawer creak', she called her husband, who checked the drawer, and believed that two florins were missing. Landlord Littlemore told Baker, 'If you don't give up the money I will give you in charge', and when Baker refused said 'I will send for a policeman and have you searched', whereupon Baker tried to leave, and was stopped by J. Sindell, a soldier home on leave. Sergeant Hawkins arrived on the scene, and a search of Baker revealed two florins, with an additional three shillings plus some halfpence. Nobody saw him take the money, and John Relf, called as a defence witness, stated that a florin had just been given in change to another customer, who had since left. Baker was found guilty, and given a light sentence of three weeks hard labour on the grounds of his previous good character. *Sussex Agricultural Express*, 10 Mar. 1874.
5.   It is not clear which of the Bartons, Egerton encountered, but presumably the rector and his sons were still filibustering about the case, described p. 145 note 20, heard on 26 Sept. 1873. George Noakes moved back to Burwash about this time; when he saw Arthur Barton passing his house in June 1874, Noakes exclaimed, 'Come on old Arthur Barton, you can have my wife', and on Barton ignoring the invitation, Noakes called him a 'hound, a swindler, and a housebreaker. . . . If I get a chance I will split your head open. I am King of Etchingham, and will do for the Bartons yet'. For this, Noakes was bound over to keep the peace in the considerable sum of £30, with two further sureties of £10 each. *Sussex Advertiser*, 24 Mar. 1874. *Sussex Agricultural Express*, 30 June 1874.
6.   The 'old man' was fifty-six-year-old George Harmer; a bricklayer, like several of his kin, he undoubtedly had to migrate in search of work in the early 1830s (as he did again in the shorter, sharp mid-century agrarian depression), and was thus an experienced tramper after work. Harmer's deposition, 26 Feb. 1852, when the victim of rabbit thieves, ESCRO. QR/E962.
7.   The Burwash branch was well established by this date. Full-time organizer Nash spoke at a branch dinner at the Admiral Vernon on 27 Feb., and further buoyant recruitment was anticipated. The first Burwash representative, presumably Shearman, to attend a delegate meeting at Maidstone, was present on 25 Apl. *Kent Messenger and Maidstone Telegraph*, 7 and 14 Mar., and 2 May 1874.
8.   The Board of Guardians decided on 8 Feb. 1874 to grant such large families in receipt of outdoor relief an extra weekly penny per child, to enable school attendance under the 1870 Act. No doubt, some pocketed the cash and did not ensure their children's attendance. Minutes, ESCRO. G10/1a/12.
9.   He meant that Mrs Isted had had to insist on Annie leaving her place in order to look after the sick mother and younger siblings.
10.   The Burwash branch, together with others in adjacent parishes were recruiting strongly. At the 7 May Burwash rally 'several farmers attended', two of whom, both unidentified, presumably unsuccessfully demanded to look at the membership books, 'promising that "every man of theirs" should be locked out on Saturday'. Shortly, three men were 'locked out' in the union's parlance, and – on the evidence of Egerton's subsequent attitude – he used the pulpit on this occasion to urge restraint on to both sides. *Kent Messenger and Maidstone Telegraph*, 2, 16 and 30 May 1874.
11.   This suggested that the club was not formally enrolled with the Registrar General of Friendly Societies, thus compromising the legal position respecting finances.

12.   Parts of the leadership of the Labourers' Union were advocating that the Union should extend its activities to include sickness benefit, which would entail a separate fund, and alter its legal position, together with making it more attractive. Hence the debate at the Club. *Kent Messenger and Maidstone Telegraph*, 27 June 1874.
13.   Thomas (fifty-six) and Eliza (forty-six) had five children under thirteen at the 1871 Census.
14.   Battle Union's ruling was certainly very strict, but perfectly legal. Different regulations in adjoining Poor Law Unions perplexed and angered claimants, and also generated arguments between and within Boards of Guardians.
15.   Hawkins, who was 'much respected by the villagers', was buried by Egerton's curate Whitaker on the 22nd. The hearse, as usual for serving policemen, was followed by Superintendent Jenner, two sergeants and seventeen constables. The brief press report also noted that his widow was 'dangerously ill'. *Sussex Advertiser*, 28 July 1874.
16.   Shearman resigned his branch secretaryship in June. His members subscribed 4/3 in recognition of his 'services', and a further 4/- for the Union's voluntary emigration fund. *Kent Messenger and Maidstone Telegraph*, 20 June 1874.
17.   The concert was held 'under the immediate patronage' of Chief Constable Mackay. Singers from Hastings joined Egerton's singing class. The money was divided between the widow, who was recovering, and an un-named woman who had 'injured her own health' in nursing the family. In Oct. the widow received a one-off payment of £50 from the Quarter Sessions constabulary committee. *Sussex Advertiser*, 1 Sept. 1874. *Sussex Agricultural Express*, 1 Sept. and 20 Oct. 1874.
18.   Neighbouring clergymen covered for each other's absence; Egerton was no doubt annoyed that his curate had seen the Anglican squire Courthope, rather than simply making the necessary respective arrangements with the other two clergymen.
19.   Weekes – described as a labourer – was not given the option of a fine, for 'riotous violent and indecent behaviour' in church during divine service. Summary returns, ESCRO. QR/E1068.
20.   Seventy-seven-year-old Harriet Skinner Thompson, bedridden with 'erysipdas' for the past six years, lived with her builder son Benjamin and his family. Among his children still at home were Hannah, four-year-old Harriet, and Benjamin aged twenty-six. Benjamin junior had been 'crazy' for three to four years, and in 1870 tried to hang himself; thereupon he was sent to a London asylum, but discharged after a week as he proved too difficult. He had violent tendencies; 'at times', said his father, he had 'threatened us all with violence. I have been afraid of him', and knives and other potentially dangerous household items, including chisels were kept under lock and key. In the mid-afternoon of the previous Sunday Benjamin was 'halloing about and making a noise . . . similar to that he frequently makes, only much worse', deposed the elder sister. Harriet junior came in crying, and on investigation the older girl discovered her grandmother had been stabbed in the forehead and was bleeding heavily. When Hannah confronted Benjamin, he threatened to kill her. Hannah got two passing men to keep watch on the grandmother, and 'took my little sister to the next door house for safety, and then went down to the chapel and fetched my mother and father'. Surgeon Combs was not called until following day, the 25th; he told the inquest jury that the wounds, inflicted by a chisel, would not have killed a younger and fitter person. The son was quickly sent as a criminal lunatic to the County Asylum, the father agreeing to pay 5/6 weekly towards the costs of committal and conveyance (£3 2s 10½d). *Sussex*

Agricultural Express, 2 Nov. 1874. Board of Guardians minute, 12 Nov. 1874, ESCRO. G10/1a/13.

21. Under the 1836 legislation commuting tithes, money payments were controlled by the average price of the relevant cereal over the preceding seven years. This could mean that tithe payments rose, when current cereal prices were falling.

22. William, aged twenty-two, son of farmworker John Holmes, married Harriet, twenty-one, daughter of labourer William Pope, on 2 Nov. 1874. ESCRO. Par.284/1/3/3.

23. Presumably Poor Law settlements, under which regulations claims for poor relief could be made. The entry suggests that even after the Union Chargeability Act of 1865, whereby the Unions rather than the parish became the units for settlement, thus carrying the financial responsibility rather than individual component parishes, the latter were still encouraged to monitor newcomers thought not to be economically stable.

24. Namely, that Egerton was uncertain whether he was legally prevented from publishing his own banns.

1875

1 Jan. . . . Commended to His Almighty care her whom in His Mercy has given to me, whose love has already been a priceless blessing to me, & in the prospect of whose consolation, encouragement & help as my dear wife, I am indeed happy. Prayed earnestly that our united lives may be to His glory, & to our own peace & joy. Prayed for the gift of comfort to all who are in trouble, especially to poor Mrs & Miss Roger in their grief thro' the fearful calamities by land & sea wh. are now in our minds, & for the poor who suffer. . . .

17 Jan. . . . to Holy Trinity Ch. Wallington [near Croydon] at 11. . . . Charles & H. Wace married us. . . . rather shaky about ye voice. Nellie looked admirably & behaved herself to perfection. . . . [After festivities] to Bath. To York House. Comfortable, but solemn & a trifle dingy.
   [Then honeymoon continued in Exeter, Torquay – 'Royal Hotel, beautiful, Hotel horribly expensive' – Babbacombe, Brixham, Bournemouth, returning to Burwash on 6 Feb.] Mr Gibbs carr[iage] met us [at Etchingham station]. Our fate prognosticated by arch of evergreens set up by Boorman children nr. Dudwell House. At Rectory West Gate, a really elegant arch, a large gathering of parishioners. Evergreen wreathing over porch. Address read by Mr. Philcox. I shortly ret[urne]d thanks. N. stood up & bowed acknowledgements. A small cheer & then ye assemblage dispersed. For the kindness of the welcome we both felt truly grateful. It was indeed encouraging. In ye hall a motto "God bless the happy pair" put up by the servants.[1] . . . Jos. Noakes this day reconciled w. the farmers w. whom he had long been at variance & also I believe w. me, & this was a great additional pleasure to me. . . .[2]

11 Feb. W. Nellie to ye Schools. Ye Infants went tho' various performances, amusing, but I doubt the educational advantages. . . .

14 Feb. Some body sent me a Val[entine] for annoyance I suppose. . . .

15 Feb. C. on old Hicks (1/-). R. & P. w. him; he has been light-headed but was sensible to day. N. meant to go w. me, but it was too muddy. . . .

17 Feb. Displayed ye presents. Only about 28 people came to see them, wh. was disappointing. . . .

18 Feb. Sch: Shewed presents again today about 70 people came, or rather more. The exhibition was really a pretty one. Our presents altogether number 114. The things are mostly useful, as well as pretty. The good wishes of some visitors quaintly expr[essed]; but nearly all included the hope of finally meeting in heaven. . . .

8 Mar. Wm. Maskell c. on me to complain of ye refusal of my nourishment to his w[ife] who is conf[ine]d. He has 8 chi[ldren] & 4 gallons & 4/- [weekly outdoor relief] & is a permanent invalid. Knowing the case & all its difficulties, I still think the authorities are severe. I gave him 2/6. . . .[3]

18 Mar. . . . On my way to ye Comm: Young John Hall met me, & stopped to ask advice as to what to do w. some roughs who had been giving him "horn fair" on a false report raised by Nairns [Norris?] Thompson that he had been "gracious" w. Mrs Th. I sent him down to Mr. Philcox. . . .[4]

13 Mar. . . . C. on Mrs G. Parsons they have agreed to try Eng[land] till after hopping & then if they are minded, to emigrate to New Zealand. . . .[5]

15 Mar. . . . Funeral of John Noakes ye old Clocksmith aged 79. I had offered to see him, but the offer was not accepted. . . .

19 Mar. . . . In morg. c. on Mrs John Hall: ye "horn fair" quiet now. . . .

22 Mar. Signed paper after personal interview for removal of Eliza Standen to Hayward's Heath asylum. . . .[6]

25 Mar. . . . Vestry meeting. Adjourned to ye Bell. Very few, but amicable. Poor rate 1s 2d. Dinner, only 8, Messrs Whatman, Jarvis, Cramp, Fuller, C.Coppard, W.Kemp, Gillham & self: pleasant & conversation brisk on various subjects by no means merely parochial. . . .

29 Mar. . . . C. on Mr. Taylor & had a cup of tea. Met Freeland, a nephew, a young man c. up about a drum & pipe band, as ye subscr[iption] not enough for brass instr[uments] 10 pipes; my goodness what a noise. I prom[ised] a sovereign. . . .

1 Apl. . . . Mrs Coleman this morg. c. w. a petition towards paying the costs of her son's conviction for leaving employer's service with 5 days notice instead of 6. I gave 2/6. . . .[7]

6 Apl. . . . met Mr. E. Smith [Poundsford Farm] & his son as also Mr. Simes, Mr. J.Fuller. Inspected the road to Burwash Comm. to 3 Cups Corner, went as far as top of Mr. Simes' River Field. To Mr. Smith's & . . . heard evidence wh. he adjudged to prove that for 25 years unquestioned use by the public made it a public road, that in years gone by, by evidence of Mr. Simes & William Budd, the parish had repaired it as far as the top of . . . River field & is adjudged that the parish liable now to keep it in reasonable repair. Mr. Smith proved to have encroached on the road in several places by putting up a wall etc, so that I said he mustn't be too strict in the question . . . w. Mr. [George] Smith [salaried parish road surveyor].[8]

10 Apl. . . . C. on PC. Girton & Segt. Tobutt [police officers newly stationed in Burwash] – both nice. . . .

16 Apl. . . . Etchingham & Ticehurst ye hundred rate in question. Truly roads are such a bore. . . .

26 Apl. . . . C. & R. w. Mrs Davis (1/-) wife of a shoemaker behind Spears; journeyman, casual work, she says his wages during a great part of the year don't average above 14/- a week: 5 ch[ildren]. . . . C. & R. w. T.Vigor Ps. 51. The pr[esent] Mrs Leaney told me wh[at] Mr. Mannings who was hung for the murder of O'Connor (?) chose to be read on the way to the scaffold.[9] . . . I heard that one of the Basses had said he didn't think he shd. sing, if I didn't let the Basses do a piece in a new anth[em] "I will lift up mine eyes". Whitfield picked Bass solo, by themselves! I had done it w. all the men, Bass & Tenor. It is hard to satisfy singers.

27 Apl. Sch. C. on old Hicks: poor old man he was past all "consciousness" as Mrs Waterhouse said. He has been a quiet, harmless, Godfearing old man, & has left a good name behind him: he was 92 last Mich[aelmas] day. . . . I c. on Ellen [Gould] at Oaklands. She a trifle better. Freelands, Tilley & Bartons, calling. A woman's rights discuss[ion] beginning & as I was in a minority of about 7 to 1, I bolted. . . .

1 May. . . . Buried old John Hicks aged 92.

3 May. Saw Mr. N.Taylor about widow Langridges relief. For self, 5 ch: she receives 5/-, 6 Gall[on]s of flour, 2 lbs of mutton, 3½ pts. of porter per week . . . is 12/7½ per week: if the flour be called 1/- per gall. 13s 1½d. She has a big boy hiding at home who only pays her 9/- per week instead of 10/- as he wd. have to any where else, so that really she ought to be having 14s 1½ per week for herself, 5 ch. & seeing now that there is no man to keep, she may be considered as well off as when her husb: was alive. Poor thing, I don't suppose she thinks so, but this is how a relieving officer calculates. . . . Ye drum & fife band took poss[ession] of ye coach house for practicing, ye results at present inharmonious & trying to ye dogs who barked vehemently.

4 May. . . . Parish meeting. Road question settled by the parish undertaking repairs down to Poundsford. I mooted the [church] bells question, & offered £25 on the one condition only that the matter was referred to Mr. Gibbs. All amicable.

6 May. . . . C. on ye Lees (1/-), ye man looked hunger striken. . . .

[10 to 22 May in Oxfordshire and Wiltshire.]

25 May. Club noisy & many members drunk. One fell into the hands of the police & was taken to the lock up; several more ought to have been; the share out was large 6/6 & others had something to do with it. I dined, no speeches, no nothing. . . .[10]

26 May. . . . Up to Mr. G[illham]'s hop-garden, & there . . . had a long t. w. him about relief. It really seems that there is not the slightest desire to be hard upon the poor people, but that there is a strong feeling, that all widows & all who can work ought to do so, & that there is a tendency on the part of many who can at any rate help to maintain themselves, to get by [escape] work altogether. I don't know how this is, but the labour test falls very heavily on some of them I am sure. . . .[11]

27 May. Sch: To ye Club on ye Comm: d. at ye Wheel Inn, only about 40 members, no band & no booth, all seemed quite sober aft. dinn. They soon left the room & I came home . . .

28 May. . . . T. w. Mr. Whatman about Mrs Honor Pilbeam. He distinctly affirms that he heard her say certain things wh. she denied, & he is supported by Mother Gorringe. Talked also w. him & Mr. Cramp about Ch: Ins[urance] wh. is to be raised to £2500. Mr. Wh. has seen ye bells, & is converted to a £100 estimate instead of a £10 one. . . .

31 May. . . . C. on Honor Pilbeam; she denies as if she was going to die, but I cannot believe her somehow. . . .

1 June. . . . Comm[ittee] meet[ing] of ye Club at ye Sch. . . . We fined 6 for being drunk & disorderly. . . .[12]

2 June. Sch: Had t. w. Mr. Anset & w. Miss Adams about making our school a mixed School. Wrote to ye Comm[ittee] of [the Privy] Council on ye subj.[13] . . . J. Vidler pleads that he stripped his jacket & squared up to R. Lulham only in self defence wh. is allowed by ye rule![14] . . . Old Ledbetter told me of a man named Pont at Brightling who was so affected by the rheumatism that his backside naturally turned round to his fore-side! but as Mr. L. added "he cd. walk about all one for that"! . . .

3 June. . . . Saw Mr. & Mrs Freeland superintending their two boys sailing boats in the river, ye boys w. tucked up trousers in ye water enjoying themselves immensely. . . .

5 June. . . . Mr. & Mrs Philcox lunched. We had much talk about Burwash of old in general. . . .

9 June. . . . Albert Hawkins leaving has got a place at Faversham as improver w. a bricklayer. . . .

Sun. 13 June. St Ph . . . good cong: Had to speak to Master Luther Leaves bef[ore] serv. as I found him brandishing ye Ch. door scraper in ye face of a young woman. It was only his fun! but the sooner Master Luther leaves off such fun & begins a reformation of his ways ye better. . . .

17 June. . . . C. on Mrs Cramp. Saw old China & some beautiful old embroidery 150 years old, & worked up by the light of a rush soaked in Mutton fat! . . .[15]

Sun. 20 June. . . . Coming home had t. w. Mr. Gibbs about ye bells; ye cost of recasting ye cracked one about £40. . . . Gave H.Noakes, 2 Honeysetts & Ahab Brown leave to fish in my pond. . . .

21 June. . . . C. on Mr. J.B. Noakes about change [cash]. He told me that some of the poor thought it hard that when I got so much money out of ye parish I shd. send round ye hat to beg money to get married with! i.e. the testimonial! . . .[16]

9 July. . . . C. on Mr. Daw, he in much trouble at ye decision of ye magistrates that Grocers having a wine licence must shut up their shops at 10 o'Clock like publicans. He wd. be quite content that no wine shd. be sold after 10, but says it is hard, as they do not sell drink to be drunk on the premises, that they shd. shut their shops up – & so it is – nor do I believe that it is the spirit of the act. . . .

12 July. . . . Overtook [Pupil Teacher] J.Sawyers & young Noakes in the Ch. Yd: JS. had just picked up in ye path one of the beastly pamphlets by wh. boys & young men are made miserable. He shewed it me & I took it & tore it up: it was by a Dr (?) Harrison. . . .

16 July. . . . C. on Mr. Barrow about acting as agricultural reporter to Sussex Daily News; he declined: spoke to Mr. Jarvis on ye subj: he decl: also. . . . C. on Mr. Daw; he suggested that if grocers with wine licences are obliged to shut up at ye same hour as publicans, they surely must be open the same time, so that on Sundays Wine Licence grocers might open all the lawful hours. . . . Mr. Courthope is puzzled about the law compelling grocers w. wine licences to close at 10 & yet the law seems clear. . . .

Sun. 18 July. . . . Had to speak to some men who were lying about at full length in the Ch: Yard smoking. It may make them cross but what am I to do. I am sure I spoke civilly. . . .

22 July. . . . c. on some poor folks to tell them to send up for some clothes wh. I had to give away. . . . C. on Master Dann (1/6) of the Square. He an anti-[trade] Unionist & his arg[ument]s were very racy & to the point. . . .

Sun. 1 Aug. . . . In aft. ye Agr: Lab. Union att[ended] Ch: ye Ch. perfectly full. I put off ye Xanings [Christenings] till next Sunday. Ye congr: admirably attentive. I pr. from Heb. xiii. 1 Let Brotherly love continue (Ext). I believe that God was with me & enabled me to pr. a sermon wh. suited the time & wh. I hope will do good. My line was that it is not the office of the minister of Xt to interfere in business matters between employer & employee, wh. is not likely that he shd. rightly understand, but that it is his office to urge strongly on both sides their common brotherhood in Xt & the duty of maintaining a Xtian spirit & temper in carrying on their trade differences & disputes. I was told that ye discourse was approved on both sides by farmers & labourers, for wh. I humbly thank God. It was a real opportunity. . . .[17]

[3 to 29 Aug. to Scotland by sea, and back via Liverpool, to Cheshire, Oxfordshire including 28 Aug. 'It seems an age since we left Burwash'.]

4 Sept. Thro' Jarvis, Honeysett's & Russells hop-gardens. Very picturesque & the hops looked beautiful. Mr. John Jarvis gave me a partridge wh. I enjoyed much. Funeral of old Joe Luck. I was sorely tried in reading ye service for ye godless old man: one can only hope that perfect justice may see more extenuating circumstances for such a life than we can. . . . Had a t. w. John Sawyers de rebus musicus; he gets on. . . .

5 Sept. . . . Young Patitt ? [Petett, Petitt or Pettitt] Edw. c. for me to sign an Emigration form. He wanted me to certify him of ye calling of farm labourer. I cd. not as he has been apprenticed to a tailor, so I signed & made a note. . . .[18]

6 Sept. . . . At Huxtable [returning from Swanley] Heard that "foot & mouth" broke out this morg. at Pockmull's Pater's tenant. . . .[19]

8 Sept. . . . Mrs J.Potten overtook me on the road, & asked me for an out-ticket order for her hus. . . . Mrs Styles stopped me & said that she had nearly lost the sight of one eye, & feared for the other poor woman. She asked for a bott[le] of port wine wh. I gave her. . . . C. on poor Mrs Pilbeam (3/6), in real trouble about her husb: who leaves her in distress. C. on John Vidler (1/6), ill out of work. . . .

9 Sept. . . . George Courthope sent me a box of grouse, 4 braces! I wrote to thank him at once. Gave Mrs Irwin a brace, Mrs Combs a brace, & Mr. Jarvis one bird wh. was all he wd. take. . . .

Sat. 11 Sept. . . . The street at turning out time quite quiet: a wonderful change from the old 12 o'Clock turning out on Sat: night years ago.[20]

13 Sept. . . . C. & P. w. Master Sinden (1/6) carter at Mottingsden. His wife a nice woman. Comes in from hopping. "Well you be mucked up mate" he . . . murmers, "I'll be all of a sweat now & I don't want you mucking about here". Spoke to young G.Pennels about his friends & himself doing apparently what they cd. to annoy me. He said they never alleged any reason, or ground of offence on my part, but there may be something. Paid Mr. Smith £6:6:0 for singing Class treat & the men are themselves to chose how to spend it.

15 Sept. . . . I wrote a note to Mr. Whatman begging of Sally Isted & c. on Sally's mother: she complained that the hoppickers were not getting on very fast & couldn't do much, & seemed to favour Sally coming up ye Rect.

16 Sept. . . . Sally Isted came, but in spite of saying that the hops were bad told Ch[arlotte, Egerton's domestic servant] that she had been earning up to 4/6 a day! If they complain of this what do they want? I had her in, paid her 4/- wh. was what she told "me" she had been earning, & I let her go.

Sun. 19 Sept. . . . heard last night was devoted to a series of free fights in ye village between Londoners & Brightonians from Honeysett's & What-mans. . . .[21]

21 Sept. . . . Just past ye Lodge Farm [returning from Hurst Green, his horse] Kitty gave her tail a swish got ye rein under tucked in her tail, & began to gallop & kick: she knocked part of ye trap to pieces & then rushed into ye hedge & thro' into ye shaw. She got hung up, her leg over ye shaft. A man fortunately came to help & I extricated her; not much hurt. . . .

23 Sept. . . . C. on Mr. Daw: he shewed me a letter just received from one Benj: Gemmy [?] who emigr[ated] to Aust[ralia] 5 years ago; he wrote from Camperdown Victoria, & gives a very tempting picture of ye country. He says "this is a free country & my wife says she never felt so free in her life". A free country is I suppose a country in wh. you haven't to touch y[ou]r hat to nobody.[22] . . . C. & R. & t. w. Mrs Rich. She says the bandage wh. I have given her does her much good, tho' she hadn't got it on as it hurt! . . . C. & P. w. poor Hannah Kemp; gave her sister 2/- as she loses her hopping in attending on Hannah. C. on old Relf; he is an old gossip, all the time declaiming agst. tittle-tattle. In ye morg. C. on old Sheather & p[ai]d him over his cheque for int[erest], & gave him ye receipt for his principal for

Lewes Old Bank, T[unbridge] Wells [branch]. He very cross because a woman told me where to find ye key to unlock ye house door wh. was locked by Mrs Pennell when she went hopping. C. on Mr. J.B.Noakes; he wanted a certif[icate] of bapt[ism] to shew that he was over 60 . . . so that he might claim exemption from jury work [service]. . . .[23]

25 Sept. Funeral of J. Pennels child. C. at ye P[ost] O[ffice] happened to look at a number of Reynold's newspaper. The Queen, Aristocracy, & Middle Classes objects of most unqualified abuse: "Nothing that is is right" really seems the motto of the paper, except that not a word is said about any possible shortcomings of the artisans & labouring class.

Sun. 26 Sept. . . . Congr: small. I shall be glad when hopping is over. No row last night I am glad to say. Had to assure some boys, Master Woodgate, Harry Isted & Wm. do, that if they disturbed the congr: again, as they had to day, they must go to H[urst] Green. Mr. Taylor saw to them & kept them in after Ch:. . . .[24]

27 Sept. . . . I c. & had a long t. w. Mrs Isted, as I understand her 74 bush[ells of picked hops] were credited the other day to Isted & Sally's bin. 74 at 2d is 12s 4d pretty good for two hands in one day, tho' Mr. Whiteheads hop garden noticed ye measures measuring very short bushels indeed. . . .[25]

28 Sept. Set out for ye Common. . . . Coppard gave me a lift part way. . . . C. on Mrs Weekes (5/-) who I found had lost her hopping, by confinement with 10th child: child dead. Thro' Mr. Simes hop-garden: hops wretched, really hardly worth picking in many cases. . . . In Mr. Robinson's garden I found old Wm. Budd & his wife at a bin 83 & 80! C. for N. at Mrs Combs, where they had been preparing decorations for harvest service. . . .

29 Sept. C. on J.Vidler (1/6). He being ill, his wife & himself have lost their hopping. . . .

4 Oct. . . . C. . . . on Mrs Hawkins to make arr[angements] about washing the school. It is now hard to get a woman to scrub.[26]

7 Oct. . . . In ye school, must speak about the filthy state in wh. it was left. Saw Mr. Gillet of Willards Hill & spoke about nephews left by death of their mother his sister very destitute. . . .

9 Oct. C. on Mrs J.Isted & set things right w. Sally whose utterances had been misrepresented somewhat to me [presumably by housemaid Charlotte]. C. on old Mrs Farley: he husb: drunk & troublesome so I had to come away. . . .

11 Oct. . . . First day of mixed school. . . .

14 Oct. Sch: mixed class did all right. . . .

17 Oct. . . . young Noakes at Fullers has left Burwash "in a hurry" for some misconduct, I am told, but I don't know what. . . .[27]

22 Oct. . . . wrote . . . a note to Sec[retary] of T.Wells Inf[irmary] a propos of a rule that they cannot receive a patient who is having parish relief.[28] Hannah Eastwood [aged fifty-seven] is the poor woman in question. . . .

Sat 23 Oct. Three weddings. Master G.Booth very cheeky indeed about ye fees. I shd. have thought little about it had he not been a young fellow who spends more than the am[oun]t on drink in a short time.[29] All ye party were more or less screwed [drunk] within a couple of hours of the marr: James Dennett & Charlotte Ellis a very resp[ectabl]e wedding. Charl. sister of my former gardener, G.Ellis. . . . C. & P. w. Mrs Fawley (1/-). Old Fawley actually knelt down at ye bed. C. & t. w. poor old Mrs Rich. She in much pain. She said "I'm glad to see you Sir, & at one time I didn't think I ever shd. be glad to see you". . . .

26 Oct. Sch. On my way thro' the village met by Mr. Whatman who asked me to take a funeral on the Common this aft: Frances Russell at 18 d. of Widow Russell, in serv[ice] w. Mr. Carey, died on Sunday [24th] night of fever. Last night the body was sent home in a coffin, & had to be kept all night in a crowded cottage. Aft. d. buried Braban child, & then Mr. Taylor drove me to St Ph: Kept waiting for some time. I had ye cart brought to ye head of ye grave, & ye coffin taken out & at once lowered. Aft: finishing this part of the serv: I went into Ch: & read ye lesson. . . .

28 Oct. . . . Funeral of Pattenden child, 6th child now dead of diarrhea within 6 weeks. . . . On my way home from Etchm. a young Mr. Birch who had come from King's Coll[ege] Hosp[ital] on invit[ation] of Mrs Holland to look at ye Parish with a view to ye practice interviewed me. I hardly knew what to say.

29 Oct. . . . sch: took a class. I wonder when the art of reading with sense will be better attained in elementary schools. . . .

10 Nov. . . . Tithe dinner, fair attendance, no speeches or toasts of any kind. "Mr." Lusted ye waiter, very free & easy & independent. Nothing remarkable in any way. I left about 5.40; ye din: was at ye Bell. . . .

15 Nov. . . . N. School; only 10 boys. I really do think they are afraid of me, & they wd. come better if I were not there, but who is to teach? . . .

16 Nov. . . . Sch. Had a renewed disturbance w. R. Thompson. On going out of school he made only the minimum of obeisance, & at the same time looked up with a certain impertinent smile. I told him to make his obeisance properly. He refused & bolted, halloaing at me most uncivilly as he passed thro' the school yard. I am sure I wish the boy no ill, & I wd. befriend him if I cd, but he has taken some unaccountable spite agst. me, because I once believed John Sawyers rather than him in the question of whether he had used bad language in church; that he did use it I have no manner of doubt. I cannot disbelieve Sawyers upon the point, as he says he distinctly heard Thompson use certain words. Thompson is in the habit of using bad language, so that that corroborates Sawyers. However nothing I can do, & no explanation that I can make will appease him, & he does all he can to annoy me. The obeisance is mere school discipline, & must be attended to. I c. on his father & stated the case; the boy is a trouble to him. . . .

17 Nov. Sch. C. on Mrs Davis wife of a shoemaker in Bell Alley. She has taught several of her children to read & write very fairly without sending them to school. She has ten! . . .

18 Nov. Sch. R. Thompson in school again, & made his submission. . . .

19 Nov. . . . To St Phillip's . . . To ye School. Took the first class. Very disheartening, great boys & girls newly come in, & hardly able to read at all. Classification almost impossible. I advised Miss Press not waste too much much time on these hopeless ones who were only keeping the rest back. . . .

20 Nov. . . . Mr. Whatman told me that ye farmers had agreed not to draw coals [from the station, without charge for the poor], "as there are now no poor".[30]

22 Nov. . . . N.S. only 12 so gave it up for the present. I am sorry, but 12 are not enough. . . .

24 Nov. . . . I c. on Mrs C[ombs] about ye coals. Ye farmers seem determined to shew by withdrawal of certain privileges in what respects the poor are beholden to charity. . . . C. & R w. T. Vigor (2/6). This family I believe in real distress, & yet T.V. has been a tradesmen for many years in good business & ought to have saved enough for old age, but here he is & what is to be done. . . . Interview with Mrs Farley about her son's conduct in church. She very excited. I C. on Mr. Philcox's manservant, who spoke in favour of young Farley's innocence. . . .

25 Nov. . . . R.R. Reeves' death after a short illness is a sad end of a life of almost unredeemed drunkenness & blasphemy; & he a farmer too whose education has been a fairly good one. . . .

10 Dec. Mr. Cramp c. on me before I had got up [convalescing after several days' illness]. he had a long t. about ye dole wh. he fears will be given up this year: he wanted to devise some plan for keeping it going, but ye bulk of ye farmers wish I suppose to show the working class that there have been certain benefits wh. have been overlooked by them in their calculations . . .

11 Dec. Mr. Whatman c. on me in ye morg. & I had a long t. about ye dole. He slightly shifted ye ground of ye farmers indisposition this year to subscribe by saying that the labourers had driven them so hard in wages etc. during the past year that they cd. not afford to subscribe. As the whole a[mou]nt subscr: by farmers is about £6 for the parish this seems somewhat untenable ground. However he was very amicable. . . .

17 Dec. Wrote out notices that the dole wd. have to be limited to Widows, Persons disabled from work, & Families where there are three children at the least. Left them at the shops. . . .

21 Dec. At ten o'Clock to ye Dole. The rules seem to have been pretty well understood & few claimants except "Widows, persons disabled from work, & families where there are 3 ch: at least". 2 women from Witherendon, but in Ticehurst parish obtained "dole" by craft. I asked ye Sergt. to suggest to them that they had better send the meat back. We gave away about 56 stones of beef at 5/4. Mr. Cramp, Mr. Fuller & Ch[arles] Coppard & self distributed, we were out about 2 o'Clock. . . .

24 Dec. . . . Blunden's party came up & sang While shepherds watched, Glorious Apollo, & the Red Cross Knight. I gave them 5/-. W.Coppard, Mepham, Hicks, Lusted & one more came up as a band of "niggers". They sang in the kitchen. The rain had begun to make their colour run and they looked piteous – 1/6 or 2/- I forget which. The Relfs ye bell ringers (hand bells) c. & played fairly, 1/6. Wet night.

Sun. 26 Dec. . . . In aft. pr. from Phil. 3. 13 Ext. Spoke of several points in wh. we need more zeal & pressing forward. H[oly] C[ommunion] Sunday Schools & brotherly love between employers & employed. . . .

28 Dec. . . . Mr. Smith ye. guardian calling me out to interview about a petition agst. a chapel at ye Union. . . .[31]

29 Dec. A Hurst Green brass band! of 13 perf[ormers] came & played, 2/-; really this band business is becoming an affliction. . . .[32]

Notes

1.   Parsons and gentry departing on, or returning from honeymoons, merited these village displays and receptions. They were invariably reported in the press, which in the Egertons' case included extra details. Philcox's speech was on behalf of the entire community, but the rectory gate arch was erected by the 'farmers and tradesmen'. No doubt members of these categories took pride in seeing their names among the long list in the county press. *Sussex Agricultural Express,* 8 Feb. 1875.
2.   Joseph Noakes was the proprietor of Tanhouse Farm; the origin of the dispute is unknown, but may derive from his serving just this year as one of the four overseers of the poor. Vestry minutes, 25 Mar. 1874, 25 Mar. 1875, ESCRO. Par.284/12/2.
3.   See above, p. 131, 16 Dec. 1872.
4.   The Noakes case detailed above was a 'horn fair'; Egerton's response, suggests that he believed that these common manifestations could be nipped in the bud through resort – actual or threatened – to legal action, at least where the accusation of adultery was false.
5.   An option probably derived from the Agricultural Labourers' Union's pro-emigration policy.
6.   Her husband, master-shoemaker, Alfred, applied to the Board of Guardians, to have his wife sent to Hayward's Heath Asylum, which was agreed on condition of his considerable weekly contribution of 5/- towards the cost. Minute, 18 Mar. 1875, ESCRO. G10/1a/14.
7.   At the Petty Sessions on 26 Feb. John Coleman, a carter's mate employed by Kitty Weller, was convicted under the notorious Master and Servant's Act of 1865, for technically leaving his work unfinished; the court annulled his contract, and imposed a fine of 1/-, plus 9/6 costs. The legislation, biased strongly in the employer's favour, prevented workers from quitting their jobs even after differences with their employers proved irreconcilable, and was despised. As non-payment of fines automatically incurred a prison sentence, the neighbourly collection reflected popular hostility to the Act, evidently shared at least in this case by Egerton. Summary returns, ESCRO. QR/E1069. *Sussex Agricultural Express,* 1 Mar. 1875.
8.   Encroachment on roads, which effectively embraced adjacent landowners or their tenants surreptitiously enclosing broad roadside verges by fencing them in, was a common occurrence. It was obviously in Smith's interest for the road leading to his farm, to be kept in good repair with public funds, which the vestry agreed in principle, but here the fact of his liability for illegal encroachment was deployed to caution him against speedy resort to litigious enforcement of parochial respons-ibility. Vestry minute, 6 Apl. 1875, ESCRO. Par.284/12/2.
9.   One of the most celebrated public executions in the entire nineteenth century, before their abolition in 1868. The double execution of husband and wife Frederick and Maria Manning for the murder of her paramour – proved the vehicle for Charles Dickens' intervention in the debate on hanging, with letters to *The Times.* H.M. Wallbrook, *Murders and Murder Trials,* (1932), pp. 100–1.
10.   On the following day, Richard Lulham was summarily fined 5/- with 8/3 costs, or fourteen days' imprisonment, on police evidence for drunkenness in Ham Lane. Summary returns, ESCRO. QR/E1070.
11.   The Labour Test represented a bastardization of the strict principles of the Poor Law Amendment Act, by which outdoor relief could be ordered – initially when the workhouse was literally full – to the able-bodied if they could prove that they had applied unsuccessfully for all available employ, or no work was available. This

strategy could be extended to all those including widows and the partially disabled (of any age) in receipt of outdoor relief, with respect to claimants having sought all part-time, or other employment, of which they were capable.

12.   See above, 25 May and note 10. Lulham was the only man before the courts, but no doubt Egerton was pleased by the Club committee's robust response to drunkenness in lieu.

13.   Under the payments by results scheme, a perennial headache for Egerton, the school lost a tenth of its grant owing to the boys' poor mathematics marks in 1874–5. Of the ninety-two boys on the books, only thirty-nine met the attendance criteria qualifying them as examination candidates. Now that the infants were segregated, mixing genders in the upper school was a logical progression, and perhaps seen as an exploratory means towards improved standards. Report, 15 Feb. 1875, ESCRO. ESC. 41/1: see below, pp. 164, 171, 11 and 14 Oct. 1875 for implementation, and 7 Jan. 1876 for further commentary on dreadful attendance records.

14.   Vidler escaped prosecution, but not disciplinary action by the Club committee, and clearly thought that these mitigating circumstances ought to have preserved him from the latter.

15.   In *Sussex Folk*, p. 121, Egerton stated that 'Within the recollection of many persons still alive, we grew flax, bleached it, carded it, spun it and wove it at home. In many of our cottages there are yet to be found sheets, table-cloths, and other articles of linen which seem to defy the power of time. Doubtless they are now kept more of curiosities than for use; still they have borne an amount of wear and tear which is certainly not expected of more modern goods.'

16.   Another example of the depth, duration and indeed realism, of anti-clericalism, still reflecting its later eighteenth-century (if not earlier) origins.

17.   By this date the now-named Kent and Sussex Labourers' Union had expanded considerably, become involved in a number of localized lock-outs, and many more local negotiations with employers over wages, hours, and other conditions. The Burwash branch was in a 'flourishing state' in May 1875, and the Union reputedly enjoyed 'the sympathy of many who have been against the Union'. The relationship between the Union and the Anglican Church was undergoing rapid reformation. Initially, Anglican incumbents had been among the Union's most prestigious opponents. Only a tiny handful of incumbents had offered any help, most notably the Revd Candy of Swanscombe (Kent), who loaned a field for an inaugural meeting way back in Aug. 1872, and had subsequently chaired branch meetings, spoken at the Union's annual rallies, and been called 'a communist or a socialist' for his pains. More seriously in Mar. 1881 he was convicted of thrashing – to the point of unconsciousness – a confirmation class lad, and sentenced to two months imprisonment without the option of a fine by the local Bench; the Quarter Sessions upheld his appeal against sentence, but imposed a heavy fine and sureties to keep the peace.

In Sussex only the Revd Eagleton at Flimwell, adjacent to Burwash, imitated Candy; Eagleton loaned the school hall for meetings, and publicly supported the Union in June 1873. If Dissenting clergymen much more actively supported agrarian unionism as elsewhere in the country, then in the south-east they received – presumably deliberately – little press coverage. Perhaps goaded by fears of Dissenters seizing the initiative, the attitude of Anglican clerics began to change, and the start of the Union sick fund in Oct. 1874 was also probably crucial, as it was with some employers' attitudes. It was said that Union branch marches to attend Church, as opposed to Chapel, services began at this time, but the evidence suggests that such events became common from June 1875, when branches were instructed to send details for inclusion in the Union newspaper. The first of those covered, involved the Burwash branch joining their Etchingham counterparts for a one-hundred-strong march led by the Hurst Green Brass Band to Etchingham church. Every Unionist sported a Union blue rosette or bow-tie, and each bandsman had 'a bouquet of forget-me-not in his coat'. After the service, they equally formally marched back to Hurst Green. Burwash branch invited the 'surrounding Branches' to a parallel occasion on 1 Aug. The procession, on which details are scarce, totalled four hundred and fifty people, who subsequently heard Egerton preach on 'Let Brotherly Love Continue'. *Kent Messenger and Maidstone Telegraph*, 29 June 1872, 28 June 1873, 23 May, 29 Aug., 5 Sept. and 3 Oct. 1874, 1, 21 and 29 May, 18 June, 2, 16 and 30 July, and 13 Aug. 1875. *Kent and Sussex Times*, 23 Apl., 18 June and 16 July 1875, 1 Apl. 1876 and 2 July 1881.

18.   Several changes to the regulations respecting assisted emigration were made during the period of the diary, and only agricultural labourers with a maximum of two children were currently eligible.

19.   A report from Burwash dated 19 Aug. stated that foot and mouth disease had spread rapidly amongst 'horned stock', but had subsided speedily and was expected to disappear completely with the current dry and hot weather. *Sussex Agricultural Express*, 21 Aug. 1875.

20.   Closing time had been changed recently from 11 to 10 p.m.

21.   A more ritualized form of violence between hop-pickers; no prosecutions derived from this mêlée.

22.   Egerton surmised correctly. Many letters home from recent emigrants, in addition to limitless work opportunities and very high real wages, also spoke very favourably of a much more egalitarian society. Charles White, from Sutton Valence, wrote to his parents from Illinois, 'My wife now has good health, and the children get so fat you would not know them . . . four hogs fattened look so nice, and all for our own use, not . . . to pay debts with'. From Brisbane, confirmed Albert Kitchenham, 'here is plenty for thousands to eat. . . . This is the place for poor people to live'. And Mark French, now in Wisconsin confirmed, 'We do not have to go and ask the farmers for work in this country, for they have to come and ask us'. *Kent Messenger and Maidstone Telegraph*, 21 Feb. 1874.

23.   Noakes was baptized on 29 June 1815, and therefore was exempt; interestingly, the ceremony was performed not by the Anglican incumbent, but by a Non-conformist minister. ESCRO. Par.284/1/2/1.

24.   Egerton was effectively threatening these juvenile delinquents with a criminal prosecution at the local Petty Sessions.

25.   In other words, Mrs J. Isted had tried to disguise her earnings by allocating the fruits of her work to her husband's and daughter's tallies, so that the mother could claim that she earned nothing during the hop-harvest, and benefit from Egerton's largesse as did others in this predicament.

26.   A reflection of competing demand for women domestics in perhaps the better working conditions, including longer hours available with more pay, in the expanding numbers of bourgeois homes.

27.   There is no record of any prosecution.

28.   Hospitals providing free treatment, and for patients referred to them by subscribers to their funds, argued that Poor Law authorities should pay for the treatment of social-security claimants.

29.   'It is only now and then that I find a bridegroom inclined to grumble in the

vestry at the amount of the marriage fee . . .'. *Sussex Folk*, p. 80.

30.   A vindictive, if common response to farmworkers who had prised out greater wages through the Union, designed – with some limited justification – to show that labourers received more than simply wages from their employers, and at this time of the year, when summer wage rates and employment levels were under threat, in reality constituted a semi-veiled thrust in the industrial relations theatre. See also below, 24 Nov., 10 and 11 Dec. 1875. Such action was widespread as the 1875–6 winter approached, with farmers withdrawing usual gifts of meat to employees who were in the Union, while those who normally did not bother with such Yuletide presents suddenly gave them to non-unionists. *Kent and Sussex Times*, 23 Dec. 1876.

31.   Eventually the workhouse was supplied with a chapel, a metallic structure – soon known as the 'iron chapel' – which was funded through a subscription rather than the poor rate. The issue soon became irrevocably embraced by the running dispute of a quarter of a century's duration, between the chaplain and at least a recurrent majority on the Board of Guardians. Revd Harrison to the Local Government Board, 1, 8 and 9 Mar. 1877, PRO. MH.12/13151.

32.   It is unclear whether Egerton is complaining at the escalating numbers of village bands in general, or the numbers performing by the rectory thus virtually demanding a donation. Some new or revived bands derived their inspiration from branches of the farmworkers' Union.

1876

7 Jan. To ye Common; on my way c. on Mrs C. Class at School. Ye Religious knowledge sadly low, but the attendance disheartedly irregular; on ye Books 155. Average for ye year 67! . . . C. on Mrs Farley, gave Mrs Joe Harmer a shilling for seeing to her, has [*sic*] her husb: has been drunk nearly 10 days . . .

Sun. 9 Jan. . . . fair congr: Ye Lab. Union meeting at Salehurst Church this morg., so few men here. . . .

[10 Jan. he journeyed to Swanley *en route* for Wiltshire, but taken ill and returned to Burwash on the 15th.]

Sun. 16 Jan. I was not able to take duty & Mr. Barker went up to St. Ph. In aft. I halloaed out to disperse Master Lester & others who in Ch. time were skating on my pond. Their "scare" was truly amusing, as they thought I was safe on ye Comm:. . . . My Bible Cl. came d[own] to ye Rect. 12 & very nice.

Fri. 28 Jan. W. up to St. Ph: took class. Our schedule here again, sad, but Miss Press has much to contend with; irregularity of attendance, ye crying evil. . . .

[31 Jan. to 5 Feb. in Bournemouth.]

16 Feb. . . . Sergt. Parkins of ye R[oyal] A[rtillery] (23 Brig.) & his wife (Ellen Fleming) c. to Burwash for a short stay, after nearly 10 years in India. . . .

17 Feb. . . . Mrs Leaney told me that her husband's father took care of & got paid for the care of one of two dogs wh. having followed a fox from the neighbourhood of Salisbury plain! ran it to a meadow in Brook's Marl Farm, where the fox & dogs were all found dead beat & unable to move any further. This was about the year 1800. I must try to trace it further, but the tradition is most common among our old people.[1] Had a long t. w. Sergt. Parkins about India. . . .

18 Feb. . . . Aft. tea Alfred Pickett came to ye Rectory & told me what grieved me terribly viz that Alfred Wells & he had come to blows at ye school on Wed. [16th] night after I left. On his ex-parte statement wh. bore on it the most manifest impression of good faith, I believe that he is not in the wrong, but it is a sore scandal, as both are communicants. The trouble rose out of an accusation agst. him by Wells of making Valentines wh. he denies. May God enable me to heal the quarrel, & not to be disheartened as I sorely tempted to be tonight. . . .[2]

19 Feb. . . . C. & had a long t. w. Wells, but I did not do much. C. on W.Coppard & heard his version of ye matter.

Sun. 20 Feb. To ye school; heard Sawyer's version. . . . Poor Wells seemed to me very vindictive; the evidence of the two others was agst. him as to what happened. . . .

21 Feb. I c. on Newton Taylor & Mr. John Fuller about ye benefit Club wh. is very low. I thought that such part of the reserve fund as had been contributed by the members themselves might be applied to such purposes as the Club might vote for, but that the am[oun]t contributed by the Honorary members shd. be retained as a guarantee agst. "sick pay" running short. . . .[3]

23 Feb. . . . C. on old Master Relf (1/-) at ye cott[age] by ye Railway. Told him his register of bapt[ism] born in 1798. His late wife's *great* grand-child Master Knowles now 21 yrs. old! Sing[ing] at ye Sch: Sawyers Pickett & Coppard of ye men. I had asked Wells to come w. ye hope of making matters up, but he cd. not appear.

25 Feb. . . . Singing boys at ye Rect. Wells came down I argued for nearly three quarters of an hour on behalf of peace, but in vain. He even refused to shake hands with or say good night to me. So little I imagine can he see any side but his own, that he thinks that because on some points I am agst. him, I am agst. him out of spite, & unfairly, but it is certainly not so.

Sun. 27 Feb. Wrote out notes of lect[ure] on Hist. of Burwash. . . . Mrs Leaney let me have a medal of Admiral Vernon dated Novr. 22 1739 "who took Portobello with 6 ships only". I gave her 2/6 for it. . . . C. on Mrs Sauter; how hopeless it is for a dirty, bad managing woman, to see anything but other people's unkindness in doing nothing for her, & everything for any body else. . . .

1 Mar. Ash Wednesday. After serv: Sawyers & Allc[orn] Hawkins w. up w. me to ye Rect. & asked whether as it is reported I had called ye Bible Class all hypocrits. Of course I denied it at once. It is not only a lie but a silly lie. . . .[4]

3 Mar. . . . Long t. w. Miss Press. I sincerely pity her: her [final teacher's] certif[icate] is not issued. She has worked hard, but under sad disadvantages.[5] . . . What a day. I had to speak to G.Lander & Eliz[abet]h Croft conduct very unsuitable to girls of 13. In ye case of ye latter a spiteful

Valentine sent to Mrs Daw bec[ause] she had complained of the 2 girls walking with her son & a young Harmer. Whom can we trust? . . .

6 Mar. . . . My lect. at 7. Admiss[ion] free. 160 persons present so J.Sawyers said who counted them. Ye Burwash "jokes" told well. People seemed interested. 1 hour 30 min . . .

22 Mar. . . . Wrote to Mr. John Bowne of Robertsbridge saying that I cd. not attend ye meeting of ye Farmers Association on Fri. as I felt that it was a clergyman's duty to remain neutral, on the ground of his inability as a non-professional man to judge rightly in ye dispute between labour & capital, & also on ye ground of his neutrality being the best chance of mediation.[6] . . . a letter from Mr. Wyndham of Sutton Mandeville Rectory, Salisbury, suggesting that ye dogs & ye "long run" might have belonged to Lord Castlehaven an Irish Peer who kept hounds at Grovely (?) House nr. Salisbury & whose hounds were notorious for speed & endurance. . . . C. on J[ames] P[hilcox], he told me that Mr. Whatman had c. on me to ask me to interview Mr. Murriéta, & to represent to him, that his giving higher wages than his neighbours rendered it difficult for others to refuse to give the same. I told James that I cd. not undertake the job. It wd. never have done for me to leave undertaken an embassage from the men of Burwash to the men who were working for Mr. Kemp last year at 2/3 [per day] & to have represented to them that their working for lower wages than the rest hindered the rest from getting more. James quite saw it. . . . He upheld my determ[ination] not to interfere. . . .

23 Mar. . . . Wrote out part of my lecture wh. I wish to deposit in ye Par[ish] Ch[est].[7]

25 Mar. . . . Coming home overtaken by Mr. Langridge late of Grantwizzle. He now managing matters for a Mr. Clement or s [Clements]. He says that the obstruction of all feeling of common interests & sympathy between man & master in his trade is complete. . . . I c. on J.P. & then to ye Parish Meeting. Adj[ourned] to ye Bell. More than [usual]. Mr. Combs, Mr. Whatman, Gillham, Crump, Taylor, Brett, H.Jarvis, J.T.Jarvis, Fuller & Coppard, also J.Coppard. Mr. Fuller got an incr[ease] of £5 [to £30] salary as highway Surveyor. Mr. Wh: quite recognising my position & agrees with my view. The meeting thought that no sentiment wd. be offended by my taking up some of ye nearly buried tomb-stones, & fixing them agst. ye Ch: wall or elsewhere so as to give more room, nor by putting ye Stone Coffins mon[ument] in a safe place, nor of shifting some of ye seats in ye tower, where ill-behaved boys do congregate. I away about 9.15. C. on JP; at ye meeting yesterday at Robertsbridge ye Burwash farmers not officially represented. Ye farmers there I believe determined to resist; we shall see. Mr. Gillham said he had just paid his men for hop-digging at wh. they earned 4/- a day.[8]

30 Mar. . . . To Mr. Gibbs at 8.30. Mr. Whitehead Snr. & Jnr. there, Mr. & Mrs Prothero. Much talk about ye labour question, & other social topics. I lent Albert Payne who was there, some pamphlets. . . .

6 Apl. . . . Had a long t. w. Frank Russell Jr. he doubted whether ye advantage of popular education, & yet he a man who has educated himself to a high degree, but ye uprising[9] of ye people frightens him. . . .

7 Apl. . . . Buried old James Edwards 77, ye man who asked me how it was that whenever he got a little too much to drink, he always felt more religion than he did at any other time! He much satisfactorily changed. . . .[10]

Sat. 8 Apl. All the morg. hunting for a text for the Unionists. . . . C. on Mr. J.B.Noakes, for change. He told me that 2 of his cats, a favourite little dog of his son's, besides a cat of Miss Hyland's had been poisoned. Ye death of ye dogs was it was supposed ye primary object, & he suspected a neighbour but I fear without reason.[11]

10 Apl. C. Day . . . a native of Leggatt ? nr. Exning, & he himself received 4/6 a week for 18 weeks during ye strike.[12]

14 Apl. Good Friday. . . . Much marble playing, but not so much I think as in years past. . . .

15 Apl. . . . Finished ye Serm[on] for Labourers Union.

Sun. 16 Apl. . . . In aft. ye Unionists attended in large numbers; very orderly & attentive. I pr. from Matt. 15, 13 (Ext). I tried by God's help to hold the balance even, & to speak for peace. I said that any movement among men in order to succeed must be based on Justice, & carried on without bitterness & malice, that merely obtaining a demand did not prove its justice, that any movement was a failure & practically rooted up wh. ceased to make men happier, & that again merely obtaining what was asked did not prove the success of the demand, as it might produce covetuousness, indulgence & wh. wd. produce in turn unhappiness. I mentioned a threatening letter sent to Mr. Burgess in Salehurst[13], & deprecated such a spirit, & I counselled arbitration of disputes must arise, & earnestly urged all classes to try to understand each others position & difficulties. The men made a collection for the T[unbridge] Wells Infirmary £1:11;4 1/4, wh. they gave me to forward. On the whole I was heartily thankful for the opportunity of speaking in God's name at such a time. . . .[14]

18 Apl. . . . I to Vestry meeting at 7. C.Coppard kept us waiting 25 min: & never uttered a word of apology. Our difficulty was to know what to do with a surplus loan rate of about £8, & how to get ye arrears of Mr. Roberts of Holmshurst & of one or two more. Adjourned meeting. . . .

19 Apl. . . . I dined w. ye singers. All very pl[easant] as long as I staid. Mr. Cramp in ye Vice Chair, dinner excellently served. Mr. Fielden[15] tackled me for not telling him about ye parish Magazine, & said that I wd. do better in the parish if I tried to be more friendly to people. I referred him to Mr. Barrow who was w. him in Mr. Smith's parlour. . . .

21 Apl. . . . I c. on Mr. Daw, he drew my attention to the state of the benefit club, apart from £25-19-1 ye revenue fund subscr[iption] almost entirely by hon: members, they have in hand only £13-0-7. He seems to think that ye sec[retary] is playing into the hands of the Union benefit Club.[16] . . . George Mepham ye Sec: of ye Labourers' Union [Burwash branch] was very complimentary to my Sermon on Sunday, & asked leave to have it printed in ye Union newspaper. I gave him the Sermon. . . .

Sun. 23 Apl. . . . Since last Sunday's sermon I seem to have noticed a marked increase of civility on the part of the men whom I meet. . . .

27 Apl. . . . C. on Harry Pagden about music. He pays 3/- a week rent for a cottage with only two rooms of any account, & wh. lets in the wet.

29 Apl. . . . 12 copies of ye Kent & Sussex Times ye Labourers Union paper sent to me from ye office [Maidstone headquarters]: about half my sermon put in. . . . Ye Union [branch] sent up Hilder w. 12 copies of ye paper, as a present. I did not need them.

30 Apl. . . . Bible Cl: Albert Honeysett has rejoined, so the secession re. Wells has only amounted to two. . . .[17]

5 May. . . . A meeting of ye Benefit Club about a feast; funds very low.

7 May. . . . in aft . . . Congr. small as a number of ye men were at a Union Ch: Parade at Heathfield. . . .[18]

8 May. Sch:. . . . meeting about 3. About 12 there. . . . Revised list of school fees. Labourers raised to 2d. each child; Ellen [Gould] & Miss Tilley represented "women's rights" by attending. . . .[19]

12 May. Burwash fair. I merely went thro' on my way to ye Common. . . . Home. Singing. 3 boys abs[ent] in ye fair, Brown, Dann, Copper. . . .

Sat. 13 May. . . . C. on Mrs Pilbeam, but her husb: was blaspheming & drunk down stairs, so I came away. . . .

[Summoned to Swanley where his father died on 15 May.]

20 May. . . . . c. on Maria Hawkins (2/-). Her father old T.Hawkins has died somewhat suddenly. I had not seem him. The refusal of parish relief except in ye form of an "order for ye house" had greatly distressed him, & till I am better informed, rightly so, for he was a deserving old man.[20] . . . C. on Bentham Fuller, & looked over his garden wh. is nice. He says some of the well to do labouring men are taking to drink 1/3 port! but the 1/6 gin is going out of fashion! . . .

23 May. . . . Yesterday had a t. w. Mr. Gillham & Mr. Newton Taylor about relief of [the recently widowed] Jane Vigor & [the case of aid denied to] Thos. Hawkins now dead. It is hard to prevent any general rule becoming oppressive at times. . . .

25 May. . . . D. w. ye Club [at the Common] only 26. D. in the big room at Hallaway's. So long as I was there, all was well. . . .

26 May. . . . A heavy Burwash day at H[urst] Green [Petty Sessions] 6 boys up for assaulting a girl, she however no acc[oun]t, still it is bad.[21] Mr. Smith of ye Bell for unlawful hours dismissed. I & others testified by writing in his favour. . . .

27 May. . . . God gave dear N. her first born child; a daughter; dear N. behaved very well I believe, & bore her pain bravely. . . . The baby, healthy & vigorous I am told. I went up & saw dear N. shortly after, she was calm & free from suffering. . . .

Sun. 28 May. To Sch: Ye Ch: Clock has taken to striking! [of its own volition]. . . .

30 May. . . . Club. I pr. from St. John 3, "Except a man be born of water & the Spirit" etc. . . . Hardly any body in Ch: but ye Children, very quiet & attentive. . . . D. w. ye Club at 1.15. Hardly any high table, very orderly, good dinner, music better than common. I sat till about 4 o'Clock. . . .

31 May. Mr. Newton Taylor came for me to go & see poor Mrs Waddell who had again attempted suicide, & whom Mr. Combs certified to need restraint. The poor woman knew [recognized] me & asked after my wife, but kept on groaning, "I am very wicked". Knowing that once before she tried to cut her tongue out, I signed the paper [committing her to the County Asylum]. . . .

5 June. . . . C. & P. w. old G. Copper (86) a true Dissenter, but says his own people don't come bec[ause] they only come for Sundays from a dist[ance] & have got to go away at once by train. To ye Marionettes, not quite so edifying, but no harm by creating laughter by antics of a drunken negro; still I really don't think any evil effect will remain. . . .[22]

7 June. . . . Ye Marionettes cleared away & gone to Robertsbridge. . . .

Sun. 11 June. . . . T. w. C.Hilder & others lounging on a tomb stone in Ch: yd. & aft. Ch. they met me again. I spoke, they said they had been to Ch; I begged their pardon sincerely for having doubted their word, but C.Hilder had told me a sad lie some Sundays ago.

[Visiting Oxford from 12 to 17 June.]

27 June. . . . C. & t[ook] tea w. John Coppard & his wife; the latter gave me a sad insight into the anxieties & troubles of a farmer w. a high rented farm (80 acres £130) borrowed capital, & a rising family. . . .[23]

28 June. . . . a letter from Mrs Pagden accusing me of tempting Children away from her school, & using language wh. I own is exceedingly hard to bear. I answered by ye mailman assuring her that she had been utterly misinformed, & that I must request her to furnish me with some proof of her assertions. I am having many disenchantments just now in my relationship with the parish, but on honestly examining my own conscience in the matter I cannot accuse myself of wrong. That I have made enemies I cannot deny, but in every case so far as I know, I have done it by speaking of matters wh. I cd. not conscientiously pass by. This particular charge is a real calumny, & I trust that I may have a chance of proving it to be so.

29 June. . . . C. on Mrs Pagden. She wd. hardly hear what I had got to say, & flatly refused to believe me. She gave me the name of Mr. & Mrs John Coppard & said that Mrs Coppard herself had accused me. To ye Comm. to ye Sch: but I was too hot to take a class of them. . . . to the Park saw Mr. & Mrs John Coppard; they both declared that there was not a shadow of foundation for what Mrs Pagden asserted. They promised to go up & see her. . . .

30 June. . . . a Mr. & Mrs Burridge (?) & others in ye street. Mr. B. had not been in Burwash over 40 years; said that he did not notice much alteration! . . .

1 July. . . . C. on Mrs Coppard. She in a great state. I can only fancy that she in her nervousness in speaking to Mrs P. about taking the boy away, had said that I had spoken about it to John, instead of John had spoken about it to me. I tried to set the poor woman's mind at ease. C. on Mr. C. in ye . . . meadow. He had been up & had expl[ained] the truth. C. on Mrs P. she very sorry, & quite exonerated me. . . . I fully forgive all, & this is set right, so now w. ye exception of ye rough boys & men I have thank God hardly any enemies, or rather people at emnity w. me.

5 July. Much letter writing, & one to Mr. Courthope for poor Mrs Heath now of Ticehurst to plead for a cottage. . . .

10 July. Sch: Beset afterwards by several poor people appealing from the decision of the Relieving Off[icer] & B[oard] of G[uar]dians. I cd. do nothing but give a shilling. The Board are evidently trying to enforce more self-reliance & to inculcate the duty of children supporting their [aged] parents. . . .

12 July. . . . Elliott Fuller c. on me; had ridden from Chalvington on his bicycle. 20 miles. Nice young fellow, but what is he to do? No great wits, & no great application. He started back about 5.30 & expected to be about 3.30 [3½ hours] on ye road. . . .

15 July. . . . C. & t. w. poor [Zenas] Clarke. He talked of applying for relief. How is it that a man who for two years has earned 15s + 5d [per day military] pension & at least 4s wife earnings, or 24/- a week is hard up 10 days after stoppage of pay [on leaving Egerton's employ as gardener].[24]

7 Aug. Bank Holiday. I drove Etty to Ye Union Workhouse. Ye Iron Ch: opened. Ye Bishop gave a capital address. Ye Collection £26-8-10. . . .

6 Sept. . . . Much excitement owing to ye mail cart having been robbed on Monday [4th] night, by ye driver it is supposed who is missing. Ye horse was tied up close to Mr. Ridedate, & about £20 was gone.

7 Sept. At 11.30 Miss Fanny Augusta Newton was married to James Fullwood Esq. of Monkstown Co. Dublin Ireland. Ch. remarkably pretty, ye decorations capital. Dear N. played ye organ & gave them Mendelssohn's Wedd. Mar. Mids[ummer] Night dr. on coming out; they gave me a two guinea fee. Etty helped, & he & I to breakfast at ye Franchise. . . . I prop. health of Bride & Bridegroom. I liked him. I suggested that as Newton was immortalized by discovering ye law of gravitation, how must F. be imm. by discovering Newton. I also hoped that the "Home Rule" wd. be mutually pleasant & that ye income of ye new married couple wd. be a satisfactory one, as an Irishman's capital is always dublin'! They away by 3.0 to Etchm., & we away soon after . . .[25]

13 Sept. Sid[ney] Irwin c. & we laid down our lawn tennis court.[26]

[14 to 28 Sept. on holiday in Bournemouth.]

30 Sept. . . . C. on Mrs Pilbeam: [husband's] escapade will cost him nearly £10, fine £3, costs 18/-, Lawyer £3-3-0, Exp. say 5/-. Loss of time 5/-; journey to Hastings to instruct counsel 4/-.[27]

3 Oct. . . . A poor discharged soldier Robt. Morgan just disch. from RA (?) found dead in W. Pennells hop garden on ye Common. Heart disease. Last seen 4.30 on Sat; if he lived to one min. past 12 on Sun. he was entitled to 1/4's pension ? When did he die.

12 Oct. To ye Comm: having c. at ye Sch. at B. Took ye class in ye hymns wh. they were going to sing & used these as texts for comment. Poor Miss Press. Ye attendance deplorable & her work very uphill. *She will leave* I fancy & I cannot wonder. . . .[28]

17 Oct. Sch. The white horse came down from Mr Taylors. My first essay in horse keeping. . . .

19 Oct. . . . New trouble. Leycester's chicken in the Ch: Yard. I spoke very civilly to his wife. . . .

20 Oct. To St. Ph. in morg. Took Class. Had to see two boys being punished by Miss Press; one had 4 stripes on hand for playing truant & telling a lie: the other, two for plain truanting. . . .

23 Oct. . . . to N. School on ye Common. . . . 19 at School. Hazelden, W. Dann & Bob Read ye teaching staff.[29]

24 Oct. To Fontridge. C. on a good many people. An interesting conversation w. old Master Payne & Mr. Osborn in ye potato field. Payne t. excellent philosophy. Such talks are pleasant. He a chapeller.[30] C. on Mrs Clear (2/6). She said her husband "bursted" as he was being carried to burial, just by the old Etchm. pay gate, also that when old Master Fellowes was being carried to be buried, the cart upset at the corner by Mr. Buss's, & that the coffin & the mourners were all thrown out. . . . C. on Mrs Gillett. I wanted to see her husb: about hop-tithe average but he not in. . . . C & R. w. Mrs Gardner, gave her 5/- towards loss of 14 chickens, killed by a dog. . . . C. on Mrs Sands (Stevenson Cottage), gave her 1/- for the potato wh. she gave me in the spring, as a specific for lumbago. . . .[31]

30 Oct. A man pleading at the meeting of the Ticehurst Board of Guardians for more relief, was addressed by the Chairman in the not unfamiliar words. "We are afraid Master Styles that yr. wife isn't a good manager" to wh. friend Styles made answer. "Well Gentlemen I dont know nowt about my wife not being a good manager, but I be quite sure of one thing, she cd. manage a good deal more if she cd. get it'.

[From 31 Oct. to 3 Nov. in Wiltshire.]

7 Nov. . . . Sent verbal description of boundaries of new district maps to Eccl[esiastical] Comm[issioner]s. . . .

9 Nov. . . . A letter of mine about Agr. Lab. Union appeared in Ye Guardian.[32] . . . In aft. c. on old Master Weston & had a long colloquy w. ye wife; curious history. 1st husb: convicted on sheep stealing & sentence of death recorded: he transported for life. She taking sentence of death being recorded to mean that her husb: was legally dead wished to be married to master Weston but Mr. Gould refused as she did not know that her husb: was dead, so she having been told by her mother that "going to church" was only a form that the children might have a settlement, proceeded being as she said young & foolish to live w. master Weston as wife, & so continued for many years, but was eventually married. Ye old man to day nearly dying.[33]

10 Nov. To ye Common. Took a cl. at ye school. Poor Miss Press in great trouble because Mrs Hartfield wanted to send her boy aged 12 to a man's school. She felt that a woman's sch: was being slighted. If it had been a man that was slighted pretty Miss Press I shd. have been quite humbled, but a woman I must leave to settle matters w. a woman. . . . C. on Mrs Hartfield. She is to make her boy keep his times this year w. Miss Press, & then he is to go to Burwash. Tithe dinner. All in good humour. Payments fair. I stopped till about 6. In answer to a bit of chaff of mine, Mr. Taylor said – We've been talking politics this aft. & have left sheep ticks alone. . . .

Sun. 12 Nov. . . . Tried heating app[aratus] in Ch: didn't act well; not understood. . . .

13 Nov. W. Mr. Gibbs to ye Ch. to try to find out what ye explosive noise in ye heating app. was yesterday aft. Cd. find nothing, so invented theories. . . .

15 Nov. Mr. Barrow c. to see me about ye field. He upset me a good deal by saying that I had been listening to people who had been poisoning my mind agst. him, an idea for wh. there was no foundation. I in my turn by being too hasty perhaps & by saying that if this was the idea in his mind it was no use our going into accounts, upsets him, for wh. I was sorry. I wrote to say that I had asked Mr. Jesse Piper to arbitrate. . . .[34]

16 Nov. Mr. Taylor c. up & spoke to Mr. Barrow. I wrote a note to Mr. B. saying that I was truly sorry if I had given him pain by what I said yesterday. . . .

[17 to 21 Nov. in London.]

22 Nov. . . . C. & P. w. Mrs Pilbeam [Snr.], very ill, expecting to be tapped for ye 2d time, tomorrow. . . .

27 Nov. . . . My letter to ye Times about pheasants in this mornings paper headed "Exchange wh. is Robbery". . . .[35]

28 Nov. Mr. Piper c. over about 11. He & I adjourned to ye field, & met Mr. Barrow. He [Piper] heard all that was to be said on both sides, & then assured Mr. Barrow that I had acted fairly & honestly in asking 30/- an acre + taxes. I fear that my tenant hardly saw it, but what cd. I do more than refer the question to a man like Mr. Piper.

30 Nov. . . . C. & R. w. Mrs Pilbeam, has been tapped for ye 3d time! 10 qts of water taken away. . . .

5 Dec. . . . Frank Thompson has a curious collection of odds & ends of ideas for a boy of 9. He told me that at Xmas some of the boys go about singing
"Poor Billy's howling & dont know what to say
So give poor Billy a halfpenny, & then he'll run away"
also about the white marks on the nails he had picked up from a book
"A gift on the finger is sure to linger
A gift in the thumb is sure to come"
a prediction with wh. I fancy the rhyme had something to do. . . .

6 Dec. C on Master Sawyers, still in bed. . . .

7 Dec. . . . Met Mr. Gillham. They have favourably considered Emma Fuller's case at the Board [of Guardians]. . . .

18 Dec. . . . C. on poor Master Sawyers: there is no hope I fear.

21 Dec. . . . Sat at distrib. of dole from 10.30 to 1.30. Mr. Cramp, Mr. J. Fuller & C. Coppard also there. Limiting ye gift to families w. 3 ch: at least, lessened the applications a good deal. . . .

23 Dec. . . . Poor Sawyers d. about 6 o'Clock this morg. I have lost a most useful helper in the parish; he was a simple-minded, God fearing, earnest man, blessed with a good understanding of Holy Scripture wh. he read & expounded in the cottages with much benefit to the listeners. He is, I humbly believe at rest in Jesus Xt. I c. on Mrs Sawyers & promised to see to ye funeral for her, arranged w. Jonathan Sinden. . . .[36]

Sun. 24 Dec. . . . Pr. in morg. from St. Luke 2. 25 "Waiting for the consolation of Israel" (Ext) applied ye text from ye bottom of my heart to Master Sawyers. I was much troubled to get along. I looked for the poor old man's grey head near the pillar in the aisle, & it was gone. In aft. Pr. from 1st S. J. 3.8 (Chandler, Peter & self). I was ashamed of myself. I had not sufficiently prepared it. The choir sang "For unto us" Handel (Messiah) really creditably, ye treble & basses best.

25 Dec. During the night the singers "rang" the bells contrary to the orders of the Ch. Warden. I must see to it, the tower will be coming down. . . . In aft. rain & very small congr. . . . D. w. Mr. Philcox & his retainers. . . . C.

on Mrs J. Barrow who has been poorly. Mr. very reserved. I wished him a happy new year.

26 Dec. Close Holyday. . . . C. on Mrs J. Isted & wished her a happy new year. Mr. Reuben Jarrett there. C. on Mr. Taylor, & did likewise. . . .

27 Dec. I dined & took the chair w. the Foresters Club at the Bear. We got on very comfortably. Mr. Newton's gardener came up drunk, & spoiled the party. Mr. Littlemore of the Rose & Crown asked him to drink, drunk as he was already. This I thought shameful, & I came away at once. Before this happened I had sung "a thousand a year" & was prepared to sing again, but I cd. not connive at drunkenness. . . .

28 Dec. Buried poor Master Sawyers ar 12 o'Clock. I have lost a good friend & a real helper in the parish. I was much affected. . . .

Sat. 30 Dec. . . . lovely night; our niggers came. I gave them 1/- & let them depart without my blessing. Poor work, & yet they have taken pains & that is something. They frightened Peter ye cat who bolted, & in his fright misbehaved himself. I caught him & impressed upon him his misdeeds. I got sadly scratched. . . .

31 Dec. . . . I had to c. to day to tell Master Sands that the bells must not be rung, only chimed; the tower will not bear the ringing.[37]

Notes

1.   Egerton subsequently published an enquiry in *The Field*, through which he received apparently confirmatory intelligence from Wiltshire. See also below, 22 Mar. 1876, and *Sussex Folk*, pp. 105–7, where the story is retold in greater detail.
2.   These were men; hence Egerton's more profound self-doubt and uncertainty.
3.   This latest problem for the Club was aggravated by successful competition from the Kent and Sussex Labourers' Union's Sick Club. When Arch's National Agricultural Labourers' Union tried to create a new branch at Heathfield (adjoining Burwash) in yet another poaching initiative, it foundered when potential recruits 'found out there was no Sick Fund'. *Kent Messenger and Maidstone Telegraph*, 5 Sept. 1874 and 30 July 1875. *Kent and Sussex Times*, 2 Sept. and 11 Nov. 1876.
4.   Allegations of hypocrisy had a strength peculiar to the district, according to Egerton, which he outlined in *Sussex Folk*, pp. 11–2, adding that 'a keen sense of the shamefulness of imposing upon good nature, and a skilful hypocrite must not expect to enjoy his success amid the applause of admiring neighbours'. However, the speedy response of a schoolboy asked to define the word – 'When a man walks lame as hasn't got nothin' the matter w' him' – suggests another interpretation.
5.   Now aged twenty-three, Priscilla Press had had six years as Pupil Teacher at Hurstpierpoint, and eighteen months at Brighton Teachers Training College, before her appointment to the National School on Burwash Common, early in 1873. ESCRO. ESC. 41/1.

6.   The recently-founded 'Farmers Defence Association' was orchestrating resistance to the Union's by now traditional wage claim advanced during the spring when demand for labour increased. Union demands were strongly resisted in villages adjacent to Burwash, namely Etchingham and Robertsbridge, together with Brede, parishes where farmworkers were 'very badly paid' in the Union's estimation, but commanding impressive average earnings through piece rates of 20 to 23/- a week according to the Association. The farmers claimed that on their refusal to pay at least 2/9 per day, their men who were Union members, struck. The Union asserted that these men were locked out, counter-claims which by this date accompanied every dispute which resulted in any stoppage of work. The Union responded with a localized propaganda campaign, led by General Secretary Simmons in person, and ostentaciously distributed cash to the members from 'a pay table' manned by branch officers outside the principal inn in Robertsbridge. The Association was also victimizing local Union leaders. *Kent and Sussex Times*, 4, 11 and 25 Mar., 15 Apl. and 3 June 1876. *Sussex Agricultural Express*, 29 Apl. and 13 June 1876.

7.   The draft lecture is amongst the parochial records deposited in the ESCRO.

8.   The Association said that their men had been earning 4-5/- daily on piece rates. *Sussex Agricultural Express*, 29 Apl. 1876.

9.   An interestingly archaic expression, more appropriate to the Swing rising of 1830 than the much more peaceful campaign orchestrated by the Kent and Sussex; nevertheless, the determination and apparent strength of the unionists, while what passed for traditional deference evaporated at this juncture, certainly frightened the more timid.

10.   Edwards was amongst the smallest farmers, with twenty acres at Little Climshurst.

11.   The killing of favourite pets was a common form of vengeance.

12.   Exning in Suffolk was an epicentre of militancy in East Anglian agrarian unionism from its inception in 1872. P. Horn, *Joseph Arch*, (1971), pp. 102–3, 108. Day was presumably an emissary, returning the earlier support his region had received from the south-east. *Labourers Herald*, 1 Jan. 1875.

13.   The sending of anonymous threatening letters was a traditional form of intimidation, which had declined considerably since its heyday during the Swing epoch. See also note 14. Robert Burgess described himself as 'farmer and hop grower'.

14.   One hundred and fifty members, not necessarily all from Burwash, attended this service at which Egerton had 'been asked to preach a sermon to the Labourers' Union' which he did 'with much pleasure. . . . I cannot help knowing that much of the friendly feeling which may have existed in happier times between employers and the employed is now gone . . .'. He went on to categorically refuse to blame either side, and said that he knew too little of the technicalities to even arbitrate, but he enjoined all to adopt a Christian approach. 'Surely . . . some means can be found out of settling these questions of work and wages without the bitterness which too often arises. . . . There can be no real comfort to an employer in counting over money which is wrung out of the necessities of starving men, nor can there be any real comfort to a man in taking home wages which have not been fairly earned, but which have been wrung from an employer, who, though he could not in justice, afford them, was obliged to give them for fear his whole business would be ruined'.

This report, which derived in part from the draft sermon Egerton gave to the Union for publication, also mentioned the threatening letter, but added that the prime suspect was a member of the Farmers' Association, angered by employers elsewhere in the district paying union rates, and was therefore 'a hoax'. Once Egerton was told, he immediately wrote to the paper to say that if true, such action was 'doubly malicious and criminal'.

In the full version, published posthumously, Egerton also denounced the 'one effect of higher earnings from what labouring people themselves tell me, and that is, the difficulty which the poor now have of getting anybody in their own class to do anything for them except they be well paid for it. Kindnesses, which used to be done for love and from neighbourly feeling, now have to be paid for . . . and this change is a sad set-off against increasing prosperity'. He addditionally warned unionists in the congregation who 'have brought anger, or ill-feeling, or pride, or covetousness into church with them . . . let them remember their Heavenly Father does not own such a spirit'. J.C. Egerton, *Village Instruction: Twelve Sermons*, (Tunbridge Wells, 1892), pp. 88–91. *Kent and Sussex Times*, 29 Apl. and 6 May 1876.

Collections for charities were usually made at such services, not least to avoid the obvious frictions if they went to the host church, be it Anglican or Nonconformist. It is worth mentioning that a significant number of Anglican incumbents were not prepared to entertain the Union. In Kent, at Puckley, for example, the rector told the union representatives that 'he could not think of such a thing . . . as a good Union sermon', and coldly 'reminded us that the wages we should get in this world was nothing compared with the world to come': the Tonbridge incumbent was advised against compliance by the churchwardens, whereupon a unionist asked 'what is a parish church for? It seems . . . that it was never built for a labouring man. I suppose it is because his coat is not good enough'.

Despite Egerton's reasoned stance, some men were locked out in Burwash early in June, and later in the year several members were blacklisted. Ibid., 18 and 25 Mar. 6 May, 13 June, and 25 Nov. 1876.

15.   The newly arrived, retired Arctic explorer, Capt. J. Leighton Fielden. had bought Rampyndene in the centre of the village.

16.   Postulating that in the event of a derisory share-out, members would join the Union's Sick Fund, unless the dividend was boosted by monies from honorary subscribers, who might then stop contributing.

17.   Altercations concerning parents in one of Egerton's groupings, could lead to children, including nephews and nieces, being withdrawn from others.

18.   This was not reported in the *Kent and Sussex Times*, indicating that the union paper did not invariably receive notifications of such events from local branch secretaries.

19.   The meeting was of the National School managers; the allusion is to the 1870 Education Act's enfranchisement of propertied women, who were also eligible to contest seats in those places where new School Boards functioned.

20.   Thomas Hawkins, a friend since childhood of the murdered Benjamin Russell, had given important prosecution evidence in the celebrated 1826 trial. (See above, p. 56, 18 No. 1859 note 17). This episode in some ways compromised all involved, and gave rise to durable inter-familial frictions, but it is impossible to say that a man with such a common name had a criminal record, though other members of his family fell foul of the law.

21.   The six adolescents accused of indecently assaulting Carey Braban on the roadside on 7 May, included Henry Isted, the son of John, who was just twelve. The other lads, George Lulham, William Butcher, Thomas Hyland, George Graham and William Langridge, were similarly aged. Their defence lawyer subjected Carey to a 'very close . . . cross examination', which revealed that she was 'rather confused

. . . as to the time, but not materially as to other facts'. The intervention of the police proved critical, as constable Comber hearing Carey's cries for help 'rushed forward' and 'rescued' her. Each defendant was fined 10/6 with 6/10 costs, or fourteen days imprisonment if not paid within two days. *Sussex Agricultural Express*, 30 May 1876. ESCRO. QR/E1074. Sectors of the Braban kinship were 'roughs', with some of the girls reputed prostitutes; hence Egerton's hostile comment. See also below, p. 230, 1/4 June 1880, and note 13.

22.   Egerton wrote a favourable report for the country press, typically spiced with some local historical reflections. After a thirty-year interval, the revived 'Middle-ton's Marrionettes' staged a week of plays, including 'The Maid and the Magpie'; 'It is a singular instance of the Conservatism of English popular taste in the matter of amusement, that an exhibition which first displayed its cleverly worked puppets when Queen Ann was on the throne, and John Cruttenden sen. and Thomas Weston were churchwardens of Burwash, should be popular still . . . what pleased in 1712 pleases in 1876'. *Sussex Agricultural Express*, 6 June 1876.

23.   According to some agricultural experts, it was precisely those farming exclusively with borrowed capital, who were most exposed as the equilibrium of agriculture was again seriously threatened in the later 1870s.

24.   Clark retired through ill-health, and on 3 Oct. died of cancer, leaving a wife and three children; *Parish Notes*, Dec. 1876.

25.   Fanny, who had taught at the National School, and also assisted with teaching the organ, was the youngest daughter of James Newton. His principal tenants, Whatman and Gillham, plus sixty others 'connected with' the estate attended, together with all the school-children. The girls symbolically wore 'wreaths of hops' and threw rice and flowers over the couple, and also went to the breakfast. The wedding attracted much interest, and 'the path to the church gates was kept clear by cords, attached to posts, which were all decorated with evergreens and flowers'. *Sussex Agricultural Express*, 12 Sept. 1876. *Parish Notes*, Dec. 1876.

26.   Lawn tennis was becoming extremely fashionable in 'parochial aristocratic' circles.

27.   The blacksmith, William Pilbeam jnr. had been prosecuted after a quite typical violent incident between locals and visiting hop-pickers. Pilbeam, in company with labourers Thomas Pennells and Thomas Dann, all of whom were drunk, spawned trouble with William Haynes, father and son, encountered walking along the Etchingham road on Sunday 17 Sept. Pilbeam represented himself as a policeman, and threatened the two with arrest, a subterfuge effectively torpedoed when Dann simultaneously laid about both Haynes's with a huge stick. On their arrest, Pilbeam claimed that one of the officers, PC Comber was himself drunk. Pennells and Pilbeam were bailed, reflecting the former's minor role, and the latter's higher social position, but Dann was held in custody until the Petty Sessions convened on 22 Sept. Pilbeam's lawyer, Jones of Hastings, claimed that Pilbeam had been summonsed only to prevent him giving testimony for Dann's defence, and insisted on separate trials for all defendants. This clearly irritated the Bench, members of which now faced an entire day in court. They threw out the charge of threatening behaviour against Pennells, cleared one of the Haynes for assaulting Dann – a case brought by Dann, not the police – and cleared Comber of the charge of drunkenness laid by Pilbeam. Dann, who had clearly used most violence, received a six-week hard-labour term without the option given to Pilbeam, the enormously heavy £3 fine with 18/- costs, or two months with hard labour. *Sussex Agricultural Express*, 26 Sept. 1876. ESCRO. Summary returns, QR/E1076.

28.   Egerton publicly addressed the issue in the next edition of *Parish Notes*, (Dec. 1876), stressing that the 'irregular attendance' of the 150 pupils on the books meant that 'only some' in standards 4, 5 and 6 qualified for the forthcoming state examinations. The note concluded – unequivocably – that 'A good education is a duty which parents owe to their children; and if they neglect that duty for the sake of a few pence which their children can earn, their responsibility is great'.
29.   All working men.
30.   For Payne see above, pp. 55, 59, 10 May 1859 and 28 Feb. 1860.
31.   A common traditional remedy, used against rheumatism in Hertfordshire in the 1870s. E. Grey, *Cottage Life in a Hertfordshire Village*, (Harpenden, 1977), cited G.E. Mingay, *A Social History of the English Countryside* (1990), p. 131.
32.   Egerton stressed that while he had rejected 'requests to attend class meetings of either employers or employed', he had responded to two Union requests to preach, knowing that farmers would still be in the congregation: he asserted that everybody had 'professed themselves satisfied' with his neutrality, and hoped that 'some day' this would enable him to be 'useful as a mediator'. *The Guardian*, 8 Nov. 1876.
33.   Neither the Assize records, nor the press, for the 1824 to 1837 period, identify Mrs Weston's first husband, possibly because the offence was not committed in Burwash.
34.   The tone of several previous entries, including 22 Apl., 23 June, 1 July 1867, and 10 July 1873, suggest that Egerton's relationship with farmer John Barrow was never easy. Recent entries, notably those of 9 Apl. and 28 June 1876, imply that Egerton's relations with at least sectors of the farmers were soured by what the latter might interpret as the Rector's pro-Union stance in his 16 Apl. sermon. But the real break with Barrow derived from the rent he paid when hiring part of Egerton's glebe, and the question of who paid the taxes levied on this land. See esp. 28 Nov. 1876, 12, 14, 26 Mar., and 6 Dec. 1877. Although Egerton spoke to Barrow at length on his wife's death (see 26 June 1878), there are many subsequent references to the squabble resurfacing, including 6 July 1881, 29 Dec. 1882, when a potential reconciliation is aborted, 20 July 1883, 13 Jan. 1884, 1 and 2 July and 16 Dec. 1885, and 18 Jan. 1886. Jesse Piper was a major farmer at Hawkhurst, just over the Kent border, who had long-term business relations with Burwash farmers, and who secured a stake in Bateman's Farm (above, 5 Sept. 1868), principally for winter pasturage of marshland sheep.
35.   According to this letter – signed 'VICTIM' – Egerton had left a clearly labelled brace of superior pheasants at the railway parcels office at a London terminus, for delivery to a friend at a metropolitan address. The birds were exchanged *en route*, and 'one old bird with only one leg, and another with its breast nearly shot away', were substituted. *The Times*, 27 Nov. 1876.
36.   Curiously, there are few references earlier in the diary to John Sawyers Snr., aged sixty-three. John Jnr. was a successful Pupil Teacher. ESCRO. Par.284/1/5/2. Sinden, like so many village carpenters, supplied coffins, and directed funerals.
37.   The order angered the ringers, and Egerton was at pains to point out that the tower dated from the early thirteenth century, had been 'several times repaired', and at least £100 would have to be spent as 'the top part is now very loose'. *Parish Notes*, 1 Jan. 1877.

1877

2 Jan. . . . C. on old [eighty-two, farmworker John] Rich. Speaking of evil ways, he said "he thought my old Man cd. leave that off if he liked", & as for himself, he had no lusts trouble him now, so why should he want a housekeeper. . . .

5 Jan. In aft. to ye Common. . . . I c. on Mrs James Pennalls, not at home, tho' her d. had just been to the Rectory & said she was not well; she had been met all the same nr. Burwash by Mr. J. Fuller. I took shelter in at Mr. Hobden's, & left 1/6 for James Pennalls, & a note for Mrs. To ye school; singing going on. Govt. music is a cruel waste of lung power on ye teacher's part, & is of no use as far as I can see to the children. C. at Oakdown; suggested no platform for penny reading on the 11th. Mrs Holland gave me a lift in her carriage as far as the Wheel; on getting out I thinking that the trap had stopped, got out but on putting my foot to ye ground I fell plump on my back into the road. Providently not hurt. C. on Mrs Hawkins & gave her dates of baptism of herself & her poor husband who d. on Wed.[3rd].

[8 to 11 Jan. in London.]

22 Jan. . . . ye men from Packham's [of Brighton] came to hot water app. on Friday [19th] & are here again today. . . .

24 Jan. . . . Penny Reading. Mr. Eley read a 27 minute piece called "The autobiography of an umbrella", the dreariest thing I ever heard. Other things good. A Mr. Bailey a Hastings Sol[icto]r, a friend of Etty's sang well. The men encored in "Huntsman's chorus" & much applauded in ye Chapers. . . . After ye concert . . . a small boy asked Fred. Holland the conductor "Please Sir did you 'squinch' your eyes at Tom Harmer because he did not sing as well as Horace Harmer. Horace's mother says she's sure you did."

26 Jan. . . . Master [Albert] Balcombe of Glyddish [Farm] c. to ask me to share with the creditors the loss wh. T. Barden's insolvency involves. I went with him to J.P. who was exceedingly angry with Balcombe for coming to me at all. As JP. is my known agent about tithes AB. it seems committed a heinous offence by coming directly to me. I ought to have sent AB. to JP & not to have gone personally, but I really did not know better, & I thought going with Balcombe was the most straightforward way. . . .

Sat. 27 Jan. Rain, rain. The men went away yesterday, leaving the heating apparatus in good order. In aft. did a little music with N. In evg. c. on JP. He all right again. W. for about an hour on ye drive by moonlight.

Sun. 28 Jan. . . . I took ye morg. duty here & pr. ye warming app. fund. . . . Coll. £4-6-3. . . .

30 Jan. . . . To our school & heard Mr. Emerson taking the 2 & 3rd standard in Reading. I was much pleased both with the reading & with the intelligence of ye children, but the former depends much on ye latter. Mr. E. lunched here. I like the man, only one boy & no girl away for bad weather.[1]

31 Jan. To ye Common. Ye women were not weeping & wringing their hands but were wringing each other's hands for joy. Miss Press will have her parchment, the two pupil teachers have passed, & about 71 p.c. of ye children presented succeeded. Miss P. flapping her hands spasmodically w. joyous motion. I fully share this satisfaction & am very thankful. . . .

6 Feb. . . . In aft. to Grantwizzle. Oh the stiles & oh the needs. C. & had a long t. w. poor Mrs J. Barden; she says it will be a case of selling up. . . . I am very sorry for Mrs Barden & her 6 children.[2] I privately baptised the infant d. of Joshua Harris; it is not likely to live. . . .

12 Feb. Very wet so wrote Lenten sermon in the morning. . . . Finished sermon a thing I have not accomplished on Monday for years.

16 Feb. . . . a letter from ye Bishop announcing promise of £50 per ann. to new distr: [namely, new parish of St Philip's] but nothing about help for ye house [new vicarage], wh. looks bad. . . .

17 Feb. . . . Some excitement in ye village as to Barden's affairs at Grantwizzle. The sale by the Sheriff's Officer is it seems restrained & the arrangements of Balcombe disappointed. He will now have to come in w. the other creditors. . . .

Sun. 18 Feb. . . . A long t. on way home w. Mr. Gibbs about ye "Cross" difficulty at ye workhouse Chapel. Mr. Harrison w. pen in hand is not judicious, & has irritated ye Guardians by a letter in addition to his contumey in replacing the Cross. It is very pitiful, for look at it either way, from Guardians point of view or from Mr. Harrison, the contention does not seem to be very important, tho' I think Mr. H. is wrong, considering his position. He ought I think to have yielded or to have resigned.[3] . . . What we suppose to be a dead rat troubling us much w. his odour in ye nursery. Shifted ye beds, & will send for ye carpenter tomorrow.

20 Feb. Letter from Mr. C.J. Trower saying that the Eccl. Commrs. have given £100 a year in all to St. Ph. so I hope the scheme is fairly safe. I wrote 12 or 13 letters in the matter, as a grant is sought from Q[ueen] A[nne]'s Bounty. . . .[4]

1 Mar. C. on JP & signed undertaking to endow St. Philips w. £130 per ann. My letter to ye Guardian asking ye authority for ye phrase "Catholic Ritual" & other questions, printed in this weeks paper. I wonder whether it will elicit any answers. . . .[5]

8 Mar. . . . To Brighton. . . . Town Hall. Ye Dioc[esan] Assoc. voted St. Philips new district £200! w. complimentary remarks about ye local exertions. Ye Bishop afterwards wished to see me about ye patronage. . . . I w. w. him to ye Railway Station. . . . I to Packham's saw Stone ye man who put up & put to rights ye heating app. . . .

10 Mar. Started soon after 8 & drove to Conyhurst; caught Mr. Piper just as he was going out. Laid JB[arrow]'s accounts before him again. He very kind & offered to go thro' them again w. Mr. B. . . .

Sun. 11 Mar. . . . St. Ph. Large cong. for morg. . . . . In aft. really exc[ellent] congr: One must be thankful to God to putting it in ye hearts of ye people to seek instruction & to worship. . . . Heard a not uncommon instance I fear of ye little practical zeal for religious education on ye part of those who clamour for it. In a neighbouring parish w. large schools [Ticehurst] Eden never teaches, but just goes into ye sch. once a week, & doesn't stop; ye curates take a class but not ye head man.

12 Mar. . . . Prepd. Mary Anne Pennalls for Conf. during part of our t. she burst into tears, touched apparently by something.[6] Tea & chat w. Mrs Whatman. Her cat jumped on to my shoulder & munched bread there. I c. on Mr. Taylor & gave him a copy of my view of ye case between Mr. J. Barrow & myself.

13 Mar. C. on JP. C. on Mr. J. Fuller & went into ye question of ye acct. w. him & Mr. Barrow. Mr. B. had c. on me just after br[eakfast]. The facts are now fairly agreed upon. The deductions from them are in dispute. . . .

14 Mar. . . . Mr. Barrow accepts Mr. Piper's argument . . . so I trust the matter is amicably settled at last. . . .

Sun. 25 Mar. . . . . Cong. thin as there was a strong counter-attraction at ye chapel, ye "circus" [a skit on circuit] preacher as J. Hyland called him, a Mr. Eldridge being there. . . .

26 Mar. . . . C. on Mr. Barrow, & went thro' figures w. him. His amended version as I make it out that in about 32 years I shd. be two or three pounds in pocket by the grubbing! However, we were amicable. . . . C. on Mrs Pilbeam; up & this after 4th time of tapping! . . . C. & spoke to a Th. Eastwood a young apprentice at Sinden's about Conf. He was being prepared by Mr. Mills at Warbleton, but now he pleads youth, 15 next May, & says that he did not expect to be at home at the time of Confirmation but thought he wd. get no harm by going to ye Classes! . . .

28 Mar. . . . d. & then to funeral of Mrs Rigglesford at 2. Being a fever case ye body was taken at once to ye grave. . . .

29 Mar. . . . Mr. Jesse Piper asked me to dine, wh. I did at 2 PM. His sheep have done better this year. A truly business man. . . .

31 Mar. . . . Kemp at Mottingsden told me that friend [Revd] Harrison at ye Union had a row w. ye Guardians & Poor Law Board in 1861 about an "alter-cloth", wh. ye Guardians would not have. Ye Poor Law Board ruled that ye Guardians were supreme on their own premises, or to that effect, & that they now refer Mr. Harrison to their letter of that date. H. has I believe withdrawn the intemperate letter wh. he wrote to ye Guardians a few weeks ago. . . .

1 Apl. Miss Hughes made two journeys to ye Rectory merely to set right some numbers of the Parish Magazine wh. the boy who delivers had dirtied; she also secured the said boy a whipping at his mother's hand, & having lectured the mother herself on her "multitude of words wh. is sin", retired home conscious of having done her duty. She is a vigorous old lady of about 77. . . . Tea w. Mr. Taylor. Parish Meeting. 5 ratepayers present at the Bear, besides the Overseer (Assi[stan]t) & Surveyor! 1/2 poor rate & 10d highway rate passed. . . .

6 Apl. Harrington declines to be nominated [to new parish of St Philip's]. His mother's health assigned as the cause, the Common not being likely to suit her. . . .

11 Apl. . . . A long t. w. Mr. Gillham about poor relief, ritualism, Darwinism, & the weather. . . .

28 Apl. . . . Met Mr. Whatman; he going to Mr. Gibbs about a man – a Benenden man – who has been trying to commit suicide in his pond. . . .

Sun. 29 Apl. . . . W. Coppard complained about ye sheep in ye Ch. yard. I don't like them, but as the Parish does nothing to help me in keeping the Ch: Yard in good order, I do not think I am called upon to spend £4-10-0 in mowing. . . .

30 Apl. Did some reading. I wish I cd. do it every day. . . . Tea w. Mr. Taylor & w. him to look over some of ye needed repairs at ye Rect.

1 May. . . . Mr. Taylor came up about 6 PM, & we looked over some of the timber on ye glebe with a view to throwing it for repairs. Singing w. trebles. Thompson & Blunden came down to take instructions about painting, whitewashing.

2 May. Sinden came down to take instructions about carpenter's work. . . .

5 May. A Mr. Purday came from Mr. Ewan Christain's office to inspect St Philips on behalf of Eccl. Comms. He lunched here en route to ye Common. I c. on Mrs Sawyers pd. her Master Sawyer's doctors bill, 11/6. C. on Js. Fuller & paid £1-6-0 for her rent. . . .

[7 to 19 May in Oxford, then London.]

24 May. . . . D. w. ye Club at Mr. Hallaways; only about 23; good dinner & only 2/6. He can't make much by that. I proposed ye health of ye Queen, & in the middle of my peroration I was baffled by Tom Fielder in a very prosaic voice addressing the waiter "sixpenworth of whiskey please". It was not easy to go on. I sang "A thousand a year" & "When the heart is young", Master Fielders commentary on wh. was, If I'd got a thousand a year I shouldn't do much work. It wd. take me all my time to spend it! & also he said "If I had a thousand a year I shouldn't be thinking much about dying". To wh. somebody rejoined Do you think never about it now Master Fielder? Ned Bourner proposed my health with musical honours & gave "For he's a hearty good gentleman" instead of jolly good fellow! All very civil. . . . Meeting at ye sch. at Burw. at 8.30 about ye Xtian young men's association & ye cricket club. Etty there; we read out ye rules etc. H. Pagden & St[ephen] Brown there, & about 5 other young men. It seems hopeful. I hope God may bless it.[7]

Sun. 27 May. Before sermon gave out notice that in Consequence of ye judgment I shd. henceforth use only ye surplice. In aft. I gave out ye same notice & preached in ye surplice. . . .[8]

28 May. . . . I had a notice that I had been elected a member of the Local Committee for Burwash "to give aid or information" to ye "Attendance Committee" under ye [1876] education act. . . .[9]

2 June. . . . Etty called to say that ye doctor in London, Lawson, calls his eye ailment "Apoplesey of the retinue"! at any rate he has to back off any work he can, & keep quiet, not play cricket or the like. Poor man I am quite sorry. . . .

5 June. Aft. br: C. on Mrs Barrow of Woodlands to see ye place for one of ye [new parish] boundary stones. A one-eyed place indeed, & almost inaccessible to a waggon. . . .

8 June. I awoke w. a touch of ye gout on ye big toe joint of ye right foot; ye result I suppose of over-eating & drinking last night [at Volunteer Camp at Lillesden, at invitation of a Colonel Ramsden]; wore a slipper & drank much pignetic saline & lemon juice. . . .

Sun. 10 June. I have had as yet no remonstrance on ye part of ye cong. about ye surplice; so that I hope that my obedience to ye judgment will not be misconstrued.

11 June. To a meeting at the Bear about ye relief list. Master Lee's relief taken off, a half of Wm. Maskells, & 6d put on to Mrs Styles, & this was all that a strict revision accomplished. . . .

13 June. . . . C. on Mr. Taylor. He told me that people are persuaded that my obedience to the judgment is only an endeavour of my own to introduce the thin end of the wedge. I cannot help it. I am very sorry, but loyalty makes me clear that I ought to obey. Sch. singing. I had to request Frank Thompson to leave as he has been growingly troublesome for some time. He was extremely insolent after school, asked me for his money at once for carrying the milk. I really had not got it with me, so I told him he must send in his bill & he shd. have it directly. I c. on his mother. I am truly sorry for his parents, as they are much troubled by some of their sons, but what can I do: it is nonsense paying a singing boy to be perpetually bothering the class & myself. . . .

18 June. Dr. to Heathfield. Put up horse at Half-moon. To Vicarage. Spent a couple of hours going through the boundaries with [incumbent] Mr. Jackson; found ye description very accurate.

19 June. . . . Sing. w. ye men. Much tried by some remarks about our always singing things over again, wh. indeed we don't do. Whoever said that "temper is nine tenths of xtianity" said what is near the truth. . . . I found Mr. Gibbs answer. Kind in spirit to me personally but bitter agst. my Ritualism! He says that tho' I do not know it, I have always been a Ritualist! as instanced by the decorations in Ch. with wh. I have never had any thing to do, & my having been asked to be a member E.C.U. Why the man who asked me knew nothing really of me. . . .

20 June. . . . Singing w. boys at 7. Fr. Thompson rejoined. I do hope he will be a better boy. I am sure I have no objection to him, if only he will behave. . . .

21 June. A letter from Mr. Gibbs written in a generous spirit accepting my disclaimers of Ritualism. I am so much relieved. . . .

30 June. . . . Looked at ye cricket. Ye Christian Association element is I fear weak; cricket has absorbed it. . . .[10]

Burwash High Street with its row of pollarded lime trees, *c.* 1910

The north side of the High Street, *c.* 1880

The watermill at Witherenden. Burwash boasted two other watermills: Dudwell Mill was demolished by Rudyard Kipling while he renovated Bateman's Mill and added a turbine

Rock Hill windmill at Burwash Common

Looking west along the High Street *c.* 1905. The cart is probably transport to Etchingham Railway Station, 2¾ miles distant

Cattle and sheep being driven along Burwash High Street, *c.* 1900

Manwaring's General Store at the top of Square Hill. It stood next door to the police station, *c.* 1905

A posed study of the staff and delivery cart of Ascott's bakery, one of three bakeries in the village, *c.* 1905

Fair Day at Burwash – traditionally held in the High Street until *c*. 1910. Farm animals are being driven along the High Street. Note the traditional Sussex smock worn by the boy in the centre, *c*. 1890

Pedestrians passing Jarvis's butchers shop. The building on the left was then the Blacksmith's Arms, *c*. 1900

The Norman parish church of Saint Bartholomew. Egerton's memorial in the form of the restored tower and new clock was funded by public subscription

A half-timbered cottage along School Hill. Although the roof is tiled, the ridge itself is still obviously thatched

The White Hart, *c.* 1908

The Bell Inn, opposite the parish church, *c.* 1905

The Admiral Vernon on the Square, *c.* 1905

Looking east along Burwash High Street, with local farmer, Walter Morris, leading his dung cart along, *c.* 1905

Ploughing a hop field at Burwash Weald, with the hop poles stacked into wigwams, *c.* 1890

A gang of woodcutters

Girls at play, Broad's Cottage, Burwash, *c.* 1908

Burwash Common – The Labour in Vain Inn is on the left, with Daw's Stores and the village reading room further along, 1905

School group at Burwash National School, *c.* 1890

The staff of Franchise House, north of the village, pose for the camera, with most of the men clutching a tool of their trade, *c.* 1900

The Misses Trower, local benefactresses to such institutions as the school and church

Top of Spring Hill, Burwash, *c.* 1905

Burwash High Street, *c.* 1880. Note the pig in the roadway. The Blacksmith's Arms is behind the man on the right

The barrels along the raised pavement of Burwash High Street indicate the presence of a cooper's shop, *c.* 1880

A Meet of Tom Pagden's beagles at The Wheel Inn, *c.* 1880

Spring Lane, Burwash, *c.* 1905

3 July. A Mrs Herbert Clifford Saunders c. about ye house [renting rectory for part of the summer]. She as far as first sight went a fascinating woman; elegant in figure, tall, good looking, easy in manner, gave me the idea of being good. She lives at 3 Bolton Gardens, S. Kensington. . . . her husb: . . . was at Ct. Ch. . . .

4 July. . . . A very trying letter from H. Dixon about the surplice. I answered it quite quietly. . . . A more trying letter from Mr. Frank Trower who because I executed ye deed of surrender of the patronage without his having seen it, thinks I meant to annoy him. Poor man. I pity his temperament. I never thought about it.

5 July. . . . To Barrows of Woodlands in ye aft. & saw ye Boundary Stone no. 3 put up at the West of his house on ye N.W. side of ye land; gave him 2/6. C. at Ellen's & took tea w. ye 13 Friendly Society girls. . . . Mr. Gibbs wrote to say that he must separate himself from Church because of the surplice. I cannot but feel that he is judging & treating me very severely & unfairly. . . . He on my representation of facts wrote that he was "both bound & glad" to receive my disclaimer of ritualism, as yet he publicly avows that he cannot worship in the ch: where I am minister. It really is hard, but it cannot be helped.

6 July. Wrote to Mr. Gibbs. A Netherfield man who sold milk accused of propagating typhoid fever by means of his foul well, argued that it couldn't be in any way his well that was in fault, as his wife's sister had sent a letter to say that they'd had titus fever in Liverpool & they hadn't had never to do wi' he's well down there, dat was very certain. 9 years before this outbreak of typhoid fever at Netherfield, a farmer's child who had died of scarlet fever, had been buried in a vault at Netherfield Ch. Yard, & three months before this typhoid fever broke out, the vault had been opened for the burial of the child's mother, & this was commonly "allowed" to be the origin of the fever! The fever was as a fact almost demonstrably traceable to the milk sent out by this man; the vessels in his dairy being cleaned with water from the foul well & some of the milk possibly diluted before sale with water from the same source . . .

9 July. Etty told me that Mr. Gibbs had been circulating his reasons. He really ought to have let me see them. Gave 10/6 to Police Benefit Fund. Mr. Gibbs sent me in the afternoon the letter wh. he has had printed. It is very civil to me personally, & the indictment agst. me is not strong. His ground of action is the necessity he feels of resisting the surplice as the first step in ritualism, but Tatham, Hayley, Eden & Foley have long since adopted it, & he was friendly with them. I wrote two or three sentences in answer. Did a swathing of mowing on Grantwizzle Farm. . . .

10 July. . . . C. at several houses but people were out haymaking.

11 July. . . . Replied to a 2d note of H. Dixon. . . .

21 July. At about 1/4 before ten was sent for to see poor G who being in liquor had fallen into the water cistern in the yard. I pulled him out, laid him down, sent to Mr. Taylor, then got G into a chair & so to bed. I am truly sorry, but it is only the outbreak of a confirmed habit. I spoke to him 2 months ago as seriously as I cd. . . .[11]

24 July. Mr. Etty brought me ye Times of July 14 to shew to me ye leading article about ye 'Judgment in Redesdale v. Clifton' wh. completely bears out my Contention that ye judgment orders ye surplice at all times of my ministration. . . .

28 July. I c. on Mr. J. T. Jarvis to meet some other farmers about ye surplice, but only Mr. Jarvis there. I defended myself to him, & I hope not without success. I made this offer that if any one will give me reasonable proof that the judgment does *not* order me to wear the surplice at all times in my ministration, I will resume the gown. . . . I c. on Mrs Whatman, & had a long t; she expressed herself as sorry that Mr. Gibbs shd. take such a strong line as to sever himself from ye church & go to chapel. . . .

Sun. 29 July. Wedding at 9 of a couple who as Wood elegantly expr: it by Virtue of lying got married here; as he said tho' nominally lodgers at Mrs Mittens, we did not believe that they had lived there at all.[12] . . . Mr. Gibbs again at chapel. I am sorry as I am sure it worries him.

1 Aug. School treat, fine day, but cloudy, & better by not being so hot. 133 chrn. 50 chrn. w. their parents, & at least 150 grown up people. Middleton's band a success; fee £1-11-6. Ye farmers attended in greater force than I have ever had them. Everybody very kind in expressing their satisfaction, so I hope ye misunderstanding about ye surplice is passing away. . . .

10 Aug. . . . C. on Mrs Henry Fuller. She gave me an interesting account of a Sussex farm servant girl's life 50 years ago. It was simple slavery. . . .

13 Aug. . . . C. & had t. w. old Mrs T. Vigor. She was not very sensible, & as Mrs Leaney remarked my talking was little more than "casting parables before swine". . . .

[20 Aug. to 22 Sept. joined family for holiday in North Wales.]

Sun. 23 Sept. . . . Shook hands w. Mr. Gibbs on his way to chapel. . . .

[26 to 29 Sept. in London.[13]]

2 Oct. [The Londoner who rented the Rectory during the summer] Mr.

Saunders c. on me & pd. me for coals, & left a donation for me to do what I like with for parochial purposes. . . .

4 Oct. Dear N. came back by ye express. I am glad as it looks more like home again.

31 Oct. Called on a number of families round ye old Pay-gate to notify them of a Cottage Lecture at John Parsons tomorrow evg.

1 Nov. . . . Lecture at Parsons: hardly any body there.

5 Nov. . . . Squibbing in a mild form going on. . . .

6 Nov. . . . Signed J. Ellis' papers for candidate for police employ in London. A curious change on life for one who began life as a farm lad in Burwash, & then shipped as an apprentice on a collier between Shoreham & Shields; then went to Africa, was for 18 months employed in elephant & Ostrich hunting, & then returned to England. . . .

7 Nov. Wedding. Stephen Sweatman & Ann Russell. He one of my most literary boys in olden days, & now Sec: of Union Club.[14] . . . Tithe dinner. Ordinary attendance. Ye Bear much renovated. Away at 5.15. . . .

8 Nov. . . . Met John Pankhurst jr. & had a long t. w. him. He had been somewhat soused by "the dole" having been denied to him some years ago while it was given to others in a better position in life. I owned the naturalness of his feelings but I pleaded our difficulty in getting at the rights of cases. Having ventilated his not unreasonable grievance, he departed I think more in peace. He is a sober hard-working fellow. Tea w. Mr. Taylor. Meeting at Parsons. Certainly an improvement, about 13 or 14. Altogether this aft. I have been encouraged & I thank God. Meeting at Sch. for Cricket Club. The xtian young men's Assoc. element has been . . . obscured, & Master R. Thompson said that ye rules were fit to light the fire with. His honesty in accepting them was not clear even to his mates. . . .

10 Nov. To ye Common. . . . Took up ye copy of ye [London] Gazette w. ye order of council constituting ye new district of St Philips. Miss Press told me Miss Emily Trowers accident & broken rib, & I talking about wounds & mentioned the value of ye skin of ye egg for broken skins, & never thinking, calmly pulled up my trouser & shewed Miss Press the bruise on my shin. I hope she wasn't scandalized. . . .

18 Nov. . . . [At church] Several regular toppers present. The state of mind in wh. they do not recognize their own habitual sin is a great puzzle to me, & yet I do not suppose for a moment that they wd. allow the sermon concerned them. . . .

19 Nov. . . . John Hyland c. in ye aft. & brought me a kindly worded testimonial from ye Common together w. £25! on giving up ye Incumbency. . . .

20 Nov. . . . In aft. read much temperance literature. Mr. Cooper c. & took tea & went w. us to ye school. A larger gathering than I expected. Etty & self spoke. Mr. Roberts & Gapp came down three parts drunk to make a row, but they failed, tho' I had to humour Roberts after ye meeting by listening for ever so long to his denunciation of drink as "the great curse of our country"! They did no harm; indeed the exhibition they made of themselves must I shd. think have been an argument in favour of abstinence. Etty, self, Miss Etty, Mother Gorringe! & possibly others signed in favour of abstinence pledge. Cramp & Taylor, young Pickett & some others a more general adhesion to ye cause. On the whole satisfactory. N. went.[15]

Sun. 25 Nov. . . . C. Etty who shewed me ye inscription for ye Corner stone of ye new parsonage; not knowing how to Latinize Burwash, & wanting to give its germitive case they had put Burwash : indicating an abbreviation; this I called cowardly as not one of them cd. tell what the : stood for. The word can't be Latinized, so let them leave it in its plain form.

4 Dec. Sch. Up to ye Common. Etty laid ye chief stone of ye new parsonage. A hymn was sung. Then ye stone was laid. Then I offered up a prayer "Prevent us O Lord" & ye rest extempore. Then a psalm was chanted. . . . Then I made an address. A Hymn was sung & then I gave the blessing. Ye day raw, but a good many people there. . . .

6 Dec. Wrote my letter of acknowledgment to ye good people on ye Common. Must get it printed. Sch. in aft; took my younger singers. The denseness of some of them disheartening. . . . Lecture at John Parsons: not many. C. on JP: he gave me 10/- to compensate for Mr. Barrow's refusal to pay more than 10/- instead of £1 to ye Ch. Expense fund, because of ye question about my land. . . .

Sun. 9 Dec. Sch. Some of ye night school boys had pulled up two posts in front of ye sch: throwing them into ye road. It is curious how they abuse their opportunities, for nobody can try more than Etty does to do them good. . . .

11 Dec. . . . C on Mr. Temple ye new Noncomformist minister. Found him a quiet average sort of man. . . .

14 Dec. St. Ph. last time. Took class, & said good-bye to ye ch; to Miss Press & to Annie Hawkes who "nearly shed a tear". . . . at ye Rose & Crown, I c. on Mr. Smith endeavouring to compose a strife between him &

Walter Hicks my gardener. Bible reading at J. Parson's: about 12. Mrs John Isted there, who 15 years ago was nearly dead.

Sun. 16 Dec. To St. Ph. H C celebrated. Mr. Cooper who was instituted yesterday at Brighton read the prayers, & assisted in the H C. He had a cold, but reads nicely. His voice not strong, but he reads leisurely. I d. w. Miss Trower, & said good-bye. I cd. hardly realize that I had ceased to be their clergyman. I c. at John Hylands, & said good-bye to as worthy a household as is to be found in Sussex. Curiously enough I heard St. Philip's bell as far off as the fir trees close by Cherry tree cottage at the entering in of Burwash. I certainly never heard it at such a distance before. . . .

21 Dec. Dole from 10.10 to 1.50. . . . This wretched perjury case against John Honeysett going on again all day, & adjourned once more.[16]

22 Dec. . . . C. on H. Dann & Mrs A. Fuller about their boys going to ye chapel magic lanthern last Wednesday [19th] instead of coming to Ch: as the singing boys are under agreement to do.

24 Dec. . . . Looked in at ye Ch. I suppressed an upright cross on ye font, out of deference to weaker [lower Church] brethren. I took a wedding at 10. A Charles Clout & Harriet Collins. Ye best man W. Britt reminded me that when he married ye bride's sister 9 years ago tomorrow he paid me partly in farthings. I quite remembered! A cheery lot & really amusing in ye vestry. In evg. ye singers came down at 6 PM. & sang in ye kitchen. 2 carols, & "Life's a bumper", the heathens. . . . I gave my usual 5/-.

26 Dec. To St. Ph. Inducted Mr. Cooper. Shortened service. I made an address after ye 2d lesson. . . . Mr. Bolton at Ch! . . .[17]

Notes

1. Advance notice of the examination had been carried in *Parish Notes*, 1 Jan. 1877, together with the injunction that all eligible examinees must 'be present without fail, unless absolutely prevented by sickness'. The report was nevertheless, unenthusiastic; in the examinations, 'a few individuals have acquitted themselves very creditably, but the majority of the children have answered, if at all, very meagerly'. The girls performed badly in both grammar and geography, but a marked improvement in handwriting was acknowledged. Dated 15 Jan. 1877, ESCRO. ESC.41/1. Reports for St Philips do not appear to be extant.
2. Grantwizzle Farm, 110 acres of which forty were pasture, was owned by William Langridge, and tenanted by Thomas Barden, who owed his landlord £352, and unspecified amounts to other creditors led by the London and County Banking Company. Barden, 'farmer and cow-keeper', kept a dairy herd of between fifteen and twenty-one cows, and sold his milk to a Hastings dealer. In a final desperate

attempt to escape from the formal declaration of bankruptcy, he claimed that he was principally a trader, not a farmer, but his suit was finally rejected by Tunbridge Wells Bankruptcy Court on 23 Mar. *Sussex Agricultural Express*, 20 Jan. and 27 Mar. 1877.

3. Egerton referred to the latest altercation between the ritualist workhouse chaplain Harrison, and the Nonconformist and Low Church dominated Board of Guardians; the letters covering this saga across more than a quarter of a century are amongst the Poor Law's successive central authorities in PRO. MH.12143–52. See also p. 190, 31 Mar. 1877.

4. A fund created in the reign of Queen Anne for the purposes of church reform, and commonly used generically to embrace the Ecclesiastical Commissioners, created by statute as a distinct body in 1836, but whose adminstrative reforming remit overlapped with that of the early body. The authority on both is G.F.A. Best, *Temporal Pillars* (Cambridge, 1964).

5. The letter enquired, but elicited no published replies, over the 'authority for the now common phrase "Catholic Ritual"', and asserted that English worshippers forced to choose between Catholicism and Puritanism, would chose the latter. He concluded by trusting that the 'broad common sense which has stood the Church of England in good stead in years gone by', would do so again. *The Guardian*, 28 Feb. 1877.

6. For Mary Ann's subsequent drift into unmarried motherhood see below, p. 286, 1 Apl. 1883.

7. The formal announcement made no mention of cricket, but stated that the 'chief rules' for YMCA members aged fourteen and over, were to 'abstain from swearing and all rough language, from all excess whatever of intoxicating drink, and from any conduct unbecoming a Christian'. Although Etty was in charge, members were enjoined only to attend public worship once a week, not necessarily Anglican. *Parish Notes*, Mar. 1877.

8. The Public Worship Act designed to obviate archaic ecclesiastical disciplinary machinery, increased episcopal powers against ritualists, but the latter exploited 'the smallest legal quibble' remaining; the present judgment removed another ambiguity exposed by ritualists. Egerton would have doubtlessly agreed with the estimation that 'a very serious stage in this Ritualist controversy', had arrived, and the warning in one leading article that if the Anglicans failed to 'adopt successful measures against' ritualists, 'the Church will soon be in a state of lawlessness which will afford a plausible pretext for . . . the most revolutionary measures', namely disestablishment. However, many Low Churchmen and especially laymen, believed that using the surplice for all official purposes, smacked of Catholicism. *The Times*, 14 July 1877. See also below, esp. 10, 13 and 19 June, 5, 24 and 28 June 1877.

9. Egerton speedily publicized the fact that the 1876 'law now makes it a punishable offence to keep children away from school without a real reason'. *Parish Notes*, Apl. 1877.

10. Egerton had in fact publicly admitted the failure of the YMCA branch. Ibid.

11. Occasionally Egerton refers to delinquents either by intitials, or some symbol; usually, other sources, if not the diary itself, reveal the identity, but in this case identification proved impossible.

12. William Fisher, aged thirty-five, a lodging house keeper, married Mary Jane Catt, aged twenty-three; as both were described as the children of mariners, Parish Clerk Wood was undoubtedly accurate. ESCRO. Par.284/1/3/3.

13. Despite Egerton's absence, he kept abreast of local affairs. The farmworkers'

union paper, *The Kent and Sussex Times*, 22 Sept. 1877, carried a leader on 'Religion and the Working Classes'; stressing the hostile 'instinctive intuition' with which especially Anglican clergymen had greeted the emergence of the Union, it admitted that this did not amount to the 'unwise and vulgar antagonism', experienced by Unionists in the Midlands. Nevertheless, South-eastern clergymen had made 'trivial stipulations' including prohibitions of labourers in the congregation wearing 'Union saches and stars', even after services for the Unionists had commenced. Egerton writing on 26 Sept. unequivocally said the leader comprised 'the truest and fairest statement of the case as I have ever seen'. Many of his colleagues feared 'that working men resent all religious teaching whatever as clerical assumptions of authority'. Egerton insisted that colleagues were 'mistaken when they set their faces against the Union'. They should – like him – have welcomed 'the opportunity of shewing the power of the Gospel of Christ in restraining passion, malice, and violence on all sides'. Ibid., 6 Oct. 1877.
14.   Literate Stephen was the twenty-six-year-old son of labourer Thomas, and Ann (twenty-one), unlike her father, the publican William Russell, also signed the register. ESCRO. Par.284/1/3/3.
15.   Twenty-one people joined after this inaugural branch meeting of the Church of England Temperance Society. Egerton argued that 'a coffee room, well warmed and lighted' was badly wanted 'for the supply of tea, coffee, bread, butter, cheese, lemonade and ginger beer, with newspapers, dominoes, chess and accommodation for writing letters, free and open to all comers who might like the public house without the beer'. Insisting that the suggestion was 'not made out of any opposition to our public houses', he realistically perceived that the proposal required a specially erected building, available rent-free. *Parish Notes*, Jan. 1878.
16.   For Honeysett's previous resort to litigation see p. 140 and note 16. This round ostensibly derived from John Honeysett's conviction and fine of £1 on 7 Sept., for working an unfit horse at Etchingham on 23 Aug., on the evidence principally of Sergeant Charles Tobutt and vetinerary Henry Jarvis, the partner of Egerton's closest friend, Charles Taylor. Honeysett farmed the fifty-five-acre Dudwell Farm, owned the adjacent mill, and also had a 'business in London'.

The horse in question, a mare, had wounds on the rump, and on the neck, in addition to 'tetters or warts'; it had been taken off farm-work in late July, and treated by both Jarvis and Taylor. Not only was Honeysett the veterinary practice's client, but Honeysett was also grazing some of Taylor's sheep, and Taylor advised on further treatment of the mare during regular visits to the farm on agricultural business.

Honeysett put the horse to work again on 22 and 23 August, collecting 'stable dung' at Etchingham station, returning with two ton loads in a 'full-sized broad wheeled' waggon, for the three-and-a-half-mile journey. On the 23rd a dressing soaked in 'blood and dirt' covering a wound as 'raw as a piece of beef' came off, and 'ten or a dozen people looked at the horse'. Among them were miller John Burgess, whose tenancy of Dudwell Mill had recently terminated in acrimony, since when Burgess went 'about public houses and markets finding out opportunities of abusing Mr. Honeysett', and now he 'put . . . people on about the horse', including Jabez Ballard, justice Gibbs's butler, Thomas Tassell, Schroeter's coachman, and George Brooker of the adjacent Temperance Hotel. They concurred in advising the two youths in charge, to walk the mare back to Burwash, and get a fresh horse to pull the cart.

They did as advised, and fortuitously a Kent horse-breaker, from Ashford, was at work on the farm when they arrived; he re-dressed the wound 'because the policemen was expected down' to examine the mare. Unfortunately, Tobutt was having difficulty with Taylor who 'would not have anything to do with the case', and partner Jarvis was prevailed upon to accompany Tobutt.

Honeysett responded to his conviction by summonsing Tobutt and Jarvis for perjury, charges heard during a marathon seven-hour sitting at Hurst Green before Courthope, Gibbs, N. Wetherell, and the Revd Luxford, on 16 Nov. Captain Mackay, East Sussex Chief Constable, was present, 'watching' the case against his colleague on behalf of the police. The Bench decided against committing either defendant for trial, and although Honeysett quickly announced that he was not going to pursue the case through privately financing their prosecution at the Assize, Honeysett himself was told that as a result of his evidence, he too would now be charged by the police, with perjury.

The same Bench, bar Luxford, presided over this case on 14 Dec., but it had to be adjourned for a week, when testimony from the seventeen outstanding witnesses would be heard. At that hearing, the prosecution, winding up its case, noted that the trial would be 'impossible to complete . . . if the court sat till midnight', and after seven hours, another adjournment was ordered.

The same three magistrates reconvened on 4 Jan. 1878; the court was crammed, and would-be spectators turned away. The ten-hour hearing proved particularly acrimonious, with justice Gibbs involving himself in a heated exchange with witness William Coppard over rumours concerning Taylor's original testimony, and also revealing that Henry Jarvis was not on speaking terms with Gibbs. A final display of acerbity involved a prosecution intervention after Honeysett's counsel described the 'unimpeachable character' of his client, to the effect that Honeysett had been 'convicted of travelling on the railway without a ticket'. *Sussex Agricultural Express*, 8 Sept., 2 Oct., 20 Nov. and 25 Dec. 1877, and 8 Jan. 1878.
17.   For Bolton see the introduction, p. 20.

1878

12 Jan. Mr Whatman told me . . . he had the following conversation with old John Russell a propos of holidays. Don't you ever get a holiday John? Well Master I doant know if ever I had a hollesday in my life without it war when I went to Craaydon to give evidence at the trial (Honeysett v. Fuller & plaintiff nonsuited).[1] I had two days an't them, & it jes was a party hollerday I can tell ye Mr. W. And when do you expect another John? I don't know as I ever shall have another – but there I'd no right to say that, for I do look for half a day before long, to bury my mother!

13 Jan. . . . C. & P. w. poor Mrs Pilbeam (1/-); doing well after 7th tapping. They took away nearly 12 quarts of water! . . . Spoke to young Edm. Langridge about behaviour at ye singing last night. . . .

14 Jan. Sch. Exhorted for tomorrow. . . .

15 Jan. Mr. Alington c. to day instead of tomorrow, & Mr. Emmerson also. . . . Ye results fair but not more.[2]

17 Jan. C. on Mrs Wickins at ye little Tot. She from Wolverhampton, he from North Wilts. T. w. old Eastwood (1/-) on ye road about Mrs Swale who has been forced I think very unfairly into ye house. . . .

Sun 20 Jan. . . . Sing. in Evg. 3 new bass volunteers, Willy Eyles, Albert Honeysett, & Jack Honeysett: most opportune, as our bass element had got very low. . . .

21 Jan. The 3rd anniversary of our wedding day, & of the completion of 3 years of absolutely unclouded happiness as far as our married life is concerned. Troubles I have had independently of domestic life, & what they wd. have been but for my dear wife. I cannot say but she wonderfully helps me to bear them. May God bless her & our child. . . . NS. A young man son in law of old Knowles, at any rate married a Prodger, lately returned from Wisconsin, U.S. . . . C. to ask me to recommend him for a place. . . .

Sun. 3 Feb. [Evening Service] . . . . Hannah Blackford attended & took ye organ. Ernest Wells reconciled & asked to join ye choir again! I am very glad.

4 Feb. Sch. Consulted w. Anset about any alteration in ye school staff. We are partly pledged to T. Jenner as pupil teacher, & if we had an assistant mistress + TJ. & Hannah Blackford, I don't know how we could stand [finance] it. . . . Some blunder about Parish Magazines, 330 too many sent! a nuisance as the cost is £1-9-0.

5 Feb. . . . To ye School, almost broken up w. whooping cough. . . .

7 Feb. . . . Buried poor Mrs Pilbeam; a good woman. I have attended her as a sick person for 16 or 17 years. Lecture at Parsons, fair attendance. . . .

Sun. 10 Feb. . . . Ye Pilbeams at Ch. in ye aft. poor people their faces sadly unknown in Ch. . . .

13 Feb. . . . Smith leaves ye Bell to day & returns into private life. Farley takes ye house, & am told that Blackford snr. takes Farley's. If he does it will be the death of him. . . .[3]

25 Feb. . . . A Burwash man explained to me his view of political honesty the following apologue. "I've got a sow in my yard with twelve little 'uns. They can't all suck at once because there aren't tits enough. So I shut six of 'em outside, while t'other six be feeding. And the six as be shut out jus to make a hem of a noise till they be let in again, & when they be let in, they be just as quiet as the rest; that my idea about politics". Another gave his view. "I be a miller & I've got rats, & I keep cats, & one day I looks into the mill & there I see cats & rats all feeding together out of one trough at my expense." C. on Mrs Weston. She told me that she & Master Weston were married at Mr. Tournay's [the Civil Registrar] at Ticehurst, & that when they went over there they didn't go together but were to meet there; however Master Weston on his way picked up a rabbit, & went back home with it! & never turned up to be married at all! The ceremony did not come off for another 6 weeks. . . .

28 Feb. . . . Lecture at Parsons; my last. Fair attendance. I am glad I have had them, & I trust that the people who have attended have done so also.

2 Mar. . . . C. & R. w. Mrs W. Kemp. "The forge" is a terribly dirty out of the way district. . . . Mrs Jas. Pennalls complaining to N. of the arbitrary conduct of the landlord said, "We couldn't get a house no one where's, so we couldn't move, but at last we had an 'injection' [injunction], & then we was forced to move in course."

11 Mar. . . . C. & P. w. old Parsons; he gets worse & suffers no pain, but he seems much more earnest about spiritual facts & realities than I thought he cd. be. C. on Mrs J. Isted; a marvellous recovery from abject weakness during many years. . . . A leak in a cracked pipe in ye heating apparatus at ye Ch. has had to be stopped. It is not right that this shd. be necessary so soon after every thing was done.

22 Mar. Uncle N. c. & I w. him to Mr. Gibbs before whom Uncle wanted to swear an information agst. a traction engine for not burning [condensing] its smoke. . . .[4]

25 Mar. . . . Vestry meeting at 7 about 45 rate payers present! Election of Surveyor of Highways, ye great point. G. Smith elected by a large majority. Mr. Bolton from South Binns made a speech. All passed off well, & no ill feeling engendered I hope between ye partizans of Mr. Robinson & of Mr. Smith.[5]

28 Mar. . . . D. w. Mr. Jesse Piper at ye Bear on ye occasion of ye Lamb treat. He in good spirits. His sheep has come up well. After d. I sang "a thousand a year". Mr. P. proposed my health very kindly. . . . Mr. P. told me that he had lately sent two consignments of rams to ye Falkland Islands. I w. to Etchm, Etty w. me for a constitutional. I to tea w. Eley. His parish is a small one but I don't envy him his vestry meetings. . . .

1 Apl. . . . T. Hubert wrote to me to lend £1000 to stock a farm wh. he wishes to take. I wrote to say yes. He offers 4 pc. I hope he will falsify an idea wh. I have, that amateur farming is a very gentlemanly way of losing money. . . .

11 Apl. Great Flood. My pond overflowed, a very rare thing. Hop-poles washed away in Mr. Whatman's brooks. . . .

12 Apl. C. on several to urge attend. at HC. on Easter day. C. on old F. Russell. John Honeysett dead. A troubled & wasted life. Has caused his neighbours almost endless annoyance by law suits & the like. . . .

15 Apl. Buried John Honeysett at 2.30. . . .

16 Apl. Buried poor Ch. Bourner. Sad to see the relations kissing the little orphan children, & saying good bye at the Ch. gate. He only 31 I think. C. on Mr. Bourne at Grove Villa: a disabled Baptist Minister late of Windsor. A much more able & intellectual man than our regular chapel pastor. Spent a very pl. hour talking to him. . . .

18 Apl. Good Friday. Good congr: In aft. much marble playing, & by older men than I have noticed before. . . .

21 Apl. Easter day. Showers in ye morg. but beautifully fine afterwards. . . . good congr: 66 comm. £2-13-7 off: ye singing capital. . . . In aft. good congr: & Etty pr. a good sermon. . . . A flock of Mr. Jesse Pipers sheep 1438 in number, came thro' obliged to travel Sunday because they cannot get food enough for more than night at a place. Home & didn't turn out again, a thing I haven't done I believe since we came back from Wales in Oct.

22 Apl. Pickett came to me. He said that the criticisms of yesterday's service were very favourable. . . .

27 Apl. . . . Etty had a nomination from Govt. to an army curacy. I fear he will go, for ye parish's sake & my own I shall be truly sorry. . . . C. on Bentham Fuller. A nephew in ye electrical instr[ument] line; has made a telephone wh. works capitally, but wh. was unfortunately just out of order when I c. . . .

Sun. 28 Apl. . . . Ye Anthem again twice [at morning and afternoon services]. It is much liked, & Amos Jenner of ye beer shop who has perhaps never been seen in church before, was there to hear it! . . .

30 Apl. My Paul Claypeddle letter appeared in ye Suss: Expr:[6] . . . I spoke to Mr. Ellis about his S. becoming a Sunday Sch. teacher. . . . young Ellis agreed to be teacher.

1 May. Etty sent a note to say that he had declined ye Army Curacy. For myself & the parish I am thankful. I hope he has not damaged his own interests. . . . A few May garlands, but there is no sentiment in the thing; it is simple begging. . . .

2 May. . . . Interviewed Harry Mepham, & asked how it was I had missed him from Ch. of late. "Why you be a Roman you be" was his answer. I tried to explain that submission to the judgment of the P[rivy] C[ouncil] was an act of separation from the Ritualists. Met poor Mrs Barden. T.B's widow; she not long ago was giving a governess £1 a week for her children! so I was told & is now receiving parish pay![7] . . . At ye meeting about ye cricket club last night, Etty yielded up a certain portion of materials to the seceders.[8]

3 May. . . . Ye tea to ye childr: who passed in ye 3 sub[ject]s: & to ye singers. 73 invited, about 61 or 62 pres. Nuts, bulls eyes, aft. tea & thin bread & butter ye great attraction. . . .

4 May. . . . Book Club, very small meeting . . . Miss Miram Combs stoutly arraigned Miss Agnes Irwin for having been up till 12.30 after some evening concert or something of ye sort at Clifton. I did not see the sin, & controverted several of Miss Combs arguments wh. then took refuge in tears; most feminine logic, or rather rhetoric, but very effective. However Miss Smith guaranteed me that I had said nothing rough or rude. I c. on poor Mrs King (1/-) who wanted to consult me as being better versed in the Script. than some, about a dream & an appearance! I said what I cd. C. on B.P. Fuller & carried on a convers: by his telephone; ye circuit now only about 200 yards; it was longer but the length was inconvenient. . . . Walter Hicks interviewed me. He thought he shd. like to find a place where his

wife cd. work or get work. I said by all means, & that he cd. stay if he liked
or go as he liked, only I hoped he will make himself content one way or the
other.

7 May. Sch. A travelling photographer taking the children en mass at dinner
hour. . . . Mainwaring told me that his S. Albert not yet 21 & still an
apprentice as a marble mason was being paid by his master 10d an hour! . . .
C. on Mrs Burgess (1/-) opp: ye Admiral; her husb: in his 82d year works at
Boarders [Farm] & still earns day wages! suffers sadly from fatigue, & the
parish (Etchingham) a week ago took off his pay; it is too bad really. . . .
[In margin, in pencil, against this entry, presumably added later: 'rubbish'.]

9 May. . . . Mr. Saunders takes our house again I am glad to say. . . .

11 May. Wrote sermon. C. on Cramp at Daw's; his boy aged 9 terribly ill
w. rheumatic fever. C. on Mrs Ballard, suffering w. two broken breasts!
her husband works at the "gyptian" digging is the gypsum digging at
Mountfield nearly 4 miles off & walks to & fro daily! poor fellow, & yet
Mrs Cramp tells me that he has worked over hours till he has bought a big
Bible to give to his daughter when she has kept her situation a certain time.
[A marginal note: '& yet 1880 conv. of poaching!'] Surely this is courage in
a good cause. He has latterly owing to break down of machinery been a
good deal out of work. The parish will not allow the doctor tho' there are 6
children, on acct. of his wages. With a willing heart I left her 10/-. . . .

13 May. Our fair. I went up & saw ye bullocks. Business fairly brisk & ye
cattle sold well. Ye boy who had been lying on his belly all Saturday [11th]
& Sunday keeping ye bit of ground in front of ye Bell rewarded, as his
people seemed doing a good bit of business, tho' I saw one young rustic lob
4 cocoa nuts off in 3 shots. . . .

15 May. Club. I pr. from 1 Cor. 3. 23 (Ext) ye are Xt's. Poor congr: Heavy
storm after Ch. Ye people in ye passage to & from ye field below ye Ch. yard
where Farley is holding ye meeting broke down ye fence; a great nuisance.[9]

16 May. Sch. Had 3 boys up to ye Rectory & sorted out ye music from 4.30
to 6. An immense collection during the last 16 or 17 years. Pr[acticed] at ye
sch. w. Trebles at 6.45. Altos c. 8 to 9; 20. Sat up finishing ye music sorting
till 1 A.M. . . .

17 May. . . . C. on Mrs Holland. The shrubs & trees all round the house
growing at a great pace, & the whole appearance of Oakdown is becoming
much more of a country seat. . . . C. on John Hyland, & had tea; ye bread
& butter delicious. . . . C. & had a chat with Mr. R. Robinson. Signed a
paper for him to get his pension. Home after a good round. My popularity
at ye Common greatly increased by my having left ye place!

Sun. 19 May. Dear N's 27th birthday. May God bless her, & give her many happy returns of ye day; all I know is that she has greatly added to my happiness. Sch. Young Ellis now a teacher. . . .

21 May. Sad weather. Thunder, lightning, & rain, & yet cold. Funeral of old Mrs Buss, 82. Ye grave not made big enough by about 2 in: at ye top, but fortunately, ye difficulties soon overcome; still it is a nuisance to have any hitch during ye service. . . .

23 May. Sch. To ye Common. C. on Mr. Daw. D. w. ye Club; 19 members. Mr. Cooper d. Mr. W. Kemp & Mr. Robinson d. also. All comfortable. Good dinn: 2/6. I sang my two songs, & then left about 3.40. Ye Club drew on ye Reserve Fund for 11/8 only this year. C. at Hollyhurst, & at Bough Villa. Mr. Pickett's photographs of St. Ph. Sch. Chrn. very fair.

24 May. At about 8 dear N. began to feel queer. We telgr. for Mrs Dadson ye nurse, & sent for Mrs Sam Watson to be ready; about 9.30 I w. up to ye vill. & telegr. for Mr. Blaker. He arrived about 12.30; dear N. kept getting worse, & ye baby was born about 12.30. A great child about 10 lbs. weight, & a daughter. Had nearly strangled itself by twisting ye cord round its neck. But dear N. & the infant all safe, for wh. I humbly & heartily thank God. Mr. Blaker C. here. Nurse c. about 4.45; a pl. person. I wrote 15 letters of announcement. In evg. c. & saw Mrs Combs. The Miss Smiths c. but were not admitted of course.

Sat. 25 May. Wrote Sermon. Old Ben Wood actually w[alked] to ye Rectory again! . . .

27 May. Little Gussey's 2d birthday. She went up to Mrs Combs & was there measured by Mr. Etty, who certified her to be 2ft 10 1/8 in; that if she lives to be full grown she will be it is said 5ft 8 1/4 in. just about her dear mother's height. . . .

31 May. . . . C. on Mrs J. I. Saw Sally; wants a place; good respectable girl. Sale of old Mrs Buss widow of "Parson" Buss's things, out in ye street. What large prices odds & ends fetch at such times. . . . C. on Etty; he seemed very happy gardening, & bedding out plants. I quite envied him his gardening tastes. . . .

1 June. . . . C. & P. w. old J. Parsons. Mrs congr[atulted] me on our 2d daughter & added Well Sir we must allow you to be a man, for they say it takes a man to get the girls, but that a lad can get boys! Plain spoken, but I remember Mr. John Cawley, at any rate the one who lived at Ridley Hall in Bunbury parish, telling me the same thing thirty years ago.

4 June. . . . I took up some jelly to Cramp's little boy. Mrs Cramp told me that poor Mrs Tom Barden who a twelvemonth ago was giving the governess of her children £50 a year! has just had an order for the house! her husb: died & left her quite destitute. It is really a sad reverse of fortune. I trafficked to the am[oun]t of ½ a lb of biscuits at Stevenson's new shop in Fontridge Lane. . . .

5 June. Sch. Funeral of H. Relf's 4th wife! & he a hearty old man still, He semed a good deal affected. . . . Derby day, tho' it made but little diff. in Burwash! . . .

6 June. . . . C. on Mrs John Vidler. Her brother's wife the d. of a publican who can't write his name won't speak to her because she is above her. . . .

8 June. In ye street one of our very thinnest little matrons met a man who was a little muddled w. drink. I suppose she had remarked this, but as they parted I heard him say "well ye flesh won't never muddle you much".

Sun. 9 June. . . . Coming home from ye evg. practice had a long t. w. some boys. R. Thompson being spokesman, who were purposefully rude as I passed. The origin of the ill feeling on his part was ye fact that some years ago I believed John Sawyers version of a matter agst. Thompson. I could not help doing so. He did not believe a word I said, so what cd. I do. I offered to call Mr. Anset as a witness as to conduct in school. Of course Mr. Anset wd. hold my way. RT was most provokingly insolent; we parted however good friends on my part, tho' I question whether my arguments made the slightest impression on him.

10 June. Aft. br: c. on Mr. F. Russell; to my surprize had rallied & was better. I . . . met his grandson Frank in the field; he is now at Lewes, & weakly as he seems, he walked home for his holiday 20 miles! & felt none the worse. C. on Mr. Nevill. His Cambridge son, Frank, at home. They w. w. me up to ye village. . . . A number of holiday makers from London & elsewhere about. . . .

[13 to 22 June at Oxford.]

Sun. 23 June. Sch. Thin thro' chicken pox. . . . Aft. serv. just by ye Iron gate opp. ye Rectory William – one of our thoroughly godless ones lingered about till I came up & then told me that my sermon on Whitsunday & my sermon to day had so touched his conscience that he cd. not help coming to tell me. He seemed very much impressed, tho' I fancied, & of his own accord he told me, that he had had a little beer. He was however in a sense perfectly sober. Still we shall see, & I earnestly pray God that the impression will remain. . . .[10]

26 June. Sch. Sun very hot again. Hicks & I brought down dear N. in a chair. She sat in ye garden & I read to her. . . . I c. & P. w. poor Mr. Russell. A weary departure from this world. C. on poor Parsons; asleep; his only refuge from bodily suffering. C. on Mrs Isted. Sally has got the place at Mrs Adamson's. Has been cook at £16, but wishes to improve herself, so goes as k. maid at £10 wh. I think very plucky of her. She is a good girl. C. & had a t. w. Henry Dann: he mentioned many Burwash boys who had risen in life; in 1834 July, his father kept sentry for 40 nights on Philcox's hill to guide persons while ye road was being mended, & ye valley filled in, at ye same time ye "dip" at ye west end of ye vill. was raised. . . . C. & had a long t. w. poor Mr. [John] Barrow. His good wife died most peacably, & in full trust in the Saviour. Sale day at ye Franchise. I wonder who has bought it.

27 June. . . . C. on JP. Mr. Lucas ye Restaurant proprietor in Parliament Strt. (?) bought ye Franchise . . . for £21000, timber at a valuation. He already owns Mottingsden Farm & Lade's Farm. His Uncle took over the business from a Mr. Henty who came down to Burwash made the acquaintance of Miss Henty [*sic*] & married her. Years afterwards, old Mr. Lucas' nephew the new owner of the Franchise, took pity on Mrs D. Haviland now a widow, & gave her shelter in Parlt. Str. Mr. Kemp of Mottingsden who has been his tenant for more than 20 years gives him a capital name as a landlord, so I hope all will be well. Pr[acticed] altos & Men in ye School. Ye Pagdens say they are working 16 hours a day tailoring. I not in till nearly 11. . . .

28 June. Sch. C. on Mr. Joseph Noakes to see if anything cd. be done to keep the well in the Square more clean & pure. I suggested a pump, but there are difficulties of all kinds. He shewed me a beautiful spring behind Mr. Philcox's cottages. . . . Asked JP to be Godfather to "Helen Mary". He agreed.

29 June. . . . C. on Mr. J. Barrow. He shewed me poor old Parson Buss Bibles, fairly worn out with study. In evg. Mr. Taylor c. on me w. a request from a poor man of ye name Tribe who years [ago] lived in ye parish that I wd. inform him how to get a divorce! as I knew all about his wife. All I cd. do was to recommend him to apply to a man of the name of John Page who had latterly got a divorce from a very bad wife. . . .

Sun. 30 June. . . . I went to Etchm. Overtook an old man with whom I talked. He lamented the neglect of Sunday, & of people's contempt for religion. He said "If they won't have it, they must stand the racket on't" by wh. I supposed him to mean, they must take the consequences. . . .

3 July. . . . C & P. w. poor Mr. Russell & poor J. Parsons; ye latter a terrible trial to his wife who is his sole nurse, as the smell is wretched. . . .

4 July. 21st Ann. of my first doing duty in Burwash. In morg. C. & T. w. old Mrs Relf (2/6) of Platts. She told me that nearly 60 years ago Mrs Carmen wife of Mr. Gould's late bailiff used to keep a day school next door. . . . C. on Mrs Ford who keeps house for Master Budd on Kings Hill. A wonderful improvement for Master Budd. His younger d. married & has one child 3 months old, & will not herself be 16 till Sept! Her name Thomas, & she is settled in a neighbouring parish. It is too bad. Charlotte ye nurse left, & tho' she is going to be married, she seemed to feel leaving Gussey & dear N. very much. . . .

5 July. Reuben Wells c. to get me to sign a pet[itio]n for a 6 day licence instead of a licence not to be dr[unk] on ye prem[ises] at Witherenden Hill.[11] He told me that not knowing his way up to the house he stood half an hour this morg. at ye door of ye passage where ye Perambulator is kept! He then ventured thro' into ye yard, thought he had come to ye front door & went back! how he got in at last he didn't say. . . . Ye County directory Canvasser C. I gave him a good deal of information, & ordered a directory!

6 July. C. on old Mrs Vigor (1/-). She told me that when Ld. Ashburnham who is just dead was married, he had in his employ a man who squinted very badly. It was thought that if ye Countess when in ye family way shd. happen to see him ye chrn. might squint, so ye man was sent to London, & had his eyes turned right! . . .

7 July. . . . W. Coppard clogmaker's S. & Lusted met me & had a t. about some singing class troubles wh. however are not I hope serious.

11 July. . . . Singing w. men at 8.30; absenteeism very trying. . . . A large black strange dog came on to the lawn while I was fiddling in the drawing room. I went out & treated him to some vigorous consecutive fifths, imperfect I dare say, but powerful. The effect was ludicrous: the dog bolted as if all the bagpipers in Scotland were screaming behind him.

Sun. 14 July. . . . Dear N. at Ch: once more, & returned thanks. Drove there & back, but still was very tired. She said ye sermon was good, & so it was. I only wish that I could write such, but do what I will, I cannot. I don't know how. Of farmers we had at Ch: to day, Messrs Whatman, Cramp, Jarvis, Boorman, John Coppard, Spencer & Honeysett, Bourner, & commonly Mr. Whitehead comes. Of course I know that Ch: going & true religion are not always synonymous, but it is something that without any coercion they put themselves under the sound of God's word. . . . Yesterday about 50 workmen from Mr. Vidlers at Hastings dined at Mr. Rose's at ye Bear. They came over in waggonettes, & departed noisily.

15 July. . . . A Mr. Clarke a dissolving view man at ye sch. I sent 1/6 but did not go. . . .

16 July. The Dissolving view men last night were drunk & cd. not go through with the exhibition. Their version this morning was that Mr. Fielden had asked them to his [private] house & had pressed them so much spirits that they got hopelessly intoxicated. If it was so it was very shameful of him. I wrote to him to ask. I married Levi Parsons Luck & Mary Pope at 11. Levi said to me "nobody never tried harder to teach me than you did". . . .

19 July. . . . Mrs John Fuller told me today . . . (a propos of old Mrs Chatfield aged 83 walking from Bodiam last week to see her sister Mrs John Parsons 7 miles, & back ye same day!) that her great gr[andmother] Mrs Button at the age of 95 wd. walk over from East Hothley to Heathfield 8 miles, to see her d. Mrs Unstead, & wd. walk back ye next day. . . . In evg. C. & P. w. old Parsons. Ye Carbolic soap was done good in quenching the smell. C. & R. w. poor Hannah Kemp (1/-); her bed room ceiling not quite 6ft from ye floor; my head all but touches it. . . . Dash restless to-night. I went out to see what was ye matter, & started a man who was apparently peeping about. I did not catch sight of him, but Sarah from upstairs announced his flight. . . .

20 July. Footsteps visible under ye servants hall window; no nails in ye shoes. . . .

22 July. . . . Mr. Gibbs c. in aft. to consult about granting an "occasional licence" at ye Franchise sale tomorrow. He obj[ects] without Mr. Lucas ye owner's consent. I sugg. telegr. at once to Mr. Lucas.

23 July. . . . N. thought she saw a man under ye beech tree, but this time it was a false alarm; it was ye rustic bench. However when we were at prayers there was a real alarm, a great bump at ye front door. Aft. pr. I opened & it was Mrs G. Noakes of Etchm. who had lost her way at our iron gate! I escorted her to ye high road; very dark night. . . .

26 July. . . . Mr. Fielden wrote a note, thanking me for "holding out the olive branch", but reasserting his views about ye Decalaguere & declining ye invitation to ye Sch. treat. Poor man. I look upon him as half cracked, but if sane culpable in ye matter of pressing drink on visitors.

29 July. . . . Fielden caught me & had a long t. about ye drealogue. I objected to its being put up, if not legible, & I don't see where it can be put up in our Ch. to be legible. . . .

[Diary breaks at 5 Aug. until 18 Sept.]

18 Sept. . . . A sad case of anonymous filthy letters before ye magistrates. Ye girl accused fully acquitted.[12] I am glad, as it is horrible to think of a girl writing such things. Bentham Fuller stuck up for her as she was in his service, & engaged Cripps ye Sol[icito]r from T[unbridge] W[ells]. I dug some potato ground in Miss Hyland's for exercise. . . .

Sun. 22 Sept. To ye Sch: & dusted ye seats re[ady] for ye teachers. Ye little girl who is paid for dusting, having excused her carelessness on the ground that she was not paid for dusting in hopping, & yet her mother & herself have been nearly kept going by charity at times.[13] . . . Etty sat during sermon under ye tower & kept ye boys & young chaps perfectly quiet: a great Comfort. . . .

4 Oct. . . . Burwash fair, but a poor do, no business & but little pleasure.

17 Oct. . . . I buried Mr. C. Gates [aged forty-five], but under the circumstances & seeing what a life the poor man had led, how he had lived for years with a woman as his wife, how he had said to me that he was ready to take his oath there was nothing wrong between them, a statement proved to be a lie by the woman's own acknowledgement to me, how he deliberately & knowingly drank himself to death, how he had refused all religious exhortation up to the last, I cd. not read words wh. I felt morally wd. be misinterpreted by the bystanders, so I omitted the "in sure & certain hope" wh. statement 99 persons out of 100 connect with the person who is being buried, & "as our hope is" to wh. people commonly attach a far higher degree of assurance than is warranted by the words. . . .

18 Oct. Sch. Young Thompson informed me that I cd. "tell lies as fast as a horse cd. gallop", a pleasant repartee elicited by the fact that I had seen him laughing when he denied doing so; living in peace with that boy I cannot, as he will not let me do so; his troublesomeness in school is astonishing. . . .

26 Oct. . . . Ye boy who last week told me that I told lies . . . came up this morg. to ask me to let him go chestnutting! Of course I let him go. . . .

30 Oct. . . . I c. on ye new miller at Russell's mill; personally prepossessing in manner & address. I hope he will do, but a pound a week rent weights him. . . . C. on Mrs Blackford; D. w. illeg. child still at home. C. on Mrs Kemp. Her son Mark just out of work for Mr. J.Coppard has nothing more for him to do; so it will be with many I fear. . . .

Sun. 3 Nov. . . . A disturbance in ye belfry before aft: serv: Master Tom Hyland holding that Belfry means Bell-free, & that it is free to all! was very "akkard" [awkward] & troublesome.

6 Nov. . . . Tithe day. . . . Tithe payers paid up better than in many parishes I believe, but I am still a long way behind. I have not exacted the additional average, about $2\frac{1}{2}$ [percent] increase on last year, but have left it as last year. No speeches. I away at about 5.15. . . . At ye tithe dinner ye old Sussex joke turned up of the man who was found toasting a piece of cheese at the end of a 12 feet hop-pole with his back to the fire & who on being asked why he cooked it like that, said that he did so to prevent the fat flying in his face (Sussex cheeses being notable for absence of fat & being better known as useful for making "pinners" for hog pounds).

9 Nov. . . . Overtaken by Mr. Whitehead & Mr Henly, riding fine horses. Mr. W. said he hadn't been able to pay a penny of tithe, wh. was true, but hunting doesn't help to pay tithe & rent. . . .

14 Nov. . . . Mr. Gibbs c. & signed Balcombe of Glyddish's testimonial for T[unbridge] W[ells] Police.

18 Nov. . . . C. on H.Dann's, long conv[ersation] about possible secession from ye Chapel. It is so hard upon Mr. J.B.Noakes who gives money & time to ye cause most freely, but is I suppose autocratic. . . .

19 Nov. Sch. In aft. a young woman c. upon me Sussanah Lloyd by name, lately housemaid at Mr. Murrieta's of Southover. She had been discharged by Mrs Noakes ye housekeeper & wanted me to interfere. I went to Mrs Noakes, & heard ye other side. Saw place where S.Lloyd had told me she had jumped from a window. Cd. not believe it, & ye alternative was her secret possession of a key. C. on Mr. Whatman; end of a shooting party; Mr. Gillham, Boorman, B.Fuller, & 2 London men there. Mr. Whatman very civil about a room for Cottage lecture.

3 Dec. [Following several days laid up with lumbago]. . . . In Evg. w. up to Parish Meeting about Highway Act. Authorized presentation of claims for road from Heathfield parish boundary to Etchm. boundary, & from Labour in Vain to Witherenden Bridge to be called "main roads". Mr. Robinson put in a claim for repairs of ye road up to Park Hill Farm at ye parish exp[ense] deferred till Lady tide. All amicable.

5 Dec. I w. to Mr. Gillham's, & he drove me to ye board [of Guardians]. My contention that the baptismal certificate & certified copies of entries from Bibles etc wh. I presented shd. be accepted as reasonable evidence of age disallowed . . .

6 Dec. . . . Cottage lecture in empty Cott: Mr. Whatman finds firing, light & benches. Not many there. I lectured from Rev. 2, ye message to Ephesus. . . .

13 Dec. Sergt. Tobutt c. to say he had orders to move. I met PC Girton last night who said he was coming here as acting Sergt. I then made up my mind to write to [Chief Constable] Col. Mackay, to say that Tobutt suited us very well, & I have written. . . .[14]

21 Dec. Dole day. I was present all ye time. Mr. Cooper came down for a bit. No difficulties. Old men widowers 2½ lbs, Widows 2½ lbs. Old couples past work 2 lbs each person. Men & women & 3 or more children, 1lb each man & wife ½lb each child.

24 Dec. . . . Singers came out; not nearly as many as last year, but they sung ye old pieces wh. Fleming & his father used to sing, & they sounded very well. I gave 5/-.

25 Dec. . . . D. with JP as usual. The old ones drop off, but the rising generation sufficiently numerous. . . .

26 Dec. Boxing day & Bank holiday. Ye thaw came on & ye day was miserable. Jonathan Sinden c. & did sundry things in ye house. He is truly handy. Lusted's "party" of singers came round 2s. 6d.

Notes

1.   See above, p. 197 and note 16.
2.   The required number of passes was achieved, partially through 'well prepared grammar' at Standard 2, but in other standards the pupils 'have shown a meagre and by no means an intelligent appreciation' of grammar and geography. A more marked improvement was observed among the infants, and Hannah Blackford was now recognized as qualified. Report, dated 7 Feb. 1878, ESCRO. ESC.41/1.
3.   Henry Blackford did take the Blacksmith's Arms beerhouse licence, registered at the 29 Mar. Petty Sessions. *Sussex Agricultural Express*, 2 Apl. 1878. He appears to have survived.
4.   David Wilder of Cranbrook, Kent, was fined 10/- with 14/6 costs, protesting that it was 'almost impossible to prevent some smoke escaping' from traction engines. Ibid.
5.   Egerton chaired the meeting. John Fuller, the relatively long-serving surveyor had resigned despite the recent increase in his salary from £25 to £30; Smith, who had to find a security of £200, was offered £32 a year for the post. Bolton attended mainly to get an agreement on a parliamentary petition for the 'amendment of certain Clauses in the County Government Bill'. Vestry minutes, 25 Mar. 1876, 3 Apl. 1877 and 25 Mar. 1878, ESCRO. Par.284/12/2.
6.   A skit, involving an imaginary conversation between rustics working at Hayward's Heath station, and the destination of labelled milk churns. *Sussex Agricultural Express*, 30 Apl. 1878.
7.   For the crises in Barden's affairs, see above, pp. 187–8, 26 Jan. and 17 Feb. 1877; he died later in that year.
8.   Which seems to denote that some members broke away from the YMCA club rules, and took some of the equipment with them.
9.   Egerton remonstrated with the 'children and other persons' responsible also for 'trampling down the graves' to save 'a few yards', in *Parish Notes*, June 1878.
10.   Another occasion in which Egerton concealed the identity; it is just possible that the man was the elder Pilbeam, the somewhat notorious blacksmith, for whom see below, 14 Feb. 1881, pp. 242–3 and note 4.

11.   Prior to transferring the beershop licence to brother Alfred. *Sussex Agricultural Express*, 30 July 1878.
12.   The case against Annie Eastwood for publishing a libel against Mrs Littlemore, the publican's wife, was adjourned from Hurst Green Petty Sessions on 30 Aug. *Sussex Agricultural Express*, 3 Sept. 1878.
13.   The term charity commonly embraced giving such jobs to impoverished villagers and their dependents.
14.   Although it was the East Sussex Constabulary's policy to move men after varying periods of service to other stations, Tobutt had recently been in trouble. Asked by the landlord of the Junction Inn, across the Salehurst border to search people suspected of thieving glasses, after a spate of such theft, Tobutt had been drinking with a man called William Mills at The Junction on 1 Nov. Subsequently, Tobutt searched Mills *en route* for Hurst Green after Mills refused to stand him 'a glass of ale'. Tobutt 'handled him very roughly', and when he discovered three decanters and four glasses in Mills' basket, 'charged him with receiving goods'; they returned to Salehurst, only to find that the landlord had lent these articles to Mills. Mills then charged Tobutt with assault, but the case was dismissed at the Petty Sessions on 6 December. Egerton's request was in vain. The twenty or so 'principal residents' subsequently framed a resolution 'to express our satisfaction with the way in which you [Tobutt] had done your duty among us since you have been stationed here, both as an officer of the police force, and as a neighbour, you have earned our confidence and esteem. . .'; this was forwarded 'through the Rev. J.C.Egerton', together with a cheque for an undisclosed sum to the Chief Constable, who authorized the payment when Tobutt transferred to East Grinstead. *Sussex Agricultural Express*, 10 Dec. 1878, and 8 Feb. 1879.

1879

1 Jan. Sch. Returns of all kinds being drawn up for H.M.Insp.

9 Jan. Mr. Emerson here early & tortured till 1.30. I went down twice but did not stop as I hate Examinations. . . .[1]

13 Jan. . . . I buried poor Walter Baker, aged 24. Has been a suffering life. I c. in at Miss Hylands, & the poor old body died while I was examining some books wh. she wished me to choose for the village library. Miss Lansdell came down[stairs] & told me.

16 Jan. . . . Answer from ye Board of Guardians that they will hereafter pay for all ye registrar's Certificates of age for Childs book. My reading of ye [Civil Registration] Act upheld as agst. Mr. Courthope & Mr. Wetherell! [also a JP] I had better be content with this unusual victory.

18 Jan. . . . Poor Miss Hyland buried today at Ticehurst, where her father & mother were buried also: she aged nearly 71. . . .

21 Jan. . . . 4th Anniv. of our wedding day. Thank God we have never had an angry word yet.

22 Jan. . . . Hicks c. my attention to footprints in ye snow in ye garden. We traced them some distance. They may have been sparrow catchers. . . .

23 Jan. Sch. C. on a number of Cottagers & told them to send for soup tomorrow. The police constable c. about 11 to say they knew who the two men were who had been in the garden; they had been sparrow catching, but they ought to have asked leave to come so near the house.

28 Jan. . . . Alfred Holland, shortly starts for Ceylon, to plant coffee poor lad. . . .

15 Feb. . . . I c. on Mrs Whatman. Mr. & Mrs Boorman there, Mr. Kemp of the Witherenden w. Mr. Lucas. I spoke about some poor law cases.

3 Mar. . . . Funeral of Leonard Grapp, aged 35 ? A simple weak young man whom drink has killed him before his time.

9 Mar. . . . C. on Mr. Bawmer, Brick House, out. His mother in law explained his absence from Church by saying that he had got into the habit of sitting in the house w. his hat on, & he was afraid he shd. catch cold if he had to sit without it in Church! Had an amusing colloquy w. Harry Mepham on ye haystack. He said I jeered at him when he came to Ch: last Club day. It was in the Coll[ection] before ye Serm. I asked him what Coll: it was; he at once replied "O Mighty God who shewest to them that be in error", wh. he accused me of pointing at him bec: I had been unable to make him see his error in leaving ye Ch: bec: I had left off ye gown & preached in ye surplice after ye Redesdale judgm[ent][2] Having my B[ook of] C[ommon] P[rayer] w. me I asked him what Sunday it was the coll: for. "3 Sund. aft, Easter" promptly, & when were you at Ch: "On Club day". When was that "3d Wed. in May 'carden [according] to the rules". I then proved that 3d S. aft. Easter was May 12th, & 3d Wed. in May . . . 15th, so I had simply used the Collect. for the week. "Well I never bear no malice" was all the amende I cd. extract; still we parted I think better friends. . . .

17 Mar. . . . Singing in evg. w. new glee club; 2 Pagdens, Coppard, J.Lusted, St[ephen] Brown. . . .

18 Mar. . . . C. on Mrs J. Isted. She shewed me W.Pope's last letter dated Helpmakaar Dec. 12. A very creditable letter. I c. at Mrs Combs to look at a Sussex Express for market quotations. Our butchers are keeping up prices unfairly.[3]

25 Mar. Quarter day. I attended ye Parish meeting; large number; 3 hours; very amicable. Increase in rates, poor & highway: Bad times & bad weather respectively ye cause. . . .

28 Mar. To Mr. Pipers Lamb feast. He has resigned his business to his two sons. He is a downright good sort, & his s. Edward whom I know, as far as I am aware takes after him. I sang "A thousand a year". Mr. P. took, I am told, in a speech later on, a gloomy view of agricultural prospects. I don't see how anybody can help doing so. . . .

29 Mar. . . . C. on Mrs Pennells ye farmer's wife. . . . A hard life hers must be as her husb: & herself try to do all ye work on ye farm. . . .[4]

2 Apl. . . . Aft. d. went out to small boys at cricket in field to East of ye garden. Irish boys seem unable to understand it; little Glasheen a hopeless performer. . . .

5 Apl. . . . C. on Mrs J. Isted; her refutation of the charges brought agst. her by Mrs Tilly on report of Newberrys, to me amply sufficient, & my confidence in no way whatever abated. . . .

Sun. 6 Apl. . . . 7 at Bible Cl: Ye morals of one are I fear not as I am told he drinks, but what can I do, I don't know as I have never seen a sign of it myself. . . .

15 Apl. . . . C. on H. Dann: he rather proud of his introduction of "Ashford" sausages into Burwash. He says he will sell 40lbs a week. . . . Spoke to young Mr. Neville in ye street. He bicycling. Had a medal for winning the race from Battle to London last year; 100 miles, time 7 hours & 40 minutes! . . .

22 Apl. . . . Long t. w. Jos. Noakes about farming. He does not see much prospect of agricultural revival under ye altered conditions of American competition. . . .

26 Apl. . . . Mr. Gregory wrote to ask me to nominate a Keeper of ye Post Off[ice] on Burwash Common, at a Salary of £4 per ann!! I sent him ye name of Henry Russell, who is recommended by Mr. Cooper & all up there.

28 Apl. . . . To ye Sch. A little boy Albert Malpas aged 6 answered almost at once ye quest[ion] "if I wanted to divide 100 marbles between 5 boys, how many apiece shd. I have to give"? Another boy in ye upper part gave an answer to "a herring & a half for three halfpence how many for half a crown?" Two bushels & a half! . . .

29 Apl. . . . I c. on Mrs T. Coleman (2/6) whose husband & son are in ye lock up on ye charge of fowl stealing. I do hope it is not true . . . . Vestry meeting, nobody came except Mr. J. Fuller, so we did not go in. . . .[5]

30 Apl. Sch. Looked in at ye Police off. Thos. Coleman & his S. Wm. up on a charge of stealing fowls. I was quite prepared to speak for them on the point of character for honesty, but ye evidence was hopelessly strong & they were committed for trial. I am really very sorry, but temptation seems to have been too strong for them. . . .[6]

[5 to 17 May in Wiltshire, barring day trip to London for a funeral on the 8th.]

21 May. Club. I pr: from last v. of 15 John 4 (Ext); very orderly congr:. . . . D. w. Club. Only 93 members. Stayed till nearly 7; very quiet then. . . .

22 May. . . . I to ye Comm. d. w. ye Club. 27 Members. Very pl. dinner, people seemed cheerful & sober. I sang my two songs. A thousand a year & When ye heart is young. . . .[7]

24 May. . . . I c. on Mrs Isted. She spoke to me about ye Prudential Assurance Compy. I cd. not admit it, as I gather from ye balance sheet that 50 per cent of premiums go in expenses. . . .

Sun. 25 May. . . . I pr. from Acts 1. 11 (Q). It is disheartening to feel how little one has improved in Sermon writing since this Sermon was written May 25 1855. . . .

[26 to 31 May, again in Wiltshire.]

11 June. . . . 4 boys only at singing – so I gave them 2d each & let them go. Ye rest at a cricket match between married & single. I went up . . .

25 June. . . . Mrs Weston showed me an apron of linen, ye flax of wh. were grown, bleached, spun & woven in Burwash in 1815 or 1816. Also a blanket in constant use over 50 years & still serviceable.

18 July. . . . c. on Mrs Corporal Hyland about her not sending her boy to sch. when the parish pays for him. She very rude. . . .[9]

25 July. . . . Bread raised 1d. I am sorry, as the farmers get no benefit having no corn to sell, & the poor people will feel the difference in their weekly outlay. . . .[8]

30 July. . . . Joseph Hall told me that ye Chicken trade was terribly dull & did not pay at present ye labour of fatting. Ye London market being invaded by Midland Counties chicken wh. are a trifle coarser but much cheaper. . . .

2 Aug. . . . Mrs John Eastwood, going w. family next week to live in London, where her husb: has got work w. B. Wood. Harry Baker also going. . . .[10]

8 Aug. . . . at 11.15 dear N. was safely delivered of another daughter. She suffered somewhat less than last time, & both she & ye child did well. God be praised. I hardly dare think what wd. have become of me if dear N had been taken from me; but thank God I need not think. . . .

13 Aug. . . . Loosemore & self to Battle; ye guard at Etchm. put us into 1st cl. carr. w. 2nd cl. tickets. To ye Deanery. Tea, & then procession to Ch. Serv. began at 7.15. Sing. ye 9 choirs, fresh, vigorous in good time & w. commendable spirit. . . . P's & F's disregarded as much as signals by a drunken engine driver. However things might have been far worse, there was no approach to a break down. . . . I pr. from 1 Cor. 14, 15 . . . 25 min. Great congr: Choirs & people at least 1000. My brethren of ye clergy after serv. v. complimentary about ye sermn, wh. they said wd. be useful. Thank God. Supper at ye Deanery. . . .[11]

16 Aug. . . . Wrote some "Sussex recollections". . . .

17 Aug. . . . The boys are found who broke ye tomb stone. Simple mischief. I hope they will be made to pay. . . .

21 Aug. Our Club went up yesterday to H. Green & somehow managed to play an innings each between ye showers; got beat by 24 or 26 runs, but H. Gr: played one or two non H. Green men. . . . Committee meeting of ye Club at 7.30. Sat till nearly 10, but did not do much. T. Pagden's little girl dead; was wheeling its perambulator yesterday. . . .

2 Sept. Lovely day. Ye wedding at 11.30. I married Charles John Etty to Fanny Tyler. Ch: nearly full in the centre aisle. Chancel very prettily decorated. . . . Serv. very reverrent & congr: very orderly. Breakfast at Mrs Combs. Only 12. I prop. Br. & Brigr. Doctor [Combs] gone to Matlock or somewhere poor man.[12] Tea to ye Chrn. at sch: nearly 200. I gave it. Marched to ye Rectory & had games, & I think enjoyed themselves greatly. So ended a busy day. Etty & his wife will be a real loss to Burwash, & to its clergyman. Read some of Old Fuller's Good Thoughts to dear N. when ye house was quiet.

[5 to 27 Sept. in Oxfordshire, Shropshire and Cheshire.]

Sun. 28 Sept. Sch. H[oly] C[ommunion] . . . Off. £2-3-7½, In aft. Etty pr. his farewell sermon. It was most touchingly real. I fairly broke down. He is a good man. Pr. in evg. Wesley's Te Deum & He counteth all ye sorrows. Dear N. at Ch: in ye morg. in ye carr[iage].

29 Sept. I Dined w. Carey at Mrs Comb's. Mr & Mrs Etty ye attractions, tho' Mrs very poorly w. bad cold. Mr. Bagdell, ye substitute for Ye Doctor, a very conversational man. To ye Sch. at 8:30; presented ye testimonial £36-5-5 to Etty. He spoke very well. Philcox proposed a vote of thanks to Anset and Dr. Harris. All very pleasant.

6 Oct. . . . Discovered my first grey hair!

8 Oct. Hard at work writing out "Recollections". . . .

11 Oct. . . . Paid ½ year's bill for [The] Times at [Etchingham] Station. . . . C. on JP re 10 perc[ent] red[uction] of tithe. I fear that my actions will get me into trouble with the brethren, but I cannot be easy till I have shown some sign of sympathy with my parishioners in these bad times. Good Loosemore [incumbent at Salehurst], the poorest man of the lot acts as I do.

13 Oct. Mr.Loosemore c. at ye Office where I met him. He is quite willing to shew sympathy with his people to ye am[oun]t of 10 p c off his tithe, so we two shall do it. I suspect rebuke from ye brethren, but I believe I am doing right, & so we must leave it. . . .

15 Oct. . . . C. on Mrs Gadd, asked after Charlie & his wife née Mary

Ragner; doing well, only lost one day all ye year as carpenter in London; earns about 39/- a week! . . . C. on Mrs Willett. She said ye farmers had had ye labourers under their thumb, but now they were suffering too. . . .[13]

17 Oct. . . . C. on JP. Mr.Micklethwaite's Sol[icito]r takes a such strong view of ye allowance of 10 p c off ye Tithes that JP. will I think advise Mr. Loosemore to alter his determination. . . .[14]

20 Oct. . . . over to Waldron, meeting & talking to sundry people. . . . Mr. John Harmer, Old Master Fuller aged 79 2/12 walking in from Heathf[ield] parish to get his pay at Burwash. . . .[15]

24 Oct. . . . Mr. Luxford c. on Justice business. . . .

1 Nov. . . . Mr. Love in a state of great excitement; somebody had of cert[ain on] purpose, broken his gate, & let his horses into ye road. It is too bad & there is a lawless knot. . . .[16]

7 Nov. . . . Two nights has N. read my "Recollections" to Aunt who says she likes them, tho' to me she has never mentioned the subject. Funny that she shd. profess to like listening to an original literary production of the host of the house in wh. she is staying, & yet that she shd. never say one word ever of commendation.

12 Nov. Tithe day; large numbers present, but I am not quite sure about ye numbers of payers. I remitted 10 p c of ye tithes as a token of sympathy; so did Mr. Cooper who however was not present. JP on behalf of ye tithe payers seconded by Mr. Gillham expressed their thanks for ye considera-tion. I shd. not have been easy in my mind, if I had not done something to show I was ready to share ye bad year w. my people & dear N. quite agreed w. me. . . .

15 Nov. . . . C. on Mrs Relf at ye Green. Her sailor son now in Ye London Fire Brigade at Paddington. She thanked me for ye remission of tithe. . . .

18 Nov. . . . I c. on Maskell at ye Forge; poor man, wife dead, & cannot yet get a housekeeper tho' his s.(15) (1/-) at home. I asked him how they got their cooking done. "We don't have none" was the answer.

19 Nov. . . . I c. on poor Mrs Boorman whose husband has failed; sad misery. I pity them all but especially ye wife & children. She thanked me for coming, so I am glad I went, but I was afraid that she might not like my doing so. C. on Mr. Gibbs; he superintending work. He had discovered that fish wh. he thought had been maliciously poisoned, had been poisoned by the overflow of a cesspool into the pond. I am glad. . . .

25 Nov. . . . C. to see Old Hilder, but he gone to ye Union Infirmary to day. Stoppage of his water. . . .

28 Nov. . . . C. on old Eastwood (1/-) at ye Tot. He said that if any body cd. get a nice Van & take the Zuloo king round in it, he might make a good living! . . .

3 Dec. . . . In aft. C. on Ellen [Gould] about soup distribution. . . .

4 Dec. . . . Gave out soup to 21 families. . . .

8 Dec. . . . Met poor old Osborn & his wife. He I fear has failed. He is a good honest hard working old man I believe, & his wife is as an industrious woman as you will find.[17] . . . Game preserving beginning to get men into trouble.[18] To "Professor Verone", a conjuror at ye Sch. Excellent; large audience. P.C.Girton c. on me, he going to Ewhurst. Hinted to me about a testimonial. I didn't take ye hint, & offered to do what I had done for Segt. Tobutt, viz. to subscribe when anybody brought me a paper.[19]

9 Dec. . . . C. on Mr. Bourner, out of health; has just lost £130 by a farmer breaking to whom he had leant the money. C. on Mr. Cramp about the dole, the St. Philip's portion of wh. Mr. Cooper wants separated from ye Burwash. He is quite agreeable, & so am I. . . .

18 Dec. . . . C. on Mr. Schroeter. He actually gives his men 18/- a week all the year round! but then possibly they have no piece work. . . .[20]

22 Dec. At ye dole. Ye Common now independent. We got finished by about 1.30. Gave old people 2lb each person. Single old men & widows 2½lbs each. Families w. 2 chrn. & upwards 1lb for father, 1lb for mother & ½lb for each child. Beef 5/- per st[one] of 8lbs. . . .

25 Dec. . . . Quite by ourselves & very happy. . . . Aft. Serv. JP told me that Mr. Jarvis was very ill. I went to see him but he was unconscious, & died at 3.30 PM of inflammation & congestion of the lungs. Terribly suddenly. He took to his bed on Tuesday [23rd] or I believe on Monday evg. I d. w. JP as usual. Same people; same jokes. . . .

29 Dec. At 3.15 buried Mr. Jarvis; large attendance, 1st Burwash funeral since Aug. 28th![21]

Notes

1. The report's principal conclusion was that teaching had been compromised by the prolonged illnesses of both Ansets.
2. See above, p. 194, 24 July 1877.
3. Populist notions of the "moral economy", part of which held that retailers should not make exorbitant profits on essential items of food, by manipulating the market, were very old and could still – be it increasingly rarely – cause traditional disturbances of the "food riot" variety in which crowds used force to compel price reductions. The survival of this ideology stipulating strict codes of practice in the capitalist market is however difficult to track, and it is interesting to see Egerton apparently comparing wholesale meat prices with those charged by local butchers.
4. Typical of the Wealden small-scale farmer using only available family labour.
5. However the vestry did convene under the chairmanship of Frederick Cramp, and came to the important decision to make the owners – rather than the tenants – of cottages rated at under £8 responsible for payments. This represented a populist victory but it is inconceivable that chicanery, rather than error, was behind Egerton and Fuller's non-attendance. ESCRO. Par.284/12/2.
6. The father, Thomas Coleman, fattened chickens on a scale sufficient to warrant description as a 'small farmer', but he represented the class of petty proprietor forced to supplement their income by labouring for more substantial neighbours. Twenty-four-year-old William was described as 'a simple-looking young labourer'. They were jointly accused of thieving four, value 14/- from farmer Thomas Bartholomew on 24 Apl., and 18 more valued at 63/- from farmer Robert Oliver on the 26th. Both Colemans had recently worked for Oliver, and William had unsuccessfully 'asked . . . for work' on the 23rd. He also conversed about the chicken trade with Oliver, who 'gave him the address where we sent the chickens when they are fatted and go to London'. Some of Oliver's birds were 'shut up . . . in a fatting Coop ready for fatting', and he also had 'a small Chicken house but it is not large enough to put all the Chicken in'; other chickens were 'sitting partly in a Dung Cart and partly on some manure under a Waggon in the Waggon lodge under the Oast: it was not enclosed'. Oliver went to the police the evening following the discovery of his loss on a Sunday morning. The reason the Coleman's were suspected is not given, but Bartholomew's birds were discovered along with Oliver's. The father protested his innocence from the moment the police appeared: on the Sat. night 'about twenty minutes to nine . . . I started up to my Club . . . and stopped till shut up time', after which he talked with John Hilder and George Woodgate in the street for some time, before returning home, whereupon he went straight to bed: 'I was not up before eight o'Clock the next morning and I never left my bed all night. . . . I am an innocent man and I cant hardly make it out'. He did acknowledge that he had asked William where the new chickens in their 'roost' had come from, but 'he made me no answer. . . . William can explain it'. William made no protestations, and offered a lame explanation; he returned home shortly before his father, fell asleep in the chair, where he remained all night: 'when I woke up it was day light I got some wood and made fire and began to get breakfast ready'. The father, who was released on bail, was found not guilty; William was sentenced to three months hard labour on each charge. Various depositions, statements, and jail calendar, ESCRO. QR/E1086. *Sussex Advertiser*, 6 May and 8 July 1879.
7. Widespread ill-health accompanied the long and severe 1878–9 winter, thereby straining the financial resources of all Benefit Clubs. *Parish Notes*, June 1879.

8.   Liquidity problems dictated the sale of wheat much earlier in the season by even the largest Burwash farmers.

9.   Some families were exempted under parochial decisions from the payment of school fees. The Board of Guardians also paid the costs of school attendance for families on regular relief. Minute, 8 Feb. 1872, ESCRO. G10/1a/12.

10.   Benjamin Wood was from the long-established Burwash family of carpenters and builders, but had migrated to London where he became a remarkably successful 'builder and contractor' based in Hackney. *Parish Notes*, Oct. 1878.

11.   Egerton eulogized music, which the 'mind of the wickedest man who ever wrote music could never pollute', the 'one art which is associated on the authority of God's Book', and which facilitated 'giving ourselves wholly to the noble task of . . . praising God'. J.C. Egerton, *Village Instruction. Twelve Sermons*, (Tunbridge Wells, 1892), pp. 24–5.

12.   This is the first reference in the diary to Combs' debilitation through alcoholism.

13.   Mrs Willett was clearly referring to the determined attempt to crush the Kent and Sussex Labourers' Union over the winter of 1878–9. Egerton did not record any detail respecting the dispute. The nearest reported lock-out and/or strike action to Burwash (whose delegates attended every meeting at the Maidstone headquarters, including emergency ones), was at Beckley and Northiam, where a hostile source said that 'many men may be seen strolling through the streets, playing at marbles, jump-back etc., evidently happy in the receipt of 15s from the . . . Union, and quite content to follow their idle life, so long as the funds hold out. But these won't last for ever'. The local outcome is unclear, but East Kent provided the principal focus of the dispute. The Union did concede wage reductions in some local negotiations, and Mrs Willett may have been referring to these, but neither side won a clear-cut victory. The funds did sustain the men, up to two thousand being in receipt of Union monies, some for twenty or more weeks, and the Union also organized an unprecedented emigration. But neither farmers nor unionists wanted a renewed struggle as the 1879–80 winter approached. *Sussex Agricultural Express*, 29 Oct. 1878. *South-eastern Gazette*, 18 Nov. 1878. *Kent and Sussex Times*, 14 Dec. 1878 and 1 Feb. 1879. Rollo Arnold, 'The "Revolt of the Field" in Kent 1872–1879', *Past and Present*, 64, (1974), esp. pp. 90–3.

14.   The Micklethwaite family were major landowners in Salehurst, and lay tithe proprietors.

15.   Heathfield was in the Hailsham Poor Law Union; Fuller was legally settled in the Ticehurst Union, and picked up his outdoor relief during the Relieving Officer's weekly visit to Burwash.

16.   William Love was proprietor of Dawes Farm. Yet another form of vengeance which, in addition to the dangers the horses ran, might also expose the owner to prosecution for animals straying on to the highway.

17.   On 17 Apl. 1880 farmer William Osborne's un-named trustee was given permission by Tunbridge Wells County Court to sell all Osborne's freehold houses and other unspecified property to A.T. Stevenson. *Sussex Agricultural Express*, 24 Apl. 1880.

18.   Hardly any Burwash folk were prosecuted at this time for poaching, except labourer Jesse Ballard, fined 30/- with 10/- costs, together with his partner, John Cook also a labourer, from Brightling, where the pair were caught with seven snares by a local gamekeeper. Ballard's 'rambling statement' in court failed to challenge the keeper's evidence at Battle Petty Sessions on 9 Dec. *Sussex Advertiser*,

16 Dec. 1879. On the other hand, Egerton's comment possibly applied to landowners' expenditure on game preservation taking an increasing proportion of incomes while the agricultural depression deepened.

19.   Egerton was clearly unwilling to initiate a collection for a village policeman being moved to another station. Unfortunately he did not spell out his reasons, but there was much residual populist hostility to the professional police, not least owing to the cost of the police rate, in addition to those whose hostility derived from being on the receiving end of police action. Egerton avoided compromising himself in the eyes of a part of his flock, which could come from launching a subscription, by quietly making his donation to a collection organized by others. See also above, 13 Dec. 1878, p. 212 and note 14.

20.   A long-standing argument held that farm labourers worked harder when paid by the piece, which enabled conscientious workers to earn more than going weekly pay rates.

21.   Farmer and corndealer Thomas Jarvis, aged 56, received glowing obituaries; 'one of' Burwash's 'leading inhabitants resident . . . for more than a third of a century, during a large portion of which time he has held a considerable breadth of land . . . and borne the reputation of being a good farmer, as well as a sound, practical, and consequently a successful man of business. In the strict sense of the phrase, he has been 'the architect of his fortune'. In the transaction of parish business, Mr. Jarvis has, for years, rendered valuable assistance, and in many local matters of a public character, his advice and aid have been freely given. The employer of a good many labourers in the various branches of his business, he will be much missed by the working class. He will also be greatly regretted by a numerous and wide circle of relatives, friends, and acquaintances; from all of whom his widow and sons will receive true sympathy for their irreperable loss'. *Sussex Advertiser*, 30 Dec. 1879. *Sussex Agricultural Express*, 3 Jan. 1880.

1880

8 Jan. C. on Thompson & Ellis. It surprises me to find how casual country tradesmen are, & how little account they take of minute [financial] accuracy. . . .

16 Jan. . . . C. on Mrs T. Pennells (2/6); husb: out of work. One of our grumblers & always running out agst. ye farmers, but now somewhat in distress. . . .

19 Jan. . . . H.Pagden lent me an orig[inal] copy of ye Burwash Xmas carols comp[osed] by James Fleming's father.[1]

27 Jan. . . . In aft. funeral of old [farmworker] Edmund Hilder 84. Kept me waiting some time owing to a family discussion in ye Bell yard, whether ye old gentleman shd. be shifted from ye parish coffin into ye better one prepared by Tom Brook. It was at last ruled that he shd. be left undisturbed! . . .

30 Jan. . . . In aft. young Mr. Stevenson of Salehurst c. over & said his father was dead, & that they wished to bring him to Burwash. I said that double fees wd. be charged for ye out-p[arishioner]. So I question whether he will be brought. . . .

31 Jan. . . . C. on Mrs Relf couldn't pay me for ye mag[azine] & her husb: always in work all ye same. . . .

1 Feb. . . . Mr. Taylor told me that Mr. Whatman's sheep were rotting fast, & that a farmer in Kent had broken, owing Mr. T. £100. It is all truly sad. . . .[2]

2 Feb. . . . C. at W.Coppard's clogmakers. . . .

3 Feb. . . . W.Ellis spoke to me about Wm. Pope's membership of Odd Fellows Lodge 744 St. Helena; wd. try & get ye club money [Pope owed]. . . .

6 Feb. . . . Buried Mr. John Stevenson of Salehurst, late of Bateman's. Enormously heavy coffin, bearers hardly up to ye weight. Catt of Robertsbridge ye undertaker paid me £2-7-0 ye double fee for stained [?] grave, & service for non-parishioner. . . .

7 Feb. Wedding of George Pennells & Harriet (?) Dodswell. Much quieter than I expected. Very wet. . . .

9 Feb. The safe came Fieldwick & his man, Hicks, & I lifted it from ye van to ye Cloak room. Ye Report of our School; they fine us £20 for insuff[iciently qualified] Staff! Poor Anset so completely acknowledged his responsibility for ye mistake that he supposed he shd. have to pay! I must write to see what can be done. . . .

11 Feb. . . . To Mr. Anset. He in a great state about ye non-qualification of ye two Assistants Misses A.J.King & M. Walters, as he had assured me they were all right; he even yesterday said he wd. have to pay ye fine out of his own pocket. Ye poor girls too much distressed, & ye case is a very hard one but I think my letter will affect ye matter. . . .[3]

12 Feb. . . . Tea w. Mr. Whatman. He is in sad distress about his sheep: he shewed me one nearly killed w. ye plaice just taken out. It is a crushing year for ye farmers. . . .[4]

13 Feb. . . . C. & R. w. old Mrs Collins (1/-), a woman whose remarks on the study of the Bible & other matters wd. well stand the ordeal of being published; they were remarkably just. C. & R. w. old Jane Vigor (1/6). She shewed me a book wh. she said she had read many times thro', but wh. now was minus binding, pages all mixed, & tied round ye middle with a piece of tape. A set of old fashioned lectures on Biblical subjects written in a scholastic language wh. doubtless wd. take many times reading to understand. Old James [Vigor] asked me to intercede with the guardians for the restoration of his pay. I had to tell him that one of the Guardians had given me as the reason why the pay had been taken off the statement that he drank more than his pay each week at the publics. . . .

16 Feb. . . . C. on Mrs J. Isted: her husb: is really a cruel man, & his selfishness is terrible. . . . C. on Mrs John Copper (1/6). Husb: has had only one weeks work for I think 3 months. Met Mr. Whatman. He told me that Mrs W. & himself had made up their minds to let their home if they cd. & live in a cottage to save expense. I greatly respect them for their resolution. I promised I wd. do all I cd. to help in finding a tenant. . . .

17 Feb. . . . News from M.C.Payne that old Mannings was bankrupt & there is to be a sale of everything. I am grieved beyond expression.

21 Feb. . . . C. on Mrs Isted. She very glad to hear of her daughter Anna's welfare at Mr. Breach's. Gave her a remittance from her d. . . .

26 Feb. . . . I to ye Evg. Entert[ainments]. Sung w. my men, save Th. Pagden who failed us, & ye two glees: fairly received. Ye readings "From Banns to Matrimony" . . . of "All ye year round" by John Fuller; good, & very amusing. "An Insurance Agent", I fancy from Max Adeler by Mr. Anset, good, but ye main feature a Mr. Grey from Hastings, a comic; he sang 5 songs! & the audience wd. have gladly heard more. Full room. It is perfectly clear that such serious performances as my concerts, are but little in ye people's tastes compared with these more lively entertainments.[5]

27 Feb. . . . attended meeting of ye Benefit Club: on its last legs, & must dissolve. . . .

28 Feb. . . . looked over Thompson's new cott[age] by ye Pay-gate. Fairly convenient. 3 bed rooms. . . .[6]

2 Mar. . . . C. on Mrs Langr[idge] S. Tommy very troublesome last Sun. after ye Chr[istenings]. Mrs Combs & Ellen [Gould] both corroborate my information. I begged him to withdraw from ye [Bible] Class. He has exhausted my patience, & I have given him every chance. Ye mother t. about partiality. I have been partial as I employed Tommy on Saturdays.[7]

5 Mar. . . . c. on Mrs Boorman, poor woman, she greatly cast down. Seeing that her husb: has Uncles & Cousins in America, who are not indisposed to welcome him, I strongly urged emigration. . . . C. on Mrs Osborne, another case of depression; poor old soul, if her story is correct, she & her husband have been done out of hundreds of pounds. C. on Morris ye fish man. A long t. He an intelligent Union man.[8] I think our argument was not without its use in helping him to see that district ladies, clergy & gentry, are in a very difficult position as regards knowing who are the really deserving. Outward appearances are fallacious, but who will give trustworthy information. I rather liked the man. . . . C. on Mrs Sands, gives up Mag: prom[ised] to pay ye 6d she owes, & Mrs Buss next door who takes up ye mag: dropped by Mrs S. . . .

6 Mar. . . . Got Mrs John Relf of ye Woodsman as a new Subscr[iber]. . . . Had two young fellows on at work in ye garden, as they were out of w[ork].

7 Mar. . . . letter from Ed[ucation] Dept. saying that ye fine of £20 is remitted! & 8/- returned wh. had been deducted, so we are better off.

9 Mar. Sch. Mr. Anset suggested that the two Assistant Mistresses were thinking of leaving. . . .

10 Mar. . . . Ye tombstone of ye family of Mr. Mann ye ancient Noncom: Min[ister] here wh. I had ordered to put straight, looked very tidy.[9]

13 Mar. . . . Lovely day. Fetched out all ye old cripples in ye Village. . . .

Sun. 14 Mar. . . . Sing: Club at 6. Fair; several new boys offered themselves, but I am doubtful, one or two withdrawn. A certain amount of persecution, so far as calling ye candidates names: "There goes another Xtian" etc. . . .

16 Mar. . . . Saw a poor bullock being dragged up ye hill by two horses on a heave gate to ye butchers. It had turned "stomach" at ye bottom of ye hill, & wd. not walk.

19 Mar. . . . C. on J. I[sted] He has been very ill, but is in a lamentably inpenitent frame of mind. His life has been notoriously bad of late, but anything I said only made him tell lies, so I came away.[10] . . . C. on poor Ada Park. She died while I was there, or at ye most a minute or two before. I prayed w. all those who were there. . . .

20 Mar. . . . C. on Mrs J. Isted, pleaded w. her s. Harry about Con-f[irmation]; wd. not come. The boy is a hard working lad, but not "spiritual". . . .

27 Mar. . . . W. down to see steam ploughing machine on ye Lodge farm; men had left off. . . .

30 Mar. W.J.Jenner to see ye ploughing machine. Certainly very ingenious, does its work capitally; ploughed 12 acres last Thursday I believe. 5 men employed. 5 shares (rope-wire). Works to 12 horse p[ower] each engine, & 2 are required, one at each end . . . C. on Mrs Gilbert & took tea. Messrs Alfred & John Kinpton there, both jolly radicals. Political meeting at ye Bull. I did not go, as I don't think active political partisanship good for a parson. Mr. Whatman told em that we have 103 Burwash Voters, & that 37 are doubtful [i.e.intended to vote Liberal].

2 Apl. . . . Vestry meeting. I went, no attendance. Mr. Piper asked me to dinner; out of about 1600 he has lost nearly 400 sheep in Burwash. Mr. A.Jarvis took in 75 [Romney Marsh sheep for wintering] & returns 6. Mr. Jos. Noakes has not sent in any as the few he has are too weak to travel. . . .

Sun. 4 Apl. . . . H[oly] C[ommunion] off. 16s 6d: collection of off. delayed by a person taking change out of ye plate! . . .

5 Apl. . . . C. on poor Mrs Elliott; he husb: can earn hardly anything at hawking & she is half starved; gave her 2/6 & 2/- for a bottle of wine. . . .

7 Apl. . . . Mrs Baitup & her husb: turned out of their cott[age] at a weeks notice after working 25 years on Mr. Vigor's farm, to make way for Balford & his wife. It is really hard. . . .

9 Apl. Aft . . . to ye Poll: no excitement, beyond Mr. Fielden w. a trumpet about 4ft. long. . . .

12 Apl. . . . Saw Guest ye miller carrying away some old hoppoles wh. he says he had bought from old Red Russell. They had never been used; had originally been 600 had dwindled away to 120 for wh. Guest was giving 6 gallons of flour [worth] about 6s. 6d. The 600 poles must have cost Russell 60/- at least.[11] . . . Political t. w. Russell (strong Cons.) & Gillham (mod. Lib.). . . .

Sun. 18 Apl. . . . Pickett at Ch. said ye sermon had done him good. It was based on one of J.H.Newman's. It is singular that nearly all the sermons that I preach not my own are noticed, while my own are passed over. How does this affect the question of preaching other people's sermons. If other people do more good, why not preach them, & yet one feels that one ought to write one's own. . . . Pickett tells me he is promoted to travelling for his house in Hastings! wh. he looks upon as a great lift. . . . Class in vestry. A. Hilder joined in. He puzzles me. . . . Had to find fault with Edm. Langridge & D. Clarke for misbehaviour, but it turned out I was wrong, so I apologized.

22 Apl. A man G. Harmer (?) c. up & asked for money to help him to London. I gave him 2/6. . . .

25 Apl. Was to have been a wedding, but ye heartless young fellow did not turn up. . . .

5 May. . . . C. on Mrs J. Isted, poor woman, hers is a joyless life. Willy at home again, & quite justified in leaving his place. . . .

[10 to 15 May in Oxford.]

18 May. C. on Cohen ye new doctor. Australian (Sydney) born of Eng. parents; favourably impressed. . . . I c. on Mr. Fuller; ye Club bankrupt. . . .

19 May. . . . I at 10.15 to ye Rose & Crown; argued ye question, & spoke my mind. They wished to come to ch. I pr. from Gal. 6.2 (Ext) & I spoke I pray . . . calmly but distinctly about the selfishness of dividing the honorary members money given to ye Club as a trustee for ye sick & aged. People at any rate very attentive. . . . I to ye tent, d. & spoke but I fear w. no effect . . . [more] there either stupidly half drunk or suffering from softening of ye brain. . . .

21 May. Ye younger members of the club held a meeting I believe to consider the formation of a new club, wh. wd. exclude all over 40 & under 18, but I do not know the result. . . .[12]

31 May. . . . Boys squabbling over cricket; big boys interfere & break up ye game.

1 June. . . . The Sergt. of Police saw me on ye subj: of a sad tale of depravity; ye girl, from ye Common, only 12 yrs old, & ye men 17 & 24: it is miserable. . . .

3 June. . . . Met ye Seargt. Two pris[oners] remanded. . . .

4 June. . . . Ye two pris: comm[itted] for trial, but released on bail.[13]

5 June. . . . Stood umpire for Burwash boys agst. Brightling boys. We beat[en] in one innings. . . . I gave 2/6 towards ye visitors refreshments. Coaching wd. do our boys real good.

7 June. . . . C. on Mr. Anset & took applic[ations] for Miss King & Miss Walters places: about 30 appl! . . .

8 June. More applications still for teachers' situation. . . .

9 June. C. on Ellen [Gould] & shewed her ye testimonials of two selected cases. . . .

12 June. . . . Coming from Ch. met St[even] Pagden who pointed out that Mr. Bourner's sheep had got into his wheat; he gave a boy 1d to go & tell him. I gave another boy a 1d to go with him, & Mr. B. I find gave them 6d between them so they did well. . . . Thomas Eastwood's last Sunday. He said good bye aft. pract[ice] in Evg. I am very sorry to lose him.

23 June. . . . In ye Evg. watched ye boys playing cricket. How much one can see of Boys dispositions in their play.

24 June. Sch. An old soldier (Penfold) tried to work me, but as his papers were not later than July 1879, I declined. "There are many Sir of yr. illustrious name" doesn't weigh with me favourably. . . .

25 June. . . . C. on ye Mistresses, Miss Anabella Janet King & Miss Marva Walters, & said good bye: they go tomorrow: we are sorry to lose them, & I only hope they will better themselves, but I doubt it.

Sun. 26 June. . . . Talked w. sundry mechanics who were here on a Beanfeast from Hastings. They all seemed satisfied with Burwash as a place for an outing.[14] (Gussey [elder daughter]) Didn't God know Mother that Father was taking the strawberries to the poor woman? (Mother) What makes you ask that Gussey? (Gussey) Because He let her die before Father got there . . .

27 June. Sch. Introd. ye new Mistresses. Small in stature, but intelligent in appearance. . . . In Evg. Sing: only one man Wm. Coppard has apparently left ye choir, if so for some reason wh. I cannot even guess, so he must take his own way, but it is trying.

28 June. A letter from John Sawyers! he is in ye G[renadier] Compy 107th Foot, now in Guernsey, but expecting to be sent to Ireland. I answered him, speaking plainly but kindly. There is not much sign of repentance. Wrote also to Charles S. Lester, Signalman, H.M.S. "Ready", Persian Gulf. . . .

29 June. Had to write a serm: for Girls Friendly Soc. Managed about 3/4 of it. In aft. serv. at 3.0. Fair congr. Girls from ye Parishes of Brightling, Salehurst, Dallington. Etchm. & Burwash. 50 pres[ent] & 9 assoc[iates]. I pr. from Gal. 6. 2. Some of the afore[mentioned] were kind enough to say that they shd. like to have it printed for ye good of ye Soc. . . .

30 June. Sch. New mistresses working apparently well. . . . The two young men yesterday . . . got 6 weeks each w. hard labour, very lenient sentence. I pray that it may do them good. . . .

1 July. . . . C. on Mrs Vine (1/6), poor grumpy old body, but she is old [seventy-three] & alone, & hard up. . . .

7 July. . . . Heavy rain, so did not go up to see ye cricket match wh. was being played in ye wet between B & B Common. Ye latter victorious by 10 runs.

8 July. In morg. C. on young Nevill & expl[ained] about Ellen's party this aft. wh. I thought was to be ye regular parochial one, but wh. is parochially aristocratic. . . .

10 July. . . . C. on Master Buss, getting better. Their child had scalded its leg badly in ye morg. The mother had pricked ye bladders wh. had become large & had let the water out, an operation wh. ye boy expressed by the elegant phrase "& they did just piddle". Talked to a poor old man by ye road side old Master Seymour, who worked for some years at Taskers' but has been in ye Union [workhouse]. No friends; poor old chap, sleeps in a barn, & hopes for haymaking. I spoke about a better world, but I cd. not find that he had any ideas beyond the coming haymaking. . . .

12 July. . . . In Evg. I c. on Mrs J. Isted: order her a bott: of wine (3/-) at Noakes, gave her 2/6 to repay John for part of adv[ance] from Ye Guardian. To ye Cricket field & watched practice. Ye batting very weak. . . . I suppose I lingered about as young Nevill passed me going Eastward & as I went into my gate repassed me having been to Etchm. Station on his bicycle. I had c. on Mr Clark, J. Park, & Master Sweatman to ask after boys' absence on Sunday. All expl[aine]d.

22 July. . . . Found ye Ch. yard again being utilised for cricket. I had to upraide, it is a great nuisance being obliged to find fault, but ye Ch: Yard must be kept from becoming a playground. . . .

23 July. Sch. C. on several poor people to tell them that there were bundles of clothes for them at ye Rect. Passing a steam threshing machine at "The Wheel" Gussey said "Mother the trains don't have a big wheel outside like . . . these engines" – her observation is very quick, & she notices likenesses & differences quickly . . .

28 July. . . . C. & t. seriously w. Willett ye carter at Brooksmarle, who was all but dead last week of bleeding after having a tooth drawn. He is still very weak (2/6). . . . C. on Miss Hughes, she gave me £1 for the poor. . . .

29 July. . . . To see ye cricket m. w. ye Comm: on ye way Cohen shewed me Bagdell's donkey wh. was nearly dead of tetanus; had been castrated; Gorringe boy had been I believe riding it, & had brought on an inflammation or something. This is the theory. W. Cohen to ye High field; our eleven weak & got a good thrashing. . . .

2 Aug. Aft. d. w. up to ye Common. Stopped to see a cricket match in High Field. A Bank Holiday between Brown's, Pagden's & Blunden's shops agst. Club. Ye Shops won by 5 runs. Large gathering. . . .

Sat. 7 Aug. Terrible rain & high wind. . . . Ye village full of people shopping. I noticed how few of ye young chaps took any notice of me. I suppose it is their independence as they know me very well, & know that at least I have never done any of them any harm.[15]

10 Aug. . . . delivered 11 mag: got paid for all & for back numbers, so now clear. . . .

13 Aug. . . . met a travelling steam sawing machine; had been sawing oak on ye Sochnersh property, & then on its way to saw fir at Rose Hill, so it saws all sorts of wood. . . .

19 Aug. . . . to ye School . . . for Schoolchildren to hear Mrs Collins make her statement of what her grandfather told her what happened to him in ye matter of ye Ghost in 1753! . . .[16]

[6 to 18 Sept. at Bunbury and elsewhere in Cheshire. Two anecdotes are entered subsequent to details of this holiday, and the internal evidence suggests that they derived from conversations Egerton had with unknown parishioners within the first three days of his return. 'A propos of the bad times in Burwash, on the Monday morning that the mob, having made a demonstration in Burwash, passed on to Hurst Green! Sam. Ledbitter, a bricklayer's labourer who was at work at the old Tot, seeing the crowd coming, ran up the ladder, & got in at the window to hide himself, but he being seen, was summarily led down & compelled to go with the rest, much to the amusement of the multitude.'

The second tale: 'Old "Donkey" Collins one morning came, accompanied by his wife & all his children & seated himself with them in a row near Mr. Gilbert the overseer's back door, & simply refused to move until he had relieved them.'[17]]

29 Sept. . . . Buried Stephen Fielder. An inquest had been held, as tho' he lived 10 weeks his death was due to swallowing Sulphuric acid. . . .

2 Oct. Wedding ought to have been at 11 but the couple were quite ready at 10.30. So as I happened to be up at the Church I married them $\frac{1}{2}$ an hour before time, a thing I never did before. Robert Blackford & Ellen Coleman, neither quite sharp, but the man sharp enough to do me out of 2/- fees, with the certif: the money was 10/- but he said he hadn't got not such money as that, & putting down 8/- he added "that's all I can do for you 'smassion". So I gave him the certificate. . . .

18 Oct. Poor Newbury died, after much suffering. Dash [Egerton's relatively new dog] tied up in the kennel, & getting tired of confinement I suppose took to howling, wh. the servants interpreted to mean consciousness of somebody dying. . . .

19 Oct. Before dinner c. on Thomas Harmer & gave his wife an order to Maidstone Infirmary for his daughter Hannah, as her eyes were very bad. C. on Mr. Gibbs & read him my version of his ideas about the licensing laws. . . .

20 Oct. . . . The Burwash newly raised drum & fife band c. up in evg. pl. 3 tunes creditably: 14 members (2/6).

21 Oct. Sch. Newbury's funeral. Coffin taken out thro's the window [of his house] – very heavy, but ye letting down into ye grave well managed. I c. on Reader ye Publican [newly installed at the Rose and Crown], seems a respectable man. . . .

3 Nov. . . . Henry Eastwood just moved in so first time for 80 or 90 years that there has not been an Eastwood of the Tott.

5 Nov. . . . C. on old Mrs Weston: hard at work (at 75 or thereabouts) in her garden. C. & had tea w. Mr. & Mrs John Coppard. I wish we had a parish full of their sort. Home; squibbing going on freely. I shd. be curious to know ye expenditure in Bur. on Gunp[owder] on ye 5th. To ye sch. Presided over Club meeting. Mr. Cohen came down & argued his case about ye scale of doctoring. 2/- a bottle medecine, shilling a mile over a mile, pills plaster etc. at a proportionate rate, accidents on poor law scale. We have only 30 members & we agreed to pay 1/6 [each] a quarter to ye medical fund. I asked ye members to let me call at their cottages & read a chapter of ye Bible in ye evenings this winter, but cd. get no response. Some said they must consult their wives. I was up at ye sch. from 6 till 9, business not having begun till 7. It is 6 proper hour.

10 Nov. Mr Gillham told me that in parishes in Kent near ye Sussex border forty or fifty years ago bad vulgar language was called "Burwash Grammar". . . .

12 Nov. . . . C. on Mrs J. Isted (1/-); pd. her this on behalf of Coleman who had got two loaves on trust & had not paid, & Mrs Isted is as poor as any one just now. . . . The James Braban family came into the village. C. at ye Police office & begged ye constable to watch ye girl closely. She will corrupt half ye village.[18]

13 Nov. Sent back ye proof sheets corrected of first number of "Sussex Folk & Sussex ways". . . .

17 Nov. . . . Entertainment. Large audience. Dr. Cohen lectured on "Ye Human frame". There was a good skeleton by way of a change & Cohen made ye lect. very fairly interesting. I read "Dora" (Tennyson), Blunden & others sang & on ye whole ye ent. was successful. £2-10-0 taken.[19]

18 Nov. . . . I wrote a note to Mr. Schroeter asking him whether he cd. give John Vigor a job. He most kindly answered in the aft. wh. is good luck for ye man. I married a master Dike & Widow Gibbs. She had sprained her ankle & was lame. Ye man joked & said that he thought I ought to throw off 5/- as a man never paid as much for a lame horse as for a sound one. I urged that he was out of court, as he had just contracted to take her "for better or for worse". Ye man smiled & collapsed. . . .

20 Nov. . . . Mrs Pope being at Widow Jenners said that Hastings & St. Leonards were all in uproar because people were saying that the world is coming to an end in 1881, & because bills to that effect were being put about in ye town.

24 Nov. . . . C. on a number of poor people to say that soup wd. begin tomorrow at 4. . . . Jane Vigor (1/-) told me she was "in queer street" again, owing 20/- for rent. John Relf has offered to let me come & read in an evg.

25 Nov. Sch. C. on Cohen to enquire about a rumoured case of small pox. All rubbish. A child had got a skin disease wh. is absolutely incommunicable. C. on some more about soup.

26 Nov. . . . C. & had tea with Mr. & Mrs Whatman. He said that apart from all other losses, he had lost £400 in Stock last year. Poor man. I did not think that he had been hit so hard. Singing w. ye boys.

27 Nov. . . . W. to ye Wheel c. on Mrs Wm. Maskell (1/-) to enquire about her brother Henry Hawkins who I want to see in ref[erence] to a letter wh. I had had from Dearsly [ex-Curate of Burwash, now vicar of Wilmington] conc[erning] a child of Hawkins in ye Eastbourne Union. Mrs Wm. M. has been married 19 years & has had 16 children! 10 alive. I found HH at Mr. Schroeter's at work. I counted I think 15 men & boys. Ye men all have 18/- a week! & lose no time! or needn't do so. Mr. Schroeter ought to be well served.[20] I c. on Mrs Dann ye bailiff's wife. She shewed me a copy of Sherlock on death sold by T. Balcomb, Burwash to St[ephen] Standen Nov. 5 1775, in wh. was the following terrible denunciation
    "If on this book a thief is thringers (fingers) liaise,
    A twisted cord shall soon end his days".
Mrs Wm. Maskell speaking of her old mother who had died in ye Union, said that her husband cd. not go to see her because he said "If she cries & hangs to me, I must have her out – it wd. break my heart to leave her in" & yet he had such a family of his own he cd. not keep her as she required somebody always to look after her.

28 Nov. . . . Mr. Taylor met me as I was going to Ch. & told me that Mr. Barrow had shewn his last letter & mine to Mr. Hyland at ye house nr. ye Bell who had said that whatever might have taken place before Mr. Barrow was bound after that letter to be friendly to me. I am glad he justifies me. . . .

29 Nov. . . . John Relf played truant & did not come in tho' I waited ever so long. He had specially asked me to come & read. Miss Tilley's fir tree at ye corner of ye house near ye road cut down. Mr. Hobden quite civil in discussing its age. My action about cruelty to his horse seems condoned wh. is satisfactory.[21]

3 Dec. . . . Mrs Flack . . . told me that ye Chapel preachers are so illiterate that she doesn't go. She doesn't care much to us, but Chapel folk are not to my taste as a rule. They trim too much. . . .

6 Dec. . . . C. on Mrs John Relf. Squabble w. neighbours & she has got to leave. C. on Mr. J. Fuller, he thinks Mrs R. is wrong. . . . C. & R. w. Bob Watson. Master Watson told me as a positive truth that about 36 years ago his father mother & 4 or 5 children lived a whole month on raw potatoes, it seems incredible, but ye man was so clear & distinct in ye point that I do not disbelieve him. All ye family had ye fever after, & his father & one brother died. . . .[22]

7 Dec. . . . Watched the two Brooks sawing timber. It must be very hard work. Mr. Gibbs says winter thrown timber is most lasting. . . .

8 Dec. . . . C. on Saml. Sweatman to ask him to punish his boy for bad behaviour in ye choir. He very civil about it. . . .

11 Dec. . . . Mr. Philcox shewed me a letter from Mr. J.H.Bolton of St Philips parish, ye London Sol[icito]r calmly asking before payment, what reduction Mr. Egerton proposed to make in his tithe. It is taking a leaf out of the Irish book to make a reduction a condition of paying the remainder.-
. . . Spent an afternoon with Mr. Gibbs trying to find an opening for the subject of his desertion of all Burwash shops in favour of Hurst Green, but without success. He is deep in farm improvements, & is going in for sheep. . . .

12 Dec. . . . Yesterday ye Ed[itor] of ye Leisure Hour sent me ye January part with the first instalment of "Sussex Folk & Sussex ways" nicely printed, & w. a good engraving or wood cut of a picture by Copley Fielding (?) c. ye Sussex Weald or Weald of Sussex.

13. Dec. In aft. went out with Home Words. C. at Mrs Osborn's, poor Mrs Boorman not in; gone with her husb. to see about something at T[unbridge] Wells: poor man, I cannot conceive his keeping any situation three months, & I can only hope I am mistaken. Sold half all my magazines. C. . . . at Vigors . . . ye wife entered into a long expl[anation] about ye quarrel w. Mrs Relf. I am inclined to think that ye latter is wrong – very.

16 Dec. C. on Mr Benjamin Barrow in the Square. Poor man, he has worked so hard & done but little in farming. I am really sorry for him. He has 9 children besides one he has lost. Mrs was a daughter of Mrs Hepworth who lived at Burnt House. . . . I c. on Mr. J.B.Noakes, & found out that it is all a mistake about Mr. Gibbs having left [stopped dealing at] his shop as well as his chapel. They are very good friends, & Mr. Gibbs professes that he cannot hear at the chapel or as I understand Mr. N. that it made his head buzz the next day, so perhaps he heard too much. I am heartily glad to find he has not deserted us altogether for trade as well as for religion, tho' even now he gets all his meat from H. Green. . . .

17 Dec. At 12 to ye Ch. to meet Mr. Davis ye organ repairer or "inside hand" from Mr. Bevington. Got him lodgings at H. Pagden's, & got Willy Eyles to help him; he said that ye organ was terribly dirty & out of order. . . . C. & had tea w. Mrs Gilbert & Miss Tozer. Mrs G. said that Watson's wife's d. had just had a child by some man at Hastings. What extra misery, as they are now almost starving.[23] . . . Told my "reading" cottagers that I was too wet to dare do it about tonight. . . .

18 Dec. . . . An inquest held today I believe at ye Workhouse on a Relf girl who died there on Thurs. I think it was about 10 mins after she had been taken out of the van from Burwash.[24]

20 Dec. Mrs C. Watson (formerly Ledbetter) c. & asked for a trifle. I couldn't help saying that she really was the last person who shd. have come, but it ended in my giving her a shilling. . . .

21 Dec. . . . ye dole given out here, as ye Sch: room was occupied. Gave the tickets in the harness room. Refused only one woman, a parishioner, as her only claim was 2 illeg. children! tho' she is now married. Old couples 4lb, widows 2½lb. Married people 1lb each & chrn. ½ each: rather fewer applicants than usual, over by 12.30. We used 20 years ago to be glad if we finished without candles. . . .

22 Dec. . . . Got cheque for £20 from ye Leisure Hour for "Sussex folk & Sussex ways". First literary money I ever earned. Couldn't send a receipt on their printed form, as that pledged me to leave the copyright as their property . . . Ackn[owledged] ye cheque. . . . Ye organ finished & Mr. Davis & Mr. Bevington left. . . .

24 Dec. . . . A "nigger" band. Danns, 2 Watsons, & 2 Brabans c. & performed. I gave them 1/6 wh. was munificent considering the perform-ance; still the perform. represented some intellectual effort during 3 weeks. "Bells" (Relf's) 1/6, one piece nice. In the others the labour involved in making perfect the wrong time & wrong notes must have been great. Pagden's party came into the kitchen, about 8. They sang better than usual (5/-). Children various.

25 Dec. Xmas day. Ye singers came under ye bedroom window about 3 a.m. & sang their carol, wh. sounded nicely. . . . I c. at J. Isted's. Saw Sally & her husband, John, & Wm – all looking well & happy. Sally's husband in ye R[oyal] Artillery. Looks very respectable. . . . I d. w. Mr. Philcox. Walter Bull chattered & got behind in his eating; his wife rebuked him, he excused his tardiness & its cause & replied, well they do say that "every time a sheep baas, it loses a bite". . . . A wedding at 9. A man living in open sin offered himself as best man! I indignantly rejected him, & afterwards spoke most plainly to him, but he absolutely hardened. Ye bridegroom very properly repudiated ye man & hoped I wd. not speak about it, but he was the bride's brother.[25]

Notes

1.   See above, 29 June, 2 and 3 July 1872.
2.   'By January 1880 large losses of ewes were recorded on the borders of Romney Marsh', and in High Wealden winter-fodder districts including Burwash. P. Brandon and B. Short, *The South-East from AD. 1000*, (1990), p. 325.
3.   The fine related to the grant overpaid in the previous year owing to some error in the paperwork respecting the qualifications of the two ladies. The report also noted that 'the absence at inspection of 25 per cent of the children on the books is unsatisfactory, being an even more distinct proof of the irregularity of attendance than the falling off in the average'. Report, 7 Feb. 1880, ESCRO. ESC.41/1.
4.   '. . . The creatures which fasten on the liver of the sheep and cause death . . . are exactly like very small plaice, and are so vigorous . . . that they will live for nearly an hour after the sheep has been killed'. *Parish Notes*, Feb. 1880.
5.   The press report, probably supplied by Egerton, did not mention the comic. Piano duets, readings, recitations, and songs were sung by individuals, including farmers and their wives. *Sussex Agricultural Express*, 6 Mar. 1880.
6.   Three bedrooms were the key consideration for advocates and their campaigns to improve rural working-class housing, as this would allow parental privacy, and separate bedrooms for male and female children. The topic was one of the very few about which Egerton wrote fiercely in *Sussex Folk*, p. 68.
7.   See above, 22 Sept. 1878 and note 13, for such 'charitably' distributed employment.
8.   Alfred Simmons, the long-serving general secretary of the Kent and Sussex Labourers' Union recognized that general labourers – including those working in the towns, and in industrial jobs in the countryside including quarrying and brick-making – were non-unionized, and membership was opened to them in the Union's first year, 1872–3. This also gave the Union a source of income from non-farming activities, which could be important in combatting lock-outs of agricultural labourers. In addition, the Union had a secure sick fund. Morris may have been an employee, but even if he was a petty entrepreneur, his economic base was probably weak, and his status not greatly different from farmworkers from whose ranks this social sector commonly came. Morris' enthusiastic membership was sensible and ideologically sound.
9.   The Revd Daniel Mann, a long-serving Dissenting minister at Burwash who died in 1787. Burwash Congregationalist Church minutes, 1810–95, annotations by J.S. Noakes, early twentieth century, ESCRO. NC.3/1/2. Mann's widow also merited a short notice on her death in 1805. *Sussex Weekly Advertiser*, 16 Sept. 1805.
10.   John Isted's deliquencies do not seem to have required any local court appearance.
11.   An eloquent testimony to both the rapid shrinkage of the local hop-acreage, and the way in which stacks of wood in the open shrank through continued pilferage.
12.   The entire fund was shared despite Egerton's 'plainly stated' entreaties; the club was re-established as the Rose and Crown Club with fifty-three members, and the press reported its first anniversary. *Sussex Agricultural Express*, 31 May 1881. *Parish Notes*, June 1880.
13.   The men involved were sixteen-year-old 'shopman', Alfred John Dann, and Thomas Copper, a labourer of twenty-two. Both were recorded as semi-literate by the prison authorities during their overnight incarceration. The lass, Thomason

Dora Braban, was indeed twelve, her birthday being in Feb., and she was unable to sign her name. She deposed before Justice Courthope that 'I was in Burwash Town last Monday night [31 May], about twenty minutes to eight I was in the village. I was coming up through the street and went into Readers at the Rose & Crown. A young man treated me with a glass of Beer. I came out again and saw Albert Dann standing at the Corner. I went back into the Rose & Crown and sat down again and he came in. Thomas Copper was in the Rose & Crown he asked me to have some Beer but I did not have any, and Albert Dann came and sat down. We all stopped in there until turn out time. About ten we started. We went as far as Mr. Gilberts, both of them wanted me to go into the Lodge. I told them I did not want to go in there, there were some Policemen about. They said the Policeman was gone home it was alright. I think they both said so.

'We all went into the Lodge they asked me to get up into a Waggon. I told them I should not. . . . Albert said "I shall down with you where you are if you don't get up into the Waggon". I got up into the Waggon and Albert had to do with me first. Thomas after. I mean they both had connection with me. Thomas had not been off a few minutes before the Policemen came, and Thomas got out of the waggon and after Albert got out. Thomas broke through the Faggots standing up beside the Lodge as soon as he heard the Policeman speak, they never paid me nor gave me anything. I did not ask them. I did not want to go, they both took hold of me and I was obliged to go. I did not scream or call out. There was only the Policeman about. I did not get out of the waggon after Dann had connection with [me] before the Policeman came. It was about a quarter of an hour after Dann had connection with me before Copper did so. Albert got up into the waggon first. Copper got up before Albert had done. I had not time to get up. I had known both these young men before. They have done the same thing to me before both of them – only once before; it was not against my wish then. Albert on Burwash Club night and Copper on Burwash Fair night; they did not give me anything then. Albert treated me with a glass of Ginger Beer. I have had connection with only one man besides them. Copper saw me first at the Rose & Crown Mr Readers on the same night', and at this point seems to be cross-examined by one of the suspects, probably Copper. 'I was not willing to go with you. I told you I did not want to go. I did ask Dann to get up into the Waggon first. Dann asked me if Copper might come up and I said yes. We all sat down together after Copper had done. Dann got out of the waggon first and said "good night", neither of them helped me to get up into the Waggon. I got up by myself. We sat down together about a quarter of an hour'.

Sergeant George Smith deposed that on 31 May 'about half past ten o'Clock in the evening, I was standing at the top of Holton Lane . . . with PC. Tappenden when the girl Braban and the two Prisoners passed by, the girl had her Arm around . . . Dann's shoulder and his arm round her waist. Copper was walking close beside of them. We watched them on the Road and when opposite Mrs Gilberts we lost sight of them. We listened for some few minutes in the road. We then could hear them in a Lodge at the back of the Barn. We walked down to the Lodge and listened outside for some five minutes. I then walked round into the front of the Lodge and saw Dann come out of the front of the waggon. Copper he went out the hind side of the waggon and ran away. The girl was lying down in the front part of the Waggon. I ordered her to get out and when outside she admitted that both . . . had connection with her that was in the presence of Dann. Dann said "yes I have had a go at you and so has Copper and twice on Burwash Club night. I shall speak the truth about it". I

saw Dann and Copper together in about ten minutes at the bottom of the Village
and I told both . . . I should report the matter'. Most of Smith's testimony was
corroborated in Tappenden's statement.

Given his comparative youth, it is not surprising that Dann made the more
forthcoming statement. 'I was standing down at the bottom of Ham Lane Mr
Smiths, she came out and saw me there, and soon as she see me she went back in
again, and me and another young Boy went up round there, and then she went for
about five minutes. She came in again and went and sat down by Mr Copper, and
we stopped till ten, and I asked before ten whether she was going out and she said no
and when she went out she went along with Thomas Copper and me and when we
got down to Spring Lane we saw two Policemen and said good night. We went up
as far as Mrs Gilberts, and went in the Lodge . . . and we stood in there for two or
three minutes and then she told me to get in the waggon and she got up next. She
told Thomas to see if any one was coming, and I asked her whether Thomas could
come up and she said "Yes", after Tom was done and me I was getting out of the
front of the Waggon and saw both Policemen. Thomas . . . ran away. I said good
night to both the Policemen again. . . .'.

Copper's brief statement included the admission that 'I said to her lets go down
into the Lodge. She was willing to go, there we had to do with her, the Police came
and I ran away. . . .'.

Both were charged with 'carnally knowing and abusing' a girl, under the age of
consent – thirteen – and were sentenced to six weeks hard labour by the Quarter
Sessions on 29 June. Neither man had previous convictions, and at the trial the only
'real question was the age of the girl'; on production of a birth certificate, 'the jury
convicted' at the same time recommending a light sentence, in reality a comment on
the lass's precocity. The age of consent was raised from thirteen to sixteen under the
Criminal Law Amendment Act of 1885. See also below, note 18. ESCRO.
QR/E1090. *Sussex Agricultural Express*, 3 July 1880.

14.   The growing rail network was increasing the numbers of easily accessible
Wealden locations for townsfolk, including Londoners; large firms, trade union
branches, benefit clubs and other voluntary organizations are found collectively
taking days in the countryside.

15.   In *Sussex Folk*, pp. 98–9, Egerton tactfully referred to the topic. 'The old
civility is now, I fear, looked upon by many as mere servility; and occasionally the
distinction between independence and impudence is apparently not very well
understood. . . . I am not . . . in the least degree complaining. . . . I cannot lose
heart about some of my own young parishioners whose tempers and dispositions as
yet do not seem especially amicable.'

16.   The press reported an 'ancient cavalcade' comprising eighty-seven-year-old
Mrs (widow of Henry) Collins, with fellow octogenerian James Weston driving a
forty year-old pony, to the National School; although the report stated that Mrs
Collins related a tale about her grandfather, Richard Balcombe (1737–1817), the
details were not included. *Sussex Agricultural Express*, 24 Aug. 1880. The details of
the story, excepting that it involved a ghost, were also omitted from *Sussex Folk*,
pp. 100–1, but Egerton did record the names of the children present, so that if any of
them lived to Mrs Collins' age – which would occur in 1959 – they would be able to
say that through her they heard the tale 'of something done by a man . . . born . . .
222 years before'.

17.   The overseer was almost certainly George Fagg Gilbert, a draper and mercer,
and farmer, an elected and leading vestryman in the difficult 1820's during which

decade he was overseer for at least one year, 1823–4. The Collins was not Henry, the husband of Mrs Collins in note 16, but probably either Samuel or Thomas; like many other labourers, both were in perennial receipt of poor relief over much of that period, and involved in various altercations with officials. Samuel was imprisoned for abandoning his family, and in the mid-1830s Thomas' request for government-assisted emigration foundered when nobody would give him a character reference. Burwash vestry minutes, various dates, but esp. 16 Mar. 1821 and 26 Mar. 1823; S. Collins, committal details, 22 Aug. 1821: ESCRO. Par.284/12/1; QR/E. Michaelmas 1821. Clerk, Ticehurst Union, to the Poor Law Commission, 5 Dec. 1836, PRO. MH12/13138.

18. Namely the sexually-experienced Thomason Dora; see note 13, above.

19. An unprecedented audience according to the press; the proceeds went towards the juvenile cricket club recently created under National School auspices. *East Sussex Journal*, 23 Nov. 1880.

20. Schroeter clearly was a model employer, as these wages were at least a fifth above average. Many employers laid off their men during adverse weather, including prolonged rain, as well as heavy snow falls. The Kent and Sussex Labourers' Union campaigned with little success against this practice.

21. However, there is no record of prosecution in the local courts.

22. See introduction, p. 16. Watson's father was not among the six heads of large labouring families at Burwash who addressed a public rally held in the village on 23 Feb. 1838, and described their extreme poverty: a petition, to the House of Commons, followed from workers 'with half filled bellied and burning hearts'. It read, in part, that 'numbers of those whose toil-cramped hands now grasp the pen to affix their names . . . are now, and for months past have been, in a state of half stavation: that through almost the whole of this inclement weather, the diet of numbers of families, has consisted almost entirely of POTATOES . . . your petitioners deem their rights, the rights of labourers who cause the earth to produce all that it *does* produce, of those without whose toil the wealthy and idle would soon cease to revel in that effeminating luxury in which they now so thoughtlessly rejoice . . .'. *Brighton Patriot*, 13 Mar. and 3 Apl. 1838. Conditions were equally appalling in 1842, and Watson could have been referring to either year, or indeed any other in the post 1835 period, as the individual circumstances of families dictated such expediences, which were widespread. However the burial registers do not record the Watsons' burials, though at this time the family may have lived elsewhere.

23. The daughter, by a previous marriage, was Caroline Pankhurst; she obtained a bastardy order against W.L. Bodkin of St Leonards, for 2/6 weekly. *Sussex Agricultural Express*, 30 Nov. 1880.

24. Eliza Sinden, née Relf, aged twenty-seven, was buried on 21 Dec., Egerton recording 'R. ye Certificate from Coroner . . . dis. of Kidneys'. ESCRO. Par.284/1/5/2.

25. Blacksmith John Bailey, twenty-six, step-son of farmer William Watkins, married labourer John Cane's daughter, Naomi, aged twenty-five. Presumably John Haffenden – who signed the register with Hannah Pennalls as witnesses – deputized for the offending Cane. ESCRO. Par.284/1/3/3.

1881

5 Jan. . . . Said good bye to Mrs Boorman. Mr. B. has got a coal business at Sutton. . . .

18 Jan. Terrible night, wind & snow, a day indeed to be remembered. The mail did not come through at all, a thing wh. so far as I know never happened before. . . .

19 Jan. Mail cart wh. ought to have come through last night, has not turned up at all. . . .

20 Jan. . . . Poor old John Sheather whom I saw last Thursday, & thought likely to live for a long time yet, & who himself was in trouble lest he shd. outlive his money (£80) died this morning . . .[1]

22 Jan. . . . nearly 50 "Snow heavers" at work today I am told.[2]

1 Feb. . . . In aft. C. on most of my singing men to ask them to supper on Monday night. H.Pagden opened my eyes about ye concerts. He said that ye bulk of ye singers grumbled at my hiring professionals, & so sending the concert money out of the parish, & that they wd. rather have a concert a house affair so that the class shd. get the praise & a supper. There does not seem to be one atom of care for music in itself, but only for praise & pudding. . . .

4 Feb. . . . C. on H. Dann. . . . I innocently enquired after Albert, wh. led unfortunately to denunciation of ye police in wh. I cd. not join. I am very sorry for ye poor man, but he ought to have exercised more supervision over his son when young. . . .[3]

7 Feb. . . . In evg. supper to my singers. Mr. Fuller & Mr. Taylor did not come as ye weather was very bad, but ye rest all appeared 13 in number I think. Supper at 7.50, than an adjournment to ye servants hall: wine drunk 4 bottles, besides ale & stout, not much therefore. A lot of songs sung. Some nice. I sang twice. Broke up about 10 min. to eleven. All seemed satisfied.

14 Feb. One Valentine, calling me an "old egg faced devil!" whatever that may mean, ye stamp not obliterated, so I bagged that. How can I be surprized if somebody in Burwash dislikes me. I think I know the reason of dislike in most cases, & if one really does one's duty, do it as humbly & inoffensively as one can, somebody or other is sure to be riled. . . . C. on old Pilbeam, & said a few words; he has had his shoulder put out by a fall when drunk.[4] . . . C. on Amos Jenner, he mooted a testimonial to Mr. Anset [who had been ill for some months]. I consented gladly. Harry Jarvis met me & quite independently suggested ye same thing by means of a benefit concert. It is pl. to see ye schoolmaster so respected. . . .[5]

20 Feb. . . . I fear that I cannot write sermons, do what I will, wh. suit the people as well as some of the old published ones wh. I occasionally preach. . . .

21 Feb. . . . C. on Wm. Maynard. I really pity the poor chap. he suffers sad pain. he has been a godless liver, but he is humbled now. . . .[6]

26 Feb. . . . C. & P. w. Mrs Js. [Fanny, aged eighty-five] Weston; quite ill, gave her 10/- as she is a worthy woman pulled down by her husband. . . .

3 Mar. . . . Mr. Gillham c. He is candidate for assistant Overseership in Ticehurst, & I wrote on his behalf to Uncle Nathan & Mr. Hussey of Scotney Castle. . . .

5 Mar. . . . C. & R. w. Mrs J. Weston, better, t. w. her husband, ignorant I fear in ye extreme, & at ye age of over 80 apparently without a thought of ye world to come; said what I cd., but oh how helpless is man to touch a really hard heart.[7] . . . Poor Gen[era]l Hinde died on Tuesday, leaving a widow & 7 children (besides two married) & about £200 a year. Tea w. Mr. Taylor. Long chat w. him & [a visiting Frenchman] Mr. Noel. Prospects of agriculture not bright certainly.

16 Mar. . . . [In Ticehurst, at Pashley, for] Supper. Looked at G. Luxford's testimonials for Ye Chief Constableship, admirable – he ought to stand a good chance. . . .

25 Mar. . . . Mr. Gillham having been elected Assist. Overseer for Ticehurst resigns our Guardianship.[8] Mr. Whatman, Mr. G. Fuller elected Guardians & Mr. Wh. resigns chairmanship. Meeting all friendly.

30 Mar. . . . Cooper pr: half an hour: monotonous & not specially interesting; very fluent extempore. I w. w. him as far as Laurelhurst, & he wanted to tell me of some parochial troubles.

31 Mar. . . . at 1.30 d. w. Mr. Piper & his son. Small gathering. I did not quite understand why fewer sheep had been put out to keep last year, but so it was. . . .

2 Apl. . . . C. at J. Coppers ye bakers, he ill. I said that of course if he liked to see me I wd. go with pleasure, but I did not offer, as he is a thorough Dissenter. . . .

4 Apl. . . . Heard that . . . poor Mrs Hinde has . . . a promise of about £300 agreed for 5 years for education of her boys by Mr. Dent & Mr. Allcroft ye glove manufacturers who were great friends of General Hinde. . . .

6 Apl. . . . C. & R. w. Js. Watson (1/-). He told me he is a Chapeler & I sincerely hope that he will stick to Chapel & get all the good he can. He needs it poor man. Cloth cutting, is cutting up old clothes, & sorting out ye pieces according to quality. He tells me there are twenty sorts of rags to be kept distinct in every sorting. He gets 3/- a cwt! for cutting & sorting ye old clothes. It seems cruelly low pay. . . .[9]

9 Apl. . . . C. on Mrs Amos Akehurst of Bowmans. She told me that she rears from 300 to 400 chickens every year. Just now the higglers are giving 3/6 for a good chick[en].

11 Apl. . . . Poor Rover Maynard gone to ye Union to day [following funeral of his wife on the 9th; he died in the workhouse on the 18th]. I shd. like to have seen ye poor chap before he went. . . .

15 Apl. Good Friday. . . . Learnt . . . that I or N. & I between us had offended Mrs & Miss J. Y[oung] by want of courtesy at the school treat as long ago as 4th of last August. I had been altogether in the dark. They had left the Church & gone to Chapel for a time, I being under the firm impression that they were genuine Chapelers. . . . Wrote to Mr. J Y & explained that our garden party does not involve a "reception" in the Rectory, & tried to make things smooth. C. on Mr. Gibbs; he is prepared to sell his place if he can. . . .

18 Apl. . . . Vestry meeting at 10, Mr. Whatman resigns office as Ch. warden being now Guardian. Mr. W. Ellis Draper & Grocer appointed his successor; good appt: at least I believe so. Deficiency in Church funds of over £16: did not seem to trouble people much. In aft. I c. on Henry Dann; ye Cranbrook Union on ye strength of my letter allowed ye 3/6 a week as before.[10] . . . Our boys cricket club & ye men's club opened with matches today . . .

20 Apl. . . . In trap from ye Establishment to dine with Herbert Newington. . . . HN instituting an enquiry as to ye antecedents & circumstances of all cases of insanity attributed to drink. He believes that hereditary predisposition to insanity producing depression makes many people drink, rather than that drinking makes them mad . . .[11]

22 Apl. . . . I buried poor Rover Maynard. He the 800th person buried in Burwash Ch. Yard since I came in July 1857. A parish coffin, without a nameplate or a vestige of furniture looks sad, tho' the moment it is covered with earth it is as good as its betters. . . .

27 Apl. . . . Back by ye road past Perch Hill & down to John Coppards. I had never been that road before, & found a cott[age] near P. Hill wh. I had never even known as being in Burwash! Home to tea, & then to ye singing. Some fresh troubles. Ye men's class collapsed. It is ye wrong time of ye year. . . .

2 May. . . . To ye Sch. Spoke seriously about ye girls teasing one another out of sch. I must put ye matter in ye hands of ye police if it goes on.

4 May. . . . In aft. c. & had long t. w., Mrs John Isted about her husband's cruel treatment of her. Her old father there. I cd. do nothing but recommend patience, grievous as Isted's misconduct is.[12] . . . C. on Mr. John Fuller & got census statistics for Parish Notes. . . .

6 May. . . . Presided at ye quarterly meeting of ye Sch. Club. 30 members. Since Aug: only 27/- (I think) spent in doctoring & only 25 days sick-pay drawn.

8 May. . . . Saml. Hazelden asked me to dine w. ye Club at St. Philips on Ascension day. I readily agreed. . . .

13 May. . . . George Luxford elected [Chief Constable of the East Sussex police on 12th] – Hurrah – I threw my hat on high. He is a capital fellow.[13] I c. on poor Mrs Flack who was hurt in her house yesterday by a lot of people rushing in after a man who had taken shelter from an attack by two Burwash Commoners. Did not see her. . . .

15 May. . . . Pr. to ye Club from St. John 3. 17 (Ext). Members wonderfully quiet & attentive, not one went out. D. w. them in booth at Rose & Crown. . . . Everybody very civil. They expected wrath, but what is one to do. It is true they took the honorary members money last year & shared it out, but they say that all, or at any rate a majority of members old as well as young agreed, so what cd. one say to one party more to another. The old members say it was done without their consent, but I imagine that that is only a way of saying that they were not very keen about the matter. Battle band, noisy, but much improved in intelligence of performance. I away about 10 min: before 6. . . .[14]

26 May. Ascension day. I up to ye Common. . . . To ye dinner. Members very warm in their greetings. Cooper there. I am sorry but do not wonder. To a person who is not used to them ye Burwash Commoners are occasionally trying. Mr. Fryer sat by me & was very talkative. He wd. have driven friend Cooper wild, as it was he gave me a text for some clear speaking about tee-totalism. Sam Hazleden R[ichar]d (?) Holmes & others very quiet & intelligent. I sang "A thousand a year" in wh. poor Fryer said "there was plenty of piety, & that was why he liked it"! & "When the heart is young": left at about 3.35. Quite touched by the kind feeling of the club. . . .

1 June. . . . JP. c. about ye "extraordinary tithe" agitation. It is too bad. There is no reason why parsons shd. suffer any more than landlords; there is no guarantee offered that ye money taken from ye parsons as tithe shd. not go into ye landlords pockets as rent. . . .[15]

3 June. C. on Mrs J. Isted, gave her a letter from Miss Coomb Superin-t[endent] of Merch[ant] Taylor's Conv[alescant] Home for ladies at Bognor, an exe[mplary] character. John Isted has gone away: good thing if he wd. stop away. . . .

9 June. Sch. Not a few boys gone to ye Bath & West of England Ag[ricultural] Show at T[unbridge] Wells. I am glad as it may open their minds. . . . [On hearing that William Hilder had hired the Mill] he must be demented, but we shall see.

13 June. W. N. to ye Village. Met Mr. Cooper in ye village, he distributing notices of ye Bazaar. C. on Mr. J.B.Noakes to get some change. I notice Miss in a very sumptuous dress, & wondered what was the matter, but Mr. Noakes never even hinted that his daughter had been married this morning at Shovers Green Chapel! Funny people. I c. on Mr. Gillham; tea & talk. It is curious how I get on so well with a Baptist in religion & Liberal in politics, but he is a good man I believe & I can mostly get on with a good man who has ideas. . . .

15 June. . . . C. on Mrs J. Isted; she seemed quite strong, thanks to ye quiet & peace of mind secured by ye absence of her husband. . . . C. on C. Brook & gave him 10/- for ye cricket club. . . .

Sat. 18 June. . . . to ye cricket field our school boys beaten in an innings. They have been wasting their time in practice by simply caring for their "hit", without troubling about fielding or careful batting. . . .

20 June. G. Harmer ye new Ch. Ward. from ye Common, c. on me to ask advice how to stop the insults of one Thomas Hicks who having been worsted in a County Court attack [i.e. a civil action, on which there are no details], revenges himself by abusing GH for rebuking his (TH's) boy in Church. I advised patience, especially as there is no law agst. mere abuse & I fortified friend Harmer with an extract from a newspaper wh. . . . two years ago contained the report of the conviction of some boys for disturbing a congregation in church. I advised him quietly to tell T.H. that if his boy or any body else's persistently interrupted in Church, he wd. be summoned to Hurst Green. G.H. went away comparatively comfortable. . . . C. on JP about ye [school]mistresses' salary, We agreed to a £10 rise for each. I c. on them & communicated ye decision. They seemed relieved in their mind. They are steady respectable women, and I think fair teachers. . . .

21 June. . . . In evg. w. in ye Glebe fields. It seems that nobody has even offered himself as a tenant.[16]

22 June. . . . To ye Common. Consulted with ye ladies about Bazaar tomorrow. . . .

Thurs. 23 June. Sch. Aft. d. w. towards ye Common. . . . Lovely day. Some capital things for sale not as it seemed to me many people. . . . I acted as an auctioneer & sold some things; not a "cheap jack" as some of my most intimate friends address me. Mrs Lee aged 51 with a baby 6 months old!

24 June. Very hot. I w. by ye Tot fields to c. on Mrs Simpson at Shrub. Lay down in ye shade for a while & considered my sermon for Sunday. Open air all very enjoyable, but not like a study table for rigorous systematic thought. C. & R. w. old Mrs Keeley (1/-) a house I have hardly ever been in; its manners & customs having long been a deterrent to a clergyman. Poor woman now ill & ready to listen. . . .

Sat. 25 June. Prep. Serm. I find great diff[iculty] in getting now much more than a leading idea. Somehow I cannot now "work it out" beforehand. . . .

28 June. . . . I c. & R. w. poor master Bassett & his wife at Turzies [Turses]. Their son seems to have been killed instantaneously as he jumped off the waggon on Friday evg. & the wheel passed over the side of his skull. He was a steady lad – [aged] about 17 10/12.[17] . . . On my way home Mrs Balcombe complained that her boy had been much caned, not for bad conduct but for ignorance, wh. grievance she said was owing to the lads having been kept away from school for a few days to work for Mr. Gillham. She pleaded that Mr. Thomson ought to have come down & caned the parents for keeping the boy away, rather than the boy for ignorance due to his having been kept away! The argument was new & not unreasonable. I wrote a note to Mr. Anset. . . .

29 June. . . . Saw my letter in ye Sussex Express about Canon Hawkins formerly Curate of Burwash & ye Revised Version, but as usual a silly Sussex Expr. misprint did it no good. . . .[18]

30 June. Interviewed a poor girl by name Clara Scrase who having kept company for five years with a young Harmer has been deserted by him, he being the father of her child, 3 months old. Let her sin be what it may I am sorry for her, as she has no father or mother, & her friends have cast her off. . . .[19]

1 July. . . . down to ye Club meeting. Members wisely agree I fancy to put off ye dinner till aft. hopping. I paid my hon[orary] memb. Subscr . . . .

6 July. . . . Ellen's [Gould] Party. . . . people seemed to enjoy themselves. I held out my hand to Mr. Barrow, but no use. Ye poor man said his was a good member & he wd. not disgrace it! I truly pity his unforgiving spirit. He surely cannot be happy with it. . . .

9 July. Mrs Russell of Holton c. to ask advice. Her husband has gone to America leaving her & 7 children destitute; poor woman, I pity her: her husb: comes of a sadly tainted, & her own mother ran away w. a man of the name of Crossingham to America, so the strain is not good. I am very sorry all the same for the woman.[20] . . . I in ye aft. to see ye boys cr. m[atch] w. ye Brightling boys eleven playing here. We were getting ye best of it when I came away. . . .

13 July. I tried a swathe with ye mowers, but my skill is on the wane. . . . C. on Wm. Weston about a piece of Burwash made linen. C. on H.Jarvis wife conf[inement] of a boy, being well. Great talk about a case of neglect on part of Dr. Cohen who wd. not go when sent for to see Mrs Wm. Maskall, who died shortly after. I do not believe that he cd. have done her any good, but it was heartless work not going. An inquest reported, but this was a fiction, tho' it wd. have been a good thing as our friend seems inclined to be somewhat selfish in the matter of visiting the poor. . . .

Sun. 17 July. Sch. Read out names of children for ye treat. . . .

18 July. Hard at work invitation writing to local gentry. . . .

20 July. . . . I c. on Mrs J. Isted & brought sweets for ye children. C. on Mrs H. Dann, very indignent w. Cohen for his bill. . . . Children at 2.45, about 115. People attended largely. I shd. say about 250; weather lovely. Farmers well represented. Dr. Cohen was active in keeping ye children amused. Ye Burwash brass band volunteered their services & quite enlivened ye afternoon. Every body seemed pleased w. ye aft.

23 July. . . . I wrote a serious letter to JB one of our young tradesmen. If persons of his rank of life make light of ante-nuptial sin, how is common morality to be mentioned among the more ignorant. It is pain & grief to me, as his wife was one of our most respectable women & a Communicant, & he himself one of our smartest young tradesmen, but I fear godless. He will be probably very cross, but I cd. not be silent.[21]

Sun. 7 Aug. . . . Largish congr. Got a box of bronchial tablets at Mr. Noakes; also he gave me out of his pocket 2 potash Lozenges w. one of wh.

I moistened my throat in ye evg. being possibly ye only Incumbent in the kingdom who preached today by aid of a lozenge & straight out of ye pocket of ye head dissenter in his parish. . . .

11 Aug. . . . c. on Mr. G. Fuller. He explained ye case of Maskell & Dr. Cohen. Want of attention of part of ye latter, but not enough to call for serious action. Dr. C's report sent to Local [Government] Board [in London]. I think it will be a lesson, as I really believe that a lesson was needed . . .[22]

23 Aug. . . . My letter to Sussex Express appeared to day . . .[23]

26 Aug. . . . Took refuge from shower at Martha Flemings; read radical newsp.

29 Aug. . . . I c. on Mrs John Isted; her husb: away 14 weeks has sent her 30/- bad man. . . . An article in ye Hastings & St. Leonards Times of Saturday [27th] abusing me, but not answering my lett: to Suss: Expr. I wrote a civil private letter to ye Editor.[24]

30 Aug. . . . To ye vill: got my paper at Jarvis . . . Ye letter in. In Saturday's two answers wh. I think I may conscientiously say were no answers to my arguments, tho' somewhat rough upon myself. It is hard to have to seem hard in such times as these, yet after the compromise under the T[ithe] Comm[utation] act, the owner of the rent charge is really not the party to the agreement who ought to suffer. The landlord ought to bear the brunt together w. ye tenant, as the owners of rent charge have for many years submitted to a considerable dimunition of income by the [Tithe] Commissioners. . . . C. on Mr. George Fuller [Guardian of the Poor] about ye emigration of a Mr. Russell. . . .

Sat. 3 Sept. . . . No further notice of my letter in ye Sussex Expr: so I am out of that, but Mr. G. Fuller & others have told me that I did not write nonsense.[25]

7 Sept. . . . fell in w. Mr. G[illham] & had a long t. about his letter in yesterday paper wh. I have not yet seen. Also about ye times. Picked up near his [hop]bin a leaf out of some schoolboy's copy book wh. had been torn out & thrown upon ye ground. By a singular coincidence the copy wh. had been written was "Bear with courage evils wh. cannot be avoided". I took it & shewed it to Mr. G., he smiled. . . . Bought ye Sussex Exp: Mr. G. very kind to me personally, & civil in ye argumentation part of ye letter. . . .[26]

8 Sept. . . . I sat up last night till 12 & till 12.45 this morg. answering Mr. G's letter privately to him, & not for print.

9 Sept. C. on old Mrs Collins; home shut up, blinds drawn. Ye poor old lady gone to her rest, aged I suppose 87. She was a quaint old being of a singularly happy disposition, a delightful student of ye scriptures, & had raised up to herself friends, so that she did not want. Her last earthly trouble was the loss of her pocket book with 2/6 in it: this she missed a few hours before her death, but as it was found again while she was still conscious, she died humanely speaking at peace. I have every reason to hope at peace with God also. . . . To Ellen's. A small garden party chiefly parochial aristocracy. . . .

[12 Sept. to 1 Oct. in Buckinghamshire and Cheshire.]

Sun. 2 Oct. I ye only teacher in ye boys Sch. no 1st cl. boy wd. volunteer to help. I spoke about it, as it was very selfish. I personally swept part of ye girls sch: wh. had been left undone. . . .

7 Oct. . . . C. on Mrs Pennells of Crowh[urst] br[idge Farm]: quite poorly; overdone, was at Ch. twice on Sunday. She tells me that for 10 years she baked two sacks of flour 8 bushel or 32 gallons every 3 weeks! She has 15 ch: alive. . . .

10 Oct. Copied out a Nil return of Marriages for the last 3 months. I am not sure that I ever did this before at Burwash. Funeral of Mrs Tracton Rochester. I buried her only daughter a few weeks ago. She was d. of "lawyer" Buss at Mayfield & latterly her husb: poor man has been drawing a chair at T[unbridge] Wells. . . .[27]

13 Oct. . . . Laurelhurst . . . then on to Vicarage. . . . Canon Puckle preached a good sermon, tho' he stirred my sense of opposition by some of ye statements wh. he made withholding corn in dear times is not the sin to my mind wh. some make it to be. If in scarcity corn was cheap it wd. be recklessly used, & thus the scarcity wd. cruelly intensify. The demanding higher prices enforces thrift, & so lengthens out the supply. . . .[28]

17 Oct. . . . In evg. waited till 7.30 & then Henry Dann appeared as the sole young Burwash man anxious to learn to sing at night; he went to look for some more who said they meant to come, but brought back word that "they didn't think they shd. come tonight"! Burrash [traditional pronunciation of the village name] all over – so ended my first endeavour to advance bona fide the knowledge of music in B . . . .[29]

18 Oct. . . . dined w. Mrs Gillett, Miss & 3 gr: ch. of Salehurst. . . . Miss G. took me to see her chickens of wh. she had as many as 500 at a time. She sold 90 last Saturday to James Leaves. . . .

20 Oct. Mr. & Mrs Schroeter c. at about 11 to speak about ye condition of ye "offices" [latrines] at ye school as some boys of parents who work for him had complained. I took him as well as Mrs to ye School. We examined the whole arrangements. Ye boys side no fault. Ye girls & infants needed seeing to. I am much obliged to Mr. & Mrs S. for interesting themselves in ye question. . . .[30]

27 Oct. . . . back at 4.30 [from Eastbourne] to ye Benefit Club, who had just fin[ishe]d d. at ye Bear. I spoke by request & was most kindly received. I feel sometimes as if such occasions give me the best chance I ever get of speaking to my working men. I enjoyed my opportunity & ye audience was most complimentary. I sung "When the heart is young" & "A thousand a year" prop[osed] health of Mr. Littlemore [licensee of the Bear] & ye band (Burwash brass) & away. A cup of tea & then lesson to music Class. . . . To Mr. Ansets; looked over testimonials of applicants for Assistant Mistresses.

28 Oct. Sch. First meeting of Musical Class for ladies: Mrs Stuart, Mrs G.Darby, 2 Miss Hollands, Fraulein Schulze, Miss Edith Russell, 2 Miss Smiths of Sea View, Miss Edith Cooper & dear N.[31] Fair results, but [music] reading powers not great . . .

29 Oct. Aft. br[eakfast] C. & R. w. old Mrs John Pennells; better; I like her: she seems a simple minded God fearing woman. . . .

2 Nov. . . . C. on JP. Cooper objects to my reduction on tithe this year. He is right in principle. Tithe ought not to be subjected to any other abatement than that wh. the law provides for. Security of income was one great motive wh. influenced the clergy in accepting the compromise in 1836 [Tithe Commutation Act]. I know that, still I do not like the thought of being perhaps the only person in the parish who receives his income this year in full. I pity Cooper. Still he overrates my income for spending purposes very largely. . . .

3 Nov. . . . said good bye to Miss Child who is leaving for a better situation in London; I am sorry she is going. If she is not a brilliant teacher, she is a persevering conscientious right minded young woman. . . .

5 Nov. A wedding, Blackford & Collins, at 11, both unfortunately happen to live in Cooper's distr[ict] but they described themselves as of Burwash. After d. round w. Magazines. . . . Much squibbing Wm. Pilbeam [junior] ye blacksmith spent so his son told me £1 in squibs. It does seem insane work.

Sun. 6 Nov. Sch. young [undecipherable] ye [pupil] teacher absent because he was out squibbing till 12 o'Clock last night & did not care to wash himself & so was late this morg. & did not come. . . . Cooper accepts my £10 towards his reduction of tithe. . . . 13 baptisms! . . . had never had so many on one Sunday. 4 chrn. of one family of Russell. . . .[32]

8 Nov. . . . C. on Mrs Collins, widow; her poor idiot d. a great trial to her.

9 Nov. . . . I w. up to the Common. Went into the sch. I fear that trouble is
before us both [i.e. National Schools in both Burwash and St Philips] for
enlargement of buildings & increased teaching staff. Miss Press showed me
her log book, reports, schedule of examinations etc.

10 Nov. . . . Tithe Audit at ye Bell at 2 o'Clock. I dined; my abatement of
10% helped to pacify the feelings of trouble due to the badness of the times.
Mr. Gillham, who moved the first resolution of the great Anti-Hop Tithe
meeting in London proposed my heath in very kind terms. I prop. ye
Queen & Tithe-payers. James Philcox, ye Parish Officers & Mr. G. Fuller. I
made a declaration on ye subj: of the Extra[ordinary] Tithe & spoke very
plainly. Mr. Gillham answered me, but we were all in good humour, & the
discussion must I think have done good. On the whole a very pl. aft. tho'
Mr. Philcox did not take so much money as usual. However people did not
refuse, they only cd. not pay. . . .

11 Nov. A bill from Mr Combs for 1878! In looking to my diary I find that
the days wh. he had chosen were purely arbitrary as in most cases I was
perfectly well; on only two days was he right in the matter of attendance. In
aft. I c. on Mrs John Isted, pd. her bill £1-5-0. . . .

12 Nov. . . . A letter of thanks from poor Mr. Whatman. His losses have
been very heavy. I am sorry for him. I wrote him as sympathetic an answer
as I cd.

14 Nov. . . . C. on Amos Akhurst at Bowmans, saw Mrs. How hard a little
farmer's wife has to work. She fats her own chicken in addition to her other
labours. . . . Singing w. men at 8. 6 now adhere. . . .

15 Nov. . . . The case of alleged medical neglect of Mrs Maskell comes on
tomorrow; adj[ourne]d Board [of Guardians] special meeting. . . .

18 Nov. . . . Met Mr. Whatman. Ye Poor Law Enquiry about Dr Cohen &
Mrs Wm. Maskell's death going on today. . . .[33]

21 Nov. . . . Read a rather spiteful notice in ye Sussex Express of [Rector of
Ticehurst] Eden's Tithe Audit. . . . a notice of my reductions.[34]

22 Nov. C & R w. old Master Edmunds at ye Tot. J. Pennells met me & wd.
make me hear his version of a matter wh. has drawn him a summons from
Mr. Love. I think the poor man is not in the wrong, but of course I have not
heard the other side.[35] Mr. Taylor met me & expressed his wonder that no
reduction of tithe was made to him for the glebe land. The truth is that the
tenant of the glebe does not pay tithe specifically, but pays it in the shape of

rent to the landlord. He really ought therefore to have come to me & have asked me as a landlord for a reduction of rent, instead of asking JP. for the 10pc on the tithe, wh. he did not pay as tithe. I begged him to accept the remission but he wd. not. . . . to Pashley [House for dinner party] . . . poor evening. All ye talk about tithes nothing new . . .

29 Nov. . . . I buried poor Mrs Butcher at 3. Saw her son George now a gardener at Streatham [Surrey], one of the most respectable of our Burwash productions, & I shd. say a thoroughly good young fellow. C. on G. Maskell, expecting to find him quite ill. I found that he had gone "up into the wood" somewhere to bargain for some hop-poles for his wife to shave. . . .

30 Nov. . . . Tea w. John Hyland. He told me that Joseph Hall had just hired 14 acres of very poor Heathfield land from Mr. Bolton the Farmers' Alliance orator at £40 a year! the landlord paying rates & taxes. . . .

2 Dec. . . . C. on Mrs Langridge. Cohen oddly enough had given no orders for isolation of her children, tho' there was scarlet fever in the house. I c. on him: he said the case had been so slight that there was no danger. To us after Mr. Combs precautions the doctrine is new. . . . Alfred Hyland stopped me to complain of Mr. Thornton's over severe treatment of his boy. I must enquire. . . . H.Dann . . . said that Mr. Quee is going to leave. I am really rather sorry as I liked the little man. . . . Tea w. Mr. Taylor he told me about poor Mr. Quee, who has offended Mr. J.B.Noakes & family. The little man has possibly not been judicious, but his position distinctly shows the difference between a Independent Minister of an Independent Congregation. The weakest goes to the wall. . . . Supper to eleven singing boys. Two Langridges did not come bec. of sore throats at home. So we sent them their supper.

12 Dec. . . . To Robertsbridge to ye George. Farmers meeting to promote ye Farmers Alliance. Leadham late fellow of BNC one of ye two principal speakers & very well he spoke. Mr. Bolton ye other orator; unpleasant & violent. I dare say 120 people present. I had a pl. t. w. Leadam. . . . Mr. Gillham gave me my invitation.[36] . . . A soup kitchen meeting here in aft . . . .

13 Dec. . . . Looked in at ye tree in Gleddish wood under wh. in 1824 ? ye man Russell was found dead, for whose murder Leaney was executed & Hannah Russell afterwards Chandler was convicted but pardoned.[37]

15 Dec. . . . I went to Mr. Verone's conjuring. Really very good, & I am as completely bewildered as when I saw him before. I the only shilling seatholder. . . .

16 Dec. . . . Singing w. boys in Ch. Sent to enquire where Ellis boy was: Ans. "please Sir he had forgot – he's gone to bed, but his mother says he shall get up at once if you like – but I said it was no matter". However ye poor boy came!

21 Dec. Gave away dole from 10.40 till 1.10. Fewer people applied than usual & we gave away nearly 60lbs less than last year. . . .

22 Dec. C. on old Mrs Collins 87 at ye Roells [?] left a small plumpudding. Sad account of ye cottage at Grantwizzle where her daughter lives. It is not fit for human occupation. . . . Said good by to Jack Honeysett. He leaves Burwash on Sat. [24th] or Sun. having finished his [tailoring] apprenticeship at Pagdens. I like the young fellow, & if he falls into good hands he will do well.

25 Dec. . . . I dined at Mr. Philcox as usual. The rising generation numerous enough. . . .

26 Dec. Performed ye marr. Serv. for Sarah Mutton our cook & Edward Henry Bull. Commercial Clerk in London. A very pretty little wedding. We lent our Brougham. Said good-bye to the new married couple. Sarah has been a faithful servant, & we wish her much happiness. . . .

27 Dec. . . . C. . . . on Mrs Simmonds ye carter's wife; not at h[ome] & children locked into ye house. . . .

29 Dec. . . . C & took tea with Mr. & Mrs John Coppard. Master Newell of ye Brightling Estate Carpenter there; an excellent memory for ye past, & we talked about ye burnings & mobbings of 1830. . . .

30 Dec. In aft. c. on Mrs Brett; both she & her husband very grateful for remission of tithe. They strive very hard & all the family work. Mr. Barton the nominee of Mr. Taylor to undertake the poor law practice vacated by Dr. Cohen obliged by Poor Law Board [in fact its successor, the Local Government Board] to resign, called on me. His manner & address pleasant. Poor Cohen it is a cruel blow, but he has really brought it on himself. He wd. take no advice or warning & his harshness to the poor has been too bad. . . .[38]

Notes

1. Sheather, aged seventy-four, was one of the smallest proprietors in the parish with a mere six acres at Budds Farm, as reflected rather pathetically in the small sum saved for his retirement.
2. By this period there was a tradition that farmworkers laid off after snow, were employed to clear the road by the parochial highway authority.

3. Local records suggest that Albert Dann's troubles involved the police elsewhere.
4. On this occasion the notorious elder William Pilbeam evaded the courts; his last conviction, when he was fined 2/6 with 20/6 costs for assaulting fellow blacksmith George Daws, occurred on 25 June 1880. Summary convictions, ESCRO. QR/ E1090.
5. The 'third evening entertainment of this season' had taken place – in Egerton's absence – on 9 Feb. Anset was ill and John Fuller presided, but the singing – 'for which this village is rather famous' – was up to standard. Egerton was present for the benefit concert on 23 Feb. which was well attended by folk from Burwash and the adjacent parishes. *Sussex Agricultural Express*, 15 Feb. and 1 Mar. 1881.
6. William Maynard, now on the eve of eighty, had at times worked for his brother John, sometime proprietor of the Bear Inn, and also a higgler and chicken fattener: William was subsequently a carrier. His godlessness in Egerton's estimation no doubt included Maynard's indecent assault on 'young widow' Fanny Ellis, while giving her a lift from Burwash to Brighton in 1864, though the Lewes Bench accepted that the lady had initially encouraged his advances. *Sussex Advertiser*, 8 Mar. 1864. Depositions of Maynard, 11 June 1842 and 15 Feb. 1846, ESCRO. QR/E885; 913.
7. At eighty-one, another elderly villain, a poacher, and petty thief, who turned to burglary, for which he was sentenced to death; it was commuted to fourteen years transportation in 1829. He returned and took up blacksmithing and led a relatively uneventful life. PRO. Assizes, 35/269/5. *Sussex Advertiser*, 17 and 8 Aug., and 5 Oct. 1829. Three summary, and one Quarter Sessions convictions 1820–9, ESCRO. QR/E Michaelmas 1820; Easter 1825; Epiphany 1827; Michaelmas 1829. See also above, 25 Feb. 1878, p. 202.
8. As we saw in the introduction, Gillham's economic interests lay across the Burwash–Ticehurst border. The fact that such men were prepared to undertake the relatively unpleasant job as assistant overseer and rate collector for very modest salaries, is another – and commonly overlooked – aspect of the agricultural depression. Gillham's sureties, of £250 each, were provided by Whatman and John Barrow, now described as a 'retired Farmer'. Board of Guardian minute, 24 Mar. 1881, ESCRO. G10/1a/16.
9. Victorian town and country shared many characteristics, including the considerable assortment of pedlers, hawkers and collectors of almost every conceivable item. Indeed, one gets the strong impression that there was no such thing as waste; almost everything could be, and was, re-cycled. Watson's testimony to the rag-collector's trade proves that to be extremely complex, and on another occasion Egerton learned that even 'the very oldest and most worn out tin pots are cut up into gardeners' labels and the cheapest kind of tin toys'.
    James was illiterate; born in 1825 he was originally a farm labourer, but subsequently became a hawker. He, unlike most Burwash men fined for poaching, spent fourteen days in Battle jail when unable to pay a 10/- penalty inflicted in 1849; he was cleared by a jury of thieving tame rabbits in 1857, and his main other brushes with authority respected his mule. Impounded for grazing in the churchyard, Watson broke it out, and was fined; two further convictions followed its straying on the highway, a charge often brought against owners who refused to stop pasturing their beasts on the time-honoured free grass of the road verges, a practice subjected to periodic police purges. Summary convictions, 1849, 1856, 1867 (twice) and Quarter Sessions trial documents, 1857, ESCRO. QR/E945; 996; 1000; 1038; 1040. *Parish Notes*, Mar. 1882.

10. Elderly people domiciled outside the Union in which they were formally settled, and therefore entitled to social-security payments, were often given outdoor relief where they lived. However, periodic reviews could lead to cases being investigated, and it seems that Dann's de facto old-age pension was renewed by Cranbrook after his case was stated by Egerton in writing.

11. For the private Ticehurst Lunatic Asylum see above, p. 66 and note 5.

12. Local records do not reveal any criminal act by John Isted at this time.

13. Capt. G.B. Luxford, aged 38, from an East Sussex landowning and clerical family, and presently of the Royal Welsh Fusiliers, was appointed as only the second Chief Constable of the County Constabulary, since its 1840 inception, succeeding the nearly eighty-year-old Capt. Mackay on 12 May. Luxford was elected from a short-list of nine selected from 140 applicants, and served until 1894. East Sussex Quarter Sessions police sub-committee report, May 1881, ESCRO. QAC/2/E4/3.

14. See above, p. 229, 18, 19 and 21 May 1880.

15. The so-called 'Extraordinary Tithe' on hops and soft fruits was a major political and economic issue, notably in the South-east during the 1880s, in which Egerton was a level-headed, if non-neutral participant. Some of his neighbouring incumbents were much more aggressive. Rector Eden of Ticehurst resorted to distress warrants against farmers who refused to pay, and ugly scenes followed. A leading Liberal, the prosperous London solicitor, Thomas Henry Bolton, who had recently purchased the Southbins estate centred on Burwash Weald, was a principal anti-tithe agitator, and in the mid-eighties, briefly an MP.

The agricultural depression of the later 1870s and early 1880s was partially caused by increased imports of all types of farm produce, including hops, and its effects were greatly aggravated by poor seasons across 1878–81. Wealden, and especially High-Wealden farmers, traditionally maintained – or claimed to maintain – a basic economic equilibrium through hop-growing's financial underpinning of their other activities. Although hops were 'speculative' in that yields and prices oscillated wildly from season to season, overall, hops retained much of their attraction, vitally affecting farmers' profits and their workers' living standards.

The depression threw exactions of extraordinary tithe into sharper profile, as it deepened across 1878–9, and in the autumn of 1881, by a Commons Select Committee's incapacity to recommend a solution. The "extraordinary" tithe lable, as Egerton pointed out publicly on occasion, was not really extraordinary at all, but part of the compromise effected in 1836 through the Tithe Commutation Act. As the value of the hop crop per acre was much greater, at least in average or good years, than other arable products, the tithe on such land was in reality a significantly higher rent charge, which varied considerably from district to district, and commonly between neighbouring parishes. Moreover, annual tithe payments were fixed on average prices across the previous seven years, which meant that payments remained high even in years when the crop virtually failed. All types of claims were made over the economic impact, including the weak argument that it prevented any expansion of hop-cultivation. Egerton believed that any reduction in tithe would encourage rent increases, thereby benefitting landowners, not tenant farmers.

16. In stark contrast to earlier days, when farmers were more prosperous, and competed to rent his glebe lands.

17. A waggoner's mate, employed by Humphrey Barton of Shoyswell, in transporting heavy loads of stone from Etchingham, to mend 'different parts of the parish highways'. The lad, and his two older companions, were all riding – illegally – in the waggon, when it suddenly met another coming in the opposite direction

along the narrow, twisting, Sheep Street Lane. He jumped out to race to the lead horse, caught his foot in the wheel, which then crushed his head, killing him instantaneously. *Sussex Agricultural Express*, 2 July 1881.

18. Recent reportage in *The Times*, respecting the newly published official, version of the New Testament claimed that the initial inspiration derived from much earlier pressure in the 1850s exerted by The Society for the Propagation of the Gospel in Foreign Parts, and its secretary the Revd Ernest Hawkins, who was briefly Curate of Burwash in the late 1820s. The irony that an incumbent of Burwash in South Saxon country – reputedly the last part of Britain to be Christianized – should have had such an historic connection, was mentioned in Egerton's letter. *Sussex Agricultural Express*, 28 Sept. 1881.

19. The child was not baptized by Egerton. But see below, p. 293, 17 Dec. 1883 and ch. 19 note 14.

20. For the Crossingham affair see above, p. 102, 26 Aug. 1870; the Russell's tainted status doubtlessly derived, at least in part, from the notorious murder of 1826.

21. Egerton typically believed that those immediately above labourers and farmworkers in the social hierarchy, namely journeymen and master craftsmen, and village tradesfolk, ought to set good behavioural examples. The identity of this couple is not known.

22. In the event a full-scale enquiry was enacted; see below, p. 252, 18 Nov. 1881 and note 33.

23. Egerton's first intervention through the press was an attack on Bolton's demand for the abolition of extraordinary tithe without compensation. Egerton wryly drew a parallel with Irish demands, for land nationalization, without compensation, aimed at the many English owners of Irish acres, and noted that Bolton as a landowner would resist extreme English radical demands for the uncompensated nationalization of land in Britain. Egerton also advanced the argument that the concept of extraordinary tithe concealed more than it revealed, and that threats to refuse its payment, ought logically to be extended to all tithes. The latter argument especially, was a real Tory challenge to a Liberal. *Sussex Agricultural Express*, 23 Aug. 1881.

24. The Liberal *Hastings and St. Leonards Times*, in a leader 27 Aug. 1881, claimed that Egerton was emerging as a 'champion' of the extraordinary tithe, attacked him for suggesting that the hop tithe was worth more if taken in kind, and ended by warning that defending 'a corrupt and rotten system' would accelerate 'the time when these vexatious ecclesiastical enactments are unconditionally abolished'.

25. The two letters came from a pseudonymist, and a Frank Piper of Hellingly. The former named Egerton, claimed that while landlords were significantly abating rents, the clergy refused voluntarily to reduce tithes, and that the only parson to do so 'was so set upon by the neighbouring incumbents that he had to abandon his just and honourable intentions'. He asserted that if hop tithes were paid in kind their value would be under a third of the commuted cash sum. He warned Anglican clergymen that they were 'losing the good feeling and friendship of those who have hitherto been the staunchest supporters of the Church'. Piper also advanced religious considerations, observing that 'in times gone by all people went to church', but that presently two-thirds of the inhabitants of rural Sussex were Dissenters, and if Anglicans maintained their fiscal exactions they would lose the remnants of their flocks.

Although Egerton's experiences as expressed in the diary reveal that the situation between Dissenters and Anglicans on the ground was much more complicated, he was no doubt offended by the thrust and vigour of his opponents. His reply advanced *laissez-faire* arguments behind his contention that if tithes were cut or abolished, the saving would accrue to landowners, not their farming tenants, and emphasized that his own tithe was rated to both poor and highway accounts in Burwash, a source of public income which, if removed, would mean larger demand on other ratepayers. He also asserted that most clergy spent their income from tithes and more, in their parishes, 'among his people'.

However, the most aggressive pro-Anglican response was a riposte from the Revd Eley, Rector of Etchingham, who claimed that newcomer Bolton farmed some of his estate directly, and rented out the remainder 'at, I am told, a higher rent than any in Burwash'. Eley would welcome a compromise, which had eluded the Select Committee; 'such would be in the interests of their [the clergy's] work among their parishioners'. Opponents 'threatened' his clerical brethren 'with robbery' and made multiple misrepresentations over the entire issue. *Sussex Agricultural Express*, 27 Aug. 1881.

26. Gillham's letter confirmed Egerton's 'uniform consistency and zeal' in the performance of 'his pastoral duties'; Gillham also very pointedly noted that calculations made in the mid-1830s were of dubious relevance owing to the subsequent abolition of a forty-five per cent hop import tariff, and excluded another factor, a doubling of farmworkers' wages across the same period. Moreover there were absentee rectors, whose duties were still performed by the traditionally underpaid curate, and he endorsed Piper's assertion of Dissent's greater strength. *Sussex Agricultural Express*, 6 Sept. 1881.

27. She was aged fifty-three, and described of Tunbridge Wells; her husband's grocery and drapery business at Burwash had collapsed. He was buried there on 19 June 1886. ESCRO. Par.284/1/5/3.

28. 'He that withholdeth Corn, the People shall curse him: but Blessing shall be upon the Head of him that selleth it'. Proverbs xi. 26. A biblical text which partially underpinned the populist view of a "moral economy", in E.P. Thompson's perception, which stipulated that producers and retailers of food should not exploit natural or seasonal shortages of essential foodstuffs, by for example under-supplying markets to drive up prices. Egerton here advances arguments associated with classical economists, including Adam Smith, and their adherents among them the Revd T.R. Malthus, which held that high prices restricted consumption, and therefore extended the availability of foodstuffs across a year following substandard yields. The latter argument was vigorously advocated by governments to combat the famines during the French Wars, 1793–1815, for which see R. Wells, *Wretched Faces; Famine in Wartime England, 1793–1801*, (Gloucester, 1988). For a brilliant discussion of ideology, E.P. Thompson, 'The "moral economy" of the English crowd in the eighteenth century', *Past and Present*, 50, (1971). However, as Egerton's earlier comments on meat prices reveal, even he was not immune from residual moral economic perceptions.

29. Egerton explained that music was 'too often looked upon as a mere amusement and not as an art which must be studied . . . before any real advance can be made'; he asserted that group activity for one hour a week, over six months, plus private study, was sufficient to learn to read music. *Parish Notes*, Oct. 1881.

30. The school inspectorate insisted in 1875 that the sharing of lavatory facilities by infant boys and girls should cease, and stressed the need for greater disinfection of the toilets in Feb. 1882. Reports, 5 Feb. 1875 and 3 Mar. 1882, ESCRO. ESC.41/1.

31.   These names read like a roll-call of a sector of the female element of Burwash society which Egerton dubbed the local 'aristocracy'.
32.   Labourer Alfred, and Almenia Russell had Charlie nine, Capel James seven, Elizabeth Ann two, and Emily Matilda six months, baptized. ESCRO. Par.284/1/2/ 4.
33.   Dr Cohen was the only candidate to replace Combs on the latter's resignation in July 1880. Cohen, then aged twenty-five, had qualified at the University of Aberdeen, and had but three months' experience. On 28 July 1881, the Ticehurst Board of Guardians ordered Cohen to report on the death of thirty-five-year-old Charlotte Maskell, after widespread rumours that the Medical Officer had not attended her properly, and had dispensed medicines irregularly. 'Many believe she died from the effects of taking the wrong powder . . . supplied . . . by Dr Cohen without having a lable on it', and 'the case has created a good deal of local feeling and excitement'. Charlotte's husband, William, initially wanted an inquest, but he 'did not have the body opened because I had no money to pay for it'.
      Cohen's report stated that the patient's seventeenth pregnancy miscarried at seven months, though he omitted that she was first attended by his fully-qualified assistant, Dr Kent on 7 July; Kent had difficulty in removing the placenta, and prescribed the 'usual' remedies namely ergot, digitalis, opium and brandy. Cohen himself called on the 8th, after the patient had had a sleepless night, and was too enfeebled to talk; as Cohen put it her 'Breath foul and the breathing laboured, sighing and yawning, nausea, vomiting, and vertigo; the haemorrage had now almost ceased . . . in a dirty condition not having been cleaned and the soiled linen had not been removed, she was cold and clamy'. Her pulse was 'Jerky and almost imperceptible', and she had lost a lot of blood. He ordered Charlotte's attendant to change the bedding, and having diagnosed peritonitis, told the attendant that 'recovery was very doubtful'.
      He decided to prescribe 'Permanganate of Potash' for external application to the abdomen, and opium, and returned to his surgery to make up these medicines. Unable to find opium pills, he prescribed some powders, when he was interrupted by an emergency case, and left immediately. On his return, a ten-year-old girl was waiting to collect Charlotte's medication, one of which was labelled, 'not to be swallowed'. On the 9th the girl returned, said that the medicines had been ineffective, but that Charlotte had not taken the powders. He ordered the lass to tell the attendant to administer the powders immediately, and then was called to another emergency. At 2p.m. he revisited the house, and discovered that the wrong substance had been taken internally, which had caused severe vomiting, and a burning sensation in Charlotte's throat. The bedding had not been changed; he instructed hourly administrations of beef tea and brandy. He called back three hours later, and while the vomiting had all but abated, he considered her 'quite beyond human aid', ordered the beef tea and brandy to be continued, and that 'while' Charlotte lived, to continue taking the powders; if these were exhausted, they were to send for more.
      On Sunday the 10th one of the Maskell boys called for more powder, which was supplied, and the boy told to inform the father 'that unless he had a nurse to carry out my orders it was no use my attending'. That evening the husband, William, called but Cohen was unavailable, and on the morrow William saw the Relieving Officer for an order for the doctor's attendance, which he took to Cohen. Cohen eventually set out at 2p.m., but was met in his road by William who said that his wife had just died. Cohen ordered an 'immediate burial as decomposition would

soon set in and the body would swell'. As the Board had ordered the Relieving Officer to collect the medicine containers, Cohen was forced to admit that these had been wrongly labelled, but he insisted that the internally taken permanganate was inadequate to cause death, which was due to peritonitis, and he duly entered this on the death certificate. He also admitted that he had overlooked Kent's first visit, and concluded that 'These particulars are only from memory, but as far as they go are *strictly accurate*'.

The Guardians forwarded the report to the Local Government Board, who asked Cohen for any detail omitted from it. Cohen merely added that on first seeing Charlotte he did not expect her to live, but that he would have visited her on the 11th but for engagements with other patients, and rather slyly added that if he had made this visit, 'I feel sure you would not have been troubled with any report'.

This failed to satisfy the Government Board's medical advisers, one of whom stated that the volume of potash consumed could easily have been the cause of death, and he was very suspicious of the real motive for ordering immediate burial: in his estimation it was 'a very serious case', and a second adviser, Dr Mouat was adamant that Cohen 'ought not to . . . retain his office and it seems very doubtful whether he has not rendered himself liable to a criminal charge'. The Board divided over what action to take, and eventually – at the end of Oct. – decided upon an 'official enquiry'.

That body heard from a number of Charlotte's neighbours, widows Casey and Hall, Mrs Relf, and an adult daughter, Sarah, all of whom had attended Charlotte in the normal way for working-class births. Ellen Casey said, 'I am a neighbour and I was sent for by Mrs Relf another neighbour', as 'A dead child had been born but the after birth had not come away'. Sarah opined that 'My mother did not lose more blood than in other confinements', and the husband said Charlotte 'was not worse than usual after this confinement'. Casey had mixed the potash with milk, Charlotte had drank the whole potion, and within half an hour told her daughter that 'They have given me the wrong powder they have poisoned me', a prophetic view she reiterated when William came home soon afterwards. To confuse such folk further, Cohen had also spoken of despatching 'some stuff to make up a syringe', and according to him Ellen not only understood the instructions, but 'indignantly replied Yes . . . she had been out nursing before and understood it quite well'. Ellen duly 'borrowed a syringe before the stuff came', though in the event these neighbours made no use of it; they did change the bedding.

Dr Mouat informed the enquiry that Cohen's performance here was 'wholly indefensible', adding categorically that 'it is usual in Poor Law and general medical practice to send remedies in the form in which they are to be used, and not to leave their admixture to the patients or their attendants, a dangerous and reprehensible practice'.

Moreover, the enquiry also revealed that when Cohen called after the potash's consumption, he immediately made Charlotte vomit with a strong dosage of mustard and water, a fact concealed in his initial report, which was compounded by leaving his patient before assessing the effects of this treatment. Interestingly the Central Board ruled that the 'carelessness' in the labelling was 'of minor importance' compared with failure to establish the cause of death, the completion of the death certificate, and the immediate burial instruction. He was ordered to resign immediately; Cohen's request for a new enquiry on the grounds that he had strong local support and confidence received short shrift.

This account is based on the extended correspondence between the Board of

Guardians, Cohen, and others, July 1881 to Jan. 1882, plus the reports, including the verbatim minutes of the official enquiry, in PRO. MH.12/13151; Board of Guardians minutes, July 1881 to Jan. 1882, ESCRO. G10/1a/16.

34.   At Ticehurst, where Eden made no concession, 'throughout' the tithe audit day, 'there were general murmers of dissatisfaction at having to pay the impost, particularly the extraordinary tithe'. Many refused to pay and an unprecedentedly small number of farmers attended the dinner. This was the first in a series of developments and events which produced violence, cases in both the civil and criminal courts, and a complete breakdown in Eden's relationships with a large sector of his parishioners. *Sussex Agricultural Express*, 19 Nov. 1881.

35.   The argument was partially caused by Love accusing Pennells of 'spoiling his hops' in undisclosed circumstances, further inflamed by Love's recent sacking of an un-named boy in his employ. During a chance encounter at the Post Office, insults were traded, and then blows, with Love defending himself lustily with his walking stick. Love prosecuted Pennells, who was fined £1 with 13/- costs, a relatively high fine for an assault, with the alternative of a month's hard labour. *Sussex Agricultural Express*, 29 Nov. 1881.

36.   Leadham argued that the Farmers' Alliance, formed only in 1879–80, had been a political success, and must hold together to achieve more. Bolton emphasized that unlike the numerous landowner-dominated Agricultural Associations, the Alliance represented tenant farmers, and its policies included the reform of rates and county government; he concluded with a ringing denunciation of tithes in general, and particularly the extraordinary, which gave German hops an advantage in British markets. Egerton did not speak. *Hastings and St Leonards Times*, 17 Dec. 1881.

37.   The date was 1826; see introduction, p. 7. The tree was one of two 'still spared by the woodcutters because of this association'. *Parish Notes*, Mar. 1882.

38.   Cohen's successor was in fact Dr William Barton, who had been practising for eighteen months; like Cohen, Barton was the sole candidate for the post at the same salary £56 per year, plus 12/- per case for 'midwifery'. While his appointment was confirmed, Dr Taylor, the Ticehurst district Medical Officer, covered Burwash. Ticehurst Board minutes, 29 Dec. 1881, 12 and 26 Jan. 1882. ESCRO. G10/1a/16. Barton's confirmation documents, PRO. MH.12/13151. Barton had local connections, the brother of the owner of Shoyswell Manor, and in 1883 he bought Cohen's private practice. See below, p. 288, 6 June 1883. *Parish Notes*, July 1882.

1882

1 Jan. Epiphany: little noticed in Burwash I am sorry to say, but week day services are not to our taste. . . . I c. in aft on J.B.N[oakes] & had a long t. Ye dissensions between Deacons & Minster in a Nonconformist Congr: seem to us outsiders pitifully paltry & spiteful.

7 Jan. . . . Had a curious request from T. Lusted to lend ye sch. room for presentations of testimonials to Mr. Quee ye Noncom: M. who having fallen out w. Mr. Noakes has got to go.[1] I met Mr. Noakes afterwards on ye road & talked to him. He said they cd. have ye Chapel. Lusted c. on me in ye evg. & I told him this. . . .

[9 to 11 Jan. in London.]

12 Jan. W. N. to ye vill. We called & arranged w. Mrs James Coppard about ye room for Mothers meeting. I c. & had a long t. w. Mr. John Fuller. Mr. F. started ye subj. Nothing can be done to get ye verd[ict against Dr. Cohen] reversed. . . .

13 Jan. I sent out about 27 orders for soup. Sch. In aft N. & self saw ye soup & tasted it; very good, peas a little hard, but more soaking wd. remedy this. . . .

14 Jan. . . . ye meeting Messrs Gillham, Cramp, C.Taylor, J.Fuller, Anset, W.Ellis, Ellen Gould: we agreed there was a deficit in ye funds that I shd. draw up a little statement, & ask for voluntary Subscr: to avoid a school board. . . .[2]

16 Jan. . . . C. on Mrs Isted; diarrhea, impending baby, sad altogether, gave her 5/- afterwards & sent down some brandy. . . .

17 Jan. . . . drew up address to Burwash ratepayers about raising further Subscr: for ye school. . . . To ye Ratepayers meeting at ye Bell. Read my statement wh. after criticism . . . I was advised to print. No difficulty foretold in collecting ye money. I hope this will be so. . . .

20 Jan. Uncle read me out twice ye judgment of ye Local Govt. Board on Doctor Cohen. What turned the decision of ye Board so heavily agst. him was his false certificate of ye cause of ye death of Charlotte Maskell. The punishment is very heavy, but he entirely brought it on himself. . . . Clarke ye "nuisance man" [Sanitary Inspector] had interviewed Uncle in morning

& I took two summonses to JP for amendment. Education Act summonses. . . .[3]

21 Jan. . . . C. on Mr. Ellis at ye shop. He offered to direct & send out circulars about ye School.

23 Jan. . . . Mr. Taylor . . . says ye man who caught ye small pox by acting as bearer at Mr. Munn's funeral at Robertsbridge, can't live 48 hours. Half Robertsbridge is getting re-vaccinated.[4]

24 Jan. . . . I c. & R. w. old Mrs Partridge. She said she often used to hear her mother state that when she was young they never thought of making a scholar of more than one in a family & that they thought they'd done a good deal if they had done that. Mrs P. is over 80 so that this dictum refers to 100 years ago (in Suffolk). . . . Mrs G. Brook in great trouble. Her husb: has got the sack from Mr. Hyland's. His generous indignation at hearing people who he respected "called over" has got him into trouble w. ye "misses" not w. ye master – but he has to go. . . .

25 Jan. To ye Sch. at 10.30. Mr. Emmerson [Schools Inspector] hard at work. . . . I soon away, as I hate examinations when I am interested in the examinees. Mr. E. lunched here; he has been at this work 19 years. I shewed him Gussy's [Egerton's eldest child] handwriting wh. he certified to be above the ordinary standard of her age. . . . To James Coppers & attended ye first mothers' meeting held in Burwash under Church auspices. Present Mrs Egerton & Mrs Gilbert as superintendents, Mrs Sands (Barn House) Mrs John Relf (deaf) Mrs James Harmer, Mrs Charles Bourner (widow) Mrs Th. Coleman. My wife had read a short prayer. Ye visitors seemed to enjoy themselves. . . . Tom Hagley (Rector of Brightling) gave me the following specimen of what a Sussex clergyman is expected to do for his parishioners. "Please Sir, my husband died just upon 6 months ago, & he always said he wd. will all he'd got to me, but he never made no will at all. So please Sir, wd. you make a will for him, & my son says he'll sign it directly"!

26 Jan. . . . John Sawyers 2nd Batt. Royal Sussex Regt. made a full Sergt. from 1 Jan. 1882. I wrote him to congr[atulate] & advice temperate use of new authority. Stephen Manwaring appointed as a waiter on board RM SS Nizan (P & O) to sail for India & China on 1st Feb.

28 Jan. In aft. to ye Common. With Mr. Smith of Seaview inspected a chicken cramming machine outside Malpas ye blacksmith's: was made as a sausage stuffing machine by Williams . . . in London. Owing to a stoppage caused by lumps of fat some time ago it wouldn't work, so old John Rich was had down as a strongman . . . to turn ye handle. This he did to so much effect that ye nozzle of ye flexible tube was blown down ye poor chick's gullet, ye man had his face all covered w. ye stuff & Rich dropped ye handle. . . .

Sun. 29 Jan. . . . aft. Ch. Had to dismiss W. Sweetman from ye choir. He is too troublesome. I c. on his father in ye evg.

31 Jan. Aft. br[eakfast] to Fontridge. . . . C. & P. w. poor Mrs Garner (Nacky's wife 5/-) who is ill of pneumonia. A more miserable tenement cannot be found I fancy out of Ireland. The poor woman may I fear die; the draughts are enough to kill her.[5] . . . Aft. d. C. on . . . Mrs James Weston (3/-). She said what you see on the fire is all the firing we've got. I told Weston [informed her husband] this morning that all the money we had was 3/4 (farthing). . . .

1 Feb. . . . mothers' meeting 8. I read & expounded 5 Matt. 5.4. . . . A large gathering, about 204 persons or probably more, to present testimonial to Mr Quee the minister who having disagreed with the deacons, had sent in his resignation. Saw J.Lusted in ye evg. as I went to post 2 letters. . . . He had done the collecting for Mr Quee; had got 144 names. Popular feeling apparently very strongly in favour of Mr. Quee & agst. the deacons. This falling out is sad whether among Ch. people or dissenters. The enemy makes capital out of dissensions among practising Xtians be they who they may.

2 Feb. Aft. br: to Fontridge. C. & R. w. poor old Mrs Garner; no worse I hope but all the discomfort. Mrs Osborn good neighbourly woman went in yesterday & changed her & made her bed, otherwise she wd. be practically unnursed. . . . To a Evg. Ent[ertainment], large audience on behalf of boys cricket club. I read "Uncle Joe's horse" a bit out of an American paper; the point being that a spiteful neighbour accusing Uncle Joe's horse trampling down his corn; doesn't wait for an expl[anation] but County Courts Joe.[6] Uncle Joe's defence was that tho' he couldn't deny keeping a horse, he did deny that his horse trampled corn, inasmuch as the only horse wh. he kept was – a "clothes horse". Relf & Blackford from ye Weald gave ye best performance viz "Avis" on hand bells. . . .

4 Feb. In aft. c. on Mrs Russell (Holt Down 2/-) 7 chrn. down more or less w. whooping cough. . . . I overtook & talked w. Mrs B. Dann. She says her husb. tells her that moles aren't running as usual this winter; that he kills only 1 where he used to catch 4 or 5. . . .

7 Feb. . . . C. & sat w. Mr. Sharpley; he gave me some very interesting details about ye Indian mutiny. . . .

8 Feb. . . . Mothers' meeting. I R. & P. A curious difficulty has arisen. Mrs Copper is ye baker & so many people owe her money that as they don't like to face their creditor, our meeting will be small! . . . . C. on G. Daw Blacksmith; has been nearly dead from a prick of a finger with a file on wh. was some red lead. I begged & entreated him to become a teetotaller, as being a bibber [heavy drinker] his blood was in a terrible state. He said he had made up his mind to abstain. . . . Mr. Whatman shewed me that Rent, Tithe, Rates & Taxes on 230.0.26 of actually available land came to £603-10-10. . . . £2-12-5½ per acre before a penny is spent on labour & manure at Franchise Farm.

17 Feb. . . . C. on H. Dann; he signified his intention of coming to church. Such intentions I don't count for much, as they originate in no change of principle or of real views, but only with some personal dissatisfaction in their own [Dissenting] community, as in this instance. HD objects to ye treatment of Mr. Quee by JBN & so leaves the chapel & comes to church. . . . Wm. Pope c. I signed for another £2-10-0 from ye War Off. making above £26 for his s. who was killed at Isandlana.

18 Feb. . . . c. on Mr. Barton ye new doctor [lodging] at Mr. Cliffords. He very busy. . . .

24 Feb. . . . C. on Mrs J. Isted & paid bill. . . .

Sun. 26 Feb. . . . not many as ye evg. was wet & it was Mr Quee Ye Ind. minister's farewell sermon tonight. . . .

27 Feb. . . . Mr. Barton ye doctor . . . overtook me & we had a chat. Certainly a diff[erent] man from our friend Cohen. . . . Singing at Sch. from 6.40 till 9.15 Boys & 15 men! we really got on.

1 Mar. . . . Mr. Bolton has I believe been making very free with myself & my income & what I gave for the living or rather what my father gave for it. I bought ye paper but wd. not read it, for fear I might get cross.[7]

Thurs. 2 Mar. . . . Singing class, only 6 present. I think I shall suspend it for a while. . . . In evg. Sing: boys . . . & 8 or 9 men. Signed a paper for John Mepham as cand[idate] for police. . . . Bradlaugh either is or is not re-elected for Northampton. I am not often so much interested in outside matters, but I do devoutly hope that a man has been rejected who having publicly stated that ye oath so help me God had no binding force on him as an Atheist, surrupticiously took it in ye H. of Commons w. ye view of taking his seat, & being ignominiously expelled from ye House after, again offered himself to ye electors. B. Thompson c. on me about ye cottage. He suggests £150–160 as ye probable cost. It seems a lot of money.[8]

3 Mar. . . . Overtook Master Burgess at 83! going home from day labour. . . .Bradlaugh re-elected. Queen shot at yesterday.

Sun. 5 Mar. . . . Referred to God's mercy in delivering ye Queen from ye hand of ye wretched lunatic who shot at her on Thursday. . . .

7 Mar. W. Mr. John Fuller in ye vill. collecting. Good success . . . I really do pity some of the ratepayers. They are hard up. Aft. d. renewed ye campaign w. equal success. Mr. Jos. Noakes argued very reasonably on ye inequality of ye payments on basis of rating, but what can we do. He has had sad times & has to pay 3 or 4 times as much as some of ye well to do tradesmen. C. on Hannah Eastwood. A good looking girl greatly disarms wrath, but in this instance I think Mrs Oake's complaint about her sudden departure is capable of being met.

13 Mar. . . . Hannah Bunkall has got a place at Mr. Stone Wiggs at T. Wells. I am glad as dear N. must have written a good 30 letters on her behalf, in addition to advertisements & telegrams. . . . C. & P. w. Mrs Waterhouse. While reading I did not notice Mr. Cohen come into ye room so ye Jew heard 3 or 4 minutes of Xtian exhortation to ye sick. He was very pl. in his manners w. his [private] patient. . . .

14 Mar. . . . C. on Mr. G. Fuller. He tells me that there is a hitch in the School Collection. Mr. Wm. Coppard refuses to pay anything, as is always the case, & some of the farmers decline on the ground that the "trade" ought to pay more.[9] I hope they will come to their senses, but I fear. . . .

15 Mar. . . . I c. on Mr. G. Fuller. he told me that things look a little more hopeful from last night. I am glad. . . . Mothers' meeting only 6. . . . ye boys began cricket.

16 Mar. Sch. A whole lot of primroses brought by ye Children gratis for ye crippled & sick children in East London Hosp[ital]s. . . . I looked in at Malpas ye blacksmith's to enquire if I had insulted his chicken cramming machine by my remarks in P[arish] N[otes]: on ye contr[ary] he seemed much pleased. . . .[10]

17 Mar. Watching ye boys at cr: Mr. J.B.Noakes & wife came by. I joined them & had long t. He of course introducing Chapel matters. Poor man. I am sorry for him ye popular feeling on behalf of Mr. Quee's very strong & Mr. N's chapel is for ye present nearly deserted. I don't see how Mr. Quee is to get a living at ye other chapel, but there he has gone for the present. . . . Sent up a large hamper of primroses picked by our children [his daughters] & ye sch. ch. "for love" to ye East London Hosp. . . .

25 Mar. . . . Spencer has broken owing we are told £1500! £800 I believe to his Uncle Mr. White of Hammerden, but a lot to our tradesmen & brother farmers. How he came to have got credit I can't conceive, as he has been notedly shaky for years. . . .

5 Apl. . . . Tea w. Mr. & Mrs Gillett very civil. He surprised to hear I was a teetotaler "Why Sir you've no reason to be". He said a friend in London had sent him a bushel of gin! i.e. 8 gallons. . . . lost my way [returning from Robertsbridge] trailed a way across a bridge up to a farm house: nobody wd. answer; staid 20 minutes or ½ an hour outside. At last a semi-tight young carter came home & didn't explain matters much. However ye moon being now up I harked back & found my way all right. A woman at ye end of tenements nearest Etchm. on north side of ye road above ye pond using ye most horrible lang[uage] I ever heard in my life. Falling out apparently w. a man who wd. not give her any money. He opened ye door & came out, so I couldn't help rebuking ye woman & ye man too. . . .

13 Apl. . . . I wrote & sent off P.N. . . . Mr. Luxford gave me leave to use a story of wh. he was the subject "I thought you was one of the gang"; sent off ms. of "Mr. Jonas Whifforn" to ye Leisure Hour. I wonder whether it will be accepted. . . .

19 Apl. . . . Mothers meeting, only 3. . . . In evg. dear N. w. me to ye Entertainment. First time she has been for two years. Mr. Nevill read a good piece. Mr. Sydney Nevill recited 2 pieces admirably. Mr. P. Nevill sang a song in good time. Mrs & Miss Nevill played. Some very weak comic songs, violently encored. Mrs Hannah (Ernest) Wells deservedly encored in a little piano piece. Ye bell ringers Relf & Blackford do. On ye whole ye standard not high. J.G. Jenner [his former star Sunday School and private tutee, later pupil teacher] imperfectly prepared owing to short notice failed in a recitation. . . .

Sun. 23 Apl. . . . Bible Cl: in evg. 6. Charles Pilbeam overjoyed; has got a place at Mr. Russells at Benenden [in Kent]. . . .

25 Apl. . . . C. at Ansets aft. ye sing: to sign a paper for Wm. Butchers to go into ye police. Fear he will not succeed as I believe him to be flat footed. Heard about Stanley "ye Machine man". A more unmitigated scoundrel it wd. be hard to find. A married man he is reported to have seduced girl after girl.

2 May. . . . To ye Bell. Fairly large parish meeting. We went thro' ye relief list & took off some relief in a few cases where it was considered that there was the capacity of earning money. . . . Wrote out ye notes [minutes?] of ye meeting.

3 May. . . . Aft. tea to ye village. Noah Cramp & Albert Dann engaged in a race. N. on bicycle AD running on foot. I cd. have run nearly as fast & he did not finish. Then Noah & P. Nevill had a race N. giving Noah 5 min start to Etchm. Noah won by a foot! . . .

5 May. Sch. Small attendance. Many boys at work. . . . Tea & away . . . to Club meeting at Burwash at ye school. Persuaded ye members to take only 1/3 [per person] out of ye box for ye dinner & to pay the other 1/3 themselves. I gave 10/-. . . .

7 May. . . . Stephen Manwaring C. at dinner time; just home from trip to Calcutta as Saloon Steward on P & O SS Nizam. Brought me an ebony inkstand from Ceylon. I think he is doing well. . . .

17 May. Rose & Crown Club day. I pr. to ye Club from S.John 3.16 (Ext). Ye members remarkably quiet & attentive. I have hope that ye Club services by God's help does good. Ye club to Laurelhurst. I ran from Ellen Gould's gate to ye Roele Cottages to overtake them & to say that I was sure that Mr. Schroeter wd. not wish them to walk all the way up there merely to pay him a compliment. He had however prepared "cakes & ale", so they went. They did not dine till nearly 3!: too late. I presided. Ned Dann sat next to me, & barely allowed any one else to speak to me all the time. I prop. health of ye Club. Mr. Wood & his band very good.[11] I away about 5.15 & w. up to Dr. Summerhayes' to tea.[12] A Mr. Buckley a Norfolk curate there & Dr. Cohen. Dr. S showed me all his improvements. I away at 10.10. Street perfectly quiet at 11.

19 May. . . . C. on Mrs J. Isted paid her baker's bill. Her husb: c. home: no better, rather worse.

23 May. . . . Met Henry Jarvis in his trap; he for some reason literally unknown to me has now twice cut me dead. I must ask him what is ye matter. [A note added 'Oct. 1882. I asked him straight why he has fallen out with me, & he confesses that the sole reason is my saying that I thought that the pew wh. he occupied in Church was a sufficiently good one – he thinking differently'.]

25 May. . . . I w. up to ye Common. Dined with ye Club. Members very civil to me. I prop. "prosperity to ye Club" and health of Mr. Hallaway ye innkeeper, who I really believe conducts his house very well. He requested me to return thanks for him wh. I did, putting virtuous expressions into his mouth wh. probably had not entered his mind. A curious opportunity of giving forth one's view about the real duties of publicans. Burwash band up. I sang "A thousand a year" just as I sang it sitting on ye music stool last Friday week at Sir Wm. Anson's ye Warden of All Souls to ye sister of ye Duchess of Argyll [during a very short visit to Oxford]. . . . Sung also "When the heart is young" (Brucker) & then away. . . .

27 May. . . . I had a long t. w. Hicks about ye [Rectory] garden. He is I am persuaded a most conscientious servant & does me justice in every way. The garden is however a heavy item of expenditure.

29 May. Bank Holiday, wh. I enjoyed in no more exciting manner than watching boys cricket. . . .

30 May. . . . I c. on J.P. & signed receipt for Miss Hughes legacy of £50 (is £45) for poor of Burwash: will be invested for poor at 2½ per c.

31 May. . . . Mothers' meeting, only 2. . . . To Evg. Ent. I was actually encored in "ye Blacksmith's Son" Hatton & I read "Homeward Bound". . . . Sidney Nevill in Pied Piper of Hamblin; very good indeed. Mr. Clarke of Brightling sang "Ye Medecine Man" in costume really humourously; very much better than most of our "Comics". Altogether best evg. we have had. . . . Charles Bourner gave me a pair of Chinese women's shoes wh. he took off the feet of two women who being wounded in the capture of Canton were having their legs amputated (in 1858). . . .

2 June. . . . T. w. Master George Harmer, speaking of a wretched girl who comes about Burwash for no good he told me that some time ago he saw the mother of the girl who told him that "if he saw the girl in Burwash again he was to cut a middling thick stick out of the hedge & drop in to her & send her home again" "for hadn't she (the mother) taken 6 acres of hops to tie, & here was this big idle girl trespassing over to Burwash" . . . not on the score of morals, but of hops. . . .

Sun. 4 June. . . . opened ye gardens to ye public. . . .

5 June. The Foresters Club; ye Burwash band came up at 1. Ye band pl. a couple of times, & then a game of cricket was had in the field beyond the wires. . . . back at 6 to ye Bell, ye Foresters dined in fair numbers. They put me in ye chair & Mr. G. Hyland himself a Forester in ye vice chair; good dinner. Speeches self Mr. Anset, Mr. Cohen, Mr. G. Hyland ye speakers. My health was kindly received, & I was able to speak in return with a freedom wh. I hope was useful. I away about 8.45. Nell from Bloxham arrived by 5.28 Expr[ess]. Seems pretty well; left her Key, so Hicks got some skeleton keys & soon opened ye box. A dangerous power tho' in this case useful.

6 June. . . . C. on Mrs Crouch & her husb. They have made the place very nice & a fair type I shd. think of a settlers clearance, as it is in ye midst of ye wood. . . .

7 June. At 2.30 dined with the School Club wh. was joined for the occasion by ye [Kent and Sussex Labourers] Union Club; d. at ye Bear. I had J. Jarvis & Amos Fenner by me. I made a speech on proposing success to ye Club, & stated my honest belief that the only countries where labourers were better off than in England were the Countries in wh. land is plentiful & easily obtainable. Contentment I suggested was not a mere lazy acquiescence in

Victorian Village

evils wh. pressed, but the spirit of making the best of evils wh. cd. not be cured, after all attempts had been made. I sang "a thousand a year". Away at 5.20. . . .

9 June. . . . I c. on Mr. John Fuller. He gave me some amusing information about Burwash 50 years ago. . . .

10 June. . . . C. on Mrs Gadd. She is in great distress of mind because yesterday's hailstorm had so damaged her hops. C. on Mrs Jones (1/-) of Brooksmarle; there are 4 Jones families, brothers in Burwash. This one, a Wm. (?) at Elphicks works for Mr. Pearson, one who married Jesse Braban's d. Eliza & works at Hoppers, & one at the Tot, who also works for Mr. Pearson. Met Mrs Bull, she becoming asthmatic; Walter [Bull] told me some interesting facts about his boy life 70 years ago.

14 June. Aft. br: to Fontridge. C. at ye Osbornes, also on Mrs Garner & Buss. Took a short cut thro' Glyddish wood, & got lost in the bush, & emerged at the lower side after much fighting with ye underwood. Maskell shewed me my way up to ye house, & I then home. Mothers' meeting only 2. I did not go in. . . .

21 June. Midsummer day. May it please God to grant us more favourable weather, or we shall really suffer. . . . Mothers' meeting a farce, only two. . . .

22 June. . . . C. & pd. a bill at Mrs J. Isted's: her husb. very ill, but not in a mood to see me. A loader at Bugsall Mill has been taking money from poor people for flour, & booking ye flour as on credit; it will go hard w. some of ye people who have been careless about receipts. . . .

26 June. . . . A constitutional round by ye old road & Etchm. P. Nevill overtook me on a bicycle. Had been to Hastings to see ye Prince & Princess of Wales open ye public park. Very pleased that on his return he had beaten recorded time, ye fastest from Hastings to ye Bell Inn Burwash hitherto 2 hrs. He did it probably 1.50 or less. . . .

27 June. Mr. Heberden takes ye house [the rectory] for 8 weeks from July 20 at 10½ g[uinea]s a week wh. includes [kitchen] garden [produce], but not potatoes. . . . C. on Mrs J. Harmer about lodgings for Mr. H's coachman. Yesterday c. on Mrs Pennells of ye Tot on ye same matter; no good, she is full. . . .

29 June. In aft. c. on poor Mr. Anset. Mrs Anset just died [after a protracted illness] about 2.15. If we are to judge people by their fruits, she was a truly conscientious as well as able teacher, & was a devoted wife & a good mother. . . .

1 July. We shall see but yesterday was we fear a fatal day for hops. The peculiar atmosphere being exactly fitted for the propagation of vermin.

Sun. 2 July. . . . H. C. 29. Off. 19s 7d; ye small number of communicants really distresses me, & I am conscious of inability to invent the means wh. some wd. discover of altering the state of things. . . . A larger number of people than usual in the garden. . . .

3 July. At 2.30 buried poor Mrs Anset aged 35. A large attendance of friends, & liberal contributions of flowers; dear N. sent a cross, & was at the funeral. . . .

6 July. I w. to Ticehurst to attend the funeral of Dr. Saml. Newington the late head of the Ticehurst Establishment for the Insane. Saw [Revd] Eden, he has returned from Ireland without getting a penny of his rents. A largish concourse of Newington friends. . . .

8 July. . . . I walked down to Etchm. for 1st d[own] tr[ain]. Saw the first railway accident I ever saw in my life. A fowl belonging to ye signalman, got in ye way of ye up train, flew up agst. the front of ye engine, was knocked down under ye wheels & killed. . . .

Sun. 9 July. A wedding at 9, ye first since Decr. 26. Joseph Malpas jr. & Emily Langridge, a Lewes girl. . . . I w. to Hurst Gn. & took ye serv. for Loosemore. . . .

10 July. . . . Master [?] called on me 3 parts drunk. He had heard I wanted a servant girl; he had a "nice young lady" "girl he shd. say". I told him he had been imposed upon, & I let him out. Somebody must have sent him up for chaff. . . . Poor little Mr. Quee left Burwash today. His congr: cd. not support him. He carries w. him the good will of many, especially of the poor.

11 July. Rain, rain, it is indeed disheartening. May God's good purpose for that He has one, thunder, lightening, storm, wind & tempest shall not make me deny, be fulfilled, be it what it may. . . .

14 July. . . . after tea w. past ye Lodge. Mr. Gibbs machine for exhausting heated air from ye haystack at work at 8.50. We must alter ye phrase in the making hay while the "moon" shines. . . .[13]

15 July. St. Swithin in his most watery mood. It rained very heavily all the morning. . . . At Laurelhurst Mr. Gibbs overtook me. I hoisted "Dash" on to ye box, & got inside. Mr. Gibbs says that his hay drying machine has not been a success so far.

[Over 19–20 July Egerton left the Rectory as his wife and children went on holiday to Swanage; it is not clear where the Rector stayed, possibly with the Gilbert family, though on 3 Aug. he put up overnight at the Bear; from 24 to 27 July he journeyed to Cheshire.]

23 July. . . . In aft. very large Congr. as Mr. Quee has gone & a good many of his followers were at Church. In ye evg. met & shook hands w. a Mr. Chowrgappak a black missionary from Madras who was preaching in ye morg. at ye Chapel. He seemed quite proud of his colour. . . .

10 Aug. . . . To lunch w. Mr Schroeter. . . . shewed me over his farm buildings saw an exhaust for cooling stacks, ingenious & effective.[14] To ye Common, to Mr. Coopers, School treat children 153. I gave away some things to old people, & to mothers of big families, for Miss S.Trower. . . .

11 Aug. . . . J. Relf gone as far as Torquay! on a professional cricket engagement, for a fortnight only. . . . Went to singing at 7.0. Boys not there but watching two bulls fighting in Mr. Jarvis's field. I cd. not be surprized at the want of punctuality. . . .

[14 Aug. went to Swanage; on 25th left his family there, and went via Nunton to Burwash, where he arrived on 26 Aug.]

29 Aug. . . . I had to call ye Police to a fight a Braban (?) & Isted (?) in ye street. . . .[15]

1 Sept. I breakf. at 7.15 thinking I may be able to go to T[unbridge] W[ells] to see the Australian cricketers, but it was raining so I did not go. . . .

2 Sept. Still very rough [wet weather]. . . . Interviewed Mr. Smith about some nuisances; must write to Mr. Clarke "ye nuisance man". . . . In ye old war [against Napoleon] Master Bull born 1806 or 7 quite remembers as a child going out into ye fields to gather charlock & nettle tops to bring home to eat or make tea of.[16]

4 Sept. Thos. Jenner & I went to T. Wells on Sat. [2nd] & saw Australians put out for . . . under 50. Game drawn, owing to wet. . . .

Sun. 10 Sept. . . . H[eberden] at Ch. twice & a Comm[unicant] so I gladly overlooked his radical politics. I to ye Rect. to say good bye to him & his two sisters who go tomorrow. He is a nice fellow. . . .

11 Sept. . . . Coming back [from the village] overtook Russell who was not sober. In his sober moments he never speaks to me, but tonight he was locquacious & wd. walk w. me. At last I had to say that he was not right. He then began to bring up my "bitterness" agst. him in ye matter of a horse wh. two years ago I found fault with on the ground of unfitness for work.

To use it was absolute cruelty & I said so, & on this he kept harping to night. His zig-zag walk was quite sufficient to prove his insobriety. Of course I felt no "bitterness" agst. ye poor man; why shd. I?[17]

12 Sept. To lunch w. Mr. Heberden. He pd. me the balance of acct. viz. £42. He spoke very kindly of ye Rectory, ye parish & ye neighbourhood & certainly people have spoken very kindly of ye Rectory tenants. . . .

13 Sept. . . . w. to Etchm. Met . . . Sally Isted that was who married ye soldier. She looked as bright & young & happy as a man cd. wish his wife to look, her husb. w. her. I shook hands wh. I fairly surprized him: he in plain clothes. . . .

15 Sept. . . . Dear N. children & nurses got back all safe. . . .

26 Sept. . . . Mr. Courthope has written an admirable letter to ye Sussex Expr: anent ye extraordinary tithe.[18] . . . I received yesterday an anonymous letter signed Parishioners, suggesting dishonesty on ye part of Walter Hicks. I at once put it in Hicks's hands. All a malicious invention I am persuaded.

5 Oct. In morg. w. my magazines. Man of somewhat superior appearance drinking at Relf's "Ye Woodsman", I go in to leave ye magazine. He offers me a drink. I decline being a teetotaller, he astonished & among other things said, Do you conscientiously say that you drink no wine or anything stronger than water (I) Nothing save tea & coffee. (He) Water, water, do you really believe that you can preach as good a sermon on that, as when you are a little elevated. . . . C. on Mrs Debley & made ye acquaintance of a Mrs Barton next door, liked her, wife of a policeman in Staffordsh[ire] police. She said that 3 Sussex men from Robertsbridge & neighbourhood had become Head ? Superintendent, Superintendent & Inspector. . . .

7 Oct. . . . I c. on Mrs Bine, poor old body her explanation for ye reasons why she left church for chapel & now chapel for church again, vague, but the secret was Mr. Quee, while he was here & cd. attend to her, she followed him. I really do not wonder, & when he left, she harked back again. She said she had been invited to go to Providence [Chapel], but "she couldn't go there if she was hired to". . . . I c. on Mrs Mepham; her husb. who is at work at Southover [Hall, for the Murriéta family] said "Madam" i.e. Signora de los Héros (?) had sacked all ye Protestant indoor servants Grandmamma Noakes included & had taken Catholics & that the Catholics at Mayfield had bought the castle & were going to turn it into "a monster". . . . Hicks entered upon his tenancy of new cott[age]. . . .

12 Oct. . . . Master Bob Turner a smith by trade & employed for some years by ye Telegr[aph] Constr[uction] but now a rag picker at Farleys stopped me to say he was all right to day. I reasoned w. him & he seemed to take it in good part, but as he finished by asking for a pair of trousers to go to London with to get a pension, I looked upon him as sadly wanting self respect. I told him that he cd. easily get an advance if he really had money to come. . . .

23 Oct. . . . A Mr. Henry Stevenson, s. of old Stevenson late of Fisher's Farm c. to get me to sign his paper for emigration w. assisted passage to Canada. C. & P. w. old Caleb Styles [an agricultural labourer, aged sixty-nine]; spent half an hour helping him upstairs. A sad instance of the remains of a wasted life. Dropsy the result of alcohol I fear, dirt, poverty. C. on Mrs Blackford who kindly sees to him. . . .

24 Oct. Longmans civilly refuse ye Sussex Folk. . . . C. on Sophy Butchers at Mrs A. Fullers. Her father has forbidden the banns between herself & John Mepham P.C. at Selmeston. I cd. not discover from the poor girl whether she wd. like me to intervene or not. All my interference cd. be seeing the father & pleading. I c. on Mr. J.B. Noakes to explain that our Evening Service was in no way my doing or intended for opposition. He quite understood. . . .

27 Oct. . . . 5 Burwash boys at Hurst Green for hedge breaking: they are very troublesome. . . .

28 Oct. The highest flood I ever remember to have seen & will be higher yet as the rain continues. . . .

29 Oct. The flood last night was higher than that of Oct. 4? (Burwash fair day) 1852. It rose to 3d step of Percy Nevill's staircase at Dudwell Mill. It was over the road at Crowhurst bridge, at Witherenden, & Etchingham. It was above the crown of the arch at Dudwell bridge. Water much gone down this morg.

3 Nov. Down to Crowhurst to see what damage had been done. Apparently ye bank round ye abutment on ye North E. side had given way. There certainly is much mischief. . . . C & had long t. w. John Pennells. He has sold 10 pockets of last year's hops, & is therefore able to talk very seriously about agricultural depression, & not in such a helpless tone of despair as some adopt. . . . Sing. w. ye boys. Had to dismiss Master John Glashen who has been pulling agst. me, & this evg. he told me a flat lie; went & saw his parents afterwards. . . .

4 Nov. Mr. [Highway Surveyor, George] Smith c. up about ye bridge. Has stopped ye [Burwash to Ticehurst] road. . . . Caleb Styles gone into ye [work]house; an unprincipled old party I fear. . . . Young W. Russell going to emigrate to Michigan c. up; was unfortunately out & he waited for me

$2\frac{1}{4}$ hours! sitting in ye kitchen hardly saying a word. I gave him 2/- & said I wd. write him out a prayer tomorrow.

7 Nov. . . . John Relf told me that he took 16 wickets of the Cambridge Wanderers at Torquay in a late match. Nearly the same eleven beat the Australians at Southampton.

8 Nov. Sch. Saw Mrs J. Copper about apartments for ye [school]mistresses. Met Mr. Whatman & W. Coppard about ye Crowhurst bridge: a bad job I fear. Met Mr. J.B.Noakes; hoped his dogs wd. not bite ye parson as I trained mine not to bite dissenters. . . .

9 Nov. Master C. Budd (6d) c. he is 5' 1" & 30 in. round ye chest but only 14 yrs. old. I wrote to ye officer in Command of ye "Dunean" Sheerness in his behalf. . . . To ye Tithe Dinner. Fair attendance, & better than I expected this year, Simes, Whatman, Gillham, Jos: Noakes, Pearson sat by me. Mr. Simes prop. my health. . . . I thanked my tithe payers for what I believe to be their honest endeavours to pay me. . . . away about 6.15.

10 Nov. . . . C. on Mrs J. Isted. [Son] John doing well.

11 Nov. . . . Ye mistresses transferred to Mrs James Copper at 7/6 a week. . . .

13 Nov. . . . At 10 o'Clock to meet Mr. Gillham at John Pennells at Crowhurst br: inspected ye bridge. Ye more I look at it, the less I like it.[19] . . . W. Mr. Gillham c. on Mr. Potts a retired nonconf. minister who has taken ye White house. Not in. Saw Mrs.

14 Nov. . . . Noah Cramp c. I gave him a recommendation to Dr. Herbert Newington. He thinks of trying for a place as an attendant [at Ticehurst Asylum].

15 Nov. . . . Mrs C. Ellis on whom I had c. after School came up & helped N. by reading to ye mothers (4). I R. & P. w. them. It seems that the mothers who come to the meeting get "jeered at". A funny world. . . .

16 Nov. . . . At 6 a meeting at the Vestry & adjourned to the Bell to consider the rebuilding of Crowhurst bridge. Mr. Gibbs, Whatman, Gillham, R.Fuller, J.Fuller, J. Cramp, Reader, W.Farley, J. Coppard, C. Coppard, A. Jarvis, H. Jarvis, & perhaps others present. Ye only resolutions arrived at were to write to ye Local Govt. Board, & to ask them with whom ye liability to rebuild now rests, & also to ask Ticehurst parish to go halves; their parish as a fact touching only 1/4 of the bridge. A Mr. Thorburn (?) ye builder [contracted for extensive work] at Southover came in to protest agst. being called upon to pay anything on a request made by ye parish for Compensation for "extraordinary traffic" damaging ye roads. . . . Things look like a shilling rate.

20 Nov. W. to Mr. Gillham's by 10 o'clock. He took Mr. Whatman self & his son George to Ticehurst; meeting at 12 instead of 11. Mr. Whatman leading had conv[ersed] w. Burwash ratepayers since our our meeting pledged Burwash to go on ye "half & half" liability question if it cost us three bridges. I was absolutely taken a back, as nothing of the sort was said at the meeting. Ye Ticehurst ratepayers firm on the 1/4 & 3/4 div[ision] of liability, & I am confident they wd. be doing only right by "sour grapes". Mr. Courthope, Mr. Wetherell present. Eden in ye Chair. Meeting adj. to hear from us again. Mr. Whatman insisted that he knew the feeling of the parish. I contended that a meeting of nearly 3 hours held for the very purpose of learning the feeling of the parish, ought to represent the feeling of the parish, & that I ought to have been told their views. . . . Mr. W. – myself parted very good friends. . . .

24 Nov. Mr. C. Ellis c. in morg. for Noah Cramps char[acter] on behalf of Mr. Raper. I strongly recommended ye young chap. Mr. Smith c. about ye bridge & ye roads. Things look bad. I wrote to Uncle N[athan] & to Mr. Murriéta mooting ye idea of ye landowners as distinct from ye occupiers finding, as an act of grace, ye disputed 1/4. . . . Met Mr. Gibbs at Miss Tilley's gate & spoke to him about ye Subscr: from ye landowners. He seemed favourable. . . .

25 Nov. . . . C. on Mrs Coleman. George, a son aged 17 just home from his place. A great burden on her for ye winter.

27 Nov. . . . Met Mr. C. Taylor on ye road in ye morg. Poor man, he gets worse. He will be a great loss to me. He encouraged me about my sermons of late.

28 Nov. . . . In aft. C. on Mrs T. Pennells. She gave me a sad account of ye moral or rather ye lack of them in ye Corner in wh. she lives. I have long known it as ye "wettest" & worst block of buildings we have. . . . Long t. w. Mr. Whatman re. bridge, just opp[osite] Mr. Philcox's.

Wed. 29 Nov. . . . I c. on Mr. Gibbs. He offered £20 to ye bridge on condition that ye County Surveyor was called in. Sing. w. ye boys. Shamefully troublesome about not coming to ye sch. till $\frac{1}{2}$ an hour late. I don't know what to do. C. Sawyers late of HMS "Ready" came down in Evg. Shewed me some shells wh. he left as a present, & a young "alligator" in a bottle, in spirits. He had supper in ye kitchen. He is a very respectable & nice mannered young fellow.

30 Nov. Meeting at ye Bell at 10 o'Clock. Mr. Standen, Mr. Rogers from

Ticehurst. Mr. Schroeter, Whatman, Gillham, H.Jarvis, J.Fuller, J. Coppard, C. Coppard, C. Taylor, G. Smith, & perhaps one or two more were present & Mr. Humphrey Barton. The offer of the land-owners to subscribe helped matters. Meeting amicable. I took a notice down to ye Sch. to get multiplied. . . . Spoke to H.Blackford in re. his singing boy grandson: he very civil. . . .

4 Dec. Mr. Smith c. Mr. Merrifield ye [Local] Govt. [Board] auditor cannot promise to allow in ye parochial accounts ye cost of rebuilding Crowhurst bridge, wh. is yet legally chargeable to Shoyswell hundred! What is the next step? . . . C. . . . on Mr. Cooper is much to be pitied as there have been & are sundry vexatious defects in ye Vic[arage] but his perpetual harping on these troubles becomes very tiresome. . . .

5 Dec. . . . Parish meeting at the Bell. Large attendance. On Mr. Merrifield's letter being read a resolution promptly carried that "Burwash parish take no further steps in the matter of Crowhurst bridge" & see how the matter stands. Mr. Gillham, Mr. Barton will have in self protection to take some steps, but the odds at present are in favour of the parishes as against the Hundred of Shoyswell. . . .[20]

6 Dec. . . . I buried poor Mrs Clear; no followers but Master Buss whose housekeeper she was & his son our Police Sergt. who was I suppose interested in seeing the poor old body "committed" to the earth. The grave unfortunately an inch or two too short. The [Ticehurst Poor Law] "Union" man explained it by saying that "the handles were in fault". The pauper coffins they are rigid, & add to ye length of ye coffin.[21] . . . Had to refuse young Charles Gorringe a character for ye R N: very sorry, but cd. not give one. . . .[22]

7 Dec. . . . C. on Mr. Farley & asked him to "correct" his boy Harry for "calling after" Miss Bates. He was civil & promised to help. . . .

8 Dec. Round w. ye Magazines. . . . Mrs Osborn showed me all over her house wh. is very roomy & with much pride her husband's joinery & cabinet work. He showed me two bullocks, 8 years old! & as big as small elephants: he expected to get £40 a piece for them [in margin: 'he got I believe £33-0-0 each']. A hard working honest man, I am sure, but not a perfect agriculturalist. C. on Bill Watson & wife (1/6), he out of work by reason of the weather [heavy snow].

15 Dec. . . . Soup given out for the first time to about 36 families. . . .

16 Dec. . . . C. on old Burgess (1/6), poor old folk; he worked for a month at ye Bough farm at 8d a day, & he says that ye others wd. not allow any body to earn 4d a day. . . . Ye Robin burying had . . . just taken place when he was there.[23] Honest old soul I believe. . . .

21 Dec. . . . Made copies of ye Quest[ion] & Answers about ye bridge, leaving one copy w. H. Jarvis & one with Mr. J. Fuller. . . .

23 Dec. . . . Took certif. of Banns to Henry Dann Jr. to his father who was not very cheerful over them, ye Son not being quite 21.

25 Dec. . . . Large Congr:. . . . Dined as usual w. JP. at 1.0. Moses Pope, wife & family abs[ent] as Moses gave notice & left sometime ago. Walter Bull talkative. George Ellis said that he had often heard his father speak of paupers being sent w. a wheelbarrow to fetch a load of beach [large pebbles from the sea-shore, used in road-mending] from Lewes, 20 miles! It seems incredible. . . .[24]

26 Dec. Burwash brass band c. up & played; they improve (5/-). . . . C. [among others, on an un-named man] came away at once, ye man sitting w. his head between his hands over a zinc pail, reaching & groaning: a sad commentary on a Xtian festival.

27 Dec. . . . A letter from W.J.Courthope asking me to write an article for ye new Nat[iona]l Review on Church work in ye Country. . . .

28 Dec. . . . Tea w. Mr. Taylor. Mr. & Mrs Whatman, Miss Boorman, & a Miss Whatman there. Mr. W. rather pernickity about ye bridge. He also startled me by saying that Mr. Gillham had told him that I had promised my consent to some arrangement about ye parish offices in Burwash in favour of his Son. Do what I will I cannot remember anything of the sort. I do not remember ever speaking about his sons candidature in Burwash. To ye meeting at ye Bell. I neatly bowled out of ye chairmanship. I had forgotten that it was a fresh meeting & so was not at ye vestry before ye meeting adj: to ye Bell. Consequently Mr. J. Fuller was elected chairman in ye vestry & was therefore chairman at ye Bell. Without a word of comment Mr. Whatman moved that ye meeting adj. for a fortnight. Mr. Jos. Noakes sec: ye motion & it was carried. Curious tactics but so it was & I disappeared. . . .

29 Dec. . . . Ellen Gould's treat. Mr. Barrow & I had some convers[ation] wh. I hope may lead to a reconciliation. I pray with all my heart that it may be so. Oddly enough last night I dreamed that we were reconciled. . . .

30 Dec. . . . C. on Widow Collins, widow of miller; she has allowed one or two [people] to get into debt & was in some trouble. I gave her 5/- on condition that she was to let me know if she ever got her money from her debtors. Her relief of mind was a treat to see. . . .

Sun. 31 Dec. . . . Miss Tilley kindly at ye end of ye sermon c[ame] out of her place & rebuked a singing boy who had been behaving badly. I dismissed him.

Notes

1.   In the twenty-six-year-old William Quee's case, the problem was even worse because he lived with J.S. Noakes' brother, John Buss Noakes. Census, 1881; see below, esp. 1 and 17 Feb., 17 Mar. and 10 July 1882, pp. 264–6, 271.

2.   Under the legislation, church schools which were unable to finance stipulated accommodation and staff-child ratios through a combination of endowment, government grants, and voluntary payments, had to make way for an elected parochial School Board, which in Burwash would certainly compromise Anglican educational hegemony.

3.   School attendance officers to enforce the compulsory provisions of the 1876 Act were commonly obtained cheaply by small augmentations to the salaries of existing local officials. Press coverage of court cases is erratic, and some Petty Sessional Clerks do not appear to have always made formal returns of convictions. On the other hand, summonses were possibly withdrawn, after parents agreed to ensure improved attendance.

4.   Although Egerton did not record much about the smallpox outbreak in an adjacent parish, events at Robertsbridge caused a panic and a scandal. Munn's burial seems to have passed off without incident, but one bearer, Henry Dobson, who went down with the disease, lived in 'a thickly populated' part of the village, and as premises for isolation purposes could not be found, the patient was ordered removed to the isolation ward at Ticehurst workhouse. His removal was delayed 'owing to the difficulty of obtaining a conveyance, and also a man . . . to drive it'. Eventually a van was procured, and Dobson, 'wrapped in a rug disinfected for the purpose' by Egerton's "nuisance man" Clarke; as the unescorted van passed through the village 'some of the children . . . climbed on to the back . . . to see (out of curiosity) what it contained', and similar events accompanied the van's passage through Hurst Green. Another waggon followed bringing Dobson's wife and children, also destined for isolation. Only the husband died, his coffin filled with limestone, and buried at midnight by the Revd Eden.

   Instructions that both these vehicles be burnt, were not quickly implemented, and Clarke had to wait five days before obtaining official sanction to burn the contents of the victim's house. The entire subject was given a vitriolic rehearsal at the next Petty Sessions, with the Revd Eley, Rector of Etchingham, castigating various officials, while members of the Bench vigorously defended them. Medical Officer, and Clerk, Ticehurst Union, to the LGB., 6 and 14 Mar. 1882, and Board's medical advisers' annotations, PRO. MH.12/13151. *Sussex Agricultural Express*, 4 Feb. 1882.

5.   George Garner and his wife Sarah, both sixty-four, cultivated sixteen acres, among the smallest farms in the parish. Grandchildren aged thirteen and eight also lived with them. Census, 1881. See also below, pp. 293–4, 296, 26 and 27 Dec. 1883, and 16 Jan. 1884.

6.   A colloquialism meaning starting a civil action heard by a County Court.

7.   A recent Chichester Diocesan Conference agreed that the extraordinary tithe ought to be negotiated away, but at a more recent Rural Deanery meeting at Hastings, Egerton argued that the tithe ought to be valued at twenty-years' purchase in the final agreement. Bolton pounced on a glaring inconsistency in Egerton's position, namely that the living at Burwash, purchased for £4000 by Egerton's father, about only four times its annual value. Yet Egerton's present proposal – to surrender his current annual £213 extraordinary tithe on hops on the payment of £4,290 from government funds – represented a huge disparity. Bolton however

noted his 'high respect' for Egerton, 'as an English gentleman, clergyman'. *Sussex Agricultural Express*, 28 Feb. 1882.

8.   Egerton was building a new cottage to house his gardener William Hicks.

9.   Farmers perennially complained that they were unfairly discriminated against, compared with tradesmen, by the rating system. Farmers' complaints reached a crescendo whenever agricultural prices moved against them, but as this was a voluntary rate (be it with compulsory implications if inadequate monies were donated), they could not be forced.

10.   Egerton had published details of the story (see above, pp. 263–4, 28 Jan. 1882) without naming anybody.

11.   The club had grown and now comprised eighty-seven members. 'The well-known Battle band gave some excellent music, the procession visiting some of the principal inhabitants of the town in its march . . .': Egerton was credited with an 'excellent sermon'. *Sussex Agricultural Express*, 19 May 1882.

12.   A non-practising surgeon, Summerhayes had recently moved from Burwash to Brightling, and was a leading local Liberal Party activist. Census, 1881.

13.   Hay stacked while inadequately dried occasionally self-incinerated.

14.   On the opposite page to this entry is an account from Horace Blunden and two other men working at Southover to whom Egerton talked. Blunden at least was a player in a hoax, played on a visiting hop-picker from London, 'a somewhat superior "Cockney"', given to 'ill-disguised contempt for "yokels" and "country bumpkins"'. Blunden and others informed the Londoner that they were going 'owl-catching' that evening, and he 'eagerly wished to join them'. Unknown to him, the others placed pails of water on a barn's rafters, invited the stranger to hold a sieve to catch the owls that they would turn out of the roof, and the cockney ended up saturated. *Sussex Folk*, p. 33.

15.   An incident which does not seem to have resulted in prosecutions.

16.   Such expedients were common during the recurrent wartime famines, when nettles fetched market prices in some locations. Bull's recollections probably derived from the 1811–13 subsistence crisis, but hard-pressed country folk possibly resorted more often to this type of measure.

17.   The incident referred to here was not recorded, but an earlier precedent was; see above, p. 113, 10 Apl. 1871.

18.   The stalwart Anglican Courthope attacked literature distributed by Bolton's organization calling the extraordinary tithe an 'unfair' and 'obnoxious impost'. Courthope, who was already a landowner at the passage of the 1836 Tithe Commutation Act, emphasized that under the legislation, landowners and clergymen agreed as to what 'portion' of land 'should be regarded as ordinary and what as extraordinary' when calculating commuted tithe payments: agreements on the distinction operated as a compromise until the onset of the depression, aggravated by imports reducing hop prices, and thereby threw extraordinary tithe payments into very sharp focus. *Sussex Agricultural Express*, 26 Sept. 1882.

19.   The bridge had 'now become a total wreck'; an elemental 'temporary foot bridge' was soon erected, by Gillham, not out of public spiritedness, but to link his two farms, separated by the Rother. *Sussex Agricultural Express*, 5 Dec. 1882. *Parish Notes*, Mar. 1883.

20.   As there were only parts of three parishes in the Hundred, making the latter responsible would have at best merely split the costs three ways. Moreover, if the third parish, Etchingham, had not agreed to such an arrangement, the resultant legal costs in establishing the Hundred's liability, or not, would amount to more than the

bridge repairs. Burwash ratepayers argued that whatever their liability, the cash should be raised by a loan, not simply to minimize the cost to current ratepayers, but to ensure that 'a burden wh. in equity ought to be spread over a number of years' – in Egerton's parlance – would also fall on future ratepayers, who would benefit from the new bridge. Approaches to the Local Government Board brought first a refusal 'to advise' Burwash ratepayers on their legal position, and secondly confirmation that the Board had no powers to sanction a loan raised on the security of either the Highways or Poor Rate.

In fact, by this date, Gillham appears to have taken a further initiative through attending as the sole Burwash representative at a Ticehurst vestry meeting on 2 Dec. This agreed that Burwash should pay half, and Ticehurst a quarter of the costs, and the landowners would voluntarily subscribe the remaining quarter – a resolution of 'excellent common sense' according to a journalist. The vestry decision, involving a record attendance of thirty-four, and chaired by Egerton, clearly torpedoed this agreement, when it was learned that Burwash's share would have to be met immediately. *Sussex Agricultural Express*, 5 and 9 Dec. 1882. Vestry minutes, 5 and 12 Dec. 1882, ESCRO. Par.284/12/2. G. Smith, and Egerton, to the LGB, 17 and 20 Nov. 1882, and endorsements, PRO. MH.12/13151.

21. Mrs Clear, a widow, had been installed by the Guardians as housekeeper when Buss senior's wife died, and no doubt in that capacity had been something approaching a step-mother to the children. Mrs Clear, subsequently returned to the workhouse, where she died. A Union official presumably arranged for the grave to be dug, and brought the coffin from Ticehurst.

22. Earlier this year, on 28 Apl., sixteen-year-old Gorringe had assaulted the elderly James Watson, and was sentenced to three weeks hard labour. The cause is unknown, but 'It appeared not to have been the first time that he had annoyed the complainant, and the police officer stated' in court that 'several complaints had been made against the boy', though this was his first appearance before the Bench. *Sussex Agricultural Express*, 2 May 1882. Summary returns, ESCRO. QR/E1098.

23. See above, p. 60, 26 Mar. 1860, and note 30, for this story.

24. There is no documentary proof on beach being carted from Lewes to Burwash in wheelbarrows, but parochial work schemes for the unemployed between 1815 and the early 1830s, often saw wheelbarrows being used rather than carts and horses to move beach in seaboard parishes, quarried materials in inland locations, and for the movement of road-mending stone *within* parishes. No doubt distances, if not details, lost nothing in the telling over fifty years or more.

1883

8 Jan. . . . Mr. Courthope . . . suggests a voluntary rate of 2d in ye £ on ye rateable property in such part of Shoyswell hundred as situate in Ticehurst & Burwash. Etchm. being commuted on score of having done much hundred work without asking help; ye rest to be made up by subscr: from landowners in Burwash & Ticehurst. . . .[1]

10 Jan. Sch. Mothers' meeting 5. . . . School audit. Messrs Cramp, Ellis, Whatman, Taylor, Albert Jarvis, Ellen Gould. Cost of cleaning cesspool only disputed item! At this end we are about £4 to ye good if Mr. Squire pays his rent £32.

11 Jan. . . . Mrs Coleman great trouble, a year's rent is owing. She has notice to quit, her husb: is unquestionably terribly selfish & spends his money on himself. She cannot get a house "no one wheres". I gave her 5/- to pacify her landlord for a fortnight & 2/- for herself.

Sun. 14 Jan. . . . In ye aft. had to speak very plainly from ye pulpit about ye misconduct of boys & girls during service. . . .

30 Jan. Sch. C. on JP. I spoke about expending the Sch. balance in substantial repairs & new furniture, ye parish will do nothing while we have a balance. . . . Taylor offered to have a committee meeting of ye sch. at his house to revise list of fees.

3 Feb. . . . JP. called to tell me that Mr. Squire had broken owing ye Sch. £20 for rent & me I think £25 for tithe. Ye Squire has done ye Parson any how. Poor man as a grocer in London he might have pulled thro' – as a Sussex farmer he is broken. I buried old Mrs Burgess, said to be 86, she died last Sat. [27 Jan.] night about midnight; her poor old husb: composed her limbs, tied up her face, & then got into bed again & slept soundly, by the side of his wife's body till morg. A somewhat touching end of a married life of 60 years. The old man is a good old soul, & till a month ago earned his living by day wages at ye age of over 80. . . .

6 Feb. At 7 Comm. meeting of ye Sch. at Mr. Taylors. Taylor, Whatman, Gillham, A. Jarvis, Cramp, John Fuller, Wm. Ellis, & self. Decreed 3 Classes of Payment (A) Farmers & Master Tradesmen (B) Journeymen Tradesmen (C) Labourers (A) 6d a week ye first & 3d for Chrn. under 7 (B) 3d a week all round (C) 2d for 1st 1d for 2d. . . .[2]

7 Feb. . . . [returning from Dallington after 10.15p.m.] Met only one human being being after Woods Corner, viz a man very drunk returning from Burwash betw[een] King's Hill & Perryman's. He swore at me roundly for saying goodnight. Home at 11.15.

9 Feb. Last night & this morg. making out lists of possible candidates for Conf[irmation] about 70 boys & 38 girls. The process nearly made me cry with disappointment when I thought of the boys & young men & realized how little even outward profession of religion there is among them. Such thoughts naturally humble me for one's own shortcomings as a pastor. . . . C. on my tenant at ye Bell.[3] He has been ill, but better. I pity a publican's calling. If a publican is not a sinner it is a mercy indeed. . . .

14 Feb. . . . Letter from Mr. Wolff ye propr[ietor] of Sussex Advertiser saying that w. my leave he wd. print ye Sussex Folk papers in ye Advers. I can't well refuse, & yet he gets a lot of matter for nothing. . . .

15 Feb. I to St. Ph. by 10.45 to marry Henry Dann & Abigail Russell. I waited till 12, but in vain. . . . Nobody coming I home. C. on Dann. He had been waiting an hour at Burwash Church. Poor man. His certif. from Mr. Balcombe ye Sup[erintending] Registr[ar] at Ticehurst gave Burwash Ch. as ye place for ye marr: Mr. Dann got it into his head that Mr. B. would send me a copy of ye Certif. of banns. Of course he did not, so according to agreement I went to St. Philip's. As ye marr. was intended to be specially quiet ye end was not obtained, ye whole village turning out w. amusement. I am sorry but I cd. not confess that I was in any way guilty. . . .

17 Feb. . . . I c. & P. w. H[arrie]t Kempe. Her cousin from ye Wheel there; said that ye drinking on ye Comm. was much less than formerly & Mr. Wm. Coppard this aft. said that a large brewery at Brighton for wh. Mr. Philcox is concerned finds trade much diminished. This is good news. . . .

Sun. 18 Feb. In evg. . . . Some but I cd. not see how many boys & young men attended in answer to my notes. I gave notice of ye discontinuation of ye evg. service in order to make way for conf. classes. . . .

21 Feb. . . . Mr. Clarke "ye nuisance man" interviewed me . . . about ye school "offices". . . .

22 Feb. W. w. Uncle to Ticehurst. He to ye Board of Guardians. I met & t. w. R[ichar]d Foley now Chairman in 79th year. . . . In aft. 1st Conf. Class for girls at 4 o'Clock in Church; about 23 pres[ent]. They were attentive & seemed in earnest. God grant that they may truly seek His Blessing, & I may be enabled to be of use to them. . . .

24 Feb. . . . In aft. C. on Mrs J. Isted about her d's conf. . . .

25 Feb. . . . In evg. at 6 my first Conf. Class for boys, 28 or 30. I was much encouraged & I was able to speak earnestly to them, & in full faith myself. . . .

27 Feb. . . . Sch. Comm. Meeting at Mr. Taylors all pres. I had to leave at 8 to go to ye singing class. Rules made that in Class A ye two first chrn. pay 6d each, each addit[iona]l one 3d, in class B ye two first 3d each add. one 2d. G. Smith & D. Blackford put into Class B. In aft. to ye Sch & dismissed it, while Mr. Anset was interviewing Sergt. Buss, who had previously tackled me. . . .[4]

Thurs. 1 Mar. . . . Class of girls in Ch. in aft: of 71, 29 pres. Enjoyed ye hour & all seemed attentive. Singing w. boys at 7. Coming out of Ch. heard 2 men playing ye fiddle in ye Bell. Stopped & listened. Spoke to 2 strangers who were also listening & happened to mention a very clever street player in Oxford to whom I gave his first engagement 30 years ago, Slapoffski by name. "I know him" said one of the men, "I worked 4 years at the New Examination Schools, & a friend of mine played in his band at balls". What a singular coincidence, that I shd. be speaking to perhaps the only one mechanic in all Sussex who has even heard of Slapoffski! Mrs D. Blackford waiting for me at 9PM to sign a certif. for her br: in law G. Blackford who is blind.

2 Mar. . . . C. on Herbert Hallaway in re. confirm. The most polite & as it almost seemed sceptical refusal possible. I pleaded but to no purpose. C. on Butler ye Shoemaker in re. Grand d's Conf: diff[erent] reception. He shewed me an old herbalists book dated 1652 by one Pennel (?) of Cranbrook. . . .

Sun. 4 Mar. . . . Aft. morg. serv. Mr. Smith interviewed me about an application for a situation as Road Surveyor for the parish of Sutton. Poor man to help him in such a matter is surely a work of charity, & I said I wd. attend to it in the evg. . . . I pr. from Gal. 3.13 (Ext) large cong. of ye mobility [common people]. In evg. 32 boys pres. 3 abs. Very attentive, & I was much encouraged. . . . Aft. to Mr. Smiths wrote out a paper for him to copy & to send, also a testimonial to be signed when copied by Mr. Whatman, Cramp, & Ellis who were pres: I cd. not sign bec: on Sat. night Mr. Gillham secured my interest for Mr. Boorman. Mr. Smith however appended a note that I wd. have signed had I not already been secured for another cand: I really do not know what the requirements of the Sutton Board are, & felt a difficulty in saying that I wd. have signed that Mr. Smith was thoroughly qualified but the pressure was great, & partly in pity, & partly thro' a disinclination to damage his interest I yielded I fear agst. my conscience. As a stranger coming in at ye last hour, he has I shd. say no more chance than I shd. have. . . .

7 Mar. . . . C. & R. w. Mrs Garner, has been ill again. How she lives at all in such a house I cannot think. The wind blows thro' it like a sieve. C. at 14 houses. John Relf & family going to move from ye beershop. He has got a permanent situation at Wellington College as cricket tutor. R. & P. w. ye Mothers (5). . . .

9 Mar. . . . C. on Mrs Collins (2/6) widow; has been ill 5 weeks & I did not know it. C. to see why Emma Relf was not at Conf. Cla: house locked up. . . .

Sun. 11 Mar. . . . Pr. in morg. from St. Luke 10. 29 (Ext). Coll. for Home Missions £3-6-10. Ye wealthy Xtians conspicuous by their absence. Wet dripping thro' ye roof by reason of melting snow; betw[een] serv. [Parish Clerk] Thompson brought Zinc pails to catch ye drips into one of wh. during aft. serv. ye rattle of ye drip was quaint. . . . At 6 Conf. Class Satisf[actory] 30 pr: 2 abs. whom I cd. hardly expect by reason of weather. 2 or 3 have I fancy refused, as I have 36 names. . . . Master G. Dann one of my singers accused on evidence apparently unimpeachable of cutting ye organ case yesterday when blowing. I dismissed him from ye choir.

12 Mar. . . . C. & R. w. Stephen Saunter, quite ill, very ignorant, can't read, aged about 21, great shame, parents seem to earn a lot of money. . . . Wrote to House Surg[eon] at T[unbridge] Wells Inf. re S. Saunter. . . .

19 Mar. . . . C. on . . . Mrs A. Hyland; long t. about ye school fees. I left her I think a little mollified. Really 3d a week for the two first, & 2d a week for each of the rest is not too much for journeymen tradesmen. . . .

24 Mar. In bed [ill for last three days] till about 12. T[homas] J[enner] c. up & copied out for me some papers in connection w. Rev. G. Barnsley's Charity to lend to Mr. John Fuller. What a poor undignified life that of a mere "clerk" seems as compared w. ye vigour & interest of ye life of a mechanic, or even of a clever day labourer, & yet tens of thousands of people look to it as specially desirable on ye score of respectability. Tom is fit for better things than merely copying. Mr. Cooper c: why shd. one curl up like a sensitive plant when he came into the room? Yet I did so instinctively. He is very kind, & means to be kind, & yet there is something unsympathetic or what seems unsympathetic in his nature. . . .

27 Mar. . . . John Isted jr. c. on me. I promised him some months ago 10/- if he staid in his place, as he is on very low wages of 1/- a week while he is learning his business as a grocer. . . .

29 Mar. . . . Met Mr. Gillham & had a talk. Ye Parish meeting passed off wonderfully quietly & ye "road" question not mooted. Ye Surveyor's Salary on ye contrary raised £3 or £4. . . .[5]

30 Mar. . . . I c. on Mrs G. Mepham; her son John coming home invalided from ye Police Force at Selmeston. . . .

Sun. 1 Apl. . . . ? [Mary Ann] Pennels brought her illeg: child by Wm. Holmes a married man to be bapt: but it was a boy & only one Godfather presented himself I was spared ye profanation of saying ye service, as this happened to be the only child presented; ye godmother was ye mother's sister. . . .[6]

Sun. 8 Apl. . . . A man put in his banns to Thompson ye clerk & paid 1/6 for them. Ye woman forbad them ye same day, saying that she had never seen ye man before that morning! . . .

12 Apl. . . . I c. & P. w. poor Mr. [Charles] Taylor; he is quite sensible tho' he had been very delirious. Oh what a comfort to minister to a sick man who fairly & honestly faces the future, humbly relying on the mercy of a loving Father thro' His Son Jesus X. Mr. Taylor has been a true friend to me, & if he dies his death will be a really grievous blow to me.

19 Apl. . . . My last class of girls. Every one now in Burwash present; gave final instructions. Have really enjoyed the 8 lectures, & I pray God that they may have been blessed both by ye candidates & myself. . . . C. on Mr. Love. He was for a moment conscious & said "Pray sit down" & that was all. His end is near. A pitiably wasted life. He was a butcher at Brighton, of the firm I believe of "Love & Myrtle". He was the youngest of 13 brothers & sisters, & the sole remnant is two nieces & a nephew, sister's children. . . . [He died on 20 Apl.]

21 Apl. . . . I w. w. ye candidates to Etchm. Ye whole viz 36 boys & 36 girls presented themselves. Ye girls brought down in Blackford's & Fieldwick's vans, & in Miss Tilley & Mrs Schroeters & Miss Gould's carriages. Good charge from ye Bishop, tho' his voice did not reach some of ye Burwash candidates. . . . Demeanour of all ye candidates very reverrent & good. . . . W. home w. ye candidates. Tea at ye Rect. 34 present. Powerful appetites, we had not fully considered their demands, however we satisfied them at least I believe. I said a few words to them & we separated. For the day on the whole, I heartily thank God. . . .[7]

Sun. 22 Apl. My good friend Mr. Taylor died this morning at about 7.30. I have lost a man on whom I relied much. Sch. I pr. from Heb. 4. 1 (V). I cd. not help an allusion to him. I trust this morning by God's mercy entered into His rest. Spoke to ye choir about ye funeral. . . . C. on Sissy Taylor. She saw me. Calm & bearing up better than I hoped. . . .

25 Apl. . . . Funeral at 3.45: large attendance, over a hundred I shd. think. One, James Cane c. all ye way from Southampton. Mr. T. had befriended him years ago. . . . friends from far & near; ye shops (many of them) shut up also ye Bear Public House. Ye Choir attended in good force. . . . singing very nice. Ye Serv. wonderfully quiet. Flowers beautiful. We sent a wreath wh. Mrs Tom Brook made in N's absence [in Surrey with her dying father]. I put on my card "In affectionate & most respectful memory of a true friend", words as genuine as words can be. . . .

Sat. 28 Apl. Fin[ished] Sermon & took it to Jos. Noakes one of ye Exec[utive]s to read for fear that my feelings might have carried me too far, but when I c. in ye evg. he passed it all as true. . . .

Sun. 29 Apl. . . . Pr. in morg. from Isaiah 6.8. Congr. all in black. I felt preaching more than I commonly do. I have lost a good friend. . . . In aft. pr. from St. Matt 5.9. . . . Congr. again in black. Really ye respect shewn to Mr. Taylor's memory very great. C. on Mrs T. She upstairs w. bad headache. Saw Sissy; gave her my sermon. . . . I do not know why but ye spirit in ye parish just now seems very great. . . .[8]

[30 Apl., having rejoined Nellie, to Oxford, returning 5 May.]

8 May. . . . C. at Nacky Garner's. He poor man very rough because I suggested his getting a woman's help in nursing his wife who is very ill, & has only a rough girl of 16 to see to her. He rated me roundly for the rubbish wh. I as a "shepherd" had put in the paper in "Sussex folk & Sussex ways" wh. Mr. Wolff in a manner compelled me to allow him to publish in ye Sussex Advertiser & for wh. I don't get a halfpenny. T. to the poor woman about other things than those of Baisden Farm.

9 May. . . . C. on Mrs C. Taylor. She in great trouble. Mr. Taylor's will very explicit, & I am sure that he acted as he thought for ye best. . . .

10 May. . . . Much movement among ye cottagers. Mrs Sands (1/6) has a new baby, tea w. Charles Coppard & wife. He lent me a book called "Confessions of a Horse Dealer"! . . .

Sat. 12 May. Burwash Fair. Held in ye two fields at ye Bear owing to foot & mouth disease.[9]

16 May. . . . I to ye Club dinner at ye Bear. Nothing very fascinating. Wm. Weston aged 82 or 83 . . . & Js. Standen aged 78 sang "ye Cottage boy" learnt from his grandfather 70 years ago. I sang "A thousand a year" & "When the heart is young". Ye Rescue fund of this club of old men with only 31 members, & only 3 years in existence is now £80 & some odd shillings. . . .

22 May. Sch. Dr. Fussell & Mr. Clark "ye nuisance men" at ye sch. They kept me 3/4 of an hour about ye drainage. . . .

23 May. . . . Club service. Full attendance of men & not one went out of
Ch. during ye service. . . . Congr. remarkably att[entive]. Home, & to tent
at 2 but dinn. not till 2.30 – too late. Club had been to Laurelhurst. I prop.
"the Queen & rest of R.F." "Medical Officer Mr. Cohen" "Hon. Memb. &
Friends & Mr. John Fuller". Club very orderly up till my departure at
5.45. . . .

24 May. . . . to Burw. Comm. Dined w. ye Club, didn't enjoy myself
much. S. Hazelden & R. Holmes good quiet & sensible as usual, but some
others not satisf[ied]. Soon away. . . .

25 May. C. on Mrs Taylor; in a good deal of trouble. C. at ye Bear, & found
I was right in thinking they closed for Mr. Taylor's funeral. . . .

4 June. At 11 to ye Bell; went over ye Relief list. Reduced a few cases, hard
to ye indivi[duals]. but really only justice.

6 June. The Foresters & the Burwash brass band came up about 10.30 & pl. 2
tunes. Creditably. I d. w. ye Foresters at 4 at ye Bell, in a booth, very
interesting.[10] . . . In evg. I to ye vill. to fetch Mr. Barton for ye Parlour
maid. Found him at Cohen's whom he has just bought out for £300, taking
also ye house. Cohen is well out of it. . . . Ye Club clearing out: did not
notice any drunken people.

7 June. . . . I c. & paid the bread bill at Mrs J. Isteds. . . . G.Noakes of
Etchm. br. to our Mr. Joseph Noakes run over it is supposed by ye
10.30PM fast down last night near ye level crossing opp[osite] Bugsall halt
& killed.[11]

8 June. . . . Inquest on G.Noakes at Robertsbridge. Acc. death. Jarvis's bull
in ye field bellowing & grumbling so I gave it a wide berth & c. down by ye
back of ye Admiral.

11 June. C. & P. w. Mr. Gibbs, very weak & low. He spoke in the kindest
way of our first relationship. I had sooner such a man fall out w. me than
many a man agree with me. Buried G. Noakes at 2.20. They kept me
waiting 20 mins. His father's funeral in 1857 kept me waiting an hour. . . .

12 June. . . . C. on Master Butchers (1/6). . . . Club at Dallington has just
broken. He takes it very philosophically. . . .

18 June. . . . On my way home met Mrs [illegible]; poor creature, given as
she is to drink I pity her, & she is so humble, & full of remorse, as it seems,
& so grateful to me for speaking quietly & without blowing up, that I was
quite touched. She in search for her husb. who was snoring drunk by ye
road side just in ye shaw. . . .

27 June. . . . R. & P. w. ye mothers (4). There is evidently a jealous feeling on the part of some of the village mothers agst. those who do come. . . .

5 July. Married Wm. Farley & Miss Mary Ann Butler. The bridegroom being in the rag & bone line, somebody . . . strewed rags & other emblems of ye trade in ye [church] path. I greatly object. Aft. l[unch] Mr Wolff propr. of Sussex Advertiser c. & had a long t. Pleasant man, but must have have been in his ancesters of no long dist[ance] a Jew. He wishes to publ. or get published ye Sussex Folk papers. I am afraid I shall get but little out of the transaction. . . .

9 July. . . . C. on Mrs George Garner, nice, but out of health, begged her to do what she cd., but ye man (old Master G.) is so abusive that ye neighbours don't like to interfere. . . .

14 July. What a scene for a painter. Poor old James Farley the clogmaker aged 83 dying, the wreck of a man of good natural ability, but of utterly wasted powers, ruined by drink, paralysed, mentioned to such attendants as he had, to put his helpless old hands together for prayers. [He was buried on 18 July.]

Sun. 15 July. . . . Congr. larger than usual tho' young Mr. Spurgeon was preaching at Chapel. . . .

20 July. Mr. Wm. Barrow of Augusta Georgia US c. & had a long chat; has been in America 41 years. Was in Engl. 22 years ago, when it seems I gave him two old coins. He gave me to understand that politics are a low trade in America. He w. round ye garden & was much pleased. He quite exonerates me in the difference between his br. & myself, & says I have done all I can to set things straight.

24 July. Mr John Fuller told me an amusing instance of the difficulties arising from lack of education in bygone days. Old Master Cottington, whom I remember at the end of his life cd. not in his youth at any rate read or write, & the young woman to whom he was paying his addresses was equally incapable. Master Cottington consulted John Payne the [radical] shoemaker & got him to write his letters for him. The young woman quite unknown to Master Cottington also consulted John Payne, & also got him to write her letters. Neither allowed a soul except John Payne to see the answers as they were received. Master Cottington took his at once to Payne to have them read, & the young woman did the same!! How Payne kept his countenance I cannot conceive, but Mr Fuller who was Payne's special friend, & who had the story straight from Payne himself has no reason to suppose that the young couple ever found out . . . or if they did it was not till after the letters had accomplished their purpose, & brought about their marriage.

31 July. . . . Committee meeting of Sch. at Mr. J. Fuller's. Salary of Miss Bates raised from £35 to £40. Sanitary matters arranged about, also repairs & painting. . . .

2 Aug. . . . colloquy w. young Mr. Spurgeon on the way [to Gillham's farm]. He is looking out for somewhere in Burwash as a convalescent home for members of his church. Tea w. Mr. G; he told me one or two good stories wh. I booked [recorded]. A German band came w. such a fearfully mutilated & discordant version of "How beautiful upon the mountains" that I went out & begged them never to play it again.

3 Aug. . . . I had a letter from Mr. Grierson of ye G[reat] W[estern] R[ailway] to say that owing to ye introduction of a simplified form of accounts of ye Railway Clearing House the work is being done w. 70 fewer Clerks & that it will be a long time before there is a vacancy for Tom Jenner. This is a great blow to me. . . .

6 Aug. Bank Holiday. A good many strangers about. . . . C. on Mrs Wm. Isted (10/-), poor woman, parish won't allow doctor, possibly justly, as her husb: earns good money, but liquidates it.[12] . . . JP. [driving Egerton to Etchingham Rectory] & I stopped below ye Lodge to see whether a man by ye roadside was drunk or ill: decided ye former.

15 Aug. George Mepham . . . told me [that] . . . many years ago, one of our rougher Burwash woman (Mrs Rigglesford) was ill, & being attended by [contracted parish surgeon] old Mr Evans. On one of his visits, thinking his patient better, he inadvisedly asked her how her appetite was. He was a somewhat shy man so I have been told, & the answer a little startled him. "O there my appetites all right again. I cd. eat a sirloin of jackass stuffed wi' "sodgers" (red herrings) if I cd. get it. Topper (her husband's nick name) brought me a basin of porridge this morning that thick that the spoon stood up in it & I ate that. . .".

20 Aug. . . . A t. w. Mr. W[hatman]. He upheld a favour shewn to a bad woman by her employ on ye gr[ounds] that she was the best hop-tyer he had. I argued that the woman's sin wd. do more harm, if it cd. be carefully traced, than her hop-tying wd. ever do good. I cannot believe in ye real benefit of a scandalous life anyhow. . . .

[27 Aug. to 1 Sept. in Wiltshire.]

3 Sept. . . . C. at Thompson's & w. him thoroughly examined ye closets & cesspool at ye school, ye outlet drain of ye cesspool must be lowered at least 2' 3". . . . W. J. Courthope c. I unfortunately out. He left a note, in it a propos of ye diff[iculty] of getting Jenner work as a clerk, he said that a

business man in London advertized for a clerk at a salary of £120 a year, &
got 1900 applications! This only a few days ago. . . .

8 Sept. . . . C. & R. w. old Mrs Wm. Pope (1/-), a typical instance of ye
old, uneducated, superstitious, shrewd, religiously somewhat callous
Sussex cottager. Told me two instances of "judgments" one where near
"Five Ashes" a man said "his wheat was doing very well if God wd. let it
alone", where it never grew any more, another where a Mrs Lavender at
Mark Cross some 50 or 60 years ago wished for her husb: who had come
home "tight" that "the next drop of drink he took might choke him"
whereupon her husb: who had just sat down to tea in trying to swallow
something choked & died at the table.

11 Sept. . . . In aft. C. & R. w. Mrs Mepham (1/6), poor thing losing her
"hopping" thro' ill health. C. on Mrs Isted pd. bill 6/8 1/4. H.H.
Newington informed me that there is a field in Ticehurst parish called in the
refined language of Sussex "Kiss-arse field". I enquired the reason, & was
told that the field was so steep that persons following one another up its
bank wd. be in the position politely suggested by the name.

15 Sept. C. in aft & R. w. Mrs Garner (2/-). I sincerely pity her as I do also
her poor gr: d (1/-) [Harriet, aged fifteen] who is a simple slave, ye husb:
sadly unfeeling. . . . Ellen [Gould] took dear N. to Pashley. Upset at seeing
a poor "Turner" woman at H[urst] Green lying insensible in ye road from a
blow. . . .

[17 to 29 Sept. in Cheshire.]

2 Oct. . . . Looked in on Mr. Love's sale. Many spectators a few buyers;
some of the things ought to go "dirt" cheap. A large oak linen chest was
bought a bargain for us 14/-. It was worth several pounds. At I believe the
last sale at that house (Daw's) I bought my oak bureau 25 years ago. . . .
T.J[enner] took tea & we studied the Civil Serv. Comm[ission] Report. . . .

5 Oct. Just before dinner out by ye iron gate I was speaking to Sergt. Buss.
He happened to mention that about a year ago he saw old Shoosmith
Uncle's gardener at Lewes. I thought the old man was in Cornwall, but at
that moment young Harry Blackford happened to come along direct from
Lewes where he keeps a public house. I said it is odd that we were just
speaking about Lewes & I asked whether he knew old S: yes he said he was
in my house a few days ago. Curious coincidence. . . . [During much of the
remainder of Oct. and into early Nov. he was confined to the house, if not
bed, by lumbago.]

8 Nov. . . . C. on Crouch ye keeper. Says he is much tempted to sell game
to people. . . . Had . . . a talk w. Mr. Potts ye ex Nonconf: preacher who

goes about visiting ye Church folk as well as his own. I said I wd. willingly resign to him any whom he liked to visit, & wd. look upon him as my helper, only I thought it was foolish both of us visiting ye same houses but he cd. not think of this, he made no distinctions & visited Ch. & Chapel folk alike; he was not bigoted. What is to be done? . . .

9 Nov. . . . Tithe dinner; nothing noticeable, all very friendly. I sang a thousand a year. When the heart is young, & The Village Blacksmith wh. I went across & borrowed at Bentham Fullers. Mr. Whatman proposed my health in the elaborate & set speech "I beg to propose the health of Mr. Egerton"! Some one sang "the Farmer's boy" a song I had never heard since I learnt the refrain of it "To plough & sow & reap & mow to be a farmer's boy" as a child in ye glebe at Bunbury. . . .

14 Nov. . . . Mothers' meeting 13. I R. & P. w. ye mothers. Master Walter Hicks aged about four came home from school very late to dinner bringing with him Miss Nellie Farley aged about 3½ whom he had persuaded to accompany him & with whom he had been pleasantly lingering. The same evening he came home also late but crying bitterly, because Miss Farley wd. not come with him, she having preferred the society of Master Walter Sweatman aged about 3!

24 Nov. . . . C. on Mrs J. Isted & on Moses Pope about places for their daughters. C. on Mr. J. Coppard at ye Park to ask their son John to be a S. Sch. Teacher; argued w. ye lad in ye barn for I shd. think nearly ½ an hour in ye pres[ence] of his father, but ye only answer "I'd much rather not", so I had to come away.

28 Nov. . . . C. on Mr. J. Fuller & Frank Russell to ask if they had Dickens' Christmas Carol wh. N. wanted to read at ye mothers' meeting: not to be had. . . . Tea w. Mr. G[illham] & some nice talk. He much exercised by a passage in a S[ociety for the] P[ropagation of] C[hristian] K[nowledge] book "Hops & hop pickers" wh. spoke of hoppers seeking matrimony "neither in holy Church nor in profane registry". I tried to explain "profane" only = to "secular", but in vain. I wrote to Chairman of ye Tract Comm. suggesting a modification of ye phrase. . . .

29 Nov. Aft. d. C. on George Daws Mr. Schroeter's bailiff. Father, mother, & sister now living w. him. Mr. S. makes all round him comfortable. . . .

30 Nov. Mrs Mepham c. & asked me to search for marr[iage] of Thos. Russell & Elizh. Park w. a view to recovery of money left by their son who had lately died in America. John Russell, who emigr. as a child w. his father about 50 years ago. I found it: Feb. 1813 & I took ye certif. to her. Ye money said to be in ye New York Savings Bank, & to be about £8000 . . .

6 Dec. Sch. Snow came on. In aft. c. on Mr. Anset & begged him to give notice that boys found making slides in the road must take their Chance of a Summons from ye Police. C. on Sergt. Buss, & on Mrs Sweatman whose boy I found myself in ye act. She thanked me. . . .

7 Dec. . . . C & had t. w. Mrs G. Hope at the Tot who has just come back to live in Burwash wh. she says she greatly prefers to Etchm. I really believe that the prospect of the "dole" beef has something to do with this. . . .

10 Dec. Aft. br: to Fontridge. C. & P. w. Mrs Garner (2/-). She cannot live long I think. Very conscious, I believe to be a poor humble minded suffering woman whose life has given her small opportunity of knowledge & less of happiness. . . .

15 Dec. Parish notes. Hard work. 600 words out of nothing. . . . C. on J.B.Noakes, shewed him pas[sage] in PN; he appr[oves].[13] . . . Ye Dudwell Mill property did not sell yesterday; only £3400 bid for 55 acres of ye best land in our parish, & a water mill wh. used to let at £75 per ann; place sadly let down in buildings & in every way. I am sorry for Mr. Nevill. . . .

17 Dec. . . . C. on a young woman at F. Harmer's. Banns asked yest[erday]. Shameful business. Father & son both have had children by ye same woman & ye old man is now asked to ye woman. I must try to escape marrying them. . . .[14]

19 Dec. . . . A traveller in bankrupt stock c. I speedily assured him that I was not his sort. . . .

20 Dec. . . . In aft. c. on Mr. Kilder new farmer at Grantwizzle. Poor man I pity him & I pity Mrs in such a slough of Despond[ency]. Has been a surveyor. His first farm I fancy. . . .

21 Dec. Mr. John Fuller, Mr. F.Cramp & myself gave out ye tickets for dole beef in my saddle room; all over in an hour & 3/4! In evg. to ye Vestry Meeting. Ye School Buildings assessed for ye first time to ye Poor rate. We put down a nom[inal] assessm. £6-10-0 the same as the master's cottage & the St. Ph. Sch. £3-5-0. Mr. J.B.Noakes there as an overseer; hasn't been to a parish meeting I fancy for years. . . .[15]

25 Dec. . . . I d. w. JP as usual. Walter Bull (77) told us about ye mobbings 1830 (Nov); terrible times. . . .

26 Dec. . . . C. & P. w. poor Mrs Garner. Pleaded w. her husb: to leave a woman in as his wife ought not to be alone as much as she is. I prom. 5/- if he consented. I c. on Mrs Sands & asked her to go up. . . .

27 Dec. . . . C. & P. w. poor Mrs Garner. I do not think she can live long. Mrs Sands was with her.

28 Dec. To Mrs Garners, for some reason or other the poor woman wd. not see me. I cannot form any opinion why. Mrs Osborn prom: she wd. send to let me know if any change of mind took place. . . .

Notes

1. It was not to be. Egerton wrote, ironically 'by common consent the Hundred rate was dead and gone', but referral to the lawyers, who 'are not so readily able to "pronounce life extinct" in . . . one of the most ancient jurisdictions in the county', saw the issue passed to the Quarter Sessions. In July 1883 the Bench ordered a hundred rate. *Parish Notes*, Jan. and Aug. 1883.
2. The school committee also had another poor – and indeed threatening – annual inspection report. Attendance was worse, 'a proof of great irregularity. If, as is reported, the Attendance Officer continues to offer no real assistance in checking this, a definite complaint should be made to the Education Department.' The grant was 'barely earned'. Attendance Officer, Clarke, went into action two days later, and on 23 Feb. prosecuted six Burwash fathers of thirteen children for not ensuring their school attendance; all labourers, they were fined 6d each, with 4/6 costs. ESCRO. Report, 2 Feb. 1883, ESC.41/1: summary returns, QR/E1101.
3. Publican William Farley was currently renting Egerton's glebe.
4. Presumably over the schoolchildren's minor delinquencies.
5. To George Smith, possibly as a consolation for not succeeding in his application for a parallel post at Sutton.
6. The baptismal register has no relevant entry, ESCRO. Par.284/1/2/4.
7. As there were also twelve candidates from Bodiam, thirty-four from Etchingham and another sixty-four from Salehurst, the service was 'somewhat long'. *Sussex Agricultural Express*, 28 Apl. 1883.
8. Taylor was fifty-two. In the burial register, Egerton wrote, 'A man whom kindness, love of truth, justice & peace, had endured him to me personally, &, as was shewn at his funeral, to the parish'. ESCRO. Par.284/1/5/3. Publicly, Egerton acknowledged that Taylor would 'tell me . . . plainly to my face . . . if he thought that I was wrong'. *Parish Notes*, Apl. 1883.
9. Vetinerary Harry Jarvis obtained a licence to permit the holding of the fair, on condition that 'no stock or sheep must be exposed for sale in the street as heretofore'. *Sussex Agricultural Express*, 1 May 1883.
10. The Foresters assembled at The Bell, and walked in procession led by the band to the Rectory, and then through the village 'stopping at the principal houses'. A cricket match preceded the dinner attended by Egerton. *Sussex Agricultural Express*, 12 June 1883.
11. Aged sixty-seven, Noakes had been to Bodiam Fair and 'was not quite sober, but he could walk alright' when he called just after 8p.m. at Robertsbridge station to buy a ticket to Etchingham, only to be told that the last train had departed. He started off, walking through fields adjacent to the railway, but soon transferred to walking along the permanent way, a common practice. The driver of the goods train following the train which killed Noakes, saw the body, stopped, loaded the

corpse on to a truck, and brought it to Robertsbridge. Once this driver reached Hastings, he inspected the engine of the preceding train, and 'found marks of blood and small pieces of flesh on the wayboard shaft'. The South Eastern Railway subsequently warned people against using the permanent way as a short cut, and eventually resorted to prosecution. Egerton recorded Noakes' accidental death on the railway in the burial register after his funeral on 11 June. *Sussex Agricultural Express*, 12 June 1883 and 28 Feb. 1888. ESCRO. Par.284/1/5/3. For scandalous episodes on Noakes' life, see above, 5 Nov. 1873, p. 141, and note 20.

12.   William Isted (born 1838) certainly had a long record of heavy drinking, being first fined for drunkenness in Oct. 1856. On 14 Feb. 1857 he left the Bear Inn about 1a.m. 'and having had a good deal to drink Henry Matthews led me to my house in Burwash and left me in the Kitchen and I fell asleep'. He had a least one poaching conviction (1857), and two for assault, both on the police. The first was a simple matter on Christmas Day 1858, and the second on very violently resisting the police when caught robbing a barn, for which he received nine months hard labour. He served another prison term, of two months, technically for vagrancy, after being found in the garden of the Revd Granville Clarke. Thereafter he was probably a more accomplished and circumspect drinker, and there is no record of further convictions in the local courts. Returns of summary convictions, and depositions in case against Matthews, Apl. 1857, ESCRO. QR/E996; 998; 1000; 1046. *Brighton Gazette*, 3 Feb. 1859.

13.   Namely the missionary meeting at the Congregational Church respecting work in India, 'illustrated by scenes from Indian life, in which some of our Burwash girls and boys, in Indian native dress, and with their faces darkened . . . took part'. *Parish Notes*, Dec. 1883.

14.   The banns respecting Frederick Harmer and Clara Scrase were read on 16, 23 and 30 Dec. In the event they were not married by Egerton. ESCRO. Par.284/1/4/1. See also above, p. 247, 30 June 1881, and note 19.

15.   Noakes had been appointed one of the overseers at the Mar. 1883 meeting. Other ratings decided at this vestry included three, and two, new cottages erected by Gillham and Schroeter, respectively, and Robert Kemp's new wheelweight and carpenter's shop. Vestry minutes, 26 Mar. and 21 Dec. 1883, ESCRO. Par.284/12/2.

1884

5 Jan. . . . C. on Mrs J. Isted. She had forgotten that it was her week to send bread up to ye Rect. . . .

11 Jan. . . . long t. w. Frank Russell about sch. fees; he is indignant bec: ye committee put him up to ye sixpenny rate. I tried to reason, but ye logic of ye pocket ignores premises & reaches ye conclusion with a directness & holds it w. a tenacity wh. are independent of the common rules of reason. . . .

13 Jan. . . . On waking this morning I said to N. I have had a curious dream. I dreamed that Mr. Barrow & I were friends again. On coming down to breakfast I found to my great surprize a note from Mr. Barrow asking me to meet friends to go into ye matters between us. I replied by note that I wd. gladly do so to consider any thing since March 1877, up to wh. date letters of his own wh. I sent him copies, fully condoned troubles. He was indeed friendly with me till June 1878, so that it is not fair to ask me to rake up all ye old accounts. I wish we cd. be friends, but except by yielding to his views, wh. I cannot conscientiously do, I fear there is no prospect of this consummation. . . .

15 Jan. . . . In evg. sing. w. 6 new boys & then w. Altos who got on capitally; only Mr. Smith's Evangelistic services at ye Chapel have perhaps taken away some of ye men; the cold accounted for others. . . .

16 Jan. . . . To . . . Garners gave him 5/- as I had prom. he ret[urne]d it me & begged me to take it to Mrs Sands. I found Mrs Sands at Mrs Crisfords, & gave it her. She gave poor Master Garner "a orful character", & said that I had luckily escaped a violent bombardment wh. had been intended for me. . . .

Sun. 20 Jan. . . . Had to refuse to church a woman whose child was born about 4 months after marriage. . . .[1]

21 Jan. Mr. N. Taylor c. . . . said . . . that it cd. not be unfair of ye parish to make ye rules for persons receiving relief as strict as ye club made for their members receiving sick pay, & there is I think something in this. I c. on ye poor woman about my refusal to church. She seemed penitent & cried & I was done. C. on Mrs Moses Pope (5/-) Ill. Schr[oe]t[er] & ye parish will not allow ye doctor. Moses her husb: earns 4½d an hour for a day of 9 hours work; allowing ½ day on Sat. this is 18-6¾ a week; no work in Xmas week. Ye parish is justifi[ed] in refus[ing] & yet Moses no better off than a good labouring man all the year. . . .[2]

23 Jan. Heavy gale last night; some to day; no mothers came. Cleared up [in] aft. . . . C. on ye singers – men – & asked them to supper for next week. . . .

31 Jan. . . . In evg. at 7 ye Choir Supper. 13 singing men, Mr. Anset & myself. Very pl. evg. Singular feature, Blunden alone beside myself sung any song. Not away till 11.30; only 4 bottles of wine drunk. The choir expressed themselves in very friendly terms towards myself. Ye servants had taken great pains to make everything nice.

1 Feb. . . . Singing boys' supper, 15. Afterwards they had Noah's ark, some drawing [room] fireworks exhibited by dear N. one of wh. fortunately ye last nearly choked us w. its fumes. Oranges, nuts etc. The small boys seemed to enjoy themselves greatly.

2 Feb. Fanny Goodman came to say Good bye. She is a brave woman. She sails for Honduras in about a fortnight. . . . C. & R. w. Master Gilbert at Platt's. He knows nearly as much about the Bible as I do. Arguing agst. ye High Calvin[ist]s who say we have no will of our own. . . . Intell[igent] old man. . . .

4 Feb. . . . Mrs Fenner at J. Budd's told a sad story of sin & misery concerning one of our Burwash Wheel girls. A certain Captn. in ye army, a married man, ought to be castrated, no other punishment wd. seem to stop his shameful treatment of other women than his wife. . . .

23 Feb. Marriage of George Thomas Braban 21 & Maria Flint widow 29. The bridegroom in a jocular humour, but I don't think he meant harm, & he owned he "forget himself" in church wh. was something for a Burwash man to own. P[rivately] B[aptized] ye illeg: child of Pennells (name Thos. Charles) wh. is likely to die.[3] . . . Fanny Goodman ought to sail to day by ye "Godalming" for Belize, Brit. Honduras. I wish her God speed. . . .

26 Feb. Poor Charles Coppard has lost his 3rd & last child;[4] also a child I think 14 yrs. of age (ye second attacked died almost right opposite Crouch's ye "Chicken fatters" on Brightling Common; also Pennell's child; a poor little Sweatman child died to day). I to ye Sch. Spoke to ye children, to tell their parents to keep them to school. Mr. Barton & Mr. Jupp c. in ye morg. I c. on H. Jarvis & authorized him to give Carbolic acid to ye am[oun]t of 5/- or 10/- to poor people on Mr. Barton's order. C. on Mr. B. to that effect.[5] . . . Looked in at ye Bell. Mr. Charles Eagleton, G. Gregory Jr, Roper ye Sol[icito]r Battle there. I did not stop as a clergyman at political meetings in his own parish is I think out of place.

27 Feb. . . . Aft. d. w. to Dallington, part way w. Mr. Britt who was going to see whether a young hop-pole shaver (Braban) had earned the money he had drawn. . . . Had a t. w. Mrs Steer; her husb: in ye Police 30 years, & they wont let him retire. . . .

29 Feb. . . . Carried up a wreath to Charles Coppard's. Saw Mrs Coppard, poor thing, to be left in a fortn[ight] w. no children at all is indeed sad. . . .[6]

1 Mar. . . . Funeral of Thomas Charles Pennells, illeg. Child of ye Wretched Mary Ann Pennells. . . .

4 Mar. . . . To Fontridge. Met & had political t. w. F.Russell. He thinks that Mr. Gladstone does not understand the English mind on its larger & more Imperial Views. . . . C. & t. w. old Garner, queer being, however we shook hands, I gave his gr: children a 1/- each for encouragement. . . . A horrible stink came as I came by the Admiral, it seemed to stick in my throat even after I had had tea.

6 Mar. W. Wilkinson in his carr[iage] to Heathfield. In passing Mockford's [?] Chapel & house, he spoke so unduly vehemently about Dissenters that I had to be very plain indeed on ye subj: of Christian Charity. He took it very well. I to his tem[perance] lodge in Heathfield House. Major Woodhead away. I interviewed "Bodle" Holmes reputed to be 104! but cd. not get much out of him. He dined at ye Burr'shers at ye public dinner in ye High Field in 1810, & had then 2 or 3 children. . . .[7]

14 Mar. . . . Sent off corrected Proofs of Sussex Folk . . . I to Gussey telling a story about a naughty boy: "I wish Gussey you cd. tell us something now & then about good boys". Gussey "But, father, good boys 'do' nothing".

17 Mar. . . . At 3.30 attended a meeting of the Farmers' Alliance at the Bell. The advertised Chairman Mr. Clarke [of Brighton] ill, & the main speaker Mr. Macer Wright did not come, so Mr. Mannington of Laughton took the chair. After a while Mr. Bolton came in & began to fire away about Extraordinary Tithe; very personal to parsons, & giving them a great deal of good advice. I spoke in return & asked him several questions as to the compatibility of the title Farmers' Friend with his £5 an acre for his own hop land, his £80 for 31 acres of brook land etc & I advised the farmers to take security that the extraordinary tithe when taken from the parsons shd. remain in their own pockets & not revert to the landlord. What I said was I think kindly received at any rate I had a candid vote of thanks along with Mr. Bolton. . . .[8]

20 Mar. . . . Wm. Russell c. & said good-bye; he sails for America on Sat. I like the lad.

21 Mar. . . . C. on widow Vidler, she shewed me a notice to quit from her landlady because she had told me about the wet coming into her room! She detailed an amusing convers. w. the landlady aforesaid. (Landl) "There are worse houses than this" (Wid: V.) "Yes but 'haps people don't live in 'em". . . .

22 Mar. Marr. of Thomas Rowley of St. Philips & Anne Elizabeth Saunter of Burwash. . . . Bridegroom, bride's mother, & bride, all signed by X; rare thing now, but bride's mother a simple Hottentot.[9] . . . Aft. d. in getting change for cheque had a t. w. Simmond Noakes about grocer's spirit licences. They are I am convinced very bad things in their working, but this of course he did not see. . . .

25 Mar. . . . I at 7 to ye vestry for ye Lady Tide meeting; adj. to Bell; large meeting, routine business. . . .

31 Mar. . . . A poor man Henry Eastwood by name, single, aged perhaps 50, found drowned this morg. in the pond by the glebe barn. Purely accidental I fancy. . . .[10]

3 Apl. . . . Funeral of poor Henry Eastwood aged 59. His br. Thomas attended. I had a t. w. him; respectable man I believe.[11]

4 Apl. Sch. Thanked ye children for ye primroses wh. they gathered yesterday gratis for ye sick children in ye East London Hospital. . . .

11 Apl. Good Friday. Good cong: 3 members of the Soc. of Friends [Quakers] there! . . . Staying at Mrs Osborn's [guest house] . . . Frank [Russell] rode down this morg. from London on his bicycle, & then went down to Dudwell Mill. I like the lad. In evg. large congr. again. . . . Ye marbles playing this year between ye Old Chapel & ye old pay-gate, not in ye vill. . . .

13 Apl. Easter day. . . . Large congr. 70 comm. off. £2-0-0. . . . Have much cause to be thankful to God for apparent earnestness of our people during Lent & on this day. . . .

14 Apl. . . . John Isted [jnr., just aged twenty-one] C. on me doing capitally at Thornton Heath. I am glad. In ye cricket field, nothing much. . . .

15 Apl. . . . To Bell for meeting Surveyors of Highways accts. all right, & yet I hardly know how. Men however like John Fuller & Mr. Gillham are not readily mistaken & they are satisfied. Anyhow I was very glad.

18 Apl. . . . C. on Mrs John Harmer (2/6). Her d. deserted very cruelly as I believe by her husb: (Dunk) leaving 4 chrn. on her hands. . . .

[Extended visit to Wiltshire, Dorset, Somerset and Oxford, 22 Apl. to 24 May.]

28 May. . . . Dined with the Old School Club. Only 30 members I think, but they have £96 in the hands of Mr. Noakes. I prop. health of ye Queen very well received. I spoke about ye franchise bill, but found that it did not create any great interest. . . .[12]

30 May. Shirked duty I fear & did not go to school. Aft. d. going thro' vill. bought a shilling copy of "Sussex Folk" at Fuller's, he had sold 5 before. Read it in a field past Mr. Gilberts; good print. C. on Mr. & Mrs Schroeter, gave the copy to him. Tea. Staid till 7.30, but I quite enjoyed my talk. He introduced me to his coachman's wife Mrs Slow, a "superior" woman. Mr. Murrieta has lent his "Scientific" water cart to water ye cricket ground. Home late.

31 May. 20 bound copies (cloth) of S.F. came from Lewes. A really pretty looking little book. . . . C. on Mrs Wm. Isted. Her d. Hannah a good looking girl of 20 wants a pl[ace] as kitchen maid in a good family, & has been maid to ye Siamese Ambassador's princess.

Sun. 1 June. . . . 2 bapt. In one case ye woman said that ye God-parents had disappointed her, so I stood as one, & Thompson was proxy for the other. Very irreg[ular] but I thought it best to do it. . . . Garden open aft. Ch. not many people came. . . .

4 June. Joseph Hall told me to day that some years ago Sam. Hayward carried 6 dozen of chickens on his back from Ticehurst Road Station to Burwash Common. The chickens wd. weigh between 1½ & 2lbs a piece, say 1½ & ye two crates at least 16lbs, being a total weight of 124lbs at the very least, & probably more! A not uncommon load for a man to carry for some miles is 3 dozen or 62lbs including ye crate.

9 June. . . . To St. Ph. Sch. Took 1st class in geography reading much pleased w. ye intelligence of ye children. Attendance like our own wretched. . . .

14 June. . . . Amos Jenner's son met me & was very cross bec: I had told Thompson that his young man was not a very brisk worker. Thompson told me that I was not ye first who had notified him of the fact. What is one to do? one cannot be entirely at ye mercy of young men.

15 June. . . . Letter . . . from . . . Mr. Thos. Hardy author of "Far from the madding crowd" apropos of "Sussex Folk".

17 June. . . . I c. & P. w. Jesse Baker. Rest of aft. taken up worse luck w. hearing a "horse" case at Mayfield fair, in wh. Tom Farley & Levi Luck are charged w. conspiracy to defraud. As far as I can make out a certain Tom Smith is the really guilty party. T. Farley spoke to me, & I then saw his father. . . .

18 June. . . . C. on old Mrs Chandler (1/6). I wish that people wd. not wish me to think them more given to Bible-reading than they are: it prevents one crediting them with possibly their due am[oun]t of good works. . . . I had a t. w. Farley pére in ye Mayfield horse case.

19 June. Madame Bodichon[13] . . . told . . . me [that] the woman's pig died, leaving a family of quite young ones behind it; one of these pigs the woman herself took & suckled it herself! afterwards in due course eating the pig when it had grown to the proper size. [added later] I mentioned this some time afterwards in Burwash & the person to whom I was speaking at once paralleled it in a case in a neighbouring parish.

20 June. I with much patience & pains, teaching my singing boys collectively Handel's air "How beautiful are the feet" heard a sound as of a boy talking. I stopped, discovered the culprit, & asked him what he was saying. He at once laid the conversation at his neighbour's door "Please Sir he asked me to give him a sparr" i.e. sparrow. His neighbour at once "Please Sir he told me he was going sparrow catching tomorrow". Cheerful subject of conversation while I was under the pleasing illusion that the two boys were singing "How beautiful the feet".

21 June. . . . Got change for a £10 cheque at J.B.N's; overheard in the shop a poor French labourer who said he was ill ordering a bottle of 1s 2d port wine. I gave the poor fellow a shilling.

30 June. . . . A very laudatory criticism of "Sussex Folk" in last Saturday's "Notes & Queries".[14]

1 July. . . . Mr. Anset at Lewes giving ev[idence] in favour of Tom Farley's char[acter]. . . .[15]

5 July. . . . To day the 27th anniv: of my first doing duty in Burwash; 27 years & oh how little good I have done. I wish I had some one to stir me up to do more.

7 July. I did my swathe of mowing as usual. Curious how one seems to remember the craft. . . . Young Burgess [who had just secured work at Northiam] c. up in the evg. & said good bye. I quite like the young fellow. I gave him Smiles Self Help. . . .

8 July. . . . My 55th birthday. . . . Wolff sent me a copy of the Spectator with a very favourable review of Sussex Folk. . . .

11 July. . . . Mrs Blackford at ye old Pay gate asked me the address of the writer of the enquiries after the Beaney family wh. I had from N. York. . . .[16]

15 July. . . . To Mr. Whatman's, had a t. about claim upon B. Thompson to refund £62 for maint[enance] of son in Hayw[ard's] H[eath Asylum][17], also about refusal by Mr. N. Taylor of order for "ye house" for d. of SW: this latter quite arbitrary & wrong. . . .[18]

Mon. 21 July. . . . our labourers have gone up to the Anti-House of Lords demonstration in Hyde Park today. Hop poles & ribbons are their insignia. I hope they know good men what they went for.[19] Harry Fawcett sent me an introd[uctory] letter to Mr. Mundella. I forw[arded] it with Mr. J. Fuller's letter to myself & on "Farm Labourer's account keeping" to The Hon. A.J.Mundella M.P. House of C. Wrote to Fawcett & Madame Bodichon who had sent me her pamphlet, able & smart, on Woman's Suffrage. . . .[20]

22 July. Wolff & Mr. J.Whelan of Daw's Place sent me copies of yesterdays Pall Mall [Gazette] w. favourable criticism of Sussex Folk.[21] . . . In my abs[ence] Madam Bodichon had c. bringing a Pall Mall! dear N. saw her. . . . Bought a penny song sheet at Martha Flemings. For meaningless ungodly vulgarity I can scarcely conceive anything more sad.

23 July. . . . I to tea at Nevills & afterwards to see his swimming class behind ye mill; very creditable to him. About 6 went in, 2 taking headers from spring board. I gave 1/- in prizes! The boys & young chaps all wear little loin cloths, & everything is nice & proper. Nevill himself is a good swimmer. . . .

26 July. . . . Mr. J. Fuller c. He is satisfied w. ye result of my 2d letter to Mr. Mundella wh. produced ye answer that Mr. M. wd. leave ye question of Farm Labourers Account keeping, as suggested to me by Mr. J.F. carefully considered before issue of next code [respecting education in agricultural parishes]. . . . C. on Mrs J.Vigor. Ye Nuisance man threatens to summons her for non-attendance of child.[22] She keeps 5 steady at school.

30 July. . . . Whole [day school] holiday. An innovation I fancy, it was begun last year. Aft. to ye vill. bought sweets. Children at 2.30., about 138. Large gathering of parishioners. I fancy old & young nearly 400. . . . games . . . Short address, hymn, 3 cheers for teachers. . . . Three cheers for Burwash parish "may it flourish root & branch for ever". "The grace of our Lord" & then all disappeared & so ended the 10th Sch. T[reat] given by dear N. & myself. The day one I think of real & general enjoyment. . . .

1 Aug. . . . C. on Ellen Morris & expostulated with her for having come to tea without an invitation, living as she is in open sin; she said some boys told her she was to come. . . .

2 Aug. . . . Boys cr[icket] m[atch] w. Etchm. in front of house. I had sorely to abrogate Master C[harles] H[icks, his gardener's son] for selfishness in refusing the use of his tumbler to the Etchm. boys, & also for arrant rudeness to myself. He sadly impertinent. I spoke to W.H. about him. I gave ye Etchm. boys some cake & 1/- to buy lemonade. We beat them in one inn. but we had 2 boys who had left sch. . . .

Sun. 3 Aug. . . . Two baptisms. I sent home one illeg. ch. wh. I had bapt. privately, as I did not want the exhib[ition] in ch. of a somewhat bold mother. . . .

5 Aug. . . . In aft. to Nevill's. Interviewed Mrs superintending a young brood of nudes paddling in the brook. One or two of the children 7 or 8 years old. I shd. think utterly unconscious of their very primitive simplicity. . . .

6 Aug. . . . Watched Will. Hicks giving a mare of Mr. Barton's her first lesson in jumping. Master & pupil both skilful. Really a horsebreaker ought to have the temper of a saint. W.H. I think very kind. . . .

7 Aug. . . . C. at Master Crisford's. He a refined & aristocratic looking labourer. Met Mr. Gibbs in his trap; he told me that poor Mr. Atherton had had a paralytic stroke. Poor man. He wd. be genuinely & greatly missed by ye labouring Class.[23] . . . Dr. Fussell came & pronounced Amos Jenner's wife to be distinctly suffering from small pox: I also believe Charles (?) Hilder's wife.

8 Aug. I bef[ore] br: to Mr. Barton's; got from him ye assurance about ye Small pox, & then to Mr. Gibbs' as he was going up to town to stop Mrs Alfred Payne from coming to Burwash if it was S.P. Home, breakfast, then to Mr. Barton's & was vaccinated. The heat keeps increasing. Refused yest[erday] an invit. to Frank Courthope at Lewes to stay a day or two at ye end of ye month to see ye Austr: eleven play a match at Brighton. Too near N's time. Sing. w. boys. I asked after Alfred Blunden. "Please Sir he's left" was all his brother said, & this was all the courtesy shewn me by a boy with whom I have taken great pains for some years. I believe it is only ignorance, but it is too bad. Standen ye sec. of ye Sch. Club, & G. Mepham ye Steward interv: me about a breach of rules by a member. . . .

11 Aug. . . . In aft. I c. on Mr. Carter JP at ye lock ups. I told him I had come hearing that he was at the lock-ups to see if "bail" wd. be any accommodation![24] A pl. chat while waiting for brother Gibbs [also a magistrate]. Some lunatic case for ye workhouse. Mr. Berkley ye [work-house] master there. . . . Had a long t. w. Mr. Newton Taylor [also district registrar of births, marriages and deaths] on my way up vill. He told me that in 13 years he has not registered in either Burwash or Ticehurst containing over 5000 souls, one death from Sm. Pox! . . .

12 Aug. . . . Settled a case of ye School Club v W.G. he pd. his fine of 3/-, I helping w. 1/- & Mrs Cane 1/-. Nevill's property not sold yesterday.

16 Aug. . . . Small pox does not at present spread beyond the two cases in the Square & the one at Knowles of the railway gate, Crowhurst St. . . .

17 Aug. . . . Knowles child has I believe died of ye Small Pox.

20 Aug. The well cleaned out. Supposed not to have been cleaned since it was sunk about 40 years ago! 60ft deep, about 3ft of mud. Stinking, but no animal matter.[25]

26 Aug. . . . C. & P. w. old Mrs Chandler: a great sufferer . . . speaking of a young woman who had gone wrong, she said "Ah she's a poor simple thing: any body can lead her any one way, its a way she's a mind to go"! There are many I thought as simple as the young woman. C. on old Mrs Relf going to hopping tomorrow. . . .

27 Aug. . . . at 8AM I buried Charles Wm. Jenner illeg. ch. of Sarah Jenner; it died at a small pox house tho' not of small pox. I thinking that the grand-parents wd. have to pay, excused the 2/6 fee, then found that the father of the child was there with a handful of silver, quite ready to pay. I was sold. Directly after ye funeral ye bell went out for another Jenner inf[an]t illeg: a cousin's child. . . .

30 Aug. . . . Mr. Combs professes that he has the Small Pox. I believe it is rubbish. Psoriasc's more likely aggravated by alcohol. . . . In aft. ye funeral of Pris[cilla] Jenner's illeg. ch. . . .

2 Sept. . . . [Returning from Robertsbridge] Blunden formerly of South-over guard on ye train to Etchm. I told him that a great change had taken place in our relations; when he was under my authority at school he was in the first class; now that I was under his authority I was in the 3rd. He seemed tickled. . . .

4 Sept. . . . down to Mr. Gillhams. . . . A poor old Frenchman (or French speaking Jersey man) who works for him in ye summer, lives in ye winter by selling roast chestnuts in ye street at Kingston-on-Thames.

6 Sept. . . . Saw poor Mrs Chandler suffering acute pain. . . .

7 Sept. . . . A review of Sussex Folk in Morning Post on Aug. 29 sent me: rather deprecatory. . . .[26]

8 Sept. . . . On to Mr. Whatman's. . . . hoppers had just arrived in two waggons from Heathfield Station being Brightonians.

9 Sept. . . . N. began to feel queer. . . . the child a boy, was born. Dear N. had a good time, & so far is doing well. O God I thank thee for thy mercies. . . . To a cr. match on the High Field. Local. A young Mr. Murriéta playing. . . . [Egerton spent the evening at the Revd Cooper's musical soirée.]

10 Sept. . . . C. on old Mrs Vine: went into the House on Monday. . . . C. on old Mrs Chandler, & yet I have not had from any one heartier good wishes over the "boy"; on coming in found that dear N. had had a sharp heart attack. God grant that it may not be anything serious. . . .

11 Sept. . . . dear N. said I must not stop on her account; to Brighton; [clergy's] meeting. . . . Found dear N. a little better, but not much. . . .

12 Sept. Mrs Gilbert told me that many years ago the wife of a very rough ungodly man (Henry Waterhouse) told her that one day she was walking in the garden when she heard a voice most distinctly calling to her "this won't do – you must alter – you must alter". She was much startled & told her husband when he came home from work. He took the voice to be a warning for himself, & his wife said from that very day he was never in a public house again. He quickly saved money to buy what he had not got before, Sunday clothes, & attended church very regularly, a thing he had never done. When I knew him he was a most consistent & well conducted old man.

13 Sept. . . . Sent up a bott. of liniment to Mrs Chandler. Another small pox case I fear viz. Will. Gorringe; has been very careless I believe in consorting w. Douch & others.

Sun. 14 Sept. . . . I up to Mr. Barton's in ye evg. [for medicine]. Sad sight in ye street at turning out time. Half our male pop. seemed to have been in "ye houses".

19 Sept. At 12.30 AM I buried Will. Gorringe. A weird scene. Two lanterns, self in surplice & hood, funeral party wheeling ye coffin on wheels to ye grave side. Nobody in ye Ch: yard exc. persons connected to ye funeral. Certainly Small Pox is dreaded. Home about 1.15.[27] . . . Ye Doctors reported dear N. doing favourably. In aft. I c. & P. w. poor old Mrs Chandler (1/6) suffering sad pain. . . .

Sun. 21 Sept. . . . I asked ye prayers of ye congr: at both services for dear N's recovery. . . .

24 Sept. Mr. Barton says the fever is gone & that dear N's temp. is normal. . . . Oh God give me a thankful heart. . . .

25 Sept. . . . I took exercise to day by digging in ye kitchen garden. Soon out of breath. However I did better the 2d time than the first, so I daresay I shd. soon mend. . . . I to ye vill. in the evg. Ye "Admiral" at pres[ent] the most popular; heard the sad sound of a woman's voice in ye tap.

26 Sept. I w. down to ye Station to fetch a bit of fish for dear N. Much touched by several enquiries after her by poor people. . . .

27 Sept. Improvement continues. . . .

2 Oct. . . . Mrs Pagden has given up her school having kept it for 57 years! . . .[28]

3 Oct. . . . Funeral of Mrs Askrill at 75 sister of Mr. Thos. Evans late Surgeon of Burwash. . . . [?] very drunk at funeral, or rather after it, as his servants very luckily delayed him coming to the service. I threatened him w. the police as his immunity is not fair to poor people who are summonsed & fined. . . .[29]

7 Oct. Mr. Barton pronounced dear N. [who had had a recurrence of 'fever'] again "Normal". . . . Sch. Only 8 fresh entries. I expected more as Mrs Pagden has retired. . . .

13 Oct. . . . C. & P. w. Mrs Chandler, cruel pain. I gave old Mrs Moon her nurse 2/-, to secure as far as may be good attendance. . . . Newton Taylor c. . . . very hard on widow Braban for having concealed from ye parish ye fact of a Son & d. having been home during ye quarantine. I asked Mr. N.T. why that was worse than ye parish concealing from widow Braban ye fact that they had no legal right to keep her in quarantine to make her lose her hop-picking. He shortly changed ye subj. . . .

14 Oct. . . . Mr S[chroeter] back w. me to ye vill. He said that if the Old Chapel & neighbouring house cd. be bought, he wd. at all events entertain the idea of buying for Parish Rooms. He is a most generous man. . . .

15 Oct. School. 33 new admissions since opening. . . . Js. Vigor at noon to day complained of my singing boys. 3 of them had broken his window, & he said that their lang[uage] was shameful. It is grievous. I must see into it. . . .

16 Oct. W. JW up to Mr. Schroeter's to lunch, & then w. him to see his cottages at the Wheel, & also the Bough Farm on the tenancy of wh. John Hyland has just entered: wished my good friend JH good luck w. all my heart. Mr. S. a most liberally minded man. Coming back I c. on Ernest Wells & his wife at "Ye Wheel". The drink trade as carried on at public houses put at its best is I fear an unsatisfactory calling. These two are too good for it at "Ye Wheel". . . .[30]

17 Oct. . . . In aft. C. on Mrs C. Pennells & on Mrs Wm. Pilbeam in ye matter of breaking of James Vigor's windows by their sons, my singing boys. Sergt. Buss had c. here this morg. about it. I had to request Mrs Sweatman, Mrs. C. Pennalls, & Mrs Pilbeam to withdraw their children. . . . Singing boys c. to ye Rect. in ye evg. (10). I spoke very strongly to them. . . .

Sun. 19 Oct. . . . good congr. Mr Combs making such a noise outside his house that I had to go to him & tell him that I must report him to the police as drunk & disorderly; he called me a condemned liar. I told Sgt. Buss's son whom I saw at ye Station to tell his father that he must keep his eye on Mr. C. No poor person wd. be allowed to go on as Mr C. does. . . .

21 Oct. . . . Sch. 42 new admissions since hopping. C. on JP to ask if a father had power to forbid the banns & prevent the marr. of a son under 21. He had never been asked during his 40 years practice & cd. not say. . . .

23 Oct. . . . Uncle Nathan c. . . . He advised me about a father's right to forbid ye banns of a son a minor. Consent of parent or guardian is necessary in such marriages before a registrar, or in getting a licence from a surrogate . . . so we assume an analogy in marr. by banns. . . .

24 Oct. N. more sleep, having taken a small dose of opium: no ill effects. . . .

30 Oct. . . . C. on Mrs Harker; certainly any labouring man who without due consid: gives up Mr. S's service seems to me to forfeit a good place. Old Knowles in evg. c. up to me to ask me to plead ye magistr. tomorrow to get his son into a Reformatory. I wrote him a letter to give to ye Chairman, ye poor fellow is too old, 17, not quite sharp I think but very mischievous.[31]

1 Nov. Dear N. had a good night without opium. . . .

2 Nov. . . . young Stephen Pope of the Marines home invalided from Suakim. [In the Sudan, garrisoned by Anglo-Egyptian forces.] He gives a sad account of the sickness, invaliding & death rate among the occupying force. It is cruel work. The Govt. thro' dread of responsibility has got us into a muddle wh. will cost us I sincerely believe far more than vigorous measures at once wd. have done. . . .[32]

6 Nov. Not much expenditure on fireworks I believe last night. Tithe dinner; about 71 guests at ye "Bell". Mr. Simes, Mr. Whatman, Mr. Gillham, Jno. Noakes, George Fuller & others near me. I prop. ye Queen & then ye Tithepayers of Burwash. Mr. Simes Mr. Gillham prop. my health & I retd. thanks & so ye speeches ended. I staid till about 5.40. Certainly I have no reason to complain of ye footing on wh. my parishioners & myself stand. . . .

14 Nov. . . . Wrote to Mr Coppard re G. Lavender who having sent us bad meat wh. cook had to return accuses cook of being in league with [rival butcher] T. Jarvis. Mr C. on me yesterday on ye matter. I wrote strongly as it is a cruel piece of injustice to cook. I ye 2 years & 9m. that cook has been with us, Jarvis has had from us £124-5-7, Lavender £137-8-5 wh. does not look much like Jarvis subsidising cook. . . .

17 Nov. . . . I was c. in by Master Barton at ye Tot to see a fine hog who had died of apparently inflammation & stoppage; about 30 stone, involv. [ing] a loss of I fear £6. I gave him 10/-. C. on Mr. Carrick ye new farmer at Border's. . . . C. on Mrs G. Watson; begged her to send her children to sch. . . . Today is the first day for many years that I have not taken in a daily paper, but Ellen [Gould] giving up ye undertaking for one, considerable [delivery] costs. . . .

19 Nov. . . . C. on Master Burgess (2/6), broke his leg larking on bonfire night! Stupid man. . . . To Mr. Gillham's to tea. In consequence of conv. Mr. G. said something about comparative evils of Establishment & Nonconformity, mentioning a newly appointed Congregationalist pluralist viz. a minister at Battle who is also minister of our chapel here preaching here once a month himself & sending supplies ye other Sundays. . . . [Also present Gillham's son, a farmer in Ticehurst, where the Baptist Chapel 'meeting is almost entirely his own family & household & just a few others who supported him, he having preached ye fine new chapel nearly empty'.] . . . . a lot of childr: making a great noise in ye lane leading to ye level crossing to Turzies; too bad of their parents to let them out so late [about 8.30p.m.]. . . .

22 Nov. . . . A new ed. of "Sussex Folk" coming out. . . .

25 Nov. . . . Had a t. w. an old man Master Cramp (2/-) aged 76 breaking stones. Had been turned away without a word from Battenhurst [Farm in Ticehurst] where he had been a sort of working bailiff for 10 years. He felt it terribly, & as far as I cd. make out justly so. It was not the turning away altogether but the heartless way of doing it wh. cut him. . . . C. on Mrs Th: Pope (1/-) Her two sons both heavy on her hands thro' weak constitutions. Ye eldest rears singing birds successfully. C. & tried to comfort poor old Mrs Waddell, who certainly has a lonely life of it. She is certainly not quite right in the head. Her husb: goes out about 6.30, & comes home at 5.30, & she sees hardly anybody during ye day. Water every where. . . .

26 Nov. . . . Poor old Mrs Dann, Tom Jenner's Grandmother, found dead in a chair yesterday aft: had been up town at noon. . . .

28 Nov. . . . Funeral of old Mrs Chandler. One of the bearers R.N. not sober. I did not like to speak for fear of a disturbance. . . .

29 Nov. Funeral of old Mrs Dann at 2 oClock. Had a long t. w. Robt. Dann her son, a very respectable young man coachman to Sir Joseph Barzalette at Wimbledon. . . .

2 Dec. . . . Sent 10/- to Mrs W.E. Caller Swanley Kent, newly married, was Mary Ann Gurr, whom I prom. to marry for nothing many years ago, when either Lucy or Gussey was married: she was then a little school child. . . .

4 Dec. Funeral of little Walter Hicks [aged five] at 3.20 shd. have been 3, but in such cases no Burwash person ever thinks of offering a word of explanation. Our four children attended. The poor parents, & indeed all present really sorrowing. Old Sam Ellis (2/6) out of Inf: says he is cured. . . . C. on J.Pennells (2/-) & wife, gave them for their s. Charles who had to keep, goodness knows how, a wife & 8 children by his day labour during this wet weather, when he loses much time.

5 Dec. . . . C. on old Gilbert (1/-); quaint as usual. He said "the devil's a mighty being, but God is almighty, & that makes all the difference". . . . C. on Mrs Delves; sad tale of trouble. Oh the drink. . . .

6 Dec. Very wet; did not put my boots on all day. Mrs Butler of ye Rocks c. to pay me my fees for 2 funerals. . . . Complained of her graves being trodden down. What can I do, they are near ye gate, & ye children run over them; gave her 1/6 towards some wire netting. . . .

Sun. 7 Dec. . . . Our 5th child [John] baptized. Sponsor Susan Margaret Darby (née Wetherell) of Pashley. Charles Reginald Egerton of all Saints School & Henry Wade DD Principal of Kings Coll: London, neither cd. be present, so they were represented by Churchwardens Cramp & Ellis.[33] Charles Thompson's son, his first child, & George (?) Blackford's son of Pug's hole were also baptized. I pr: from St. Matt. 13. 31. 32 (Ext). Meant fully to have alluded to poor little Walter Hick's death but ye subj: of my sermon being ye training & cultivation of ye seed of ye grace of God in a living child's heart. I utterly forgot the poor dead child. I was very sorry when I remembered after church. . . .

8 Dec. . . . In aft. c. on Burgess (1/6), his leg better, long t. on "religion". He had been disgusted by various ultra Calvinistic utterances of a man for whom he used to work, but I question whether his disgust w. high Calvinism had made him a good Arminian. . . .

19 Dec. Sch: gave viva voce instr[uctions] to all ye school re Christmas & our Lord's early life. W. to Etchm. for constitutional. Saw Mr. Gibbs & Mr. & Mrs Schroeter on ye road. Helped old Master Burgess home w. a load wh. was too heavy for him, as he is over 80 years old.

21 Dec. Shortest day. I always feel thankful when ye turn of ye days from shorter to longer has come.

22 Dec. Dole. We gave it out in my harness room. Almost same as normal. Mr. John Fuller cd. not come having bad feet, but sent two grandsons who were very useful. Mr. Cramp helped me; finished before 1 o'C. Price of beef 5/- per stone, same as 2 years ago, too bad seeing ye depression of prices. . . .[34]

24 Dec. . . . Wm. Coppard's party of singers c. at about 8. Had not practs. enough & one or two funny mistakes were ye consequence. . . . Some hand bell ringers also, but mercifully no boy singers. To post letters before 10. Street noisy.

26 Dec. Burw. brass band; creditable "considering" but as music doubtful. I c. at Mrs C[ombs]'s. Ye doctor opened ye door. I on ye spur of ye moment wished him a happy new year, & he returned it, I believe! . . .[35]

Notes

1.   The relevant registers are inadequate to an identification of the parties.
2.   The implication is that model employer Schroeter's altruism did not extend to paying for, or towards, his employees' extraordinary expenses (which was not unusual among the more responsible masters) on the grounds that above-average wages should enable recipients like Moses Pope to meet such demands either from savings or through benefit club membership. Clearly parochial officers, including the Guardians took a similar view, and this consideration appears to have underpinned Taylor's attitude.
3.   Egerton did not record the baptism, but he entered the ten-month-old's burial on 1 Mar. 1884. ESCRO. Par.284/1/2/4; 1/5/3.
4.   Coppard's house was the 'first infected' by diptheria; although 'tenanted by a farmer of a relatively superior education to many of those in the Weald . . . yet from his remarks to the [Local Government Board] Inspector, he could not, or would not recognise the seriously contagious nature of the disease, until it carried off his three children'. While 'there is no stable, Cow-yard of Pig-styes close to it [the farmhouse] as one often sees', a newly-installed lavatory was badly fitted, and effluent went direct

to an unventilated cesspool, which polluted the water in the well. However, the Inspector concluded that the disease was 'probably . . . imported from London' by a railway worker whose children were shortly afflicted. Sanitary authority, medical officers' reports, 5 Apl. and 16 Aug. 1884, PRO. MH. 12/13152.

5. Although the sanitary authority had powers to close schools during an epidemic, the Ticehurst officials had used them only once in their eleven-year existence; 'generally speaking if many cases of an infectious disease occur in a Village the School practically closes itself without Authority from any-one'. The epidemic proved quite serious, but fatalities were restricted to two children in addition to the Coppards'. Ibid.

6. The Coppard children were not buried at St Bartholomew's.

7. The 1924 edition of *Sussex Folk*, opposite p. 78, contains a photograph of Holmes, smoking his pipe, and dated 1885. Holmes was the object of some publicity in 1883 when the Relieving Officer confirmed that Bodle, or rather Richard Holmes' baptism ninety-seven years previously was entered in the Heathfield parish register. However, Bodle claimed that he was baptized as a child of six or seven and remembered the occasion. The report added that Holmes' brother, Henry, aged about ninety 'goes to work on the roads every day'. Bodle 'is said to have consumed a great deal of beer in his time, and can even now discuss a pint with considerable relish. Beer drinkers, with this example of longevity . . . may fairly challenge their teetotal friends to produce a champion who has lived so long'. *Sussex Agricultural Express*, 7 Apl. 1883.

8. In fact an inaugural branch meeting, and Bolton not only publicly dissected Egerton's income, sector by sector, forcing Egerton to correct some of the figures, but also asserted that the clergyman possessed 'the best house in the parish . . . grounds equal to a park', and eighty acres of glebe. Egerton accurately summarized the rest of his argument in the diary, though not the shrewd thrust that he was certain that Bolton, 'as a business man got every farthing' possible from his investments. *Sussex Agricultural Express*, 22 Mar. 1884.

9. Thomas, twenty-six, and Elizabeth, twenty, were unable to sign their names; nor was Stephen Saunter, but the other witness Lizzie Rowley had a brave stab at signing her's. ESCRO. Par.284/1/3/3.

10. Harry Eastwood worked for William Farley of the Bell; Eastwood was last seen late on Sun. 31 Mar. making his way to the 'Rectory barn' where he 'used occasionally to sleep'. 'There were no marks of a struggle, and in the deceased's pockets were found three eggs which were not even crushed'. The body was discovered the next morning by a lad, Frank Davis, sent to fetch a horse. The jury returned an accidental death verdict as 'owing to the [exceptional] dark he must have stumbled into the pond'. *Sussex Agricultural Express*, 8 Apr. 1884.

11. However, Thomas Eastwood had been in trouble in his earlier days; at the age of twelve he had served two weeks in Battle House of Correction for breaking his contract as a carter's mate, in 1860 had pleaded guilty to the theft of underwood, and in 1868 was fined – with three others – for an assault. Henry Eastwood had been charged, but acquitted on charges of passing counterfeit money (1841), theft (1843) and rape (1849). He served a three-month sentence for opportunistically filching a flitch of bacon being smoked up the bar-room chimney of the Admiral Vernon in 1855, and was fined under the game laws in 1852, 1857 and 1869. Returns of summary convictions, and depositions re. theft cases (1843 and 1855), ESCRO. QR/E875; 890; 907; 965; 985; 999; 1042–3. *Brighton Gazette*, 23 Feb. 1843, 2 Aug. 1849, 1 Apl. 1852, 4 Jan. 1855, 4 June 1857 and 5 July 1860.

12.   The legislation extended the vote to all male householders in county constituencies, thus effectively putting the rural working class on a equal footing with
their borough counterparts. One possible cause of the apparent lack of interest
derived from the fact that relatively few could be expected to vote Conservative, and
were unprepared to talk about their Liberal preferences, notably with the solidly
Tory Egerton.
13.   Bodichon, the sister of the Arctic explorer Benjamin Leigh Smith, lived at
Scaland's in Robertsbridge, and is best known for her support of Girton College.
Sussex Agricultural Express, 9 June 1883.
14.   '. . . . There is no pedantry, theological or social. . . . From first to last it is
full of genuine humour; all the better in some cases, perhaps, because it is
unconscious'. One doubts the latter suggestion, but the anonymous reviewer was
impressed by the 'pathetic document' detailing the budget supplied by John Isted's
wife, and attributed 'a most retentive memory' to Egerton; in fact, much of *Sussex
Folk*'s contents were entered in the diaries across the years. *Notes and Queries*, 6th ser.
IX, (28 June 1884), p. 518.
15.   The nineteenth-century horse market was the literal antecedent to its
twentieth-century successor, that in used cars. The horse trade embraced professional full and part-time dealers, including Farley, occasional speculators, swindlers
(and Levi Luck was no saint), and individuals who bought and sold their own
mounts. In addition there were significant numbers of stolen animals on the market.
Farley and Luck were charged with fraudulently obtaining a pony, valued at £10,
from one Frederick Tester on 30 May. Both sides employed lawyers at the
committal hearing on 10 June at Mark Cross Petty Sessions, the report of which,
was brief, but typified such insights into the market. 'The alleged transaction took
place at the fair at Mountfield, when a worthless animal was exchanged between
defendants and prosecutor'.
   At the Assizes, the judge rather unusually more or less directed the Grand Jury to
find that there was a case to answer, but the defendants never reached the dock, as
the prosecution dropped the charge. It is significant that local efforts respecting
character witnesses were made only for Farley, the son of the landlord at the Bell,
and not the rougish Luck. *Sussex Agricultural Express*, 14 June and 5 July 1884.
16.   Peter Beaney's wife left him in 1829 for another man, and they emigrated to the
USA, leaving Peter with two sons; 'Soon after', Peter abandoned his boys, 'and was
not heard of for some time', during which period the mother arranged for the
children to join her in the States. Peter returned to Burwash, and on learning of his
wife's death in 1834, he remarried, and had three more boys by 1838, 'with the
prospect of a large family'. However, his sons by his first marriage were 'prospering',
and invited their father to join them. His emigration costs were met from Poor Law
funds. Vestry case for assisted emigration, 1838, PRO. MH.12/13140.
17.   Since son Benjamin's incarceration following his killing of his grandmother,
(see above, p. 151 and note 20, another son, Thomas, had also been declared insane
and hospitalized in the county asylum. Father Benjamin's maintenance payments
were now in serious arrears, and having failed in two attempts to have Thomas
released to reduce financial obligations, he was now forced to pay off the debt by
instalments. Board of Guardian minutes, 15 May, 12 and 26 June, 10 and 24 July
1884, ESCRO. G10/1a/17.
18.   As this matter was not referred to the Board of Guardians, it would appear that
Egerton's lobbying of Guardian Whatman resulted in overturning Relieving Officer
Taylor's decision.

19. The still buoyant Kent and Sussex Labourers' Union had campaigned by holding over a thousand local meetings, and sent numerous petitions to parliament supporting Gladstone's Liberal government's Franchise Bill, whose principal provision would enfranchise many farmworkers. The Union's annual rally for 1884, held in Rochester, was pre-occupied with the issue, notably the burgeoning opposition in the Lords, and the Tory leader Salisbury's claim that agricultural labourers were uninterested in the vote. In late May and early June, the Union's General Secretary, Alfred Simmons 'arranged with several of the most powerful political and trade organizations in London' to hold a massive pro-Franchise Bill rally in the capital, eventually held on 21 July after the Lords rejected the Bill.

Although nearly one thousand 'societies, clubs and associations' took part in the procession, it was led from the Embankment to Hyde Park by the Kent and Sussex contingent, symbolizing the largest sector of workers to benefit from the franchise. Special trains were laid on, and more than five thousand farmworkers, among them the Burwash contingent, led the march. Over one hundred branch representatives carried 'the new white and blue branch banners', and these '"long blue lines" . . . and their hop-poles' were effective. Among 'the hundreds of thousands of London working men who lined the streets . . . enthusiasm knew no bounds. They grasped the hands of the labourers as they marched along . . . shouted and cheered "Bravo, Kent", "Bravo, Sussex", "Bravo, hop-poles"'. Contingents of farmworkers from other Home Counties, and representatives from regions across the country, were also present, and Simmons insisted that his fellow leader, Joseph Arch of the depleted National Union, was also given an opportunity to speak. Estimates of the numbers eventually rallied in Hyde Park ranged from a half to one million. In some eyes the demonstration 'will be remembered as the battle of the Peers and Peasants'.

Salisbury's dismissive assertion, was echoed by local Tories. Farmer Heater of Robertsbridge typically claimed, 'that the labourers who went from that parish. . . . did not know what they went for', slightly more assertive than Egerton's reserved tone in this diary entry. *Kent and Sussex Times*, 24 May, 7 and 28 June, 5, 12, 19 and 26 (in which extensive reports from the *Daily Chronicle* and *The Echo* were reprinted) July, 2, 16 and 23 Aug. 1884.

20. Mundella was radical MP for Sheffield constituencies, 1868–95, a leading figure in the passage of the 1870 Education Act, and currently vice-president of the Privy Council Committee on Education; he soon piloted the 1885 Compulsory Education Act.

21. It was anything but favourable; entitled 'A Book of Rustics', it claimed that several of the 'best stories . . . illustrate rather the stupidity than the wit of the genuine rustic', while sarcastically observing that 'taken fresh from the lips of the unenfranchised [*sic*] county householder himself' – or – 'that little studied member of the British fauna, Hodge'. *Pall Mall Gazette*, 21 July 1884.

22. Earlier, a campaign had been launched against absentees because 'many children are sent out by their parents to gather primroses to be sent to the London markets, and brings in a goodly sum for several weeks, and a great help to those with large families'. Labourer John Vigor had been fined sixpence with 4/6 costs, for not ensuring John, eleven, and ten-year-old Lily's attendance, in Aug. 1883, though there is no record that Inspector Clarke implemented his threat this year. *Sussex Agricultural Express*, 1 Apl. 1884. ESCRO. QR/E1103.

23. For Atherton see above, 24 Mar. 1870, p. 97, and ch. 6 note 7.

24. The Hurst Green Bench made increasing use of premises adjoining the Burwash Police Station to hold the divisional Petty Sessions and on occasions

magistrates attended to grant bail to prisoners. Egerton, however, appears to have been joking with justice Carter.

25. Although renowned for 'quality' and 'abundance', the current 'pollutions . . . were very serious', and Egerton seized on the issue to exhort the owners – not the tenants – of adjacent cottages supplied from this source, to finance the installation of a proper pump. *Parish Notes*, Aug. 1884.

26. Deprecatory because, like the *Pall Mall Gazette*, it seized on the chance to ridicule the enfranchisement of farmworkers, like many of Egerton's characters, who had 'waited for years without betraying the smallest anxiety to possess . . . the franchise'. It also asserted that 'the humour is frequently extremely difficult to discover'. *Morning Post*, 29 Aug. 1884.

27. Aged twenty-one; the register records the 12.30a.m. burial. ESCRO. Par.284/1/5/3. Gorringe's brothers, James and Frederick, respectively thirteen and nine, also contracted smallpox, and were transferred immediately to the isolation ward in the workhouse infirmary, where their lives were reputedly saved through treatment.

28. For Mrs Emma Pagden, see above, 28–9 June 1876, p. 179. The real cause for her retirement was the end of her daughter Frances' supportive role, on the eve of the latter's marriage to James Methven, head gardener at Southover Hall. *Parish Notes*, Nov. 1884.

29. Curiously, the burial register records her as a niece of Thomas Abel Evans (died 1846), and that her corpse was brought from Trinity Square, Southwark, where she died. These contrary statements respecting her lineage renders impossible the identification of the drunken relative. ESCRO. Par.284/1/5/3.

30. Ernest Wells took the notorious Wheel over from Stephen Barden in Sept. Interestingly, at the Brewster Petty Sessions on 29 Aug. Superintendent Jenner had informed the Bench, that over the past year there had been no complaints against licencees and only nine prosecutions for drunkenness, deriving from, he said, the 'much less inclination among the labouring classes to visit public houses owing to the various temperance movements'. None other than the crusty Gilbert-Cooper acknowledged that the formation of a branch of the Blue Ribbon Army had reduced drunkenness in St Philips. *Sussex Agricultural Express*, 2 and 30 Sept. 1884. *Parish Notes*, July 1884.

31. Knowles came across from Tunbridge Wells to Ticehurst and spun a totally spurious tale to Mrs Ann Field about her lad – also working at the spa – sacked for 'taking drink', and now needing his fare home. Mrs Field gave Knowles three shillings for her boy and an equal sum to the messenger, 'to go back by the afternoon omnibus'. Knowles was sent for trial at the Quarter Sessions, where in Jan. he received a six-month hard-labour term, the chairman observing that since 'out on bail', Knowles 'had been frequently obtaining money in the same way'. *Eastbourne Express*, 4 Nov. 1884. *Sussex Agricultural Express*, 4 Jan. 1885.

32. A reference to Britain's continued tortuous North African involvement, and in particular to Gladstone's cabinet's delay in sending an expeditionary force to extricate General Gordon, cut off in Khartoum; the force began fighting its way up the Nile between Oct. and Dec. 'while all England counted its daily steps'. Gordon was killed in the siege, three days before the relief troops arrived in Jan. 1885, and precipitated perhaps the lowest moment in Gladstone's second ministry. The quote is from R.C.K. Ensor, *England 1870–1914*, (Oxford, 1963 edition), p. 82.

33. Only the eldest Egerton child Helen Mary (born 7 July 1878), and John, were baptized at Burwash. ESCRO. Par.284/1/2/4.

34.   Egerton again complains that retail prices for meat had not fallen commensurately with the prices commanded by livestock.

35.   Combs' alcoholism by now had turned him into a social reject, though his wife – Louisa – whom he married in June 1857, was a daughter of lawyer James Philcox, and this guaranteed that she remained part of Egerton's 'parochial aristocracy'. Her husband continued to practise until the mid-1880s, but in 1887 was listed as a gentleman instead of surgeon in the *Post Office Directory*.

1885

1 Jan. Brought in ye new year by reading over my ordination vows. It is humiliating reading. I prayed God earnestly for strength to do better for the coming year. He has been very merciful to me. O may it please Him to continue His mercy & to spare me my dear dear wife [who had recurrent fever, developed an abscess, and had been periodically bed-ridden since the birth of the last child].

3 Jan. Marriage of Henry James Budd 19 & Ann Alice Eastup 21, at 9 a.m. I had to give ye fee as ye girl pleaded abject poverty on ye part of both & I believe truly. She said she had got a place at Maidstone or near it. . . . Ch[arles Breach, a London-based doctor, Nellie's relative, whom she periodically consulted] told me a terrible story of a judge who I knew died suddenly some time ago on circuit, but I did not know that he was found dead of heart disease in a common brothel. . . .

9 Jan. . . . On ye road today by Mr. Philcox's I tried to compose a violent strife between a party of drunken tramps. Tramp humanity is of a low type certainly.

13 Jan. . . . C. on Master Budd & Mrs Jenner. His S. Charles No. 1843 Training Ship St. Vincent Portsmouth did not c. on me at Xmas time as both his father & Mrs Jenner asserted; he did not wish me to think that he came "cadging". The first time that I have had this honourable reason given for a boy's not coming to see me! . . .

14 Jan. . . . I looked at ye Times. One really loses a great deal by not seeing it. . . .

16 Jan. Sch. When will children understand that guiltless is not guilty. I instance shameless – nameless – but it will all have to be explained again next week. . . .

19 Jan. . . . J[ames] B[raban] & G[eorge] L[avender, the master-butcher]! in custody for stealing & ye latter for receiving some geese belonging to Mr. Gillham. If ye receiver is convicted he ought to get double punishment; still it is very sad to see one of our tradesmen in ye hands of ye police.[1] I c. on Mrs Langridge about her relief. She is not having fair play.

28 Jan. . . . In ye aft. c. on ye various members of ye Sing. Cl. to remind them of ye supper tomorrow. It is hard on me; nobody had taken ye trouble to ask H.Pagden as on Sunday night I begged them to do. . . . Sing. w. men 17, 4 B: we really got on.

29 Jan. . . . Ye Singers c. at 7. 13 & myself. A really pl: party. Good dinner; we adj[ourned] to ye housekeepers room, & there sat talking, drinking 4 bott. of wine among 13, or about 3 glasses apiece & singing. J.B. Blunden. Cottage by the sea & Good news from Home. H. Pagden & P. Nevill & self A thousand a year & When ye heart is young (Boucher) & "ye jolly miller" . . . Away at 11.20. I believe that ye evg. was enjoyed. . . .

31 Jan. Wedding at 11. All tainted, but what is one to do. Ye bride & bridegroom repented as father & mother before marr: Groomsman's child born almost immediately after marr: bridesmaid had illeg. child. Certainly ye Serv: seems not to have been constructed for such, but there is no other.[2] . . . C. on Mrs White, in bed again. She certainly a superior woman, curiously in that she speaks of matters & of them in terms wh. indicate out of the way thought & reading. . . . In evg. a Mr. Osterbury (?) a highly intelligent & well educated mechanic working at Southover c. at 8.45 PM to see if I cd. do anything towards obtaining mitigation of sentence for Lavender. I shewed him the impossibility of my believing him innocent.

5 Feb. . . . C. on Lizzie Isted, [who had been seriously ill for some weeks] too ill to see me. C. at poor Harry Pagdens; had been badly shot in both legs out rabbiting by a man of ye name of Eaton. In much pain. Yesterday a man at Brightling had his face so badly shot that he was taken to London at once. Yesterday a man from ye Comm. broke his leg wrestling at ye Bell: roughish times altogether.[3] C. on W. Ellis's. An objectionable song (Comic) sung last night at ye entertainment, as an encore, by a mechanic from Southover. Wretched things ye Music Hall Comic Songs. I must have protested hard had I been there. Annie Ellis ye Shoemakers d. sang w. much applause I believe; dangerous accomplishment in her rank of life I fear. . . .

9 Feb. . . . Thos. Eastwood, Carpenter, formerly a young lad apprenticed in Burwash & a worthy young fellow, a blue ribboner, c. to say good bye on his way to Brisbane, Queensland, Australia. He ought to do well. I recommend him to God in prayer. After d. to St. Philips school. . . . Miss Press consulted me about Pupil Teachers. . . . my clear opinion that no teacher ought to be requested to punish children in school for things done amiss out in the road or street after they have left the school. I interview Mr. Morrison . . . came in & soon began to advance wonderful doctrines about land & taxation. . . .

12 Feb. . . . After lunch at 12 w. to Totingworth. Saw Mr. Pirie, his school will not be opened till after the hopping holidays, so we must wait at present. He shewed me all over his new house in course of building. His brick yard, hothouses, farm buildings, roads, quarry etc. all carried on on a scale indicating a command of large capital. . . .[4]

18 Feb. . . . Sch. report, wretched, Grant £110-4-0 inst. of £145 last year. Wrote to Anset. Left ye letter w. Philcox for approval. . . .[5]

19 Feb. . . . C. & P. w. Lizzie Isted. Ye mother gave me a sad acc[ount] of prevalent immorality, chiefly of women drinking. I know it is horrible, ye more sad because I can do as far as I know absolutely nothing. . . . Sing. w. boys at Ch. & then w. 4 altos & 1 T[enor]. . . . A Shoe Club (S.Ellis's) dinner going on wh. took my men.[6]

26 Feb. . . . Got change at Noakes. Even Simmons Noakes studying a map of Egypt ye clearest testimony to ye interest created by ye war I have yet found.

27 Feb. . . . C. on old widow Dann (1/6). A lonely life certainly & sometime ago her clock stopped & she missed it terribly "because a clock is such company". . . .

Sun. 1 Mar. . . . Pr[actised] w. Choir aft. Serv. Had to suspend W. Blackford for ye evg. for bad behaviour.

3 Mar. . . . Got a special rat-trap from London to try & circumvent a wary old rat wh. is very troublesome. . . .

7 Mar. . . . C. on Alfred Bowmer & signed his pension paper; he is bad; spoke seriously to him. His hope seems to be in the fact that he never tried to hurt anybody. . . . W. with Mr. John Fuller ex[amine]d ye old chapel, & in the Evg. wrote to a Mr. Beeching, a banker at T[unbridge] Wells whose father marr. a d. of ye Mr. Thos. Blundell who died May 31 1813, & who acc. to a tablet in ye chapel purchased & presented ye chapel to ye congr: of Protestant "Desenters" [sic] of ye Ind: denom[ination] therein assembling.[7] I wrote to Mr. B. to ask about ye ownership now that ye chapel is disused, & all ye trustees dead. . . .

9 Mar. Gussey a propos of Alfred Holland's marriage: during rehearsal "Wilt thou have this Dutch doll for they husband?". . . . Gussey "Are they called 'groom's men' because they rub the bridegroom down?".

11 Mar. . . . C. on Mrs Hook; d. been primrosing, 6d a doz. bunches given. Sad enemy to schooling.[8] C. on Mrs Maskell, new comer next door, tidy young wife. C. on Mrs Crouch, husb: says Sundays is just the day when a [game]keeper is obliged to be especially on ye alert. "If every body else wd. go to church he cd".

Tues. 17 Mar. . . . C. on Sergt. Buss, not up, met him at 12 & reported 4 boys for annoying Mrs Blake; two boys laid down in the dark for her to tumble over them. The boys were no longer school boys. . . .

20 Mar. . . . C. on JP. & on Mrs Barton of the Tot about her child going primrosing in school time. She pleaded that it wasn't for no money, but only for flowers to send to friends at Hastings. . . .

21 Mar. . . . C. on Harmer. Chrn. all ill, drains stopped up, well I fear polluted. A Jarvis' cottage. . . .

25 Mar. . . . C. on Mr. J. Fuller. He at his wits end to think of a 2d guardian. Messrs. Whatman & R. Fuller resign. Mr. George A. Hyland will serve, but who will be ye 2d. . . .

28 Mar. In aft. c. on Mr. W. Ellis; he told me that Mr. Whatman had consented to serve again as Guardian. I am very glad. . . . C. & P. w. Lizzie Isted (1/6) very ill. C. on old Mrs Hyles at Ashlands. Hard to introduce any subject non-secular. . . .

29 Mar. . . . Dear N. had her clothes on except her outer garmets for ye first time since Sept. 9. God be thanked. Miss Noakes lent her a walking stick like ye ones w. wh. witches are always pictured. N. w[alks] much more easily w. it, but ye children are amused. . . .

2 Apl. "A huge" rat ct. at last. . . .

6 Apl. . . . Met young John Isted, so respectable, now a general assistant in a grocer's shop [elsewhere; home for Easter holidays]. He has been most plucky in his determination to raise himself. Stephen Burgess also in ye vill. nice young fellow. . . . Vestry meeting at 7. Appointed committee to go on w. Willingford bridge w. all speed. Harry Jarvis told me he had to dismiss summarily a young pupil [Sunday school teacher] who was on a months trial [in Jarvis' employ]. He having been found in company of one of our wretchedly immoral girls, & having taken up w. one of our shakiest young fellows as a companion. Mrs Jesse Braban c. in evg. for an out p[atient's] ticket for her child. I never remember such a rush for out p. tickets [about which he recorded no detail]. . . .

9 Apl. W. up to St. Philip's to wedding of Alfred Holland youngest son of Honble. Mrs F. Holland of Oakham, & Edith Gilbert-Cooper d. of Revd. W.W. Gilbert [Cooper], Vicar of St Philip's; very pretty wedding indeed. Church full of people. Ye congr. included ye school children, very remarkably quiet & reverrent. I signed ye register. Old Mrs Fairway, aged 90 last Decr. (?) & a baby in its mothers arms were close to me, so that all ages were represented. Dr. Summerhayes played ye organ very well, &

played out ye Wedd. March from ye music to Mids: Night's dream Mendelson. I to ye breakfast at ye Vic[arage]. I had to propose health of bride & bridegroom wh. I did w. good conscience as they are both much respected in ye parish. A very cheery wedding.

11 Apl. Aft. d. c. on Rd Head at Mrs Hendsden. C. on Mrs G. Maskell next door. Owing to a scarcity of cottages, married d. & child & husb. quartering there. Interv. Mr. Kemp & son hard at work in ye hop-garden. Poor man: he has hard work to live.

Sun. 12 Apl. . . . I had to speak to some men, London mechanics I think, who were lolling about on the tombstones smoking as we came out of church. I put it to them whether I was asking any thing unreasonable in asking them to chose some other place to smoke in. They were civil as not to answer, & I think they moved.

13 Apl. Set to work w. account of ye wedding. In aft. took it up to ye Vicarage & read it to Mr. Cooper who approved. . . .[9]

15 Apl. . . . Letter from John Sawyers Corp. 1st R[oya]l Sussex Regt. thanking me for Sussex Folk recd. at either Sakdue Wells or Karti. C. on Harry Noakes to enquire about an old Clocksmith Dadswell by name. Mr. G.A.Hyland c. me in to shew me 2 candelabras & a silver teapot presented to his wife & himself by his associates in ye G.P.O. wh. he has just quitted after 40 years service. Very handsome, & must be very gratifying to him.

16 Apl. . . . At noon c. on JP & looked at an old clock by Thomas Dadswell Burwash to see if there was any date, as a Mr. B.C. Scammell, London & County Bank Lewes who is looking up Sussex Horologists has written to me to enquire. No date visible.

17 Apl. . . . C. on Mrs Schroeter, & had a cup of tea. She complains as do other people that trained nurses have their drawbacks. They are members of a profession & it is absolutely unprofessional to put their hand to anything not immediately connected with their profession. This one has been in waiting a fortnight, & will of course not do anything whatever till the baby arrives. . . . C. on George Lavender. Came out of prison yest. I at once shook hands, & told him that I wished him well, but that I devoutly hoped that he wd. become a teetotaller & earnestly seek God's help to continue so. I am not at all sure how it will be. I was quite touched by his wife's thanks for kindness.

18 Apl. Wrote sermon. I dont know why I have not written more lately than I have done, but writing is necessary. Too much extempore is I am sure not good.

21 Apl. Sch. Had to hand over ye names of some extra careless readers to ye tender mercies of Mr. Anset [just returning after protracted illness]. C. on Mr. Gibbs, very kindly. Mrs A. Payne there, wondered why her children were not strong. I didn't like to suggest that the children of 1st cousins seldom are strong. . . . C. on Mrs T. Pennells (2/6). Long t. w. husb. out of work even at this time of year. . . .

23 Apl. Funeral at 3. Illeg. ch. of [Mary Ann] Pennells & Wm. Holmes. Parents as bold as brass. . . .

[28 Apl. to 5 May in Oxford, returning on 9 May via Essex for funeral of Uncle Charles, aged 87.]

11 May. . . . C. on Mrs Isted. Lizzie worse. Met poor H. Dann Senr. has been in the Univ. Coll. Hosp. where he was plainly told that he is hopelessly ill of cancer in ye cheek or side of his face, poor fellow, he had long feared it. . . .

12 May. Fair day; up to ye vill: good deal of stock changed hands at low prices. . . .

15 May. . . . Wrote & posted P.N. Hard work word spinning with no materials. . . .

22 May. . . . C. on Mrs W. I[sted] (2/6). She gave me a sad account of several instances of female depravity in ye vill. It troubles me much & ye more because I feel absolutely helpless. C. on Mrs J. Isted; poor Lizzie [just eighteen] died either last night or this morg: a sad sufferer.

Sun. 24 May. . . . Sch. Had to send home Js. Glaskeen. His refusal without any cause to sing ye hymn too gross to be overlooked. I c. on his father & mother. They had nothing to say in ye boy's defence. He has I am sure long been pulling agst. me & in ye singing. Too bad of him & I am sure he cannot allege that I have done anything else than my best for him for years. . . .

25 May. . . . Buried poor Lizzie Isted. C. on George Watson (2/6); poor chap & his wife have gone hungry I fear, but they are a very reticent couple, & one over looks them I fear. . . .

26 May. . . . D. w. ye old Sch. Club at ye Bear. 37 old cripples in ye Club, but they have managed to put by £100 in 4 years. I sang "A thousand a year" & "When the heart is young". Tried to elicit any ideas the men might have about votes, but with the enc[ouragement] of "A Cheap Loaf" I utterly failed.[10] . . . Ye Etchm. Brass band (celebrated!) eng[aged] at Club at 5.45. Ye Burw. brass band gone ye way of all such instit[utions] when at public houses, & has collapsed. . . .

27 May. Dear Gussey's birthday (9th). She is a dear good child, & very helpful to her mother. Old John Chandler c. about relief. It wd. be a shame to drive him into ye workhouse. . . . Ambrose Pilbeam (2/6) c. for a character for ye Royal Engineers. I gladly gave him one & wished him well. I think he is doing wisely. . . .

28 May. Sch. but too late to take a class, as Mr. Hyland hindered me on Guardian business. C. on Mrs Bourner: her husb. (Alfred) died this morning; had he lived till Sunday night [31st] at 12 PM he wd. have been entitled to £8:2:0 a quarter's pension. To ye Club at ye Common. . . . C. on Ernest Wells at ye "Wheel" he better & I w. w. him to Hallaways [licensee of the Railway Inn]. . . . Ye Club much as usual. T. Fielder & myself led as usual a bout of questions & answers. I was lucky & fixed him, much to ye amusement of ye club, to whom he is rather a bore. I sang "A thousand a year" & "When the heart is young". . . . C. on J. Hyland, & w. him a farming walk. His crops promise beautifully. . . .

29 May. Sch. C. on Mr. Gibbs. Pl. chat. He much at a loss of ye report of ye Commission on "Housing ye poor". I feel almost in despair on ye subj:. . . .[11]

30 May. Not feeling very brisk. Took exercise for nearly 2 hours in ye drive. Long t. w. Frank Russell about affairs of ye nation. An old John Fairway said many years ago to Mrs Gilbert one day in the hop garden "There was a time when I hadn't got a rag to my back, & now I'm all rags": one of our old incorrigibles. . . .

31 May. Trinity Sunday. . . . Every member of ye choir at Ch. . . . & we did Boyce in A w. ye organ. . . .

2 June. . . . In aft. I went to call on Master Mallin of Brooks Marle about the burial of his unbaptized child. I met him in the field & agreed that we wd. go straight to the grave, as the child has never been brought into the visible Church at all, & as therefore some difference ought to be made. The man was very civil. Met Mr. Js. Noakes & Mr. G. Taylor. Mr. J.N. said that Master Edwards bailiff at Shoyswell has declared that he has sown 16 acres of oats himself in a day: this at 7½ bushels per acre wd. mean scattering 120 bushels of seed, & allowing a weight of 38 lbs per bushel, this wd. mean 4560 lbs or two tons & 8 cwts of seed! If the man's statement is true, the days work a very good one. A man of the name of Hook who used to be on Holton Hill is also reported to have mowed 9 acres of oats in a day, mowing round & round like a mowing machine, & never going twice over the same ground & having men to sharpen his scythes for him, so that he need not stop. . . . if true it was also a remarkable piece of work. . . . Met T.C. I said I was sorry Tom to see you drunk yesterday. Well sir he said "it wasn't what I bought, but my sons happened to be along w. some loads of faggots

& they had their 'lowances,[12] so they gave me some drink, & I b'aint used to it & it got over me, but it did me quite a lot of good". Oh Tom I said you musn't say so. "Well Sir", he replied, "it worked me uppards & downwards at such a rate that it was better than goin' to any doctor, & that shows I wasn't used to it". . . .

3 June. . . . Suggested by J B Noakes steps to be taken about ye old chapel now in ruins. C. to see if Elizabeth Eastwood was staying w. Mrs Burgess at ye Tot. Lond[on] Sch. Board wants her & ye girl out of there; her mother wife of Jack Eastwood late of B. now in Hackney has 8 chrn. eldest 16 & 5 eldest girls. This one I dare say is at work, & said to be in ye country. . . .

4 June. Foresters Club w. two men on horseback & w. ye Etchingham band c. to ye Rect. at 1.20. To ye Club booth at 2.0. Fair number at dinner. I prop. health of ye Queen & rest of R.F. & Prosperity to ye Court Hearts of Oak. C. away a little before 5. Ye band pl. For he's a jolly good fellow as I left, set me wondering what popularity of that sort is worth; not much I fear as a trifle wd. turn the feeling the other way. . . .

5 June. . . . C. on Mr. Fielden to ask where ye enclosures were wh. he said I had made. He was very cross w. me at first wouldn't shake hands, acc[used] me of acting maliciously, wh. however I think he half retracted, & altogether very contrary. Wouldn't tell me anything about ye enclos: so I am honestly ignorant what he means. He calmed down at last & shook hands. He seems utterly incapable to understand that I have any right to question his enclosure of our village green. . . . then to ye School Club. Admitting new members, some of the very drinkingest members of our community admitted bec. they were never known to have nothin' the matter wi'em. I don't know what is to be done. . . .

10 June. . . . I c. on Mr. J. Fuller to ask whether it wd. in his opinion be agst. the feeling of the parish if I tried on my own account the question of legality of the inclosure.[13] He thought certainly not.

11 June. . . . C. & R. w. old Mrs Dann (2/6). Poor lonely life. Her canary & her clock being her only society, save Master Packham ye half wit who comes up occasionally & worries her by his silly chatter. . . .

13 June. . . . Had a t. w. J. Vidler who is not unjustifiably aggrieved by his employer's not allowing him after 6½ years' service, even a month's holiday to recover his health. . . .

15 June. . . . Curious run upon Out patients. . . .

17 June. . . . C. aft. d. on Mr. Gibbs; he endorses my action re. enclos:. . . . I to ye Weald. . . . Ye chapel anniversary at ye weald . . . a largish number of ye cause, & had much t. They begged me to join them at tea. I declined plainly on ye ground of ecclesiastical discipline, not on ye ground of lack of brotherly love. Mr John Hyland told me that old "Donkey" Collins used to say that "he never knowed but one good Russell, & he was hung for murdering a man" . . .[14]

26 June. . . . From ye Pagden's garden watched mowers in ye Chesnut meadow, & wondered what ye constitutions of some men must be, who can drink lie about indelecti, & yet work hard for years. . . .

28 June. . . . Ambrose Pilbeam here for Queens Coron. holiday. His new R. Engineer uniform splendiferous. He tells me that he maintains his teetotalism, if this is so he will do. C. on Alfred B came out of prison yesterday. I shook hands, as I believe that his crime was really no worse than the result of an ordinary drunken bout. Spoke very seriously about Sundays & teetotalism. Poor fellow, the drink is his ruin. . . .[15]

30 June. Old Master Copper . . . throwed his scales & weights into the water, when the inspector was coming, but they were so light, they wouldn't sink.

1 July. To Ellen's garden party. Mr. J. Fuller & myself were sitting on a bench chatting; poor J. B[arrow] came up from ye other side of ye lawn, spoke to & shook hands w. Mr. Fuller, but quite ignored me. I put out my hand & asked him to shake hands; he angrily refused & began to open ye old questions. Poor man if he cd. but forgive he would be much happier I am sure. . . .

2 July. . . . C. on Mr. J. Fuller & consulted him about a further endeavour on my part to set things right with Mr. Barrow. I determined to leave myself unreservedly in the hands of Mr. J. Fuller, Mr. W.J. Whatman, Mr. Gillham, & Mr. Jas. Noakes, & I wrote an identical note to each of them asking them to act as mediators. . . .

4 July. . . . In aft. took my swath as usual in ye field near the west gate; got on very comfortably. George Brook (1/-) furnished my scythe. . . .

6 July. . . . A wall being built enclosing a bit of ground between ye Admiral & Manwaring's ye result I believe of a disagreement between Hawkins & Manwaring. It is truly sad.

7 July. . . . C. on Mr. Gibbs. He let me have the Times of last Friday [3rd] w. ye report of a case "Langley-appellant Cherton-Respondent" in wh. L.C.J. Coleridge gives judgement singularly analagous to our view of Mr. F's encroachment. Uncle N. had sent me the cutting wh. I lent to Mr. Js Noakes . . .[16]

9 July. I w. over to Scalands gate. . . . C. on Mrs Whitfield Pennells, so rejoiced at her husb: living up there away from ye publics. . . .

10 July. . . . C. on B.P. Fuller: he tells me that the new act will raise the number of Burwash voters from about 130 to 500! H.Jarvis in ye shop detailed his experiences yesterday of having two teeth out under gas. Never no more for him. . . . Long t. w. George Braban manager of Mr. Seamen's fish ship "The Mermaid" in Lewes . . . has got on well. . . .

14 July. . . . Bastile destr[oyed] in 1789 & Bodle Holmes now alive in Heathfield was then 9 years old!

15 July. . . . Sent for to see a poor man who I fear is dying, Th. Kemp (2/6) at ye Rocks. Has been a R.N. seaman. Pens[ione]d. C. from Yarmouth to see broth: Jesse Kemp & others; taken ill on Sunday [12th] I think. I gave 5/- to Mrs. J.K. for ye poor wife trav[elling] exp. from Yarmouth. . . .

16 July. . . . C. on G. Blackford (1/6) blind & paralytic at David Bs at Southover. Intell[igent] man, tho' a pauper in Clerkenwell Workhouse. "He thought Mr. Fleming wd. have made Dean of Westminster when Dean Stanley dies"![17]

21 July. . . . I c. on Mrs Jesse Kemp, ye poor man's widow . . . her late husb. [whom Egerton buried on 23rd] 25 years in navy & coastguard two years ago invalid[ed] from C. Gd. good cond[uct] medal. . . .

24 July. . . . Much excitement in ye vill. over ye sale of Mr. Coney's property where Sissy Taylor lives 10a 1r 22p. Mr. Fielden ran it up to £3000! & Mr. Schroeter then bought it for £3050-0-0 + £23-10-0 timber! I met Mr. & Mrs Schr. in ye street returning. He very pleased w. his victory, & I must say I am delighted. The price is of course beyond all reason, but he will do the vill: more good than Mr. F. cd. have done. I c. aft. dinn: to say good bye to poor Charlotte (5/-). She returns home today. We lent her the air bed. She was a truly faithful servant to us, & I cannot forget it. Mr. Gillham has bought Biggs' [Farm] where they live for £2500 & timber £101-0-0. 88A 1R 23P. He must have done about right.[18]

29 July. . . . Bought sweets & made ye final preparations. Children came at 2.40 just as I got back from ye funeral of old George Dawes ye Bl. smith. About 135, all S. Sch. Chrn, ye people later; large number, I dare say 200. Several remarked that there seemed to be a greater sense of unity in the party than usual. What a comfort that it is so. . . . Thanked ye people for their sympathy during dear N's long illness. Thanked ye S. Sch. teachers. . . .

1 Aug. . . . Aft. d. I c. on H. Jarvis; better. He lent me a copy of ye new Voters list; a real reductio & absurdum of ye theory of representation. . . .

3 Aug. . . . Took Henry Jarvis ye new list of voters wh. I had corrected for him. 405 on ye lists & 1 claim! Some of ye names make the extension of ye franchise a mockery in their case. . . .

11 Aug. Aft. d. c. on Mrs Essey at ye cott. below ye old chapel. Her father there, a Devonshire man complains sadly of ye "uncouthness" of our Burwash natives. There must I fear be something in it. C. on Mr. & Mrs Whatman & had tea. . . . I was greatly distressed by ye troubled state of Mr. W's mind over farming prospects. I tried to speak seriously & to put ye duty of patience, trust on ye true grounds. Mr. W. thanked me & I think that our poor friend was relieved by ye talk. Times are critical, & the future of agriculture is very difficult to forecast. Back to ye sch. for singing, but nobody came so I had an hours private grind [on the organ]. . . .

14 Aug. . . . C. on Mrs H. Dann. Curious instance of the confidence with wh. people who feel that they have been unjustly accused of something, speak of getting justice in the world to come, as if there were no other matters than this particular one in wh. justice might not perhaps bring them in very guilty. C. on Mrs Edwards; she has her oven in ye kitchen, so that baking days make a great mess. . . .

15 Aug. . . . Burwash boys club pl. & beat Brighting boys club on ye gr. opp. ye Rect. We sent them out tea.

19 Aug. . . . C. on Mr. C. Coppard. H. Jarvis there, & we agreed about posting ye notices of ye Vestry meeting to take into consideration ye Enclosure of ye footpath. . . . Mr. Coppard's brother a miller at Mayfield is able to sell flour at 7d a gall[on] & can buy wheat at 30/- per q[uarte]r; what chance have farmers?

21 Aug. To ye school & wrote ye names of ye 27 prize children in their respective books. At 3 Mr. Pirie & myself went down to ye sch. Not many people there, still enough for encouragement. I gave some statistics. Sch. open 279 times from 5th Jan. to July 30. 4 chrn. att. 279, 27, incl. ye 4, 271 & upwards. Mr. Pirie made a nice address, nothing very striking, but sensible & business like. He gave away ye prizes. . . . C. on ye Evangelist ladies Misses Green, at Littlemore's; long t. & ended with prayer. Good women I do not doubt. . . .

Sat. 22 Aug. Ye good ladies c. to ask for ye Sch. room tomorr. evg. I gave them ye use of it, tho' I cd. clearly see that our agreement wd. be impossible except in a common desire to make people better Xtians. . . .

26 Aug. . . . C. on H. Jarvis & sat till ye meeting. Mr. Inderwick MP for Rye & cand. for Rye div[ision of East Sussex] spoke for an hour & a quarter claiming every political virtue on earth for Liberal princ[iples]. Good temper, & free from abuse, & quietly received. Dr. Summerhayes in ye chair. A Mr. Macer Wright spoke, a far more full bloodied Radicalism was his. Mr. Hoadly started ye subj: of Extraordinary Tithes, & a Mr.— said to have been in prison some years ago [endorsed '& truly so Decr. 1885'] for stealing at ye Hare Mere sale, came all ye way from Kent to rail at ordinary tithe. Mr. I. neatly shunted ye question w. some general platitudes. A certain number of labouring men there, but not a great number. One drunken voter outside caused interruption, but I got near him & was able to quiet him. Altogether a quiet & orderly meeting, but whether it made many converts I don't know, Over about 9.30.[19]

27 Aug. . . . Posted & otherwise delivered 26 letters of thanks to subscr. to Prize Fund. Old scholars, am[oun]t £2-2-6 plus 10/- from T. Jarrett & 5 from T [?]. . . . at 7.30 to vestry meeting at Ch. Adj. to Bell, about 12 there; they carried 2 Res[olu]tions one that the fence was an encroachment, & an obstruction to the public; the other that this being so the Surveyor on my agreeing to pay all Expenses, be instructed to take the necessary legal proceedings to have it removed. All perfectly amiable. No opposition whatever, tho' one or two did not vote.[20]

1 Sept. Not much shooting as far as I cd. hear. . . . C. on Mrs J. Isted. Sad story of immorality & trouble. I doubt whether there is much odds [difference] between town & country. C. & R. w. poor Mr. S. Watson (2/-), very suffering, but great humility, peace & comfort. I don't know why it is, but there is something inexpressibly more satisfactory to me in the way in wh. the piety of a humble minded Ch. person shows itself, than in the corresponding way of Dissenters. Poor H. Dann for inst: He forgets the days of the week but hopes "he may never forget 'the blood'". . . . In ye morg. Mr. G.A. Hyland c. asking me to take ye chair at ye Conserv[ative] meeting on ye 9th. As a clergyman I declined, as I always have done. I sent him up to Mr. J.H. Nicholl, he sent him to Mr. Forsyth . . . at Oakdown, ex MP for Marylebone, whom he secured.

2 Sept. . . . Mr. Dalton at ye Police off. committing a man for trial for a stupid burglary at H. Green; also a man remanded for stealing a coat. . . .

3 Sept. . . . In aft. I w. up to St. Philip's. . . . To ye Vicarage, quite a pleasant gathering. Mr. Forsyth, Author of a well-known Life of Cicero . . . a man whose conversation in these parts a godsend. . . . C. on John Hyland. Went up into ye Oast & saw ye hop pressing apparatus. James Fairway said "never no more treading for me". Several of Mr. H's gardens, a really beautiful sight, but ye price offered disheartening. . . . gave a traveller 6d said he was a plumber, a gas fitter by trade, w. from Brighton to day. I never knew so many travellers! C. on Mr. G.A. Hyland, & t. about ye meeting for Wed.

[7 to 12 Sept. on a visit to Cheshire.]

25 Sept. [Blacksmith] William Pilbeam snr. fined only 10/- for so disturb-[ing] ye congr. at ye Wheel West Ch[apel] that ye serv. was given up. Mr. Courthope said that if ye disturbance had been in a church, he wd. have had heavier punish[men]t. I own I can't understand it, as a known offender for drunkenness. . . .[21]

2 Oct. . . . conversed w. Mr. Pennells. I was much pleased w. his sentiments about giving a man a chance who had come out of prison.[22] . . . On return c. on Mr. G.A. Hyland re political meeting here. . . .

6 Oct. . . . Found letter from Mrs Goschen, enclosing one from Sir H. Ponsonby saying "The Queen will be much pleased to accept a copy of Sussex Folk & Sussex ways from Mr. Egerton". I wrote to Mrs Goschen. Sir H. Ponsonby, & to John Carrington [domiciled in London] about getting a copy of ye book bound. . . .

22 Oct. . . . at 2 o'clock Mr. Roberts c. & negotiated about ye encl. I renewed an offer of £20 but wd. not entertain any compromise as ye inclosure remaining. He left, but returned in about an hour w. a note from Mr. Fielden agr[eeing] to remove ye encl. for £25 & exp: already incurred. We adjourned to Mr. Philcox, who drew up an agreement wh. I signed, & gave to Mr. Roberts. Encl. to be removed by 27th. I hope ye agr. will stand bec: tho' I am advised that ye case must have gone agst. Mr. F., he wd. have put me to a lot of annoyance, & even if I had won a lot of expense. . . .

26 Oct. . . . Sent for to bear testimony to ch[aracter] of Henry Isted who is in custody for stealing chickens. I c. on his mother & shewed how I cd. do no good. He was convicted for being drunk & riotous [disorderly] in Ticehurst at the last [Petty Sessional] sitting at H. Green, & yet poor lad this I believe his first act of "dishonesty". His brother (2/-) & sister in great trouble. I am much grieved. A few years ago he was a Sunday Sch. Teacher, then went to a master who drank [George Lavender], & was himself convicted of receiving stolen goods, learnt bad habits, & gradually sank. I had done my best to keep him straight poor lad. . . .[23]

27 Oct. Ye enclosure in process of demolition, but Mr. Fielden has planted a tidy-sized tree on ye ground. I c. on him to say that this was not in accordance w. ye agreement. He somewhat rough in language, but nothing more. On coming outside I said that simply as a protest I must pull a twig off ye tree. I did so, whereupon he dealt me a savage kick, fortunately on ye most kickable part, so that it did not hurt. I believe that I took no notice, & that I went on talking to Kitty Weller who knew nothing about my agreement. However, on this point ye bystanders cd. testify better than I can. Anyhow Mr. Gillham who saw it said to me

"Well you've a better temper than I have". It is too bad Mr. F. to have planted ye tree as his doing so involves the whole question of right, wh. was my main contention. . . . My "Sussex Folk" came, bound in ye most lovely manner for ye Queen. I had suggested vellum, & gilt edges, & ye style suits capitally.

28 Oct. Up town. Fence, tree & all clear gone! I am thankful, & I only hope that ye question may not be raised again. . . . To Edmunds', Mr. J.B. Noakes had just been reading so I did not stop. . . . C. on Mr. Smith & told him he need not appear ar H.Green on Friday. . . .

29 Oct. . . . Did not go to ye Dioc[esan] Conference for fear of my contingences re enclosure. In aft. to St Philip's [Cooper on holiday]. John Hyland stopped me & told me of poor Hallaway's illness at ye Railway Tavern. I at once c., but he was unconscious. Had been ill nearly 5 wks. & I have never heard. . . .

30 Oct. Petty Sessions. I staid at home till they were over. . . . Our two poor lads got 3 months. Curious instance of what I believe to have been a sudden impulse of evil, as neither up to that moment had ever been suspected of dishonesty, tho' they were given alas to drink. H.I. had been quite sober for a fortnight, & only that evg. had given all his money exc. 2/- to his mother, & bought a new coat. When I got home Master Essery ye blacksmith had brought up his S. Samuel to sign papers for ye RN. Ye boy a nice bright lad. In ye evg. I c. & answ[ered] in pers[on] a note from Mrs W. Pilbeam complaining of something I had said to her boy in sch. Misinterpreted quite. . . .

3 Nov. . . . C. & sat w. Mr. & Mrs Smith at Sea view. A sad gloomy politician, everything going to ye dogs at once. Calvinists can hardly be cheerful. C. on Mr. Simes, good old man but poorly. . . . ye sad times have beaten this worthy old man & he said that he cd. not pay me [tithe] this year. . . . To Burwash by 7. Presided at an open political meeting at ye Bell. Room crammed, people very good humoured. A Mr. Harrison, a London mechanic Chief Conserv. . . . Mr. John Fuller ye Liberal opponent. I cd. gather nothing to ye effect produced. . . .[24]

4 Nov. . . . C. on Mr. G.A. Hyland. He says that ye times are affecting his rents in London. . . .

10 Nov. . . . Mr. Hyland interviewed me about ye meeting next Tuesday [17th]. . . .

12 Nov. . . . Some careless carter has bodily overthrown the right head stone pier of my East-gate. Similar thing happened 40 years ago I am told. Master King reset it. . . .

17 Nov. . . . At 6.40 to Mr. Hyland's. Mr. Bird & some more came in.
Meeting at ye sch. Well attend: about 200. I took ye chair. Mr. Bird, a good
speaker for his audience; he a self made man, has property in Brixton. A
couple of working men speakers (from Hastings I believe) effective. Mr.
John Fuller took ye opp. side. I was told I was a little too quick in disposing
of a diff. of statement between myself & Tom Brook about canvassing, but
I was sure that every body who knew John Fuller must be convinced that it
was a case of misunderstanding somewhere, & as misunderstandings can
seldom be cleared up so well in public as in private, I ruled that the matter
shd. pass. I am truly sorry if there was any seeming unfairness to Mr. J.F.
Mr. Nicoll Jr. spoke well. My cold so bad that I cd. scarcely speak. Order &
attention very good. . . .[25]

18 Nov. . . . C. & P. w. H. Dann, poor man, his tenacity of life
wonderful. . . .[26]

20 Nov. . . . Tithe dinner; good attendance, tho' I don't know much about
payments! Mr. Gillham prop: my health in most hearty terms, & nothing
cd. be kinder than ye reception of his speech. I feel sure that my tithe payers
will do their best poor tho' that may be, I proposed ye health of dear N. &
Mr. Philcox. Thoroughly good feeling in every way. I away about 5.20
very smoky & hoarse.

Sun. 22 Nov. Thought it was wiser not to go to S. Sch. [though took
morning and afternoon services; at the latter] Large congr: got along better
than I expected. In evg. at Bible Class. T.C. was very troublesome; what a
nuisance it is that a young fellow old enough to know better, won't give
himself a chance. . . .

24 Nov. T.C. came & apologized. A remarkable fact in ye history of Sussex,
but it was due to ye good advice of W[alter] H[icks]. . . . C. on JP. ye
deficiencies [in tithe payments] I am sorry to say serious. . . . C. on John
Fuller. He introd: me to Mr. Inderwick w. whom I had a pl. chat for I
daresay 20 mins. Mr. Sheppard (?) w. him. Mr. I. thinks that ye class sitting
will be actually re-elected, & will not be very different from ye class sitting
in ye old House [of Commons]. . . .[27]

25 Nov. Mrs Schroeter c. w. but a sad account of Mr.S. N. & I advised
promptly best London advice.[28] . . . C. on Mr. J. Fuller. Wm. Ellis jr. is
posting up each morning ye state of ye elections: this morg. C.36. Lib.30
Indep. 2. Parnellites 2. . . .

26 Nov. . . . I w. up to Laurelhurst. Mr. S. opened ye door to me, but I
was much grieved to find him so ill. He did not say one single word
while I was there. I saw Mrs. S. . . . & earnestly adv: best Lond.
adv: . . .

27 Nov. . . . Elections so far reveal a Cons: reaction, tho' not an absol. Cons. majority. . . .

30 Nov. St Andrew's day. . . . Not a large congr. but I enjoyed ye service. Alms offered £1-10-9. Burwash people do not understand week day services, & also a week's mission by ye Evangelization Soc. began I believe at ye Chapel.[29]

1 Dec. . . . First signs of hot feeling on politics in ye vill. Bentham Fuller put out a very big loaf labelled Gladstone, & a little two penny one labelled I think Salisbury. Telling but most fallacious. . . . by Blackford [a fly and van proprietor, whom Egerton usually hired, commonly to go to Etchingham station] to St. Ph. Ye room crammed, little trouble caused by H.F[uller] forcibly preventing a young Daw, not an elector, & supposed [annotated '(w. good reason Decr.14th)'] to be the leader of an organized body of interrupters, from coming in. He created excitement outside & when eventually he & his fellows got in they certainly made a noise. Mr. Bird again adv. protection. Mr. Brookfield [Conservative candidate, Rye division] spoke well, in good temper, in gentlemanly tone. & with fair arg[ument] & created a very good impression. Ye Hastings "working men" not so successful. Mr. H. Nevill made a capital chairman. I was much pressed to take ye chair, but I steadily refused. I think I was fairly successful in quieting a noisy young Scotchman & one of our own folk at the back where I stood. "God save the Queen" sung at ye end. Mr. John Fuller again pluckily upheld ye Liberal cause. Ellen Gould & other ladies there. I argued with young Daw that at all events as a non-elector he had no "right" to come into "a public meeting of electors", ye parrot cry of "Vote for Inderwick" ye chief interruption. B[rookfield] & I drove home, & had some sandwiches, & he had a glass of whiskey & water. We had a very long & pl. chat in ye study. I took a great fancy to him. He is a son of Mr. Brookfield ye well known H.M.Insp. of Schools. Cambr[idgeshire] Cavalry Regt, retired & lives at Rye.

2 Dec. I got up early & polled at 8 o'Clock. Mr. G.A. Hyland, Tom Brook & I ye first three. Brookfield rode down to Etchm. for 10.24. Ye children liked him much & I am very glad he came here. . . . [After visiting Stonegate] home about 7, but no disturbance whatever beyond boys shouting chiefly "Hinderwick for ever". My children having a half holiday held a political meeting. Ye oldest, most decrepit, & worst dressed dolls in their collection represented ye Liberals! but ye meeting collapsed for want of opposition.

3 Dec. Mr. Gregory in all right for East Grinstead div. I am glad; wrote to congratulate him; 960 ? maj:. . . . Mr. Brookfield elected by majority of 223 Hurrah. I home, rang a peal on ye dinner bell & Gussey played "for he's a jolly good fellow" . . . on ye piano. We all, children & all, delighted. . . .

I c. to congrat. Mr. Barton, Mr. Ellis jnr, Mr. H. Jarvis & Mr. G.A. Hyland on ye success of their efforts wh. have been unremmitting. Wrote to B[rookfield] to congrat.

8 Dec. Signed papers for James Joseph Gorringe 14 9/12 to go into R.N. In aft. had conv. w. John Fuller about Free Trade & ye [Co-operative] Stores. He confessed that on principle of Free Trade dealing at ye Stores is perfectly correct. It is hard then for those to be called fools who talk about Fair Trade, & yet be called unfair to local tradesmen if on simple Free Trade principles they deal at ye Stores. . . . C. on Mrs J. Isted. Sally at Yarmouth, still ill. I sent her 2/6. Stephen aged 10½ having tried a newly sharpened bill hook on a tree in front of Bentham Fuller's had to pay 3/6 or go to H. Green. I gave 2/6 to save ye boy.[30]

10 Dec. . . . To see JP. . . . Mr. Murriéta one of ye wealthiest men in ye county calmly claims ye offer of 10% reduct. on ye tithe!

11 Dec. . . . C. at Noakes Bros. for change. Mr. J.B.N. introd. me to Mr. Murch ye Missioner of ye Evangelization Soc: now here. He complained to me that his having his mission at ye chapel had crippled ye effect. I liked ye man. . . .

14 Dec. Capital letter from A.M. Brookfield MP. Old J.Chandler brought me a sad account of ye roughness & unfeeling cond[uct] of —— I am sorry, as I hear ye same tale in several quarters. It is not right. . . .This morg. trying my old revolver cautiously pointing it at ye floor, one chamber was loaded & went off. Shortly after dear N. came in & seeing something black on ye ceiling, got a chair & took it down. It was ye bullet! How had that rebounded from a Turkey carpet?!'

15 Dec. . . . C. on Mrs Parsons & saw old Bodle Holmes her br: who had come over for ye day from Heathfield; reputed age 106 last May (1/6). . . .

16 Dec. . . .R. & P. w. ye mothers m. [in abeyance during Nellie's prolonged illness] only 4. It really is hard on poor N. . . . C. on Mr. J. Fuller, & asked him about a letter wh. years ago Mr. J. B[arrow] wished me to read aloud at a Penny reading, but which Mr. J. F[uller] in JB's interest advised me to suppress. Mr. JB had told Mr. Gillham that Mr. JF denied having advised me to withhold it. Mr. JF "to the best of his belief & recollection advised me as I said, & Mrs JF distinctly recollects her husb: at the time telling her that he, had advised me not to read it". 7 men under notice to leave Southover on Sat. . . .

18 Dec. J.N[oakes] supr[ised] me by saying that Mr. Brookfield had not yet written to thank H. J[arvis]. The thanks are really deserved. . . .

21 Dec. . . . Dole day. I down to harness room at 10. Mr. J. Fuller & Mr.

Cramp. We had finished practically by 12.5. I remember when we used to fetch candles! but then we had the Common & Witherenden Hill. Still a great change. About 5 fewer appl. this year, & ye meat 4/6 per 8lb inst[ead] of 5/-. . . .

22 Dec. . . . C. on Mrs Cramp (2/-), Sellers br; husb. 76 working for 7/- a week. . . . To Mr. Whatman's to tea. He in rather better spirits, has been killing & selling his own sheep, making about 12/6 a head more than the [wholesale] butchers wd. give him. Home w. him & Mr. Hicks ye miller going to ye market at ye Bell.

24 Dec. C. on Mr. J. Fuller for dole ticket for G. Copper: he gave me one for 4lb. . . . Ye singers at 8.40 (6/-) . . . Ye sing. much as usual. I can't say improved.

25 Dec. . . . Some singers c. at 2.30AM, but we did not hear them, as they sang opp. ye fr[ont] door & Dash barked only as they went away. Ye regulars Wm. Coppard & party came I supp[ose] about 5. No Pagdens this year, the first year in wh. none of the family have sung probably for 90 years. . . .

28 Dec. [At Pashley] . . . . Ye Volunteer band c. & played to my mind surprisingy well. Old Mr. W.W. Leaney still ye band master. It is many years since I heard him conducting his band of niggers in "Jimming crikey, blow me tight" to the wonderment of Lady Herchal, Mrs Hardcastle & other tip-toppers in Flimwell Sch. room.

29 Dec. . . . At 5 to Martha Flemings tea party to her little Sunday school tots. 16 or 18 of them, as happy as ever cd. be. I quite enjoyed myself. Miss Littlemore sang really very nicely, & Annie Ellis also on a smaller scale. Ye little ones had learnt "I have to hear the story to sing to me". I gave Martha 2/6 for prizes, & my blessing. . . .

31 Dec. . . . J. Fuller c. & went thro' our soup list w. him for his advice. . . . Spent ye transition from ye old to ye new year in reading my ordination vows & in prayer for God's help to keep them better. A humbling time. How is it that one makes so little progress in good things. . . .

Notes

1. The two geese involved were valued at 10/- each by their owner; they disappeared from the 'plat near his house' overnight on Sat. 17 Jan. In customary fashion, he tracked the single set of footprints – 'One had nine rows of nails, with four or five heads missing' – to the vicinity of Braban's house. Gillham then went to

the police, and Sergeant Buss and PC Tappenden retraced the footprints, searched Braban's house, and arrested him on discovery of boots matching the tracks. It is not clear whether Braban told Buss that Lavender had bought the geese, but the police soon found the birds in the butcher's cart. At a special court sitting on 23 Jan., Braban pleaded guilty to theft, but Lavender's story, that he bought the geese at the suspiciously low price of five shillings each from Braban, with whom he had not dealt before, and made no enquiry as to their origin, not surprisingly failed to convince justices Courthope and Carter of his innocence of receiving stolen goods. Both men were sentenced to three months' imprisonment. *Sussex Advertiser*, 26 Jan. 1885. *Sussex Agricultural Express*, 27 Jan. 1885.

2.   William Jenner, twenty-four and son of labourer Charles Jenner Akehurst, married Sarah Maria, twenty, daughter of Amos Jenner. The witnesses were Edward Douch and Priscilla Jenner Akehurst. ESCRO. Par.284/1/3/3.

3.   Additional incidents coming into this category, included Henry Mann 'pointing a loaded gun' at one of Lord Ashburnham's gamekeepers, which earned Mann a three-month hard-labour term, without the option of a fine, and labourer Alfred Mepham's assault on carpenter George Brook at the Rose and Crown. Mepham – who claimed to be 'only larking' – 'struck him with a glass bottle in the mouth' after Brook had spent some time talking to Mepham's 'sweetheart . . . in the scullery'. *Sussex Agricultural Express*, 3 Feb. and 3 Mar. 1885. Summary returns; depositions, Mepham case, ESCRO. QR/E1109.

4.   Newcomer Logie Pirie had recently purchased land in St Philips; an Anglican, he vowed not to tolerate the absenteeism experienced by the parochial National School. *Parish Notes*, May 1885.

5.   While the report granted that some absenteeism derived from illness, there was 'much preventable irregularity' of attendance, while 'the apparent inability of the children to concentrate their attention, on what they have in hand' was partly owing to their permitted 'talkativeness'. Report, dated 16 Feb. 1885, ESCRO. ESC.41/1.

6.   Subscription clubs for relatively expensive items including clothes and shoes were popular among working families, and in the countryside were commonly run by traders like the bootmaker Samuel Ellis.

7.   The last surviving trustee, James Lade, died at Heathfield aged seventy-two on 11 Jan. 1883. Plans were being made for re-building for the purposes of a reading room and library; ironically a new lending library had recently been opened at the Congregational Church, with 109 volumes, and appeals for subscriptions to increase stocks. ESCRO. NC.3/1/2.

8.   Indicating that last year's legal offensive had been remarkably ineffective; see above, 26 July 1884, and note 22.

9.   'There are few occasions', Egerton wrote, 'which show a country parish to greater advantage than a marriage, when both the bride and bridegroom happen to be . . . well-known and respected for the interest they have taken in the parish, its people, and its schools . . .'. He also remarked on 'the quiet and absence of restlessness among the children themselves . . . not one of the least remarkable features of the day'. His final reflection, ran; 'As we left the church we could but feel that all who had known this part of Sussex forty years ago must be sharing our thankfulness and wonderment at having lived to witness such a scene on Burwash Common, as Buckle's Farm, this particular spot, was indeed ignorant of church, school, brides and bridegrooms, triumphal arches, carriages and horses. All its experience was of heath and hoth, and very scanty crops of anything valuable'. *Sussex Agricultural Express*, 18 Apl. 1885.

10.   With the first general election under the 1884 Reform Act looming, the Tories were nervous over the county seats in which a proportion of working men would exercise the franchise for the first time. The Tories made some forays into the new rural electorate, as at Lamberhurst with Conservative Working Men's meetings, but with little success; alternatively, the Tories 'constantly reiterated assertions . . . that the labourers are lukewarm on political matters'. The party also had protectionist elements eager to help depressed farmers through import tariffs, which was why the Liberal's rigid adherence to free trade produced the sloganizing over cheap bread, leaving Egerton feeling so helpless. The Kent and Sussex Labourers' Union General Secretary, Alfred Simmons, had recently been adopted as Liberal candidate for the St Augustine division of Kent, which bordered Canterbury. *Kent and Sussex Times*, 28 Feb., 21 Mar. and 9 May 1885.

11.   The sixty-eight page report of the Royal Commission was principally concerned with London and the larger cities, gave a vivid but depressing picture, and emphasized the total inadequacy of especially sanitary legislation, passed during the previous forty years. *The Times*, 8 May 1885. Gibbs held rigid *laissez-faire* ideals, even over housing; see above, p. 138, 20 and 23 June 1873.

12.   Carters commonly had stipulated amounts of beer paid for by their employers, sometimes through exchanging hay with innkeepers. Carters are regularly encountered in heavy drinking sessions, all the more likely when routine business saw sons from away meeting up with their father, whose identity cannot be ascertained from the initials given here.

13.   Fielden had erected a fence 'in front of his premises called "Rampyndene" . . . enclosing a portion of the footpath and Sweard in "Burwash Street". . . . the grunsward has been removed and . . . the highway has been left from time immemorial free'. Vestry minutes, 27 Aug. 1885 and 25 Mar. 1886, ESCRO. Par.284/12/2.

14.   Ironically, Collins inverted the truth; a Russell was murdered and a Leaney hanged.

15.   Probably bricklayer Alfred Banks, heavily fined for a drunken assault on a man at Ticehurst at the end of 1884, and subsequently imprisoned for non-payment. Summary returns, ESCRO. QR/E1108.

16.   Coleridge ruled – or rather reiterated an old judgement – that verges were part of the highway. The litigant's enclosure was twenty-six feet wide, and 177 yards long. *The Times*, 3 July 1885.

17.   Blackford presumably had returned to Burwash to visit family and friends. A further example of Fleming's (for whom see above, p. 47, note 3) revered status in the village.

18.   The Coney family were long-term, non-resident owners of lands, farms, and other properties, in the district. The lots mentioned by Egerton were among more properties in Ticehurst, Whatlington and Pevensey, sold in a huge auction at the Royal Kentish Hotel, Tunbridge Wells. The property bought by Schroeter included a substantial house, and four cottages. Bidding commenced at £1200, and the competition between Schroeter and the socially aspirant Fielden for these central Burwash properties was intense. Egerton no doubt felt that Schroeter would make a more philanthropic cottage landlord.

Biggs Farm, in Ticehurst, was one of the farms tenanted by Gillham, who seized this opportunity to buy; bidding commenced at £2000.

Bowman's Farm, 160 acres and a substantial farmhouse, went to W. Button domiciled in Robertsbridge; bidding started at £2000 and the farm made £2750. *Sussex Advertiser*, 27 July 1885.

19. The Liberal *Sussex Advertiser*, 31 Aug. 1885 tartly noted the meeting, and explained that as the paper had not been forewarned, no reporter attended.
20. Fourteen people were present, but Fielden – the encroacher – was not among them. Burwash vestry minutes, ESCRO. Par.284/12/2.
21. The costs, however, were an additional pound, paid to the prosecutor Edward Simes, for Pilbeam's 'violent and indecent behaviour' in the Wesleyan Chapel on 6 Sept. Pilbeam had stormed in, 'with his dog in the midst of the evening service to loudly insult . . . the congregation, to tell the minister to come down, as he himself could preach better than that, and that they were hypocrits': 'after enduring for upwards of half an hour . . . this sacriligious treatment the congregation simultaneously dispersed'.
     Curiously, somebody who had known Pilbeam for thirty years, as 'always . . . a straightforward, honest, hardworking man, and one whose skilled labour as a shoeing and general smith, but he always attends to it himself, and his character will stand the strictest test and enquiry', said so in the press. It provoked a riposte, printed anonymously 'that a reference to the records of Hurst Green Petty Sessions, during the time stated would show that this man . . . has appeared there on occasions' before. The evidence does not invariably discriminate between the William Pilbeams, father and son; the father – aged seventy-four – had at one time combined his smithing with running The Stag beershop, and had been prosecuted at least three times for opening during prohibited hours. He had at least four convictions for assault, including on the police, and on a licensee, and another for drunk and disorderly. The son appears to have been first convicted of drunkenness at the age of nineteen in 1863, and subsequently picked up convictions for drink-related offences, including assaults and refusing to leave licensed premises. Both Pilbeams paid the relatively huge fines – including one of £3, with 18/- costs – imposed on them, and their relative prosperity preserved them from alternative spells of imprisonment. Summary conviction returns, ESCRO. QR/E901, 1023, 1053, 1066, 1069, 1075–6. *Brighton Gazette*, 8 Apl. 1847. *Sussex Agricultural Express*, 3 and 13 Oct. 1885. *Kent and Sussex Times*, 17 Oct. 1885.
22. Many employers would not give regular or permanent work to ex-prisoners.
23. Henry Isted had at least three convictions for drunkenness since 1880, including that in Feb. 1885 when he was fined 10/- with 12/- costs for being drunk at the Bell; then, he claimed that he was subject to epileptic fits, and 'felt a little queer on this occasion, and [William] Meopham put him in a stable'. In 1883, he was also fined 5/- and 7/6 costs along with William Maskell for the traditional Guy Fawkes's Day offence of rolling ignited tar barrels in the street.
     On the current occasion, Isted, accompanied by Edmund Langridge, had raided fellow labourer William Pope's chickens, from his residence at Shrub Cottage. Pope kept six hens and eighty chickens, and Isted and Langridge took four hens and thirteen chickens. As the pair returned at 2a.m. they were seen on the Burwash–Ticehurst road by PC William Windsor. He stated that 'When they caught sight of me . . . Langridge, dropped a bag in the hedge, and they kept coming towards me. I went to the . . . bag . . . and found some chickens in it warm. The two . . . passed me. I . . . overtook them. I asked them how they accounted for the chickens. Both of them said "We don't know anything about them". I told them I would apprehend them. . . . Isted took his belt off his waist, and said "If you put your hand on me, I will show you". I told them both that if they attempted to run away, I should knock them down. After a lot of persuasion, I got them to the station'. Here Windsor removed the prisoners' shoes, and later that morning found tracks made by them

near Pope's cottage; Pope later identified the stolen birds as his. In court Isted's current employer gave him a good character reference, but Courthope chairing the Bench, and sentencing them both to three months hard labour, caustically stated that 'it was all they could give, otherwise they would have given them more'. See also below, p. 329, 30 Oct. 1885.

Summary conviction returns, ESCRO. QR/E1089, 1104, 1109. *Sussex Agricultural Express*, 30 Oct. 1885. *Sussex Advertiser*, 2 Mar. 1883.

24. There is little independent, or even partisan, information on these meetings, as the press focused on those addressed by the candidates themselves. Inderwick spoke at Ticehurst, Robertsbridge, Burwash Common and Burwash, between 16 and 28 Nov. to audiences principally comprising agricultural labourers and small farmers. He advocated a 'system of peasant proprietorships', not least to keep labour on the land, and an end to tied cottages and arbitrary evictions. *Hastings and St Leonard's Times*, 21 and 28 Nov. 1885.

25. The Liberals later alleged that Egerton said in a reference to them, 'Confound their politics'. Ibid., 28 Nov. 1885.

26. Henry Dann, aged fifty-seven, was buried on 30 Nov. A grocer and draper, 'by years of untiring industry and perseverance . . . raised himself from the position of quite a poor boy'. *Parish Notes*, Jan. 1886.

27. Namely, that the abolition of specific representation of seventy-nine towns, the reduction from two to one MPs sitting for another thirty-six, and – much more importantly – significant change in the county constituency electorate, and the radical restructuring of many constituencies, would not be reflected in any marked shift in the type of men elected. Property qualifications for MPs were abolished in 1854, but even in 1885, there were only a few working-class members, including the National Agricultural Labourers Union's leader, Joseph Arch. As Arch said during his election campaign in Norfolk, 'The two millions of new voters wanted some one of their own class to speak for them. I was ready'. Cited, P. Horn, *Joseph Arch*, (1971), p. 168.

28. That medical opinion should be speedily obtained from a London, as opposed to a provincial, doctor; the Egertons consulted both local and metropolitan practitioners during Nellie's prolonged illnesses.

29. In fact a series of 'special religious services' went on over three weeks, and were 'fairly well attended'. Congregational Church, Burwash, minutes, Dec. 1885, ESCRO. NC3/1/3.

30. Minor criminal offenders still commonly compounded with their victims, both sides preferring to avoid the courts; Fuller's exaction of a relatively large sum for a prank by a poor neighbour's child was severe, though perhaps under half the sum in a fine and costs which might have been imposed by the local Bench.

1886–7

1 Jan. Took ye soup tickets to Gorringe boy for distr[ibution]. . . . C. on Mrs J. Isted; not in; gave Annie 2/6 for her m[other] in lieu of soup. C. on Harry Eastwood (2/6) at Elphick's. Sad story of short work & d[aughte]rs bad health. . . .

4 Jan. . . . A capital photograph of Mr. & Mrs Charles Ellis in their shanty in Colorado. In evg. a young man George (?) Kemp of Mottingsden c. on me to consult me on spiritual matters. I advised staying at home for a while & doing what he cd. among his own sort. . . .

7 Jan. . . . C. & P. w. poor Mrs W. Isted, bronchitis & expecting confinement any day; poor woman she is to be pitied. No fire place in ye room. I ordered her a blanket at Ellis', as a loan. C. on Mrs T. Coleman, suffering & her husb: out of work. . . .

8 Jan. . . . In aft. went w. Hicks to look at ye ground near ye barn, to see if anything cd. be done in giving work by searching for gravel. Agreed to set a man on tomorrow.

9 Jan. . . . C. & P. w. poor Mrs W. Isted. 7 months child born last night, & she racked w. bronchitis. I gave Caroline Vidler 2/- on Mrs I's acc. & 1/6 on her own. Sad case. . . .

11 Jan. . . . C. & P. w. Mrs Wm. Isted, very ill; sent some beef tea, soup for ye children, & some meat for himself, poor fellow I pity him. He hates the drink I sincerely believe, but his moral power is "nil" & his poor wife & chrn. suffer. . . .

12 Jan. . . . We had to day a loin of mutton direct from our farmer Mr. Whatman at 8d instead of 10d. It was excellent meat, & I cannot in reason see why I shd. not buy more of him.

18 Jan. . . . C. on Mr. Jos. Noakes. Ye JB question apparently insoluble. C. & took tea w. Mr. Gillham. Son has had much bad luck in his new business in London. No fault but has fallen into a partnership in wh. "sharp practice" has worsted him; he leaves £100 in ye business & comes home. I am truly sorry, as he was hoping to be married this Xmas. C. on Mr. J. Fuller. His son Ivan just going into business at Eastbourne. . . .

19 Jan. . . . N. Taylor ye Rel[ieving] Off. c. on me. . . . He says that ye distress is not quite so great as expected.

21 Jan. . . . Met Mr. Kemp of Mottingsden who tackled me about my interv: w. his Son George, but relieved when I told him that I had advised his son to stay at home. & not at present seek missionary work. . . .

22 Jan. . . . Ye Choir boys supper 12. They seemed to enjoy themselves much. Our 4 children amusingly useful in shewing games etc. . . . Ye surplus bread & butter, cake etc. from ye choir treat brought down . . . to [night] sch. . . . & soon disappeared.

25 Jan. . . . A long t. w. Th. Pennels in my sand pit on ye land question. He cannot be brought to believe he says that farming won't pay.

26 Jan. Dupl[icates] Sched[ule, respecting school registers] only 72 & the nearest fraction per cent at passes. It is really serious. Ye sch. ought to do better.[1] . . . C. & P. w. Mrs W. Isted (2/6). The paraffin stove costs her 3/6 a week poor woman, but she is . . . better.

29 Jan. Sch. Aft. came on wet, but luckily cleared up for the poor people to come & get their soup at 4. N.S. 20. . . .

Sun. 31 Jan. Very wet . . . Congr. very small. . . . Coming away slipped up & fell ignominiously at ye left of Bell Alley, just opposite ye "Bell". . . .

2 Feb. . . . C. on Mrs J. Coppard. Mr. told me that nearly £1400 is due for the Land Tax, Prop[erty] Tax, Inc[ome] Tax & Poor Rate from Burwash before Mar. 25! I don't envy him his job of collecting it. C. on Maskell's housekeeper at ye Forge. Illeg. Ch. w. her. Ye man (at Godstone) "had to marry" another woman, soon after this ch: was born. Miserable work, as I am not sure whether ye misery has ceased. . . .

4 Feb. . . . The old chapel being rapidly renovated. I hope ye reading room scheme will answer.[2]

8 Feb. . . . C. on Mrs J. Isted (1/6). Ye acc. wh. she gave me of her son's exp[eriences] at Lewes Gaol of ye hard labour, & low diet, indicate considerable misery, & I shd. think ye system sufficiently deterrent. A Mr. Brook from Heathfield trustee of a chapel there, tackled me about ye repairs. Used some strong lang. about stolen property. I cd. not help bantering a little about ye new-born zeal for a building wh. had been in ruins for years. We parted very good friends. C. on poor Winnie Relf (2/6) ye old body shivering by an apology for a fire wh. however burnt up more brightly afterwards. C. & P. w. Mrs Charles Kidder (1/-) gr. d. of old Master Wickham whom I knew so well in his long illness years ago. . . .

10 Feb. . . . Monday's [8th] Socialist riots in London in every body's mouth. Truly the war between bottoms & tops seems likely to intensify itself. Hyndman & Burns ought to be locked up. Mother's meeting 8. I P. w. them. Mothers opinions mixed. Miss Wontres [?] said between the uselessness of sacking jewellers shops & the necessity of doing something when a wife & family are starving. . . . Ye drum & fife band represent[a-tive]s c. & I gave them 10/-, & a note to the 2 princ: fifers viz. Thomas Bourner & Walter Lusted, holding them responsible for ye good behaviour of ye band (12 in all).

12 Feb. . . . C. at Martha Fleming's to see what view the penny weekly papers took of the riot. Reynold's the most republican had not come down, but Lloyds, the Weekly Times & I think the Despatch took really a very fair & unprejudiced view of the situation, reprobating utterly Hyndman & his lot, while sympathising w. ye really distressed operatives. . . . C. & sat w. Mr. G. Fuller. He very strong agst. the thriftlessness of the poor, but he lives opposite ye "Bear", & sees enough to make him angry. . . .

15 Feb. . . . C. on Mr. Pearson. Mrs attending her 200 chickens; her son shewed me over ye buildings; ye steam engine 2 h.p. very handy. . . .

17 Feb. . . . in aft. C. on Jesse Baker ye decayed tailor, & had a t. semi-scientific, semi-religious. He of opinion that the planets have a good deal w. our good or ill fortune. . . .

22 Feb. . . . To ye Reading room. Very successful institution, now of 4 years standing, self-managed, but not, of course, self-supporting.

23 Feb. . . . Ye expense of Ye Fife & drum band too much for them. . . .

24 Feb. . . . C. on Mrs Wm. Isted; her doctor's bill for 5 weeks . . . £2-13-0; how is she to pay?'

25 Feb. . . . Harry Isted (William's son) & John Burgess c. for me to fill up papers for free passage to Western Australia.

1 Mar. Gave a Mrs Jones 10/- on her representation of a fire. I hope that I was not unduly credulous. . . . I wrote to Mr. W.A. Raper Sol[icito]r Battle, my views of a draft bill for the abolition of Extr[aordinary] Tithe, to be introduced by Col. Brookfield. We ought rather in interest of both sides to agitate for delay in legisl. till prospects of Engl. Agr. are clearer.

2 Mar. . . . C. on Mrs Wm. Jones; saw remains of burnt things. Her tongue one of the most vigorous clappers I ever knew. . . .

3 Mar. Sch. Aft. c. on Mrs Louisa Collins by her request. Child w. terrible water on the brain. I did not give ye woman anything bec: her husb: is in steady work. She keeps her child away from sch: & is herself a steady customer of ye public houses. She very cross, but to help her wd. not be fair to others. . . . I have 5 men now at work on ye glebe.

6 Mar. . . . Poor Tommy Weston wd. speak to me to "vindicate" his character. I said "friend you have had just two pen'orth, & you had better go home or you will be overcome": he replied "Oh no Sir, I've only had a pint of twopenny". . . .

Sun. 7 Mar. . . . 2 Baptisms. In one case ye mother brazened it out that she was married to the man with whom she lives, but I believe that she lied unto me. . . .

8 Mar. . . . Tea w. Mr. Whatman. Times are bad, wh. nobody can deny. In aft. I formed in ye street part of a conclave of Guardians, Mr. Joseph Handley, Mr. Whatman, & Mr. Hyland, & we took counsel on one or two relief cases. . . .

11 Mar. . . . Henry Isted & John Burgess c. I gave them 5/- each toward outfit. . . .

13 Mar. . . . Mrs C. Vidler c. me in about Jane Weston who had taken refuge there. I foolishly gave Mrs V. 1/6 for keeping J.W. for several days. JW has money to pay for herself. I then to her sister Mrs Littlemore. A sad tale of family strife. So delayed that I cd. not take the boys for singing. . . .

Sun. 14 Mar. . . . In ye evg. at 6.30 no less than 43 boys for conf; one too young. I was startled. O God give me Thy grace in dealing with the hearts of this number, ye demeanour & apparent earnestness all that I cd. wish. . . .

15 Mar. . . . C. & took tea w. Mr. Gillham. He spoke much of ye grief brought upon a neighbour & his wife by ye misconduct of a child. . . .

21 Mar. . . . In evg. 4 boys away. 2 only without reason assigned: one fresh one pres[ent] + 39. Quiet outside & demeanour inside all that I cd. wish. . . . I have much just now to encourage me. . . .

24 Mar. Poor Mrs Dann interv: me & pleaded so hard with me to use my infl[uence] agst. her being obliged to go into "ye House", that I wrote a note to Mr. Hyland ye guardian begging him to hear her state her case herself. I am convinced that the House wd. be better for her, & yet it seems hard to force an old body in agst. her will. She is poor creature old, very dirty, very helpless, & very incapable, & yet I don't expect her to live long in ye House. She might however most easily set a light to her present tenement. . . . C. on Mrs R? Keely. Most unaccountably had never been to see her before, tho' she has been married 13 years! & is quite reputable. I felt very much

ashamed of myself, & the good woman did not spare me, as indeed she had
no need to do. One thing was that she had never been ill, so I had never had
her called to my attention for that reason . . . parted good friends. . . .

25 Mar. To ye school. Martha Fleming told me that a little boy had been in
& out of her shop in the vain attempt to buy a pencil just like Mr Thornton's
(Our Assis. Master) because then he was sure he shd. get his sums right! but
the money (6d) was too much . . . Found Mr. Whatman trying to persuade
Albert Jarvis to be Guardian. . . .³

Sun. 28 Mar. . . . Mr. Philcox thanked me for ye [morning] sermon. A
very rare thing, but encouraging when it comes. . . . Confir: Cl. only 2
abs. 40 pres: & again all that I cd. wish for in demeanour & attention. . . .

31 Mar. . . . In aft. funeral of Wm. J. Isted aged 24. Ye Foresters attended &
Brother George Ellis read ye customary prayer at ye end of ye service. Ye
young man's father told me that his son had never used a bad word in his
life, nor had ever been in a passion. . . .

1 Apl. W. Wm. Ellis Jr. to look at ye incipient reading room; will I fear hang
fire for want of funds. . . .

3 Apl. Wrote to friend Cooper an answer to a letter on ye old question of St.
Philip's its area, population & disproportionate inc[ome]. I urged that all
this was thoroughly known before he took the Living. . . .

8 Apl. In all day – a rare thing. . . . N.S. 14. Last night of ye season. . . . I
spoke a few words & shook hands w. each boy as he went out. N.B. Not a
"thank you" from any one. I am sure it is not because they do not mean
"thank you" but because they do not think of it. . . .

16 Apl. Kind letter from Captn. Pierson Adjt. of 1st Royal Sussex re J.
Sawyers. S. has elected to stay another 6 years w. ye Colours. Oddly enough I
had just written to him advising him to do so. . . . Ye two lads H. Isted & J.
Burgess have to start for Swan River on Monday! They c. on me. . . .

Sun. 18 Apl. . . . At 5 . . . Henry Isted & John Burgess c. I gave each a
Bible, & we had prayers together. I gave each of them also 2/6, as evidence
of my good wishes. They start tomorrow to embark at Plymouth on Wed:
on board ye "Oriano" 2000 tons. . . . Conf. Cl. 36 or 37. . . .

20 Apl. Yesterday & today ye Chrn. have been out primrosing for All Saints
Bloxham & for Mrs York for Greenwich Hospital School Church. I c. on
Mrs Weeks (?) ye new constable's wife. . . . Saw Sergt. Buss after Ch. on
ye subj: of ye unruly boys in ye street. The constable has been watching
premises in Ticehurst.

21 Apl. . . . As for ye walk [to Park Hill] I quite enjoyed getting off ye beaten track of my ordinary rounds. . . .

26 Apl. . . . Read some . . . art[icles] in ye Quart[erly] Rev. Democracy seems inevitable. I can only hope that ye antecedents of English national & political life may give some qualifications to democracy wh. may save England from ye consequences wh. democracy has hitherto entailed upon ye countries in wh. it has prevailed. I cd. freely trust the common sense of the people, but now I am called upon to yield my unhesitating allegiance to the sense of the common people wh. is a very different thing to do.

30 Apl. One of the Pilbeam boys wished . . . to join ye Cricket Club. Mr Anset called his particular attention to ye rule agst. swearing & told him that if he joined he wd. have to obey it. Master P. objected to this rule, & asked whether he couldn't pay a little more & swear as he liked! . . . Gave poor old [agricultural labourer, Robert] Cramp 1/6; he nearly 78 & out of work.

8 May. . . . I met ye boys at ye old Chapel & w. them to St Ph. & very orderly & well behaved. Very hot & dusty w[eather]. . . . Ye Church was prettily decorated. Ye Bishop arr[ived] at ye door about 11.30; good congr: His address from Heb. 4. 16. very fatherly & simple, not exciting certainly, & I fear not likely to be remembered long, still at ye time decidedly good; all our Burwash cand. 43 boys & 28 girls were confirmed. God only Who knoweth the hearts knoweth how many came in ye right spirit. All we can do is hope for ye best & to pray for ye blessing. . . .

Sun. 9 May. . . . In evg. one's disappointment began. Only 9 at Bible Class. Ye Sing. however very good; gave notice to day of Early Celebrations next S. for Cand. & par[ents]. I wonder whether any will come.

10 May. . . . A letter from Thos. Eastwood at Brisbane: doing well. . . .

12 May. Burwash Fair. I cursorily inspected ye show. Very good one, but very few buyers. . . .

13 May. W. up to St Ph. . . . To ye sch. Numbers low & a general sense of depression wh. I have rarely observed in ye sch. . . . Ye whole atmosphere of ye Common seems now to be one of unrest & discomfort. . . .

14 May. . . . a club meeting for fixing ye dinner day; 9th of June. Ye other club thro' its Sec. J. Lusted informs me that it will not come to church this year.

15 May. . . . C. on J. Lusted who told me that ye Club thinks it is mocking to go to church when some of ye members are ye worse for liquor. . . .

Sun. 16 May. Early celebration at 8. Comm[unicants] 26 Off. 12s 4½d. A few of ye newly confirmed girls, but not a single boy out of the 43. It is to me mysterious. . . .

[17 to 29 May at Oxford.]

2 June. In ye evg. I to ye vill. to post ye results of hours searching of registers for two applicants. Nearly got my head knocked off by a cricket ball on ye glebe.

8 June. . . . In aft. funeral of poor George Pope aged 18, 7th child ye Popes have lost. . . .

9 June. To ye Club dinner, ye "Old Men's Club", dinner at ye Bear. After dinner Harry Mepham [a farmworker, aged sixty-two] & myself had a talk about Parsons, Deans, Bishops, & other people who get thousands a year & did nothing. He firmly believed that the Income of Bishops & Deans & other dignatories came out of the taxes. I sang "A Thousand a year" & "When the heart is young"; during ye latter performance Walter Morris Snr. at my elbow was fast asleep. His somnolescence secured him not a little chaff. . . . Ye Etchm. band (2/6) came to ye Rect. at 6.15 on its way to ye Club room. Vigorous to say the least of it, but very creditable to a parish no bigger than Etchm.

Mon. 14 June. Grand wedding at 11.30. Wm. John Ellis of Mr. Wm. Ellis ye Stonemason at Etchm. & Miss Harriet Thompson Skinner d. of our Benjn. Thompson Builder. Kid gloves & tobacco smoke ye prom[inent] features of ye bridal party. Very nice, orderly, & reverent. I was at ye breakfast. Capitally managed in ye carpenters' shed. About 24. I prop. ye health of ye bride & bridegr: I hoped that when his calling summoned him to ye scaffold, he wd. go not as a martyr, & that ye scaffold wd. mean to him not death, but a living. Mr. Ch. Thompson prop. my health. In returning thanks I pulled out of my pocket a telegr: wh. I had just had from ye House Surg: at T. Wells "No room for Parson" wh. I shewed as proof that my health rendered me an unsuitable case for ye Hosp. It was meant that there was "no room for Thomas Parsons". Funeral at 3 of Keely's little . . . child. I then to ye cricket gr:. . . . Saw . . . Mr. Ostenburg, a radical Cabinet maker, much employed at Southover. He talked rad: pol: to me for I shd. think ½ an hour. He believes in ye Daily News. . . .

18 June. . . . Last night ye Hop Tithe Redemption Bill . . . read third time in H. of Commons. To my mind eminently unjust, but parsons are not as powerful as landlords & farmers, in such matters. Mr. Bolton having got up ye agitation have pleaded the agitation as proof that the bill was necessary. The change will not improbably make living in the Rectory an impossibility.[4] . . . Measles now an epidemic.

19 June. . . . Funeral of Mr. Trayton Rochester (63) late grocer & draper here. Had buried 6 chrn. & his wife in our yard. I c. on Herbert Pope, no better. He said he liked "rather roughish" books to read. Adventures I suppose & such like. . . .

21 June. . . . C. on Master Debley: long t. on politics; he dead agst. Home Rule & Disestablishment! . . . Mrs Relf ye deaf old lady blew me up for not calling oftener. They ought to have let me go on distributing ye magazines! On my way home devoted some exertion to beheading thistles by ye road side w. my w[alking] stick. Every body's business is nobody's & these wd. have seeded ye parish. Ye band pr[acticed] in ye Sch. R[oom]: they certainly improve. . . .

22 June. Writing serm. & calculating effect of ye Tithe Redemption bill. Kept me in most of ye day. . . . Two poor crocks of Farley's, newly bought from a fair, stood ye whole of ye time I was out, without moving, with their heads on each other's necks, as if poor brutes they were confiding to one another, the miseries of their lives, wh. must have been great. The idea once in my head, the sight of the poor brutes quite touched me. My loss by ye Tithe Red: bill be from £120 to £150 as ye terms made are good or bad.

23 June. . . . C. & P. w. Mrs Pattenden (2/-), very ill of Infl[amation] of ye lungs.. Husb. has had to sacrifice work & mowing.

24 June. C. on Mrs Bull, & had a t. w. Walter: he told me that ye dung cart wh. he was filling was in part to his knowledge more than 60 years old as Mr. Jos. Noakes' father bought it at Lewes so long ago. . . .

28 June. Telegr: from Mr. Aitkens at Ticehurst asking me to be chairman of Col. Brookfield's meeting on Fri: [2 July] I answered "yes" if the meeting was a "public" one. . . . C. on a newly married couple Heselden & wife. He a brickmaker at Mr. Gillham's yard. She seemed quite nice. He mends clocks & watches. At 7 to ye Sch: Meeting did not begin till 7.45. Mr. Reuter son (2d) of ye telegraph Reuter, ye cand. (Gladstonian) present. He, Mr. Slade music seller of St. Leonards, & Mr. Macer Wright Ed. of Hastings Times (?) ye speakers. I spoke, but they, in ye Chairman (Mr. Hallaway) wd. not allow me more than about 3 minutes. Mr. M.W. very sarcastic about ye clergy. . . . "Gladstone" ye one word with wh. they conjured. My speech almost unique . . . in that I did not once use his name. A very typical meeting. Bottoms & Middles & Tops & so it will be. Democracy seems imminent, & flattery is the only key to power w. ye democratic element in politics. No man who wishes to win with the multitude, must even hint that it can be wrong. So it was certainly tonight. I was freely listened to, & had no right to complain of the reception given to me personally.[5]

29 June. A Mr. ? from Mr. Atkins c. to suggest practically that Mr. Scott of Heathfield Park shd. be Brookfield's Chairman. Wont make a halfpenny odds to me, only probably I cd. keep order in Burwash as well as any stranger. I gladly acquiesced in Mr. Scott's presidency. He is a layman & in many respects more suitable, only I doubt his power of control of ye "Common" people. Lois [Egerton's servant] had forgotten poor girl to tell me last night of a funeral to day at 3, so I was 15 mins. late. I explained ye reasons to ye poor people. Ye child to be buried (Agnes Isted 3m.) was d. of ye poor Wm. [John] Isted who died a month or two since [31 Mar.]. . . . "Bateman's" I believe sold to Henry Noakes, Albert Jarvis & Tom Jarvis. So we don't benefit much by new blood there.

2 July. . . . to ye tent in Farley's field. C.A. Egerton in ye Chair. Brookfield, Dr. Gray of Hastings (?) Last year a thorough Inderwickian, Mr. Earle (?) Bird, Mr. Harrison (paid agent) & Mr. John Fuller (Gladstonian) ye princ: speakers. John Burgess who had had just two glasses too much caused a great deal of interruption, tho' humouress rather than ill-natured. . . . Otherwise ye meeting almost painfully dull. Brookfield spoke sensibly, Earle Bird flew to ye high branches of ye rhetorical tree. Dr. Gray spoke very well, tho' rather clerical in his delivery. Cd. not say whether a single voter was converted either way. Brookfield staid ye night w. us at ye Rect: we sat up past 12 Chatting, & I found him a very pleasant companion.

8 July. . . . sch. Offered a prize of 2/- for the best & 1/- for the next best list of Burwash folks now abroad in ye colonies & elsewhere. . . . I was asked to go straight to ye "Wheel" to speak on ye Irish question, at a Brookfielden meeting, as ye Testallers [?] had "jacked up". I politely declined & ye orator turned up at last. . . .

9 July. . . . voted. . . .

10 July. . . . C. on Mrs Mallion of Brooksmarsh. She out haying all ye week! . . .

12 July. I to ye sch. & read out the names of children. Two families send their children to ye chapel [Sunday] school as well as ours. It is not fair that children by going to chapel shd. get two treats, whereas by sticking to us they only get one, so I do not ask them to ours, but it is a nuisance. Saw John Burgess. He so cross w. me because somebody had told him that I sent the policeman to him on the night of Mr. Brookfield's meeting. I had of course done no such thing, as the constable to whom I went at once bore me out. . . .

14 July. . . . At 2.30 ye children came up. . . . Large party. 200 I am sure besides ye children (102). Our own children to Miss Tilley's to avoid chance of measles. . . . Joseph Noakes wanted to find some man of his weight to run him a race! I at once accepted. . . . I won it amidst much laughter, as two such barrels are not often seen trundling along at that pace. . . .

22 July. Staid at ye Rect. till 10. Ye B.B.B. i.e. Burw. Brass Band c. w. a few Foresters, a somewhat draggle-tailed display, & pl. They blew really very creditable blasts. . . . At 2 to Forester's dinn: very small att: I was called to ye chair; a Mr. Ward was in ye V[ice] C[hair]. Toasts aft: "ye Church" prop. by Mr. Ward, & ye band struck up "for he's a jolly good fellow". The fact was they did not "hear 'the Church'", & heard only my name wh. was coupled with it, hence ye honour. Ye company very kindly disposed to me personally. . . .[6]

24 July. . . . A herd of goats in ye village for sale, in charge of a genuine Taffy from Pembrokeshire.

26 July. . . . C. & R. w. Mrs Keeley, but ye old story, utter inability to see her past life in its real light as needing repentance, so what is one to do? It seems useless to offer the comforts of religion when there is no humility, no acknowledgment of sin, & yet it is hard to be obliged to re-open old sores, a process wh. only ensures angry denials, & observations that "God knows the truth" etc. I came away disheartened. . . . C. & had tea w. Mrs Gillham . . . [who] assured me that the result [of the race with Noakes] gave very widespread satisfaction! People seem delighted to be able to chaff ye village "boss" about something in wh. for once he was not head man! . . . Made a copy of reg[istration] of a Henry Collins marr: in 1766 for an eager pursuer of some lost property.

27 July. . . . C. on Mrs J. Isted (2/6). Her cup full of trouble. . . . To ye Glebe barn to see a colt of Farley's. Young Farley having a gallop on an old pony wh. was going to be killed because it was "old & wore out", so I suppose he thought it cd. do no more harm galloping it up to the last minute. I heard ye gun go off & Rudkin said death was instantaneous. . . .

29 July. . . . Mrs Bowner told me that Mr. Willsher of Squibbs told her that last year he raised 2,700 chicken. He has a machine wh. hatches "by paraffin or something of that".

31 July. . . . c. on Mrs Diplock, spoke about her boy not going to sch. She said he was the only one left out of 12! & that he bled at the nose if he went to sch, or rather she was sure he wd. do so if he did go! . . .

9 Aug. All ye Burwash world . . . to see H.R.H. & the Duchess of Teck at Etchm, whence he was going to open a Barnado's "Babies Castle" at Hawkhurst. I sent evergreens, but I told Mr. Smith ye Surveyor of Highways to tell HRH that I did not expect to be made a Bishop any the more for the greens. . . .[7]

11 Aug. . . . Buried poor old Mrs Collins formerly Pettit. Her claim to fame is an age of 92 years & the survival of 22 confinements! [Annotated later: 'this statement I find doubtful'.]

12 Aug. . . . C. on old widow Jenner (1/-). She said that old Mrs Keely who is still alive had had 14 children, that not one had died, & that they all married. . . .

[23 Aug. to Swanage where met up with family, and on to Bournemouth and Torquay; returned to Burwash on 4 Sept.]

10 Sept. . . . Some hoppers making a terrible noise at night in ye road. It sounded as if murder was imminent, but after a while they went away as if nothing had happened.

16 Sept. . . . C. at Mr. Johnson's at ye little shop; he hammered down a nail in my boot wh. was troubling me; he talked about the isolation of Fontridge Lane & it's distance from any place of worship. I liked ye man. Looked in at Master Batups; he told me that Wm. Relf next door, for whose sake I had made this long round, was out hopping & was standing it very well. It certainly is astonishing to see how ye hop garden draws out anybody who can hold together to get there. . . .

Sun. 19 Sept. . . . Mr. H. Ward of Holmshurst c. upon me in ye vestry to make arrangements about ye funeral tomorrow of old John Rich [shoemaker] aged 73 who committed suicide by hanging himself last Wed. [15th] but in what state of mind ye jury cd. not determine. Ye body was not taken into Church, & I omitted the "Almighty God with Whom to live" as the language does not seem so absolutely pertinent to those who have presumably not died in faith. Mr. Ward accompanied me to the grave & said ye responses. The old man had no kith or kin to follow. . . .

21 Sept. . . . C. on Mrs Pennells of ye Tot. She & her husb. argued that they always used to get on better w. Irish hoppers at Bodiam than w. Engl[ish] roughs. If you were civil to ye Irish they were civil to you. If they used bad language it was in their own tongue & not understood of others, & if they fell out it was among themselves . . .

24 Sept. . . . to Pashley . . . Mr. Courthope c. on his way home from ye Petty Sessions.[8] . . . Ellen Hollist took me . . . as far as ye Station. . . . Two hoppers in custody, going to Lewes for their evil deeds.[9]

27 Sept. . . . Offered a reward of 5/- for discovery of ye mischievous person who let ye sheep out of ye Ch. Yard.

28 Sept. . . . In aft. at 1.25 buried James Eastwood (Totty) ye imbecile aged 38. They left me waiting 25 mins. & never said a word. . . .

7 Oct. . . . Sing. at 7. Ye boys troublesome: a noise while I just went into ye vestry. I asked who caused it. Frank Ellis said "all of us" so I dismissed them all & said I must find them tomorrow. It is a great nuisance. Two of ye men later told me who the culprits were. . . .

8 Oct. . . . Sing. w. boys. Fr. Ellis owned to having started ye noise, so I condoned ye offence, & paid ye boys. . . .

13 Oct. . . . 3 men, staying in Burwash c. to take a total abstinence pledge. One for his own sake & ye others for his sake. I t. w. them some time & was much interested. I asked God's blessing w. them on their resolution. . . .

16 Oct. . . . While I was in ye post office at Wadhurst writing a telegr. to Hicks, I heard some curious criticisms of parsons, "They give such a lot of trouble" "They do think themselves such kings". . . .

29 Oct. . . . C. on Sands of Burnt House; out of work after 11 years steady employ on one farm. It is very sad. To ye Ch: dear N. c[ame] w. me & pl. org[an] w. ye boys. They sang steadily enough, tho' weak.

5 Nov. . . . Very wet. Only 4 boys at ye Singing, gave them 2d a piece. T. Jarvis our butcher having fitted out his small boy with a stock of squibs, suffered accordingly. Ye young hopeful or those with him having watched Mr. Jarvis out of ye shop inserted a squib in ye carcase of a pig & retired a judicious distance to watch ye effect. When Jarvis' man came out to find ye offenders ye street was quite clear. . . .

6 Nov. . . . C. on Mrs. J.Isted & paid her 2/- for Stephen singing. She agreed w. me that he is troublesome. . . .

10 Nov. . . . Sch. Tested ye registers. One little infant marked present wrongly. Supposed that another answered for her. 1st case of error I have ever found.

16 Nov. . . . At 8 PM, I to ye Bell. Meeting of rate payers to go thro' ye relief list. Positively only one case considered that of [sixty-eight-year-old, farmworker] G.Copper. . . .

17 Nov. A note from Mr. G.A. Hyland our Guardian saying that he looked upon ye decision of ye meeting last night in ye case of G. Copper as a vote of a Want of Confidence, & that he shd. resign his office on ye 25th![10] I wrote a civil answer. Copper had been so Mr. H. stated personally offensive to him & Mr. H. had determined that he shd. go into "the House". Last

night Mr. Barton cd. not certify Copper able to walk, & ye meeting voted
out-door relief. . . .

18 Nov. . . . At 2 my tithe audit dinner. Good attend. & I have good results!
Ye personal feeling towards myself most kindly, & that is worth much. Ye
farmers unquestionably badly off & I am sure that they may do their best for
me. I sang "A thousand a year" as usual & "When the heart is young". I left
about 5-10 having spent a very pl: afternoon. Poor JP much overcome in his
speech. . . .

Sun. 21 Nov. Sch. I told ye girls to go in at ye South aisle to avoid running
ye gauntlet of ye boys in ye porch. . . . Got Miss George to sit in ye N.W.
corner to keep order; asked for volunteers in ye same cause. Ye Church
much quieter. . . . I wonder whether boys of ye Natl. Sch: rank have any
sense of humour. 3 of my bad boys were reported to me by H. Pagden to
whom I am sincerely obliged, as playing tricks behind my back. I had to
speak very strongly. What curious old school memories "Stir up" Sunday
recalls.

22 Nov. . . . Coming home [from Dallington] w. w. William Budd who
most determinedly shunted any conv: on other than secular matters. . . .

29 Nov. . . . Blunden to inspect ye WC. cd. find nothing to account for
some violent odours. Must get a London man if evil goes on. . . .

3 Dec. . . . Mrs Hollands dog poisoned to day. She sent a note into ye
Vestry asking me to see ye police. I did so, & saw Segt. Buss. He said he
wd. look round after midnight, when ye moon was down. . . .

4 Dec. . . . House startled in ye evg. by a fearful noise at 10.25. Some said a
traction on ye roof. Others a bursting of all ye waterpipes, foul air pipes, &
ventilatory shafts belonging to ye house, others gunpowder. It was really
the breaking of ye winding cord of ye striking part of ye cuckoo clock wh.
had just been wound up for ye week. . . .

6 Dec. . . . C. on Mrs Pope of Holten whose son Walter died very suddenly
on Thursday [2nd] by breaking a blood vessel. Her last surviving child of
the 10 she has had. . . .

7 Dec. Sch: tested registers; all right. Took Infants. . . . My 1st question
was, "who was the first man who ever lived on the earth?". Ye answer was
prompt "God". I suppose ye 2d quest. is "Who made the first man?".
Funeral of Walter Pope aged 16. . . .

9 Dec. . . . To ye Concert. Ye Children (3) made their first appearance on
a platform; they sang a little duett . . . in good tune, & said their words

very clearly. I pl[ayed] by heart & did not make a slip. . . . Mr. Caine Sch. M[aster] from Battle sang a really good comic song by Grossmeth. . . .[11]

21 Dec. St Thomas's day. Gave out the dole. Mr. J. Fuller & F. Cramp helped. Finished it in about two hours. Nothing special except that I withheld my vote for several cases of illegit. children. . . . In evg. attended a meeting at ye Bell to go thro' ye relief list. Sundry cases discussed. Ye general result being ye addition of about 10/- a week to the whole list. Ye writer of an anonymous letter agst. one case took nothing by his endeavour to lower one widows pay, one or two of his statements not being supported by evidence.[12]

24 Dec. Funeral of Mr. Sone at 83. Had been a voluntary inmate of "Ye House" for sometime.[13] Great influx of singing companies, mainly boys by twos and threes. An irregular cohort of performers for While Shepherds watched led by Edwin Honeysett.

25 Dec. For the first time in perhaps the memory of any living person, no singers at the Rectory in ye morg. to sing "Hail happy morn". Wedding at 9. Saml. Vigor & Mary Tootes. No teachers at Sch, so children went home. . . .

28 Dec. . . . C. on Mrs Gilbert, worse. She told me a terrible story of W[illiam] I[sted] coming home drunk turning his wife out of doors & eating up ye whole of ye dole beef, wh. she had cooked for ye children on Sunday [26th]. Really a man who gives way to drink is worse than a beast, for no beast wd. eat its childrens food in such a way. . . .[14]

1887

Sun. 2 Jan. . . . Large Congr. I bapts. Bressie Dodswell. C. on J. Jarvis & T. Pagden to complain of their boys going out after ye 2nd Hymn in Church, presumably to skate [in the snow]. . . . Saw Ambrose Pilbeam & Banks (Alfred) ye two R. Eng[ineers]. Looked well & Ambr. P. has his first stripe for Corporal wh. is good.

8 Jan. . . . C. on Mrs Sands; her d. coming home [after going on trial as housemaid a month earlier]; it is too bad. She will not get such a chance again as Mrs Schroeter's, & only because the mother fancied that the girl was not well. . . .

11 Jan. . . . First day of giving out soup, but a nasty day for the poor people. I did not turn out till sing. w. boys in evg. Pay night. I asked whether they wished to leave no one spoke.

15 Jan. . . . So dark that on leaving the town, in groping my way I actually turned round, & without knowing it walked some way towards the Weald! . . .

21 Jan. . . . In aft. a meeting here of ladies in Burwash Parish & St. Philip to organize a canvass for the Jubilee Women's offering to the Queen. . . . Old W. Pilbeam found drowned in ye Touching [?] pond has been missing a week; sad end of a sad life.[15]

26 Jan. . . . C. on poor B. Thompson, & had a long & interesting t. w. him. I fear that there is not a little scepticism on religion amongst us, but I cannot find the ye sceptics offer any better alternative than that wh. xtianity does. . . . In evg. read my Hist. of Burwash at the Reading Room to members only. 51 present & reading lasted just under two hours! & there was no sign outwardly given of weariness.

27 Jan. To ye sch. at 9.20. Mr. Emmerson [HMI] there but no Mr. Allington. I went round, & put pressure on some of ye parents of absentees. . . .[16]

28 Jan. . . . I to ye sing. H. Pagden sadly troublesome. I reasoned w. him by himself when ye others had gone, but without apparent effect. I c. in ye aft. on Brown ye coachbuilder. His son who told me that his father wished him to leave the singing had told a simple lie. It is very sad.

1 Feb. Started for school, but found I had on my old overcoat the torn condition of wh. sent me home. In aft. C. on Sam. Ellis, burnt his foot with a hot brick in bed. . . . Mrs Pennells of ye Tot consented to take our cat whose nuances & customs have become unbearable.

3 Feb. . . . Meditated on ye ways of boys, why they shd. be so troublesome, but came to no satisfactory conclusion. . . .

5 Feb. . . . John Burgess just going over to a Liberal meeting at Brightling to hear Mr. Macer Wright on Ireland; he (JB) will I imagine be lively, it is a pity.

6 Feb. . . . Sissy Taylor interv. me after Sing: to say that she thought that ye Dissenters had been overlooked in asking persons to become collectors for ye Jubilee fund. I am much obliged to her; will set to it tomorrow.

7 Feb. I c. on Miss Kate Noakes & asked her to act as a collector. She was very willing to do so. . . .

19 Feb. Funeral of Mrs Gilbert at 2. Being ye boys & girls half holiday, they were many & unruly, tho' Mr. Cramp ye Ch: W[arden] kept them out of ye Ch. during ye service. . . .

24 Feb. . . . a young woman of ye name of Wilmshurst, servant at Mr. Pednarns [?] c. to ask me if I cd. help ye formation of a branch of "ye Xtian Progress Soc." formed for reading ye Bible. She is a Brenchley young woman, & seemed much in earnest. Burwash is I fear an unlikely parish, but I shd. rejoice if she cd. do anything, or if I cd. help her. I down to ye Sch. to hear ye Brass band practice. I was really much pleased. The absence of gradations of tone was of course very noticeable, but the tune was good, & they played w. much spirit. . . .

26 Feb. Found that I had carelessly read a request from Mr. Hayler at Robertsbridge that I wd. preside at a public lecture on ye Irish question in ye Conserv. Interest, as a request from ye Radicals for ye use of ye sch. room for a lecture on ye Irish question! I humbly apologized.

2 Mar. . . . In aft. went w. Dr. Barton & Mr. Newton Taylor ye Relieving Officer to Mrs Leaney's at Mr. Gibbs lodge. Interviewed her husbands mother who has been for sometime under delusions, & violent. Signed ye order for her removal to Haywards Heath. . . .

21 Mar. To Sch. at 9.30 & staid till 12. Sad number of men standing about with nothing to do. . . .

25 Mar. In aft. a meeting of ye Jubilee Collectors to see if they could undertake visiting work. . . . There seemed to be a fair amount of readiness & districts were allotted to those who were present. . . . Vestry meeting at 8. Adj. to ye Bell. Some diffic: about Parish Officers. Mr. G.A. Hyland kindly stood again as Guardian, & Mr. Whatman offered himself as Overseer wh. was kind as the office this year is important owing to a new valuation of ye parish. . . .[17]

Notes

1. The annual inspection report mentioned 'some improvement', but of greater moment for the first time asserted that 'the Discipline ought to be better'; the observation that 'The attendance is miserable, but bad attendance does not justify the Managers in removing names from the Register', was equally disheartening. Dated, 1 Feb. 1886, ESCRO. ESC.41/1.
2. The reference is to the relocation of the Working Men's Institute and Reading Rooms in the Old Chapel; Egerton did not mention its 1882 foundation, and although it shortly opened (see below, p. 340, 22 Feb. 1886), further funding was needed for shoring up the building. See below, pp. 350–1, 9 Dec. 1886.
3. Whatman, who had served as Guardian since 1881, failed, and stayed on for another year, when Alfred Jarvis served. Vestry minutes, 26 Mar. 1886 and 25 Mar. 1887, ESCRO. Par.284/12/2.
4. Bolton, since Dec. 1885 MP for St Pancras, a seat he lost in 1886, was the principal architect of the 1886 Extraordinary Tithe Redemption Act. He claimed

that 'if fairly carried out' it would 'satisfactorily dispose of the question'. Episcopal pressure in the Lords gave the Commissioners extra powers, including a brief to decide whether hop-land at the time of the redemption was likely to remain so. When these commenced, hops had experienced a further drastic price fall, and Bolton and others campaigned to ensure that the Commissioners were alerted to an anticipated further and major shrinkage in hop acreages. However, the Commissioners visits to the localities did not start until the summer of 1887, a period not covered by the diary, and Egerton predeceased their deliberations in Burwash. *Sussex Advertiser*, 10 Jan. and 11 July 1887. See also below, p. 360.

5.   According to one press report 'The Rector . . . and a few Tories were also present, and although expressions of dissent were frequent, the proceedings passed off in an orderly manner'. Reuter attacked pressure for tariffs to protect the agricultural interest; if these were imposed, manufacturing interests would demand parallel measures. Reuter asserted that the recent Extraordinary Tithe legislation had been forced on the Tories, but he devoted most of his speech to the support of Gladstone's position on Home Rule for Ireland. Egerton formally but unsuccessfully moved a motion that Home Rule 'in the form currently proposed would be dangerous to the country', and was seconded by surgeon Barton. *Sussex Advertiser*, 3 July 1886.

6.   The Hearts of Oak No. 5332 of the Ancient Order of Foresters was however in a relatively flourishing state. Over the year only £25 had been paid in sickness benefit, and there had been no deaths other than a member's wife, and expenditure was £10 less than in 1884–5. The fund had increased by £52. Following three resignations, and fifteen recruits, membership currently stood at seventy-nine. Schoolmaster G.E. Anset was secretary. Dinner was at the Bell as landlord Farley was a member.

7.   Etchingham was the nearest railway station to the thirtieth and last of the proposed Barnardo's homes. The special train from London arrived at the station, 'very prettily decorated with evergreens, flowering and foliage plants'; the Tecks were escorted by four mounted Kent County policemen, and a detachment of the West Kent Yeomanry. 'The whole countryside turned out and lined the road for the seven miles. . . . at nearly every cottage some kind of decoration had been hung out. . . . At Hurstgreen . . . an arch of evergreen had been erected across the road, bearing the inscription "God be with you"'. *Sussex Agricultural Express*, 14 Aug. 1886.

8.   Where the sole Burwash case involved labourer Thomas Vidler, convicted on Sergeant Buss's evidence for being drunk and disorderly on the 11th, and fined 5/- with 10/- cost, or two weeks hard labour in the event of non-payment. Summary conviction returns, ESCRO. QR/E1116. *Sussex Agricultural Express*, 28 Sept. 1886.

9.   They typified hop-pickers and their customary offences. Thomas Williams 'of no fixed abode' received a one-month term for opportunistically stealing ten pounds of raw meat from a Hurst Green abattoir on 21 Sept., and sailor William Sullivan, of Brighton, was sentenced to a total of six weeks hard labour for the theft of an ornate walking stick, and then an ounce of tobacco on 20 Sept. at Bodiam. Williams' protestation of innocence – 'he did not smoke, but when apprehended he had on him two pipes and tobacco dust in his pockets' – was lame even by such offenders' standards. *Sussex Agricultural Express*, 28 Sept. 1886.

10.   The threat to resign from 25 Mar. 1887 was not implemented, and Hyland occupied the office from 1885 to 1888. Vestry minutes, 26 Mar. 1885 to 26 Mar. 1888, ESCRO. Par.284/12/2.

11.   The concert was in aid of the 'Burwash Working Men's Institute and Reading Rooms', opened on 6 Nov. 1886, after recurrent delays in repairs to the old Independent Chapel, which had closed on the 1864 erection of a larger church in the centre of the village. In the summer of 1886, William Ellis jnr., described as an 'active young tradesmen', orchestrated yet another subscription, as the building was thought likely to collapse entirely over another winter, which financed the final rebuilding, with the premises divided into three rooms. In the first month another seventy joined, 'chiefly young tradesmen and farm labourers. Daily and weekly newspapers, magazines, and apparatus for many harmless amusements are provided'. The concert at the National School attracted the enormous audience of 250. Other performers included several farmers and tradesmen, principally Dissenters, who – unlike the Noakes' family – had little to do with the Rector. Presumably they comprised the anti-Noakes faction of Dissenters, and these people may have seen the institute as a rival to the Congregational Chapel Lending Library, run by W.H. Noakes, with a collection of 278 volumes to date. *Sussex Advertiser*, 15 Dec. 1886 and 24 Jan. 1887.

12.   Which nevertheless reveals that the contents of anonymous letters in these delicate matters were taken seriously.

13.   George Sone was described as a resident 'hostler' at the workhouse in the 1851 census; presumably he simply retired at some point and went to the 'old men's ward'.

14.   On 28 Jan. 1877 Isted was again fined (10/- and 11/- costs) for drunkenness on 27 Dec. on the evidence of Sgt. Buss; summary conviction returns, ESCRO. QE/E1117.

15.   William Pilbeam was seventy-five, and 'for more than half a century a blacksmith in' the village; the press reported that on 14 Dec. 1886 he 'wandered away from his son's house . . . which had been his home for some years and from that time until . . . Friday [21st] nothing was known of him' when he was discovered in the 'large pond' on Franchise Farm. 'The body was very little decomposed, when taken out of the water, owing possibly to its having been covered for several weeks with ice'. *Sussex Advertiser*, 24 Jan. 1887.

16.   Dated 14 Feb. 1887, the report showed a distinct improvement, with the mixed school's results indicating 'creditable progress', while in the infants 'the Children are orderly and seem interested in their work'. ESCRO. ESR.41/1.

17.   He omits Albert Jarvis's nomination as the second Guardian, following a year's stint as one of the overseers. In fact Richard Fuller, Thomas Brook, and James Bourner, were also appointed overseers, following the doubling of elected overseers introduced in 1885, possibly in anticipation of a revaluation, one of the most emotive and contentious exercises. Vestry minutes, 26 Mar. 1885, 25 Mar. 1886, and 25 Mar. 1887, ESCRO Par.284/12/2.

Epilogue and Evaluation
Epilogue 1887–1888

Egerton's arrival in Burwash coincided with the first few years of the most sustained period of relative agrarian profitability since the end of the war, way back in 1815. At the time of his death in March 1888 there was no apparent end to yet another agricultural depression deriving from the later 1870s, but the situation in Burwash was becoming particularly acute, notably for the farmworkers. The village had not experienced the pronounced depopulation seen elsewhere in the rural districts; its population stabilized, with 2,232 inhabitants in 1871 and 2,285 in 1881, before a slight fall to 2,093 by 1891. These figures obscure a modicum of structural population change, with a perceptible if not substantial fall in labourers, being compensated for by an increase in semi- and fully retired affluent folk, and their household servants. Their households and gardens absorbed some local labour. One of two long-standing wealthy residents speculated in this market by building new houses. When Albert Jarvis finished one such house at the end of 1889, it was hoped that he would soon attract a tenant, and that he and others would 'be encouraged to build more . . . and induce people to come to Burwash to reside'.[1] But this was hardly a short-term measure. The immediate and principal economic problem in agriculture was the rapid collapse of hop-growing.

   Hop-acreages increased during the first half of Egerton's incumbency, with 250 in 1864 rising to nearly 400 in 1874. Thereafter lower prices, slightly higher labour costs, and competition from imports, led to considerable apprehension that the 'hop-land' was being driven 'largely out of cultivation'. Planters were already reducing labour and manure inputs and were reputedly 'indifferent as to the cultivation of their grounds'. As a result, in 1887, 'The earnings of pickers, polepullers, and dryers, have been . . . very small'. No longer did 'hop-picking with its earnings furnish the' means for working families to obtain replacement 'winter garments and winter comforts'. Over the winter of 1887–8 the only 'slight improvement' in the parochial 'labour market' came from better than expected wood sales on a Brightling estate, and major repairs to the main road which 'found work for some hands, though not for long'. At the start of the following winter 'too many . . . little children . . . show by their pale and hungry looks that there is but scant fare at home'.[2]

   'Where employment is to come from when hops are gone', Egerton wrote in January 1888, 'no-one can tell us'. At this moment he started plans to finance a significant round of emigration – principally of labourers – through a public subscription. Egerton's interest in the achievements of

Burwash folk who had either migrated or emigrated was perennial and natural, but he had built up quite a reputation for encouraging young, and enterprising men and women to start careers elsewhere; as one of those who had benefited, said after the Rector's death, 'I might have spent a life of drudgery but for him. I was not the only one he sent out of Burwash; most all, I think, have done well'. Egerton also drew public attention to these achievements, and at the end of his life, he helped project his proposed new emigration, by subtle emphasis on its long tradition. For example, he cited a letter of 1838 vintage from William and Elizabeth Russell, in New South Wales, to William's brothers, Sam, George and Reuben, Elizabeth's father, and her two brothers Job and Levi Mepham: 'if you mean to do yourselves any good, this is the only place for you to come'. This was penned shortly after William and Elizabeth, with an infant son, refused workhouse accommodation, but accepted poor-law assisted emigration. George Russell, his wife, and three children under six, went in 1839, also aided by public funds, and while none of the other recipients of this letter left Burwash in the same manner, they all departed. Now, Egerton asked whether any current residents were still in communication with these people, and what had become of them.[3]

Egerton's scheme possibly died with him, though the dour Gilbert-Cooper at St Philips, with typical clumsiness, initially tried to maintain the momentum. 'The separation and scattering of families to distant lands may seem a hard measure', he wrote, 'but it is a hard necessity'. And he continued in a even more frigid utilitarian style, worthy of Malthus yet replete with Old Testament undertones:

> Emigration in due course is quite a law of the very existence of nations. It was so in old times, it is so in our days. When a country is over-populated in proportion to its extent and means of feeding and supporting its people, emigration . . . is the obvious remedy for relieving the state of congestion.[4]

Nonetheless, the situation is clear; for at least many working people and their families in Burwash – the source of all 'congestion' – during the final year of Egerton's career, economic prospects were bleak, the suggested remedies radical and traumatic. They were 'hard' alternatives to the continued inadequacy of employment, wages, and available social-security benefits: the results were visible in the faces of the children.

This economic malaise, and its social potential, was responsible for gloom, dampening notably the celebrations of Queen Victoria's Jubilee. Problems over preparations recorded during the last three months of the Rector's diary, recurred; 'It would be more easy to rouse enthusiasm if times were better and money more abundant', asserted Egerton in May 1887, and the whole thing remained essentially low-key. Some said the organizing committee was 'not representative'. Members of the Burwash Brass Band, accurately read the signs, and offered their services which were seized upon by those charged with festivities at Dallington. On the day, the service at St Bartholomew's drew a record congregation, ironically symbolized by those unable to get in. Only the parish church 'and its approaches' were decorated with evergreens and flowers, though many houses sported Union Jacks. The schoolchildren had an unprecedented breakfast in the school room, and were joined for a tea later in the day by their mothers. The children also had customary sports in front of the Rectory; youths played cricket, while the shopkeeper Miss Fleming provided a 'meat tea', for old people living in the village. Mrs Holland maintained the discrimination against cohabitees, with another tea at Oaklands for 'all the young married people of the parish', while ninety elderly folk from the west had their tea courtesy of the Trower spinsters. Celebrations terminated with a bonfire, and fireworks. Perhaps the real calibre of the day was best revealed by the solitary policeman who materialized right 'at the end of the evening', while people were dispersing, as Gussey Egerton swept up some embers from the fire to keep as a momento. Her father composed a short eulogy on Britain's triumphal imperialism coincident with Victoria's half-century on the throne.[5]

Otherwise, Egerton's last year was relatively uneventful. The Anglicans retained their educational hegemony, though it took a hefty voluntary collection to increase St Philip's school capacity by forty-eight places, to avoid recourse to a School Board. Despite appeals for 'a good pull and a *pull all together*', over half the cost came from donations by the Rector, Gilbert-Cooper, and the Trowers. Although some improvements were noted in educational achievements in 1887, absenteeism went largely unabated, and in 1888 adverse effects were reported deriving from Anset's prolonged 'feeble health', although it had already precipitated his early retirement.[6]

The Congregationalists' fund-raising campaigns for overseas missions continued unabated, but once again the response proved economy-related, and a mere £5-13-4 was raised during the whole of 1887. Financial considerations were hardly relevant to the major religious development in Burwash in that year, namely the creation of a Catholic Church at Southover Hall, by the immensely rich Madame de los Heros. Both chapels and chancel had 'circular apsidal ends', and whatever the skill lavished in the execution of the building, the provision of a Presbytery presaged the imminent arrival of the new Catholic parish priest. Publicly, the Anglicans appear to have ignored this entire initiative, though it comprised a logical extension of the earlier replacement of all Protestant by Catholic domestic servants at Southover, recorded by Egerton, at the same time as it outdated the reasons behind his view that the hoary question of Anglican–Catholic differences could be totally and safely ignored in Burwash.[7]

The most notable resident to die in this period was the Amazonian, seventy-five-year-old, spinster Kathy Weller. A superb obituary – which volunteers the tantilizing fact that she was also the long-term keeper of a daily diary – charts her remarkable career. The daughter of the draper,

Robert Weller, who failed, and turned his hand to gardening, Kathy's first employment was as a miller's 'warehouse-woman and gardener', an extraordinary dual-occupancy even by Wealden standards. Villagers recalled regularly encountering Kitty making light of carrying standard two and a half hundredweight bags of flour. Enterprise on her own behalf at this early stage included 'filling up her odd time by building a lodge, a fence, or a pig-pound', and soon after her father's death she took the twelve-acre Little Bateman's Farm.

She subsequently became a general shopkeeper, but when the tenancy of the Bell became vacant, took it despite its repute as 'a rather disorderly house'. Here she imposed her will, was reknown for physically ejecting drunks, took some hard knocks herself, and on occasion prosecuted the most rowdy, awkward, or violent. Edward Fuller, who dealt in fruit when not labouring, was one local roughneck, whom Kathy prosecuted on two occasions; in the second, in 1865, she stopped Fuller organizing a raffle, whereupon he 'threw her down . . . and struck her . . . tore her clothes very much, and made use of bad language'. However, other cases reveal that she did permit more favoured customers to illegally gamble on licensed premises, and if she herself evaded conviction for after-hours opening, she came perilously close to it in 1871. Indeed, the formal record of this episode, when the Grand Jury refused to sanction the prosecution that Kitty sought, probably conceals the fact that she had, effectively, fatally compromised the renewal of her licence. She certainly surrendered it, but she had towards the end of the 1860s taken on the lease of a seventy-acre farm, employing four men and two boys, which enabled her retention of an entrepreneurial profile. Her departure from the farm was in virtual anticipation of the deepening of the agricultural depression, and she then put her capital into cottage properties. She supplemented her income as a rentier by gardening, and seasonal labour, including haymaking, virtually till within days of her death, and as her obituary writer put it, 'for a female, a somewhat extraordinary life'. The same could hardly be said of the builder Benjamin Thompson, who also died in 1887, but his stable business was taken over by his sane sons; two remained in mental institutions.[8]

Along with the customary trickle of convictions for poaching and drunkenness, most offences in Burwash during Egerton's last year were minor; James Watson was again fined for obstructing the highway with his horse and cart, and grocer Stephen Mainwaring's incaution in letting his horse stray on the road 'near the Police Station' also resulted in a court appearance, while one of the Harmer family was proceeded against for moonlighting thereby preventing his landlord's seizure of furniture for £4 rent arrears. Levi Luck was in trouble again, but only for having an unlicensed dog. Later in 1888 a crackdown on petty bread retailers for sales other than by weight, netted five offenders. Much more serious, both legally, and doubtlessly morally in Egerton's eyes, were the rape charges levied against Alfred Watson and Henry Farley, and Frederick Dann for aiding and abetting. All three men were in their early twenties, as was their victim, Harriet Hawkins, Watson's sometime 'sweetheart'. Harriet, an orphan, had been brought up partly in a Barnardo's Babies Castle, but subsequently 'passed a great portion of her time in . . . [Ticehurst] Workhouse', from whence she periodically discharged herself for a few days, before returning to regale other inmates with stories of her sexual exploits while out and about. On this occasion, the alleged offences occurred after she drank heavily with all defendants before noon. Such prosecutions reinforced, rather than counteracted, male jurors' chauvinist prejudices, and the case at the Assize had visibly collapsed when it was formally abandoned.[9]

If concerts once again contributed to the funding of both the cricket club and the literary institute, other important elements of Egerton's world were changing. Given his repeated ridicule of the increasing democratization of politics, he surely would not have been happy with the radical changes to county governance with the coming of the county councils. Henceforth, the magistracy retained only their criminal administration; the justices were even denied an automatic majority on the county police committee, as half the members were now elected councillors. Yet where contested, the first elections to the new East Sussex Council were not on party lines. Burwash, which was joined by Ticehurst to form a constituency, was one of the minority of sixteen seats contested.[10]

The current head of the Ticehurst Asylum Dr Herbert Hayes Newington, a somewhat reactionary Tory, was opposed by T.H. Bolton, the ex-Liberal MP. A Conservative Association had been formed at Burwash but one week previously, with G.A. Hyland as its first president. Ironically Hyland publicly supported Bolton, who seems to have aimed to the point of concentration on working-class voters, urging 'the mechanics and agricultural labourers to elect men who could sympathise with and do something for the benefit of the masses'. Instead of focusing on those aspects of local administration the new county councils would take over, Bolton prophesied a broadening remit as the new bodies 'became little local parliaments'. Bolton speculated that they would take over and reform educational provision, with an emphasis on vocational and technical training, address the question of abysmal working-class housing, and displace the Local Government Board thus removing social-security matters from centralized control. Newington attacked Bolton's 'visionary' perceptions, and warned that their implementation, especially education, would greatly inflate the rates, to the disadvantage principally of farmworkers. Newington romped home by 446 votes to 299.[11]

By then Egerton was dead, one week before the Tithe Commissioners appointed under the 1886 Act piloted through the Commons by Bolton, were scheduled to visit Burwash. Egerton died on 19 March, supposedly from 'gout of the heart' after a month's serious illness. He was fifty-eight. On 30 May, the senior congregationalist deacon, John Buss Noakes died, aged seventy-three, after four years' retirement from business. On 27 June, the seventy-seven-year-old Andrew Gibbs died; although the first part of the burial service took place at St Bartholomew's, in which parish he had lived since 1854, and therefore preceded Egerton, it was significant that the body was returned to London for burial in the family vault at Kensal Green Cemetery.[12]

Egerton's death moved the somewhat colourless Gilbert-Cooper to a dramatic account from the perspective of St Philip's parsonage on the Common. On 19 March,

> The news soon spread, not only over his own parish, but also over Burwash Weald . . . It was like the spreading of a dark cloud wherever it reached. Gloom and sorrow filled all dwellings, all hearts. A stranger passing through Burwash later in the day was struck by the stillness and hush which prevailed all the street down. No children's mirth, yet children there were to be seen; no hum and stir of business and work. A few here and there stood about talking, but with bated breath. It was like a village of death – all inhabitants thinking, speaking of grieving for one whom they should see no more in the flesh, but whose familiar form, kindly smile, and cheery greeting seemed so present with them, as hardly to enable them to realise that death had removed him from them.[14]

He was buried at St Bartholomew's four days later; the coffin, covered with flowers, was carried into the church by eight members of the choir. A procession, estimated between two and three hundred, included most members of Egerton's 'parochial aristocracy', several neighbouring incumbents, 'the leading ratepayers and tradesmen', the rest of the choir, the schoolchildren, and miscellaneous parishioners. The seating proved inadequate, for the numbers attending the service, performed by his brother, the warden of All Saints, Brixham, the Revd P.R. Egerton, and Dr Wace, the man who had married John Coker, and still principal of King's College.[15]

He was replaced temporarily by the Revd Western until the new Rector C.F. Maude, took over in November, after Nellie and the five children had moved from the Rectory. At almost the same time, Gilbert-Cooper, resigned the thin living at St Philips, ostensibly on the grounds of age, and was replaced by the Revd C.M. Saunders. The new incumbents launched a minor shake-up. The district visitors were reorganized on a sounder, more practical footing, and *Parish Notes*, previously comprising separate reports from the two parishes were amalgamated, though neither of the new incumbents was able to imitate Egerton's power of sensitive, but sociologically informative, capacity for obituary. Maude immediately launched a crusade against small boys using the churchyard as a playground, and embarked on a campaign to plant flowers and rose trees by the walls; Egerton's utilitarian grass-cutters, the sheep, were an automatic casualty.[16]

On her departure, Mrs Egerton presented each pupil in St Bartholomew's and St Philip's National Schools with 'a memorial card of the late Rector', and choir members of both congregations with a 'cabinet portrait' of John.

Somewhat later, nearly a year after Egerton's death, a committee comprising some upper-class women, including Misses Tilley, and Gould, the lawyer James Philcox, and farmers and tradesmen, decided to launch a subscription to fund a memorial to Egerton, namely a clock, to be installed in the church tower. The response exceeded expectation, not least through contributions from a number of people who had prospered, having taken Egerton's advice to migrate. The additional monies were to be spent on full restoration of the tower, and buying the 'much needed' replacement churchyard gates at St Bartholomew's. If the clock came from the metropolitan makers of Big Ben, village tradesmen benefited from the other components, builders Thompson from the tower, while the relatively recently arrived blacksmith Malpas forged the new gates.[17]

The unsigned obituary published in the parish magazine, was naturally, laudatory, but its stuffiness suggests Gilbert-Cooper's authorship. He stressed Egerton's capacity as 'a steady and wise counsellor' in both spiritual and temporal matters, qualities reflected in the volume of mail he received from past and present parishioners. Somewhat more questionable, was the assertion that Egerton was 'a loving student of human nature', and those who were denied christenings, Christmas beef, and other charitable assistance, would hardly have concurred that Egerton 'could always enter with true sympathy into the daily lives of the people he loved so well'. And the diaries only partially confirm another observation:

> Music was the one relaxation which he allowed himself in his busy life. . . . The unusual excellence of the church choir, taught and trained by himself, and the quiet behaviour of its younger members, which has been much commented upon, have been a source of real happiness to him.[18]

Evaluation

Diary editors commonly make fundamental errors, even to the point of insulting various categories of prospective readers. The highlighting of personality factors, or of points of serious academic import, in introductions can be pre-emptive, to the degree of preventing readers from making their own evaluative assessment of character, or being denied the excitement of identifying matters of historical significance for themselves. Similarly, conclusions composed by editors, can be repetitive to the point of boredom. The introduction in the present volume aimed to avoid these pitfalls, through the presentation of an historical picture of Burwash, from the perspective of about the time that Egerton arrived in the place. Only the briefest biographical detail of the man was provided, together with the slightest anticipation of the contents of the diary text, in order to round off this part of the book. A brief mention was also made in the introduction of Anglican claims to have played a major role in essentially civilizing a notoriously unruly, insubordinate and, at times, desperate majority of the population. This evaluation primarily addresses that question.

Egerton himself went to considerable lengths to try to build up his uncle Gould's achievements, which he suggested as late as 1882, had 'never . . . been fully understood'. Of course, elements of this reputation were undeniable. Gould was responsible for the rebuilding of St Bartholomew's church, simultaneously terminating the ancient and socially divisive system of private pews, and he was also the prime mover behind the the erection of the first National School in the village. Gould's efforts respecting the Common, the initial adaptation of the old workhouse, and the subsequent building of St Philips and another schoolroom were equally obvious, and as Egerton liked to stress on occasion, all this building was funded to the tune of over £6000 'without a penny being spent in printing for the purpose of soliciting subscriptions'. Egerton also emphasized that his uncle spent a disproportionate amount of energy, and his own money, on 'this far off part of his parish', and claimed that this 'work bore fruit before the advent of the railway station' in 1851.[19]

Gould's interests were not exclusively pastoral. He was a keen hunter, who enjoyed shooting, and so was presumably hostile to some of his parishioners' incessant poaching. He appears to have directly farmed his glebe, and although he was responsible for the development of the rectory gardens, this also facilitated his horticultural interests. A regular exhibitioner and competitor at the Ticehurst Agricultural Association shows, he won prizes for livestock, root-fodder crops; his gardener also engaged successfully in the 'professional', as opposed to cottage garden produce prize-category, for vegetables. Early in the diary, Egerton recorded Gould's apparent irritation that his, then new, curate was not simply unfamiliar with agricultural method, but was also apparently indifferent. If John Coker's indifference persisted, he maintained the expensive finery in the Rectory gardens, and made recommendations of Burwash folk for the non-agrarian prizes awarded annually at Ticehurst.

The latter comprised part of the paternalist dimension to the Society's activities. It was no accident that it was formed almost simultaneously with the implementation of the Robbery Bill, and sought to bolster the independent labourer ideology of the system's architects by awarding prizes for working folk, who brought up large families without recourse to public aid, in addition to further cash awards for tidy cottages, and model gardens. Gould also provided allotments – there were seventy-three in 1859 – and prizes were given annually for produce raised by their plebeian cultivators. Interestingly, Gould tacitly admitted problems over juvenile deliquency and youthful irreverence, by his assertion in that same year that he would provide more land to ex-national schoolboys 'so that he may see them, and watch over them on the precarious period from school to manhood'. Moreover, Gould had a modest appreciation of his own efforts, for it was in 'temporal matters' – which he curiously limited to the restoration of St Bartholomew's and the building of the school – in which he detected a degree of success. Otherwise, after thirty-five years 'among them . . . it grieved him to see so little good from his labours'. In this context, he asserted during a speech at a friendly society anniversary, that

> he wanted to see less drunkenness, fewer illegitimate children, more religion among them. He had laboured, and should continue to do so, but he could not say that his was a model parish, he wished he could.[20]

By inference, Egerton himself, endorsed his uncle. As might be expected, given his pragmatic ecumenicalism, he acknowledged that it was the Wesleyans who constructed the 'first building dedicated to . . . public worship' in that 'wild part', namely the Common, and announced that whenever he got a sight of it he reacted with feelings of 'thankfulness and respect'. He also believed that the efforts of lay folk – both Anglican and non-conformist – had had a beneficial respect, especially the Anglican Miss Trowers who did not arrive until the mid-sixties, and Mrs Holland, who finally became resident in 1871; the only non-conformists he appears to have accepted into this category were the Wesleyan farming family, the Simes's. While Egerton's diary revealed some respect for the Congregationalist leadership, he was scathing about their capacity for destructive in-fighting, and probably incensed that the divisions in the Anglican church – which were certainly not of his making – nevertheless operated to reduce his own flock, members of which had the temerity to resort to the Congregationalists. Egerton is strangely silent on any socially ameliorative impact which the latter may have had. When coupled with his own, private doubts about his lack of achievement, what he perceived as his inadequate energy, the impression conveyed is that he himself did not seriously entertain the view that religious endeavours had had a particularly fundamental impact on sanitizing his Victorian village. He does seem to have believed that a curious combination of clerical and lay Anglicans, Methodists, more intensive agricultural exploitation of the Common district, and education – child and adult – had ameliorated the moral condition of Burwash Weald. If Egerton had been asked, he would have almost certainly agreed that the professional police were also important in this context. Egerton certainly campaigned relentlessly to erode previous notoriety, through a long-term and continuous exercise in public relations, especially in parts of the county press, which we have cited fairly extensively in the footnotes.[21]

The sheer persistence of those contemporaneously identified in Burwash, as elsewhere in the Victorian countryside as the 'roughs', also impresses. Egerton periodically acknowledged – be it privately – that a considerable sector of especially working-class folk were beyond not simply the pale of organized religion, but outside 'respectability', however defined. The best evidence here undoubtedly derives from Egerton's efforts with the Isted brothers, whom neither he, nor their wives, nor for that matter the police, could seemingly permanently tame. Moreover, the 'roughs' were not exclusively working class. Blacksmiths – in the persons of at least the elder Pilbeam, and his rival Daws, who oscillated between drunken binges together, and interchanges of fisticuffs – deserved something of their general characterisation as insubordinates, and equally warranted alignment with the roughs. In the main, these people were hostile – on occasion openly so – to the village 'boss'. While it is interesting that Egerton was not in his own village when he experienced open denunciation in old-style radical politicized terminology, or overheard – probably designedly – two women discoursing on parsons thinking themselves 'such kings', it is surely equally symbolic of social relationships that his temporary offer of a refuge at the Rectory for the youthful Sally Isted spawned hostile, accusatory, sexual innuendo, while his church services for the men of the Kent and Sussex Union stimulated a marked increase in respectful acknowlegement by farmworkers of his reverence's passage along the street. But the latter was almost certainly temporary; more enduring, is the type of social ostracism incurred, as Egerton occasionally noted, by working people, or their children, who participated in Anglican ventures, be they the choir or the mothers' meetings. It was the rebellious, irreverent and coarse comics, who were encored, not the seemingly sanctimonious 'Christian' performers at village concerts.

Gilbert-Cooper's successor, the Revd Saunders soon appreciated that his energetic provision of more church services, drew in very few parishioners. School attendance, even after the compulsory provisions of the 1876 Act, also remained problematic, and rudimentary literacy difficult to achieve. But there were changes. Most noticeable were the stark contrasts between the early and later nineteenth-century agricultural depressions. Certainly poverty remained a major factor; it more or less forced some to the Rectory to receive hand-outs of soup, a telling rural variant of the soup-kitchens featured in the Victorian city. The prolonged serious crime waves, interspersed with covert and especially open social protest, experienced earlier were not repeated. There was, perhaps, less despair, reduced feelings of sheer hopelessness in the later Victorian village. Some of this might be attributed to shades of optimism induced by agrarian trade unionism, and the extension of the vote, whatever their illusory future. Moreover, many of the new generations had for decades been voting with their feet, and getting out, with or without Egerton's direct encouragement.

Egerton entertained no romantic misconceptions over the realities of life for the majority of continuing rural inhabitants in the later nineteenth century. One of his most incisive observations, committed to the diary on 1 September 1885, sadly noted that there was little difference over public morality, between town and country, except presumably scale. He also knew the human realities behind the picturesque qualities of the outward veneer of the Victorian village. Among many other revealing observations about social conditions was his rider about Gussey's eventual height, namely dependency on her reaching adulthood. Infant and child mortality remained relatively pronounced, and of course, in the diaries (and else-

where), he recorded the burials of many children, including the observation
with the burial register entry respecting nine-year-old Ruth Marshall, four
days after Christmas 1882; 'Was at a children's tea party on Friday & died
the following Monday'. The fact, also recorded, that he felt moved over the
deaths of people in the prime of life, as opposed to the elderly, or babies and
children, speaks for itself.[22]

The question of social-security clearly perplexed Egerton to the point of
distraction. Like so many of his class, and with his education, he was
committed to free-market economics and the self-help principles popula-
rized by Samuel Smiles, a copy of whose classic he gave to a youngster
departing from Burwash. In theory, Egerton believed in the essentially
laissez-faire principles of the New Poor Law. He was bugged by its practice.
He clearly thought it immoral that the invalided Maskall should raise an
enormous family on outdoor relief, but on occasion fractured his belief in
the paramountcy of independence when he saw the inadequacy of wages
paid to hard-working folk with enlarged family responsibility, and tried to
intervene in order to secure them public aid. Egerton also resented some
decisions to send old folk, usually the widowed, to the workhouse, though
on occasion he thought that perhaps they would be better off in the material
sense if they were in care.

In March 1883, Egerton penned a brief obituary notice of Caroline
Burgess, aged eighty-six; she was survived by her husband John, who had
worked for the parish on Bough Farm during the bad years after the war,
but who subsequently maintained Caroline and himself by day-labour till
he attained eighty-three, the previous year. John now went to live with a
son. The Rector continued strongly:

> we feel sure that in such a case there is no more degredation attaching
> to an allowance from the parish than there is to a pension earned by
> long and faithful service under the county, the government, or private
> employers. The degredation of parish pay belongs to those persons
> who have had their chance of doing well, but who by carelessness or
> wilfulness having thrown them away, have become beholden to
> neighbours who have had no better chances than they have had
> themselves.

Ironically, privately, Egerton had great difficulty in deciding who imposed
through misrepresentation, and who were genuine candidates to benefit
from the judiciously warped principles of the Victorian Poor Law he
enunciated here.[23]

Finally, the fact that there was no repetition of the serious social malaises
of the 1820s, in the depressed 1880s, owed probably more to the professionalization and institutionalization of the County Police, than it did to
religion, education, and exhortation. Egerton himself had sufficient resort
to the police, even over delinquent schoolchildren, whom we should
remember were all under thirteen, to suggest that he would have gone

someway at least privately, to according a major role to the police in whatever sanitization had been achieved. Moreover, he had some faith in the prison system, remarking publicly after a visit to Parkhurst on the Isle of Wight, that where 'moral principle' failed to stop crime, the 'sight of . . . gloomy walls, solitary cells, the absolute silence, the prison clothing, the cropped hair . . . the cutlasses and rifles of the warders', should suffice.[24]

But the 'roughs' remained, with another generation invariably in the making. The street provided one venue, with anti-social behaviour denounced yet again by the Rector in 1886; he threatened:

> "the lads of the village" on the subject of rough and unruly conduct in their evening play. . . . Their heedless selfishness has for some time been causing annoyance. . . . if a quieter and less objectionable form of play is not adopted, strong measures, for . . . the public peace and comfort, will . . . be taken to enforce order.

The arrival of the police was not invariably the occasion for rapid dispersal; youthful members of the Pennells, Hilder and Langridge families, 'and other young men [who] have given the police a good deal of interruption while on duty . . . and had frequently interfered with the police in the village', stated a reporter from Hurst Green Sessions, as the chairman – the Revd Luxford – imposed fines, and announced that anybody subsequently convicted would get a taste of prison without the option of a fine. Luxford would have repeatedly encountered young men lolling about in groups on Sundays in his own parish, for this seems to have been a long-standing and very widespread practice; only the degree of insult offered by these parties to churchgoers – including the minister, as Egerton recorded – seems to have varied.[25]

The imposition of discipline, and then of a sort, up until the onset of adolescence, was as much as could be achieved even under compulsory education, and where it retained Anglican domination as in both Burwash parishes. For once, Egerton's colleague Gilbert-Cooper's, showed an element of incisiveness. 'It is very sad', he wrote in 1884, 'to see the falling off in decent and orderly conduct' in children 'no sooner than they have passed away from School influence and discipline'. He filibustered over working-class parents who 'screened' their offspring from complaints of 'ill-conduct, by referring to other children and attributing favouritism or some worse motive' to the complainant. And he detected major class distinctions. The comparatively 'disadvantaged' comprised 'the children of working men'. It was they who left school 'early', and 'practically in most cases' became 'their own masters', whereas the offspring of the middle-classes, whether at boarding school or not were there longer, well into their teens, and 'not allowed to behave amiss and defiantly'. Egerton's diary recurrently testifies to the gaps between him and at least considerable sectors of the working-class majority. That this testimony is there, is an eloquent expression of Egerton's honesty and essential realism. In his study of the Victorian Anglican Church, the distinguished historian of religion

Owen Chadwick concluded his chapter on 'The Country Parson', by noting that 'The list of interesting incumbents of villages could go on for many pages. The work bred remarkable men'.[26]

Egerton was certainly an interesting character. But for historical reasons, the social sanitization of Victorian villages like Burwash could not derive from Anglicanization; it was precisely the breeding of most incumbents which maintained fundamental class barriers too. Even a man of Egerton's intelligence and sociological perception took years – and even he needed to be directly told – about some fundamental class-based barriers. Among the exemplars in the diary which spring to mind are his complete failure to perceive why his use of professional musicians was resented by those lowly folk who he had interested in music; they believed that the proceeds would be better spent on them: free dinners in their own parish, not the payment of fees to distantly-domiciled bourgeois. Again, his reverence never really could understand why the crudities of the penny-dreadfuls and the plebeian concert comics were much more attractive than anything directly under his auspices. Moreover, he was too much of a boss, denouncing drunks, cohabitors, and pregnant brides, which for many represented the unacceptable attempted imposition of alien, middle-class Victorian values. And, although it is largely concealed in the diary, Egerton had a quick temper, and was prone to speedy resort to physical chastisement, cuffing ears, and using the cane to thrash, possibly to excess. Certainly, some parents thought so, and within a year of his death the schools committee ruled that only the headteacher was empowered to cane, and all others were to desist from 'cuffing' or 'boxing ears'.[27]

Not surprisingly Egerton scored relatively few triumphs with his working-class parishioners. And those he might claim, commonly involved migration and upward social mobility. There was the son of one of Egerton's night school teachers, Samuel Hazleden junior, who secured a job in a London Library; 'a young man, who in culture and bearing would do credit to any village in England'. Edward Manwaring, son of William the carrier and sometime simultaneous tenant of the Admiral Vernon, died at the age of forty-three, in 1884. By then he was a very successful

> pickler and jam manufacturer in Peckham . . . another of the instances
> of our parishioners doing well when they come into competition with
> the outside world.

Hence the affluent arrived, some to commute, most to retire. At least some of the more adventurous, and aspirant, sons and daughters of the toilers in the fields, the workshop, and the petty-proprietors of beer-houses, departed this Victorian village.[28]

Notes

1. *Parish Notes*, Jan. 1890.
2. Ibid., Jan. 1888, Dec. 1889 and Jan. 1890. *Sussex Advertiser*, 10 Oct. 1864, 12 Sept. 1874, 11 May 1885, 3 July 1876 and 26 Sept. 1887.
3. *Parish Notes*, June 1887 and Apl. 1888. Burwash ratepayers' meeting respecting emigration, 4 Nov. 1836; Ticehurst Union Clerk to the Poor Law Commission, listing Burwash emigrants, 12 Feb. 1838; May 1839, list Burwash emigrants, PRO. MH.12/13138–40; Census, 1851.
4. *Parish Notes*, Apl. 1888.
5. Ibid., May and July 1887. *Sussex Advertiser*, 27 June 1887.
6. School inspectors' reports, 14 Feb. 1887 and 11 Feb. 1888, ESCRO. ESC.41/1. *Parish Notes*, Mar., Apl. and Aug. 1887.
7. *Sussex Advertiser*, 24 Oct. and 12 Dec. 1887.
8. Stylistic evidence suggests that the obituary writer, who got some details wrong, was not Egerton. *Sussex Advertiser*, 29 Aug. 1865 and 17 Oct. 1887. Census, 1851, 1861, 1871. Summary returns, and other criminal documentation, ESCRO. QR/E.1002, 1013, 1017, 1020, 1031, 1040. *Parish Notes*, May 1887.
9. *Sussex Advertiser*, 1 and 15 Aug. 1887. *Sussex Agricultural Express*, 3 Jan. 1888. Summary returns, ESCRO. QR/E.1118, 1120, 1122, 1124.
10. *Sussex Agricultural Express*, 4 Feb. and 4 Aug. 1888, and 19 Jan. 1889.
11. Ibid., 24 Nov. 1888, 5, 12, 19, 22, 26 and 29 Jan. 1889.
12. Ibid., 11 Aug. 1888. *Parish Notes*, Feb., June and July 1888.
13. *Parish Notes*, Apl. 1888.
14. Ibid.
15. *Sussex Agricultural Express*, 24 and 31 Mar. 1888.
16. *Parish Notes*, Nov. 1888, Jan. and Mar. 1889.
17. Ibid., Mar., June, Sept. and Oct. 1889. *Sussex Agricultural Express*, 4 Sept. 1888.
18. *Parish Notes*, Apl. 1888.
19. Sermon, 19 May 1882, in J.C. Egerton, *Village Instruction; Twelve Sermons*, (Tunbridge Wells, 1892), p. 116. Egerton, jotting in parish register, 1868, ESCRO. Par.284/1/1/6. *Sussex Agricultural Express*, 28 May 1867.
20. Ibid., 24 May and 15 Oct. 1859. *Sussex Advertiser*, 18 Oct. 1864 and 10 Oct. 1865.
21. Egerton, op.cit., pp. 115–9. *Parish Notes*, June 1885.
22. Burial register entry, 29 Dec. 1882, ESCRO. Par.284/1/5/3.
23. *Parish Notes*, Mar. 1883.
24. Ibid., Apl. 1886 and Nov. 1888.
25. Ibid., Apl. 1886. *Sussex Agricultural Express*, 5 Aug. 1876. R. Wells, 'Social protest, class, conflict and consciousness, in the English countryside, 1700–1880', in M. Reed and Wells (eds.), *Class, Conflict and Protest in the English Countryside 1700–1880*, (1990), p. 226.
26. O. Chadwick, *The Victorian Church*, 2 vols, (1966 and 1970), II, p. 181.
27. *Parish Notes*, Aug. 1889.
28. Ibid., Apl. and July 1884. Census, 1851.